LABOR ECONOMICS
and
LABOR RELATIONS

7th edition

LABOR ECONOMICS
and
LABOR RELATIONS

LLOYD G. REYNOLDS
Yale University

PRENTICE-HALL, INC., *Englewood Cliffs, New Jersey 07632*

Library of Congress Cataloging in Publication Data

REYNOLDS, LLOYD GEORGE, (date)
    Labor economics and labor relations.

    Includes bibliographies and index.
    1.–Labor economics. 2.–Industrial relations—
United States. I.–Title.
HD4901.R47 1978   331′.0973   77–14600
ISBN 0–13–517706–5

Printed in the United States of America

10 9 8 7 6 5 4

PRENTICE-HALL INTERNATIONAL, INC., *London*
PRENTICE-HALL OF AUSTRALIA PTY. LIMITED, *Sydney*
PRENTICE-HALL OF CANADA, LTD., *Toronto*
PRENTICE-HALL OF INDIA PRIVATE LIMITED, *New Delhi*
PRENTICE-HALL OF JAPAN, INC., *Tokyo*
PRENTICE-HALL OF SOUTHEAST ASIA PTE. LTD., *Singapore*
WHITEHALL BOOKS LIMITED, *Wellington, New Zealand*

For Anne, Penny, and Bruce

Contents

THE TRANSITION FROM SCHOOL TO WORK
PUBLIC EMPLOYMENT AND TRAINING PROGRAMS

8

Labor Market Policy: Discrimination   158

WOMEN WORKERS   NONWHITE WORKERS
ANTIDISCRIMINATION POLICIES

III

WAGES AND INCOMES

9

Wages at the Company Level   183

WAGES: MEANING AND MEASUREMENT
WAGE DIFFERENCES AMONG EMPLOYERS
THE CHOICE OF A WAGE LEVEL
THE INTERNAL WAGE STRUCTURE: JOB EVALUATION
SUPPLEMENTARY INCOME PAYMENTS

10

Money Wages, Prices, and Employment   203

A CENTURY OF RISING WAGES
WAGE–PRICE RELATIONS: A SIMPLE VIEW
WAGES AND UNEMPLOYMENT: THE PHILLIPS CURVE
ISSUES IN WAGE–PRICE POLICY
DIRECT PRESSURE: INCOMES POLICY

11

Real Wages and Labor's Income Share   228

THEORIES OF LABOR'S SHARE
CHANGES IN RELATIVE SHARES: ANALYSIS
CHANGES IN RELATIVE SHARES: EVIDENCE

VII

THE FRAMEWORK OF PUBLIC CONTROL

Preface

Labor economics and industrial relations are distinct but overlapping subjects. Labor economics is linked to the central core of economics by the theory of labor markets and wage determination; but unionism alters market structure and market results. Industrial relations is a multidisciplinary subject to which economics has made important contributions; but major contributions have come also from law, history, psychology, sociology, and industrial administration.

The effort to cover both subjects in a single text raises problems to which there is no agreed solution. While the notion of synthesizing them throughout the book is attractive in principle, it can lead to undesirable distortions in coverage. On one hand there is a temptation to focus the economic analysis on the unionized 25 percent of the labor force, and on the other a tendency to analyze industrial relations systems in overly economic terms.

This book follows the alternative course of treating the two subjects somewhat at arm's length. This raises the question of which should come first, and again there is no "correct" answer. Each sequence has advantages and disadvantages. I choose to place the economic analysis at the beginning of the book partly because "this is where the action is" on the frontiers of research and policy discussion.

Any author must realize, however, that his own preferences on organization will not be universally shared. So I have tried to make each chapter of the book a self-contained teaching unit, which users can rearrange to suit their own preferences. The material on trade unionism and collective bargaining in Parts IV and V, for example, could be used effectively *before* Parts I–III by teachers who prefer an institutional introduction to the course.

Parts I–III have been extensively rewritten for this edition. Those who have used the book in the past will find new material on the economics of education and human capital, the dynamics of labor markets, race and sex discrimination, the unemployment-inflation trade-off, the reasons for differences in individual earnings, and alternative approaches to the poverty problem. These are important research frontiers in labor economics, and I have tried to incorporate the latest theoretical developments and research findings. At the same time, by diligent pruning, I have managed to make this edition somewhat shorter than its predecessor.

I am grateful for advice and help from many quarters. John Turnbull, University of Minnesota and Thomas Barocci, Sloan School of Management, MIT, reviewed the previous edition and made many helpful suggestions for improvement; but the usual disclaimer concerning their responsibility is in order. Nantanee Vacharasiridham compiled the new statistical data. My greatest debt, as always, is to Gail Ross for her skill and precision in drafting charts, tidying up the manuscript, and double-checking proofs.

In addition to those whom I can thank by name, I should like to express appreciation to the hundreds of students and teachers in the United States and elsewhere whose suggestions have contributed to the continuing improvement of this book.

L.G.R.

LABOR ECONOMICS
and
LABOR RELATIONS

INTRODUCTION

1

Labor in Industrial Society

Labor is always and everywhere the largest factor of production; and labor income always constitutes a large part of national income. Historically, this income has taken a variety of forms. In economies permitting slavery, it is mainly the subsistence of the slaves and their dependents. To the isolated peasant of Nepal, it is whatever he can produce and consume on his plot of land. Where the peasant markets part of his output, it is cash income plus his subsistence production.

Strictly, only part of the peasant's income can be regarded as labor income. Part of it is a return on his ownership of buildings and equipment, and part may be a rent arising from superior quality of his land. But where landowner, capitalist, and worker are rolled into one, these distinctions may not seem important.

Labor income becomes separable and measurable when the worker is hired for a wage or salary. His contribution to production then consists of his physical or mental effort, and the price of this effort is his wage. Modern labor economics focuses on economies in which a large part of the population consists of employees and analyzes major dimensions of the employment relation: the number of people who will offer themselves for employment, the number of hours they will work per week and per year, the deployment of the labor force among the many specialized occupations in the economy, the determination of wage rates and other terms of employment for each occupation, and the distribution of total national income between employees and others. It is concerned also with the special institutions that have grown up around the employment relation, notably trade unionism and collective bargaining, and with the degree to which these institutions modify the supply and compensation of labor. Labor economics is not confined, however, to workers who happen to be organized or to the

3

lower occupational strata of the population. It is concerned with *all* labor effort, with employees at every occupational level, including the effort exerted by employers and self-employed persons.

The predominance of employer–employee relations is associated with the rise of modern industry and large production units, which is still limited to certain regions of the world. Most of the world's population remains in the preindustrial era. In most countries of Asia, Africa, and Latin America, half or more of the labor force is engaged in agriculture. The remainder are mainly petty traders, service workers, or independent artisans. Only a small fraction of the population works in factories and other modern enterprises.

The great transformation which ushered in the industrial society began in Great Britain in the latter half of the eighteenth century. During the nineteenth century the movement spread to a dozen other countries. Accelerated industrial development began around 1830 in France, Belgium, and the United States, around 1850 in Germany, around 1870 in Sweden and Japan, and around 1890 in Canada and Russia. Today the industrialized world includes almost all of Europe (including the USSR), North America, Australia, and Japan. Mexico, Brazil, Argentina, and Chile are also nearing this stage of development.

SOME FEATURES OF
THE INDUSTRIAL ECONOMY

Today's industrial countries differ widely in size, climate, geographic characteristics, language and cultural traditions, and form of government. Yet they also have many features in common. Similarities in the economic matrix give labor problems a family resemblance throughout the industrial world. These common features include:

1. *The pattern of employment.* Most of the labor force is employed in manufacturing, construction, public utilities, and government. Agriculture employs only a declining minority; and while employment in trade remains substantial, trade is carried on increasingly by mass distributors rather than small shopkeepers. The economy is characterized by large production units, which employ hundreds or thousands of people and often use large amounts of capital equipment per worker. Occupations are highly specialized and diversified, with many jobs requiring substantial skill and training. Many people work in clerical, technical, and professional occupations, and this white-collar segment of the labor force grows considerably faster than the blue-collar segment. A description of the United States? Yes, but a description also of Sweden, the USSR, and Japan.

2. *The level of output and incomes.* Large, capital-intensive production units applying modern technology yield high output per worker, and this provides higher real incomes and living standards. This accounts for the mys-

tique of industrialization throughout the underdeveloped world. One can argue over the question of how much more the American worker produces than the Soviet worker. But there is no doubt that either produces more than the average worker in Uganda or Indonesia. A large and growing national output, of course, may produce controversy over the division of the gains. How much should go to employees as against owners of capital? How much should go to each group of wage and salary earners? These issues are more intense under industrialism than in a static, agricultural society where incomes are assigned by tradition and paternal authority.

3. *The dependent status of employees.* From one standpoint, the shift from self-employed farmer or artisan to employed wage earner liberates the individual. He is free to move about in search of work, to better himself, to work his way up the occupational ladder. But in other ways it reduces his independence. The wage earner must find work in order to live, while the farmer can always live after a fashion from his own output; and when the wage earner is employed the details of his work are closely regulated. Someone else specifies the times at which work is to be done, the nature of the task, the materials and equipment to be used, the pace of work, and the expected quantity and quality of output. Above the worker stand all the layers of management, from first-line supervisor to company president.

4. *Administration and the web of rules.* Dependence does not stop with the worker. The supervisor is himself under higher authority, and so are the general foreman, the plant superintendent, and the vice-president in charge of production. Even the company president is responsible to a board of directors. A large enterprise is bound together by an elaborate hierarchy of authority, which specifies the powers and responsibilities of everyone from company president to laborer.

It is bound together also by a network of rules governing output and cost targets; products, equipment, and production methods; types and amounts of compensation; employment, promotion, discharge; and many other things. At a particular time most of these rules are taken as fixed, and changes are occurring only at the margin; so one is apt not to realize their extent and complexity. But reading a fifty-page union contract reminds one how complicated the internal government of a large business can be. When we say that the industrial worker must learn discipline, we mean that he must know and observe this web of rules, in addition to submitting to the personal authority of the supervisor.

5. *Worker protest and labor organization.* Workers new to industry often find it difficult to submit to rules that they have had no hand in creating and that may appear harsh and arbitrary. So the early stages of industrialization are usually attended by labor unrest and spontaneous individual protest. This may show up in high absenteeism and turnover, disobedience to the foreman, and underperformance on the job. There may also be sporadic strikes and riots by large numbers of workers. This was common in early British and American industry and is common today in the newly industrializing countries.

Eventually, however, protest is channeled into continuing organizations and takes a more effective if less violent form. Prominent among these organizations are the trade unions, whose tactics normally include both political action and defense of the workers' interests in the plant. Fitting trade unions into the social structure and defining their functions relative to those of industrial management and of government is a characteristic problem of industrial society.

6. *Insecurity and mobility.* An industrial economy is by definition a changing economy. Products, methods of production, the location of industry, and the demand for specific skills are in constant flux. Without these changes the economy cannot continue to advance to ever higher levels of productivity and income.

These dynamic shifts keep open the frontier of opportunity. The new plants and industries are typically more efficient than those that they supplant. They provide more productive jobs at higher wages. But the opposite side of the coin is a high degree of personal insecurity. Plants fail and are shut down, products and services become obsolete, jobs disappear through technical change, location shifts leave stranded populations in depressed areas. The worker has to be quick on his feet to avoid being stranded and to seize new opportunities as they appear. Even if he is quick and lucky, this enforced job-hopping involves anxiety and dissatisfaction, and it leads workers and unions to be preoccupied with the problem of job security.

7. *The pervasiveness of labor markets.* Under slavery or feudalism workers can be ordered to the places where they are needed. But in a complex industrial economy, coercion is inefficient, quite apart from its infringement on human dignity and independence. Even in planned economies, direct allocation of workers to jobs has been used only in periods of national emergency. The general rule is that each worker hunts his own jobs and each plant recruits its own workers. Employers use wages as the main magnet for attracting labor, and income is a major consideration in workers' minds when choosing jobs. There are markets for labor, though usually not very efficient ones. The wage for each kind of labor is heavily influenced, if not fully determined, by supply and demand conditions in the market. This is what brings the study of labor into touch with the central core of economic theory.

In stressing the resemblance among industrial economies, one should not overlook important points of difference. There are differences, for example, in the strength and activities of trade unions. There are differences also in the balance of power among unions, industrial managers, and government officials. In some countries management still lays down the rules of industrial employment with little hindrance from any source. In others management is forced to negotiate with strong unions but is largely free of government control. In still others, government participates actively in setting terms of employment, and in some countries it has the dominant voice.

SOME KEY ECONOMIC ISSUES

What major issues arise from the employment relation? At least seven such issues can be distinguished:

1. *Maintaining adequate total demand for labor.* This is a chronic problem for economies in the early stages of industrialization, which usually have a surplus of underemployed labor in agriculture. It is a recurrent problem for industrialized capitalist economies, whose growth is interrupted occasionally by

general depression. Depression cuts national output and reduces the incomes of workers along with those of most other people. It usually means a sharp reduction of new investment, the major source of economic progress and higher living standards. It reduces the opportunity for people to change jobs and make occupational progress. It leads to adoption of unwise government policies, which are presented with plausible arguments as depression remedies.

For these reasons almost everyone now subscribes to "full employment" as an economic goal. But how full is "full"? Does full employment mean an average of 3 percent of the labor force unemployed between jobs, or an average of 5 percent? Does it mean trying to maintain about as many vacant jobs as there are unemployed workers, or an actual excess of vacancies? The higher the employment target, the more likely it is that there will be consistent upward pressure on the price level. Should one worry more about unemployment or about inflation? One can scarcely expect union leaders to give the same answer as pensioners or insurance executives.

2. *Developing effective labor markets.* Ours is a market economy. To a greater degree than most other countries we have succeeded in establishing free choice of occupation by individuals, free choice of goods by consumers, and free access to markets by businessmen. The market mechanism is far from ideal, however, and labor markets are less efficient than most others.

Workers presently market their labor under serious handicaps of ignorance, misinformation, and uncertainty. Employers are not much better off in their effort to locate the best workers available. Job hunting will always be something of a game of blindman's buff because of the innate complexity of the employment process. It should be possible, however, to enlarge and improve the state employment services and to find other ways of raising the plane of competition in the labor market. A better matching of individual capacities with job requirements would improve productive efficiency and increase national output.

Access to markets for technical, managerial, and professional occupations usually requires education beyond high school. For young people and their families, this poses a problem of weighing the costs of such education against the prospective returns. In social terms, it raises a problem of estimating social returns to education, and of achieving an efficient allocation of resources among levels of education and courses of study. The economics of education is a subject in its own right; but because of its bearing on the selection of workers for high-level occupations and on earnings in those occupations, it can also be regarded as a branch of labor economics.

3. *Training, organizing, and motivating the labor force.* The labor market is supposed to achieve a distribution of the labor force among industries, plants, and localities which corresponds to the detailed pattern of demand for labor. But this is only a first step. Workers as they come through the hiring office are a conglomerate of isolated individuals, not a working team. They have to be trained, organized, supervised, and motivated to perform efficiently in the production process. They must be subjected to a new network of rules and controls, a new industrial discipline quite unlike that of an agricultural society.

The importance and generality of this problem have been well stated by Kerr and Siegel:

The process of industrialization may then be seen as involving in the productive sector the addition or the changing of a complex body of working rules . . . concerned with the recruitment of a labor force, with the training of that labor force in the myriad skills required by the advanced division of labor, with the locating of workers in some appropriate pattern of geographical, industrial, and occupational dispersion. It involves the setting of rules on times to work and not to work, on pace and quality of work, on method and amount to pay, on movement into and out of work and from one position to another. It involves rules pertaining to the maintenance of continuity in the work process (so intimately related to the maintenance of stability in the society)—the attempted minimization of individual or organized revolt, the provision of views of the world, of ideological orientations, of beliefs, the introduction of some checks on the individual insecurity inherent in an industrial order. The structuring of this web of rule must be undertaken regardless of the form of industrialization, in Russia and the United States alike.[1]

4. *Determining wage rates and labor income.* This set of rules has such a venerable tradition in economics that it may be singled out for special mention. The wage problem comprises at least four subproblems:

a. *Determining the general wage level.* Within the enterprise, how much of sales revenue can fairly be claimed by labor as against other operating expenses and profits? When should the company's wage level be raised, and on what grounds? Looking at the economy as a whole, what should be the level of money wages and real wages? What is a proper split-up between labor and property incomes? How fast should the national wage level be raised over the course of time, and why?

b. *Determining relative wage rates for different types of work.* How is the national wage total to be divided among the individuals comprising the labor force? Within a particular plant or industry, should the most skilled job pay 20 percent more than the least skilled, or 50 percent more, or 100 percent more? Should some industries pay higher wages than others, and how much higher? Should workers earn more in some geographical regions than in others, or more in large cities than in small towns? The relationship among wages in different occupations, industries, and areas is commonly termed the problem of *wage structure* or *wage differentials.*

c. *Deciding the method of wage payment.* The leading issue here is between payment on the basis of hours worked and payment on the basis of output (*piece work* or *incentive* payment). This issue arouses strong feeling among workers and is decided differently in different industries and countries. Piece-rate payment is used more widely in Russia than in the United States. Within the United States, some industries use piece-rate payment exclusively, while others do not use it at all.

d. *Deciding the form of workers' income receipts.* The national wage bill may go almost entirely into direct wage payments, or a substantial share may go into old-age pensions, family allowances, medical and hospital services, unemployment compensation, and other indirect benefits. In some European countries these indirect benefits are one-third to one-half as large as direct wage payments. In the United States, where they are less fully developed, the proportion is approaching one-fifth.

---

[1] Clark Kerr and Abraham Siegel, "The Structuring of the Labor Force in Industrial Society: New Dimensions and New Questions," *Industrial and Labor Relations Review* (January 1955), p. 163.

5. *Balancing producer and consumer satisfactions.* There is an obvious conflict of interest between the workers engaged in producing a particular product and the consumers of the product. It is to the workers' interest to work short hours, at a leisurely pace, amid pleasant surroundings, and to receive high wages plus ample fringe benefits. These things raise costs, however, and must be paid for by consumers through higher prices. How can one strike a proper balance between the interests of the two groups?

Wage earners, moreover, form close to half of the consuming public and salary earners another quarter.·There is thus a conflict of interest *within* the wage and salary group. People can work longer and harder as producers in order to enjoy more goods as consumers, or they can take things easier and consume less.

Two "automatic" solutions of this problem appear in economic writings. The independent producer consuming his own product—Crusoe on his island— can presumably strike a direct balance between effort and consumption. He can judge the point at which the effort of knocking down another coconut or catching another fish would outweigh the satisfaction from eating it. Subsistence farmers, who form a large part of the world's population, are in much the same situation.

In a complex industrial society, it can be argued that the problem is still solved by the normal working of the labor market. Each worker, by choosing his employer and occupation, can get long hours or short hours, heavy work or easy work, pleasant or disagreeable conditions. Greater effort or unpleasantness will presumably have to be compensated by higher wages. The worker will choose the combination of wages and working conditions that best meets his personal preferences.

There is something to this line of argument, but one should not rely on it too heavily. The labor market is a rather blunt instrument even for determining relative wage rates. It is even less adequate for determining optimum hours, proper work speeds, and desirable working conditions. Despite our best efforts to improve the market mechanism, it will remain necessary to supplement it by institutional regulation.

6. *Protecting against predictable risks.* The industrial worker depends heavily on a regular flow of money income. This dependence is increasing with the growth of credit facilities and installment buying. Anything which cuts off the weekly paycheck threatens not only the worker's dinner table but also his house, car, furniture, and household appliances.

The reasons why the stream of income may fail are well known and many of them are predictable. It is certain that everyone must grow old, and probable life spans can be predicted fairly precisely. There are good figures on the incidence of industrial accidents and on various types of disabling illnesses. We know that there is a certain minimum of unemployment even in good years. It seems sheerest common sense to develop ways of protecting workers' incomes against such contingencies. This not only benefits the people concerned but also increases the stability of the economy. There is room for argument over the desirable level of protection, the proper balance between private insurance funds and government systems, and the percentage of cost that should be borne by workers instead of by employers or consumers. The need for a comprehensive network of protective measures, however, is no longer seriously questioned.

7. *Assuring a minimum level of living.* There is also increasing consensus that no member of the community should be allowed to fall below some minimum level of subsistence. Social security and private insurance systems,

minimum-wage legislation, farm income supplements, and state and local relief systems are all expressions of this concern. Arguments are not so much over principle as over feasible support levels and detailed institutional arrangements.

This issue is usually discussed in a labor course because it touches many wage-earning families. But it is not exclusively or even mainly a problem of manual workers. The group below the poverty line also includes rural families living on inferior land, who have lower living standards than any sizable group in the urban population; broken homes containing no wage earner, or in which the principal wage earner is disabled; and many older people drawn from all occupational levels. Inability to work and produce, rather than low wage levels, is now the main source of poverty in the United States.

MECHANISMS OF ADJUSTMENT: INSTITUTIONS AND THE MARKET

Two main mechanisms are available for resolving these issues—the competitive labor market and institutional rules imposed by business concerns, trade unions, and government. Though these may be regarded as alternatives at a theoretical level, in practice they will always be found operating together. Even Russia, which might seem to be an extreme case of government control, has important elements of a competitive labor market. Individual establishments recruit labor as best they can; workers move about the country in search of better jobs; occupational and regional wage differentials are adjusted to lure workers to the place where labor is scarcest.

One should also not assume that market forces and institutional rules necessarily conflict. They may do so, but they may also work in the same direction, and institutional regulation may simply ratify a market decision. We shall argue at a later point that this is largely true of wage determination in the United States. Both the general wage level and relative wage rates for different jobs are determined mainly by supply-and-demand pressures in the labor market. Unions largely take credit for wage increases that were "in the cards" on economic grounds. It is politically necessary for a union to do this, just as it is necessary for whichever party holds power in Washington to take credit for business prosperity which it may have done little to create. But the fact that under collective bargaining the union is entitled to *announce* a wage increase does not constitute evidence that it *caused* the increase.

The question of how far labor conditions are or should be determined by institutional rules rather than by market pressures rouses strong emotions and leads people into extreme positions. One school of thought tends to glorify the market, to assert that it does or could adequately regulate terms of employment, and that institutional "interference" is bound to be either ineffective or harmful. At the other pole, some people write off the market as ineffective and defend the necessity and beneficence of institutional controls. Reality is certainly more complicated than these extreme views would suggest. The labor market seems to perform some functions quite effectively, while in other areas its performance is less satisfactory. Starting with as little bias as possible, we must try to discover where the market performs well and where it breaks down, to explain why the relative importance of market and institutional regulation differs from country to country and time to time, and to analyze what happens when the two mechanisms pull in opposite directions. This is the task of the whole book; but a few preliminary comments will help to set the stage.

The Role of the Labor Market

Elementary economics texts describe the operation of a competitive labor market and the results it might be expected to yield. The broad argument is that, given free and informed competition among workers and employers, each worker must be paid the value of his contribution to production. He cannot be paid more, because the employer could not continue to operate. He will not be paid less, because the employer would be making abnormal profits and some other alert businessman would enter the industry and bid up the price of labor. There is thus little scope for controversy or bargaining over the price of labor.

This is of course a very simplified and idealized picture. It assumes many small employers competing for labor, no collusion among employers or workers, adequate channels of information, and a number of other things. It is no secret that actual labor markets depart considerably from this competitive ideal. Many employers are large and the worker's choice is often restricted to one or a few companies; employers often get together on wage rates and on policies which make it hard for workers to change employers; channels of information are poor and there is no effective central clearinghouse for labor; the exchange of a machinist's labor for a "package" of wages and working conditions is a more complicated transaction than setting a price on a loaf of bread; workers dislike changing jobs and, when forced to do so, they hunt new jobs in a haphazard and ill-informed way; during periods of heavy unemployment the worker's bargaining power—which depends basically on his power to change jobs—is seriously reduced.

Despite these deficiences, the labor market is a reasonably effective instrument both for determining relative wage rates and for raising the general wage level as national output rises. The great increase in real wages in the United States over the past century has not been due in any large measure to collective bargaining or government decree. It has occurred mainly because employers were able and impelled to keep raising their wage offers in the market year after year: able because development of new machinery and production methods was steadily increasing output per man-hour; impelled because the labor market forces each employer to bid against others to hold his share of the labor supply. The labor market is the main mechanism by which increases in productivity have been translated into higher wages and living standards.

The market also does reasonably well in determining relative wage levels for different plants, industries, occupations, and regions. One can always find many queer or inequitable wage rates; but viewed broadly and over the long run, the national wage structure is not unreasonable. Moreover, it is evolving over the course of time in a way that is understandable on economic grounds. Wage inequalities of every sort are diminishing and this is due mainly, though not exclusively, to changing supply and demand conditions.

Finally, the labor market is the only device we have for sorting out many millions of workers with varying skills and interests among the multitude of different jobs in the economy. Any attempt to do this by administrative methods, in addition to encroaching on personal liberty, would be hopelessly cumbersome and inefficient. Even communist countries, as noted earlier, rely mainly on wage inducements in the market to secure a desirable allocation of the labor force.

Recognition that the labor market does some things well, however, should not blind us to the things which it does poorly or cannot do at all. It is not highly effective, for example, in regulating working conditions— physical conditions, safety and sanitation, work speeds, treatment by supervisors, and other personnel policies. The market still sets limits in the sense that, if plant conditions become too bad, workers have the option of leaving. But these limits may be quite wide. Working conditions are hard for the market to evaluate and control because they are intangible, qualitative, hard for the worker to discover before he is on the job, and hard to bargain about on an individual basis. Workers conclude that the effective remedy is not individual bargaining or quitting (the market solution) but group pressure through a union.

The market cannot provide security against arbitrary demotion or discharge by supervisors, nor can it establish equitable rules concerning layoff, rehiring, and promotion. These require administrative procedures within the enterprise. The market is not very good at bringing about marked changes in employment practice, such as a shift from a ten-hour to an eight-hour-day. It is not good at establishing minimum standards which, in order to survive, must be enforced on all employers simultaneously. Examples are rules concerning work by women and children, safety and health standards, and minimum wage legislation. Nor is it a good device in areas where there are substantial economies in collective action. Pensions, unemployment compensation, and other income security devices could be set up entirely by individual employers, and if enough employers adopted them, the market might force others to follow. There are clear economies, however, in applying insurance principles to the entire labor force through government security programs. Finally, the labor market obviously cannot improve itself. Organized effort is required to mitigate the structural defects noted earlier and to enable the market to perform its natural functions better.

An important and irremovable source of difficulty is that most workers regard resort to the market—that is, a change of employers—as a disaster rather than an opportunity. They typically want to continue with their present employer. Advice that they can improve their employer's behavior by leaving him they regard as academic. They prefer to change the employer's behavior without leaving him, and for this they need union organization.

The Place of Institutional Rules

Organizational rules may be imposed to override market determinations that are displeasing to workers or employers. More importantly, however, they are a way of reaching decisions at points where the market is imprecise or ineffective. They supplement the market mechanism at least as much as they compete with it.

The main contenders for rule-making authority are the business firm, the trade union, and the state. Adherents of each of these often regard it as the normal rule-making body, entitled in principle to exclusive authority. Many businessmen still regard management as the proper group to decide on terms of employment and resent "outside interference" by unions or government. To the trade unionist, it is an article of faith that conditions of employment should be regulated by union–management agreement. Socialists tend to regard government as the logical guardian of workers' welfare.

Looking at the world as a whole, however, it is clear that no one system of rule making can be regarded as inevitable. This point has been cogently argued by Kerr and Siegel:

> Given these three contestants, there are several general systems for distributing the essential power to make rules governing the labor force. Three of these possible rule-making relationships may be designated as monistic, in the sense that the rules . . . are set primarily by one of the contestants. . . . (1) The employer may set the rules, and . . . may follow a policy of paternalism, as in Japan before World War II, or a policy of forced worker self-dependence, as in England in the early period of industrialization. A conceivable, though much less likely actual possibility is that (2) the worker may give the directions. His "union" then becomes more or less of a producers' cooperative (as in sectors of the Israeli

economy). . . . (3) The state may issue the commands, as it does in Russia and in all the nations within the Russian orbit. The "unions" there are essentially "agents of the state" with only such authority as may be granted them by the state.

Three additional systems may be called dualistic, since two of the contestants share rule-making power in the industrial sector. (4) The power may be shared, as in the United States prior to the recent rise in state interest, primarily by the employer and the unions whose relationships may range from reserved tolerance to secret collusion. (5) Or the employer and the state may divide the authority between them. The power of the state may be ranged alongside that of the employer, as in Nazi Germany, or in opposition, as in Mexico or Argentina or Guatemala in recent years; or the state may vacillate back and forth as in France and Italy. . . . (6) Or the state and the worker may participate jointly in rule-making, as in the nationalized industries in Great Britain.

Finally (7), the three contestants may share rule-making power in a pluralistic system . . . as evidenced in Scandinavia, the United States, and several of the member nations of the British Commonwealth.[2]

This last situation, where all three parties have a finger in the pie, seems to be characteristic of countries with a long history of democratic government and industrial development. This group includes the Scandinavian countries, the Netherlands, West Germany, Britain, Canada, the United States, Australia, and a few others. Taking the world as a whole, it is an exceptional rather than a typical situation, though a number of other countries—France, Italy, Mexico, Japan, India—may evolve gradually in the same direction.

Though all three groups share rule-making power in these economies, each has certain areas of decision within which it has a comparative advantage and therefore a preponderant voice. Even in strongly unionized economies management retains a large measure of administrative authority. It typically has exclusive control over, or at least the right to take initial action concerning, production organization, production methods, production volume and labor requirements, recruitment and hiring of labor, assignment of workers to specific jobs, appointment of supervisors, determination of work speeds, establishment of shop rules and application of penalties for violating them, layoffs, and other personnel matters. Management acts; the union protests or appeals. The union may eventually secure a reversal of the decision, but the power to act retains much of its pristine potency.

The specific function of unionism is to police in-plant decisions and actions of management. This means negotiating a general framework of rules within which management action is confined (the union contract) and ensuring equitable application of these rules to individual cases (the grievance procedure). Rules concerning the conditions under which a

---

[2] Kerr and Siegel, "The Structuring of the Labor Force," p. 163.

worker may be penalized, demoted, or discharged are of prime importance, as are rules concerning layoffs, rehiring, promotion, and other matters of job tenure. Though unions also do much to influence wages and working conditions, their distinctive function is to establish a system of industrial jurisprudence through which the individual can seek redress from harmful decisions by management.

Government has a comparative advantage in establishing minimum standards which are considered sufficiently important to be enforced on everyone. This may mean either bringing laggards up to the market level or establishing standards in areas where the market is not very effective. Government is an efficient mechanism for devising protection against loss of income through unemployment, old age, total or partial disability, and other causes. It is now generally agreed that government has responsibility for maintaining adequate total demand for labor. Finally, only government can prescribe rules to govern union and employer conduct in collective bargaining.

The Order of Discussion

In such a complex area there is no preordained sequence of discussion. One can deal with institutional arrangements first and market phenomena later, or vice versa. Much thought and experimentation has convinced the author that it makes most sense to start with the economics of labor markets—the determinants of labor supply and demand, employment and unemployment, wage rates and income distribution. These matters are examined in Parts I to III. The discussion is not limited to unionized workers or even to manual workers, who are now a minority of the American labor force. It covers the full range of occupations and earnings, from farm laborers to brain surgeons. It uses the standard tools of microeconomic analysis with due attention to the ways in which labor markets differ from commodity markets. It ranges sufficiently far afield to deal with such issues as the relation between equality of occupational opportunity and the financing of higher education, and the reasons for the unfavorable occupational and income position of black workers relative to white workers. It incorporates the growing volume of sophisticated research on employment and earnings. And it explores policy issues in such areas as wages, hours, poverty, employment discrimination, economic insecurity, training and retraining, and labor market organization.

In Parts IV to VII we examine trade unionism and collective bargaining as economic institutions: the development and characteristics of American trade unions, bargaining arrangements and bargaining tactics vis-à-vis employers, the content and administration of the resulting agreements, the economic impact of collective bargaining, the legal framework within which collective bargaining operates, and proposals for changes in this framework by further legislation. A chapter on industrial relations in other countries underlines the point that industrial relations systems are the result of historical circumstance rather than abstract logic. Our own arrangements are not fixed or inevitable but have changed and are continuing to change over the course of time.

DISCUSSION QUESTIONS

1. What features of modern industrialism give rise to labor problems? What kinds of labor problems might arise even in a purely agricultural economy?

2. During the nineteenth century some writers predicted that with the growth of industry the population would soon consist mainly of manual workers. Why has this not happened?

3. "Development of strong trade unions usually takes a half-century or more after the appearance of modern industry." Do you agree? If so, what reasons can you give for the slow development of union strength?

4. What are the principal "labor problems" in a general social sense? Would you expect these problems to differ substantially in the United States, the USSR, Japan?

5. Why is the labor market usually supplemented by institutional rules in determining wages and conditions of employment?

6. "The operation of the labor market has done more over the past century to improve wages and working conditions in the United States than trade unions and government together." Discuss.

7. Looking at the whole range of occupations and earnings in the American economy, which, in your opinion, are:
    (a) the most important phenomena to be explained?
    (b) the most important issues of government policy?

READING SUGGESTIONS

The best brief introduction to the range of issues discussed in this book is probably E. H. PHELPS BROWN, *The Economics of Labor,* New Haven: Yale University Press, 1962. For a comparative view of the impact of industrialization on employment relations, see C. KERR, J. DUNLOP, C. MYERS, and F. HARBISON, *Industrialism and Industrial Man,* Cambridge, Mass.: Harvard University Press, 1960. On labor problems in the less developed countries, see WALTER GALENSON, *Labor and Economic Development,* New York: John Wiley & Sons, Inc., 1959. Also see GALENSON's *Labor in Developing Economies,* Berkeley and Los Angeles: University of California Press, 1962. On wage setting and labor mobility in the USSR see ABRAM BERGSON, *The Economics of Soviet Planning,* New Haven: Yale University Press, 1964.

I

THE LABOR FORCE

In any society some people work and some do not. Schoolchildren and retired people are not in the labor force; but the definition of school-leaving age and retirement age varies from country to country. Adult males normally work, but employment of women outside the home is conditioned by cultural as well as economic factors. In Chapter 2 we examine who works in the United States and how labor force participation rates have changed over time. We look also at decisions about hours of work, which are a major dimension of labor supply. The trend of working hours in the United States has been downward for more than a century. We ask why this has happened and speculate about the future.

Labor force is a matter of *quality* as well as *quantity*. Workers in the American economy today are much more educated, skilled, and productive than their grandfathers. This improvement in work capacity is called *human capital formation* and may contribute as much as physical capital formation to long-run economic growth. It occurs partly through formal education, and partly through on-the-job training and work experience. Education and on-the-job training involve substantial costs; but they also bring substantial returns, to the individual and to society. In Chapter 3 we examine how these returns can be estimated, and look particularly into the economics of higher education, asking such questions as: How much is a college education worth? Is higher education in the United States presently overexpanded or underdeveloped? Is the present system of financing higher education equitable?

In Chapter 4 we look at the deployment of the labor force among areas, industries, and occupations. The pattern of employment shifts over time in response to changes in product demand and technology. Thus each year many people change jobs, some because they have to, some in response to greater opportunities elsewhere. In a typical year, about one-sixth of all wage and salary earners shift to new employments. This massive flow of people through the labor market poses major problems: for the individual, problems of job search, opportunity, and insecurity; for the employer, problems of labor recruitment, screening, and training; for society, problems of improving labor market efficiency by reducing the time spent in job search, and by achieving a better matching of individual abilities with job requirements. Chapter 4 thus provides a transition to Part II, where the operation of labor markets is analyzed in detail.

2

The Labor Force: Quantity

WHAT IS LABOR?

Labor resembles nonhuman agents of production in some respects but differs from them in others. First, man is the object as well as the author of economic activity. The test of an economy's performance is the net satisfaction that it yields to the population. The relevant satisfactions (and dissatisfactions) include those associated directly with work as well as those derived from consumption. A machine used in production does not experience pleasure or pain. A human being does. In appraising a change in working hours, work speeds, or work methods, one must consider the effect on workers' satisfaction as well as on production costs and prices to the consumer.

Second, land and capital are owned by outside agents, but except under the unusual condition of slavery, the worker owns himself. He decides the direction in which his productive capacity is to be deployed. He decides (or his parents do) how much to invest in general education and vocational training, and receives any increased income resulting from such training. Because of limited knowledge and foresight, limited facilities for educational loans, and the fact that individuals must reckon in terms of posttax income, there is probably less investment in human beings than would be desirable from a national standpoint.

In other respects, however, labor is analogous to capital. Like capital, it can be defined either as a *stock* of productive instruments existing at a point of time, or as a *flow* of services yielded by these instruments over time. In the stock sense, *labor* is the totality of people counted to be in the labor force, with whatever skills and productive capacity they possess at the moment. This is the "human capital" of the nation, a very old concept

21

in economics. The individuals included in this stock are heterogeneous and difficult to add up in any meaningful way; but this is equally true of machines, buildings, and other capital goods.

In the flow sense, *labor* is the number of man-hours available or used in production over a period of time. Over *what* period of time? We usually say a year, and with a good reason. Hours per year may change without any change in weekly hours of work because of changes in vacation allowances, paid holidays, sick leave, and other arrangements. A yearly calculation is helpful also in taking account of seasonal workers, part-time workers, and others whose activity needs to be measured over a full annual cycle.

The flow of labor services available to an economy normally rises over time, but in a complicated fashion. There are four main dimensions of labor supply:

1. *The population base.* We do not attempt to explain differing rates of population growth, taking them simply as a datum. The population of the United States has increased continuously throughout our history, but the rate of increase has fluctuated considerably—low in the 1920s and 1930s, unusually high from 1945 to 1960, and lower again since that time. These fluctuations in population growth are reflected in fluctuations in labor force growth; but there is a long lag, because it takes time for young people to grow up and begin work. Thus the "baby boom" that began in 1946 meant that, beginning about 1964, the rate of increase in the labor force also rose substantially. The marked drop in birth rates beginning about 1957 meant that the rate of increase in labor force also began to drop in 1975. This pattern stands out clearly in the annual rates of increase charted in Figure 2–1.

2. *Labor force participation rates.* A second variable is the proportion of the population who choose to engage in gainful employment. Even with a stable population, the labor force might rise or fall because of changes in participation rates. There have been large changes in the United States since 1900—upward for adult women, downward for people under twenty and over sixty-five—and we must explore the reasons for these changes.

3. *Hours of work.* The flow of man-hours has risen less rapidly than the labor force because of a long-term decline in hours worked per week and per year. This decline has been going on since the mid-nineteenth century, and a reasonable economic explanation can be given for this.

4. *Labor force quality.* While the aggregate flow of labor services measured in man-hours is a significant figure, it veils the fact that these services are extremely heterogeneous. The flow includes man-hours of corporation presidents' time, research chemists' time, bricklayers' time, farm laborers' time. In recent decades the percentage of managerial, professional, and technical workers has risen substantially, while the proportion of low-skilled workers has declined. The average *quality* of the man-hour flow has increased.

This qualitative dimension is sufficiently important that we shall devote an entire chapter to it. In the present chapter we concentrate on the quantitative aspects of labor supply—specifically, labor force participation rates and working hours.

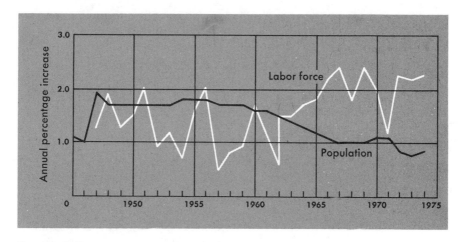

Figure 2–1

Annual Rates of Increase in Population and
Labor Force, 1947–1974

SOURCE: *Statistical Abstract of the United
States* (Washington, .D.C.: Government
Printing Office, 1975).

INDIVIDUAL VERSUS FAMILY DECISIONS

Microeconomic theory has traditionally been highly individualistic. "The consumer" maximizes his or her utility from consumption. "The worker" maximizes his or her utility from work, consumption, and leisure.

Most adults, however, are members of families; and theorists have recently begun to explore the implications of treating the household as the decision-making unit. The approach has proven fruitful and has produced a rapidly growing stream of research often referred to as "the new home economics."

There are several features of this approach. First, the household is viewed as deciding simultaneously on purchase of goods from the market, use of the time available to family members, consumption patterns, and savings rates. These decisions are interrelated and none can be fully understood without the others. Moreover, decisions of different family members are interrelated. Even though each member sells labor time individually in the labor market, a wife's decisions about working are influenced by the husband's earnings, the availability of other family income, the number and age of children, and so on.

Second, the family does not purchase final consumption goods in the market. Consumption goods are produced within the household by combining purchased goods with the time of family members, and time and purchased goods are substitutable. This is most obvious in the case of do-it-yourself activities: you can buy a bunk bed for your children, or you can buy lumber and make it yourself at home. But the principle applies to a wide range of consumption activities. Cooking meals at home uses more family labor time than bringing in a meal from McDonald's or Kentucky Fried Chicken.

This has implications for the allocation of time by family members. Instead of a simple choice between work and leisure, there is a four-way allocation among: sale of labor time in the market; use of time for education and training which will raise earning power in future; use of time in home production of consumption goods; and leisure (which often means combining time with purchased goods to produce "recreation").

Finally, time allocations, consumption patterns, and other aspects of household behavior vary systematically over the life cycle. Investment of time in education and training occurs mainly in early life, when the future payoff period is longest. As the person shifts from learning to doing, and as hourly earnings rise with increasing age and experience, people tend to offer more time in the market to take advantage of the higher wage. This time is made available, not just through a reduction of leisure, but through a reduction of education time and of time devoted to household production. Theoretical speculation on this point has been confirmed by research findings. Ghez and Becker report that, for all employed white men, average hours worked per year rise rapidly to age 25, then less rapidly to a peak at about age 40, then fall gradually until about 60, and decline sharply after that point.[1] The age–hours curve differs somewhat by level of education, and for nonwhite as against white men, but retains the same general shape.

The household approach will prove useful in later sections in explaining changes in labor force participation rates and trends in working hours.

PARTICIPATION IN THE LABOR FORCE

Definition and Measurement

The percentage of a country's population, or of a subgroup in the population, that is in the labor force at a particular time is termed its *labor force participation rate,* usually shortened to *participation rate.* Measurement of the labor force involves complicated problems, which

---

[1] Gilbert R. Ghez and Gary S. Becker, *The Allocation of Time and Goods over the Life Cycle* (New York: National Bureau of Economic Research, 1975).

can only be suggested here.[2] In the United States, a complete enumeration is made every ten years in connection with the decennial census.[3] Between censuses the Bureau of the Census conducts a monthly survey of a small sample of households carefully selected to represent different sections of the country. On the basis of information obtained from these households, estimates are made of the total labor force, employment, and unemployment in the country as a whole. This *Monthly Report on the Labor Force* is the standard source for current labor force information, although it is not quite as accurate as a complete census count.

An individual is counted as being in the labor force if he is able to work and either has a job or is "actively seeking" work. This apparently simple definition leaves considerable room for doubt in many cases. What about a man who says he is able to work, but whom employers judge to be so incapable that they are unwilling to hire him? What about a man who is not "actively" seeking work because he believes that there are no jobs available in his area, but who would accept a job if offered? What about a coal miner in a depressed mining area who is willing to take a mining job but no other kind of work? Added to these logical problems is the fact that the census interviewer may see only one family member and has to take that person's word about the status of other people in the household. This leaves room for a good deal of misunderstanding and faulty reporting. Another problem is that millions of workers in the United States go into and out of the labor force quite frequently.

As a result of these and other difficulties, there is a considerable range of error in published reports on the size of the labor force. While we shall follow the convention of using a single labor force figure, it would be better to think in terms of a zone around the reported figure, which in a country as large as the United States may number several million people.

Participation Rates in the United States

What is the evidence on actual labor force participation in the United States? Table 1 shows participation rates for subgroups in the population in 1890, 1947, and 1975, with estimates for 1990.

---

[2] The reader interested in these problems and the efforts of statisticians to overcome them should consult Clarence D. Long, *Labor Force, Income and Employment* (New York: National Bureau of Economic Research, 1950); John D. Durand, *The Labor Force in the United States, 1890–1960* (New York: Social Science Research Council, 1948); and A. J. Jaffe and Charles D. Stewart, *Manpower Resources and Utilization: Principles of Working Force Analysis* (New York: John Wiley & Sons, Inc., 1951).

[3] The census is rightly regarded as one of the most accurate of statistical sources. A July 1953 issue of the *New York Herald Tribune*, however, reported that a Chicago census enumerator had added several thousand nonexistent names to his lists during the 1950 census and made up fictitious characteristics for these nonexistent people. When asked the reason for this, he replied, "I thought we had a quota to meet."

Table 1

Labor Force Participation Rates by Age and Sex, United States, 1890, 1947, 1975, and Projections for 1990

Sex and Age Group	1890	1947	1975	Projected 1990
Males				
Total	89.3	86.8	78.5	78.4
16–17 }	61.5*	52.2	49.0 }	55.4
18–19 }		80.5	73.0 }	
20–24	90.8	84.9	85.9	82.1
25–34 }	99.0	95.8	95.5	94.4
35–44 }		98.0	95.8	94.7
45–54 }	98.2	95.5	92.1	91.5
55–64 }		89.6	75.8	77.5
65+	74.1	47.8	21.7	19.3
Females				
Total	21.0	31.8	46.4	45.9
16–17 }	26.9*	29.5	40.2 }	47.0
18–19 }		52.3	58.3 }	
20–24	32.1	44.9	64.3	66.2
25–34 }	18.0	32.0	54.6	51.5
35–44 }		36.3	55.8	55.2
45–54 }	15.7	32.7	54.6	58.0
55–64 }		24.3	41.0	45.8
65+	10.7	8.1	8.3	8.3
Total, both sexes	56.1	58.9	61.8	61.5

* These rates cover all persons aged 14–19, while subsequent rates cover those 16–19 only. If we had a comparable 16-19 rate for 1890, it would presumably be considerably higher than that shown.
SOURCE: Data for 1890 are from Long, *Labor Force, Income and Employment,* Appendix A. Data for 1947 and 1975 and Bureau of Labor Statistics projections for 1990 are from *Employment and Training Report of the President* (Washington, D.C.: Government Printing Office, 1976).

Reading across the table, we see the marked changes which have occurred over the years. Among men, labor force participation in the youngest age groups has declined considerably because young people on the average now complete more years of education. The sharp decline in participation rates among older men suggests that retirements are now occurring at a considerably earlier age. The most striking feature of the table is the sharp increase in the proportion of women who are in the labor force. In 1890, only one-fifth of women aged sixteen and over were at work. Today the proportion is more than two-fifths, and in the age group twenty-five to fifty-four it is more than one-half.

Table 2

Shifts in Labor Force Composition, 1951–1975

	Percent of Labor Force in Each Group	
Sex and Age Group	1951	1975
Male		
16–19	3.8	5.4
20–24	6.4	8.6
25–64	55.2	44.8
65+	3.9	2.0
Female		
16–19	2.8	4.3
20–24	4.4	6.5
25–64	22.6	27.3
65+	0.9	1.1
Total male	69.2	60.9
Total female	30.8	39.1

SOURCE: *Employment and Training Report of the President* (Washington, D.C.: Government Printing Office, 1976).

These changes in participation rates, plus the population upsurge of 1945–65, have produced marked changes in the composition of the labor force (Table 2). Men aged twenty-five to sixty-four, once considered the core of the labor force, now form less than half the total and their percentage is still falling. Women, who as recently as 1951 were only about 30 percent of the labor force, now form about 40 percent. Young people sixteen to twenty-four also bulk proportionately larger—almost one-quarter of the total. True, a higher *proportion* of people in this age range now finish high school and go on to college. But the total *number* in this age group has increased so greatly because of the earlier "baby boom" that they provide many more workers as well as more students.

The considerations affecting decisions to work or not to work differ substantially for men and for women, for young people and older people. We shall look briefly at two interesting groups: married women and older workers. We shall also explore the disputed issue of how labor force participation responds to fluctuations in the demand for labor. The results reported come mainly from a major study at Princeton University by William G. Bowen and T. Aldrich Finegan.[4]

---

[4] William G. Bowen and T. Aldrich Finegan, *The Economics of Labor Force Participation* (Princeton: Princeton University Press, 1969). This study is based on data from between 78 and 100 metropolitan areas for each of the census years 1940, 1950, and 1960, which were subjected to both cross-section and time-series analysis.

Married Women

Married women compose a large and growing component of the labor force. In 1975 about 21 million married women were in the labor force, of whom three-quarters were full-time workers. To understand the reasons for the rapid increase in working wives, let us first examine *which* wives work and which do not. The most important characteristics appear to be:

1. *Color.* The participation rate for black wives, after adjusting for education and other personal characteristics, is about 7 percentage points higher than that for white wives. This may be related to the traditionally matriarchal structure of black families. It may be also that employer discrimination in the range of occupations sought by black women is less severe than it is for black men.

2. *Age of children.* Participation rates rise as child care responsibilities decrease. For wives with children under six, the participation rate is in the range of 15 to 20 percent. This rises to 35 percent for wives with children aged six to thirteen, and to about 55 percent when there are no children under fourteen in the home.

3. *Education.* This factor operates in the expected direction, and even more strongly than for men. Among wives with no children under six, those with four years of education or less have a participation rate of only 27 percent. But for those with seventeen years or more of education, the rate is 77 percent. Bowen and Finegan estimate that two-fifths of this difference is really a "wage effect." More education opens the door to higher occupations with greater earnings opportunities. The rest of the gap, they think, must be due to such things as the fact that women with very little education have difficulty finding and holding jobs, which discourages labor force participation; the fact that the jobs open to highly educated women are more varied and interesting, providing considerable psychic income as well as higher money income; and the fact that education itself may develop a strong "taste for work."

4. *Other family income,* which means primarily the husband's earnings. This effect is strong and in the expected direction. In families whose income apart from the wife's earnings is below $3,000, about 50 percent of the wives are in the labor force. This falls to 21 percent for families with income of $11,000–$15,000, and to 12 percent for families with $15,000–$25,000.

5. *Occupational level of husband.* One might expect that the "pure" effect of this factor, after adjustment for income level and other variables, would be for the wife's participation rate to fall as the husband's occupational status rises. To some extent this is true. Wives of sales and clerical workers, service workers, and factory operatives have adjusted participation rates in the 38–41 percent range. For wives of professional, technical, and managerial

---

The results for 1960, which we emphasize here, correspond in most cases to those for 1950; but 1940 shows different behavior on some points. Those interested in the wealth of detailed findings and the thorough discussion of statistical methods should consult the original source.

workers the range is 32–34 percent. Surprisingly, however, wives of laborers have a participation rate of only 32.5 percent. There is no obvious explanation for this, except possibly that laborers marry women with limited work capacity.

6. *Labor market variables.* Comparing different cities at the same point of time one finds, as expected, that wives' participation rate is higher where wage rates for women are relatively high and where the industry mix contains a high proportion of "women's jobs." On the other hand, the participation rate varies *inversely* with the supply of women in the community and with the wage level of domestic servants. To the extent that working wives must hire household help, higher wage rates for domestics increase the opportunity cost of working and thus discourage participation.

The rapid increase in working wives has been one of the most dramatic labor market developments of recent decades. Between 1947 and 1975 alone the participation rate for wives more than doubled, from 20 percent to 45 percent, and the trend is still upward. How can one explain this large change in such a short period?

Several developments have helped to raise the participation rate for married women. The general wage level has risen greatly since 1945, and women's wages have risen even faster than men's. This would naturally induce women to offer more time in the market and reduce the amount of time allocated to household production. This has been made possible by a rapid mechanization of household operations. Bowen and Finegan point out that prices of household appliances have risen much less rapidly than the wage level since 1945. Substitution of capital for labor time in household production is a rational response. There has also been a rapid growth of coin laundries, fast-food establishments, and other places selling goods which were formerly produced at home and took a good deal of women's time.

For women as for men there has been a marked increase in average years of education and, as we have seen, greater education makes for higher labor force participation. The clerical, sales, teaching, and other white-collar occupations in which women have traditionally been employed have been expanding faster than the blue-collar occupations traditionally regarded as "men's work." Perhaps partly because of rapid growth of demand for white-collar workers, employers have been willing increasingly to redesign jobs on a part-time basis, which makes them easier for married women to handle. Currently about one out of four employed women works part-time, and part-time work is especially prevalent among married women living with their husbands.[5]

---

[5] On this point, see Richard Morgenstern and William Hamovich, "Labor Supply of Married Women in Part-Time and Full-Time Occupations," *Industrial and Labor Relations Review* (October 1976), pp. 59–67.

The rapid decline of birth rates since the early sixties and the current preference for small families has also reduced household production and made more time available for market activities. In addition, there seems to have been a marked shift in preferences, an increase in women's "taste for work," associated partly with the women's liberation movement and campaigns to reduce sex discrimination in employment. The old convention that women vanish from the labor force after marriage has been replaced by expectations of a lifetime career, interrupted at most for a few years by child–rearing. This shows up in the rising enrollment of women in law, medicine, and other postgraduate programs which imply a long career commitment.

Older People

While labor force participation declines from fifty-five onward, there is an especially sharp break at age sixty-five. For men, the adjusted participation rate drops from 80 percent at age sixty-four to 44 percent at sixty-five. Why the sharp decline at this point?

Sixty-five is a conventional age for compulsory retirement from business concerns, universities, and government agencies. This convention, however, is strongly reinforced by the operation of the Social Security systems, under which a woman becomes eligible for full benefits at age sixty-two and a man at age sixty-five. Moreover, if one continues working beyond sixty-five, any earnings in excess of $3,000 a year lead to a reduction of one dollar in pension payments for each two dollars earned. This obviously discourages anything like full-time work. The penalty for work disappears at age seventy-two, however, and sure enough, labor force participation rates rise a bit at age seventy-three, indicating that some people are still healthy enough to hold a job.

The work penalty in the Social Security Act was inserted at the insistence of organized labor, to make sure that older people were forced out of employment. The idea that there are never enough jobs to go around, and that it is necessary to keep some people out of employment in order to create jobs for others, is deeply embedded in union thinking. This is true especially in industries experiencing a long-run decline in demand for labor, such as steel and automobiles, where the unions have tried to counter rising unemployment by forcing down the retirement age from sixty-five to sixty-two, sixty, or even lower.

At the same time paradoxically, the medical profession is working with considerable success to prolong the normal life span. Thus the period during which a person is healthy and capable of work, but is not allowed to work under existing rules of the game, is steadily lengthening. This poses a serious question of social policy.

The Impact of Unemployment

The issue of unemployment, which cuts across all groups in the labor force, has been left to the end because it is important and because economists have been arguing about it since the 1930s. Some have argued that a rise in unemployment will increase labor force participation by wives and young people, who are forced to go to work to support the family when the husband is unemployed—the "additional worker" hypothesis. On the other side it is argued that, as unemployment rises and the chances of getting a job diminish, many workers will give up and leave the labor force—the "discouraged worker" hypothesis. An individual might respond in either of these ways; but the question is which predominates for the labor force as a whole.

Bowen and Finegan marshal convincing evidence that the discouraged worker effect predominates. The relation of unemployment to labor force participation is negative and significant for every subgroup studied. The effect is particularly strong for married women (where a 1 percent increase in unemployment [6] is associated with somewhat more than a 1 percent decrease in labor force participation), for men sixty-five and over (where the decrease is 1.6 percent), and for male teenagers (where the decrease is 1.9 percent). These groups, whose attachment to the labor force is looser than that of prime-age males, are precisely the groups which one would expect to be most responsive to variations in employment opportunities.

An important implication of these findings is that, in periods of less than full employment, there is a substantial amount of "hidden unemployment" in the economy. Many more people would look for work if the demand for labor were higher. The amount of "labor slack" in the economy is thus larger than the unemployment figures indicate. Bowen and Finegan estimate that, in the census week of 1960, hidden unemployment was about 1.3 million persons, of whom more than half were women.

The opposite of hidden unemployment may be termed "induced participation." When the demand for labor is unusually high, jobs come seeking people. Many people who would not normally seek work will yield to the blandishments of the recruiter when he appears, literally or figuratively, on their doorstep. Bowen and Finegan estimate that the additional workers drawn into the labor force between 1963 and 1967 by the high demand associated with the Vietnam War totaled 1.9 million, of whom again more

---

[6] There is a possibility of confusion here. If the national unemployment rate rises from 4 percent to 5 percent, we sometimes call this loosely "a 1 percent increase"; but it is of course a 25 percent increase. In the Bowen–Finegan study, a 1 percent increase means that the unemployment rate rises from, say, 4 percent to 4.04 percent.

than a million were women. To ignore these expansion joints in the labor
force can lead to serious miscalculations in macroeconomic policy.

What determines how many hours a person will want to work per
week or per year? Among the many influences at work, we single out two
for special examination: the effect of the hourly wage rate, and the effect
of other income available to the family. We shall assume that the decision
is an individual one and involves only allocation of time between work
and leisure. This is oversimplified because it ignores the fact that work
decisions are usually made in a household framework. But the simple
model nevertheless gives useful predictions.

Wage Rates and the Supply of Hours

As usual, precise reasoning forces us to assume a higher degree of
introspection and rationality than most workers probably achieve. We
assume also throughout this section that there are no institutional constraints on working hours and that workers have full freedom of choice.

Decisions about working hours are usually analyzed by constructing a
preference map relating income and leisure. An indifference curve on this
map, such as I_1 in Figure 2–2, shows different combinations of income and
leisure that would be equally acceptable to the worker. Put differently, it
shows how much leisure the person is prepared to sacrifice for additional
income of x dollars per week. This is the only precise sense in which one
can speak of "desire for income." Naturally, everyone "desires" income if
it can be had for nothing. The strength of this desire can be tested only by
asking how much leisure the worker is prepared to give up in return. The
answer will differ at different *points* on the indifference curve. If the person is already working fifty hours a week, it will doubtless take more income to induce him to put in an extra hour than would be the case if he
were working thirty hours a week. We show this by drawing the indifference curve concave upward.

Higher indifference curves, as usual, represent successively higher
levels of satisfaction. I_2 in Figure 2–2 is preferable to I_1. Why? Because a
worker moving up from, say point A toward I_2 can have as much income
as before and more leisure (point C), or as much leisure as before and
more income (point B), or some intermediate combination yielding more
of both income and leisure. By the same reasoning, I_3 is preferable to I_2
and so on.

Knowing a worker's preference map does not tell us how many hours
he will actually work. To discover this we must also know the hourly wage
rate for his job. Suppose that this is $5 an hour. Then if he worked the
physically feasible maximum, say one hundred hours per week, he could
earn $500 (point A in Figure 2–3). If he does not work at all, he will

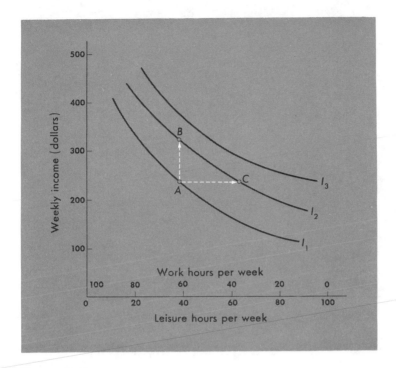

Figure 2–2

Preference for Income Versus Leisure

earn nothing (point *B* in Figure 2–3); and he can do anything in between. The line *AB* indicates his *budget constraint*. The market permits him to choose any point on *AB*—or, for that matter, any point *below AB*. But he will not choose a point below *AB,* because this would mean working for less than the market wage. Nor can he choose any point *above AB,* because the market wage for his job is not high enough.

Now what point will he actually choose? He wants to achieve maximum satisfaction, that is, to reach the highest indifference curve that his budget constraint permits. In Figure 2–3, this is I_2. The point *C,* at which *AB* just touches I_2, is the point of maximum satisfaction.

The fact that this is the best he can do can be demonstrated in either of two ways. First, note that at the point of tangency, *C,* the *slopes* of *AB* and I_2 are equal. These slopes have a special significance. The slope of I_2 at any point indicates how much income the worker is willing to sacrifice in order to get a little more leisure. It measures his (subjective) *marginal rate of substitution* between income and leisure. The slope of *AB,* on the other hand, is an objective fact given by the market. It indicates the rate

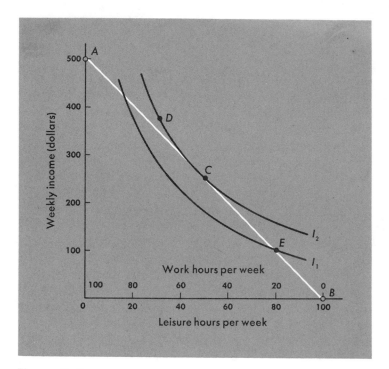

Figure 2–3

The Choice of a Workweek

at which he can actually substitute income for leisure. When the two slopes are equal, the subjective marginal rate of substitution exactly equals the objective or feasible rate. This defines a position of maximum satisfaction.

Second, consider what will happen if the worker tries to move away from point C. Any other point on I_2, such as point D, would yield the same level of satisfaction. But point D is unattainable because it lies above his budget constraint. Indeed, all points on I_2 other than C are unattainable. The worker is free to move up or down AB, say to a point such as E. But E lies on a lower indifference curve, indicating less satisfaction, so he will not want to do this. Since any feasible move away from C will reduce his satisfaction, this point indicates his optimum workweek.

How will the worker respond to a *change* in the market wage? Suppose his wage rate rises from $5 an hour to $6 an hour. We show this in Figure 2–4 by drawing a new budget constraint, A_1B. If he works the maximum possible hours, he can now earn $600 a week instead of $500. The new budget line lies above the old one. This enables him to reach a

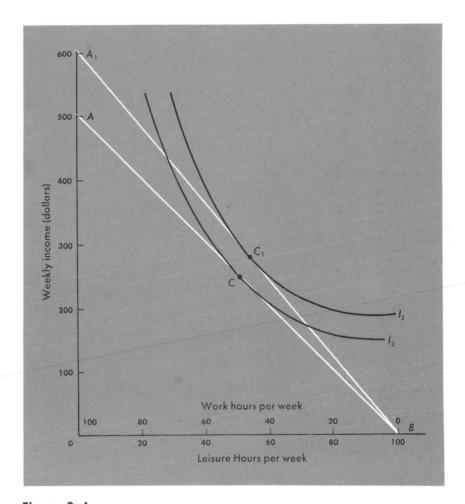

Figure 2–4

The Effect of a Wage Change on Hours

new and higher indifference curve, I_3. His point of maximum satisfaction is now C_1, where A_1B is tangent to I_3.

Note that at C_1, he is working *fewer* hours than before. He has more leisure as well as more income. But this result depends on the shape of I_3. A little pencil experimentation will convince you that it would be possible to draw I_3 so that it was tangent to A_1B somewhere to the *left* of C. One would then conclude that the worker had responded to the wage increase by working *more* hours than before.

We cannot be sure on purely logical grounds whether a wage increase will incline a worker to work more or fewer hours. The reason is that the wage increase has two effects that pull in opposite directions. It means, first, that the price of leisure has risen. To take an hour off from work now costs the worker $6 rather than $5. Following the principle that one usually buys less of a good when its price has risen relative to other goods, one might expect the worker to "buy" less leisure, that is, to work longer hours. This is called the *substitution effect*.

On the other hand, the wage increase makes the worker better off than before. He can afford to buy more of everything, *including* leisure. This *income effect* will incline him to work less and enjoy more leisure as he becomes more affluent.

If the substitution effect predominates, the worker will work more hours than before. But if the income effect predominates, he will work fewer hours. In drawing Figure 2–4 as we did, we *assumed* that the income effect predominates and that a shortening of hours is the normal response to rising wages.

Some statistical evidence in support of this view will be cited in a moment. In addition, an interesting logical argument has been developed by Gary Becker.[7] He argues that we do not actually consume goods directly. Rather, we buy goods that, *when combined with time,* yield consumer satisfaction. Services such as education, travel, spectator sports, outdoor recreation, TV viewing all require substantial amounts of time. Goods and leisure, in short, are *complementary* inputs into consumption. We cannot actually raise our standard of living without having more leisure. According to this view it is natural that, as rising wage rates permit higher levels of consumption, people should decide to work less.

Other Income and the Supply of Hours

In Figures 2–2, 2–3, and 2–4 we assumed that all family income came from the earnings of the person whose decisions we were examining. But often this is not the case. One or more other family members may be employed. The family may have income from rents, interest, and dividends. A low-income family may be receiving welfare or other transfer payments from government. It is thus important to examine how income available from other sources will affect individual decisions about work.

Suppose in the first instance that Mr. G's family, graphed in Figure 2–5, has no source of income other than his earnings. He can get a job at an hourly wage shown by the slope of the line *AB*. The highest indiffer-

---

[7] Gary Becker, "A Theory of the Allocation of Time," *Economic Journal* (September 1965), pp. 493–517. See also Staffan B. Linder, *The Harried Leisure Class* (New York: Columbia University Press, 1970).

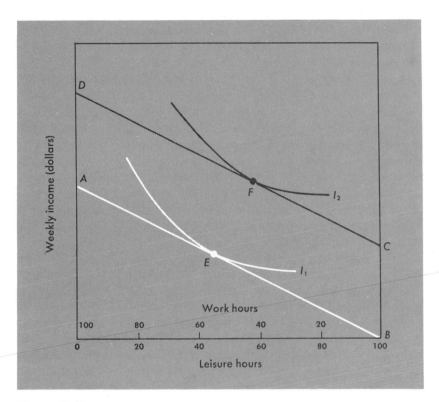

Figure 2–5

The Effect of Other Income on Hours

ence curve he can reach is I_1, and he will choose to work the number of hours corresponding to point E.

But now suppose that the family has income of BC dollars from some other source. Mr. G's family have this much income even if he does nothing; but of course it will have still more if he chooses to work. His budget constraint is shifted upward from AB to CD. Note that the two lines are parallel. The reason is that their slope depends on the wage rate, and the wage rate has not changed.

The G family, being richer, can now reach the higher indifference curve I_2. By our usual reasoning, Mr. G will choose the point at which his budget constraint is tangent to this curve, that is, point F. Note that he is now working fewer hours than he was before. This result is not logically inevitable, but it is plausible. All it says is that leisure is a "normal good," which yields satisfaction, and will therefore have a positive income elasticity of demand. Or, following Becker's reasoning, one could reason that a higher level of consumption *implies* greater use of time at home for this purpose. At point *F*, the family has higher cash income than at point *E*, and can buy more market goods; and it also has more time at home to convert these goods to consumption use.

We could repeat this experiment by giving the *G* family larger and larger amounts of "other income," enabling it to reach still higher indifference curves I_3, I_4, and so on. In this way we could trace out a locus of intersection points, which would run upward to the northeast, with work hours declining steadily with increasing affluence.

These ideas are helpful in explaining such things as the apparent negative relation between husband's income and wife's hours of work. Wives of high-income husbands often choose to work part-time rather than full-time. It also explains why a poor family, if given a guarantee of a minimum income without working, would be expected to offer fewer hours of labor in the market. Some experimental evidence on this point is reported in Chapter 13.

Evidence on the Supply of Hours

The ideas in the last two sections are useful also in interpreting the historical record. In the United States over the past century, rising wage rates and income levels have been accompanied by a marked decline in hours of work.

The trend of weekly hours in manufacturing since 1890 is shown in Figure 2–6. Hours fell gradually until 1929, then more sharply during the Great Depression. The forty-hour workweek, in lieu of the previous forty-eight-hour norm, was promulgated in the National Recovery Administration codes of 1933 and 1934 and later in the Fair Labor Standards Act of 1938. The Fair Labor Standards Act does not prohibit work beyond forty hours, but the provision that such work must be compensated at 150 percent of the normal rate gives employers a strong incentive to avoid it. Hours averaged considerably less than forty during the thirties because of depressed demand, rose well above forty during World War II under inflationary demand conditions, then settled back to an almost constant level since 1945. While there have been small cyclical variations around the forty-hour norm, the norm itself has not changed.

Hours worked *per year,* however, have continued to decline through the spread of paid vacations and holidays. Most workers now receive paid vacations of one to four weeks, and the length of service needed to qualify for these benefits has been steadily reduced. In addition, seven or eight holidays are usually paid for, and this list also tends to grow longer over the years.

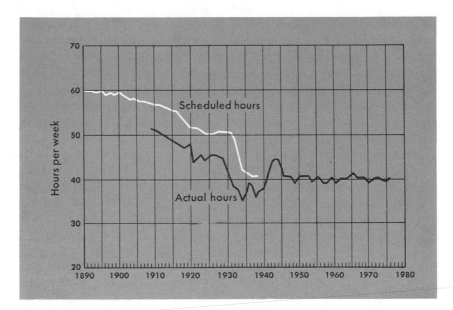

Figure 2–6

Average Weekly Hours in Manufacturing
1890–1976

The trend has been similar in other high-income economies. In Canada, for example, average weekly hours in manufacturing fell from sixty-four in 1870 to fifty-three in 1910, to forty-four in 1945, and to about forty at the present time. In all countries, workers' increasing productive power has been translated into greater leisure as well as higher incomes.

One cannot be sure that hours actually worked at any time correspond precisely with what workers would prefer. It seems certain, however, that trends in workers' preferences and in actual hours have been similar. It is unlikely that many workers today would prefer the fifty-hour week of 1900; or alternatively, that most workers would prefer only twenty-five hours, with the reduction of weekly income that this would necessarily entail. If either statement were true, one would expect more public outcry over the hours issue than there has been in recent years.

There have also been cross-section studies designed to test the wage–hours relationship for different groups of workers at the same point in time. T. A. Finegan analyzed average wage level and average hours worked by census occupational groups in 1940 and 1950. He concludes that "in general, the findings of this study support the orthodox construct of a negatively inclined supply curve of labor. When other things are held constant, adult males with higher hourly earnings work fewer hours per week." [8] Gordon C. Winston reached similar results from an international comparison of thirty-one countries. He calculated a labor effort index for each country by combining weekly hours of work and labor force participation rates and analyzed the relation of this to per capita national income and the level of manufacturing wages in each country. The relation, as expected, was negative and statistically significant. It appeared that a 10 percent increase in income was associated typically with about a 1 percent decrease in work effort. [9]

What Scope for Preference?

Some may think that we have overstated the role of individual preferences in determining working hours. Given the fixity of employers' operating schedules, union contracts, and wage–hour legislation, does the individual have much scope to adjust hours to his own preference system?

There are two broad answers to this question. Even at a particular time, there is more scope for variation of hours than might appear at first glance. And over the course of time, employer and union policies are responsive to worker preferences.

Elements of flexibility include, first, the fact that the labor force includes self-employed business and professional men with considerable freedom to adjust hours and income. Second, while business concerns usually have a scheduled workweek, the schedule differs considerably among establishments and industries. Some are on thirty-hour schedules, while others continue to work forty-eight hours or more. Thus people who prefer shorter hours can to some extent shift toward shorter-hour firms.

Third, there is wide and growing scope for part-time work by students, housewives, or people who just want to avoid the "rat race." As of 1974, one out of six nonagricultural employees worked less than 35 hours a week, compared with one out of eight in 1964. Part-time work is particularly common among women, one-quarter of whom are on part-time schedules.

Fourth, there is the possibility of overtime work. In May 1974, about 4.5 million people were working beyond their normal weekly hours. When

---

[8] T. A. Finegan, "Hours of Work in the United States: A Cross-Sectional Analysis," *Journal of Political Economy* (October 1962), pp. 452–70. Among the "other things" that must be held constant are sex, color, education (positively related with hours of work), and marital status (increased family responsibilities also being associated with longer hours).

[9] Gordon C. Winston, "An International Comparison of Income and Hours of Work," *Review of Economics and Statistics* (February 1966), pp. 28–39. See also M. S. Feldstein, "Estimating the Supply Curve of Working Hours," *Oxford Economic Papers* (March 1968), pp. 74–80.

business activity is high, many employers find it cheaper to pay overtime rates to some of their present employees than to bear the cost of recruiting and training new workers. Research studies show that those most eager to put in for overtime are workers with large families and high income needs. Men are about three times as likely to work overtime as are women.

Fifth, it is possible to hold two jobs. In 1975 about 3 million men and 1 million women were "moonlighting." Economic motivation is strongly evident here. One study found that a 10 percent increase in the moonlighting wage produced an increase of about 26 percent in the supply of hours—7 percent from people who decided to take a second job, and 17 percent from an increase in average hours worked by moonlighters.[10] Other studies have shown that moonlighting increases with size of family, from 5.4 percent of married men without children to 10.3 percent with five or more children. It decreases as earnings on the primary job rise, from 12.5 percent for married men earning less than $60 a week to 5.5 percent for married men earning more than $200 a week. Moonlighting is especially prevalent among teachers, policemen, firemen, farmers, and service workers.[11]

Finally, it seems clear that many people reduce their *annual* working hours by taking time off during the year. They follow the advice of an airline television commercial to "sneak a week" now and then. T. A. Finegan found that all employed males in a recent census year averaged about forty-three weeks of work during the year.[12] They were unemployed, on the average, for two weeks and spent the remaining seven weeks in "nonparticipation." There was also much variation among individuals in the amount of time spent at work. Only about one-third of this variance was attributable to differences in unemployment, the remainder being associated with personal characteristics. Thus married men averaged more weeks of work per year than single men. Additional years of schooling, increasing age (up to age forty), and urban rather than rural residence were also associated with more weeks of work per year.

Over the course of time, changes in workers' views about the desirable workweek and workyear influence union and management policies. In the case of the union, this influence is exerted through political channels. Union officials are elected leaders who need the support of their members to remain in office. When the bulk of the membership becomes convinced, say, that a thirty-five-hour week is preferable to a forty-hour week, this will soon become official union policy.

[10] Robert Shisko and Bernard Rostker, "The Economics of Multiple Job-Holding," *American Economic Review* (June 1976), pp. 298–308.

[11] For a more detailed analysis see Harvey R. Hamel, "Moonlighting—An Economic Phenomenon," *Monthly Labor Review* (October 1967), pp. 17–22.

[12] T. A. Finegan, "The Work Experience of Men in the Labor Force: An Occupational Study," *Labor and Industrial Relations Review* (January 1964), pp. 238–56.

As regards employers, workers' preferences operate through the labor market. An employer competing for labor offers a "package" of wages, hours, and conditions that is attractive enough to recruit the number and quality of workers he wants. The hours component of the package will conform to prevailing practice—say, a forty-hour week, six paid holidays, and two weeks' paid vacation for those with five years of service. Suppose now that workers' preferences shift, so that many want a thirty-five-hour week or four weeks' vacation. Some employers incorporate these new specifications in their package, but some do not. Those who do not will find—wage rates and other components remaining equal—that they are attracting fewer workers and have a higher quit rate. There will be pressure on them to come into line, particularly during periods of high employment when labor is scarce. The older concept of a "normal" work schedule will be eroded gradually by the force of competition for labor.

The prospect for the future is a continuing gradual decline in hours worked per year; but just how this will occur is less certain. There is some indication that workers prefer more time off in solid blocks rather than through shaving small amounts off the working day. An increase in length of vacations is naturally popular. The idea of an occasional "sabbatical" of several months for long-service workers, introduced some time ago in the steel industry, may grow in popularity. The three-day weekend is obviously attractive, as witness the legislative provision that standard national holidays *must* fall on a Monday. Some companies have experimented with a regular four-day week, without necessarily reducing weekly hours of work; and workers have been willing to work as much as ten hours a day to achieve the longer weekend.

It is important that worker preferences be allowed to operate as freely as possible, in this area as in others. There is some tendency for union officials to push for premature reduction of hours as a supposed "solution" for unemployment. But this is a defeatist approach to the problem. The constructive approach, in industries such as steel and automobiles where labor demand is declining, is to speed the movement of workers out of the industry through retraining and placement programs. General unemployment should be countered by monetary–fiscal policy rather than by revising the definition of full employment downward through reduction of hours.

DISCUSSION QUESTIONS

1. "As a country's per capita income rises, one might expect a gradual decline in the labor force participation rate. In the United States, however, the overall participation rate is somewhat higher today than it was in 1890, despite much higher income levels." Discuss.

2. Draw an aggregate labor supply curve for the United States as of the current month. Explain why you drew the curve as you did.

3. How can one account for the rapid increase in women's labor force participation rate in recent decades?

4. What would be the main consequences of reducing the standard workweek in manufacturing from forty hours to thirty hours
    (a) during a period of heavy unemployment?
    (b) at a time of full employment?

5. "In a full-employment economy, the worker's freedom to change jobs protects him against excessive hours just as it protects him against substandard wages. Government intervention to establish a standard workweek is likely to be harmful rather than beneficial." Discuss.

READING SUGGESTIONS

On labor force participation, in addition to the Bowen–Finegan study, see CLARENCE D. LONG, *The Labor Force Under Changing Income and Employment,* Princeton: Princeton University Press, 1958. Also see GLEN G. CAIN, *Married Women in the Labor Force*, Chicago: The University of Chicago Press, 1966; and "Unemployment and the Labor-Force Participation of Secondary Workers," *Industrial and Labor Relations Review*, January 1967, pp. 275–97. Current labor force data appear each year in the *Employment and Training Report of the President,* issued by the U.S. Department of Labor.

On hours of work, see the Industrial Relations Research Association symposium volume edited by CLYDE E. DANKERT, FLOYD C. MANN, and HERBERT R. NORTHRUP, *Hours of Work*, New York: Harper & Row, Publishers, 1965.

3

The Labor Force: Quality

Two centuries ago Adam Smith observed that the capital stock of a nation consists partly in

> the acquired and useful abilities of all the inhabitants or members of the society. The acquisition of such talents, by the maintenance of the acquirer during his education, study, or apprenticeship, always costing a real expence, which is a capital fixed and realized, as it were, in his person. Those talents, as they make a part of his fortune, so do they likewise of that of the society to which he belongs. The improved dexterity of a workman may be considered in the same light as a machine or instrument of trade which facilitates and abridges labour, and which, though it costs a certain expence, repays that expence with a profit.[1]

Smith's insight was forgotten by the economists who followed him and the capital concept was narrowed to nonhuman instruments of production. Only in the 1950s did the concept of human capital reappear as an apparently fresh discovery. Its rediscovery was associated with growing interest in the long-term growth of national output. Economic growth, a central concern of the classical economists, dropped almost completely out of the conventional literature from roughly 1840 to 1940, surviving only in the underworld of Marxian economics. But beginning in the 1940s a number of scholars, led by Simon Kuznets, attempted careful measurement of the growth of national output in the Western industrial countries since about 1850. The new measures were intriguing. They challenged both economic theorists and statisticians to *explain* why the growth rate has varied from country to country and time to time.

One obvious source of growth is an increase in inputs. The labor force is growing, mainly because of population growth. The stock of physi-

---

[1] Adam Smith, *The Wealth of Nations,* 1776 Book II, Chap. 1.

cal capital is also rising, since construction of new capital goods typically exceeds the wearing out of old ones. But the striking fact is that output rises a good deal faster than inputs. An early study by John Kendrick found that, in the United States from 1919 to 1957, labor and capital inputs rose at an average annual rate of 1.1 percent per year. Gross national product, however, rose at a rate of 3.2 percent a year. The input increase thus accounts for only about one-third of the output increase; and similar results have been reported for other economies.

The gap between the growth rates of inputs and output is often termed *the residual*. This label, of course, does not explain anything—it is simply, as Moses Abramovitz has noted, "a measure of our ignorance." It has also been termed a measure of *total factor productivity*. It indicates that, for one reason or another, the productivity of the factors of production has increased substantially over time.

Subsequent research has turned up a variety of factors that may help to explain the residual. The one which is relevant here is that, over the decades, the factors of production increase in *quality* as well as *quantity*. In the case of physical capital, invention leads not just to more machines but to different and better machines. As old equipment wears out, it is replaced by equipment with greater productive capacity. The effort to take account of this in growth theory has led to the concept of *vintage capital*. Each part of the nation's capital stock is dated by its year of origin, and it is estimated that each year's capital is, say, 3 percent more productive than that of the year before. When you sum up the nation's capital stock year by year on this basis, you get a faster rate of increase than appears from crude measures with no quality adjustment.

Labor as well as capital has improved over time in the American economy. There has been an increase in the nation's stock of *human capital*, resulting from a combination of formal education, on-the-job training, and work experience. Americans today have, on the average, more than twice as many years of education as their grandparents. Their skills have also been substantially upgraded. About 45 percent of the labor force is now employed in professional, technical, managerial, and clerical occupations, compared with 25 percent in 1930. At the lower end of the ladder, the percentage of farmers, farm laborers, and other laborers has fallen from 33 percent in 1930 to about 8 percent today.

MEASURING LABOR QUALITY

Can we measure this kind of improvement in labor force quality? Efforts at measurement have taken two main forms. One starts from changes in the amount of *education and training* embodied in the labor force, the other from changes in its *occupational composition*.

No one has ever seen a unit of human capital, so there is no way of measuring it directly. But if we assume that education and training are worth what they cost, we can use expenditures on them to arrive at an indirect estimate of the human capital stock. The most ambitious study of this kind is by John W. Kendrick.[2] He estimates that as of 1969 the nation's human capital stock was almost four-fifths as large as its stock of tangible physical capital. Moreover, over the forty years 1929–69, human capital grew considerably faster than physical capital. In 1929, gross investment in tangible physical capital—structures, equipment and inventories—was 23.1 percent of GNP. In 1969, this figure was virtually unchanged at 22.9 percent. Meanwhile, however, gross investment in intangible human capital had risen from 12.1 percent of GNP in 1929 to 19.4 percent in 1969.

To put the same arithmetic differently: over the period 1929–69, the gross stock of physical capital rose at 2.4 percent per year. The gross stock of intangible human capital, however, rose at 3.6 percent per year. By 1969 the gross stock of intangible human capital was estimated at $3,890 billion, compared with a value of $5,010 billion for the physical capital stock. While such estimates cannot be precise, they are probably of the right order of magnitude. They suggest that to ignore human capital is greatly to underestimate the amount of investment going on in the American economy. Moreover, human capital is growing steadily more important relative to physical capital and, if past trends continue, will soon exceed it in absolute size.

The second approach to measuring labor force quality starts from the occupational composition of employment. This has obviously improved over time. The percentage of farmers and laborers is much lower today than it was in 1900. The percentage of professional people, technical workers, managers, and executives is much higher. The increase in the average skill level of the labor force can be measured, provided we are willing to assume that the wage rate for each job indicates the productive contribution of workers on that job.

We then proceed as follows: instead of totaling man-hours of every type indiscriminately, we first subdivide them into occupational groups— laborers, auto workers, plumbers, schoolteachers, typists, lawyers, and so on. The subdivision can be as fine as the statistics permit. We then "weight" the number of man-hours in each group by a factor based on the

---

[2] John W. Kendrick, *The Formation and Stocks of Total Capital* (New York: National Bureau of Economic Research, 1976). Kendrick's estimates of intangible human investment, in addition to education and training costs, include half of medical and health expenditures (the other half being treated as maintenance rather than investment) plus certain costs associated with labor mobility. Education and training costs, however, form about 80 percent of the total.

relative wage rate for the group. Suppose we take the lowest-paid group in the economy (farm laborers or whatever) as our base. Each man-hour of that kind of labor has a weight of 1. Then each hour of auto assembly-line labor might get a weight of 3, high school teachers 4, electricians 5, college teachers 7, lawyers 10—depending on what the wage statistics show. Finally, we add up these "adjusted" man-hours for all occupations to get a figure for total labor supply.

Having done this for 1977, we redo it for 1978, 1979, and so on into the future. What shall we find? If the number of people in the more highly skilled groups, which receive heaviest weight in this procedure, is rising faster than the number of low-skilled occupations, then our total of "adjusted" man-hours will rise faster than a total of "crude" or "unadjusted" man-hours. The growing gap between the two totals over any period of years tells us how rapidly the average skill level has been rising.

There is clear evidence that the average skill level of the American labor force has risen substantially over time. John Kendrick found that over the period 1909–57 total man-hours worked in the U.S. private economy increased by 31 percent. When man-hours were weighted by skill level as described above, however, this "adjusted" total rose 56 percent over the same period—almost double the rate of increase in the crude total.[3]

PRIVATE RETURNS TO EDUCATION

The importance of human capital as a determinant of productivity raises problems for individuals and for society. Can we estimate how much additional education is worth to the individual who receives it, in terms of extra earnings over his or her working life? From a broader standpoint, how does the return to *society* from additional education differ from the return to the individual? Can we estimate the social rate of return to different levels of education? And does this provide any indication of whether U.S. governments have been investing too much or too little in education?

There is abundant evidence that earnings rise with educational level. Figure 3–1 shows an education–earnings profile for white, nonfarm, male workers in the United States, in 1959. A chart for a recent year would doubtless look quite similar, though the dollar amounts on the vertical axis would be larger. Indeed, charts for countries as diverse as

---

[3] John W. Kendrick, *Productivity Trends in the United States* (New York: National Bureau of Economic Research, 1961). For another set of estimates by somewhat different methods, see Edward F. Denison, *The Sources of Economic Growth in the United States and the Alternatives Before Us* (New York: Committee for Economic Development, 1962).

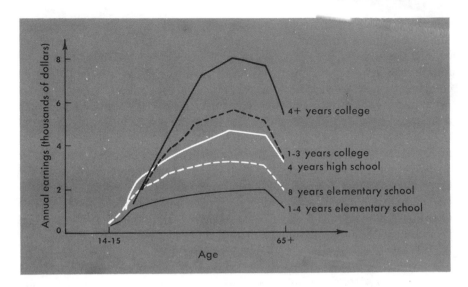

Figure 3–1

Years of Education, Age, and Earnings

SOURCE: Adapted from Mark Blaug, *An Introduction to the Economics of Education* (London: The Penguin Press Ltd., 1970), p. 23.

Britain, Mexico, and India show this same characteristic shape. Several principles seem to hold good for a wide range of countries:

1. Earnings normally rise with age until somewhere beyond the age of 40, then level off, and eventually decline.
2. The higher the educational level, the higher (usually) is the starting salary and the steeper the rise of earnings during the early years of working life.
3. The higher the educational level, the later the year at which maximum earnings are reached and the higher the retirement income.

Characteristics 2 and 3 account for the higher lifetime earnings of the more educated.

The fact that more education is *associated* with higher earnings, of course, is not conclusive evidence that the education *causes* the higher earnings. Part of the higher earnings of the more educated may be due to greater mental ability, and part may be due to superior home background and other advantages. Thus from the *gross* increase in earnings associated with increased years of schooling one should deduct the amount attributable to these other factors in order to estimate the *net* effect of education alone. The net increase is the difference between the earnings of, say, a college graduate and a high school graduate who are identical in measured ability and in all other relevant characteristics.

There have been many efforts to estimate the difference between gross and net returns, and we shall have more to say about this in Chapter 12. Meanwhile, we shall simply assume that the net return to education can be estimated; and whenever we speak of "the return to education" in this chapter, it is net return that we have in mind.

Education, of course, involves costs as well as benefits. By "buying" an additional year of education, you can assure yourself of higher earnings year after year until retirement. On this basis, you can calculate the rate of return on your educational investment.

Consider, for example, the return on a four-year college education. On one side, we total up all costs incurred during the four years. The largest cost item, often overlooked, is the opportunity cost of the student's time—how much he could have earned during the four years if he had *not* gone on to college. To this must be added tuition, fees, books, and incidental expenses. Since one has to live in either case, living costs should *not* be included, except to the extent that they are higher at college than they would have been at work. Suppose that the total cost of the four years of college comes to $30,000.

How much is this education worth? Suppose that college graduates earn, on the average, $3,000 per year more than high school graduates over a working life of, say, forty years. It might seem that one could simply multiply $3,000 by 40 and conclude that the value of the college degree is $120,000. But this would be wrong. Why? Because these are *future earnings*, whose actual receipt is from one to forty years away; and because a dollar a year from now is not worth as much as a dollar today. The psychological reason is that future income shrinks in people's minds, and the farther away it is, the smaller it appears. There is also an objective reason. If the market rate of interest is 5 percent, and if I put about $95 in a savings bank today, this will grow to $100 a year from now. Thus $100 to be received a year from now is worth only about $95 today. To be precise, it is worth $100/1.05 = $95.23. The *present value* of an income due one year hence is obtained by *discounting that income by the rate of interest.*

Income due two years from now must be discounted more heavily, since it is farther away. And we apply the same principle. If the rate of interest is 5 percent, $100 put out at interest today will in two years be worth $100 \times (1.05)^2$. To get the present value of income two years hence, we throw this into reverse. The $100 due two years from now is worth today $100/(1.05)^2 = 90.70.

Now back to our college graduate. His training yields him a *stream of future income* over a forty-year period. We want to find out the present value (PV) of this income stream. Let us call the market rate of interest i. Then, applying the above reasoning,

$$PV = \frac{3,000}{(1+i)} + \frac{3,000}{(1+i)^2} + \frac{3,000}{(1+i)^3} + \ldots + \frac{3,000}{(1+i)^{40}}$$

$$= \sum_{n=1}^{40} \frac{3,000}{(1+i)^n}$$

Now what rate of return is the graduate earning on his educational investment of \$30,000? This is the same as asking: at what rate of interest will the present value of the future income stream just equal its cost?

The rate of return on an investment is the rate of interest at which the present value of the income stream yielded by the investment is equal to its cost. It must satisfy the condition that the cost of education (C) equals the present value of education (PV).

Call the rate of return in this case r. Then, applying our rule, r must satisfy the condition that:

$$C = PV = \$30,000 = \frac{3,000}{(1+r)} + \frac{3,000}{(1+r)^2} + \frac{3,000}{(1+r)^3} + \ldots + \frac{3,000}{(1+r)^{40}}$$

$$= \sum_{n=1}^{40} \frac{3,000}{(1+r)^n}$$

Solving for the value of r, which can be done with a compound interest table, we find that this educational investment yields a bit under 10 percent per year.[4] So, if you can borrow money at 5 percent to acquire an education that yields 10 percent, you are making a profit. More generally, additional years of education are profitable so long as the rate of return exceeds the market rate of interest.

Before rushing out to get a loan, however, you may want to consider two points. First, what the statistics usually show is the *average* rate of return to everyone who has achieved a certain educational level. But there is a great deal of variation around the average. Some people will earn 20 percent on their college education, while others will earn nothing. So, if you are averse to risk, the *uncertainty* of future earnings may cause you to set a lower value on them.

---

[4] This is usually called the *internal rate of return*. We should note, however, that its calculation depends on the assumption—reasonable in this case—that *each item in the future income stream is positive*. If one or more of these items is negative, it may not be possible to calculate a unique, positive, internal rate of return. We simplified the illustration also by assuming that the earnings premium attributable to education was the same in each future year. This is not at all necessary. We could have varied the amounts in the numerator, as Figure 3–1 suggests they actually do vary in practice.

Second, to estimate the return to college education today, we need to know how much the class of 1980 will be earning (and how much those with only a high school diploma will be earning) in *future* years from 1980 to about 2020. But all we actually know is how much *past* college graduates, educated as long ago as 1930, are now earning compared with past high school graduates. With the supply of college graduates increasing rapidly, their earnings premium may be smaller in the year 2000 than it is today. So, if we base our estimates on today's relative earnings, we may be overestimating future returns to education.

The numbers used in our illustration were pulled out of the air. But there are numbers in the real world corresponding to these hypothetical numbers. The economic journals are full of studies reporting estimated returns to different levels of education at various points in time. Research to date suggests several conclusions:

1. The view that "education pays" is well founded. Private net rates of return to college education are usually estimated in the range of 10 to 15 percent. This is in line with returns to investment in physical capital goods.
2. The marginal private rate of return seems to decline with the level of education. College education yields a lower rate of return than high school. M.A. and Ph.D. training yield lower rates of return than the B.A., though returns to training in law and medicine remain high. Returns fall because the opportunity cost of the student's time rises substantially in college and graduate school, and also because he usually has to pay some part of education costs, which are free at primary and high school levels.
3. There appears to be a "diploma effect." The rate of return on the final year needed to get a college degree is higher than the return on the first three years.
4. There are considerable differences in rates of return by sex, color, and region (which will be discussed further in Chapter 8 in connection with discrimination in employment). The return to college education, for example, is higher in the South than in other regions, suggesting a relative shortage of college graduates.
5. There was a marked turnaround in the market for college graduates in the late sixties. The great increase in college enrollments during the sixties added to supply, while a leveling off of the uptrend in managerial and professional jobs meant a less than proportionate increase in demand. The result was a relative deterioration of starting salaries for B.A. graduates, which fell in real terms between 1969 and 1974. Freeman estimates that the private rate of return to B.A. training fell from 11.5 percent in 1969 to 8.5 percent in 1974.[5] This may be partly responsible for a marked decline between 1969 and 1974 in the percentage of each high school class going on to college.

It should be emphasized that rate-of-return calculations based only on earnings *understate* the private benefits from additional education. They

---

[5] Richard B. Freeman, "Overinvestment in College Training?" *Journal of Human Resources* (Summer 1975), pp. 287–311.

should be regarded as a lower limit rather than as an accurate estimate of total benefits. This is true for several reasons. First, the managerial, professional, and technical jobs populated mainly by college graduates provide larger fringe benefits as well as higher annual earnings. They are also more creative, secure, prestigious, and satisfying. Second, there is much evidence that more education increases a person's ability to cope with the various markets in which he is involved in adult life. More educated people have more job information and make better career choices, and they are also more efficient as consumers and as investors.[6] In addition to earning more dollars, they get greater value from each dollar. Finally, education is a *consumption good* as well as an investment good. It broadens mental horizons and increases enjoyment from leisure time in later life. Some students even get enjoyment from education while it is going on!

It is reasonable to assume that private rate-of-return calculations have a major effect on demand curves for education. This assumption yields testable predictions, which stand up well against the evidence. For example, since the size of the returns to higher education depends partly on ability, the more able students have a stronger incentive to go on and one would expect them to attend college in disproportionate numbers. This expectation is confirmed by the evidence. Among the least able one-quarter of graduating high school seniors, as indicated by test scores, only about 30 percent go on to college. But of the top one-quarter, 70 percent go on; and for the top 10 percent in order of ability, 90 percent enter college.[7]

One would expect also that college students would consider economic returns in choosing among fields of study. A recent study by Richard Freeman concludes that students have quite accurate information on the attractiveness of various fields, and also on opportunity costs and direct costs of education:

> Students appear to be well informed about economic opportunities in the market for college graduates. Subjectively, most consider the information available at the time of their career decision to be adequate for a sensible selection. Objectively, their evaluation of the economic characteristics of such well-known professions as medicine or law and of specialized doctorate fields is in accord with economic reality. The perceived position of careers with respect to starting salaries, growth of income over the life cycle, and changes in job opportunities are nearly perfectly correlated with statistical measures of these characteristics.

---

[6] See several interesting papers in F. Thomas Juster (ed.), *Education, Income, and Human Behavior* (New York: McGraw-Hill Book Company, 1975).

[7] Paul I. Taubman and Terence I. Wales, *Mental Ability and Higher Educational Attainment in the Twentieth Century,* National Bureau of Economic Research, Occasional Paper 118 (1972), p. 19.

Further:

> The supply of young men to high-level occupations is governed by economic incentives. All else being the same, increased wages attract students to a field and add to the supply of specialists several years later. Lags in supply are due primarily to the length of educational programs. Both econometric and survey data indicate rapid response to changes in market conditions.[8]

Economic theory does not, of course, suggest that individuals will always choose the career offering highest *monetary* returns. The prestige of an occupation, the degree of independence it affords, the ease or difficulty of the work, its inherent interest and satisfaction will all influence the decision. But *all other things being equal,* an increase in earnings in one occupation relative to others will incline more people toward that occupation.

SOCIAL RETURNS TO EDUCATION

Although the demand for education depends on private decisions, the supply of educational facilities depends mainly on government decisions. As with other kinds of government output, the question of how much education should be produced depends on a calculation of *social* costs and benefits, which will usually differ from their private counterparts.

The social return to education is the addition to national output arising from the worker's increased productivity. We assume that productivity is measured accurately by money earnings. (Everyone recognizes that, because of labor market imperfections, earnings and productivity do not always correspond; but there is little agreement on the size of the discrepancy, or how to adjust for it.) Note also that we should take gross income, with no reduction for income tax, since the tax influences only the distribution of output gain and not its size. In estimating private returns, on the other hand, we take posttax income, since this is what the individual actually receives.

On the cost side, the private calculation includes only costs borne by the student or his family. But in a social calculation we must count the full cost of buildings, teachers' time, and other inputs into education, regardless of how these costs are financed. At the elementary and high school levels, these costs come almost entirely out of public funds. Even at the college

---

[8] Richard Freeman, *The Market for College-Trained Manpower* (Cambridge, Mass.: Harvard University Press, 1971), pp. xxiii–xxv. See also, by the same author, "Supply and Salary Adjustments to the Changing Science Manpower Market: Physics, 1948–73," *American Economic Review* (March 1975), pp. 27–39; and "A Cobweb Model of the Supply and Starting Salary of New Engineers," *Industrial and Labor Relations Review* (January 1976), pp. 236–48.

and graduate school levels, student tuition covers only a minor part of total educational costs. In 1968, for example, direct total instruction costs per student averaged $1,630 in public colleges and universities and $2,270 in private institutions. Tuition and fees, however, averaged only $1,030 in private institutions, or about 45 percent of educational costs; and $250 in public institutions, or about 15 percent of educational costs.[9]

The procedure for calculating the social rates of return is exactly the same as that illustrated earlier for private rates. The internal rate of return is that which makes the future income stream, discounted to the present at that rate, exactly equal to the full cost of education. Because full cost is substantially *above* private cost, the social rate of return to education is considerably *below* the private rate—often by 3 or 4 percentage points, at the college level. If Freeman's estimates are accurate, the social rate of return to college education today is well below 10 percent. The return to postgraduate training in the arts and sciences is even lower—very low indeed for Ph.D. programs in some areas.

What can one conclude about whether higher education is presently over- or underexpanded? This requires some criterion, some standard for judging what is an adequate social rate of return. The two criteria most often suggested are (1) the market rate of interest on long-term government securities—if the government can borrow money for, say, 6 percent, it can afford to invest in any project yielding more than this rate; and (2) the rate of return on physical capital in the private sector, usually estimated in the range of 10 to 15 percent. Economic resources, it is argued, should be allocated so as to equalize the rates of return on investment in the private and public sectors.

If we adopt the latter test, it seems clear that the higher education establishment has been expanded somewhat beyond optimal size, particularly at the M.A. and Ph.D. levels. We must be cautious about such a conclusion, however, because of intangible benefits of education not reflected in earnings. Some of these accrue to the educated individual, and form part of private rather than social returns. In addition, however, there are *external effects,* that is, benefits to others in the economy which are not registered through the price system.

Perhaps the most important of these is the effect on the next generation. There is evidence that the amount of time mothers spend with their children varies directly with the mother's educational level.[10] Children of more educated parents receive more preschool education in the home and

---

[9] Theodore W. Schultz, "Optimal Investment in College Instruction: Equity and Efficiency," *Journal of Political Economy* (May–June 1972), Part II; p. 4.

[10] Arleen Leibowitz, "Education and the Allocation of Women's Time," in Juster, *Education, Income, and Human Behavior.*

more guidance and encouragement in the later school years. The fact that children of more educated parents typically score higher on IQ tests must in part reflect home environment rather than genetic endowment.

There are other external effects as well. More scientists and engineers should accelerate research and invention, a major factor in productivity growth. More highly educated managers and supervisors add to the productivity of those working under them. More educated citizens should be more informed and active participants in public affairs. Education apparently reduces the propensity to engage in crime, partly by raising the prospective rewards from legal as against illegal activities.[11] Since some of these effects are not measurable, however, one cannot say just how much they add to the social return to education. Thus there will always be room for differing judgments about whether education is under- or overdeveloped.

WHO SHOULD PAY
FOR HIGHER EDUCATION?

In addition to the question of how much resources should be devoted to higher education, there is the question of who should pay for these resources. As higher education becomes steadily more expensive, there is increasing concern over how the costs should be distributed between students and taxpayers.

One school of thought regards higher education as essentially a private investment good, whose possession benefits the owner through higher lifetime income. Why should this good be provided at public expense? Why shouldn't it be sold at cost, like any other capital good? The argument for pricing human capital at full cost is similar to that for pricing physical capital at full cost. Unless supply reflects all relevant costs, there cannot be the matching of costs and benefits required for efficient allocation of resources. Further, most of the higher earnings resulting from college education come as private benefits to the individual. So he, and not society, should bear the costs of his training.

Under the present system, most students in public institutions pay tuition covering only a small fraction of the cost of their education. They are thus receiving a substantial scholarship and—this is the main point— they receive this *without regard to financial need*. The scholarship benefits rich families in the suburbs along with poor families in the slums. Indeed, some studies indicate that students attending state-supported colleges and universities come from families whose average income is higher than that of the average taxpayer in the same state. Subsidizing of higher education

---

[11] Isaac Ehrlich, "On the Relation Between Education and Crime," in Juster, *Education, Income, and Human Behavior.*

may thus involve an income transfer in the "wrong" direction, from lower to higher brackets.

It is argued also that, under the present system, there is "unfair competition" between public and private institutions. The latter, having no direct access to tax funds, must charge relatively high tuition to survive. In order to admit students from low-income families, they must "buy" them with scholarships, and their limited resources prevent doing much of this. Thus for students of modest means, the choice among institutions is unduly restricted. This is undesirable *per se*, and it also puts the public institutions under less pressure to do a good educational job. This could be corrected by setting tuition at a full-cost level in both public and private institutions, while taking care of the "ability to pay" problem by publicly financed scholarships adjusted to parents' income.

Another school of thought argues, however, that higher education should be priced below cost for all students on the ground that such education has large external effects on the community. This argument is used to support free elementary and high school education. Why stop at grade 12? Why not extend the same reasoning through the college level? This is clearly the kind of argument in which no one can be proven right.

The closer education is priced to full cost, the more severe the problem of where students from low-income families can find the necessary funds. The family which wishes to buy an item of physical capital, such as a house, can wait until it has saved part of the purchase price and then borrow the remainder, putting up the house as collateral on the loan. But for investment in human capital, these options are much less feasible. If the student himself has to save the necessary funds, this takes time, during which he is growing older and passing beyond the normal college age-group. He might find himself entering college at the age of twenty-five instead of eighteen. If, on the other hand, he tries to borrow for education, what can he put up as collateral? In a nonslave state, an individual cannot mortgage himself to guarantee repayment of the loan.

The private capital market, in short, is not well suited to financing educational investment. Any system of educational finance which implies heavy student borrowing must specify how borrowing facilities are to be provided.

There are numerous federal, state, university, and private loan schemes for students. But total loan volume is still small relative to potential need. Efforts are underway, in Congress and elsewhere, to develop a more comprehensive federal program. Several issues are involved:

1. Should a federal agency lend directly to students, or should it merely guarantee loans made by others? (The main federal program at present is a guarantee program, which reinsures other lenders against risk of loss.)

2. Should students be allowed to borrow up to the full amount of direct educational expenses, including living costs? Or should there be a lower ceiling?

3. Should interest rates be at market levels, or at some lower level? Loans below the market level would amount to a subsidy to higher education and, like any other form of subsidy, would have to be justified on the ground of external effects. (The present federal guarantee program allows lenders to charge what they choose. There is a proviso that, if the lending rate rises above 7 percent, the federal government will pay the interest above that level, but this proviso has not been used to date. Further, for students from families with "adjusted income"—adjusted for number of children, number in college, etc. —below $15,000 a year, the federal government pays the interest on loans *during the years of study.*)

4. What are appropriate repayment arrangements? Some present programs have short repayment periods—say, ten to fifteen years beginning soon after graduation. This imposes a burden on the borrower at precisely the time when costs of buying and furnishing a house and rearing children are also high. Most families can repay with less effort at a later stage when child-rearing costs have declined. Repayment periods of twenty to thirty years, comparable to those for mortgage loans, would seem more efficient.

An interesting feature of some present loan plans is that repayment obligations are calculated, not as a fixed amount, but as a *percentage of future income.* Those for whom education (or education plus ability) turns out to have a high income payoff are charged more, while those with lower future earnings pay less. This raises questions of equity, since it involves some redistribution of (future) earned income. It also raises interesting questions about what might lead a student to choose one system rather than the other. Percentage repayment might be attractive in terms of reducing risks. If you do poorly in later life, you pay little; if you do well, you pay more, but you have the money to make the payments. On the other hand, students who feel confident that their abilities will bring them above-average incomes in future years should logically prefer flat-rate repayment.

The "negative dowry" objection to loan plans for women students is not as serious today as it might have been in earlier times. It assumes that women who marry are out of the labor force and that the husband will have to repay their loan obligations as well as his own. This is no longer a generally valid assumption. Most married women now resume work after their children are in school, and the proportion who do so is rising over time. The fact that a woman's career is likely to be interrupted for some years when children are small might, however, warrant a different timing and duration of loan repayments.

What about outright scholarships, covering part or all of educational expenses, for children from low-income families? Subsidizing higher education through low-cost tuition, as we have seen, involves a substantial scholarship element *unrelated* to financial need, and apparently involving an upward redistribution of income. A more restricted system, limited to

Table 1

College Entrance of High School Graduates, by Ability and Socioeconomic Status, 1966

Ability Group	Socioeconomic Status of Family	Entering College		Not Entering College	
		Number (Thousands)	Percent	Number (Thousand)	Percent
Highest fifth	1. Highest	192	95	11	5
	2.	120	79	33	21
	3.	82	67	40	33
	4. Lowest	30	50	30	50
Next highest fifth	1. Highest	109	84	21	16
	2.	90	63	53	37
	3.	78	52	70	48
	4. Lowest	34	36	60	64
Total (top 40 percent)		735	70	318	30

SOURCE: *Toward a Social Report* (Washington, D.C.: Government Printing Office, 1969), p. 21.

families in the lowest-income brackets, would redistribute a smaller amount of income in a downward direction.

There have been many sample surveys indicating that, for students at the same level of measured ability, the percentage going on to college is much higher from high-income families than from low-income families.[12] Some estimates for the entire U.S. high school graduating class of 1966, prepared by the U.S. Department of Health, Education, and Welfare, are shown in Table 1. The table includes only the top 40 percent of graduating seniors, ranked by measured ability, and shows the percentage who went on to college from families at various socioeconomic levels. These students were presumably all capable of college work. Yet 318,000 of them, or about 30 percent, did not go on to college; and of these two-thirds came from families in the two lowest economic groups.

This clearly involves a substantial waste of talent. It seems both efficient and just to channel a larger proportion of talented people from low-income families into the higher educational system.

But would not an adequate loan fund system do the job? Why should anything more be required? A case for scholarships would have to rest on

---

[12] A review of such studies, and additional analysis relevant to this section, will be found in Seymour M. Lipset and Reinhard Bendix, *Social Mobility in Industrial Society* (Berkeley and Los Angeles: University of California Press, 1963).

some combination of the following arguments: (1) that low-income families are more myopic and poorly informed about education than high-income families; and that on this account they would underborrow from the loan fund; (2) that the present distribution of personal income is too unequal and that, in addition to redistributing cash to low-income families, we can reasonably redistribute goods such as educational benefits; (3) that subsidies to higher education are warranted by consumer benefits and external effects, and that this form of subsidization is preferable to others.

The federal government presently supports work–study programs, which make payments in return for part-time work at the college; and a system of "educational opportunity grants" to students from low-income families. But these grants still cover only a minority of low-income students, they average only about $500 per student per year, and they do not differentiate effectively among families at different income levels.[13]

On the assumption that a scholarship system is desirable, the present system needs revision to achieve more complete coverage of low-income families, larger grant amounts, and a sliding scale providing full support at the bottom and reductions as family income rises. To the extent that higher education is to be subsidized, it seems most efficient to do this through loans and grants *going directly to the student*. By raising effective demand for education (that is, demand backed by ability to pay), this will enable colleges and universities to raise tuition closer to full educational costs with the favorable results outlined earlier.

TRAINING ON THE JOB

Although formal education may provide background skills and enhance learning ability, much of the specific skill related to productivity is acquired after graduation. The medical graduate spends several years as an intern and resident. The young college teacher learns to teach by teaching. The skilled craftsman often serves a three- to five-year apprenticeship. Semi-skilled operatives and clerical workers usually go through a training period, designed to familiarize them with the organization, to inculcate job skills, and to weed out those unsuited for permanent employment. Learning continues informally beyond the training period, through day-to-day instruction by foremen and supervisors.

The total cost of on-the-job training, including the opportunity cost of trainees' time, is very substantial. Jacob Mincer estimates that, for U.S. males, the aggregate annual investment in on-the-job training in 1958 was

---

[13] For discussion of this and other federal programs, see Robert W. Hartman, "Higher Education Subsidies: An Analysis of Selected Programs in Current Legislation" (Washington: Brookings Institution Reprint Series, 1972).

$13.5 billion, compared with an annual investment of $21.0 billion in formal schooling. He also estimates that the rate of return to on-the-job training is in the neighborhood of 10 percent, that is, of the same order of magnitude as returns to college education.[14]

The skills acquired in this way are of two types: some are specific to a particular employer, while others are transferable among employers. A carpenter or electrician can work for numerous building contractors or can set up in repair work on his own. An illustration of firm-specific skill might be a worker engaged in fabricating some component of a Xerox copying machine. (There are several other producers of copiers, but they are not located nearby and their machines are not identical.) In this case he can practice his acquired skill only with his present employer.

To the extent that workers and employers calculate economically, the costs of these two types of training will be differently distributed. The employer who trains a worker in a transferable skill cannot count on benefiting directly, since the worker can leave him at the end of the training period or at any time thereafter. There is thus no reason why the employer should bear the cost of the training; but it is rational for the worker to bear it, since the "human capital" which he thus acquires is a personal possession which he can carry to any job. Given full information and competitive conditions, then, the employer will pay the trainee a wage equal to his productivity per time period *minus the cost of training him during that period*. The employer's total cost for wages plus training equals the worker's productivity, so he does not lose. The worker takes a reduced wage during the training period, comparable to the reduced or zero earnings of a college student; and he expects to be repaid in the form of higher earnings over his working life.

The case of a firm-specific skill is different. Here the worker is not acquiring a transferable skill. There is no reason for him to pay for something that could be lost overnight if he loses his job. So the market will not permit the employer to shift training costs to the employee through a reduced wage. He will have to pay him as much as any other employer in the market would be willing to do. In this case it is the employer who makes the investment during the training period. His total cost for wages plus training is *above* the productivity of the trainee.

Why is the employer willing to do this? Because he expects the worker to stay with him, and expects to recapture his training investment in future years. The training raises the worker's productivity *in this specific employment,* though not in others. In later years, then, the employer will pay the

---

[14] Jacob Mincer, "On-the-Job Training: Costs, Returns, and Some Implications," *Journal of Political Economy*, Supplement, *Investment in Human Beings* (October 1962), pp. 50–79.

worker somewhat *less* than his productivity at that time, the difference going to repay the initial costs of training. Why will the worker accept this? Because the higher productivity acquired through training cannot be carried with him to another job. Although he is being paid less than he produces in his present job, he is earning as much as he could produce and earn anywhere else, that is, he is getting his transfer price. This is all that the competitive market requires.[15]

There is doubtless some element of skill specificity in any job. Even the apparently transferable clothing cutter or steel rolling-mill operator, once he is hired, learns to find his way to a particular workplace, learns the limits of the foreman's temper, the performance standards of the company, and minor differences in products, methods, and equipment. The fact that the employer usually has an investment in a particular worker, and that the worker has an investment in his existing job, makes the labor market operate somewhat differently than it otherwise would.

DISCUSSION QUESTIONS

1. In what respects is "human capital" similar to, and in what respects different from, physical capital?

2. What methods are commonly used to estimate the rate of quality improvement in the nation's labor force over time? Do you see any possible sources of error in these methods?

3. Explain the method of calculating the private rate of return on an investment in education.

4. Why do most studies show a considerable difference in private and social rates of return to education? For what purposes is each measure useful?

5. Suppose someone concludes that the social rate of return to four-year college education is 10 percent.

(a) What are the possible sources of bias in such an estimate?

(b) Assuming that you could get an unbiased estimate, how would you use it in judging whether the allocation of resources to higher education is too large, too small, or about right?

6. Explain and criticize the idea of pricing higher education on a full-cost basis, accompanied by an adequate loan system for students.

---

[15] The reasoning in the last few paragraphs derives from Gary Becker, who first emphasized the differing market consequences of transferable as against firm-specific skills. See his *Human Capital* (New York: National Bureau of Economic Research, 1964).

7. Draw up an ideal loan system, specifying such things as public or private management, source of finance, loan ceilings, interest rate, and repayment period.

8. Higher education can be and is subsidized in a variety of ways:
   (a) Below-cost tuition
   (b) Loans at below-market interest rates
   (c) Scholarships for students from low-income families
Appraise the relative merits of these different techniques.

READING SUGGESTIONS

Basic studies in this area include GARY BECKER, *Human Capital*, New York: National Bureau of Economic Research, 1964; RICHARD FREEMAN, *The Market for College-Trained Manpower*, Cambridge, Mass.: Harvard University Press, 1971; JACOB MINCER, "On-the-Job Training: Costs, Returns, and Some Implications," *Journal of Political Economy*, Supplement, October 1962; JACOB MINCER, "The Distribution of Labor Incomes: A Survey with Special Reference to the Human Capital Approach," *Journal of Economic Literature*, March 1970; and THEODORE W. SCHULTZ, *Investment in Human Capital: The Role of Education and of Research*, New York: The Free Press, 1971. See also a special journal issue devoted mainly to financing of higher education: *Investment in Education: The Equity-Efficiency Quandary*, *Journal of Political Economy*, May–June 1972, Part II.

Most recently, the Carnegie Commission on Higher Education has published a series of major monographs in this area. Especially relevant to this chapter are MARGARET S. GORDON (ed.), *Higher Education and the Labor Market*, New York: McGraw-Hill Book Company, 1974; F. THOMAS JUSTER (ed.), *Education, Income, and Human Behavior*, New York: McGraw-Hill Book Company, 1975; and PAUL TAUBMAN and TERENCE WALES, *Higher Education and Earnings*, New York: McGraw-Hill Book Company, 1974.

4

The Labor Force: Deployment

The last two chapters have depicted the national labor force in broad brush strokes. In this chapter we focus on the fact that these workers are deployed over tens of thousands of specific jobs, in specific locations, with specific characteristics and training requirements. If the labor market problem were merely to provide 90 million undifferentiated jobs for 90 million homogeneous workers, life would be much simpler than it actually is.

Life would be simpler, too, if the distribution of workers among occupations, industries, and areas remained stable over the course of time. One could predict future labor requirements at each point in the economy, and workers and young people preparing for employment could plan accordingly. But in the growing, technically dynamic, and geographically dispersed economy of the United States, the pattern of employment is constantly shifting. The structure of jobs in 1980 is different from that of 1950, and the job pattern of 2000 will again be different. The labor force is continuously being reshaped to fit new patterns of labor demand.

Shiftability of demand increases the volume of traffic through the labor market, increases the amount of unemployment between jobs, and intensifies the need for efficient labor market organization. Data compiled by the Bureau of Labor Statistics suggest that about one-sixth of all wage and salary earners change jobs in a typical year. For young people, women, and black workers the percentage is substantially higher.

The reasons for this movement are complex, and we shall have more to say about them in later chapters. They include cyclical and seasonal fluctuations of demand, the rise and decline of particular businesses, instability of some workers, and the perennial (and rational) search for better jobs. But a major contributing factor is the gradual shift in patterns

63

of labor demand in response to changes in product demand, production methods, and location of economic activity.

DEPLOYMENT BY INDUSTRY

It would be useful to know how many new jobs appear each year, what kind of jobs they are, and where they are located; and also to know the characteristics of jobs that disappear. This information we do not have. We can draw conclusions about *net* shifts in demand, however, by observing the behavior of employment; that is, by comparing the *stock* figures for two dates we can infer something about the *flows* between these dates. An industry in which employment has risen must have had an excess of new vacancies over vanishing jobs.[1] If employment has declined, job disappearances must have exceeded job creation. Similar conclusions can be drawn from data on the occupational and geographical distribution of employment. It will be useful, therefore, to look at the changing pattern of employment in recent decades and the statistical projections that have been made for the future.

Study of many countries over long periods shows that, as a country's per capita income rises, there are systematic shifts in the relative importance of different industries. These shifts are confirmed by cross-section comparison of countries at different income levels at the same time.[2]

There are two main reasons for these shifts: (1) differing income elasticities of demand (as per capita income rises, demand for medical care rises faster than demand for potatoes); (2) differing productivity trends. If productivity is rising unusually fast in industry A, its unit cost of production will be falling unusually rapidly. This will be reflected in prices, and the products of industry A will become cheaper relative to other products. This will encourage consumers to buy more of A's products than before, and less of other things.

The clearest tendency is a long-run decline in the relative importance of agriculture. The proportion of the labor force engaged in agriculture falls from 70 percent or more in the least developed countries to 10 percent or less in the most advanced. This does not, of course, mean any

---

[1] Note, however, that *gross* changes in demand, which determine the volume of unavoidable labor mobility, cannot be ascertained from employment data. If employment in an industry has risen by 100,000 over a certain period, this could mean 100,000 new jobs with none disappearing, 200,000 new jobs with 100,000 disappearing, or any similar combination.

[2] See in particular Simon Kuznets, *Modern Economic Growth* (New Haven: Yale University Press, 1966), and Hollis B. Chenery, "Patterns of Industrial Growth," *American Economic Review* (September 1960), pp. 624–54.

decrease in agricultural output. It means rather such a great rise in agricultural productivity that the population can be fed by a much smaller segment of the labor force. One farm family, instead of feeding few more than itself, can now feed ten other families as well.

Industries engaged in commodity production—manufacturing, mining, construction—increase sharply in importance as economic growth proceeds, but this increase does not continue indefinitely. After a certain point, the proportion of the labor force engaged in these industries levels off and moves along on a plateau. In most advanced industrial countries this plateau level is between 30 and 40 percent of the labor force, though in a few countries (Britain, Sweden, West Germany) it approaches 50 percent.

With agriculture continuing to decline in relative importance as development proceeds, and with commodity production leveling off, what takes up the slack in the labor force? The answer is found in industries producing services of every sort—wholesale and retail trade, banking and finance, recreation and entertainment, professional and other personal services, and government. Except for domestic service, which declines in the long run, the proportion of the labor force employed in service activities rises steadily as national income rises. More than 50 percent of the labor force in Canada, and almost 60 percent in the United States, is now employed in the service industries.

The trend in the United States from 1870 to 1930 is shown in Table 1, while Table 2 gives a more detailed picture for selected years since 1929.[3] Agriculture, which as late as 1880 still employed half the labor force, today employs less than 5 percent. This has come about partly because of the low income elasticity of demand for food, partly because of a spectacular rise in agricultural productivity since 1940. Over the last

Table 1

Distribution of Employment (%) by Major Sectors, 1870–1930

	1870	1880	1890	1900	1910	1920	1930
Agriculture	50.8	50.6	43.1	38.1	32.1	27.6	22.7
Industry	30.0	30.1	34.8	37.8	40.9	44.8	42.1
Services	19.2	19.3	22.1	24.1	27.0	27.6	35.2

[3] Table 1 and the first two columns from Table 2 are from Victor R. Fuchs, *The Service Economy* (New York: National Bureau of Economic Research, 1968), pp. 19–24. The 1974 data and 1985 projections in Table 2 are from *Employment and Training Report of the President* (Washington, D.C.: Government Printing Office, 1976), p. 336.

Table 2

Employment (%) by Sector and Major Industry Group, 1929–85

	1929	1947	1974	1985 (Projected)
Agriculture	19.9	12.1	3.8	2.1
Industry	39.7	42.1	34.0	31.6
Services	40.4	45.8	62.2	66.3
Industry				
Mining	2.2	1.7	0.8	0.8
Construction	5.0	5.2	5.3	5.3
Manufacturing	22.8	26.7	22.5	20.6
Transportation	6.6	5.3	3.3	2.8
Communications and public utilities	7.2	2.1	2.1	2.1
Government enterprise	0.9	1.2	...*	...*
Services				
Wholesale trade	3.8	4.5	5.0	4.7
Retail trade	12.9	13.9	16.7	16.5
Finance and insurance	2.6	2.2 }	5.0	5.4
Real estate	0.8	1.0 }		
Households and institutions	7.0	5.2 }	19.9	22.1
Professional, personal, business, and repair services	7.3	8.3 }		
General government (including armed forces)	6.0	10.6	15.6	17.7

* Included under other categories.

three decades more than 25 million people have left the land, and those remaining are more than capable of meeting our food requirements.

The industrial sector increased in relative importance until 1920, reaching a peak of 45 percent of total employment in that year, from which it has receded to somewhat under 40 percent at present. Manufacturing has remained rather stable in the long run, at around 25 percent of the labor force, and construction has held steady at 5 percent. But there has been a sharp decline in mining employment (mainly in coal) and in transportation employment (mainly on the railroads).

The really striking development since 1920, and particularly since 1945, is the rise of what Fuchs has labeled "the service economy." In 1920 the proportion of the labor force employed in service industries was less than 30 percent. Today it is more than 60 percent and still rising. In the goods-producing industries, including agriculture, *there has been virtually no increase in total employment* since 1947. In that year some 31.3 million people were employed in the goods-producing industries. The total in

1974 was 29.4 million, and the projected figure for 1985 is 31.5 million. This means that the net increase of more than 30 million in the labor force since 1947 *has been completely absorbed in the service industries.*

It does not mean that no one has been hired in the goods-producing industries since 1947. Since workers retire each year, there is considerable hiring for replacement purposes. But *net expansion* has been concentrated almost entirely in the service sector. Within this sector, the most rapidly growing areas have been government service and professional, personal, and repair services. These two areas alone now employ close to 30 percent of the labor force.

What are the reasons for this growing preponderance of service employment? It is often asserted that the income elasticity of demand for services *as a group* is higher than that for goods *as a group*. After reviewing the evidence for the United States, Fuchs finds little support for this view. Indeed, commodity output in real terms has risen just about as fast as output of services since 1929. The decisive factor, then, is the differing movement of output per worker in the two sectors. Fuchs finds that over the period from 1929 to 1965 output per man rose at an average annual rate of 3.4 percent in agriculture, 2.2 percent in industry, and 1.1 percent in services.[4] Put differently, the amount of labor needed for a given volume of output has been shrinking much faster in industry and agriculture than in the service industries. This leads to a steadily shrinking proportion of the labor force in the agricultural and industrial sectors.

William Baumol has put this point in a dramatic parable.[5] Consider an economy with two sectors. In one sector (which we may call *S* for services, though Baumol does not), productivity never rises. In the other sector (which we call *G* for goods), productivity rises at a constant rate. Wages in *both sectors* rise at the same rate, geared to the rate of productivity increase in the *G* sector.

What will happen? (1) If the ratio of real output in the two sectors remains constant, the proportion of the labor force employed in the *G* sector will approach zero, while the proportion in the *S* sector will approach 100 percent. As this happens, the rate of productivity increase in the economy will also approach zero. (2) Cost (and hence price) per unit of output in the *S* sector will rise without limit. Output of goods with a demand that is price-elastic will decline and perhaps ultimately vanish. As examples, Baumol cites fine handmade goods, fine restaurants, live theatrical and concert performances, and "stately homes" requiring domestic servants. (3) Activities for which demand is income-elastic and price-

---

[4] Fuchs, *The Service Economy*, p. 51.

[5] William J. Baumol, "Macroeconomics of Unbalanced Growth: The Anatomy of Urban Crisis," *American Economic Review* (June 1967), pp. 415–26.

inelastic, such as education and marketing services, will absorb a steadily increasing proportion of the labor force and of GNP. Since many of these are public-sector activities, pressure on state and local government budgets will be intense.

The rise of the service economy has other implications for economics, and especially for labor economics. (1) Economic evolution is often portrayed as a movement toward ever larger and more impersonal production units. This view is based almost entirely on the (now declining) goods sector. Most service activities have a relatively small scale of plant, and self-employment is common. (2) In the same vein, it is often said that the impersonal, routinized, and mechanized conditions of modern industry have squeezed the intrinsic interest out of labor, and that the worker must increasingly find his satisfactions off the job. But in the growing service sector, many activities require a high level of skill and training, involve personal contact with the consumer, and permit a wide variety of satisfying work activity. (3) Service industries employ a high proportion of white-collar workers, a high proportion (almost 50 percent) of women workers, and a high proportion (more than one-quarter) of part-time workers. This is reshaping the composition of the labor force and the character of labor markets. Economists need to devote relatively more attention to white-collar labor markets than has been true in the past. (4) Less than 10 percent of workers in the S sector are unionized, compared with more than 50 percent in the G sector. Unless unionism succeeds in penetrating the service industries, it will be a declining influence in the economy; and if it does succeed, the character of the union movement will be considerably changed.

DEPLOYMENT BY OCCUPATION

A different classification of the labor force is in terms of the kind of work done—unskilled, semiskilled, clerical, professional, and so on. Trends in the occupational distribution of the labor force stem partly from the industry shifts just described. If industries employing large numbers of clerical workers, salespeople, and professional people are increasing in relative importance, these groups will form a growing proportion of the labor force. A second factor, however, is changes in work methods within particular industries. Thus manufacturing now employs a considerably lower ratio of production workers, and a higher ratio of clerical, supervisory, and other nonproduction workers than was true a generation ago. Automation of production processes in both factory and office has altered the skill composition of the labor force.

Changes in the occupational distribution of the labor force since 1930 and Bureau of Labor Statistics projections for 1985 are shown in Table 3.

Table 3

Occupational Distribution (%) of the U.S. Labor Force, Selected Years, 1930–85

	1930	*1960*	*1975*	*1985* *(Projected)*
Service-type occupations	36.5	55.5	63.6	65.6
Professional, technical, and kindred workers	7.1	11.4	15.0	15.5
Managers, officials, and proprietors (excluding farm)	7.7	10.7	10.5	10.5
Clerical and kindred workers	9.3	14.8	17.8	19.4
Sales workers	6.5	6.4	6.4	6.1
Service workers	5.9	12.2	13.7	14.1
Goods-type occupations	63.3	44.2	36.4	34.4
Craftsmen, foremen, and kindred workers	13.4	13.0	12.9	13.3
Operatives and kindred workers	16.4	18.2	15.2	14.7
Laborers (excluding farm and mine)	11.4	5.4	4.9	4.6
Farmers and farm laborers	22.1	7.8	3.5	1.8

SOURCE: Data for 1930 are from *Historical Statistics of the United States* (Washington, D.C.: Government Printing Office, 1965), p. 76; for 1960, 1975, and 1985 from *Employment and Training Report of the President* (Washington, D.C.: Government Printing Office, 1976), p. 336.

The most striking feature of Table 3 is the growing predominance of the service-type occupations (which are largely, though not entirely, synonymous with "white-collar" employment) over goods-type occupations. As a percentage of total employment, the former group pulled ahead of the latter around 1955 and the gap has been widening ever since.

This is a general tendency in all advanced industrial countries. For example, Table 4 compares the occupational distribution of the Canadian labor force in 1901 and 1961. Note that more than four-fifths of women workers, and more than half of all workers, are now engaged in white-collar occupations.

There has been an especially sharp increase in demand for professional and technical skills. In the United States, professional, semiprofessional, and technical workers have quadrupled in numbers and more than doubled in relative importance over the past half-century. This is due mainly to a great rise in consumer incomes and living standards, which has permitted consumers to spend much more on education, health, entertainment, and other professional services. A high proportion of national income spent on professional and personal services is, in fact, almost a definition of a high

Table 4

Occupational Distribution (%) of the Canadian Labor Force, 1901 and 1961

Occupation Group	Male Workers		Female Workers		Total Workers	
	1901	*1961*	*1901*	*1961*	*1901*	*1961*
Primary production	50.5	17.6	3.8	3.9	44.3	13.8
Blue-collar	27.4	34.1	29.8	10.8	27.9	27.9
White-collar	17.0	38.6	66.0	82.1	23.4	50.5
Transport and communication	5.1	9.7	0.4	2.1	4.4	7.7
Total	100.0	100.0	100.0	100.0	100.0	100.0

SOURCE: Adapted from H. D. Woods and Sylvia Ostry, *Labour Policy and Labour Economics in Canada* (Toronto: Macmillan of Canada, 1962), p. 324.

standard of living. Another factor is the increasingly complex and scientific character of industrial operations, which requires large numbers of research scientists, engineers, and technical assistants. It is estimated that there were 7,000 engineers in the United States in 1870. Today there are more than half a million, and the number is still increasing.

Clerical and kindred workers have increased from 2 million in 1910 to over 15 million at present. Almost two-thirds of these workers are women, and this is the main point at which women have increased their participation in employment. The rapid growth of clerical employment reflects partly the expansion of service industries in which clerical workers are especially important—government, finance and insurance, trade, communications, and so on. It reflects also the growing size, complexity, and mechanization of industrial operations, which require more and more people to distribute and keep records on the goods produced, and relatively fewer people to produce them.

Until recently, semiskilled factory operatives formed an increasing proportion of the labor force because of the growing importance of manufacturing in the economy and the accompanying mechanization of production. Increased use of hand-operated machinery created a great array of jobs that required a short period of specialized training but did not require the craftsman's all-round knowledge and experience. One should perhaps term this *incomplete* or *partial mechanization*. The more complete automation of many production processes since the late forties has reduced the need for semiskilled operatives, and their importance in the labor force has begun to decline.

Interestingly enough, the proportion of skilled workers in the economy has remained roughly constant over the past half-century instead of declining as might have been expected. The proportion of skilled men on production work in manufacturing has indeed fallen as production processes have been subdivided, mechanized, and downgraded. This has been offset, however, by a great increase in repair and service jobs—maintenance mechanics needed in factories to keep the more complicated machinery in good repair; automobile and airplane mechanics and repairmen; telephone, telegraph, and power linemen and servicemen; and a wide variety of other groups. Skilled building trades workers have increased in relative importance with the high level of construction activity since 1940; and foremen and subforemen, whom the census classifies with craftsmen, have also increased in number.

Farmers and farm laborers have diminished in importance with the relative decline of agriculture. Domestic service has declined sharply as high labor demand has enabled domestics to shift to better-paid jobs in manufacturing and elsewhere. There has also been a sharp decline in the proportion of the labor force engaged in urban unskilled labor, which has been cut more than half since 1930. There is much less "back work" in industry today than there was fifty years ago, owing partly to the development of mechanical lifting and moving devices—conveyor systems, gravity feeds, mechanized hand trucks, overhead cranes, and so on. Much of the work that used to be done by people with strong muscles is now done by a machine operated by a man who needs less strength but more intelligence and experience. In this respect, then, industrial employment has become more skilled and more pleasant.

Although the classification of jobs used in Table 3 is conventional, it is not entirely satisfactory. One tends to assume that all jobs in the professional–managerial categories are more skilled than those in the sales–clerical categories, and that these in turn are more skilled than most kinds of manual labor. But this is not entirely true. *Within* each of the standard occupational categories there is a wide range, from jobs requiring little skill or training up to the most complex and demanding kinds of work. For this reason James Scoville developed a new fivefold classification based on richness of job content—complexity of the operations involved, amount of general educational background required, and length of specific vocational training.

Scoville's classification cuts across the standard occupational classification. Thus some clerical workers (auditors, librarians) fall in class one, while others (telegraph messengers, office boys) fall in class five. Some administrative workers (personnel managers, editors) are assigned to class one, but others to lower classes down to building managers (class five). Similarly for each other major category. Although this classification is ad-

Table 5

Distribution of Employment (%), by Job-Content Level

Level	1940	1950	1960	1970 (Estimated)
1	6.1	6.8	8.7	9.4
2	9.6	11.5	14.2	16.1
3	28.5	32.5	34.2	34.7
4	24.5	20.8	17.0	15.8
5	31.6	28.4	25.9	24.0

SOURCE: Data are from James G. Scoville, *The Job Content of the U.S. Economy, 1940–70* (New York: McGraw-Hill Book Company, 1969), p. 54. Since the study was published in 1969, the 1970 data are estimates, while those for earlier years are actual magnitudes.

mittedly experimental, it is logically superior as an indicator of skill level and training requirements, and we saw in the last chapter that it correlates well with earnings level and educational attainment.

Scoville's results, some of which are shown in Tables 5 and 6, confirm that the skill composition of employment in the American economy has been rising very rapidly. More than 25 percent of all jobs now fall in the top two skill classes, compared with only 15 percent in 1940. There has been a corresponding shrinkage in the relative importance of the lowest two categories, from 56 percent of employment in 1940 to 40 percent in 1970. The implication of these shifts for *rates of increase* in labor demand are shown in Table 6. The less skilled occupations have had very low rates

Table 6

Rate of Increase in Employment (%) by Job-Content Level

Level	1940–50	1950–60	1960–70 (Estimated)
Total	24.5	10.8	19.2
1	39.2	41.7	29.5
2	50.6	35.9	35.7
3	41.7	16.5	20.9
4	12.5	−9.1	10.3
5	12.0	10.8	10.3

SOURCE: Data are from James G. Scoville, *The Job Content of the U.S. Economy, 1940–70* (New York: McGraw-Hill Book Company, 1969), p. 54. Since the study was published in 1969, the 1970 data are estimates, while those for earlier years are actual magnitudes.

of increase since 1940, with class four showing an actual decline from 1950 to 1960. Classes one and two, on the other hand, have had very high rates of demand increase.

In order to achieve supply–demand balance over this period, it has been necessary to deflect a high proportion of young people entering the labor force into the upper occupations, requiring more prolonged education and training. How successfully this has been accomplished and whether failure of training levels to rise as fast as demand requirements has created structural unemployment will be examined in Chapter 7.

Automation and Skill

It is desirable to add a word on automation because of the prominence of this subject in popular discussion and the numerous misconceptions surrounding it. In popular usage, automation is a loose term covering a variety of different things. Baldwin and Shultz have distinguished (1) "continuous automatic production" or "Detroit automation"—the linking together of separate production operations along a continuous line through which the product moves unaided by human hands; (2) "feedback technology"—use of built-in automatic devices (servomechanisms) for comparing the way in which work is actually being done with the way in which it is supposed to be done and then making automatic adjustments in the work process; (3) "computer technology"—use of computing machines for recording and storing information and for performing both simple and complex mathematical operations upon it.[6]

These devices can be used separately or in combination. The hypothetical "automatic factory" of the future would employ all three in various proportions. Computer technology is farthest developed at present. Its main impact will be in the office, where it will displace a large amount of clerical labor and possibly even junior management personnel. Information technology may structure many management jobs in the future, just as Taylorism structured hourly rated production jobs in the past.

The other two types of automation are less fully developed but have a large potential impact on factory production over the next two or three decades. Broadly speaking, these processes operate to reverse the labor force trends produced by the partial mechanization of earlier times. Old-style mechanization, as we have seen, made for a rapid multiplication of semiskilled machine tenders at the expense of skilled craftsmen. But once materials handling and machine operations have been sufficiently sub-

---

[6] George B. Baldwin and George P. Schultz, "Automation: A New Dimension to Old Problems," *Proceedings of the Seventh Annual Meeting of the IRRA* (1954), pp. 114–28.

divided and routinized, they can be taken over completely by automation and the need for the semiskilled man disappears. In some industries, then, the semiskilled operative may turn out to have played a temporary and transitional role on the way from old-style handicraft production to fully automatic production.

As automation gathered force during the fifties and sixties, there were frequent expressions of alarm over its possible consequences. Here, it was said, is a "second industrial revolution," moving at a much faster pace than the mechanization of earlier decades. Whole categories of employment will be laid waste. The aggregate man-hour requirements of the economy will shrink. Reduction of the workweek and other special measures will be needed to avert massive unemployment. These predictions were disputed by others, and there was a large outpouring of literature, including a full-scale examination by a national commission.[7] The dust has now settled to the extent of producing considerable agreement on several points.

First, there are indications that—at least in the United States—the pace of technological change has been faster since 1940 than it was in earlier decades. There is no direct measure of the rate of technical progress. But the rate of increase in output per man-hour, or perhaps better, in output per unit of combined labor and capital inputs, reflects technical progress in a broad sense. Both types of productivity index have risen considerably faster in recent decades than in earlier decades. The National Commission found also that the time lag between discovery of a new production process and its commercial application has fallen considerably. For a sample of technological innovations, the "development period" averaged twenty-four years in the era from 1920 to 1944, but only fourteen years in the period from 1945 to 1964. Expenditures on industrial research and development have risen at a sensational rate since 1945, both absolutely and as a percentage of GNP.

Second, the view that accelerated technical progress leads to *general* reductions in labor demand has been convincingly refuted. If this view were correct, one should observe an uptrend in the national unemployment rate. But in actuality, since 1945 the unemployment rate has fluctuated mainly within the range of 4 to 8 percent, with no perceptible long-run trend.

Third, displacement of labor in particular firms and industries is clearly a possibility. Indeed, it seems likely that changing technology is

---

[7] See the multivolume *Report of the National Commission on Technology, Automation, and Economic Progress*, particularly Vol. 1, *Technology and the American Economy* (Washington, D.C.: Government Printing Office, 1966). See also Jack Stieber (ed.), *Employment Problems of Automation and Advanced Technology* (New York: Macmillan Publishing Co., Inc., 1966), proceedings of a conference held at Geneva by the International Institute for Labour Studies.

now eliminating jobs at a (moderately) faster rate than was true before 1945. This hypothesis is difficult to test statistically. If a new process reduces the cost and price of a product substantially, and if demand is sufficiently elastic to produce a large increase in sales, there may be no absolute decline in employment. One can still speak of "labor displacement" in the sense that the number of people employed with the new process is less than would be required for the same level of output with the old process. In some cases there has doubtless been absolute displacement as well. But these cases are confined at any time to limited sectors of the economy.

Even when total employment in a firm is not reduced by automation, the distribution of skill requirements may be considerably altered. The results of research to date suggest that the net effect of automation is usually an upgrading of skill requirements.[8] The skills eliminated tend to be of a routine or semiskilled character. On the positive side, automation increases the need for skilled workers in the machine-building industries, for skilled maintenance men to keep the automatic equipment in steady operation, for "machine watchers" who must be able to respond quickly and correctly to machine errors, and for computer programmers and other technicians. But this is cold comfort to the displaced bookkeeper or machine operative unless he is enabled to learn to the new skills.

DEPLOYMENT BY AREA

A final important characteristic of labor demand is its geographic location. In a country as large and diversified as the United States, job opportunities may be expanding rapidly in some areas while they are stagnating or declining in others. This may be due to the decline of an industry (coal mining in Appalachia, agriculture in many southern and midwestern states), to the geographic shift of an industry (textiles from New England to the South), or to spectacular expansion of an industry that has become localized in a certain region (automobiles in Michigan at an earlier period, aircraft and electronics in California in more recent years).

---

[8] See, for example, George P. Shultz and Arnold Weber, "Technological Change and Industrial Relations," in an IRRA symposium *Employment Relations Research* (New York: Harper & Row, Publishers, 1960); the March 1962 issue of the Annals of the American Academy, devoted entirely to automation; and Roy B. Helfgott, "Electronic Data Processing and the Office Work Force," *Industrial and Labor Relations Review* (July 1966), pp. 503–16. This study of seven large companies that had installed computerized data processing showed an overall increase of employment because of the rapid increase of workloads. There was, however, considerable displacement of labor in the lowest clerical grades, with a more than offsetting increase of employment in higher grades.

Table 7

Average Annual Percentage Change in Population, Selected States, 1960–70 and 1970–75

	1960–70	1970–75		1960–70	1970–75
Arizona	3.1	4.4	Illinois	1.1	0.0
Florida	3.2	4.1	Iowa	0.2	0.3
California	2.4	1.1	Massachusetts	1.0	0.4
Texas	1.6	1.7	Pennsylvania	0.4	0.0
Wisconsin	1.1	0.8	New York	0.8	−0.2
Ohio	0.9	0.2	West Virginia	−0.7	0.6
New Jersey	1.7	0.4	Rhode Island	1.0	−0.5

SOURCE: Bureau of the Census, *Current Population Reports*, Series P-25, No. 640 (November 1976).

Recent population trends for selected states are shown in Table 7. Some states are obviously growing more rapidly than others—in population, labor force, and economic activity. The rate of expansion in Florida, the Pacific Coast, and the Southwest is well above that in the Northeast and North Central States. The rising demand for labor in the more rapidly growing regions is met in good measure by migration from stagnant or declining areas.

The statistics of migration reveal a large amount of geographical movement.[9] In a typical year, about 6 percent of the American people move across county lines. About half of this is movement within the same state, while the other half is across state lines. The movement is broadly "economic"; that is, it is toward areas of relatively high wages and expanding employment. Unemployed men are about twice as likely to move as employed men. Young people are much more mobile than older people. Mobility also increases with level of education. By occupation, much the highest migration rate is for professional people, followed at a considerable distance by sales workers and management people. The high mobility of professionals results from a combination of high education level, wide geographical scope of the market for professional skills, and good channels of market information.

On one hand, this large-scale migration connotes opportunity for personal advancement. On the other hand, it involves personal and social costs and provides opportunity for mistaken choices. How far the move-

---

[9] For an analysis of migration since World War II, see Eleanor G. Gilpatrick, *Structural Unemployment and Aggregate Demand* (Baltimore: The Johns Hopkins Press, 1966), Chap. 7.

ment could be rationalized by improved labor market institutions is an important question to be considered in Chapter 7.

SOME CONSEQUENCES OF DEMAND SHIFTS

Shifts in labor demand have major consequences, for workers and for the economy. First, trends in labor demand are the main force operating to reshape the pattern of employment. People learn the skills and move to the locations that production requirements impose on them. If, in the aggregate, jobs are becoming more pleasant and satisfying over the course of time, this increase in welfare should be included in any assessment of economic progress. This source of increased welfare—"producer satisfaction" as distinct from "consumer satisfaction"—has certainly been important in the United States over the past fifty years.

Second, the larger the shifts in demand, the more members of the labor force will have to change jobs one or more times in the course of their working lives. This involves costs that must be set against the advantage of a dynamic economy. An enforced job change strikes the worker as a misfortune rather than an opportunity, so subjective costs are involved. The period during which the worker is unemployed while seeking a new job involves a production loss to the economy; and the employment service activities, training programs, and other measures needed to speed the readjustment of the labor force also involve economic cost.

The dimensions of this problem depend partly on the rate at which population, labor force, and national output are growing over time. With a static labor force, a *relative* decline of employment in any sector would have to mean an *absolute* decline as well. But if total employment is rising, a redistribution of the labor force can occur without anyone's losing his job. Employment can decline relatively in some sectors simply by rising less rapidly than employment in general. In this sense a high rate of economic growth eases the difficulties of labor force readjustment.

The problem of the employed worker is different from that of the young person preparing for employment. The worker committed to a particular occupation and industry need worry only about an *absolute* decline of employment in his sector of the market. If there is no decline, his position will become increasingly secure through formal or informal seniority arrangements. Those still in the educational pipeline, however, need to know the composition of the job vacancies that will be available *at the time they enter the market.* More correctly, they should know the distribution of both prospective vacancies and prospective labor supplies, since this will determine the tightness or slackness of particular submarkets.

Third, the magnitude of demand shifts will affect the unemployment level in the economy. A larger volume of movement through the labor market, even assuming the same average time between jobs, must itself raise the unemployment rate. In addition, there is the possibility that many of the workers who lose jobs because of demand shifts will not have the qualifications required for the vacancies that are appearing at the growth points of the economy and may on this account suffer unusually long periods of unemployment. This kind of maladjustment is often termed "structural unemployment." Structural unemployment, however, does not have to be accepted as a fact of nature. It can be attacked by various measures of manpower policy, which we shall analyze at a later point.

Finally, the heavy volume of traffic through labor markets raises important questions about how these markets operate and whether they could operate better than they presently do. By "better" we mean an increase in either the *speed* of placement of unemployed workers in vacant jobs, or in the *quality* of placements—appropriateness of workers' tastes and abilities to job requirements, leading to mutual satisfaction of employer and employee, leading presumably to greater permanence in the job. Because of the complexity of the hiring transaction, we should not expect to see anything approaching a "stock exchange for labor." But the level of information could be improved, and organizational improvements may also be possible. To this range of problems we now turn in Part II.

DISCUSSION QUESTIONS

1. The rise of the "service economy" has increased the service industries' share of total employment but has apparently not increased their share of national output. Can you explain these divergent trends?

2. Over the past several decades there has been a marked shift of demand toward jobs with higher educational and skill requirements. What kind of labor market maladjustments might result from this shift, and how could one determine whether such maladjustments have in fact occurred?

3. From your previous training in economics, can you explain why accelerated mechanization and automation need not raise the level of unemployment?

4. How is continued progress of automation likely to affect the occupational composition of the labor force?

5. "Steps should be taken to spread the growth of new industry more evenly over the country, thus reducing the need for expensive interstate migration." Do you agree? Why, or why not?

6. What are the main economic costs arising from a more rapid, as against a less rapid, rate of shifting in labor demand?

READING SUGGESTIONS

The Fuchs, Gilpatrick, and Scoville studies cited in this chapter contain useful analyses of trends in labor demand over recent decades. Current data on the distribution of employment are published in the *Monthly Labor Review* and in the annual *Employment and Training Report of the President*.

II

THE LABOR MARKET

The demand for and supply of specific skills meet in the market to determine wage rates for particular jobs. Here as elsewhere in economics, demand, supply, and price are interdependent. Wages help to call forth labor supply and to determine where particular workers will seek employment. Wage rates also, given particular demand curves for labor, determine how much labor each employer will be willing to hire.

Apart from its wage-determining functions, the labor market is important in other respects. Whether employers who need labor and workers who need jobs are able to locate each other quickly, whether square pegs drop readily into square holes, whether workers' skills adapt themselves slowly or rapidly to trends in labor demand—all affect the efficiency of the economy. We shall examine how well our labor markets perform in these respects, and the reasons for this performance.

We begin in Chapter 5 with the simplified market models that should already be familiar to you from elementary economics, but that nevertheless merit a brief review. The main simplifications are: the wage rate is the only dimension of the hiring transaction; all vacancies are filled by outside hiring rather than internal promotion; workers are interchangeable in the eyes of employers and are of equal efficiency; information on both sides of the market is perfect; training costs are ignored; job changes are instantaneous; and there are always as many jobs as there are people willing to work at existing wage rates. Within this framework we examine (1) wage determination under purely competitive conditions; and (2) the wage effects of supply restrictions, government regulation, and market power exercised by employers or trade unions.

In Chapter 6 we remove the simplifying assumptions of Chapter 5 and examine the operation of actual labor markets. Key features of actual markets include

81

complexity of the employment "package"; limited information, leading to search activity by workers and employers; importance of firm-specific training and experience; filling of many vacancies through promotion in the "internal labor market"; and the existence of unemployment. We shall ask *who* is most frequently unemployed, and why there are still so many unemployed when the economy is operating at "full employment."

We do not have to take labor markets as we find them. There has been much research on possible improvements of these markets, and many government programs are operative in this area. In Chapter 7 we examine improvement of *information* through manpower forecasting, improved counseling of young people, and strengthening of the public employment service; and efforts to improve workers' employability through *training* programs. Chapter 8 examines labor market *discrimination* against women and against black workers, and efforts to reduce such discrimination.

5

Simple Labor Market Models

What do we mean by *the labor market?* Is it a mere abstraction, or is it something we can see and touch? How does it operate? In which respects does it resemble or differ from commodity markets?

These are complex questions that will occupy us for the next four chapters. In this chapter we examine how labor markets would operate under highly simplified conditions. The next three chapters explore some of the complications that appear in actual labor markets.

The Scope of Labor Markets

A market is not necessarily, or even usually, a single place. True, there are places that are directly involved in labor recruitment and place-ment—union offices in the building or printing trades, the central hiring hall for longshoremen or seamen, the local office of the state employment service in each community. But these places are not synonymous with *the* labor market, since their use is usually not obligatory and much of the flow of labor bypasses them.

The standard definition of *market* is an area within which buyers and sellers are in sufficiently close communication that price tends to be the same throughout the area. Such an area may vary in size from a neighbor-hood to the whole world. In the case of labor, the size of the market area varies with the skill level involved. Top administrators and professional men enjoy a national (even to some extent an international) market. The number of qualified people being small, employers find it feasible and desirable to recruit from all parts of the country. Accurate information about openings, salaries, and so on, is usually available through personal contacts and professional associations. The cost of moving from one part of the country to another is small relative to potential gains in income and professional advancement.

For most manual, clerical, and subprofessional jobs, the locality is the relevant market area. A worker who is settled in one community is unlikely to know much about, or to be much interested in, jobs in other cities. Homeowners, in particular, are usually unwilling to move except in response to prolonged unemployment. Their market horizon is limited to the area within which they can readily commute to work. As auto transport has increasingly superseded public transport, however, commuting areas have become larger and more flexible. Towns that at one time were quite distinct are now merged into a common market. Moreover, nearby localities are linked by the *possibility* that people might move in response to a substantial divergence in wage levels or employment opportunities.

A locality is not a *single* market, but contains many specialized markets. In Seattle there are markets for typists, for aircraft welders, for schoolteachers, for janitors, and for hundreds of other occupations. Again, markets for "neighboring" occupations are linked by the possibility of labor transfer from one to the other. Occupationally as well as geographically, markets are linked in an intricate network, within which one can distinguish certain ridgelines at the boundaries of commuting areas and clearly defined skill groups.

In a certain sense, each employing unit can be regarded as a separate market. The specialized production jobs in a large manufacturing plant, for example, are typically filled by internal promotion rather than outside recruitment. The employer looks to present employees as his source of supply, and workers look to this "internal market" for their prospects of advancement.

The Simplified Labor Market

All the labor markets discussed in this chapter have the following characteristics:

1. The attractiveness of a job is measured by its hourly wage rate. Other job conditions are taken as given and constant. The wage is the sole variable that the employer can manipulate to attract additional labor.

2. All job vacancies are filled through the market. We ignore the fact that in practice many vacancies are filled through internal promotion.

3. Workers are interchangeable in the eyes of the employer and are of equal efficiency. We overlook the facts that in practice employers have hiring preferences based on sex, race, age, experience; that workers differ in efficiency; and that to achieve full efficiency on a particular job usually requires a training period.

4. There are always as many jobs available as there are workers who choose to work at prevailing wage rates. There is permanent full employment.

5. Workers and employers are perfectly informed. Workers know about vacant jobs, the wage rates, and other job characteristics. Employers know about workers who might be attracted to the firm and what wage it will take to attract them.

6. It follows that vacancies can be filled instantaneously. "Frictional unemployment" does not exist.

The warrant for these assumptions consists, not in the fact that they correspond closely to reality, but rather that they yield results with considerable predictive power. The economic forces that operate in these simple markets are operative also in actual markets. Moreover, by removing these assumptions one by one, as we shall do in Chapter 6, we can build up a picture of actual labor markets more systematically than could be done otherwise.

One other point should be emphasized before we proceed. In analyzing wages in a particular plant or company, we assume that *everything else in the economy remains constant.* More specifically, all product prices, interest rates, and wage rates offered by other employers remain constant. This technique was developed by Alfred Marshall of Cambridge, who called it "the method of *ceteris paribus"*—other things equal. By using it, we separate out the market in which we are interested from all the other markets to which it is related. Another term for this technique is *partial equilibrium analysis,* as distinct from *general equilibrium analysis,* which views the market network as a whole.

When we draw a supply–demand diagram for a particular company or industry, we show the wage rate on the vertical axis and the quantity of labor employed on the horizontal axis. The assumption that *all other wages are constant* gives this vertical axis a special significance. As we move up the vertical axis, this means that the wage rate is rising *relative to all other wages in the economy;* and conversely for a reduction in wages.

Unless this is borne clearly in mind, one can readily fall into misstatements and confusion. For example, it is *not* correct to say: "If company A's wage rate rises, more people will prefer to work there." But it would be correct to say (under our assumptions): "If company A's wage rate rises *relative to other wage rates,* more people will prefer to work there." Again, it is *not* correct to say: "If company A's wage level rises, it will hire fewer workers." But it is generally true (under our assumptions) that "if company A's wage level rises, *all prices and other wage rates remaining unchanged*, it will hire fewer workers."

EMPLOYERS' DEMAND FOR LABOR

Employers hire labor to produce a product. Demand for a particular kind of labor is *derived* from demand for its product and is related to the *productivity* of the labor in question.

The Law of Variable Proportions

Without reviewing the whole of production economics, we can restate one of its central principles. This describes what happens as increasing quantities of labor are applied to a fixed quantity of capital goods—a *plant*. The principle is:

As increasing quantities of a variable factor are applied to a fixed factor of production, the resulting additions to output will eventually decrease.

The classical economists called this the *law of diminishing returns*. They derived it by applying more and more labor to a fixed acreage of land, and thought of it as associated particularly with agriculture. But it is in fact a general principle, applicable to any kind of production. It is now usually called the *law of variable proportions*. It could also be called the *law of diminishing marginal productivity*.

The operation of the principle is illustrated in Figure 5–1. *The added product resulting from the use of one more unit of labor is its marginal (additional) product.* The *MP* curve in Figure 5–1 shows marginal productivity rising in the early stages. One man turned loose in a complicated plant will not produce much. The marginal product of a second man will be higher, because the work can be subdivided more effectively. A third and a fourth man will also add increasing amounts to the product. As

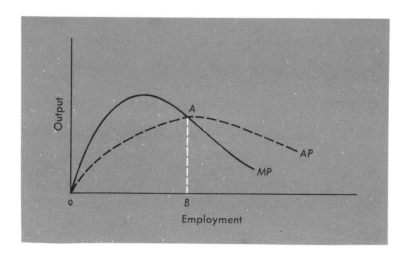

Figure 5–1

The Law of Variable Proportions

more and more men are added, however, the marginal productivity of labor must eventually begin to decline, since each man is working with less and less equipment. The *MP* curve turns downward.

The average productivity curve, *AP*, which shows *average* output per worker at each level of employment, has a gentler upward and downward slope. Note that *MP* intersects *AP* at the point where *AP* is a maximum. This is no accident, as can be shown by a simple illustration. Take a football team averaging 6 feet in height, and add a player of 6 feet 6 inches. The average of the group will now be higher than before. But if we had added a man of 5 feet 6 inches, the average of the group would fall. The same principle holds here. So long as *MP* is above *AP*—that is, so long as each new worker adds more than the average output of the workers previously employed—this keeps pulling the average *up*. But when *MP* falls below *AP*, it begins pulling the average *down,* and *AP* begins to fall.

We can show also that it will never pay to operate this plant with fewer than *B* workers. Why? Because up to this point the average productivity of labor is still rising. This means that, up to *B*, the fixed factor is not being fully utilized. So it cannot pay to operate to the left of *B*. Rather than do this, it would be preferable to abandon part of the plant and concentrate labor on the remainder, in order to reach the top of the *AP* curve. But this will rarely be necessary. The producer will normally operate the plant somewhere to the right of *B*, that is, somewhere on the declining section of the *MP* schedule. *So only this part of the schedule will be shown in later diagrams.*

Demand for Labor:
Competitive Product Markets

What we have been calling marginal product is more correctly described as *marginal physical product* (*MPP*). But business calculations are made in dollar terms. What the producer is interested in is how much *revenue* he will get by employing an additional worker.

The additional revenue secured by using one more unit of a factor is called its marginal revenue product (MRP).

If the marginal physical product of labor is declining, however, we can be sure that its marginal revenue product is also declining. This is true regardless of competitive conditions in the market for the company's product. Suppose first that the product is sold under conditions of pure competition. Here we must introduce the concept of *marginal revenue*:

The amount which an extra unit of output adds to a producer's sales revenue is called marginal revenue (MR).

A producer under pure competition is by definition such a small part of total industry output that it can vary its rate of sales without affecting the market price. So there would be no point in cutting price below the market level. The company can sell as much as it wants to *without* doing that.

Think about what this means. It means that the *demand curve for the company's product is horizontal at the prevailing price.* It means also that, under pure competition, *price and marginal revenue are equal.* If the company can sell an additional unit with no reduction in price, then its revenue is increased by the full price of that unit. In graphic terms, the marginal revenue schedule is horizontal and identical with the demand schedule.

Labor's marginal revenue product curve, however, will still be downward sloping. Why? Because beyond a certain point the marginal physical product (*MPP*) of labor is declining. Since additional units of output are sold at an unchanged price, physical product and revenue product are strictly proportionate. As *MPP* falls, labor's *MRP* will fall at the same rate.

Demand for Labor: Producers with Market Power

Pure competition is unusual. Most producers have some degree of *market power.* A seller has market power if he is able to influence the price of his product. In this case he must choose a price and, other things equal, this price will determine how much he is able to sell. *His demand curve slopes downward to the right.*

Market power may exist for one of several reasons: (1) A company may be the only producer of a particular good. (2) There may be only a few producers, each with a sufficiently large output to affect the market price. (3) Each company's product may not be *quite* the same as that of others. Company *A* makes Wheaties while company *B* makes Krunchies. So company *A* sets the price of Wheaties and can set it higher or lower than the prices of competing brands.

In all these cases—monopoly, oligopoly, and monopolistic competition—the producer is faced with a downward-sloping demand curve. Having set his price, he can sell only the quantity demanded at that price, as shown by the demand curve. If he wants to sell more, the price must be lowered.

This has an important consequence: *marginal revenue is no longer identical with price.* For a downward-sloping demand curve, *marginal revenue is always less than price.* Remember what marginal revenue is: the addition to revenue obtained by selling an additional unit of product. Why isn't this equal to the price obtained for that additional unit? Because in order to sell an additional unit the producer must reduce his price, not just for that unit, but for all the goods he is selling. The price cut on the goods he could have sold anyway is a loss in revenue, which must be deducted from the sales price of the additional unit.

Thus at any point on the demand schedule, marginal revenue is less than price. This means that the *marginal revenue schedule lies below the demand schedule* throughout its length, and slopes downward more steeply.

What does this mean for labor's marginal revenue product? It means that, as more and more workers are employed, their marginal revenue product (*MRP*) now falls for a double reason: (1) each worker adds less to output—marginal *physical* output is falling; and (2) each additional unit of output adds less to sales revenue, because of the downward slope of the marginal revenue schedule. Thus labor's *MRP* schedule falls more sharply than its *MPP* schedule.

Productivity, Wage Rate, and Employment

We conclude that, for producers operating under pure competition as well as for those with market power, labor's *MRP* schedule will slope downward, as shown in Figure 5–2. Now how many workers will the

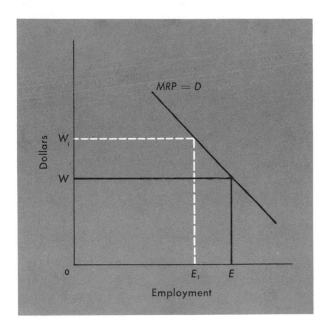

Figure 5–2

Labor's *MRP* Schedule Is its Demand Schedule

employer hire? To determine this, we need additional information namely, the rate of wages. Suppose this is W. The employer who wishes to maximize profit will observe the following rule:

> *Increase employment up to the point at which the marginal revenue product of labor equals the cost of labor.*

Up to E in Figure 5–2, the additional revenue brought in by an additional worker is greater than his wage; so he is adding to profit. Beyond E, however, an additional worker would bring in less than his wage, so profit would be reduced.

If instead of W, the wage were W_1, then the correct level of employment would be E_1. In fact, we can find the correct employment for any wage rate simply by moving along the MRP schedule. So we conclude that, for a single employer buying labor in a competitive market:

> *The demand schedule for labor is its marginal productivity schedule.*

This is sometimes wrongly called "the marginal productivity theory of *wages*." This is incorrect, because it does not specify how the wage rate is determined. The wage can be set by market competition or collective bargaining or legal regulation. All it says is that, once the wage is determined (by whatever means), the employer will try to adjust employment and output to maximize profit. It is a theory of *labor demand*.

Suppose there are many employers of a particular kind of labor in a particular market, and we wish to add up their total demand. We do this by horizontal addition of the individual companies' demand schedules,[1] just as we add individual consumers' demand schedules to derive total demand for a product. This gives us an *aggregate demand schedule* for this kind of labor. It must slope downward, because the individual schedules from which it is derived slope downward.

Elasticity of Demand for Labor

The slope, or more precisely the elasticity, of the labor demand schedule differs from one kind of labor to another. What determines elasticity of demand in a particular case?

The answer can be important—for example, to a union considering

---

[1] One complication, however, should be noted. Suppose that the companies are also producing the *same product*. Then a wage change, by changing employment and output, will also change the *price of the product*, which will shift each company's MRP schedule. We can still construct a labor demand schedule for each company and for the group; but in so doing, we must take the price effect into account.

the possible impact of a wage change. Would an increase of 10 percent in an industry's wage level (everything else in the economy remaining unchanged) reduce employment by 5 percent? Or only by 1 percent? The answer may make considerable difference to union and employer strategy.

The demand for labor is derived from the demand for its product and so follows the general principles of derived demand. These should be familiar to you from elementary economics but may be restated here. Elasticity of demand for labor depends on:

1. *Elasticity of demand for the product.* Suppose that a 10 percent wage increase raises total unit cost 5 percent and that product prices also rise 5 percent. If elasticity of demand for the product is low, say 0.5, sales will fall by only 2.5 percent. But if elasticity were higher, say 2.0, sales and employment would fall 10 percent because of the same wage increase. The more elastic the demand for the product, the more elastic the demand for the labor used in making it.

2. *The proportion that labor costs form of total production costs.* If labor is only 10 percent of the total, then a 10 percent wage increase will raise total unit costs only 1 percent. The effect on product prices, sales, and employment will be small. But if labor forms 80 percent of production costs, the impact will be greater. On this account, a skilled craft union covering only a small part of an employer's labor force is in a stronger bargaining position than a plant-wide union. The cost of buying off the craft group is small, and this lessens the employer's resistance; and the employment effect is too small to deter the union from an aggressive wage policy.

3. *The difficulty of substituting other factors for labor in production.* In some cases the existing technique of production may be the only known method, and the possibility of modifying it to save labor may be small. But in other cases, there may be alternative methods involving greater mechanization. At a higher wage, one or more of these methods will become profitable and will be brought into use. The greater the number of known alternative methods and the more labor they save, the greater the elasticity of demand for labor.

4. *The supply curves of productive services other than labor.* (This is harder to grasp than the previous three points.) Look at it this way: one reason for lower employment at a higher wage is that production costs rise, product prices rise, sales and output are reduced, and purchases of productive services are reduced. Suppose, however, that the industry uses some factor— say a specialized raw material with no other uses—with a supply curve that is highly inelastic. As the industry's demand for this material falls, its price will go down. This reduction in the industry's costs serves as an offset to the higher costs resulting from the wage increase. So the increase in total cost and price will be smaller, and the drop in sales and employment smaller, than they would be without this cushioning factor. In this case, labor's gains are partly at the expense of the owners of this other factor.

To sum up: The demand for labor will be more inelastic—that is, a wage increase will produce a *smaller* drop in employment—in proportion as: (1) demand for the product is inelastic; (2) labor costs form a small proportion of total costs; (3) the known possibilities of substituting capital and other factors for labor are small; and (4) supply of one or more non-labor factors is inelastic.

LABOR SUPPLY TO AN OCCUPATION

Turning to the other side of the market, let us look at a worker trying to choose among alternative occupations. We assume that he is not only free to choose but has the information needed for accurate choice. In addition, if the occupation is one requiring extended training, we assume that the choice is being made at an age when this is still feasible. A hypothetical choice among law, business administration, architecture, or accounting is not meaningful for a forty-year-old plumber; but it is a realistic decision for a college sophomore.

The wage rate is not the only criterion of occupational choice. Occupations differ in many other respects—in public esteem, in working hours and degree of effort, in regularity of employment, in the pleasantness of the work, in the scope that they offer for originality and initiative. Each person will evaluate these characteristics differently, depending on his preference system. But each person will tend to select the occupation that on balance seems to offer him greatest *net* advantage.

Suppose now that we wish to chart a labor supply curve for a particular occupation. Having just said that the wage rate is far from the only consideration in job choices, it may seem arbitrary to single it out for special consideration. But there are reasonable grounds for doing so. First, wages are *measurable,* while many other dimensions of an occupation are not. Second, income is for most people an *important* consideration in job choices. Third, the wage rate is one of the more *flexible* characteristics of an occupation. Some characteristics, such as the intrinsic difficulty and pleasantness of the work, are deep-rooted and change only slowly. The wage can vary from month to month. So it is plausible to take it as variable in our analysis, and to assume that other characteristics of the job are constant over the period in question.

Remember also that the characteristics of all other jobs in the economy, including their wage rates, are given and constant. A movement up the vertical axis in Figure 5–3 is an increase in the wage for this occupation *relative* to all other occupations. The upward sloping supply curve S says that the higher the relative wage for this occupation, the more people will choose it over other occupations. A higher wage for an occupation will increase its net advantage relative to other occupations. So some people who previously did not think it quite attractive enough will now switch

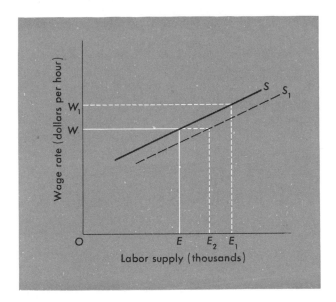

Figure 5–3

The Labor Supply Schedule

over and choose it in preference to something else. If the relative wage rises still higher, some more people will switch over, and so on.

A rising supply curve is still more plausible if we bring in educational and training costs. There are few occupations that do not involve some training cost, and for the higher occupations the cost is very substantial. The returns may also be substantial, but they are uncertain, so they will be evaluated differently by different individuals. People will differ in their estimate of the most likely rate of return, in their attitude toward risk and uncertainty, in their actual ability for the occupation in question, and in their confidence in their own ability. Therefore, if the true (but unknown) return to investment in training for an occupation is 10 percent, some people will choose it and some will not. But we can be reasonably sure that, if the rate of return rises to 12 percent, returns to all other occupations remaining unchanged, *more* people will choose it than previously. Supply is positively related to prospective earnings.

We must observe the usual cautions in interpreting the supply schedule. Suppose the wage in Figure 5–3 rises from W to W_1, everything else remaining unchanged. By looking at the supply curve, we see that the number who prefer this occupation will rise from E to E_1. *This is not an increase in labor supply.* It is simply a movement to another point on the same supply schedule.

An increase in supply means that the whole schedule has shifted rightward to a new location, such as S_1, so that at every possible wage more people now prefer this occupation. At a wage of W, for example, the number wishing to enter the occupation is now E_2 rather than E.

While labor supply curves normally slope upward, their shape differs from one situation to the next. An important consideration is that supply adjustments take time. This is especially characteristic of professional and technical occupations with a long training period. At any moment the number of trained chemical engineers is fixed, and a higher wage will have no immediate effect on numbers. In the short run, the supply curve is vertical. An increase in the relative wage for chemical engineers will, however, lead more college freshmen to enroll in this specialty, and this will increase supply four years later.

In addition to vertical (short-run) supply curves, there are also examples of horizontal supply curves. Professor W. A. Lewis, a leading student of economic development, argued that new industries setting up in a largely agricultural economy will be able to attract as many workers as they want at a constant real wage.[2] There is an "unlimited supply of labor," arising from the existence of large numbers of underemployed people in agriculture, handicrafts, petty trade and services, and other traditional activities. The income yielded by these activities is very low. By paying a moderately higher industrial wage, employers in the "modern" sector can get all the labor they need. Their labor supply curve is a horizontal line at the industrial wage.

DEMAND, SUPPLY, AND WAGES

Labor demand and supply schedules interact to determine how many will be employed in each occupation and how much they will be paid. Let us ask first how this would work out if all labor markets were purely competitive. This will provide a useful benchmark against which we can measure the effect of deviations from competitive conditions.

In addition to the general assumptions listed at the beginning of the chapter, the assumption of pure competition means that:

1. There is full freedom of occupational choice. This implies, among other things, that a young person choosing an occupation that requires training can always obtain the necessary funds to undertake training.

---

[2] W. A. Lewis, "Economic Development with Unlimited Supplies of Labor," *Manchester School* (May 1954).

2. There is full freedom of exchange. Any employer may hire any worker, and any worker may work for any employer.

3. There are many employers and many workers in the market, so that no one can influence the market price.

4. There is no collusion on either side of the market. Employers do not unite to drive down the wage level, nor do workers form unions to drive up wages.

Equilibrium Under Pure Competition

In this context we now ask how many people will be employed in occupation *A,* and at what wage rate. The demand and supply schedules for the occupation are shown in Figure 5–4. Then, by the usual reasoning, we can predict that the market will move toward equilibrium at point *A*. *E* workers will be employed in this occupation at a wage rate *W*. Any employer who wishes to hire this type of labor will have to pay the market wage.

Similarly, we can draw demand–supply diagrams for occupations *B*, *C*, *D*, and so on, through every type of work performed in the economy. There will be an equilibrium wage and employment for each occupation.

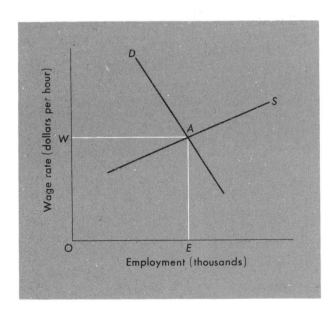

Figure 5–4

Equilibrium in a Competitive Labor Market

Thus the structure of relative wage rates is completely determined, and so is the occupational distribution of the labor force.

This may seem no great feat until one thinks about how labor would be allocated in the absence of a competitive market. Suppose some federal official had to decide, for the American economy as of 1980, how many people should be schoolteachers, how many should be bricklayers, how many should be accountants, and so on. This would be a staggering problem. Yet a competitive market system solves the problem rapidly and inconspicuously.

We can show also that the competitive market solution is optimal, both in terms of national output and in terms of people's satisfaction from work. In output terms, correct allocation requires that the marginal revenue product of a particular kind of labor be the same in every employing unit. The need for this condition is obvious. If a bricklayer has a higher marginal revenue product in company A than in company B, then national output can be increased by shifting labor from B to A. As this goes on, marginal productivity will fall in company A and rise in company B. When it becomes equal in the two companies, nothing can be gained by further shifting.

The proof that this condition is satisfied under pure competition is straightforward. The market price of any type of labor will be the same to all producers. But each producer, to maximize profit, will employ labor only up to the point at which $MRP = W$. Since W is the same for all producers, MRP must also be the same.

Output is not everything. It is desirable also that the tasks performed by members of the community should be so allocated among them as to involve a minimum of sacrifice, because everybody is doing the work in which his net advantage is highest.[3] If this condition is met, we can be sure that no switching of two people between jobs could benefit one person without either harming the other or causing a drop in output. And this condition will be met if people are able to make a free and informed choice among jobs.

Consider Mr. A, whose income is below Mr. B's. Then A must have chosen his job, in preference to B's, either because, lacking aptitude for B's occupation, he could not have earned B's income in it; or because he sees other disadvantages in Bs' job that more than offset the higher wage. In neither case would there be a gain from moving A to B's job. In the first case output would fall, and in the second case A would feel worse off than before.

---

[3] This point was drawn to my attention by a passage in Tibor Scitovsky, *Welfare and Competition*, rev. ed. (Homewood, Ill.: Richard D. Irwin, Inc., 1970).

Shifts in Demand and Supply

We can show, then, that competitive labor markets yield an optimal allocation of the labor force *at a specific moment*. We can show also that the competitive market is an effective mechanism for *reallocating the labor force over time* in response to changes in demand and supply conditions.

Suppose, for example, that the supply curve in Figure 5–5 shifts from S to S_1. At any given wage, more people than before are now available for this kind of work. This could happen for several reasons. This could be a white-collar occupation requiring high school graduation, and the proportion of each age group who finish high school could be rising. Or the job could have become easier, or other nonwage conditions could have improved. Or certain groups (women, black workers, and so on) formerly excluded from this kind of work may now be admitted, increasing the available supply.

Remember that everything else in the economy is being held constant. Moving to the right along the employment axis means an increase in employment in this occupation relative to all other occupations. Moving upward on the wage axis means a higher wage for this occupation relative to all others. If supply shifts from S to S_1, employment will rise to E_1 and the

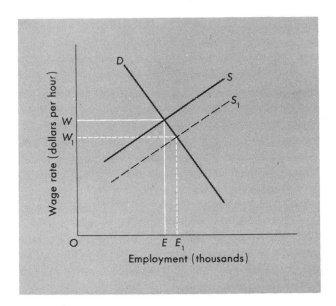

Figure 5–5

Supply Shifts, Wages, and Employment

relative wage level will fall to W_1. This result may seem odd, because we hardly ever see a wage rate falling in actuality. We live in an expanding economy, in which most wages are rising continually. But this means that a particular wage can fall relatively by *rising less rapidly* than wages in general.

We conclude that *increased labor supply to an occupation, other things remaining unchanged, will raise employment and lower the relative wage in that occupation. A decrease in labor supply will reduce employment and raise relative wages.*

Now consider the effects of a shift in demand. Demand for the occupation shown in Figure 5–6 rises from D to D_1, the supply curve remaining unchanged. What will happen? We can predict that employment and relative wages will both rise. But employment may not rise at once if it takes time to train workers for the occupation. In the short run, with the number of trained workers fixed at E, the equilibrium wage level will shoot up to W_2. As new trainees enter the occupation, however, employment will expand and relative wages will subside toward the equilibrium level W_1.

The effect of a decline in demand could be seen by sketching in a demand curve to the left of D. Employment and relative wages will both decline.

We conclude that *increased demand for a particular occupation, other*

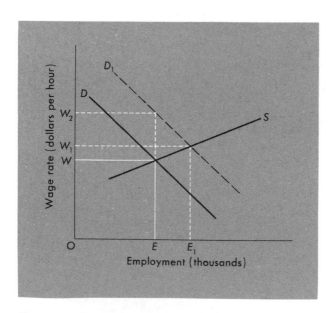

Figure 5–6

Demand Shifts, Wages, and Employment

things being equal, will raise both employment and the relative wage in that occupation. A decline in demand will reduce employment and relative wages.

Demand shifts, as we saw in Chapter 4, are large and frequent in the American economy. Over a period of years, demand schedules for some kinds of labor will have risen sharply, some will have risen moderately, some will have fallen. These shifts produce both a reallocation of employment and a change in relative wage rates.

DEPARTURES FROM PURE COMPETITION

At this point, while retaining the general assumptions listed at the beginning of the chapter, we drop the assumption that the labor market is purely competitive. Among the many possible departures from pure competition, we select three for examination: (1) restrictions on entrance to an occupation; (2) wage fixing, through collective bargaining or legal regulation; (3) situations—of which the "company town" is the stock example—in which one employer is so large relative to the size of the market that he can set his own wage rate.

Restrictions on Labor Supply

We assumed earlier that anyone can enter any occupation, but this is not always true. If the occupation requires extended training, as in science, law, or medicine, the capacity of training institutions may limit the number who can enter. There are state licensing systems for many occupations, usually managed by those already in the field, and this can be used to restrict admissions. Some of the literary, scientific, and artistic professions require natural talents that only a few may possess.

In Figure 5–7, D is the demand schedule for a certain occupation, while S shows the number who would *prefer* to enter it at various wage levels. If entrance were free, E people would be employed in this occupation at a wage level W. Because of some supply restriction, however, only E_1 people can actually get into this field. Running up to the demand schedule, we see that this number can be employed at a wage of W_1, well above the competitive level.

Note that where supply is fixed, *the wage level is determined solely by demand.* An upward shift of the demand schedule would raise the wage rate, while a downward shift would reduce it; but in neither case would there be any effect on employment. The control of supply blocks the normal allocative function of the market.

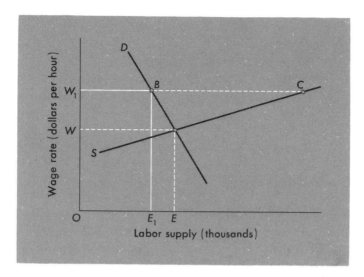

Figure 5–7

A Restriction on Labor Supply

Those who would prefer to work in this occupation but cannot gain admission, shown by the distance E_1E, will not remain unemployed. They will have to seek employment in other occupations, and the increase in labor supply to these occupations will lower their equilibrium wage. Thus the wage structure is distorted on two counts: an artificially high wage for the occupation in which the supply restriction occurs, and an artificially low wage in other occupations in which entrance is unrestricted. Moreover, the forcing of people into occupations in which their marginal productivity is lower reduces national output.

Regulation of Wages

Let us use Figure 5–7 to illustrate a different type of market intervention. Suppose that, with the demand–supply situation as shown, some outside agency simply decrees that the wage rate shall be W_1. At this wage, employers will be willing to hire only E_1 workers instead of E workers they would have hired at the competitive wage. The number employed in the occupation is reduced, not by restriction of entrance, but indirectly via wage regulation. As before, those who would prefer to work in this occupation but are not able to do so will have to seek work elsewhere, driving down the relative wage in other occupations. Both the structure of wages and the allocation of labor are distorted.

The "outside agency" could be a trade union. We cannot assume, however, that organization of a union necessarily raises wages above the competitive level. The union might like to achieve this result; but employers have an incentive to resist. Depending on the relative strength of the parties, the bargained wage may or may not be higher than it would have been in a competitive market. In Part VI we shall examine evidence on the actual impact of unions on wage rates in the United States.

Even if a union succeeds in establishing a wage level such as W_1, it may encounter an additional difficulty. By projecting a horizontal line from W_1 across to the labor supply curve, we see that a large number of workers (shown by the distance BC) would prefer to work in this occupation but are unable to do so. Many of them, indeed, would be willing to work for less than W_1. This creates a possibility that nonunion employers will spring up to employ them at less than the union scale. Thus the union must not only overcome the resistance of employers who are already unionized, but must be able to organize new companies as rapidly as they appear. A high-wage policy has to be supported by an effective organizing policy.

Employers' Monopsony Power

Under pure competition, each employer is too small a buyer of labor to influence the wage. He can buy as much or as little labor as he requires at the market rate. His labor supply curve is horizontal.

Suppose, however, that the company's employment is a large part of total employment in its area. At the extreme, suppose, it is the dominant employer in a "company town." In this case it can no longer assume that unlimited labor is available at a standard wage. It will normally have to raise wages to attract additional workers from other companies and areas. It is faced with an *upward sloping labor supply curve* such as S_L in Figure 5–8.

What does the curve S_L show? For any level of employment, it shows the wage rate—the *average cost of labor*—needed to attract that number of workers. But if the average cost of labor is rising, the *marginal cost* must be rising even faster. Look at it this way: to attract an extra hundred workers, the employer must offer a higher wage to those workers. But since it is impractical to have two wage levels in the same plant, he must also pay the higher wage to everyone he was previously employing. So the cost of additional labor is higher than appears at first glance. The marginal cost of labor rises along the line MC_L.

The employer's labor demand schedule, as we saw earlier, is identical with labor's marginal revenue productivity schedule. It is shown in Figure 5–8 by $D_L = MRP_L$. What will it pay the employer to do in these circumstances? To maximize profit, he should hire only up to the point at which

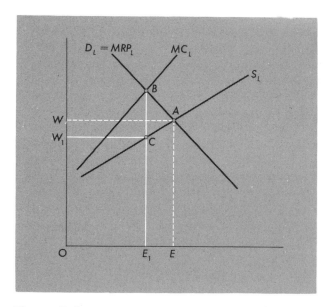

Figure 5–8

A Monopsonistic Buyer of Labor

the cost of hiring an additional worker equals that worker's revenue product. In Figure 5–8 this is point B, where $MRP_L = MC_L$, and corresponds to an employment of E_1. If he goes beyond this, so that $MRP_L < MC_L$, he is losing money on each additional man employed.

Looking now at the labor supply curve, we see that E_1 workers can be hired at a wage rate W_1, so this will be the company's wage level. There is now a gap, shown by the distance BC, between labor's marginal revenue product (BE_1) and its wage (CE_1). The size of this gap depends on the elasticity of labor supply. It is easy to see that if the supply curve in Figure 5–8 were steeper, the MC curve would also rise more rapidly, B would be higher up on the demand curve, both wages and employment would be lower, and the gap BC would be larger. The common sense of this is that the more firmly workers are tied to a particular occupation or area, the greater is the employer's power over the wage level.

The one-company town is perhaps not as common today as in former times. In small communities, however, there are often a few substantial employers who cooperate closely on personnel matters. In such cases, a monopsony wage might result from open or tacit agreement among employers to hold down the wage level. Adam Smith thought that employers were "always and everywhere" engaged in this sort of conspiracy. While "always" is too strong, "commonly" might be accurate.

We can draw a further conclusion from Figure 5–8. Suppose the workers organize a union and persuade the employer to agree to a higher wage—for example, the wage W. The employer's freedom of decision is now restricted. Any portion of S_L lying below the bargained wage is irrelevant. S_L, and therefore MC_L, become horizontal along the line WA. The employer will now move to the point at which this line intersects the demand curve, which will mean an employment of E.

Thus we reach an apparently paradoxical result: starting from a monopsony situation, it is possible to raise the wage rate with no reduction in employment, and in fact with an increase in employment. Note, however, that this is true only up to the wage W. Above this level, employment will begin to decline, though up to point B it will still be higher than the monopsonistic level E_1.

The disagreement among economists over the economic impact of unionism is partly a difference of opinion over whether unions are more monopsony-reducing than monopoly-creating. Where wage rate has been depressed by employers' monopsony power, a union may bring it closer to the level that would exist under pure competition. But a union may also, as we illustrated in Figure 5–7, use its power to push wages above the competitive level. Which situation is more common in practice is a question of fact.

THE LEGAL MINIMUM WAGE

The United States has had a federal minimum wage since the passage of the Fair Labor Standards Act of 1938, commonly known as the Wage Hour Act. This set a minimum wage for workers engaged in interstate commerce, exclusive of agriculture and a few other types of industry. The standard workweek was set as forty hours after 1940, with limited exceptions for certain seasonal industries. Employers were required to pay time-and-a-half for work beyond this limit.

The original minimum wage levels, 25 cents an hour in 1938 and 40 cents an hour in 1945, quickly became obsolete because of the rapid rise of money wages following 1945. The Fair Labor Standards Act has accordingly been amended several times, raising the minimum to $2.30 an hour as of 1976. At the same time, the concept of what constitutes "interstate commerce," and the consequent definition of workers covered by the act, has been considerably broadened. Virtually all workers in mining, construction, manufacturing, public utilities, and government service are now covered. In addition, trade and service enterprises with annual sales of $250,000 or more are covered, and so are workers on large farms (roughly, farms with seven or more wage workers). The main groups still excluded are some 7 million workers in trade and service establishments that do not meet the dollar volume criterion for coverage, plus 2 million domestic servants and 1 million wage workers on smaller farms.

Thirty-eight states, including all the major industrial states, also have minimum wage laws covering intrastate activities; but in fourteen states the law covers only women and minors. The minimum wage is often not specified in the act, but is left for administrative determination on the basis of recommendations by industry wage boards. The minima vary considerably from state to state, being lower in states where the general wage level is low. The minima are generally below, and sometimes substantially below, the federal minimum.

The federal minimum has typically been set well below the *average* level of hourly earnings at the time. The intent is not to raise the general level, but to bring up workers who are judged to have lagged too far behind the general advance of wages. Typically, each amendment has set a new minimum at around 50 percent of actual average hourly earnings in manufacturing. As the general money wage level continues to rise, the percentage relation of the minimum wage to average earnings declines. When it has fallen to one-third or so, Congress gets busy again and raises the minimum.

The impact of the minimum wage system is uneven. It has virtually no effect on durable goods manufacturing, construction, or public utilities. But it does affect trade, services, and low-wage branches of manufacturing, such as cigars, fertilizers, sawmills, seamless hosiery, men's and boys' shirts, footwear, and canning. Within this sector, it impinges on the least-skilled groups and on the lowest-wage areas of the country. The effect on plants in the southern states is considerably more severe than in the North. Much of the pressure for continued increases in the minimum comes from unions that have succeeded in organizing most northern plants in their industries but have not been equally successful in the South. Their only effective tool for bringing pressure on the southern wage level and sheltering union plants from lower-wage competition is through the minimum wage.

There is no doubt that the Fair Labor Standards Act has achieved its direct purpose of raising wages in the lowest-wage areas and industries. Unskilled workers must be brought up to the new minimum; and this often leads to increases for higher job classifications, in order to give them a reasonable differential over the unskilled. Studies of the 1956 and 1963 increases indicate that, in low-wage branches of manufacturing in the southern states, plant-wide average hourly earnings were often increased by 10 to 20 percent.

If wages are raised, and if the labor demand curve has its usual shape, one would expect a reduction in employment. The higher wage level will encourage capital–labor substitution, so that less labor is demanded per unit of output. Moreover, output itself will fall because of the higher level of production costs, which under either monopolistic or competitive assumptions leads to higher product prices and reduced sales. Unemployment may show up particularly in the demise of marginal producers who cannot survive at the new wage level.

An exception to this occurs when the employer is a monopsonistic buyer of labor. In this case, as explained earlier, he has an incentive to restrict employment in order to hold wages below the level for comparable work in other markets. Here a forced increase in the wage rate can, in principle, raise wages and employment simultaneously. The one-company town is the traditional example.

Reliance is also sometimes placed on the "shock effect." This assumes that, in labor markets where supply conditions permit a low wage rate, management is apt to become lazy and inefficient in its use of labor. A forced increase in wage rates will rouse it from its lethargy and lead to improvement in personnel and production management. These may be sufficient to raise labor's marginal physical productivity schedule by as much as the wage rate, so that unit labor costs are no higher than before.

This may indeed happen. But the conclusion that *employment* will remain unchanged does not follow. Consider first a purely competitive industry. A company in which management adjusts as described will end up with unchanged employment; but because of the rise in labor's marginal productivity, its output will be greater than before. This is all right, since by definition a competitive producer can sell as much as he wishes at the market price. But this is not feasible *for the industry as a whole*. If total industry output rises, demand remaining unchanged, the price of the product must fall. This lower price is unprofitable, since unit production costs have not changed. The least efficient producers will presumably vanish from the industry, and employment will decline.

Now consider a monopolist, who is following the marginal-revenue-equals-marginal-cost rule for maximum profit. The minimum wage raises his *MC* curve by, say, 10 percent. Now, by strenuous economizing he raises labor's physical productivity by 10 percent and forces the *MC* curve back to its previous level. His equilibrium output, price, and profit are the same as at the beginning. But his employment is lower, because labor requirements per unit of output have fallen.

What the "shock effect" argument really demonstrates is that a forced wage increase need not permanently reduce an industry's output level or profit level. But this is different from saying that employment will remain unchanged. Management's economizing efforts usually involve using less labor per unit of output, so that employment declines.

There have been numerous statistical studies of the impact of the minimum wage system on employment.[4] They differ considerably in methodology and results, and cannot yet be regarded as conclusive. The bulk of the evidence, however, supports the theoretical prediction that a relative wage increase in certain establishments and industries is associated with a relative decline of employment in those industries. This does not necessarily mean a rise in unemployment for the economy as a whole. So long as part of the economy is not covered by the minimum wage system, workers displaced in the covered sector can seek employment in the uncovered sector. This increase in labor supply will depress relative wage rates in the uncovered sector and produce a wider wage gap between the two sectors.

If all occupations were covered by the minimum wage, however, the effect would be to raise the general standard of employability and to squeeze some workers out of the labor force. There are always people who, because of youth and inexperience, advancing years, limited intelligence, or physical handicaps, are unable to produce at the normal rate. Where there is no legal minimum, employers can hire these people at a wage proportionate to their productivity. With a minimum wage, this is no longer possible. The employer cannot afford to keep on his payroll anyone who cannot produce enough to be worth the minimum wage. Workers of low productivity are discharged. If they then leave the labor force, they will not be counted as unemployed. But the practical result is the same—they become dependent on private or public support.

Several recent studies conclude that the minimum wage system has had a particularly adverse effect on the employment of young people and has contributed to the rise of the teenage unemployment rate.[5] Many econ-

---

[4] See, for example, J. M. Peterson, "Employment Effects of Minimum Wages, 1938–1950," *Journal of Political Economy* (October 1957); David E. Kann, "Minimum Wages, Factor Substitution, and the Marginal Producer," *Quarterly Journal of Economics* (August 1965), pp. 478–86; Jacob J. Kaufman and Terry G. Foran, "The Minimum Wage and Poverty," in Sar A. Levitan and others (eds.), *Towards Freedom from Want* (Madison, Wis.: Industrial Relations Research Association, 1968), pp. 189–218; Arnold Katz, "The Employment Effects of State Minimum Wages," *Journal of Human Resources* (Spring 1973), pp. 250–56; and Robert Goldfarb, "The Policy Content of Quantitative Minimum Wage Research," *IRRA Annual Proceedings* (1974), pp. 261–68.

[5] Thomas G. Moore, "The Effect of Minimum Wages on Teenage Unemployment Rates," *Journal of Political Economy* (July–August 1971), pp. 897–902; Marvin Kosters and Finis Welch, "The Effects of Minimum Wages on the Distribution of Changes in Aggregate Employment," *American Economic Review* (June 1972), pp. 323–32; Douglas K. Adie, "Teenage Unemployment and Real Federal Minimum Wages," *Journal of Political Economy* (March–April 1973), pp. 435–41.

omists now believe that, if the minimum wage system is continued, teen-agers should be given special treatment. At the time of the minimum wage increase in 1973, the administration proposed such a split-level system. This would have permitted young people to be hired at a rate below the general minimum for a limited period of time, during which they could be screened, trained, and brought up to normal productivity levels. The proposal was strongly opposed by organized labor, however, on the ground that any increased employment of teenagers would simply displace older workers, and was voted down in Congress. The idea still seems worthy of consideration for the future.

DISCUSSION QUESTIONS

1. Discuss the geographic size of the labor market for a bituminous coal miner, a computer programmer, a high school mathematics teacher, an aeronautical engineer.

2. (a) What are the main assumptions used in constructing the simplified market models of this chapter? (b) What additional assumptions are required to define a purely competitive labor market?

3. Explain why a union may move the wage rate either closer to, or farther away from, the rate that would prevail under pure competition.

4. What is meant by employers' monopsony power? Under what conditions might one expect such power to be substantial?

5. What determines the elasticity of demand for a particular kind of labor?

6. What are the main factors to be considered in making a rational choice among occupations?

7. Is it plausible to assume that the supply curve of labor to an occupation always slopes upward? Explain.

8. Explain why, under pure competition, the allocation of labor among occupations and the relative wage rates for these occupations are simultaneously determined.

9. In what sense can the allocation of labor that would be achieved under pure competition be regarded as optimal?

10. Explain the meaning and the main effects of:
    (a) an increase in demand for a particular kind of labor.
    (b) an increase in supply of a particular kind of labor.

11. "It is quite possible for a minimum wage system to benefit some workers while at the same time harming others." Discuss.

READING SUGGESTIONS

The operation of competitive labor markets is analyzed in any text on intermediate price theory. See, for example, C. E. FERGUSON, *Microeconomic Theory* (rev. ed.), Homewood, Ill.: Richard D. Irwin, Inc., 1969; SIR DENNIS ROBERTSON, *Lectures on Economic Principles*, Vol. 2, London: Staples Press, 1959; TIBOR SCITOVSKY, *Welfare and Competition* (rev. ed.), Homewood, Ill.: Richard D. Irwin, Inc., 1970; and GEORGE STIGLER, *The Theory of Price* (3d ed.), New York: Macmillan Publishing Co., Inc., 1966.

6

Labor Markets in Operation

The market model described in Chapter 5 has come in for heavier criticism than has any other part of neoclassical economics. Critics have emphasized the many ways in which the underlying assumptions differ from labor market realities. Some have concluded that the theory, far from being helpful, is actually misleading.

Here we must recall the principle that any model should be judged by the predictions that can be drawn from it, and by the correspondence of these predictions with events. The apparatus of Chapter 5 was designed to make predictions about relative wage rates and employment levels in particular occupations and industries. For example, it predicts that, if demand for a particular occupation rises faster than demand for other occupations, there will be an increase in relative employment in that occupation, and at least a temporary increase in its relative wage. Again, an increase in labor supply to an occupation will increase employment in that occupation and reduce its relative wage. These are important predictions, and they are in general accord with the facts.

The correct criticism of the simplified model is not that it is *wrong,* but rather that it is *limited* or incomplete. There are many aspects of reality that it cannot illuminate because of the simple framework within which it operates.

Suppose, for example, that we are interested in such questions as: Why is there a substantial amount of unemployment in the American economy even at business cycle peaks? Why do some groups in the labor force have much higher unemployment rates than others? Why do different employers typically pay different wage rates for the same kind of labor in the same locality? Why do money wages continue to rise even when unemployment exists? And why do they rise faster when unemployment is low than when it is high?

We clearly cannot get any explanation from the models of Chapter 5, in which these phenomena are excluded by definition. Rather, we must develop a more complicated labor market model that is capable of coping with a wider range of phenomena. Specifically—and contrary to the assumptions of Chapter 5—we must take account of the following features of actual labor markets:

1. *Labor demand shifts frequently.* The fortunes of individual companies and industries rise and fall. There are general fluctuations in aggregate demand for output and hence for labor. This means that the traffic through the labor market is heavier than it otherwise would be. Moreover, the labor market operates differently when total employment is rising than when it is falling.

2. *Labor supply is heterogeneous.* Workers differ in physical abilities, intelligence, education, job training, age, sex, color, and other respects that employers regard as significant.

3. *Labor market information is inadequate.* Workers have limited information about available jobs, and employers have limited information about available workers. Both workers and employers have to search the market to increase their information and range of choice. This search activity is time-consuming and expensive.

4. *Unemployment is normal.* Shifts in demand plus inadequate information means that there will usually be some unemployment between jobs. This would be so even if there were always as many job vacancies as workers looking for jobs. In addition, there is usually some "excess unemployment" due to an inadequate number of vacancies, that is, an inadequate level of aggregate demand for output.

5. *Labor mobility is limited.* The tie connecting a particular worker to a particular job is more than a matter of wage rate. Workers do not flit from job to job for a one-cent-an-hour difference in wages. Nor do employers typically lay off existing employees because they could replace them by new workers at a lower hourly rate. This behavior is economically rational. An employer who has spent money on locating and hiring a worker, on putting him through a probationary screening period, and on training him for specific operations in the company has an *investment* in the worker that would be lost if he left the company. For similar reasons, the worker has an investment in his present job. Thus worker decisions about changing jobs and employer decisions about changing workers have an investment aspect as well as a current-rate-of-pay aspect.

FLOWS THROUGH THE LABOR MARKET

The main flows into and out of the labor market are shown in Figure 6–1. The large size of these flows is suggested by Figure 6–2, where we chart hirings, separations, layoffs, and quits as a percentage of employment in manufacturing industries.

At the bottom of Figure 6–1 we show the production apparatus of the economy. Total demand for output rises at an erratic pace over the course of time, requiring additional labor for production. As labor demand rises

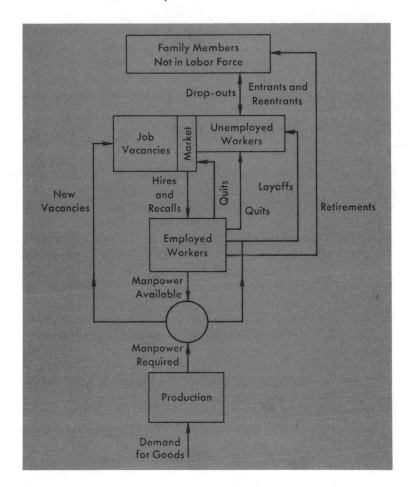

Figure 6–1

Flows and Stocks of Workers and Jobs

SOURCE: Adapted from Charles C. Holt, "Improving the Labor Market Trade-off Between Inflation and Unemployment," *American Economic Review* (May 1969), pp. 135–46.

above present employment, new vacancies are created, which appear on the left side of the diagram. Vacancies are also created continuously through quits and retirements.

On the supply side we see some workers who have quit to take new jobs without ever becoming unemployed. The unemployed include those who have quit without a job in sight, those who have been laid off, and new entrants to the labor force.

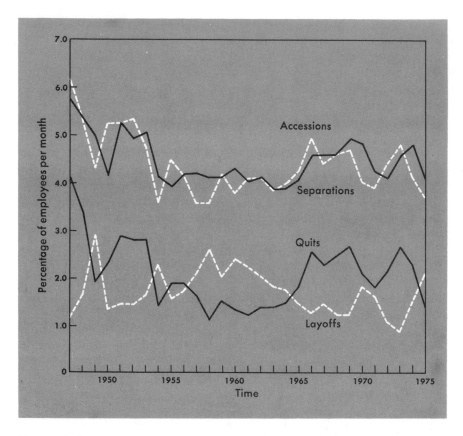

Figure 6–2

Accessions, Separations, Quits, and Layoffs: Annual
Average of Monthly Rates, U.S. Manufacturing

SOURCE: *Employment and Earnings* (Washington, D.C.: Government Printing Office, 1976).

The families at the top of the diagram are the ultimate source of labor supply. Here there is a continuous two-way movement of people into and out of the labor force, for reasons outlined in Chapter 2. The diagram assumes that all those entering or reentering the labor force pass through a period of unemployment, though in fact some of them may obtain jobs right away.

Although the apparatus is readily understood, several features of its operation should be underlined. First, unemployed workers and job vacancies normally coexist, and in large numbers. One tends to think of the unemployed as a surplus, as people "left over" after all vacancies have been filled. It is more accurate to think of them as people in motion through the market, people in course of being fitted into vacancies that are thus destroyed although the supply of vacancies is constantly being renewed. The relative sizes of the "vacancies box" and the "unemployed box" vary, of course, with fluctuations in aggregate demand. During an economic upswing, the vacancies box expands and the unemployed box shrinks; and conversely in recession.

Second, the flows in the diagram are not independent of each other, but are strongly interrelated. More specifically, the system exhibits *negative feedback;* that is, a change that by itself would raise (or lower) the level of unemployment produces other changes that tend to move unemployment back toward the initial level. For example, an increase in vacancies resulting from a general increase in labor demand tends to reduce the unemployed pool. But an increase in vacancies also tends to increase the quit rate and the flow of new workers into the labor force, which tends to replenish the pool. Again, an increase in layoffs during recession raises the number of unemployed; but this lowers the quit rate and increases the number of "discouraged workers" dropping out of the labor force, which brakes the increase in unemployment.

Third, and partly because of this negative feedback, the net change in the *stocks* of vacancies and unemployed workers is small relative to the gross *flows* of people through the market. The year-to-year change in the number of unemployed is typically less than a million. The flow through the market, however, is of the order of 30 million per year. Interestingly enough, the size of the flow during prosperity does not vary much from its size during recession. During recession, the layoff rate rises but the quit rate falls; and conversely during expansion. These opposite fluctuations, which stand out clearly in Figure 6–2, roughly offset each other, so that the "total separations" line moves along rather smoothly.

EMPLOYERS' SEARCH BEHAVIOR

How do employers and workers adjust to limited information about the environment? We begin with the employer because, as demander of labor, he in a sense takes the lead in the market. Much of workers' search behavior, indeed, can be interpreted as a response to employer behavior.

Note first that wage costs are to some extent substitutable for search costs. A company that is known to pay above-average wages can count on a stream of good-quality applicants for work. A company toward the bottom of the area wage structure will have to spend more on advertising and recruitment, and may also find that its applicants are of inferior quality.

This is one reason why a high-wage policy may be económically rational. We shall have more to say about this when we discuss company wage policies in Chapter 9.

A second important consideration is that the company knows more about its present employees, who have been sifted out over the years, than it does about potential recruits. This alone would make it rational to hold onto present employees. It also explains the tendency of employers, when they need additional labor, to pass the word first through present employees. The employer reasons that, if the present employees are satisfactory, their friends and relatives are likely also to be more satisfactory than a random sample from the labor market. In addition, people who already have friends in the company are more likely to accept jobs and to settle down as permanent employees.

Another comon policy is to fill vacancies arising in the company by promoting present employees rather than by outside recruitment. This is good for morale and makes employment in the company more attractive. It is also less risky, because the company knows more about the worker being promoted than it could possibly know about a newcomer. Recognition of this tendency has led to development of the concepts of "inside" and "outside" jobs, and "the internal labor market."

The Internal Labor Market

Different industries have different employment patterns. In some cases, the worker's attachment is to a *craft* rather than to an *employer*. A skilled electrician will count on working for many electrical contractors over the years. For him, "the labor market" usually means the union office. This is a common pattern, not only in industries hiring craftsmen, but in other industries such as longshoring, where employment is intermittent and involves a single type of labor.

But in other industries there is a *hierarchy* of jobs, ranging from unskilled labor to highly skilled and specialized operations, and the worker expects permanence of employment and a chance of occupational progress. The large manufacturing plant is the prototype of this situation, although it exists also in white-collar industries and in government employment. It is here that the concept of an internal labor market becomes relevant.[1]

In a large, hierarchical organization there will usually be dozens or hundreds of different jobs. Many of these are highly specialized, existing only within one industry or even one firm. The employer may not be able to find experienced workers in the outside market, but must provide the necessary training on the job. Moreover, employers usually consider it

---

[1] See Peter B. Doeringer and Michael J. Piore, *Internal Labor Markets and Manpower Analysis* (Lexington, Mass.: D. C. Heath and Company, 1971).

good personnel practice to offer present employees first choice of vacancies on "higher" jobs, and outsiders are considered only after inside sources have been tapped. Union contracts often contain elaborate rules governing which employees shall be entitled to "bid" for a particular vacancy, and how much weight shall be given to length of service, personal efficiency, and other factors in selecting among bidders.

Thus the number of jobs that are open to outside hiring may be much smaller than the number of jobs in the plant. In each production department, new workers may be hired as trainees at the bottom of the skill ladder. From that point they work their way up to more desirable and better-paid jobs as vacancies arise, and in accordance with company policies or union contract rules. Jobs on these promotion ladders are open to outsiders only in the event that no insider wants the job.

Clerical workers, and even executive personnel, also tend to come in at the bottom and work up the ladder in a similar way. The main exceptions are professional, technical, and skilled jobs requiring extended training: doctors and nurses for the company's medical department, computer programmers in the office, skilled maintenance and repair men in the plant. Vacancies on such jobs will be filled by outside recruitment.

Dunlop has termed the jobs that are normally filled by outside recruitment the *ports of entry* into the company. He emphasizes that the number of such ports is limited and may change over time with changes in company organization and collective bargaining practices. The rules and procedures governing interjob movement within the company define the *internal labor market*. Direct linkage between the internal and external markets occurs only at the ports of entry.[2]

A vacancy arising anywhere in the plant will still, if total employment remains unchanged, require recruitment of a worker from outside. But the point of hiring may be quite remote from the point at which the vacancy occurred. A vacancy on a skilled production job may lead to hiring of an unskilled trainee, several insiders having meanwhile moved up the ladder. To the extent that this is true, the employer is hiring *trainability,* rather than a preexisting job skill.

Important consequences follow from this. A worker who has climbed some distance up a promotion ladder in one company and is then thrown out of employment by shifts in demand has suffered a real hardship. He is unlikely to be able to move horizontally to the same level of skill and earnings in another company. More probably he will have to start near the bottom with a new employer and work up once more. A displaced worker may also lose accrued pension rights and other benefits earned by length

---

[2] For a good statement of these concepts, see John T. Dunlop, "Job Vacancy Measures and Economic Analysis," in *The Measurement and Interpretation of Job Vacancies* (New York: National Bureau of Economic Research, 1966), pp. 27–48.

of service. Thus it is rational for workers to show attachment to their present jobs and to regard a forced change of employers as a misfortune.

For jobs that are ports of entry for many companies, the concept of a general labor market makes sense. Workers can move from one company to similar jobs in other companies; and each company's terms of employment must be sufficiently in line with those of other companies to attract the number of recruits it needs. For jobs that are typically filled from within, the concepts of an area-wide market and an equilibrium wage make considerably less sense. Such jobs are not fully insulated from the tides of labor demand and supply in the outside market; but they are a good deal more insulated than the port-of-entry jobs. Wage rates on them are not precisely determined by the market, but are set by rule-of-thumb procedures that will be examined in a later chapter.

Hiring Standards and Screening

Not every applicant for work gets equal consideration. The employer normally has a set of hiring standards that are used to *screen* out the candidates who will be considered seriously.

These standards serve a double purpose. First, companies normally have more applicants than they can hire. This is true of the "best" employers almost all the time, and it is true of almost all employers in recession periods. To interview, test, and check references on every applicant would be quite expensive. Screening devices reduce the flow to manageable proportions and thus hold down preemployment costs.

Further, in the face of uncertainty about how an applicant will perform on the job, the employer falls back on characteristics that he regards as reasonable *proxies* for trainability and job performance. He knows—or thinks he knows—that high school graduates perform better than dropouts, that a married worker of 30 is more likely to stay with him than a teenager, and so on. These beliefs are related to the company's past employment experience, though they may rest partly on noneconomic preferences.

The specifications that may be important in a particular case include:

1. *Sex*. Jobs tend to be ticketed as "men's work" or "women's work."
2. *Age*. The preferred employee is usually one with some, but not too much, work experience—someone in his twenties or early thirties. People younger than this not only have less experience but are more prone to change jobs, while older people are often regarded as less vigorous, less trainable, more subject to illness and accident.
3. *Color*. The fact that in the past white workers have normally been preferred to black workers of equivalent qualifications is apparent from casual observation. The reasons for this discrimination and the efforts to curb it by law will be considered in Chapter 8.
4. *Education*. In some cases educational requirements are built into the

job. A lawyer should have finished law school, a chemical engineer should have at least an undergraduate degree, and so on. But even when education is not strictly essential, it is normally preferred. Large companies want their potential executives to have at least a college degree, and many prefer graduate training in business administration. High school graduation is generally required for white-collar employment, and to an increasing extent even for good manual jobs.

The fact that employers' educational specifications are often higher than is required for job performance does not necessarily mean that they are irrational. Completion of a certain educational level is an indication of intelligence, energy, motivation, and future learning potential. More highly educated employees may also be considered socially more cooperative and adaptable, "nice people to have around." At any rate, employers' educational preferences are real and they confront the school dropout with substantial problems.

5. *Experience and proficiency.* Experience enters mainly for professional, technical, and skilled manual jobs on which the employee may be presumed to continue learning and improving his productive capacity for some time. For low-skilled jobs with a short training period, the employer may actually prefer less experience to more, on the ground that the worker has less to unlearn and "we can teach him to do it our way." Even when experience is not important, however, the personnel office will usually put the applicant through proficiency tests. Prospective assemblers of radio parts may be given tests of manual dexterity, bookkeepers tests of arithmetical aptitude, typists and stenographers tests of speed and accuracy.

6. *Present job attachment.* A common situation, particularly in small towns and cities, is the existence of a tacit understanding among employers that they will not hire away each other's workers. These understandings, often termed "antipirating agreements," operate as follows. An applicant at plant *A* is asked what he is doing now. He replies that he is employed at plant *B* but wants to move. The personnel manager of plant *A* then calls the personnel manager of plant *B* and asks whether he is willing to release the worker in question. If the personnel manager of plant *B* says that his company still needs the worker and does not wish him to leave, plant *A* will usually decline to employ him. In line with this view, employers usually object to the public employment service's registering a man for work if he is currently employed. These practices mean that a worker may be forced to cut his ties with his present employer before seeking a new one. This increases the risks of movement and reduces the number of workers willing to take the risk.

Hiring preferences, related in part to differences in labor quality, have several interesting consequences. First, "labor supply" to the firm includes only those workers whom the employer is willing to count as part of the supply; and this changes with the overall demand–supply situation. In a recession period, when many unemployed workers are available, an employer may be able to set high standards and get exactly the characteristics he prefers. But in a tight labor market he may have to reduce his requirements substantially. The available labor supply depends on how low the employer is willing to dip into the manpower barrel.

If we suppose that, when he lowers his standards of age, experience, education, and so on, he thereby gets workers of lower productive capacity, then his cost of labor *per unit of standard efficiency* will increase. There is little evidence on how far hiring specifications are in fact related to efficiency, but some relation must surely exist.

A further consequence is that the pool of unemployed at any time is biased toward the least preferred members of the labor force; and a particular worker's chances of reemployment depend partly on his personal characteristics. The unemployed can be regarded as arrayed in a queue, with employers hiring from the top of the queue and working downward. At the head of the queue are white high school graduates aged twenty to forty, with good work experience and good scores on proficiency tests. Toward the tail of the queue come the teenagers, the oversixties, the unskilled, the illiterate.

The use of screening devices can involve either or both of two types of discrimination: (1) There is "statistical discrimination" when a worker who is fully qualified for a job, perhaps better qualified than the one actually hired, is screened out of consideration on the basis of color, sex, age, or education. This is unfair to the individual; but the employer can rationalize it on the ground that the cost (to him) of making some mistakes of this kind is less than the cost of putting every applicant through the full interviewing and testing procedure. (2) Alternatively, the real purpose of the screening test may be to discriminate—the employer just doesn't want women, or black workers, or some other group. Even when this is the intent, however, the hiring rule will usually be explained on economic grounds. To penetrate behind the procedure to the intent is difficult, as we shall see in discussing employment discrimination in Chapter 8.

The "Dual Labor Market" Hypothesis

Some economists have extended the internal labor market approach to the point of asserting that there are two distinct types of labor market: *primary* and *secondary*. The primary sector involves relatively large employers with well-defined internal promotion ladders, which offer stable employment, good promotion possibilities, and (usually) relatively good wages and working conditions. In the secondary market these features are absent. Jobs are short-term, low-skilled, low-paid, and offer little scope for promotion. The distinction is between a steelworker employed by Bethlehem Steel and a dishwasher employed by Charlie's Quick Lunch.

Piore has characterized the two sectors as follows:

> The basic hypothesis of the dual labor market was that the labor market is divided into two essentially distinct sectors, termed the *primary* and the *secondary* sectors. The former offer jobs with relatively high wages, good working conditions, chances of advancement, equity and due process in the administration of work rules and, above all, employment

stability. Jobs in the secondary sector, by contrast, tend to be low-paying, with poorer working conditions, little chance of advancement, a highly personalized relationship between workers and supervisors which leaves wide latitude for favoritism and is conducive to harsh and capricious work discipline, and with considerable instability in jobs and a high turnover among the labor force. The hypothesis was designed to explain the problems of disadvantaged, particularly black workers in urban areas, which had previously been diagnosed as one of unemployment.[3]

Other economists, however, have questioned whether this adds up to a new theory of the labor market.[4] Jobs cannot be sorted into two distinct boxes—"good" and "bad." They range from best to worst jobs in a continuum, with no clear dividing line. Wage determination in secondary markets does not require a new and different explanation—indeed, these markets are unusually competitive, as compared with the administered wage structures in the primary sector. Secondary sector workers are not blocked off permanently from primary employment. There is substantial upward mobility, particularly during a business cycle upswing.

The dual market theorists have made a contribution, however, in emphasizing the negative feedback mechanisms operative in casual, low-wage employment. Employers in this market offer little stability of employment, opportunity for learning on the job, or prospect of advancement. They may also be unusually prone to hiring discrimination and harsh discipline. Thus workers employed on these jobs get a low yield on such human capital as they do possess. This gives them little incentive to invest in further education and training; and this reinforces the employer's conviction that they are unproductive and undeserving of better treatment. The lack of skill and work motivation which makes it hard for low-wage workers to find better jobs cannot be taken as inherent characteristics of the workers themselves. In part, at least, they result from the feedback mechanism in which the worker finds himself involved and from which it is not easy to escape.

WORKERS' SEARCH BEHAVIOR

The fact that a worker has a job, and a certain investment in the job, does not mean that he is entirely out of the market. He may be able to move to a higher-wage company at his present job level; or he may be able, by

---

[3] Michael J. Piore, "Notes for a Theory of Labor Market Stratification," Working Paper No. 95 (Cambridge, Mass.: Massachusetts Institute of Technology, 1972).

[4] For a variety of views, see Glen C. Cain, "The Challenge of Dual and Radical Theories of the Labor Market to Orthodox Theory," *American Economic Review* (May 1975), pp. 16–22; Michael L. Wachter, "Primary and Secondary Labor Markets: A Critique of the Dual Approach," *Brookings Papers on Economic Activity*, No. 3 (1974), pp. 637–80; Paul Osterman, "An Empirical Study of Labor Market Segmentation," *Industrial and Labor Relations Review* (July 1975), pp. 508–23; Glen G. Cain, "The Challenge of Segmented Labor Market Theories to Orthodox Theories: A Survey," *Journal of Economic Literature* (December 1976), pp. 1215–57.

moving, to get promotion to more responsible and better-paid work. An alert worker will keep his eye out for such opportunities and, if he sees another job with estimated future advantages exceeding those of his present job, he will switch. Each year many workers go directly from one job to another without passing through the unemployed pool. This is especially common in professional and managerial employment, where people usually have the new job lined up before leaving the old.

There are two difficulties, however, particularly at lower occupational levels. First, having to put in eight hours a day on one job reduces the time that can be spent looking for another. Company employment offices and the state employment service are usually open only during business hours on weekdays, which may be precisely the time one has to be at work. Second, employers discourage job-switching, which is often stigmatized as "labor pirating." An employer will engage in this "ungentlemanly" practice only for unusually well-qualified workers whose desirability outweighs the probable animosity of fellow employers.

For these reasons a worker will often find it expedient to quit his job and engage in a period of full-time job search. If he is being rational rather than impulsive, a decision to quit involves a probability estimate of the characteristics of the new job that he may be able to find, and how long it will take him to find it. He will quit only if the estimated value of the hypothetical new job outweighs the value of the present job, plus the income loss during the period of job search, plus (if he is averse to risk) the costs of uncertainty.

These estimates are influenced by the state of demand for labor. In a year of economic expansion, when jobs are plentiful and wages are rising, workers' estimates of how well they can do in the market will also rise. So quit rates show a marked cyclical pattern, rising in prosperity and falling in recession. Quit rates also vary widely among occupations and industries, and are related to the worker's investment in job-specific training. Turnover is highest in such occupations as casual labor, domestic service, low-skilled jobs in hotels and restaurants, retail stores, hospitals, and other service industries. Here the degree of skill is so slight, the relative wage so low, and the prospect of advancement so small, that the future value of the present job is low, and is often outweighed by the lure of the bird in the bush.

The pool of job seekers includes not only those who have quit but also those who have been laid off or discharged and those who are just entering or reentering the labor force. The search for work goes on through many channels, differing somewhat with the skill involved. Skilled craftsmen tend to work through the union office. White-collar workers make considerable use of private employment agencies. Branch offices of the state employment service, help-wanted advertising, and other media play their part. The commonest channel, however, is applying directly at the company or following up leads from friends and relatives.[5] This is in part a response to the fact that employers rely heavily on these informal channels.

An unemployed worker is not simply in limbo. Job search is a productive activity, with costs and potential benefits. The direct cost is the income lost by not working. The cost is reduced if the worker is eligible for unemployment compensation benefits, but it may still amount to half or more of his normal earnings. The benefits consist of the fact that further search will reveal additional job openings, some of which may be superior to those he encountered at first. He probably has a vague idea of the range of wage rates available in the area; but he does not know which wage is offered at which place, or which employers are hiring at the moment. Job search, then, is like drawing slips of paper from a black box, each with a wage rate written on it and a "Yes" or "No" prospect of employment. As he continues to draw, there is always a chance that a high-wage job will pop out of the box.

The worker typically has only one job offer before him at a time, which he must accept or reject very quickly. So he needs a *decision criterion,* which will tell him whether an offer should be accepted or rejected. This criterion is determined by weighing the costs of continued unemployment against the possible gain from continued search.

The criterion is most easily formulated as a minimum acceptable wage rate, though in practice other dimensions of the job will be relevant. At the beginning of unemployment, the criterion will be framed mainly in terms of past experience. If a worker has been earning $5.00 an hour, he may set his asking price for a new job at $5.50 in order to improve himself. This price will be influenced also by what he knows about the range of rates prevailing in the area, and by whether jobs appear to be plentiful or scarce.

As he continues to search, two things happen. His expectation of gains from further search are likely to fall. He will not apply entirely at random, but will start with the places that he believes have the best jobs in the area. As he works down the roster from better to poorer employers, his estimate of the wage he can get will tend to fall. At the same time, the cost of an extra week of unemployment is likely to rise. Studies of how people adjust to income lost during unemployment indicate that for a month or two the main adjustments are some reduction in expenditure levels (presumably by postponing purchases of durables and semidurables), some reduction of liquid assets, and some accumulation of unpaid store bills. As time goes on, however, the burden of debt increases, and the squeeze on consumption becomes more severe.

As the cost of continued unemployment rises and the estimate of potential benefit declines, the workers' minimum acceptable wage falls over

---

[5] For statistical data see Carl Rosenfeld, "Jobseeking Methods Used by American Workers," *Monthly Labor Review* (August 1975), pp. 39–42.

the course of time. The hypothesis that the acceptable wage is inversely related to length of unemployment has been tested and confirmed by numerous research studies.[6] Eventually, the worker comes across a job that meets his minimum standards at that time, and his unemployment ends.

How long this takes is much influenced by the overall state of the market, that is, the relative numbers of vacancies and unemployed. Visualize the market as a basketball court containing thousands of red and blue balloons. Each red balloon is a vacant job, with a wage rate attached. Each blue balloon is an available worker, with a minimum acceptable wage. If a blue balloon hits a red balloon, and if the offered wage is equal to or greater than the acceptable minimum, the two balloons explode and disappear from the scene. During a cycle upswing, the number of vacancies is rising and the price tags that they carry are also rising; for both reasons, the speed with which acceptable jobs are found tends to increase.

In years of high labor demand, the average time required to find a new job is about a month. In recession years, this may rise to six or seven weeks. Even during recession, however, most of the unemployed have been unemployed for relatively short periods.

This theory of job search has interesting implications. As Stigler pointed out initially, it provides one reason for coexistence of different wage rates for the same skill in the same labor market. Such differences would be eliminated only if workers continued to search the market so long as any wage differences remained. But workers will not do this because it does not pay them to do it. They will search only up to the point at which the marginal cost of further search equals the marginal benefit; and this is quite consistent with permanent wage differences.[7] Search theory is helpful also in explaining the volume and characteristics of unemployment.

UNEMPLOYMENT: TYPES AND SOURCES

The Level of Unemployment

Unemployment is the difference between the amount of labor offered *at present wage levels and working conditions* and the amount of labor hired at those levels. The most obvious aspect of the problem is full-time

---

[6] For a review of findings in this area, see Charles C. Holt, "Job Search, Phillips' Wage Relation, and Union Influence: Theory and Evidence," in E. S. Phelps (ed.), *Microeconomic Foundations of Employment and Inflation Theory* (New York: W. W. Norton & Company, Inc., 1970). See also William F. Barnes, "Job Search Models, the Duration of Unemployment, and the Asking Wage: Some Empirical Evidence," *Journal of Human Resources* (Spring 1975), pp. 230–40.

[7] George J. Stigler, "Information in the Labor Market," *Journal of Political Economy*, Supplement, *Investment in Human Capital* (October 1962), pp. 94–105.

unemployment—the situation in which people are willing and able to work but have no jobs. Determining the size of this group is not as easy as may appear at first glance. How does one judge whether a worker has the necessary ability to find or hold a job? What exactly is meant by "willingness to work"? Despite these problems of measurement, we have relatively reliable information from the Census Bureau's "Monthly Report on the Labor Force," based on a sample survey of households throughout the country.

This survey also collects information on part-time workers, who are divided into (1) those who are working the number of hours they prefer, and (2) those who are working fewer hours than they prefer. The latter are said to be "working part-time for economic reasons." The amount of time they are losing, when added to that of the full-time unemployed, yields a measure known as "labor force time lost."

There are, in fact, a considerable number of different "unemployment rates," each of which might be useful for judgments of economic welfare and formulation of employment policy. Following the custom of labeling different money supply measures as M_1, M_2, and so on, we might distinguish U_1, U_2, and so on up to U_7.[8] Here are the definitions and magnitudes for the year 1975:

Concept	Definition	Percent, 1975
U_1	Persons unemployed 15 weeks or longer, as percent of civilian labor force	2.7
U_2	Unemployed job losers, as percent of civilian labor force	4.7
U_3	Unemployed household heads, as percent of household head labor force	5.8
U_4	Unemployed full-time job seekers, as percent of full-time labor force	8.1
U_5	Total unemployed, as percent of civilian labor force (*standard official measure*)	8.5
U_6	Total full-time job seekers plus half part-time job seekers plus half those on part-time for economic reasons, as percent of civilian labor force less half of part-time labor force	10.3
U_7	U_6 plus "discouraged workers," as percent of civilian labor force plus discouraged workers less half of part-time labor force	11.5

See also J. J. McCall, "Economics of Information and Job Search," *Quarterly Journal of Economics* (February 1970), pp. 113–26.

[8] Adapted from Julius Shiskin, "Employment and Unemployment: The Doughnut or the Hole?" *Monthly Labor Review* (February 1976), pp. 3–10.

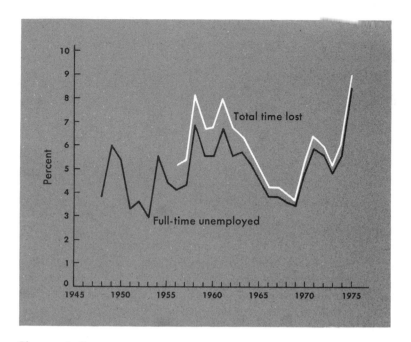

Figure 6–3

Full-Time Unemployed, and Total Time Lost
Through Unemployment, 1948–75

SOURCE: *Economic Report of the President* (Washington, D.C.: Government Printing
Office, 1977).

Figure 6–3 shows the movement of the full-time unemployment rate
(U_5) and the figure of total time lost (close to U_6, though not quite identical with it). The unemployment rate has fluctuated mostly in the range of
4 to 7 percent of the labor force. Total time lost is typically about 1 percent
higher—more than this in recession years, less than this in boom years.
    Unemployment rates in the United States are rather high compared
with those in other industrial countries. A comparison over several years,
adjusted to U.S. definitions of unemployment, is shown in Table 1.[9] Canada has unemployment rates at roughly the U.S. level. The Italian rate is
explained mainly by the existence of a large depressed area in southern
Italy. The five other countries in the table typically have unemployment
rates less than half those of the United States, with the rates of Japan and
West Germany especially low. The reasons are not fully known but prob-

---

[9] Data are from Arthur F. Neef and Rose A. Holland, "Comparative Unemployment Rates, 1964–66," *Monthly Labor Review* (April 1967), pp. 18–20.

Table 1

Full-Time Unemployment as Percentage of Labor Force, Adjusted to U.S. Definitions, Eight Countries, 1959–66

	United States	Canada	France	West Germany	United Kingdom	Italy	Japan	Sweden
1959	5.5	6.0	2.8	1.6	3.1	5.7	1.9	—
1960	5.6	7.0	2.6	0.7	2.4	4.3	1.4	—
1961	6.7	7.1	2.0	0.4	2.3	3.7	1.3	1.5
1962	5.6	5.9	2.0	0.4	2.8	3.2	1.1	1.5
1963	5.7	5.5	2.4	0.4	3.4	2.7	1.1	1.7
1964	5.2	4.7	1.9	0.4	2.4	3.0	1.0	1.6
1965	4.6	3.9	2.3	0.3	2.1	4.0	1.0	1.2
1966	3.9	3.6	2.4	0.4	2.3	4.3	1.1	1.6

ably would include the following: (1) These are relatively small countries, in which people do not have to move so far to get from declining to expanding regions. (2) Most of them have long had active labor market policies designed to accelerate retraining and relocation of labor. Such policies were not seriously pursued in the United States until the mid-sixties. (3) These countries have in general maintained a higher level of aggregate demand—a level that produced fuller utilization of labor and other resources.

Unemployment and Aggregate Demand

The bulk of unemployment in the economy can be classified as either long-term or short-term, and can be associated either with inadequate total demand or with frictions and maladjustments in the labor market. This yields the four-way classification shown below.[10] Although these categories are not entirely independent, they provide a useful framework for our discussion.

	Short-Term	*Long-Term*
Inadequate demand	Cyclical unemployment	Growth-gap unemployment
Labor market maladjustment	Frictional unemployment	Structural unemployment

---

[10] While this conceptual framework is familiar, the terminology used here is borrowed from Eleanor Gilpatrick, "On the Classification of Unemployment: A View of the Structural-Inadequate Demand Debate," *Industrial and Labor Relations Review* (January 1966), pp. 201–12.

Cyclical unemployment is a familiar fact of life. Although we have had two long economic expansions (from 1938 to 1945 and from 1961 to 1969) associated with war conditions, these are unusual. An upswing typically lasts only two to four years, after which the economy turns down into recession. Hours of work tend to fall. Many workers are reduced to part-time work. Many others are laid off entirely. Even the mild downswings of 1953–54, 1957–58, 1960–61, and 1969–70, added about 2 million workers to the unemployed. Many people become discouraged about the prospects of finding work, and leave the labor force or decide not to enter it. Thus during recession, in addition to those visibly unemployed, there is a substantial amount of "hidden unemployment" consisting of people who would seek work if the chances of finding work were better.

Demand unemployment is not just a cyclical phenomenon. It would be so if each upswing carried all the way to full employment before toppling over. But this need not happen. From 1929 to 1941 the American economy remained well below full employment even at cycle peaks, and this was true again on a less dramatic scale from 1958 to 1965. An economy can experience periods of prolonged sluggishness during which demand unemployment is present continuously. In such periods there is a "GNP gap." The economy's productive capacity is rising faster than actual output, and part of the capacity remains unutilized. "Growth-gap unemployment" seems a good term for this longer-run demand deficiency.

The amount of demand unemployment at any time cannot be measured precisely. One tends to think of demand unemployment as the excess of actual unemployment over the irreducible minimum that would exist anyway because of frictional and structural factors. If this minimum is estimated at 4 percent, while the actual rate is 6 percent, then by subtraction we conclude that there is 2 percent unemployment due to deficient demand. If demand can be raised enough to absorb an additional 2 percent of the labor force, we shall arrive at "full employment."

Unfortunately, this line of reasoning is not tenable. The reason is that the level of frictional and structural unemployment is itself a function of aggregate demand for labor. As demand for labor rises, enabling jobs to be found more rapidly, the "irreducible minimum" of unemployment shrinks. But as the level of unemployment falls, the rate of wage and price increase tends to accelerate. Unemployment can be reduced, not merely to 4 percent, but to 3 percent or even lower if we are willing to accept a sufficiently high rate of inflation. Full employment is not a matter of labor force measurement but a matter of choice among conflicting economic goals. This issue, one of the major policy issues in contemporary economics, will be analyzed further in Chapter 10.

Frictional Unemployment

Frictional unemployment arises partly from short-term irregularities in the demand for labor by particular industries and enterprises, which occur apart from general cyclical fluctuations. In such industries as merchant shipping and longshoring, the number of men needed in a particular port varies from day to day. Orders coming into a manufacturing plant in a particular month may be larger or smaller than expected. Although employment fluctuations can be smoothed out by use of inventories, overtime work, and other buffers, they cannot be avoided entirely.

Seasonality of operations is a familiar phenomenon, especially in agriculture and building construction. In the colder regions of the country, building activity tapers off during the winter months. In crop raising, there is a peak of activity during the harvest season. The men's and women's clothing industries work hard while getting out the spring and fall styles, but slacken off in between. Seasonal industries tend to attract enough labor to meet their peak requirements during the rush season, which means that some of these people are unemployed in the slack season. In a competitive labor market, this failure to obtain a full year's work would be compensated by a higher hourly rate. But the idle time is still wasteful from a social standpoint.

In the United States during the early sixties, seasonal unemployment seems to have constituted about 15 percent of total unemployment, or somewhat less than 1 percent of the labor force. In Canada, where the climate is more severe and seasonal activities are relatively more important, the figures were roughly twice as high—30 percent of all unemployment and close to 2 percent of the labor force.[11] These figures are substantial enough to cause concern. In Canada, the Dominion government has attempted to shift some of its own construction to the winter months, has encouraged the provincial governments to do the same, and has agreed to pay 50 percent of the direct labor cost on some municipal projects not usually carried out in winter. Moreover, it has encouraged housing starts in the autumn by providing funds at reduced interest rates through the Central Mortgage and Housing Corporation. There has not yet been a thorough analysis of the impact of these programs on seasonality in the construction industry.

But even if seasonal and irregular fluctuations were absent, the large flow of workers through the labor market would involve some unemploy-

---

[11] See David C. Smith, "Seasonal Unemployment and Economic Conditions," in Arthur M. Ross (ed.), *Employment Policy and the Labor Market* (Berkeley and Los Angeles: University of California Press, 1965), p. 196.

ment between jobs. Workers need time to inquire of friends and relatives, visit the state employment service, apply directly to companies, weed out acceptable from unacceptable jobs; and the employer needs time to interview applicants, administer preemployment tests, and decide whom to hire.

Suppose, for example, that 30 percent of the labor force must find new jobs each year, and suppose that job hunting requires an average of one month. This would produce an average unemployment rate throughout the year of $30/100 \times 1/12 = 1/40$, or 2.5 percent of the labor force.

The level of frictional unemployment depends partly on the efficiency of the labor market, and is in fact the best index of efficiency. If the average job-hunting period could be cut from four weeks to two weeks through improvements in information and clearinghouse facilities, frictional unemployment would be cut in half. How much can actually be done in this direction will be discussed in the next chapter.

But the level of frictional unemployment is also affected by the state of demand, by the relative number of job vacancies and unemployed workers. It makes a great difference whether the number of vacancies equals the number of unemployed, or whether it is only one-half or one-quarter of that number.

George Perry has estimated [12] that, at a national unemployment rate of 3 percent, a prime-age (twenty-five to forty-four) male worker would take an average of 4.3 weeks to find a new job. At an unemployment rate of 6 percent, however, the average length of job search would be 6.6 weeks. This is why one must regard frictional unemployment not as a fixed amount but rather as a function of aggregate demand for labor.

Structural Unemployment

The unemployment we observe at cycle peaks is typically in the range of 4 to 5 percent. Clearly, not all of this is frictional in the sense just described. The reason is that, instead of a single labor market, we have a great number of submarkets for particular jobs, with specialized skills and qualifications. Most of the interaction between workers and vacancies occurs within these submarkets. The walls between submarkets are rather impermeable in the short run, and are not easy to penetrate even in the longer run. Thus it is possible, even normal, to have an excess of vacancies over unemployed workers in some markets coexisting with an excess of workers over vacancies in others. Vacancies and unemployed cannot get together and cancel out, but simply coexist. Unemployment arising in this way is usually called *structural*.

---

[12] George L. Perry, "Unemployment Flows in the U.S. Labor Market," *Brookings Papers on Economic Activity*, No. 2 (1972), pp. 245–78.

To take an extreme example: suppose all the new jobs becoming available in a particular year are professional jobs requiring college training, while all the new workers becoming available are high school dropouts. Then the vacancies would presumably continue unfilled and the workers would continue unemployed. Such structural unemployment is more serious than frictional unemployment. It is likely to continue for a longer time, and its reduction requires greater effort and expense.

The distinction between frictional and structural unemployment can be illustrated by a simple diagram (Figure 6–4). The vertical axis shows the number of job vacancies in the economy, the horizontal axis shows the number of unemployed workers. Along the 45-degree line *OF*, the number of vacancies equals the number of unemployed workers—one possible definition of "full employment." Above the line there is excess demand for labor, while below the line there is excess supply.

Over the course of the business cycle, the economy can be regarded as moving up or down a curve such as B_1. On the upswing, vacancies are increasing and unemployment is falling, so we travel up the curve to the left. On the downswing, we move back down to the right. Such a curve is usually called a *Beveridge curve,* after Sir William Beveridge, who first ex-

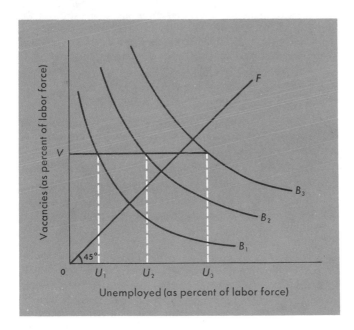

Figure 6–4

Beveridge Curves Indicating Differing Levels of
Structural Unemployment

pounded the full employment concept during the 1940s.[13] Beveridge, incidentally, defined full employment as a position to the left of the 45-degree line, involving an excess of vacancies over job seekers.

What, then, is the significance of the higher curves B_2 and B_3? These correspond to progressively worse *structural* conditions in the labor market. They are worse because, for a given level of vacancies such as V, the level of unemployment rises from U_1 to U_2 to U_3 as we move up to higher Beveridge curves. The higher curves represent increasingly severe obstacles to movement of unemployed workers in some submarkets toward vacancies in others.

Measures to reduce structural unemployment, then, involve trying to shift leftward, closer to the origin, the B-curve on which the economy is presently operating. To the extent that this is possible, the amount of unemployment corresponding to a given level of aggregate demand will be lower. Measures to raise aggregate demand, on the other hand, reduce unemployment by moving the economy upward to the left along the *same* B-curve.

What determines the severity of structural unemployment in an economy at a particular time? Relevant considerations include:

1. *The rapidity of shifts in labor demand.* Over the past generation in the United States such shifts have been quite rapid. The direction of shift has been away from jobs with low skill and education. The number of farmers and laborers has fallen, while the number of professional, managerial, and technical workers has risen. The demand for schoolteachers rose rapidly during the fifties and sixties as the "baby boom" swelled school enrollments; but demand ceased to rise in the seventies as falling birth rates brought a decline of enrollments.

2. *The speed and accuracy of supply adjustments.* The fact that demand is shifting does not necessarily mean a mismatching of demands and supplies. If demand trends could be accurately forecast, if young people preparing to enter the labor force were perfectly informed concerning them, and if the necessary educational and training facilities were always available, one could imagine a situation in which the qualifications of those emerging from the educational system just matched the pattern of new job vacancies. But these requirements can never be entirely realized. So it is quite possible that new entrants to the labor force will be undereducated, in the sense that their average educational level falls below the average educational requirements on new jobs. And it is very likely that they will be miseducated, in the sense of oversupply of some skills and undersupply of others.

3. *The flexibility of skill coefficients.* This depends on production technology. If a certain line of production requires exactly so many people at each skill level, with no possibility of substitution among skills, then a shortage of any one skill will shut down production, causing unemployment among workers whose skills are complementary to the one in short supply. If, on the

---

[13] See in particular the famous "Beveridge Report," *Full Employment in a Free Society* (New York: W. W. Norton & Company, Inc., 1945).

other hand, a shortage of one skill can readily be compensated by substitution of others, structural maladjustments are less likely. Fortunately, a shortage (and associated high price) of one skill sets up a search for substitution possibilities. When fully trained, all-round machinists become unavailable, there is greater effort to break down jobs so that they can be performed by partly trained men. When doctors are very scarce, some of their work can be taken over by interns, nurses, and technicians.

4. *The transferability of skills.* How much time is required for an adult worker whose skill has become obsolete to learn a new skill that is in active demand? This depends on such things as whether his old skill is part of a larger skill-family within which transference is relatively easy; whether his educational and training background has been broad or highly specialized; whether adult retraining facilities and programs are readily available; whether the jobs for which demand is expanding have a long or a short training period. Geographical considerations are also important. If the geographic location of new jobs is shifting rapidly, if information does not filter readily from one area to another, if costs of movement are high, the likelihood of structural maladjustments is increased.

5. *The fixity of employers' noneconomic hiring specifications.* Employers tend to specify higher educational requirements than are strictly necessary for job performance. They tend to prefer white workers over equally qualified black workers, and often to prefer male workers (who may be scarce) over women workers (who may be more readily available). These preferences soften up as demand for labor rises, but they rarely vanish entirely. They may create a problem of labor transferability on social grounds even where there is no real problem on economic grounds.

6. *Geographic diversity of the economy.* Each area has its own complex of industries and, depending on the fortunes of these industries, area shortages and surpluses of labor can readily develop. Information flows between areas are even less adequate than those within areas, and interarea movement is also expensive. Thus disparities in unemployment rates among areas get corrected only with a considerable lag. The long-standing unemployment problem of the Appalachian coal-mining areas and the New England textile towns are classic cases in point.

Robert Hall has pointed out [14] a continuing difference in unemployment rates among major metropolitan areas. Chicago, Houston, and Washington have consistently low unemployment rates, New York and Philadelphia are considerably higher, while Los Angeles and San Francisco are still higher—typically twice as high as the lowest cities in the group. These differentials were not reduced appreciably even under the boom conditions of 1965–69. Unemployment fell substantially in all cities, but the differentials among them remained. Interestingly enough, there is a marked positive correlation between a city's relative *unemployment* level and its relative *wage* level. A plausible hypothesis is that surplus workers do not leave the high-wage cities because the wage advantage, if and when they do get a job, compensates for the higher probability of unemployment.

Although structural unemployment is unresponsive in the short run to

---

[14] Robert E. Hall, "Why Is the Unemployment Rate So High at Full Employment?" *Brookings Papers on Economic Activity*, No. 3 (1970), pp. 369–402.

fluctuations in aggregate demand, it is somewhat responsive over a longer period, particularly a prolonged period of unusually high demand such as 1941–45 or 1965–69. Under the pressure of high demand, obsolete skills get "melted down" and cast into new molds. Workers have a stronger incentive to learn new skills or to change localities when jobs are obviously available. Employers facing labor shortages also have a stronger incentive to invest in training and to modify noneconomic hiring requirements.

But structural unemployment does not vanish even at demand peaks. The number of unfilled job openings at the state employment services rose from around 200,000 in 1962–63 to more than 400,000 in the period from 1966 to 1968. Moreover, about 50 percent of these jobs—and 75 percent of the professional, technical, and managerial jobs—had remained open for thirty days or longer, an indication of genuine shortage. Considering that only a minority of vacancies are listed with the employment service, there were obviously widespread shortages in specific occupations at this time. During these same years there were typically about a half-million workers who had been unemployed for fifteen weeks or more. Considerable mismatching of supplies and demands is indicated.

The effect of structural unemployment is to raise the unemployment rate corresponding to a certain rate of price increase. Suppose that, at a certain level of aggregate demand, frictional unemployment alone would amount to 4 percent of the labor force. In addition, however, there are long-term unfilled vacancies equal to 1 percent of the labor force, and a corresponding number of workers who cannot fit into these jobs because they lack the necessary qualifications. Total unemployment, then, is 5 percent. Prices are rising at, say, 5 percent per year.

Now suppose that the unemployed who lack qualifications could be "melted down," transformed instantaneously into proper candidates for the available vacancies. Then employment could be raised by 1 percent and unemployment reduced to 4 percent. Aggregate demand would have to be raised sufficiently to absorb the increased output. But one could then have a higher level of output and consumption, and 4 percent unemployment, with prices rising no faster than they used to rise with 5 percent unemployment.

The Differential Impact of Unemployment

Unemployment is distributed unevenly over the labor force. Laborers experience much more unemployment than skilled manual workers, and the latter have substantially higher rates than clerical workers. Nonwhite workers experience substantially more unemployment than white workers—partly, but not entirely, because they fall in the lower occupational groups. Teenagers have much higher unemployment rates than older workers.

Table 2

Variation in Unemployment Periods by Sex and Age, with an Overall Unemployment Rate of 5 Percent, 1972 Economy

Sex and Age Group	Group Unemployment Rate (Percent)	Unemployment Spells	
		Average Length (Weeks)	Number per Year
Males			
16–19	14.0	4.0	1.82
20–24	8.4	4.8	0.91
25–44	2.9	5.8	0.26
45–64	2.5	6.9	0.19
Females			
16–19	14.4	3.9	1.94
20–24	7.9	4.0	1.03
25–44	5.1	4.4	0.60
45- 64	3.3	5.4	0.32

SOURCE: Adapted from George L. Perry, "Unemployment Flows in the U.S. Labor Market," *Brookings Papers on Economic Activity*, No. 2 (1972), pp. 245–78.

What accounts for these differentials? Are the disadvantaged groups unemployed *more frequently,* or for *longer periods,* or both? Some estimates on this point by George Perry are shown in Table 2. Young people do not have longer *spells* of unemployment than older workers, nor are women unemployed for longer periods than men—the reverse is true in both cases. The difference is entirely in the *number* of spells per year. Young workers are in the market more frequently than older workers, partly because of more active job shopping during the early years of employment. Women are in the market more frequently, partly because of withdrawal from and reentry into the labor force for personal and family reasons.

The situation for black as compared with white workers is a bit more complicated. Estimates by Robert Hall,[15] not reproduced here, indicate that black workers do have longer spells of unemployment than comparable white workers—about one-third longer in the case of black men, almost 50 percent longer in the case of black women. Again, however, the biggest difference is in number of spells of unemployment per year. Black men become unemployed almost twice as frequently as white men, and black women more than twice as often as white women.

These findings simply push the question one step back: *Why* do young

---

[15] Robert E. Hall, "Turnover in the Labor Force," *Brookings Papers on Economic Activity*, No. 3 (1972), 709–56.

Table 3

Unemployment Rates by Reason, by Color, Sex, and Age, 1968–71

Color, Sex, and Age	Unemployment Rate by Reason (Percent)				Ratio of Unemployed Entrants to Total Unemployment (1)/(4)
	All Reasons (1)	Lost Job (2)	Left Job (3)	New Entrant or Reentrant (4)	
White					
Male					
16–19	12.24	2.60	1.41	8.23	0.67
20–24	6.61	2.85	1.12	2.64	0.40
25–64	2.24	1.61	0.30	0.33	0.15
Female					
16–19	13.04	1.65	1.37	10.02	0.77
20–24	6.66	1.67	1.44	3.56	0.53
25–64	3.62	1.59	0.51	1.53	0.42
Nonwhite					
Male					
16–19	24.35	5.01	2.68	16.66	0.68
20–24	11.39	5.98	1.71	3.70	0.32
25–64	4.01	2.90	0.45	0.65	0.16
Female					
16–19	31.57	3.32	2.97	25.28	0.80
20–24	14.12	3.85	2.31	7.96	0.56
25–64	5.58	2.24	0.83	2.51	0.45

SOURCE: Adapted from George L. Perry, "Unemployment Flows in the U.S. Labor Market," *Brookings Papers on Economic Activity*, No. 2 (1972), p. 272.

people, women, and black workers have more spells of unemployment per year? A person may come into the market in one of three ways: he may be entering the labor force for the first time, or reentering it after a period of absence; or he may have quit his job; or he may have been laid off or discharged. The relative importance of these three sources is indicated by Table 3, drawn from the Perry study cited earlier.

For young people, much the commonest reason for being in the unemployed pool is entry or reentry to the labor force. There has to be a first time for everyone; and young people also go into and out of the labor force more frequently than older workers—because of discouragement at inability to find work, because of return to school, or for other reasons. Women, and even women of mature age, are also in and out of the labor force more frequently than men. Note that almost half of the women aged twenty-five to sixty-four who were in the unemployed pool were reentering the labor force.

Quitting is the least important source of unemployment; but quit rates are still substantial, and again show a characteristic pattern: Young people quit jobs more frequently than older people, and black workers more often than whites. For young people, this can be interpreted as fumbling one's way toward a satisfactory job through a trial-and-error process. For black workers, it may reflect the fact that many of them are in low-skilled and low-paid jobs. Since these jobs are relatively unattractive and impermanent, and have no future, it is natural that workers should quit them frequently in hope of better luck next time.

More significant, however, is the difference in layoff rates. Workers who are young and/or black and/or unskilled are the most marginal members of the labor force—first to be laid off on a cycle downswing and last to be rehired during expansion. This shows up in Table 3, and also in a study by Lester Thurow. He calculated "marginal disabsorption rates"— that is, the marginal propensity to be laid off in recession—and the corresponding marginal absorption (rehiring) rates on the upswing, for specific groups in the labor force. By occupation, layoffs hit laborers five times as hard, and skilled manual workers three times as hard, as white-collar workers. Black workers' marginal layoff rate is more than double that of white workers in the same skill category; and the rate for men aged eighteen to twenty-four is more than double that for those aged thirty-five to sixty-four.[16]

There is a widespread impression that the unemployment picture has worsened over the past decade or so; that is, that the level of unemployment corresponding to a given level of labor demand (and job vacancies) is higher than it used to be. In terms of Figure 6–1, the Beveridge curve has shifted upward to the right.

Recent studies of labor market dynamics tend to confirm that this has happened, and to suggest how it has happened. Perry, in the study cited earlier, finds that, for the same unemployment rate of prime-age males, unemployment among young people is now substantially higher than at earlier times. The change is in *number of spells* of unemployment, rather than in *duration* of each spell. Young people are unemployed more frequently—their attachment to the world of employment is more marginal.

At the same time, because of the population upsurge noted in Chapter 2, these young people are now a considerably larger percentage of the total labor force than in earlier times. When this larger proportion is multiplied by a higher unemployment rate, the *national* unemployment rate comes out at a characteristically higher level. A 3 percent unemployment

---

[16] Lester C. Thurow, "The Changing Structure of Unemployment: An Econometric Study," *Review of Economics and Statistics* (May 1965), pp. 137–49.

rate for prime-age males constitutes a quite tight labor market. In 1960 this degree of labor market tightness would have meant a national unemployment rate of perhaps 4 percent. Today, the same degree of tightness would mean a national rate of at least 5 percent. This intensifies the unemployment–inflation dilemma.

The rise in youth unemployment rates is something of a mystery. We do not really know why it has happened, to what extent it is a transitional rather than a continuing problem, or what policy measures might help to reverse it. Possible reasons for the relative increase in youth unemployment include:

1. The rapid increase in the relative supply of young people since the early sixties, together with a less rapid increase in jobs customarily assigned to young people, and a reluctance among employers to alter their assignment practices.
2. An increase in the importance of job-specific training, strengthening employers' preference for employing workers who already have such training.
3. Substantial increases in the real minimum wage, which may make young workers more expensive (relative to their productivity) than mature workers. Research studies of this effect were noted in Chapter 5.
4. Changes in the work attitudes of the young. Greater "choosiness" among jobs may have raised the amount of voluntary turnover during the early years of employment. Changes in work–leisure preferences, and the general rise in family income levels, may have made unemployment appear as less of a disaster and more of an opportunity than it used to be.

DISCUSSION QUESTIONS

1. What are the key differences between actual labor markets and the simplified models discussed in Chapter 5?

2. Explain the concept of the "internal labor market." Under what conditions will an employer find it expedient to fill a vacancy by internal rather than outside recruitment?

3. The employment package includes many things in addition to wage rates. Discuss the consequences of this for:
    (a) the worker's search for employment.
    (b) employers' adjustment to growing scarcity of labor during an
        economic expansion.

4. Why do employers use a variety of personal characteristics to screen out workers who will be considered for employment? In what sense may these screening standards involve employment discrimination?

5. In what sense may a job seeker be regarded as productively employed?

6. What factors have a bearing on the minimum terms of employment that an unemployed worker will accept?

7. Is informal search for work (and for workers) necessarily less efficient than more formalized procedures such as a state employment service? Explain what you mean by "efficiency" in this connection.

8. Explain the main interactions among labor market flows that occur:
   (a) during a decline in aggregate demand for labor.
   (b) during an upswing in aggregate demand for labor.

9. Explain why some frictional unemployment is unavoidable in actual labor markets.

10. Distinguish clearly between frictional and structural unemployment.

11. Why is it impossible to determine precisely how much of the unemployment in existence at a particular time is attributable to frictional, structural, and demand factors?

12. What are the main reasons why:
   (a) young workers have more spells of unemployment per year than older workers?
   (b) black workers have both more spells and longer periods of unemployment than white workers?

13. How would you account for the growing divergence of teenage unemployment rates from those for older age groups?

READING SUGGESTIONS

Most of the empirical work on labor markets has focused on manual labor. See in particular CHARLES A. MYERS and GEORGE P. SHULTZ, *The Dynamics of a Labor Market,* Englewood Cliffs, N.J.: Prentice-Hall, Inc., 1951; SEYMOUR M. LIPSET and REINHARD BENDIX, *Social Mobility in Industrial Society,* Berkeley and Los Angeles: University of California Press, 1963; HERBERT S. PARNES, *Research on Labor Mobility,* New York: Social Science Research Council, 1954; and LLOYD G. REYNOLDS, *The Structure of Labor Markets,* New York: Harper & Row, Publishers, 1951. On the volume and behavior of unemployment, see ELEANOR G. GILPATRICK, *Structural Unemployment and Aggregate Demand,* Baltimore: The Johns Hopkins Press, 1966; CLARENCE D. LONG, *The Labor Force Under Changing Income and Employment,* Princeton: Princeton University Press, 1958; National Bureau of Economic Research, *Measurement and Behavior of Unemployment,* Princeton: Princeton University Press, 1956; National Bureau of Economic Research, *Measurement and Interpretation of Job*

138 The Labor Market

Vacancies, New York: Columbia University Press, 1966; ARTHUR M. Ross (ed.), *Employment Policy and the Labor Market,* Berkeley and Los Angeles: University of California Press, 1965; and *Measuring Employment and Unemployment,* Report of the President's Committee to Appraise Employment and Unemployment Statistics, Robert A. Gordon, Chairman, Washington, D.C.: Government Printing Office, 1962.

Important recent contributions include ALBERT REES and GEORGE P. SHULTZ, *Workers and Wages in an Urban Labor Market,* Chicago: The University of Chicago Press, 1970; and EDMUND S. PHELPS, (ed.), *Microeconomic Foundations of Employment and Inflation Theory,* New York: W. W. Norton & Company, Inc., 1970.

7

Labor Market Policy: Information and Training

Economists first became interested in labor markets rather incidentally, because of an interest in wage determination. The original issue was whether labor markets are sufficiently competitive, so that the wage structure emanating from these markets could be considered approximately right, and interference with this structure by unions or government presumptively harmful. Controversy over this issue has produced a long series of empirical studies of labor market behavior, continuing to the present.

Gradually it became apparent that the labor market is important, not just as a forum for wage determination, but in other respects as well. Imperfect labor marketing can lock up in frictional unemployment people who might otherwise be productively employed. Round pegs allocated to square holes reduce national output. If educational bottlenecks unduly restrict entrance to certain occupations, the result is not just wage distortion but frustrated ambitions and economic waste. Since the job is such an intimate part of most people's lives, labor market imperfections reduce welfare more than limited information in product markets.

Labor market engineering is thus an important policy area in its own right. Moreover, while earlier labor market studies focused mainly on manual labor, it is now recognized that major issues arise at higher occupational levels. When one views manpower policy as embracing all occupational levels, and as focused on effective matching of individual skills and preferences against changing demand requirements, several basic problems come to mind.

1. There is the problem of limited information and poor clearinghouse facilities in each locality. This suggests the question of how far these deficiencies can be corrected by improvements in the U.S. Employment Service.

2. The information problem is especially critical for young people in school and college. Decisions made at this time determine the student's general occupational and income level for the rest of his life. There is every indication that these decisions at present are poorly informed and every reason to think that better occupational forecasting and occupational counseling could contribute much to economic efficiency.

3. Even if a student recognizes the advantages of higher education, he may not be able to pursue it because of his parents' financial position. Whether higher education is priced at cost or below cost, and how far scholarships and loan funds are available to low-income students, has a major impact on labor supply to the higher occupations. This range of issues was explored in Chapter 3.

4. Many people who thought they had acquired a marketable skill discover in later life that their skill has been rendered obsolete by shifts in product demand, production technology, or location of industry. This poses a problem of retraining adult workers so that they can enter occupations in which demand is growing, thus reducing the volume of structural unemployment. In some cases, movement to a different geographic area may also be required.

5. A further problem is labor market discrimination, based most commonly on sex or race. Women tend to be segregated in a limited range of occupations, and are poorly represented in managerial and most professional fields. Black workers are seriously disadvantaged compared with white workers. A disproportionate number are in low-skilled and low-paid jobs, and they also suffer disproportionately from unemployment. The whole of the next chapter is devoted to this problem. In this chapter we focus on issues of information and training—areas 1, 2, and 4 above.

INFORMATION AND ORGANIZATION:
THE LOCAL LABOR MARKET

For most subprofessional occupations—factory work, construction work, clerical and sales work, service occupations—the labor market is a locality. It is the area within which people can conveniently drive from home to work, and their movement is normally restricted to this area.

The market imperfections emphasized in the last chapter can never be removed entirely. But the fact that we shall never see a purely competitive labor market—a "stock exchange for labor"—should not deter us from doing anything at all. Much could be done to make labor markets function better, even if still imperfectly. First, however, it is necessary to ask just what we are trying to do: What are the economic objectives of labor market policy?

From a general economic standpoint, there are several shortcomings in the present movement of labor. First, there is probably too much movement—more quitting of jobs and shifting about than there would need to be if things were better organized. Unnecessary movement is a hardship to the worker and involves recruitment and training costs to the employer. Second, workers take more time to locate a new job than would be necessary in a better-organized market. Again, this is both a hardship to the individual worker and a loss of labor power to the economy. Third, there is considerable mismatching of individual abilities and job requirements. People do not necessarily end up in the jobs for which they are best suited. The ideal allocation of the labor force described in Chapter 5 is not attained.

What could be done to provide workers with better job information? Considering the importance of this matter, it is rather surprising that there is no place where a worker can get an accurate picture of the full range of occupations, wage rates, and working conditions available in the community. The nearest thing to an information center is the local office of the state employment service, which can provide information about vacant jobs registered by employers. Since employers are not required to register vacancies, however, and since many of them prefer to recruit labor directly, this gives an incomplete picture of the opportunities available. In many cities, the chamber of commerce or some other employers' organization collects periodic information on wage rates, and in some cases also on fringe benefits and other aspects of personnel policy. This information is compiled for the use of employers, however, and is not open to others in the community.

It would seem desirable that somewhere in the community, possibly at the local employment service office, there should be a roster, not simply of the jobs that happen to be vacant at the moment, but of the principal types of work offered by each employer in the community. This should include the wage rates paid, qualifications required, and other key items of information about each job; and it should be open for inspection at any time by workers interested in a change of employment. This would work some hardship on employers whose jobs are relatively unattractive and whose existence depends partly on the fact that their workers do not know about attractive opportunities elsewhere. Any competitive market penalizes those unable to meet the market price. Employers offering superior wages and conditions, on the other hand, would find it easier to recruit labor than they do at present. From a community point of view, workers would be able to seek jobs in a more informed way, the chances of each job change being in the "right" direction would be greater, and there would be a consequent gain in economic efficiency.

Central to any effort to improve labor market efficiency is the system of public employment offices. This system was established by the Wagner–Peyser Act of 1933. This act provided that states that established employ-

ment service systems and appropriated funds for their support would receive from the federal government an amount equal to that supplied by the
states. In return for this grant of funds, the federal government reserved
the right to prescribe minimum standards of personnel and operating procedures, which the state services must meet. Between 1933 and 1937, employment service systems were established in all the states and the District
of Columbia. These state employment services were "lent" to the federal
government during World War II and, as the main operating arm of the
War Manpower Commission, exercised extensive influence over the movement of workers into and out of essential industries. Shortly after the end
of the war, the employment offices were returned to state control. The
federal government, through a small overhead organization known as the
United States Employment Service, continues to prescribe minimum operating standards and to share the administrative costs of the state systems.

Most cities of ten thousand or more now have a branch of the state
employment service staffed by at least one full-time official, and larger
cities have proportionately larger offices. Smaller towns and cities are
usually served one or two days a week by a traveling official of the employment service. The function of the public employment offices is to
provide a meeting place for buyers and sellers of labor. Any employer with
a vacant job may place an order at the employment service, specifying the
nature of the work, the qualifications required, the starting wage, and
other relevant facts. Any unemployed worker may register for work at the
employment service, and workers who have applied for unemployment
compensation are required to register. The registration form, usually filled
out with the aid of a trained interviewer, contains key facts about the
worker and about his last few jobs.

The problem of the employment service official is to match orders and
registrations as best he can. When an order is received, he looks through
the active file of registrants for workers who appear qualified for the job
in question. He makes a tentative selection, talks with the worker to find
out whether he is interested in the job, and if he is interested, passes him
on to the employer. The employer need not hire workers sent out by the
employment service, nor need workers accept the jobs to which they are
sent, though there is some pressure on workers drawing unemployment
compensation. The employment service checks a few days later to find out
whether the man was hired or not. If he was, this is counted as a "placement" by the local office.

The number of placements made by the state employment services
in private industry remained low throughout the thirties, largely because
of the low level of demand for labor. There was a great increase in placements during the war years, due partly to the active demand for labor by
employers, and partly to the control regulations that required most place-

ments in essential industries to be made through the employment service. Total placements reached a peak of more than 11 million in 1944. Placements have fallen considerably since the end of the war, but remain well above the prewar level. The volume of placements naturally fluctuates with the level of business activity. The placements made by the public employment offices are also concentrated rather heavily in certain occupational groups—domestic and other personal services; farm labor, construction labor, and unskilled labor in general; and semiskilled factory work. There is relatively little placement of skilled tradesmen or white-collar workers, most of whom prefer to seek work directly.

There is no reliable way of estimating what proportion of all placements in private industry is made by the state employment services, but the proportion is probably less than one-fourth. Why is the employment service not more widely used? The main reason is that employers can usually fill a good vacancy quickly without resorting to the employment service. Word of the vacancy gets passed on to friends and relatives of people already in the plant, the foreman remembers someone who used to work on that job and looks him up, or the union has a suggestion to make. Thus a worker with good contacts can usually locate a job through "the grapevine," and feels little need for the employment service. Where employer and worker are able to locate each other directly, there is no need for the employment service to intervene. It exists to supplement other methods of work seeking, not to supplant them.

The employment service is hampered somewhat by the inherent complexity of the placement job. It is hard to become familiar enough with all the jobs in an area, and with the idiosyncrasies of each employer, so that one can tell whether a particular worker will be acceptable for a particular job. It is difficult also to gauge accurately the experience and abilities of each registrant. When a man says that he is a toolmaker, is he really a toolmaker or only a grade B machinist? A failure to judge accurately both the man and the job leads not merely to a lost placement, but also to a loss of prestige with the employer and worker involved.

The employment service is also under a certain amount of pressure to refer workers to vacancies even against its better judgment. Employers keep asking, "Why don't you send me someone?" Workers keep asking, "Why can't you find me a job?" A worker drawing unemployment compensation must be willing to accept work at his usual occupation under reasonable conditions in order to remain eligible for benefits. The only way of testing his willingness to work is by referring him to a job. The fact that the local offices of the employment service have to administer this "willingness to work" requirement has an unfortunate effect on their placement activities. It means that a large proportion of registrants at the employment service are unemployment compensation recipients. This causes many workers to look on the employment service as virtually a relief office, while others regard referral to work as simply a formality that must be gone through to earn eligibility for unemployment compensation. It also leads to employer complaints that the employment service refers many unqualified workers, and that employment service registrants constitute the least desirable segment of the labor force.

This point can be generalized. The employment service is widely regarded as a social welfare agency whose task is to find work for the unfortunate. It is put under pressure to give priority in referrals to disadvantaged groups in the labor force—the long-term unemployed, members of minority groups, people with physical or mental disabilities. But the employment service cannot push people into employment in the face of employers' natural desire to find the most efficient candidate for each job. Ill-conceived efforts to do so may sacrifice the respect and cooperation of employers, on whose job orders the service ultimately depends.

Considering these difficulties, the efficiency of employment service operations in most states is surprisingly high. But the gap between performance and potential remains wide. There is need for clearer recognition of the service as an *economic* agency rather than a *welfare* agency. Its task is to perfect the labor market mechanism, to serve all members of the labor force rather than merely the hard-to-place, to reflect employer requirements accurately and objectively, to locate the man most suited to a particular job rather than the man who needs work most. It cannot hope to correct the distress resulting from inadequate demand for labor, or from personal handicaps, or from mistaken hiring preferences. It can hope to reduce frictional unemployment, to cut employers' hiring and training costs, and to secure a more efficient matching of individual capacities and job requirements.[1]

Effective performance of these functions calls for educational and entrepreneurial activity by the employment service. Not only the unemployed but also young people on the point of leaving school and people who already have a job but want a better job should be encouraged to register. The usefulness of the service to employers must be demonstrated in action. This may require changes in internal operating procedures, such as exposure of each vacancy to several workers, and of a well-qualified worker to several vacancies. There is evidence that vigorous action along these lines can increase the service's placement volume and its acceptance in the community.[2]

---

[1] For an eloquent and well-reasoned statement of this view, see E. Wight Bakke, *A Positive Labor Market Policy* (Columbus, Ohio: Charles E. Merrill Publishing Company, 1963).

[2] See, for example, the account of a very successful experience in Madison, Wisconsin, in Eaton H. Conant, "Public Employment Service Operations in a Clerical Labor Market," *Proceedings of Fifteenth Annual Meeting of IRRA* (1962), pp. 306–14.

There is considerable agreement that administration of un[
compensation should be separated from employment service (
They should be in separate physical locations, and the quite diff
tions of their staffs should be emphasized. This would help to r
welfare taint which has hung over the employment service in the past.

A further requirement for effective operation is adequate salaries.
Employment service personnel are not on federal, but rather on state salary
scales, which vary widely from state to state and are typically below the
levels offered by private industry for comparable skills. An employment
service officer who does a good job and becomes favorably known to employers is quickly hired for personnel work in industry. This means high
turnover of employment service personnel and a tendency for the less able
to remain while the best people depart. Without an attack on this problem,
other efforts to improve employment service operations may be ineffective.

The focus of this section has been on movement of workers within
an area, but we should note that for some occupations the market is regional or national in scope. This is true for most professional, technical,
and managerial occupations, and even for some skilled manual trades.

To serve such occupations, the state employment services have organized an Interarea Recruitment System. Under this system an employer
order that cannot be filled within the locality is first cleared with other
employment service offices in the state. If it remains unfilled, it is passed
on to other states that seem likely to have the kind of labor in question.
Employment service headquarters in these states pass the information down
to their local offices, until eventually some office pulls out the card of a
suitable candidate from its file of registrants. Particular attention is given
to orders for professional personnel. There is a special Professional Office
Network, which now includes 121 offices strategically located in cities
throughout the United States.

These activities face the usual difficulties of employment service
operation, and there are additional obstacles of time and distance. But these
may be removed increasingly by computer hookups and other means of
high-speed communication.

THE TRANSITION FROM SCHOOL TO WORK

Information and placement facilities are especially important for high
school students, who face educational choices which will heavily influence
their later careers, and most of whom will enter the labor market on or
before graduation.

---

[3] See, for example, "Placement and Counseling: The Role of the Employment
Service," a report to the Secretary of Labor from the Employment Service Task
Force, reprinted in R. A. Gordon (ed.), *Toward a Manpower Policy* (New York:
John Wiley & Sons, Inc., 1967).

From the ninth grade onward, most students find themselves in one of three high school programs: an *academic* program oriented toward college entrance, a *vocational* program which inculcates job skills along with general education, and a *general,* or catch-all, program. Assignment to one or other of these tracks seems to be relatively efficient in terms of student ability as measured by test scores.[4] The bulk of students in the academic program are above the fiftieth percentile in measured ability, while the bulk of vocational students are below the fiftieth percentile. Students in the general program have test scores intermediate between the other two groups.

Classification is not perfectly accurate, however, especially when one considers that test scores in the ninth grade are imperfect indicators of future potential. We should note also that students in the academic program are mostly above the fiftieth percentile in terms of socioeconomic status of parents, while the reverse is true of vocational students. This suggests that test score achievement, and assignment to one educational track rather than another, are strongly influenced by home background. To a considerable extent, then, the educational system serves as a transmission belt, preserving the position of advantaged and disadvantaged families from generation to generation. But it also serves as a channel of opportunity. Some bright children from poor families do climb the educational and occupational ladder. Some less intelligent, wealthy children do flunk out and sink to lower levels. The policy problem is to increase the element of opportunity in the system.

Each of the three high school programs presents labor market problems. Most serious is the case of the one-quarter of high school students enrolled in a "general" program, which does not prepare either for college entrance or for a specific vocation. In terms of ability, students in this program rank higher on average than those in the vocational program. They also tend, however, to be relatively aimless. Most of the high school dropouts come from this group, and they form the bulk of those who later need remedial training. Assignment of students to this program can be regarded as a failure of students, parents, and school officials to face up to the eventual need for occupational choice. Avoiding the problem at this stage leads to worse problems later. A number of national advisory panels of educators have recommended that the general program be abolished.

Most graduates from the academic program enter college, which postpones facing the labor market. But by no means all go to college, and the proportion has recently been declining. The proportion of all high school graduates entering college peaked at 62 percent in 1969. By 1973, it had

---

[4] See Rupert N. Evans and Joel D. Galloway, "Verbal Ability and Socioeconomic Status of 9th and 12th Grade College Preparatory, General, and Vocational Students," *Journal of Human Resources* (Winter 1973), pp. 24–36.

fallen to 50 percent and was still declining, perhaps partly in response to an apparent oversupply of college graduates to the labor market.[5] A graduate of an academic program who does *not* go on to college faces the problem of entering the labor market without specific job skills.

Students enrolled in a vocational program would seem to have the clearest path ahead; but there is still the question whether the skills in which they have been trained correspond to the skills demanded in the market. This has often not been true in the past. For many years Congress, in appropriating funds for support of vocational education, imposed restrictions that forced heavy emphasis on domestic science and agriculture. As late as the early sixties only one-sixth of vocational school students were classified as studying "trades and industries," where the expanding opportunities mainly lie.

The situation was improved considerably by the Vocational Education Act of 1963 and the 1968 amendments to this act. Federal appropriations for vocational education were increased substantially and the previous occupational restrictions were eliminated. Federal support is now available for all occupations except those requiring four years or more of college training, as well as for construction of new vocational high schools and technical colleges. This has produced a substantial increase in the numbers being trained. Between 1964 and 1974, high school enrollments in vocational programs rose from 2.1 million to 8.4 million, post-high school (technical college) enrollments rose from 0.2 to 1.6 million, and adult enrollments in part-time programs rose from 2.3 to 3.5 million. There has also been a realistic shift in type of training provided. Between 1964 and 1974, agriculture and domestic science declined from 63 to 30 percent of the total. In 1974, 20 percent of students were enrolled in office occupations, 21 percent in trades and industries, 6 percent in distribution, and 10 percent in health services and other technical fields.

The labor market problems which arise at the college level resemble those at the high school level. Here, too, there is a problem of choice among alternative curricula, a problem of graduates from nontechnical programs who enter the labor market without specific job skills, and a problem of dropouts who may also have placement problems. College students, however, are in a better position than high school students to face these problems. They are older, are better prepared to seek out and use labor market information, have a higher quality of counseling, and have a preferred position in the eyes of most employers. So, without meaning to minimize college-level difficulties, we shall focus here on problems at the high school level.

These problems are of three kinds: first, provision of occupational

[5] Richard B. Freeman, "Overinvestment in College Training?" *Journal of Human Resources* (Summer 1975), pp. 287–311.

information and counseling during the high school years; second, institutional arrangements for bridging the gap between school and work; and third, "second-chance," or remedial, programs for those who fall through the meshes of the system and end up among the teenage unemployed.

A good deal of occupational information is already available. The Department of Labor projects demand for a large number of occupations, and prepares occupational handbooks for use by employment service staff, school counselors, and others. These projections, however, are subject to a considerable margin of error. Technological change gradually alters the skill proportions required for any type of production. The size of such shifts is hard to predict. Further, there is usually some substitutability among skills. If skilled craftsmen become scarce, jobs can often be redesigned to be done by less skilled men. Finally, demand is not independent of relative wage rates, a fact that tends to be overlooked in physical manpower projections. Failure of supply of a particular kind of labor to keep pace with demand leads to a rise in its relative wage; and this leads employers to economize by substituting machinery or other types of labor for the scarce skill. Indeed, shortage or surplus of a skill cannot be defined except by reference to its wage.

A further difficulty is that, for most occupations, projections must be reduced to a local level to be really useful. A high school student in Scranton, Pennsylvania, needs to know the outlook for various occupations in Scranton rather than in the continental United States. This requires estimates of shifts in the geographic location of production. For short periods ahead, each employer in an area can be asked to forecast his hiring needs at various skill levels. But such forecasts rapidly lose precision as the period is lengthened and are probably useless beyond two or three years.

There is need also for careful individual counseling. Most large high schools now have one or more vocational counselors, but it appears that more than half of all high school students still leave school without having had systematic occupational advice.

Counseling involves testing the student's aptitudes, discussing his interests and preferences, and providing accurate occupational information. During their last two years of high school, students should become familiar with the occupational structure of the economy, prospective earnings in various occupations, the nature of the work and other nonwage characteristics, the amount and type of specialized training required, the trend of demand and the chances of securing employment, employers' hiring methods and requirements, and the operation of the employment service and other placement agencies. This might be done through regular classroom courses, supplemented by class visits to stores, offices, factories, and other places of employment, and by guest lectures by employers and others familiar with particular fields. This would help students to form their own job preferences, to discuss job possibilities with school counselors in a more informed and realistic way, and to set about seeking work more effectively.

At the end of the student's school career, unless he continues to college, he needs a job. For skilled manual trades, apprenticeship programs provide part of the answer. As of 1974, about 100,000 young people were entering apprenticeships each year, and some 300,000 were in course of being trained. About 40 percent of these were in the construction industry. The printing trades and metal trades are also traditional areas for apprentice training. But one also finds apprentices scattered through a wide variety of industries and trades—for example, 6,536 prospective automobile mechanics as of 1974. Even so, only a small proportion of skilled workers (who now number some 11 million) pass through formal apprenticeships, and there is little doubt that the system could usefully be expanded. One difficulty is that the employer makes a considerable investment in training an apprentice, with no assurance that the worker will stay with him after completing his course. This is a more serious problem than union restrictions on numbers.

For other high school students entering the labor market, there is a problem of exploring the needs of employers in the area, routing students to places with job possibilities, following up on what happens, and making additional placement efforts as needed. This could conceivably be done by school counselors, by state employment service placement officers, or by collaboration between them. In some localities close and effective collaboration already exists; but in other areas this is not true. In addition to the problems posed by unclear division of responsibility there is the difficulty, noted in the previous section, that many employers do not have enough confidence in the state employment service to use it as a major recruitment channel. So the problem of bridging the transition from school to work often turns out to be no one's responsibility, and the student is left to sink or swim.

Some of the European countries have better institutional arrangements in this respect, which we might well study and emulate. Placement of school leavers is accepted as an important social responsibility. Procedures are clearly defined and, most important, the responsible officials follow up and continue their efforts until a satisfactory placement is achieved. Apprenticeship systems are more fully developed than in the United States; there is usually a provision that young people start out at a relatively low wage, and work up to the adult wage over several years.

Actual work experience during the school years is one of the best ways to help young people sort out their interests and abilities. A good deal of this goes on informally at present through teenagers' simply hunting out part-time or summer jobs. There is also a substantial federal program which provides funds, channeled through state and local governments, to employ young people from low-income families during the summer months. In 1975, for example, Congress appropriated $473 million for this program, which provided summer jobs for 888,100 youths aged fourteen to twenty-one. These were mainly in public and nonprofit agencies, such as schools, libraries, hospitals, and community service organizations. Typical jobs included nurse aide, teacher aide, summer camp aide, typist, cashier, library aide, clerk, nutrition aide, and day-care aide.

A school leaver's first job may not last very long. It is normal for young people to change jobs frequently in the early years of employment, as they develop and test their skills and preferences. "Shopping for jobs" by trying them out is unavoidable in a market where preemployment information is fragmentary and imperfect. One should expect, therefore, that young people's unemployment rates will be substantially above those of older workers.

Actual unemployment rates for young people, however, and especially for young black people, are higher than would be expected on the basis of normal turnover. This reflects the presence of a group of young people, composed largely of high school dropouts, whose limited training and other personal characteristics cause employers to put them at the end of the employment queue. They need a "second-chance" program designed to raise their employability and to integrate them into the regular labor force.

Young people as well as older workers are eligible for the training and employment programs to be described in the next section. There is also one program aimed specifically at disadvantaged young people aged sixteen to twenty-one. This is the Job Corps, which dates from 1965 and which currently enrolls about 50,000 young people per year. About three-quarters of the enrollees in the most recent year were men and one-quarter women, and slightly more than one-half were black. About 90 percent had not completed high school, and 80 percent were from families with incomes below $5,000 a year.

A distinctive feature of the program is its use of residential training centers, which are intended to offer a healthful learning environment. In addition to job skills, the program involves remedial training in English and mathematics, in personal care and appearance, and in job application techniques. The placement record is good. In fiscal year 1975, about two-thirds of those completing the program were placed in jobs, and another 25 percent either returned to full-time school work, qualified for some other training program, or entered military service. Among government training programs, this one seems to have a relatively high payoff.

PUBLIC EMPLOYMENT AND TRAINING PROGRAMS

The federal government has been heavily involved in training activities since the passage of the Manpower Development and Training Act of 1962. It has been involved in special programs of public employment since the Emergency Employment Act of 1971. Most of these programs were brought together for purposes of authorization and funding by the Comprehensive Employment and Training Act (CETA) of 1973. Since the training and employment activities differ substantially in purpose, content, and clientele, it will be well to discuss them separately.

Special Public Employment Programs

Title II of CETA authorizes transitional public service employment programs for areas of "substantial unemployment," defined as areas with an unemployment rate of 6.5 percent or higher. Conceived during the 1970–71 recession, this program has now assumed an aura of permanence. Even in years of general prosperity, there are depressed areas which meet the 6.5 pecent unemployment criterion. In 1975–76, with the national ememployment rate in the neighborhood of 8 percent, most parts of the country qualified for assistance. Funds under this Title, and indeed under the additional programs described below, are allocated to and administered by state and local governments; and the new public service jobs are also at those levels.

The severe recession of 1973–75 seemed to require additional action and funding. Title VI of CETA, created by the Emergency Jobs and Unemployment Assistance Act of 1974, provided for a temporary program of public service employment to ease the impact of high general unemployment. Funds under this Title are also distributed to states and localities, primarily on the basis of the number of unemployed people in the area.

These programs are of substantial size. Appropriations for the fiscal year 1975 were $770 million for Title II and $875 million for Title VI. As of June 30, 1975, 147,000 people were employed under Title II and an additional 94,500 under Title VI. The intent is to provide temporary employment, income, and maintenance of work skills for people who will eventually be reabsorbed into the private sector. The clientele, except for the fact of having been unemployed, are not especially disadvantaged. The 1975 enrollees, compared with the unemployed population in general, had a substantially higher percentage of men, of high school graduates, and of people of prime working age—a group, in short, which might be expected to be relatively productive in either private or public employment.

There is an additional route by which people can get into special public service jobs. Title I of CETA, which authorizes the training activities to be described in a moment, gives state and local governments block grants with wide discretion as to the type of training to be provided. The main options are classroom training, on-the-job training in private industry, and "work experience," which in practice means work for state and local agencies. During a recession it becomes difficult either to place classroom trainees or to induce employers to hire workers for on-the-job training, and there is a natural tendency to shift toward improvised public sector employment. As of June 30, 1975, 329,800 people were getting work experience under Title I, compared with 127,200 in classroom training and 41,100 in on-the-job training. As compared with the Title II and Title VI employees, this group has a considerably larger percentage of young people, black people, and those with less education.

All told, then, upward of a half-million people were employed in special public service jobs in mid-1975. This compares with a total of some 12 million "regular" state and local government employees. As compared with training programs, which may or may not lead to jobs, public service jobs do provide assurance of work and income. The work done is of some value and, on the assumption that private-sector jobs are not available for these people, the social opportunity cost is low. At the same time, these programs involve several difficult problems.

First, are all these jobs a net addition to employment? Or do they in part replace "regular" state and local employees? There are usually rules prohibiting this possibility; but these are not easy to administer. It is simple enough to prevent layoff of existing regular workers and their replacement by "emergency" employees. But suppose that a city agency is expanding and needs additional workers. Since special public service workers are "free" in the sense of being paid from federal grants, while regular workers must be paid from the city budget, there will be a natural tendency to prefer the former. Moreover, if one could enforce the principle that special public service workers should never be used on jobs which could be done by regular government employees, it might be hard to find useful work for them and they might be relegated to leaf-raking.

Second, what should special public service workers be paid? The lower their wage, the stronger will be their incentive to seek out and accept jobs in the private sector. On the other hand, a low wage strengthens the tendency for state and local agencies to substitute them for regular employees. Further, a low wage carries the implication that the money is really relief rather than payment for services performed, and this is not conducive to good job performance.

Third, can (or should) the supposedly temporary character of special public service employment be maintained? Economic upswings do provide additional jobs in the private sector. But even at cycle peaks there are usually not enough jobs to go round. This poses a possibility that special public employment may become a semipermanent occupation for the least preferred members of the labor force, and a continuing supplement to regular state–local employment. If one believes that output of state and local services is presently too low, expansion of those services through a permanent corps of special service workers could be regarded as desirable.

This is a different rationale, however, from that embodied in present legislation, which emphasizes the temporary and countercyclical character of the special programs.

Finally, to what extent should public service employees be eligible for "regular" public sector jobs as vacancies occur? Even if there is always a group of special employees around, individuals who have shown unusual ability might be selected and upgraded in this way. This would conflict, however, with established channels of recruitment and promotion, which usually require competitive examinations under civil service commission auspices, and are often negotiated with a union of public employees.

These questions, to which there are no easy answers, need to be considered in designing and evaluating public service employment programs.

Training Programs

Title I of CETA provides training grants to state and local governments, leaving them discretion to allocate funds among various types of training. Apart from the work experience option, the main possibilities are *institutional* training versus *on-the-job* training. Institutional training involves some combination of classroom instruction and practice work, often using the facilities of local vocational schools, but sometimes involving construction of new training facilities. On-the-job training (OJT) involves contracting with an employer to train workers in his plant, with government bearing a share of the training costs.

Choice between these is sometimes dictated by the kind of skill in question. For manufacturing operations that involve complicated and expensive equipment, and where employers are large enough to staff training programs, OJT is indicated. But in small-scale service, repair, or construction activities, where no one employer has adequate training facilities, institutional programs are necessary. OJT has the advantage that people who show good ability during the training period can often go directly into regular jobs, so that there is no placement problem. But under OJT the employer usually screens and selects the trainees, and he will naturally select the most trainable and resist the seriously disadvantaged. Moreover, the willingness of employers to contract for OJT varies with the business cycle. During a recession most companies are not seeking new employees, so an OJT program can have no payoff for them.

About 175,000 people were enrolled in training programs as of June 30, 1975; but since most programs last less than a year, the total number enrolled at one time or another during the year was about 365,000. Enrollees under Title I are not a cross section of the unemployed, but are a relatively disadvantaged group with special employment difficulties. Of the 1975 enrollees, 62 percent were less than twenty-two years old, 61 percent had not completed high school, 37 percent were black, and 87 percent were from low-income families. These are the kinds of people, of course, for whom remedial training was primarily designed.

In addition to CETA, there are two other substantial training programs. The Job Corps program, limited to young people and carried on in residential training centers, has already been described. In addition, there is a Work Incentive Program (WIN) for people receiving Aid to Families with Dependent Children (AFDC, or "welfare"). A 1971 amendment to the Social Security Act required all persons sixteen years or older in AFDC families to register for employment or training, unless exempted for reasons of health, age, home responsibilities (children under six), or other special circumstances. Registrants are required to accept available employment, training, or other services necessary to prepare them for jobs, under penalty of being disqualified for welfare. In fiscal year 1975, there were 839,000 new WIN registrants, of whom 328,000 were certified as available for employment or training. The program is administered by cooperation between local WIN offices and local welfare staff, and also involves CETA since many of the registrants are referred to CETA programs for training.

The need for the most disadvantaged members of the labor force to acquire skills and increase their employability is scarcely to be questioned; and large-scale training activities will doubtless continue. It should be emphasized, however, that their success depends on availability of jobs at the end of the training period. In recession periods when aggregate demand for labor is falling, the placement rate is bound to be low. Of the people terminated from CETA Title I programs during fiscal 1975, more than one-third dropped out before completion of training, and another third did not succeed in finding regular jobs. Only about one-third were placed in unsubsidized private or public employment. Of the people certified as "available" under the WIN program, about half either found jobs or were placed in OJT training programs leading to regular employment. This emphasizes the need for a vigorous full-employment policy to complement and validate training programs, which can help to adapt labor supply but are powerless to create demand.

How can one evaluate the benefits and costs of a retraining program? Several kinds of calculations can be made, each of which is important for different reasons:

1. *Private costs and returns.* How much is the worker paid during the training period, how much would he have received otherwise from earnings or transfer payments during this period, how much additional income will he receive in later years because of the training? From this standpoint, earnings must be estimated *after* income tax, since this is what the worker will actually get. An informed worker will not enroll in a training program unless the prospective private return is satisfactory.

2. *Social costs and returns.* These are the real resources used up in the training program compared with the resulting addition to national output. This is the basic test of worthwhileness from a public standpoint, and provides a basis for ranking training projects in order of their prospective payoff.

3. *Budgetary costs and returns to government.* What cash outlay is required by the training program? What will be the offsetting savings in unemployment compensation and welfare payments? Assuming that the trainee will earn more and work more regularly in future years, how much will this add to government revenue through income taxes, and how much will it save in unemployment payments? Budgetary costs cannot be ignored, since they limit the number of projects that can be undertaken in a given year. A project with low social costs but high budget costs may prevent the government from launching a half-dozen other desirable projects. Budget considerations can be overlooked only if enough funds are available, from tax revenues or borrowing, to undertake *all* projects for which social benefits exceed social costs.

Since social costs and benefits are basic, and since their estimation raises numerous problems, it will be useful to say some more about them. Trainees normally receive a living allowance during the training period. This is a budgetary cost but not a social cost, since it does not use up any productive resources. The social costs are, first, the value of the trainee's time, that is, the amount he might have produced by working instead of studying. If we assume that, in the absence of training, he would have continued unemployed, this cost is zero; but this is not a safe assumption. A common estimating procedure is to take a control group of nontrainees with personal characteristics similar to those of the trainees, observe how much the nontrainees earned over the same period, assume that the trainees could have earned this same amount, and count this as the value of their time. In addition, the costs of training include the time of teachers, supervisors, and employment service officials; interest and depreciation on the buildings, machinery, and other equipment used in training; and paper, books, chalk, electric power, raw materials for experimental work, and other supplies used up currently in training activities.

Several problems arise in evaluating benefits. Not all of those who start a training program finish it, and not all of those who finish get precisely the jobs for which they were trained. One can argue that only graduates placed in relevant jobs should be counted. But this may yield an overconservative estimate, since even dropouts or people placed in other kinds of work have probably derived *some* value from the time spent in the program.

Now take a particular graduate, who is doing the kind of work for which he was trained. We can observe how much he is earning; and we assume that his output at least equals his earnings, otherwise he would not be employed. For this purpose earnings should be taken *before* taxes, since we are interested in the addition to national output rather than in how much of this the worker receives. The difficult problem, however, is to estimate how much more he is earning that he would have earned if he had not entered the training program. What can we use as a basis of comparison? We could take his earnings on his last job before becoming unemployed, which assumes that without training he would eventually have been reemployed in the same kind of work. Alternatively, earnings of graduates of a training program can be compared with those of a control group with comparable personal characteristics but who have not had the benefit of training. Full comparability, however, may prove impossible. The participants in a training program, by virtue of having applied and been selected, are an untypical group rather than a random sample of the unemployed.

There are other difficulties: the labor market may have improved between the time the worker was trained and the time of the follow-up study (as was happening over the period 1962–69, when many follow-up studies were made). This could partly account for more regular employment and higher earnings by trainees. Alternatively, if the labor market has worsened, as in 1973–75, a poor employment record would not prove that the training was useless. It is difficult also to judge how far any benefits to trainees resulted from training *per se,* and how far the program simply called them to the attention of employers and helped to overcome employer resistance to hiring people with their personal characteristics.

It is not surprising, then, that cost–benefit studies have produced a wide variety of conclusions.[6] The verdict is generally favorable, but more study is needed. In particular, we need to know more about how the return to training varies with personal characteristics of the trainee and with content of the training program.

DISCUSSION QUESTIONS

1. What sectors of the labor market (by industry and occupation) can public employment offices realistically hope to serve?

2. What modifications in the employment service system would help it to serve these sectors more effectively?

3. Under what conditions may a high school graduate (or dropout) face unusual employment difficulties?

---

[6] See studies reported in Gerald G. Somers, (ed.), *Retraining the Unemployed* (Madison: University of Wisconsin Press, 1968); *Cost–Benefit Analysis of Manpower Policies* (Kingston, Ontario: Industrial Relations Centre, Queen's University, 1969); Daniel S. Hammermesh, *Economic Aspects of Manpower Training Programs* (Lexington, Mass.: Heath Lexington Books, 1971); and Charles R. Perry and others, *The Impact of Government Manpower Programs* (Philadelphia: Industrial Research Unit, Wharton School, University of Pennsylvania, 1975).

4. Can you (on paper) devise a system which would effectively bridge the transition from school to work?

5. What kinds of vocational information did you receive from high school counselors or others? What additional information would you have found useful?

6. At the end of 1976, there were about 8 million unemployed. About a half-million were involved in emergency public employment programs. Should this number have been larger? Why, or why not?

READING SUGGESTIONS

In addition to the references cited in the text, see LEONARD P. ADAMS, *The Public Employment Service in Transition, 1933–1968* (Ithaca: New York State School of Industrial and Labor Relations, Cornell University, 1969); E. WIGHT BAKKE, *A Positive Labor Market Policy* (Columbus, Ohio: Charles E. Merrill Publishing Company, 1963); and RICHARD A. LESTER, *Manpower Planning in a Free Society* (Princeton: Princeton University Press, 1966).

8

Labor Market Policy: Discrimination

It is no secret that black workers are disadvantaged in the labor market relative to white workers, and that women are disadvantaged relative to men. The disadvantaged groups hold a disproportionate number of the poorer jobs in the economy, and earn less per hour and per year.

This could be due, in whole or in part, to discrimination in employment. Discrimination occurs when a black (or female) worker, equal to a white (or male) worker in objective measures of ability, training, and experience, receives poorer treatment as regards recuitment, hiring, training, promotion, or wage rate. In addition to such direct discrimination, there are important indirect forms of discrimination—notably, differential access to educational institutions, apprenticeships, and training programs.

Economic analysis of employment discrimination has moved back and forth between two worlds, a world of theory and a world of facts, which have not made very effective contact. The earliest theory, advanced by Gary Becker, posited a "taste for discrimination." "If an individual has a 'taste for discrimination' he must act as if he were willing to pay something, either directly or in the form of a reduced income, to be associated with some persons instead of others. When actual discrimination occurs, he must, in fact, either pay or forfeit income for this purpose." [1] This definition applies to an individual discriminator—an employer, fellow worker, or consumer. *Market discrimination* is defined as the difference between the actual black/white wage ratio and the ratio which would exist if no one had a taste for discrimination. If black and white workers are equally

---

[1] Gary S. Becker, *The Economics of Discrimination* (Chicago: The University of Chicago Press, 1957), p. 6.

productive, if employers are the only ones who discriminate, and if perfect competition prevails in both product and labor markets, the size of the black/white wage differential depends on the distribution of employers' tastes for discrimination and on the relative supplies of black and white labor.

Under these conditions, a company would hire either all black or all white workers, depending on whether the employer's taste for discrimination exceeds or falls short of the market wage differential. There would be complete segregation in employment. Further, employers with a relatively low taste for discrimination, and who employ black labor at lower wage rates, would achieve lower production costs. If product markets are competitive, one would expect these low-cost firms to expand at the expense of others, which would raise the demand for black labor and eventually eliminate the wage differential.

This prediction led other economists to inquire: Why is it that competitive forces do not serve to eliminate discrimination in the long run? Kenneth Arrow, in particular, suggested several possible answers [2]:

(1) At any time an employer has a substantial investment in the recruitment and training of his present work force. Thus as black workers move into the white economy, an employer will be hesitant to replace his present workers with blacks even at lower wage rates.

(2) In a world of limited information, an employer may *believe* that black workers are less productive than whites, even if this is not true. He may use skin color as a convenient screening device, just as he uses education level and other observable characteristics. Note, however, that while these two considerations would *slow down* movement toward an equal-wage equilibrium, they would not prevent it indefinitely.

(3) There is, however, a third possibility which might prevent it. Suppose that white workers initially have more education and training, better work habits, and superior productivity. Employers thus prefer them and are willing to pay them more than blacks. This means that whites get higher returns than blacks for investing in education and training. Hence they continue to invest more and to maintain their productivity advantage, which reinforces employers' preference for them. This feedback mechanism, essentially the same as that used by "dual labor market" theorists, could postpone wage equalization indefinitely.

Turning to the world of fact, we observe that black (and women) workers have a different occupational distribution than white (or male) workers, and that they earn less money. The next step is to explore how far

[2] Kenneth J. Arrow, "Models of Job Discrimination," in Anthony H. Pascal (ed.), *Racial Discrimination in Economic Life* (Lexington, Mass.: D. C. Heath and Company, 1972).

these differences in earnings can be explained by factors other than color and sex—that is, by differences in education, on-the-job training, work experience, degree of unionization, and other variables that we know to be correlated with earnings. Differences which can be explained in this way tend to be regarded as "normal," though they may be attributable in part to indirect discrimination in education and other respects.

Suppose that by drawing on these variables we can explain 60 percent of the earnings gap between men and women or black and white workers. (This figure is pulled out of the air for illustration—actual magnitudes will be discussed later.) What about the remaining 40 percent? This is often taken as measuring the effect of "pure discrimination," the penalty for being black or female. Strictly speaking, however, it is just an unexplained residual. It may reflect race or sex discrimination in employment. But it may also include the effect of other personal characteristics which are related to earnings but which we are unable to measure, and which are at any rate not included in our regression equation. We thus have no *direct* measure of the effect of discrimination on earnings. Statements about its probable size rest rather on indirect inference.

One other preliminary comment is in order. Both black workers and women workers face discrimination in employment, and it is convenient to assemble everything we have to say about discrimination in one chapter. But this should not be taken to imply that the employment problems of the two groups are entirely similar. It takes little reflection to recognize that the problem of establishing equal employment opportunities for men and women is inherently more complex and difficult than that of establishing racial equality. Effective equality for men and women in the world of employment would require changes in male attitudes and behavior, in the division of labor within the household, and in a wide range of social institutions. It is thus not surprising that we have made less progress in the area of sex discrimination than in that of racial discrimination.

WOMEN WORKERS

The growing labor force participation of women was described and explained in Chapter 2. Continuing employment throughout the working years has now become the rule rather than the exception. A woman often withdraws from the labor force for a few years while her children are small; but even this temporary withdrawal is far from universal—about 30 percent of mothers with children under six are in the labor force. This proportion rises rapidly as children attain school age, and more than half of all wives aged thirty-five to sixty-five are labor force members.

Women's Employment: Job Segregation

The most striking feature of women's employment is their concentration in a limited number of occupations, and the relative absence of men in those occupations. Job segregation on the basis of sex is even more severe than that based on race; that is, the occupational distribution of white men is more similar to that of black men than to that of white women. Nor does the situation seem to have changed materially since 1900. Edward Gross has calculated an index of job segregation, based on the percentage of women (or men) who would have to change jobs in order for the percentage of women in each occupation to equal their percentage in the labor force. Since 1900 this index has moved in the narrow range of 66–69 percent. (A comparable index of *racial* segregation as of 1960 works out to 47 percent.[3])

About 38 percent of all those classified as professional workers are women. But this means a large number of school teachers, librarians, and nurses, and a thin representation in most other professions. The percentages given in Table 1 of all employees in selected fields who were

Table 1

Sex Distribution of Employment in Selected Professional Occupations, 1960 and 1970

Occupation	Women as a Percentage of Employment		Occupation	Women as a Percentage of Employment	
	1960	1970		1960	1970
Engineers	0.8	1.6	Computer specialists	29.8	19.6
Architects	2.0	3.5	Vocational and educational counselors	41.0	43.6
Lawyers and judges	3.4	4.8	Secondary school teachers	49.3	49.1
Physicians	6.9	9.2			
Pharmacists	7.5	11.9	Health technicians	68.2	69.6
Scientists, life and physical	8.3	13.1	Librarians	83.2	79.2
Accountants	16.4	26.0	Elementary school teachers	85.8	83.6
Teachers, college and university	23.7	28.4	Dieticians	92.8	92.0
			Registered nurses	97.5	97.3

[3] Reported in Mary Stevenson, "Women's Wages and Job Segregation" (Conference on Labor Market Segmentation, Harvard University, March 16–17, 1973; mimeo). This is a valuable source on the segregation problem.

women as of 1960 and 1970 illustrates both the degree of segregation and the limited progress in reducing it over the decade.[4]

The situation is similar in lower occupational strata. Mary Stevenson [5] classified occupations into seventeen levels, on the basis of the amount of general educational development (cognitive skill) and specific vocational preparation (training time) that the job requires. She then compared men and women within each occupational level. These men and women typically had different jobs, but these jobs all required equivalent amounts of education and training. Several interesting findings emerged:

1. Women with a given amount of education tend to be at a lower occupational level than men with the same amount of education. In this sense, women tend to "work below their ability." An implication is that the rate of return to education is lower for women than for men.

2. Within each occupational level, women are more concentrated into a few occupations than are men. The range of occupational choice open to a man is substantially wider.

3. There is segregation by industry as well as by occupation. ". . . Women's industries tend to be less profitable and have less market power than men's. . . . The labor market assigns women to the industries which are not capable of paying higher wages because of the economic environment in which they operate." She estimates that industry characteristics such as concentration, profit rate, and unionization account for about one-third of the male to female earnings differential at the semiskilled level.

What kinds of job tend to get typed as "women's work"? The sociologist Harold Wilensky concludes that women are concentrated in jobs

that involve one or more of the following characteristics: (1) traditional housewives' tasks—cooking, cleaning, sewing, and canning; (2) few or no strenuous physical activities and hazards; (3) patience, waiting, routine (receptionists, sales workers, telephone operators); (4) rapid use of hands and fingers, such as in office machine operating and electrical assembling; (5) a distinctive welfare or cultural orientation; (6) contact with young children; and (7) sex appeal." [6]

The classification of particular jobs as "men's work" or "women's work" is largely traditional and cultural and does not reflect sex-related differences in abilities. Most jobs done by men could equally be done by

---

[4] Data are from Victor R. Fuchs, "A Note on Sex Segregation in Professional Occupations," *Explorations in Economic Research* (N.B.E.R.), 2 (Winter 1975), pp. 105–11.

[5] In addition to the report cited earlier, see Mary H. Stevenson, "Relative Wages and Sex Segregation by Occupation," in Cynthia B. Lloyd (ed.), *Sex, Discrimination, and the Division of Labor* (New York: Columbia University Press, 1975).

[6] Harold Wilensky, "Women's Work: Economic Growth, Ideology, Structure," *Industrial Relations* (May 1968), pp. 235–48. See also, in the same issue, Valerie K. Oppenheimer, "The Sex-Labeling of Jobs," pp. 219–34.

women, and there is no reason why men cannot be librarians, primary school teachers, or airline cabin attendants. The arbitrariness of conventional classifications is suggested by the variation of practice among countries. In the USSR, for example, large numbers of women are employed as doctors, economists and statisticians, engineers, agriculturalists, and veterinarians, as well as in many types of heavy manual labor.

A further aspect of segregation is the tendency toward exclusion of women from supervisory and managerial positions. This is true even within the sphere of "women's work": the school principal, the chief librarian, the director of hospital services tend to be men. It is even more true of situations in which a woman, if promoted, would be supervising male employees. The explanation commonly offered is that men would resent a woman supervisor to an extent that makes her use unfeasible.

The great increase in employment of women over the past several decades has *not* occurred, for the most part, through entry of women into traditionally male occupations. Rather, clerical and service occupations traditionally dominated by women have experienced an unusually rapid increase in demand; and at the same time a number of new "women's occupations" have appeared. One could perhaps find a few occupations that have shifted from the "men's work" to the "women's work" category over the course of decades. But there are few cases in which an occupation has been successfully integrated, continuing to employ large numbers of men *and* women workers.

The persistence of job segregation raises a puzzling question. Assume for the moment that women cost less than men of the same ability, education, and training. It would seem that employers could reduce costs by substituting lower-cost for higher-cost labor. In a fully competitive market, this substitution would continue until men's and women's wages were equalized. What prevents this from happening? What maintains the segmentation of the market?

There is no agreed answer at present; but there are several possibilities:

1. Women's labor may not be as cheap as it appears. Additional costs of training, turnover, and absenteeism may bring the full cost of female labor up to that of male labor, even though the hourly wage rate is lower. We shall comment further on this in the next section.
2. Employers, blinded by stereotypes, may consider women less efficient for the job in question, even though this is not so in fact. If they believe that there is a male–female productivity gap that exceeds the wage gap, employment of women may appear unprofitable.
3. Women may also have stereotypes, instilled in them by sex-role socialization from childhood onward. This may deter them from even applying for traditionally "male" jobs.
4. Male employees may oppose intrusion of women into their job territory. This is rational in that free admission of women would tend to lower male

wage rates. If this opposition is severe, the employer may consider that the realistic alternatives are to maintain the status quo or to shift to an all-women labor force. This would be a drastic shift, and the supply of women workers in the area may not be sufficient to permit it.

5. Finally, the salaried personnel managers and other executives who do the discriminating suffer only indirectly, if at all, from the lower company profits which may result. Modern theories of corporate management emphasize that profit maximization is only one of numerous influences on management decisions.

Women's Earnings: The Wage Gap

Measurement of male–female wage differentials should involve rates of pay for "similar work." But accurate comparison is harder than may appear. The results are much influenced by the width of the occupational classification used. If one uses very broad categories—professional and managerial people, sales workers, factory operatives—the results are not very informative. Any such category includes hundreds of specific occupations, most of which will be either predominantly "male" or "female." If, on the other hand, one uses a very narrow classification—men and women doing identical work in the same establishment—one is examining an unusual situation, in which sizable wage differences are virtually excluded by definition.

A number of such narrow studies have been made. Donald McNulty, who analyzed eleven occupations employing substantial numbers of men and women, found that for most occupations two-thirds to three-quarters of the people were employed in establishments employing only men or only women for the occupation in question. In these segregated establishments, the occupational wage level in men-only establishments was usually one-quarter to one-third higher than in the women-only establishments. In the minority of establishments where men and women shared the same occupation, differentials were considerably smaller—of the order of 8 to 14 percent.[7] Direct discrimination is obviously difficult. The presence of male co-workers tends to pull women's wages up toward the male level.

An analysis of census and Bureau of Labor Statistics data by Henry Sanborn reaches similar conclusions.[8] When comparison is narrowed to men and women in the same occupation in the same plant, the differential in earnings is typically less than 10 percent, and such difference as remains is not necessarily discriminatory. Where workers in an occupational class

---

[7] Donald J. McNulty, "Differences in Pay Between Men and Women Workers," *Monthly Labor Review* (December 1967), pp. 40–43. The study covered accounting clerks, order clerks, payroll clerks, office boys and girls, tabulating machine operators, elevator operators, janitors, and shipping packers.

[8] Henry Sanborn, "Pay Differences Between Men and Women," *Industrial and Labor Relations Review* (July 1964), pp. 534–50.

move up within a rate range with increasing experience, the fact that male workers usually have longer average length of service may give them some wage advantage. There may also be productivity differences, though evidence on this point is scanty. Sanborn reports an analysis of pieceworkers' earnings in the shoe and furniture industries, indicating that women pieceworkers earned (and presumably produced) about 10 percent less than men; but one would expect productivity to vary with the kind of work in question, so that this result cannot safely be generalized.

Further evidence comes from a study by Albert Rees and George Shultz of individual workers' earnings in a dozen occupations in the Chicago labor market.[9] Four of these contained enough men and women to permit analysis of the relation between sex and earnings. They found that, after controlling for age, education, seniority in present job, and total work experience, women punch press operators earned about 8 percent less than men, women accountants 11 percent less, women tabulating machine operators 14 percent less, and women janitors 18 percent less.

An interesting study of science and social science Ph.D.'s in academic institutions found that men and women normally receive their first appointment at the same academic rank—instructor or assistant professor. In the natural sciences, women are promoted about as rapidly as men; but in the social sciences (and presumably also in the humanities) they are promoted more slowly. There is also some adverse salary treatment of women. Comparing those of the same academic rank, women receive on the average 90–95 percent as much as men.[10] A study of the legal profession, on the other hand, found salary discrimination of 10–20 percent on initial hiring. Women lawyers' relative earnings also declined with increasing age, probably reflecting slower promotion to junior and senior partnerships.[11]

Two studies of a broader type have already been mentioned. Mary Stevenson, relying heavily on education as an indicator of labor force quality, found that women typically work below their ability, and also earn below their ability; that is, earnings differences between "male" and "female" occupations are larger than can be explained by differences in education and training time. Fuchs finds interesting differences by marital status, age, and type of employment.[12] In government employment, women

[9] Albert Rees and George P. Shultz, *Workers and Wages in an Urban Labor Market* (Chicago: The University of Chicago Press, 1970), Chap. 11.

[10] Alan Bayer and Helen Astin, "Sex Differences in Academic Rank and Salary Among Science Doctorates in Teaching," *Journal of Human Resources* (Spring 1968). See also George E. Johnson and Frank P. Stafford, "The Earnings and Promotion of Women Faculty," *American Economic Review* (December 1974), pp. 888–903.

[11] James I. White, "Women in the Law," *Michigan Law Review*, 65 (1967), p. 1051.

[12] Victor Fuchs, "Differences in Hourly Earnings Between Men and Women," *Monthly Labor Review* (May 1971), pp. 9–15.

earn 81 percent as much as men; but in private wage–salary employment the ratio is only 58 percent, and in self-employment only 41 percent. Single women earn on the average 88 percent as much as men; but the widowed–divorced–separated group earns only 69 percent as much, and married women living with their husbands only 58 percent as much. For all groups, and particularly for married women with husbands present, the female–male wage ratio declines with increasing age. This is another way of saying that men's earnings rise more steeply with age than do women's. Fuchs surmises that this may be due partly to larger amounts of investment in formal and on-the-job training by men or their employers.

Two general impressions emerge: (1) Even within a narrowly defined occupation, where men and women work side by side, there is usually an earnings differential in favor of men. This usually arises from existence of a rate range for the job, within which men are rated higher, or promoted faster, or simply survive longer than women, eventually reaching the top of the range through seniority. But this kind of differential is moderate in size and does not account for most of the earnings gap. (2) More important is the fact, emphasized by Stevenson, Oppenheimer, and others, that "women's jobs" pay less than "men's jobs" that seem comparable in terms of education and training requirements. This is the main phenomenon to be explained.

There are several possible explanations, not necessarily mutually exclusive. The first is that job segregation itself would be sufficient to explain a differential in earnings. If jobs and workers are divided into watertight compartments, then wages in one compartment may be permanently higher or lower than those in other compartments. Wages in the different compartments are not *unrelated* to each other; but they are related *via* product markets rather than through the labor market. Relative earnings are determined in the same way as the terms of trade between trading nations. For a given technology, they will depend on relative rates of increase in labor supply within each group, and on rates of increase in demand for the products of each group.

This is essentially J. E. Cairnes' theory of "noncompeting groups," based on his observation of the class structure in nineteenth-century Britain.[13] It is today often referred to as "the crowding hypothesis." It holds that the growing supply of women's labor is dammed up within the boundaries of traditional "women's work" and has difficulty spilling over into male-dominated occupations. This tends on one hand to depress wage rates for women's occupations, and on the other to raise wages in male occupations that are protected from female competition. Although labor market

---

[13] J. E. Cairnes, *Some Leading Principles of Political Economy Newly Expounded* (New York: Harper and Brothers, 1874).

segmentation is not complete, and while some of the dikes have been crumbling in recent years, this line of reasoning carries considerable force.

A second hypothesis is that hiring women is more expensive than hiring men. In a competitive market, this must be offset by a lower wage rate. Some of the statements made in this connection seem to be unfounded. For example, there is no evidence of significantly higher illness or absenteeism rates among female workers, nor do women move from job to job more frequently than men. But women do leave and reenter the labor force three or four times as frequently as men.[14] This arises partly from the convention that a husband is free to seek new jobs that may involve a change of residence, and that the wife then moves even at the sacrifice of her own job. It arises also from the exigencies of child bearing and child rearing. Most women who have children count on being out of the labor force for at least a few years during this period.

Several consequences follow from this. Quitting a job does impose costs on the employer in terms of disruption of the work team and added recruitment and training expenses. So, if the probability of quitting is substantially higher for women than for men, it is rational for the employer to take this into account at the time of hiring. Moreover, higher turnover means that female workers typically have a shorter length of service with a particular employer. Given that advancement in responsibility and earnings is significantly related to seniority, this could explain somewhat lower earnings for women.

Perhaps most important is the possibility that female workers may receive less on-the-job training than men. As we saw in Chapter 3, the cost of firm-specific training is borne in the first instance by the employer, and he will expect to recover this cost in the future. If the employer's estimate of probable future years of service is substantially lower for women than for men, his incentive to provide training is correspondingly reduced. Moreover, a good part of on-the-job training consists simply of continued experience, and women who have on the average a shorter period of service with each employer accumulate less experience. So, to the extent that earnings differences reflect on-the-job training and experience rather than formal education, one would predict a differential in favor of men.

The fact that women living with their husbands are especially disadvantaged in terms of earnings suggests that additional factors may be at work in their case. These could include: (1) A lower supply price: women who are only partially responsible for family support may be willing to work for less than unattached women or men. (2) What may amount to the same thing, they may have a marked preference for work that is close to home or that is pleasant and interesting, and may be willing to trade a

---

[14] George L. Perry, "Unemployment Flows in the U.S. Labor Market," *Brookings Papers on Economic Activity*, No. 2 (1972), pp. 245–78.

certain amount of income for these things. (3) A sizable proportion of this group work part-time. To the extent that organizing work on a part-time basis involves higher costs for employers, a lower wage may be part of the price for having the schedule one prefers. (4) Since most of this group will have had their work careers interrupted one or more times, they will usually have less accumulated experience and job training than men or women who have been continuously in the labor force.

Is the male/female earnings gap increasing or diminishing? Here the evidence is encouraging. Fuchs concludes [15] that, over the decade 1959–69, the ratio of women's to men's earnings rose by 4.8 percent. This is all the more striking in that the ratio of women to men workers also rose by an unprecedented 20 percent. The explanation must be that the occupaions employing mainly women were expanding fast enough so that demand more than kept up with the rapidly rising supply. It is interesting also that the increase in women's relative earnings was largest (11.4 percent) for women with college training. This may reflect a reduction in discrimination against women at the higher managerial and professional levels.

NONWHITE WORKERS

Discrimination in Employment

As in the case of female workers, discrimination in *wage rates* is a minor part of the problem. The main problem is discrimination in *employment*. This occurs when black workers of equivalent training, ability, and work experience are denied equal opportunity to be hired, retained, and promoted. This can occur in several ways. Black workers may be excluded entirely from the more desirable jobs in the company and restricted to those at the bottom of the skill structure. They may be hired as laborers and janitors, but not as operatives or craftsmen. Even if they are admitted to production work, they may be placed on a separate seniority ladder with a low cutoff point, so that they cannot move up as high in the job structure as those on the "white ladder." In the case of skilled crafts, black applicants may be excluded from apprenticeship or other training programs which provide the necessary skills. This has been a long-standing complaint in the construction industry.

"Statistical discrimination" may result also from the screening effect discussed in an earlier chapter. For example, employers often require a higher level of education than is really necessary for the work in question.

---

[15] Victor R. Fuchs, "Recent Trends and Long-Run Prospects for Female Earnings," *American Economic Review* (May 1974), pp. 236–42.

Given the lower educational level of the black labor force, this automatically excludes many black workers who could in fact do the job satisfactorily.

Discrimination, correctly defined, has no productivity basis and must therefore rest on noneconomic preferences. Many employers, other things being equal, simply prefer white workers to black. And white workers, partly through social prejudice, partly through fear of economic competition, resist the introduction of black employees into their plant or occupation. The relative weight of these factors is difficult to determine, since an employer who wishes to discriminate can always find objections among his white labor force to serve as an excuse.

The effect of union policies appears to vary with the type of union in question. Industrial unions cannot directly regulate admission of black workers, since they have no control over hiring; and in steel, automobiles, and other mass-production industries, black workers typically form a substantial part of actual and potential union members. This being so, the union must be somewhat responsive to their interests. The drift of the evidence, to be detailed in a later chapter, is that industrial unions tend to raise the wages of unskilled workers relative to those of skilled craftsmen. Since black workers are overrepresented in the unskilled ranks, this tends to raise black wages relative to white wages. Ashenfelter concludes that, in the industrial union sector, blacks are unionized as highly as whites relative to their numbers in employment, and that the wage ratio of blacks to whites is perhaps 4 percent *higher* than it would be in the absence of unionism.[16]

The situation in the craft union sector is quite different. Here the unions do have a voice in admission of new workers to the trade, and have in general fought a delaying action against admission of blacks. In construction, for example, the percentage of black workers in the skilled trades is very low— typically in the range of 0 to 2 percent—while they tend to bunch up in such jobs as plastering (where they form 14 percent) and construction labor (where they form 30 percent). The percentage of black workers unionized is only about half that of whites. Ashenfelter estimates that, in the craft union sector, the wage ratio of blacks to whites is 5 percent *lower* than it would be in the absence of all unionism.

The effect of employment discrimination (plus educational disadvantages and other factors to be noted in a moment) is to bunch up nonwhite workers in a limited range of occupations—primarily laboring and service occupations. It is clear from Table 2 that there has been progress in this respect over the past generation. Note particularly the sharp increase in

---

[16] Orley Ashenfelter, "Racial Discrimination and Trade Unionism," *Journal of Political Economy* (May–June 1972), pp. 435–64.

Table 2

Employed Persons by Occupation Group and Color, 1948 and 1975

Occupation Group	1948 Nonwhite (Percent)	1975 Nonwhite (Percent)	1975 White (Percent)	1975 Nonwhite as Per cent of White
White-collar	9.0	34.2	51.7	66.2
Professional and technical	2.4	11.4	15.5	73.5
Managers, proprietors, and officials	2.3	4.4	11.2	39.5
Clerical	3.3	15.7	18.1	86.7
Sales	1.1	2.7	6.9	33.1
Blue-collar	39.7	37.4	32.4	115.4
Craftsmen and foremen	5.3	8.8	13.4	65.7
Operatives	20.1	20.0	14.6	137.0
Laborers (except farm)	14.3	8.7	4.4	197.7
Service	30.3	25.8	12.3	209.8
Private household	15.1	4.9	1.0	490.0
Others	14.7	20.9	11.3	155.0
Farm	21.0	2.6	3.6	72.2
Owners and managers	8.5	0.6	2.0	30.0
Laborers	12.5	2.0	1.5	33.3
Total	100.0	100.0	100.0	—

SOURCE: *Employment and Training Report of the President* (Washington, D.C.: Government Printing Office, 1976), p. 237. For a review of recent progress, see Richard B. Freeman, "Decline of Labor Market Discrimination and Economic Analysis," *American Economic Review* (May 1973), pp. 280–86.

the proportion of nonwhite workers in clerical, technical, and professional occupations, and the sharp decline in those employed as farm laborers and domestic servants. Progress has been due partly to the very tight labor markets in the years from 1942 to 1945, and 1966 to 1969, during which black workers were pulled upward in the occupational structure. Legislation against discrimination in employment, pressure from civil rights groups, and increased political representation of the black community must also have contributed, but to an extent which is difficult to determine.

Despite substantial progress there is still a striking disparity in the occupational distribution. Only about 34 percent of black workers are in white-collar occupations, compared with about 52 percent of white workers. The converse of this is an overrepresentation of black workers in unskilled, semiskilled, and service occupations.

This concentration of black workers in the lower occupational strata—the "crowding effect"—has wage consequences similar to those noted earlier for female workers. The supply of labor to these occupations is enhanced, since supply cannot readily spill over to the higher occupations, and so their equilibrium wage rate is artificially depressed. The result is that predominantly "black" occupations requiring a given level of qualifications pay less than "white" occupations at the same level. Moreover, black workers tend to be employed "below their ability," in the sense of having more education and job experience than white workers employed at the same occupational level.

How can this situation persist? The supply–price of black labor is lower, or—what amounts to the same thing—a given wage rate will attract black workers with qualifications superior to those of white workers. So why don't employers proceed to substitute cheap labor for dear? There are several possible reasons—mistaken employer stereotypes, black workers' reluctance to apply for jobs that they believe they cannot get, actual or potential opposition by white employees, nonmaximizing behavior by lower-level executives—but we do not know the relative weight of these influences or the interaction among them.

White and Nonwhite Earnings

Some indication of how far black workers fall short of the average earnings of all workers in each major occupational grade is provided by Table 3. It should be noted that these are not nonwhite—white ratios but nonwhite—average ratios, the average including the nonwhites.

Black women clearly do better relative to white women than black men relative to white men. Indeed, in most occupational categories, there is little difference in women's earnings on the basis of color. Black men do

Table 3

Median Nonwhite Income as Percentage of Median Income for Total Labor
Force, by Occupation and Sex, 1949 and 1969

	Male Workers		Female Workers	
Occupation	1949	1969	1949	1969
Professional and technical	57.5	72.3	84.9	102.3
Managers, officials, and proprietors	50.0	66.0	44.6	95.3
Clerical workers	83.6	84.7	95.2	98.1
Sales workers	54.8	64.2	74.5	112.7
Craftsmen	62.6	72.4	78.7	87.9
Operatives	72.1	81.6	76.9	92.6
Service workers (except private household)	77.6	85.5	86.8	117.5
Private household	91.1	102.9	100.5	116.8
Laborers (except farm and mine)	81.0	90.5	88.5	98.0
Farm laborers and foremen	71.6	72.5	88.0	71.6

SOURCE: Adapted from Richard B. Freeman, "Decline of Labor Market Discrimination and Economic Analysis," *American Economic Review* (May 1973), p. 281.

relatively best in the clerical, service, and laboring categories, and less well
as executives, professional and technical workers, and skilled craftsmen.
There was clearly substantial improvement for most categories between
1949 and 1969.

Other studies confirm that black women have made substantially
greater progress in recent decades than black men. This reflects the rapid
movement of black women out of domestic service and laboring occupations into clerical, sales, professional, and technical jobs with markedly
higher earnings.

An additional dimension of the problem is *regional* differences in the
nonwhite–white income ratio. The gap is substantially larger in the South
than in the North. The heavy northward migration of black workers since
1940 has thus produced a (statistically) automatic increase in their relative
earnings. Indeed, for male workers, this has been the major source of income gain.

Despite recent gains, black women are still disadvantaged in terms of
occupational distribution and relative earnings; and for black men, the disadvantage is substantially greater. But before ascribing this entirely to employment discrimination, we must take account of the somewhat lower
educational level of the black labor force. While the education gap has
shrunk markedly in recent decades, black workers still have on the average

somewhat less education than white workers as well as a lower quality of education.

To put the same point differently: additional years of education have in the past had a lower payoff to blacks than to whites. Moreover, the black/white earnings ratio *declines* with rising level of education, being lowest among college graduates. This is a phenomenon which Finis Welch has termed "discrimination against education." [17]

Important changes, however, have recently been occurring in this respect. This becomes clear when one analyzes black/white differentials by age as well as by educational level. For older "vintages"—people who finished their schooling and entered the labor market ten or twenty years ago—the traditional relations hold good; but this is not true for more recent vintages. For black high school and college graduates who have entered the market recently, the payoff to additional years of schooling is as high as for whites. Indeed, the greatest relative gains in earnings over the recent past have been made by black college graduates.

One possible interpretation is that the *quality* of black education has been rising, and rising faster than that of white education. Figures on average class sizes, educational level of teachers, and average expenditure per pupil in the public school system support this supposition. It seems likely also that government antidiscrimination programs have led to some relaxation of discrimination against black college graduates in managerial, professional, and technical employments.

One implication is that, as older black workers retire and are replaced by younger ones who are less disadvantaged in education and earnings, this will by itself contribute—indeed, has already begun to contribute—to a reduction in the overall black/white differential.

Numerous studies have attempted to determine how much of the white–nonwhite earnings gap is attributable to schooling, and how much results from other factors, including labor market discrimination.[18] The consensus appears to be that years of schooling alone account for only a small part (of the order of 10 to 20 percent) of the earnings gap. When we include lower *quality* of black schooling as indicated, for example, by performance on standardized tests, we can account for somewhat more of the difference in earnings. There remains a large residual, however, pos-

---

[17] Finis Welch, "Labor Market Discrimination: An Interpretation of Income Differences in the Rural South," *Journal of Political Economy* (June 1967), pp. 225–40.

[18] See Joan Gustafson Haworth, James Gwartney, and Charles Haworth, "Earnings, Productivity, and Changes in Employment Discrimination During the 1960's," *American Economic Review* (March 1975), pp. 158–68; and Finis Welch, "Black–White Differences in Returns to Schooling," *American Economic Review* (December 1973), pp. 893–907.

sibly as high as two-thirds of the total gap, which must be traced to other factors. Among these, labor market discrimination is doubtless most important.

Unemployment and Family Income

Lower wage rates alone would make for lower incomes in black families; but in addition, black workers have a substantially higher unemployment rate that white workers—typically about twice as high. This is true especially of black teenagers, whose unemployment rate in the most recent recession rose above 30 percent. In recession years black workers are more than twice as likely to be laid off as are white workers. Part of this results from the adverse occupational distribution; that is, a high proportion are unskilled and semiskilled, and these groups have high layoff rates. But even after adjustment for this factor, the layoff rate for black workers remains well above that for whites, suggesting some degree of discrimination against them.

Less regular employment, plus lower wage rates, plus (for black men) somewhat lower labor force participation rates, all help to depress family incomes in the black community. The distribution of incomes of white and nonwhite families in 1974 is shown in Table 4. Here again there has been modest progress. In 1950, black families averaged 54 percent as much as white families. By 1970, this had risen to 64 percent. But the distributions for the two groups are still strikingly different. In 1974, almost 30 percent of black families had incomes below $5,000 a year, while only about 10 percent of white families were at this level.

Table 4

Annual Income, White and Nonwhite Families, 1974

	1974	
Annual Income	*White (Percent)*	*Nonwhite (Percent)*
Under $3,000	4.3	13.6
3,000– 4,999	6.8	16.0
5,000– 6,999	8.4	13.0
7,000– 9,999	13.5	16.2
10,000–14,999	25.1	19.0
15,000 and over	42.1	22.4
Median income	$13,356	$8,265

SOURCE: *Statistical Abstract of the United States* (Washington, D.C.: Government Printing Office, 1975), pp. 390–91.

ANTIDISCRIMINATION POLICIES

Federal efforts to check discrimination in employment go back at least to the 1940s, but were intensified from the early 60s onward. The federal government is itself a large employer, and in this respect a superior employer. We have already noted that the female/male wage ratio is substantially higher in federal employment than in the private sector. Nondiscrimination is official policy, and there has been a serious effort to move women and black workers up the ladder to senior positions. Though women and blacks are still much underrepresented at the Cabinet and sub-Cabinet levels, they occupy a growing number of positions at the level of bureau chief, division chief, and senior staff adviser.

An important statute, especially for women workers, is the Equal Pay Act of 1963. This applies to all occupations covered by the Fair Labor Standards Act and is enforceable through the same machinery. The inspection staffs that check establishments for violations of the minimum wage and overtime provisions can at the same time check complaints of wage discrimination against women. Between 1963 and 1970 about 1,400 court cases were filed in this area, and back-pay orders were issued running to many millions of dollars.[19]

The two major lines of attack on employment discrimination, however, have been: (1) equal employment opportunity statutes, applying to the entire labor force; (2) directives prohibiting employment discrimination by government contractors, applying to a highly visible and strategic portion of the labor force.

Equal Employment Opportunity Laws

Some twenty-five states, including virtually all the northern and western industrial states now have fair employment practice laws on the books. In some states these are not supported by an adequate budget and enforcement staff, and are virtually dead letters. The large industrial states however, such as New York, New Jersey, and Pennsylvania, have sizable staffs and an active enforcement program.

At the federal level, the guiding statute is the Civil Rights Act of 1964. Title VII of this Act makes it an unlawful employment practice for an employer "to refuse to hire or to discharge any individual, òr otherwise to discriminate against any individual with respect to his compensation, terms, conditions, or privileges of employment, because of such individual's race, color, religion, sex or national origin . . ." and also "to

---

[19] Robert D. Moran, "Reducing Discrimination: Role of the Equal Pay Act," *Monthly Labor Review* (June 1970), pp. 30–34.

limit, segregate, or classify his employees in any way which would deprive or tend to deprive any individual of employment opportunities. . . ." Similar prohibitions apply to employment agencies, labor organizations, or joint labor–management committees in charge of apprenticeship or other training programs. Title VII applies to all employers in interstate commerce with twenty-five or more employees, and to unions with more than twenty-five members.

Enforcement of Title VII is entrusted to a five-man Equal Employment Opportunity Commission (EEOC). The commission has authority to receive complaints, to try to resolve these by discussion and persuasion, and where this fails to seek enforcement through the U.S. Attorney General. Civil suits may also be filed by aggrieved individuals, and the Attorney General may intervene in such suits where he finds this to be in the public interest. The EEOC does not supersede existing state or local FEP laws. Indeed, when it receives a complaint from an area that has such a law, it is obliged to notify the appropriate state or local officials and to allow them a reasonable time to investigate the complaint. For states with FEP laws, then, the EEOC operates mainly as an appeal tribunal to handle tough cases which could not be adjusted at lower levels. For states without FEP laws, on the other hand, it operates as a court of first resort. Its authority is limited to employers engaged in "interstate commerce." The interpretation of interstate commerce, however, has become more liberal over time, and now covers more than 75 percent of all workers in private employment.

Until recently suits under Title VII could be brought only by private parties or by the Justice Department. Expense is a serious barrier to private suits, while activities by the Justice Department have been limited by a small staff and lack of coordination with the EEOC. A 1972 amendment to the Act permits the EEOC to bring suits on its own motion where it believes that a violation of Title VII has occurred. A stronger proposal, considered but eventually defeated in the Senate, would have empowered the EEOC to issue cease-and-desist orders. Thus once the EEOC ruled that discrimination had occurred, the employer (or other institution) would not have been allowed to continue such discrimination pending trial.

The definition of discrimination under Title VII is gradually being worked out in the EEOC and in the courts. The Act prescribes a policy of color blindness (and sex blindness). The employer must not discriminate against members of minority groups, but neither may he discriminate in their favor. He is entitled to set tests and other objective standards for hiring; but these must be related to job performance, and not serve merely as a discriminatory screening device.[20]

A recent Supreme Court decision held that the employer is prohibited

---

[20] *Willie S. Griggs* v. *Duke Power Company* (U.S. Supreme Court, No. 124, March 9, 1971).

from requiring high school graduation or passing a general intelligence test as a condition for employment in or transfer to a job when: (1) neither standard is shown to be significantly related to job performance; (2) both requirements operate to disqualify black applicants at a substantially higher rate than white applicants; and (3) the job in question formerly had been filled only by white employees as a matter of company policy. The courts will clearly become involved increasingly in the tricky question of what hiring standards actually are related to job performance.

An employer's *recruitment* policies as well as his hiring requirements are subject to scrutiny. Suppose that, because he recruits through current employees or through the union office, he gets few or no black applicants. The courts have generally held that such recruitment procedures are illegal if they result in a workforce whose racial composition is significantly different from that of the community.[21] The natural remedy is for the employer to list his vacancies with the state employment service and to advertise them in media serving the black community. But how much of this new recruitment activity must he undertake? Here again the EEOC and the courts are involved in a difficult question.

Discrimination is forbidden not only in hiring but in transfer, promotion, and other aspects of employment; and this leads the courts still deeper into internal personnel procedures. Seniority is a common basis both for promotions and layoffs. Suppose that, because black workers have not been hired in the past, they have had no chance to accumulate seniority. Or suppose that they have been assigned to a separate seniority ladder, with no possibility of transfer to the "white ladder." In some steel mills, for example, the practice has been to maintain dual seniority systems, which keep some lines of work reserved for white workers and other (generally less desirable jobs) reserved for blacks. In 1973 the Federal District Court in Birmingham, Alabama, held that this practice in the Birmingham mill of the U.S. Steel Company was unlawful. It ordered that the two ladders be integrated into a single seniority system, which would permit any steel worker to move into any job if he has the seniority and can qualify to do the work. Detailed arrangements for doing this were worked out subsequently by union–management agreement.[22]

Discrimination by Federal Contractors

Every president since 1940 has established a body charged with preventing employment discrimination by government contractors. Enforcement efforts have been particularly active since 1960. The administrative

---

[21] On this and other aspects of employment discrimination, see "Employment Discrimination and Title VII of the Civil Rights Act of 1964," *Harvard Law Review*, 84 (1971), pp. 1114 and ff.

[22] Vincent L. Matera, "Steel Industry Equal Employment Consent Decrees," Industrial Relations Research Association, *Proceedings* (1974), pp. 217–224.

body is the Office of Federal Contract Compliance (OFCC), where author- ity extends to all activities of companies holding federal contracts, rather than only to direct government production. This includes most large com- panies in the country; and it also includes bodies such as universities, which usually have some federal research contracts. The sanction, rarely invoked but potentially powerful, is cancellation of federal contracts with persistent violators of OFCC directives.

The OFCC has gone beyond the EEOC in not merely prohibiting dis- crimination but in also setting up quantitative targets for minority group employment. Compulsory quotas are specifically prohibited by the Civil Rights Act of 1964. Instead, the OFCC sets up—or requires the con- tractor to set up—advisory or "target" quotas, to be reached at a specified future date. An employer who fails to reach the target is not necessarily in violation. But he must demonstrate that he has made a serious effort to do so through an "affirmative action program."

OFCC Revised Order No. 4 of December, 1971, requires contractors with 50 or more employees or contracts of at least $50,000 to have an affirmative action program which includes: (1) a self-analysis to determine whether women and minority-group members are being underutilized; (2) proposed action, including goals and timetables, to remedy any deficiencies; (3) affirmation of an equal opportunity policy, and dissemination of the policy both internally and externally; (4) establishment of a director of equal opportunity programs, with responsibility for developing programs and checking on accomplishments.

Special programs have been developed in the construction industry. Since construction workers usually have no long-term connection with any one contractor, an effective program must be area-wide and, as a practical matter, must involve the unions as well as the contractors. In the earliest of these programs, the "Philadelphia Plan" initiated in 1967, the OFCC itself set goals for admission of black workers to apprenticeship training and to employment as craftsmen. More recently, emphasis has shifted to development of "hometown plans," agreements negotiated among unions, employers, and minority-group representatives to increase minority-group employment on construction projects in the area. Failing effective local action, however, the government can fall back on the Philadelphia Plan approach. The government's right to institute such programs has been up- held by the courts.[23]

The "affirmative action" approach has been criticized on several grounds: that it may pressure employers to hire less efficient rather than more efficient workers, with a reduction in national output; that establish-

---

[23] *Contractors Association of Eastern Pennsylvania* v. *Shultz* (District Court, Eastern Pennsylvania, March 13, 1970). The Supreme Court refused to review this case.

ment of hiring quotas amounts to "reverse discrimination," which is unfair to white, male employees; and that the approach is so controversial that it may undermine political support for the civil rights movement. Supporters of the approach would argue that a carefully constructed program need not be either inefficient or inequitable. Some black leaders would add that, even if some reverse discrimination is involved, that is no more than appropriate compensation for past injustices to the black population. This will no doubt continue to be one of the more controversial and tension-ridden areas of employment policy.

The total impact of these equal-opportunity programs is hard to judge, because it is hard to separate their influence from that of other labor market developments. There has certainly been substantial alteration of employers' hiring and promotion practices. Some areas of skilled employment largely closed to blacks in the past have been opened up. Women and black workers are beginning to penetrate the best-paid and most prestigious levels of professional and managerial employment.

Part of what has been achieved was no doubt due to the prolonged economic expansion of 1961–69; and part was achieved through education, persuasion, and voluntary alteration of employer practices. But this does not mean that the legislative measures outlined above were unnecessary or ineffectual. Persuasion works better when government has laid down clear standards of public policy, when noncompliance with these standards leads to adverse publicity, and when legal sanctions are lurking in the background without complete certainty that they will not be invoked.

DISCUSSION QUESTIONS

1. Explain the meaning of: wage discrimination; employment discrimination; job segregation; the "crowding hypothesis."

2. How would you explain the persistence of job segregation for female workers, when employers could apparently save money by abandoning it?

3. The earnings of married women living with their husbands are considerably lower, as a percentage of men's earnings, than the earnings of single women. How would you account for this difference?

4. "Equal pay for equal work is not necessarily in the long-run interest of working women. Willingness to work for less is one way that women can outcompete men and take over additional areas of employment." Discuss.

5. Many educational institutions now profess to follow a "sex-blind policy" in college and graduate school admissions.

(a) What does this mean?

(b) How could one test whether such a policy is actually being followed?

6. To what extent does reduction of employment discrimination against women require:

(a) additional legislation?

(b) improved enforcement of existing legislation?

(c) other social and cultural changes?

7. To what extent can the earnings gap between white and nonwhite workers be attributed to:

(a) smaller quantity and poorer quality of education?

(b) employment discrimination?

(c) wage discrimination?

8. What evidence would you examine to determine whether an employer has engaged in employment discrimination against nonwhite workers?

READING SUGGESTIONS

In addition to the references cited in the text, see ARTHUR M. ROSS and HERBERT HILL (eds.), *Employment, Race, and Poverty* (New York: Harcourt, Brace and World, Inc., 1967); LESTER C. THUROW, *Poverty and Discrimination* (Washington, D.C.: The Brookings Institution, 1969); ORLEY ASHENFELTER and ALBERT REES (eds.), *Discrimination in Labor Markets* (Princeton: Princeton University Press, 1973); SAR A. LEVITAN, WILLIAM B. JOHNSTON, and ROBERT TAGGART, *Still a Dream: The Changing Status of Blacks Since 1960* (Cambridge, Mass.: Harvard University Press, 1975); CYNTHIA B. LLOYD (ed.), *Sex, Discrimination, and the Division of Labor* (New York: Columbia University Press, 1975); and STANLEY H. MASTERS, *Black–White Income Differentials* (New York: Academic Press, Inc., 1975).

III

WAGES AND INCOMES

Part III covers issues that at first glance may appear quite diverse. The common thread is the determination of wage rates in the American economy. These rates are set in the myriad markets in which employees seek workers and workers seek jobs. The analysis of Part III thus builds upon our analysis of labor markets in Part II.

Wage decisions are usually made at the company level. In an imperfect market, an employer has some discretion in choosing (or bargaining about) a wage level. In Chapter 9 we examine how this discretion is exercised, and also the problem of setting rates for "inside" as against "outside" jobs.

Millions of wage decisions cumulate into the movement of the *money wage level*. This level normally rises every year, but at a variable rate linked to the movement of employment and prices. In Chapter 10 we attempt to explain why wages rise faster when unemployment is low, a relation usually labeled "the Phillips curve." In recent American experience, any effort to approach "full employment" has led to an undesirably rapid advance of wages and prices. We consider attempts to cope with this problem, including direct wage and price controls.

Of greater interest to workers over the long run is the movement of the *real wage level*, that is, money wages adjusted for changes in consumer prices. Increases in real wages result mainly from increases in national output; but there has also been a moderate increase in labor's share of national output over the past half-century. In Chapter 11 we look at alternative theories of what determines labor's share of output, and review the evidence on long-run changes in this share.

The general level of wages is a statistical fiction. The reality is thousands of wage rates for specific jobs, ranging from very high to very low. In Chapter

181

12 we examine the size of wage differences and whether these differences seem to be increasing or decreasing over time. The conventional explanation for them rests on demand and supply schedules for specific skills. But we also examine a newer approach based on "human capital" theory, which tries to relate differences in earnings directly to differing investments in education and training.

Because of differences in labor incomes, and even larger differences in property incomes, the size—distribution of incomes among American families is quite unequal. In Chapter 13 we examine the present degree of inequality, ask whether inequality is increasing or decreasing over time, and explore the impact of the tax system on inequality of *spendable income*. There is particular concern about families at the low end of the income scale, those who fall below the "poverty line." We look at what is now being done to improve their situation through transfers of cash and commodities, and examine proposals for changes in the present system.

9

Wages at the Company Level

After a detour into labor market policy, we resume where we left off in Chapter 6: how the labor market operates, and in particular how it operates to determine wage rates for particular jobs.

To speak of "wage decisions" or "company wage policy" implies some latitude for choice. In the simplified markets of Chapter 5, there is no such latitude. The wage is given by the market. There is no need for any employer to pay more, and it is not possible for him to pay less. In actual labor markets, there is room for choice; and some employers pay more than others for the same type of skill in the same market. This is the first puzzle that we have to untangle.

WAGES: MEANING AND MEASUREMENT

It is necessary at the outset to say something about the numerous possible meanings of *wages*. The term is not as simple as it appears, and some of the disagreement that arises in discussing wages is due to the fact that people are talking about different things.

Most wage earners have an hourly rate of pay, usually referred to as the *base rate,* but this is not necessarily the amount which the worker actually receives. Many people work on a piecework or incentive basis, under which the amount they receive depends on how much they produce. Under an incentive system a worker is expected to earn a good deal more than his base rate—indeed, it is this expectation which gives him the incentive to maintain a high rate of output. For jobs above the unskilled level, there is usually a *rate range* rather than a single rate, and workers move up within this range on the basis of seniority and merit. A worker may work overtime, which is usually compensated at one and one-half times the regular wage; or he may work on a second or third shift and receive a premium for this.

For these and other reasons, a worker's *average hourly earnings* may be considerably above his base rate of pay. The distinction is important, because the wage statistics collected and published regularly by the U.S. Bureau of Labor Statistics relate to earnings rather than to wage rates.

A still higher figure is *total hourly compensation,* which includes a variety of fringe benefits paid for by the employer: paid vacations, paid holidays, other payments for time not worked, payments for medical and hospital insurance, payments into pension funds, employer contributions under the Social Security and unemployment compensation system, and other possible items. This is what an hour of labor actually costs the employer, and what the worker receives, in cash or in benefit rights, per hour worked. This figure, in short, corresponds most closely to the concept of "wages" in theoretical labor market analysis. This is also what unions and employers bargain about—a total "package," including improvements in fringe benefits as well as in wage scales, but which can be reduced to a cents-per-hour equivalent. In later sections, when we use the term "wages" without qualification, we mean total hourly compensation.

While this is the key figure, certain other calculations are important to employers and workers. The employer is interested in two things: how much it costs him to hire a man-hour of labor, and how much output he is able to get from this man-hour. It is not wages as such that matter, but wages in relation to productivity.

Hourly compensation divided by hourly output yields *labor cost per unit of output.* This figure, and its movement over time, is very significant in business calculations. If compensation rises faster than productivity, labor cost per unit will be rising, and it is a reasonable prediction that the product price will rise to cover the higher costs. For the economy as a whole, an index of commodity prices parallels quite closely the index of unit labor costs.

The worker is interested in how much he actually receives in his pay envelope, and in how much this money will buy. His weekly *take-home pay* is influenced not only by total hourly compensation, but by how much of this comes in the form of cash rather than benefits, by the number of hours worked per week, and by the size of deductions for Social Security, personal income tax, and other purposes. Because of these additional factors, take-home pay can change considerably even without any change in hourly compensation.

How much the paycheck will buy—*real* wages, as distinct from *money* wages—depends on the movement of consumer prices. Most of the time money wages are rising more rapidly than retail prices, so that real wages are also rising; but this was not true during the rapid inflation of the early seventies. Between 1970 and 1976, the average weekly money earnings of all private nonagricultural workers rose by almost exactly the same percentage as the Consumer Price Index—a bit over 50 percent in both cases. Thus in terms of real weekly earnings the average worker was no further ahead in 1976 than in 1970.

WAGE DIFFERENCES AMONG EMPLOYERS

We said at the outset that employers do not pay identical wages for the same skill in the same market. What is the evidence for such a statement?

At a qualitative level, there is the testimony of practitioners and informed observers of wage determination. Anyone who has discussed wage setting with company executives has encountered such statements as "We pay the highest wages in town," or "We keep up with the average of rates in our area," or "We try not to fall more than ten cents an hour below the area average." Executives take it as obvious that they have some room for maneuver, and can usually give a reasoned account of their wage strategy. Again, anyone who has engaged in arbitration of labor disputes has been presented with tables showing the rates paid by different employers for supposedly similar work. Intercompany equity is usually taken as one of the more compelling arguments in wage negotiations, and evidence of intercompany differences is used to document claims of inequity.

There is also a large amount of statistical evidence. The U.S. Bureau of Statistics has made many city-wide wage surveys, aimed at analyzing the rates paid by different employers for the same occupational title. These commonly show a rate range of the order of 20 to 30 percent. Wage dispersion appears to vary inversely with skill level—least for the most skilled jobs, greatest for "common labor." A summary of these studies by Robert Raimon found that, for all the skilled occupations studied, the quartile deviation averaged 11 percent; that is, one-half the rates for the occupation fell within a range of 11 percent on either side of the median. In the case of semiskilled occupations, however, the quartile deviation was 24 percent.[1] Such results might be rationalized on the ground that, as one goes down the skill ladder, job information becomes poorer and placement channels less adequate.

A serious difficulty in such studies is lack of full comparability in the data. Even though different plants use the same job title, the work may differ considerably. "Welding" is not the same in an aircraft plant and a shipyard; and even "common labor" is not as standardized as the term implies. Particularly troublesome is the question of worker quality, which

---

[1] Robert L. Raimon, "The Indeterminateness of Wages and Semiskilled Workers," *Industrial and Labor Relations Review* (January 1953), pp. 180–94.

is undoubtedly important but difficult to measure, and in any event not measured in most wage comparisons. Studies that have tried to get at this problem typically conclude that higher-wage companies do get a somewhat higher quality of labor. The Rees–Shultz study of a number of occupations in the Chicago labor market found a positive relation between workers' earnings and such proxies for quality as years of schooling, years of work experience, and (for typists and accountants) scores on performance tests.[2]

But are the differences in quality as large as the differences in wages? Do the higher-wage employers get as much as they pay for? Most scholars, including Rees and Shultz, have concluded that the answer is probably negative. An explicit test was made by Eaton H. Conant, who analyzed the aptitude test scores and hiring salaries of female high school graduates placed as typists by the state employment service in Madison, Wisconsin. He found a statistically significant difference between the test scores of girls hired by employers in the top third of the salary range and those hired by employers in the bottom third of the range. The average quality differential, however, was only about 5 percent; and it was sufficient to account for only about one-tenth of the difference in starting salaries.[3]

There is a strong probability, then, that wage differences are not fully offset by quality differences, and that the high-wage employers are paying more *per efficiency unit of labor.*

What are the characteristics of relatively high-wage companies as against relatively low-wage companies? Studies by Slichter and others [4] suggest that several factors are important:

1. *Size of establishment.* Other things being equal, larger plants tend to pay higher wages than smaller ones.
2. *Profitability of the company.* Where profits are high, wage decisions are likely to be more generous than where they are low.
3. *Ratio of labor costs to total costs.* A low ratio, so that wages are not a major factor in management's profit calculations, makes for a relatively high wage level. Oil refining is a notable example.
4. *Degree of industrial concentration.* While the evidence is not entirely

---

[2] Albert Rees and George P. Shultz, *Workers and Wages in an Urban Labor Market* (Chicago: The University of Chicago Press, 1970), p. 219.

[3] Eaton H. Conant, "Worker Efficiency and Wage Differentials in a Clerical Labor Market," *Industrial and Labor Relations Review* (April 1963), pp. 428–33.

[4] Sumner H. Slichter, "Notes on the Structure of Wages," *Review of Economics and Statistics* (February 1950), pp. 81–92; Melvin W. Reder, "Wage Differentials: Theory and Measurement," in *Aspects of Labor Economics* (Princeton: Princeton University Press, 1962), pp. 257–311; Leonard W. Weiss, "Concentration and Labor Earnings," *American Economic Review* (March 1966), pp. 96–117; Stanley H. Masters, "Wages and Plant Size: An Interindustry Analysis," *Review of Economics and Statistics* (August 1969), pp. 341–45.

clear, it appears that tight oligopolies with "cooperative" pricing arrangements pay higher wages than companies in more competitive industries.

5. *Degree of unionization.* A difficulty here is that large plant size, a high concentration ratio (as indicated by the percentage of industry output produced by, say, the four largest companies), and strong unionization tend to go together. Thus it takes careful statistical analysis to separate out the effect of each factor. The indications, however, are that unionization by itself is significant, and so is concentration by itself.

For these reasons there appears to be a wage hierarchy among companies, related partly to the industry to which they belong; and this ranking seems to remain rather stable over long periods of time.

THE CHOICE OF A WAGE LEVEL

Granted that employers have some latitude in choosing a wage level. how do they choose? Why do some prefer to be high-wage companies and others low-wage companies? How is wage level related to hiring strategy, and how does strategy change over the course of the business cycle?

The High-Wage Employer

Occupying a high rank in the local wage hierarchy is not always a matter of choice. If the plant is part of a national organization, major wage decisions will be made at headquarters and will be influenced by company policy as well as by local labor market circumstances. If the company is unionized, the union will usually try to achieve a uniform wage scale in all the company's plants, wherever located. Thus a steel mill in Birmingham, Alabama, may find itself paying wages that, while only average for Pittsburgh, are well above the average in Birmingham.

Next, there are several economic gains from a high-wage position, which serve to offset the higher wage costs:

1. The probable gain in worker quality has already been noted. The high-wage plant, with an ample supply of applicants, can impose stricter hiring standards. Its recruitment costs will also be lower, since workers came to it instead of the company's having to search the market.

2. The high-wage company can also demand superior performance after employment—regular attendance, consistent effort, high output standards. Workers who know that they have a job above the area level will be anxious to keep it and will be willing to put in a good day's work in return for good pay.

3. Quit rates will be lower, since the worker's estimate of the probability of finding a better job will be lower if his wage is already high. Quits are expensive because of the cost of recruiting and screening a replacement, train-

ing him, and bringing him up to full proficiency. Reduced turnover, then, is a substantial offset to higher wage costs.

4. The extra elbowroom resulting from a high-wage position means that the company does not have to reconsider its wage level at frequent intervals. If the labor market tightens, it will have to adjust eventually, but not immediately. This economizes the time of management officials.

5. In the case of a nonunion company, a high-wage policy may be regarded partly as insurance against unionization. The argument that "the union can't get you any more that you're getting now" is more effective when backed by high wages.

6. In a unionized company, a high-wage policy may reduce losses from labor disputes and work stoppages.

7. If we interpret *economic* broadly to include psychological satisfaction of executives as well as company profits, there are other gains from a liberal wage policy, such as prestige in the community and popularity with employees.

The Low-Wage Employer

How does an employer judge whether he is close to "the prevailing wage" for his area? One source of information is area wage surveys conducted by the local Manufacturers' Association or Chamber of Commerce. These reveal, among other things, the average straight-time hourly earnings (*a.s.t.h.e.*) of each company of significant size. These can be ranked from top to bottom, and any company can see where it stands in the ranking. Average hourly earnings is a fallible standard, however, because it depends partly on the skill mix of the establishment. A plant in which the work requires a large proportion of low-skilled workers could reasonably be expected to have *a.s.t.h.e.* below the area average.

For this reason, employers also pay attention to hourly rates for specific jobs for which there is an active "outside market." Maintenance electricians, carpenters, and other craftsmen, as well as watchmen, guards, janitors, and elevator operators, are jobs of this sort. (In the clerical realm, rates for bookkeepers, cashiers, typists, stenographers, and secretaries would provide useful comparisons.) Particularly significant is the starting rate for new production workers. In manufacturing, this is the port of entry into the company for most employees, and this rate is thus especially important in the competition for labor.

Since this survey information is available only at intervals and is not entirely easy to interpret, employers tend to attach special importance to the highest-wage companies in the area. These are the largest and most visible competitors for labor, and it is their rates that are most likely to be known and gossiped about by workers. A lower-wage company, then, may gauge its wage position partly by how far it is below the top of the ladder.

How can an employer sink in the wage structure? A prime consideration is the level of employment needed to meet production requirements in, say, the six months immediately ahead. Even if this is the same as present employment, some hiring will be necessary to replace losses through quits and retirements. The minimum feasible wage can be defined as the wage that will produce just enough applicants (or, more correctly, enough acceptances of job offers) to maintain the desired employment level. This wage will be related to the rate of change of desired employment—higher if employment is rising than if it is stable or falling. It will be related also to nonwage characteristics of the jobs.

This minimum wage, however, will not necessarily be the most *economic* wage for the company, for reasons already suggested. The workers who would accept jobs at this wage would be of relatively low quality, and they would have little motivation to perform effectively. Moreover, the lower the wage, the higher will be the quit rate and the resulting costs of recruitment, screening, and training.

A wage somewhat above the bare minimum, therefore, may actually lower labor costs per unit of output. To maximize profit, the employer should raise wages so long as the gain from improved labor quality and reduced turnover exceeds the addition to the wage bill. When marginal wage costs and benefits are exactly equal, he has reached the economic wage.

Even the low-wage employer, then, has to choose a wage level; and the economic wage will differ from one employer to the next. Companies will differ in rates of desired employment expansion, in nonwage characteristics of jobs, in susceptibility to quits, and in efficiency in recruitment and training. They will differ also in their appraisal of the imperfect information available. For these reasons one should expect dispersion of company wage levels, rather than the identity that would occur in a simplified market model.

The characteristics of low-wage employers are the reverse of those of high-wage employers. They tend to be relatively small, selling their products in competitive markets, with low profit margins, and frequently of nonunion status. They are to be found mainly in light manufacturing, trade, and the service industries. They are not low-wage employers because they prefer to be—indeed, a position near the bottom of the area wage structure is precarious and uncomfortable. The situation is rather that their wage-paying ability is severely constrained by product market conditions.

Over the course of years, there is turnover of employers as well as workers. Many low-wage companies are companies en route to elimination from their respective industries. Their profit margins are declining because of falling product demand, poor management, antiquated equipment, or locational disadvantages. As downward pressure from the product market continues, they sink gradually lower in the area wage structure (not by cutting wages, which is a rare occurrence, but by giving smaller increases than other employers). They are forced to test how low they can sink and still maintain a work force. Eventually, they find out. They are forced through the floor of the area wage structure or squeezed against the union scale or the legal minimum wage. At this point the game is over.

Response to Cyclical Fluctuations

A major feature of actual labor markets is fluctuation of aggregate demand for labor. These upswings and downswings of demand affect employers' wage strategy and the size of intercompany wage differences.

The strategy of high-wage employers is relatively deliberate, sluggish, acyclical. They are far enough above the area level so that they are not constrained by short-run changes in the labor market. They count on making wage increases year after year. They are usually monopolists or oligopolists, and tend to set prices by a percentage markup over average unit cost of production. An orderly and predictable upward movement of wages contributes to orderly, controlled price adjustments. When a trade union is in the picture, wage schedules will usually be adjusted only once a year; and union leaders, like employers, prefer a regular pace of increases. This serves as a demonstration to the members that the union officers are "delivering the goods" and deserve to be kept in office.

Fluctuations in labor demand, then, show up mainly in the distance by which low-wage firms find it feasible to lag behind the leaders. During an upswing of demand, the high-wage firms will not only be raising wages according to usual practice, but will also be increasing employment. They will be encouraging applications for work and accepting a higher proportion of applicants than usual. Firms toward the bottom of the wage structure will find their applications declining in numbers and quality. They will also find their quit rates rising because of the increased opportunities for job-hopping to the higher-wage firms. To hold down turnover costs and achieve *their* desired rate of employment, they will have to raise wages by *more* than the high-wage firms are doing, thus narrowing the gap between them. During periods of nearly full employment, then, the area wage structure tends to contract like a squeezed accordion.

During a downswing, the reverse tendencies come into play. The higher-wage firms will be laying off workers or at any rate ceasing to hire. Laid-off workers and new entrants will be forced lower down in the wage structure in the search for work. The low-wage firms find their queue of applicants growing longer and improving in quality, while at the same time their quit rate is falling. They will thus find it feasible to lag farther behind the wage leaders. They need not cut wages to achieve this result. Since the leaders are raising wages year in and year out, all the low-wage firms need do is give smaller increases. Thus the wage structure expands again in response to a general decline of employment.

This cyclical compression and expansion of the wage structure is confirmed by a number of statistical studies.[5] Reduction of intercompany differences is particularly noticeable under war conditions, such as 1942–45, 1950–53, 1966–69. During World War II and the Korean War, the compression was intensified by wage controls, which operated to allow low wages to move up faster than high ones. If American labor markets were consistently as tight as they have been during these periods of peak demand, we would move toward a narrower band of intercompany differences than has prevailed in the past. But most labor markets are rather loose most of the time, with a considerable surplus of unemployed over vacancies. This is a major reason why intercompany differences remain large.

The other major effect of cyclical fluctuation is on employers' hiring standards. We noted earlier that employers use a variety of screening criteria to determine acceptability for employment. If a company finds its pool of acceptable applicants running down, the pool can be enlarged in either of two ways: by raising its relative wage rate to draw in more applicants, or by lowering its hiring standards so that a larger proportion of applicants are rated as "acceptable." To the extent that the lowering of standards means accepting workers of lower productivity, this amounts to an increase in the wage *per efficiency unit of labor*. This tendency, plus increased use of overtime and rising quit rates, is one reason why unit labor costs of production tend to rise toward the top of an economic upswing.

Pressure to reduce hiring standards during an upswing impinges in the first instance on the low-wage firms, who are the first to feel the pinch of labor shortages. In a strong upswing, however, the tendency will extend eventually to most employers. During a downswing, the tendency goes into reverse. As labor supplies become more ample, hiring standards are raised again and only members of preferred groups of workers are kept in or added to the work force. The fact that adjustment of hiring standards is so rapidly reversible may cause employers to prefer it over wage increases as a means of attracting labor in a tight market. Wage increases are in practice not reversible, and cause a permanent escalation of labor costs.

The variety of adjustments open to the employer have been well described by Hildebrand:

> For instance, suppose that the local labor market becomes progressively tighter. To avoid raising wage rates, the employer may intensify his recruiting efforts, perhaps improving nonpecuniary conditions as well.

---

[5] Michael L. Wachter, "Cyclical Variation in the Interindustry Wage Structure," *American Economic Review* (March 1970), pp. 75–84.

In some cases he may be able to simplify certain jobs, breaking them up into multiples requiring a lower grade of labor. If necessary, he may reduce his standards for hiring and for promotion, deliberately accepting candidates of lower efficiency on the premise that the enforced rise in unit labor costs will be temporary, that poorer workers can later be laid off or demoted. For the same underlying reasons, he may tolerate some rise in costs of turnover, and some fall of efficiency among the already employed, the second expressed by increases in absenteeism, tardiness, and bad work, and possibly by slow-down tactics.

Together, these responses serve as expansion joints for absorbing the shock of a change in market forces, one that enables the employer to put off raising wage rates, mainly by tolerating a decline in labor efficiency and a rise in indirect employment costs. Although unit labor cost will still rise, to some extent its course will be reversible when the market loosens up. By contrast, a rise in wage rates for practical purposes is irreversible.[6]

A corollary of this mechanism is that the fate of the less preferred groups in the market—young workers, black workers, the relatively unskilled, uneducated, and unproductive—depends on maintenance of high aggregate demand for labor. In a very tight market, employers will follow the maxim, "If the body is warm, hire it." The less preferred groups will have a chance to be hired and to get training and work experience. In a slack market, on the other hand, many of them will be ruled out of employment by conventional hiring criteria. It is no accident that black workers have made their greatest occupational advances in periods of very high labor demand, such as 1942–45 and 1966–69.

The Vacancy Model and Queuing

It will be useful to formalize the kind of labor market we have been discussing and to explain how it differs from the simplified model of Chapter 5. The key structural features of the market are heterogeneity of workers as well as employers, limited information leading to search activity by employers and workers, unemployment as a normal feature of the market, and cyclical fluctuations in aggregate demand for labor.

A key behavioral characteristic is that the company's wage level, instead of being dictated by the market, is a matter of policy. Most companies most of the time are *not* paying the bare minimum required to meet their employment objectives. There is considerable difference in the wages offered by different employers in the same market for the same type of skill.

The short-run situation of a typical employer in such a market is

---

[6] George H. Hildebrand, "External Influence and the Determination of the Internal Wage Structure," in L. J. Meij (ed.), *Internal Wage Structure* (Amsterdam: North-Holland Publishing Company, 1963), pp. 277–78.

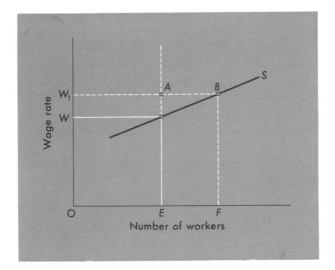

Figure 9–1

Combination of High Wages and Job Rationing

shown in Figure 9–1. The S curve shows the number of workers whom the employer could attract and retain at alternative wage rates. E is his desired employment level for the next planning period. The minimum wage required to reach this target is W. Instead of this, the employer chooses to pay the higher wage W_1. At this wage, the number of workers wishing to work at the company (F) exceeds the number required (E). The company rations the number of jobs available among the larger number of workers by applying selective hiring criteria. Its wage–employment position is at point A—off the supply curve.

The workers applying at this company—and at other companies in the market—can be regarded as arranged in a queue, with the most preferred groups at the head of the line and the least preferred at the tail. Employers hire from the front of the line and work their way down as far as necessary to meet their employment targets. The result is that the least preferred workers are the last to be hired on an upswing and the first laid off on a downswing.

This is often called a *vacancy model* of the labor market. The reason is that, with a surplus of applicants at most companies, a company need only announce a vacancy in order to get a new employee. Consider the problem of reallocating labor among companies and industries, a process that is going on all the time. In the simplified models of Chapter 5, with continuous full employment and each firm operating on its labor supply curve, any reallocation of labor would involve a change in relative wage rates. Wages in expanding firms would rise relative to those in contracting firms.

But if many firms are in the situation of Figure 9–1, these results do *not* follow. Firms can expand employment simply by opening their doors. Labor can flow from lower-wage to higher-wage sectors without any change in the structure of relative wages.

Research studies suggest that there is something to the vacancy model. Ulman notes that there was little correlation between percentage wage changes and percentage employment changes in fifty-seven industries over the years 1948 to 1960. What mainly happened was that industries whose wages were already relatively high in 1948 increased their wage advantage over the period. The dispersion of industry wage levels increased. These results, he concludes, run counter to the competitive hypothesis: ". . . since the relatively high-wage industries did not tend to increase employment more rapidly than the others, they did not on the average have to raise wages more rapidly, as in fact they did, in order to attract additional labor." [7]

At the same time there is evidence that *major* changes in supply–demand relations are associated with relative wage shifts, even though moderate ones may not be. Ulman notes that there was an association between wage and employment changes for the extreme cases in his sample, that is, the 10 percent of industries in which wages rose most and the 10 percent in which they rose least. Phelps Brown also found such an association in the United Kingdom for industries in which the male labor force declined by more than 5 percent or expanded by more than 30 percent. He concludes: "Thus, within a wide range, the rate of growth of an industry seems to have imposed no particular requirements on the relative earnings it offered but outside that range it did." [8]

The cyclical behavior of wages and hiring standards can also be explained in terms of Figure 9–1. The distance WW_1 can be termed the company's *wage margin,* which determines how quickly it will have to adjust to a tightening of the labor markets. The high-wage employers described earlier have large wage margins. The low-wage employers have small margins—at the bottom of the structure, no margin at all.

During an economic upswing, low-wage employers will be trying to expand employment like everyone else. E moves to the right. At the same

[7] Lloyd Ulman, "Labor Mobility and the Industrial Wage Structure in the Postwar United States," *Quarterly Journal of Economics* (February 1965), pp. 73–97. See also Alan K. Severn, "Upward Labor Mobility: Opportunity or Incentive?" *Quarterly Journal of Economics* (February 1968), pp. 143–51. This study lends support to the vacancy model in the sense that an industry's quit rate is strongly associated with the general unemployment rate as well as with the industry's relative wage position.

[8] E. H. Phelps Brown and M. H. Browne, "Earnings in Industries of the United Kingdom, 1948–59," *Economic Journal* (September 1962), pp. 517–49.

time, S is shifting leftward as labor is drained off to expanding high-wage companies. The wage margin shrinks, and in time W_1 *becomes* the minimum that must be paid just to achieve desired employment. The company must then raise W_1, or try to shift S back to the right by lowering hiring standards, or (usually) use some combination of both. As the market continues to tighten, this pressure, felt initially by the low-wage employers, is transmitted up the line to the higher-wage firms, until eventually the process of wage increases plus reduction of hiring standards becomes general throughout the market.

The reverse process, which comes into play as aggregate demand for labor declines, can be traced out in the same way and need not be detailed here.

THE INTERNAL WAGE STRUCTURE: JOB EVALUATION

Thus far we have concentrated on the *average* wage level of a company. Most companies, however, hire dozens or hundreds of different types of skill. Each of these jobs has its own wage, varying from the entrance rate or "common labor rate" to the highest-skilled jobs in the plant. How does management determine proper relative wage rates for these many kinds of work? And how does the presence of a union alter the process?

Some kinds of labor may be in general demand throughout the area and hence have an *outside market*. This is likely to be true for jobs at the bottom and top of the skill ladder, for unskilled labor on one hand and skilled maintenance craftsmen on the other. It seems also to be true of standard office occupations. Turnover of women in these occupations is rather high, a new crop comes into the market each year through high school graduation, and the new graduates are able to get good information about company salary levels from high school vocational advisers, the public employment service, and shopping around. This puts pressure on each employer to remain within a reasonable distance of prevailing area rates.[9]

But the outside market impinges only at certain points in the company wage structure. There is a great array of semiskilled and skilled production jobs that are specific to a particular industry or even a particular company. Workers are usually not hired into these jobs from the outside, but work up from within the company on a seniority basis. It is not easy for them to

---

[9] For an interesting analysis of competition and salary determination for certain clerical occupations in Boston, see George P. Shultz, "A Nonunion Market for White-Collar Labor," in *Aspects of Labor Economics* (Princeton: Princeton University Press for the National Bureau of Economic Research, 1962), pp. 107–46.

transfer to other companies, since the same job may not exist elsewhere, and since other companies also prefer to promote from within. Thus there is an *inside market* for these jobs, but no outside market. The precise ranking of jobs, and the determination of proper wage differences between them, becomes a matter for administrative discretion and collective bargaining.

A pattern of job rates develops in the first instance through shop custom. Certain jobs come to be regarded as related to each other on the basis of physical contiguity, sequence of production operations, or a learning sequence in which workers progress from lower to higher rank in a work team. Workers and foremen develop ideas about how much more one of these jobs should pay than another. Once established, these wage relationships tend to persist through custom. When asked to explain why their wage schedule looks as it does, most plant managers will say, "We have always done it that way," or "It just grew up that way."

Reliance on custom alone, however, is not always satisfactory. It is particularly unsatisfactory as an answer to workers or union officials who contend that a particular rate is too low and should be raised. Management has thus turned increasingly to systems of *job rating* or *job evaluation* that purport to provide a scientific basis for determining the relative worth of different jobs. There are several reasons for the popularity of these systems. Some managers believe that they provide an absolutely fair and incontrovertible basis for determining relative wage rates. Even those who recognize that no wage scale can presume to absolute justice seek the definite standards provided by job evaluation, because they make for administrative uniformity and simplicity in handling wage matters. Job evaluation provides a yardstick by which management can judge the merit of complaints by workers or the union; at least, it enables management to answer these complaints and to provide a rational explanation of its wage decisions.

Job Evaluation Procedures

Job evaluation procedures cannot be discussed in any detail here, and the student interested in them should consult the standard works on the subject.[10] In general, however, the procedure is as follows:

One must first select a set of *factors,* or criteria to be used in rating jobs, and set a maximum point score for each factor. An example is the widely used rating scale of the National Metal Trades' Association. The factors used and the maximum possible score for each are as follows:

---

[10] See, for example, C. W. Lytle, *Job Evaluation Methods* (New York: The Ronald Press Company, 1946); F. H. Johnson, R. W. Boise, Jr., and Dudley Pratt, *Job Evaluation* (New York: John Wiley & Sons, Inc., 1946).

education (70), experience (110), initiative and ingenuity (70), physical effort (50), mental and visual effort (25), responsibility for equipment and processes (25), responsibility for material or product (25), responsibility for safety of others (25), responsibility for work of others (25), working conditions (50), and work hazards (25). More briefly, these factors may be summarized as: education, experience, and skill (250), responsibility (100), effort (75), and working conditions (75). This relatively heavy weighting of skill and light weighting of effort is characteristic of most of the other rating scales in current use.

The next step is to make a careful description of each job in the plant, and to rate each job in terms of the selected factors. The rating applies to *the job itself,* not to the workers who happen to be doing the job at the time. The result is a total point score for each job, which enables one to rank all jobs in the plant in order of importance. These scores are not precise measurements, but contain a large element of judgment.

The next step is usually to group the different jobs into a limited number of brackets or *labor grades.* Thus, jobs with a score of 450 to 500 may be put in labor grade 1, jobs with a score of 400 to 450 in labor grade 2, and so on down. In some systems the numbering is the other way round, so that the *lowest* jobs are in labor grade 1.

It is necessary next to decide what shall be the highest and lowest wage rates in the plant.[11] What rate shall be paid for, say, class 1 tool-makers, and what shall be paid for sweepers, laborers, and janitors? In a nonunion plant, this decision is usually made on a comparative basis, that is, by surveying the rates currently paid for class 1 toolmakers and laborers by other plants in the area or industry. Under trade unionism, of course, determination of the high and low rates becomes a matter of bargaining, though rates in other plants will probably still be used as data for bargaining purposes.

It must be decided, finally, how rapidly the rates for intermediate labor grades shall rise; that is, what the shape of the *rate curve* shall be. Two very different rate curves are shown in Figure 9–2. Employers tend to favor a schedule similar to curve *B,* under which rates rise rather slowly for the first few labor grades in which the bulk of the labor force is concentrated, and then more rapidly in the higher labor grades where there are few workers.

As a practical matter, the decision will be influenced a good deal by the shape of the existing wage schedule of the plant. At some stage in the

---

11 The company may also select several intermediate jobs that exist in other plants in the area, so that there is an "outside market" for them. A survey is made of the wage rates being paid by other companies for these jobs, and the average wage for each job determined. These averages, or "peg points," can then be used as a guide in determining the company's own rate structure.

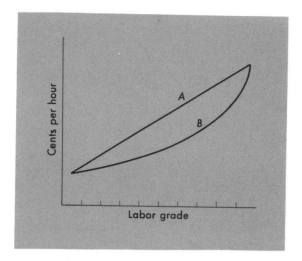

Figure 9–2

Occupational Rate Curves for a Plant

procedure, it is usual to take the existing rate for each job, chart it against the point score for the job, and fit a curve to the scatter diagram thus obtained. The rate curve finally adopted under the job evaluation system will not necessarily have just the same shape as this empirical curve, but is likely to resemble it rather closely. Custom and established wage relationships provide a powerful argument; and if the present wage structure of the plant resembles curve *B,* management is unlikely to agree to a new schedule resembling curve *A*.

It is clear from this brief description that rate setting based on job evaluation is not "scientific" in the sense of mathematical precision. Judgment must be exercised at each step in the procedure—the choice of rating factors, the assignment of the point weights to each factor, the actual description and rating of jobs, the determination of the top and bottom of the wage structure, and the determination of the shape of the rate curve between these points. The judgments of different individuals on each point are bound to differ somewhat, and the final outcome is a working compromise. Job evaluation does, however, make the exercise of judgment more deliberate and systematic than it might be without definite rules of procedure.

Unions have usually been skeptical of job evaluation. They feel that it tends to freeze the wage structure too rigidly, to reduce the role of collective bargaining, and to restore the setting of job rates to unilateral management control. Unions typically resist the introduction of new job evaluation plans. When a plan already exists, however, they will usually work under it while at the same time insisting on their right to bargain over the structure of the system and the rating of specific jobs. In a few cases the union has cooperated actively with management in designing a new evaluation program. The outstanding example is the rationalization of wage rates in basic steel, carried out jointly by the United Steelworkers and the major steel companies during the late forties.[12] Here the union secured reduction of an unmanageable load of grievances over wage inequities, some overall increase in earnings for its members, a standard wage structure applicable throughout the industry, and a gradual phasing out of regional wage differences.

SUPPLEMENTARY INCOME PAYMENTS

The modern union agreement has been described as "a contract with a fringe on top." But the term *fringe benefits,* coined in a period when such provisions were minor, is no longer appropriate. These items now constitute a large and growing proportion of workers' incomes and employers' payroll costs.

A survey of 761 companies by the U. S. Chamber of Commerce reports that in 1975 employee benefit payments averaged 35.4 percent of payroll, or 193.2 cents per payroll hour, or $3,984 per year per employee.[13] There was substantial variation, however, among companies. While 10 percent of firms had benefits of less than 25 percent of payroll, another 10 percent had benefits of 45 percent or more. On an industry basis, textiles and clothing had lowest benefits (27.3 percent) while the chemical industry was highest (41.0 percent).

In interpreting these figures, one must remember that the sample consisted of large companies, and that fringe benefits are positively related to size of company. An average for all companies in the country would be lower than that shown by the Chamber of Commerce survey.

Whatever the correct figure for the current year, there is no doubt that the trend has been upward. The Chamber of Commerce survey reports that benefit payments for a sample of 152 identical companies increased from 22.7 percent of payroll in 1955 to 40.3 percent in 1975.

Quantitatively most important are:

---

[12] For a detailed analysis of this case, see Jack Stieber, *The Steel Industry Wage Structure* (Cambridge, Mass.: Harvard University Press, 1959).

[13] U.S. Chamber of Commerce, *Employee Benefits 1975* (Washington, D.C., 1976), p. 5. A similar survey is conducted and published every year.

1. *Retirement pensions.* Virtually all wage and salary earners are now covered by the Social Security system. In addition, about 75 percent of plant workers and 80 percent of office workers are covered by company pension programs.[14] Employer contributions to Social Security and to company retirement plans averaged 11.2 percent of payroll in 1975 for companies included in the Chamber survey.

2. *Paid vacations and holidays.* These are now enjoyed by more than 80 percent of plant employees and 90 percent of office employees, and cost 8.5 percent of payroll in 1975 for companies covered by the Chamber survey. Paid holidays have increased from four or five per year some time ago to an average of eight per year at present. In addition to the standard national holidays, there has been increasing use of *floating holidays*—for example, to provide a long weekend when a national holiday falls on a Thursday or Tuesday, or to give each employee a holiday on his own birthday.

Vacations are almost invariably linked to length of service. A common formula at present is one week after one year of service, two weeks after five years, three weeks after ten years, and four weeks after twenty years. Such formulas can be, and in fact have been, liberalized gradually in the course of time by reducing the years of service required for each length of vacation.

3. *Insurance and health programs.* More than 90 percent of both plant and office employees have company-financed life insurance, hospitalization insurance, and surgical insurance. A majority also have illness and accident insurance. About one-third of plant employees and two-thirds of office employees have specified periods of sick leave on part or full pay. These programs cost 6.4 percent of payroll in 1975 for companies included in the Chamber of Commerce survey.

These are only the more important items. The Chamber of Commerce survey identifies and costs twenty-one types of fringe payment. The list includes such things as employer contributions to state unemployment compensation and (in a few industries) to union-negotiated private unemployment benefit funds; paid rest periods, lunch periods, wash-up time, travel time, and other time not actually worked; and various types of profit-sharing and bonus arrangements.

The rapid growth of supplementary benefits has been attributed variously to:

1. Their preferential treatment under the personal income tax. A dollar that the employer contributes to a pension, health, or insurance fund is a full dollar, while a dollar increase in direct wage payments may yield the worker only seventy to eighty cents after taxes.

2. The fact that life insurance or health protection is cheaper when purchased on a group basis. Again, a dollar spent by the employer in this way yields more benefit than if the dollar were paid to the worker and he had to purchase his own protection.

---

[14] James N. Hoff, "Supplementary Wage Benefits in Metropolitan Areas," *Monthly Labor Review* (June 1968), pp. 40–47. This survey is more comprehensive than the Chamber of Commerce survey, so we rely on it to estimate the coverage of various benefit programs.

3. A belief among employers that benefits with value that increases with length of service will attach workers more firmly to the company and reduce costly turnover.

4. Union pressure for larger supplements.

An analysis of manufacturing industries by Robert Rice [15] revealed a consistent positive relation between benefit levels and both level of direct wage payments and size of company. The wage level alone explained more than 70 percent of the variance in benefit levels. Not only do supplementary payments vary positively with earnings, but the *ratio of supplements to earnings* also varies positively. This means that wage differentials progressively understate the differentials in total compensation as one moves up from lower-wage to higher-wage companies.

There was no significant relation between turnover rates and the level of supplementary benefits, which suggests that the turnover-reducing effect of benefits may have been exaggerated. Neither was there any significant relation between benefit levels and extent of unionization. This suggests that much of the increase, particularly in areas such as pensions and insurance, can probably be attributed to voluntary employer action.

DISCUSSION QUESTIONS

1. (a) Explain the main alternative concepts of *wages.* (b) When we talk about *company wage policy,* which concept are we using?

2. As personnel director of a company, you are responsible for recommending to top management how large a wage increase should be made for the year ahead. What kinds of information would you need to prepare your recommendation?

3. What characteristics of actual labor markets permit companies to pay different wage rates for the same job in the same market?

4. What company characteristics are likely to put a company in the low-wage rather than the high-wage category?

5. Over the course of a business cycle, how will the wage–employment strategy of a high-wage company differ from that of a low-wage company?

6. "Job evaluation provides a firm scientific basis for determining correct wage rates for each job in the plant, and removes any need for judgment or bargaining on this issue." Discuss.

---

[15] Robert G. Rice, "Skill, Earnings, and the Growth of Wage Supplements," *American Economic Review Proceedings* (May 1966), pp. 583–93.

7. Company *A* is willing to make a wage increase costing twenty cents per man-hour and, in allocating this between basic wage rates and fringe benefits, it would like to follow employee preferences. How would you design an experiment to discover what these preferences are?

8. Are there any labor market constraints on Company *A*'s allocation between wage rates and benefits? Explain.

READING SUGGESTIONS

For general discussion of company wage policies, see RICHARD A. LESTER, *Company Wage Policies,* Princeton: Princeton University Industrial Relations Section, 1948; SUMNER H. SLICHTER, *Basic Criteria Used in Wage Negotiations,* Chicago: Association of Commerce and Industry, 1947; SUMNER H. SLICHTER, JAMES J. HEALY, and E. ROBERT LIVERNASH, *The Impact of Collective Bargaining on Management,* Washington, D.C.: The Brookings Institution, 1960. Other useful sources on wage determination at the company level include JOSEPH W. GARBARINO, *Wage Policy and Long-Term Contracts,* Washington, D.C.: The Brookings Institution, 1962; JACK STIEBER, *The Steel Industry Wage Structure,* Cambridge, Mass.: Harvard University Press, 1959; GEORGE W. TAYLOR, and FRANK C. PIERSON (eds.), *New Concepts in Wage Determination,* New York: McGraw-Hill Book Company, 1957.

10

Money Wages, Prices, and Employment

We shift now to the behavior of the general level of money wage rates. A key feature of this behavior is that the rate of increase in money wages is related to the level of economic activity. The wage level rises every year, but it rises faster when unemployment is low than when it is high. There is also a complicated interaction between the money wage level and the price level.

This poses important policy issues. Full employment is a generally accepted objective of macroeconomic policy. Reasonable stability of prices is also considered desirable. But each time we approach full employment, we observe that the price level rises at an undesirable rate. Are we forced, then, to choose between an undesirably high level of unemployment and an undesirable rate of inflation? Can high employment and reasonable price stability be reconciled?

A CENTURY OF RISING WAGES

Wage movements in the United States over the past century are summarized in Table 1, and year-to-year changes since 1947 are shown in Figure 10–1. The trend of money wage rates is strongly upward. This is no recent development, but goes back as far as our records exist. The rise was most rapid during the three war periods covered in Table 1; but a rising wage level is normal in peacetime also. From 1880 to 1914, a long period of peacetime industrial expansion, money wages rose about 70 percent. On a year-to-year basis, wage rates rose in twenty-five years of the period,

Table 1

Money Wages, Consumer Prices, and Real Wages in Manufacturing, United States, 1860–1970

	Percentage Change		
	Money Hourly Wages	*Consumer Prices*	*Real Hourly Wages*
1860–70	+ 53	+41	+ 8
1870–80	− 10	−22	+11
1880–90	+ 18	−11	+32
1890–1900	+ 3	− 8	+12
1900–10	+ 29	+16	+14
1910–22	+141	+78	+37
1922–30	+ 12	0	+13
1930–40	+ 26	−16	+50
1940–50	+131	+72	+34
1950–60	+ 57	+23	+28
1960–70	+ 49	+31	+13
1970–76	+ 52	+46	+ 4

SOURCES: 1860–1929: Clarence D. Long, "The Illusion of Wage Rigidity: Long and Short Cycles in Wages and Labor," *Review of Economics and Statistics* (May 1960). This study draws on basic research by the author and by Albert Rees at the National Bureau of Economic Research.
1929–57: Albert Rees, *New Measures of Wage Earner Compensation in Manufacturing, 1914–57* (New York: National Bureau of Economic Research, Occasional Paper 75, 1960).
1957-70: Standard Bureau of Labor Statistics series, as published in *Economic Report of the President* (Washington, D.C.: Government Printing Office, 1973).

remained stable in five years, and fell in only four. Since the bottom of the Great Depression in 1933, there has not been a single year in which wages failed to increase.

Movements of real wages are shown in the final column of Table 1. Note that there are no minus signs in this column. There has been no period in which real wages have failed to advance, though the pace of advance has varied.

Note also that there is no apparent relation between the rate of increase in real wages and in money wages. Real wages have risen rapidly at times when money wages were also rising rapidly (1910–22, 1940–50); but real wages have also risen rapidly when money wages were moving upward rather slowly (1880–90, 1930–40).

The explanation, as will appear in Chapter 11, is that increases in real wages depend mainly on increases in productivity, which are not closely related to money wage movements.

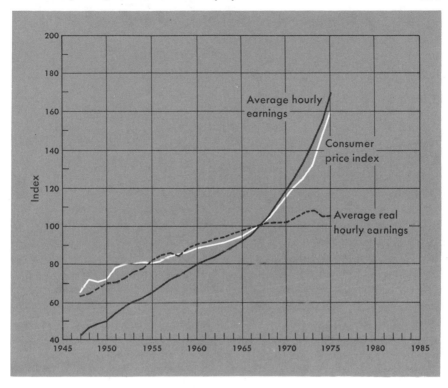

Figure 10–1

Hourly Earnings, Cost of Living, and Real Hourly
Earnings in Manufacturing, 1947–75 (1967 = 100)

SOURCE: *Economic Report of the President,* (Washington, D.C.: Government Printing Office, 1976), pp. 204, 220.

WAGE–PRICE RELATIONS: A SIMPLE VIEW

Until recently, inflation was regarded as a problem in monetary theory. Inflation arose, it was argued, when the level of money demand rose above the productive capacity of the economy—"too much money chasing too few goods." According to the "demand-pull" theory, prices were pulled up by excess money demand, and wages were pulled up after prices, as workers strove to avoid a cut in real wages.

This view was called into question by two aspects of reality: the fact that the price level typically rises well before the economy has reached full employment; and the fact that unions and business concerns have market power, hence some discretion in deciding on wage and price increases. This led in the 1950s to theories of "cost-push inflation," under which a wage-price spiral could be generated by sheer exercise of market power, independent of demand considerations. There was considerable controversy between adherents of this view and of the older demand-pull approach.

Today, most economists would agree that this dichotomy has not proven fruitful. At a theoretical level, pure cost-push in the absence of demand changes does not seem a very likely occurrence. But the course of an ordinary demand-induced inflation may be influenced, in greater or lesser measure, by the existence of market power.

Forgetting about causation, and looking simply at observed behavior, the following things seem to happen:

1. The rate at which the money wage level moves upward is related to the tightness of the labor market. Wage increases are relatively large at cycle peaks, smaller (but still substantial) during recession. This wage behavior can be explained through the normal working of the labor market, as described in Chapter 9, without resorting to union "monopoly power."

2. Output per man-hour in the private economy typically rises year by year. The movement is not perfectly regular, which again is due partly to the operation of labor markets. During a recession that is expected to be temporary, employers are reluctant to lay off experienced workers in whom they have a substantial investment. There is "labor hoarding" in the sense of people kept on the payroll even though there is less work than usual for them to do. This shows up in reduced productivity, or at least a below-normal rate of increase in productivity. Conversely, during an upswing, this slack in the labor force permits a substantial rise in output with little increase in employment. Productivity rises unusually fast.

Averaging out these short swings, the annual increase in labor productivity is of the order of 3 percent. If, then, the hourly cost of labor to employers (including payments for fringe benefits as well as direct wage payments) is also rising at 3 percent, *labor cost per unit of output* will remain unchanged. Unit labor cost will rise only if labor costs rise faster than productivity.

3. Leaving aside farm prices, in which movements are somewhat different, the *prices of nonagricultural products move very closely with unit labor costs*. If labor cost per man-hour in a particular year rises by 6 percent, while output per man-hour rises only 3 percent, then unit labor cost will rise by 3 percent. It is a good guess that nonagricultural prices will also rise by about 3 percent. Figure 10–2 shows an index of unit labor cost and of non-agricultural prices from 1947–72. The close parallelism of the two series is evident.

Why should prices behave in this way? The behavior is compatible with the hypothesis that industrial prices are set by a percentage markup over unit labor cost, and that this percentage is relatively stable. Many companies, particularly oligopolists with substantial market power, seem to behave in this way. But we do not assert that all prices are determined in this way—simply that the price level behaves *as if* the principle were widely followed.

Nor need we assert that the margin between price and unit labor cost remains completely unchanged. There is some tendency for margins to expand during a cycle upswing and to contract during a downswing; and this change in margins, together with changes in sales volume, accounts for the cyclical

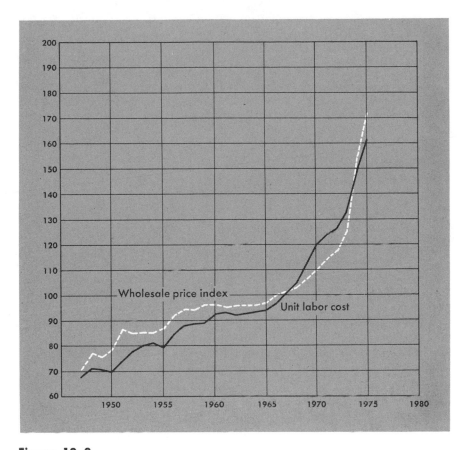

Figure 10–2

Unit Labor Costs and Wholesale Price Index,
Private Nonfarm Economy, 1947–75 (1967 = 100)

SOURCE: Data are from *Economic Report of the President,* 1976, and *Employment and Training Report of the President,* 1976 (Washington, D.C.: Government Printing Office).

swings in business profits. Over a period of years, however, these short swings average out, leaving the parallelism of labor costs and prices as the dominant fact of life.

4. To round out the picture, the rate of increase in prices—specifically, retail prices to consumers—feeds back into the rate of wage increase. If prices have been rising at 4 percent a year, and are expected to continue rising at this rate in the year ahead, then workers will expect larger wage increases than if prices had remained stable, in order to "stay ahead of the cost of living." They may expect increases of, say, 7 percent. If they get these increases, and if productivity rises at the normal 3 percent, then prices will indeed rise at the

expected 4 percent. The expectation is self-fulfilling. It is this circular reaction which leads to use of the phrase "the wage–price spiral." A strong upward spiral of this sort is difficult to curb, as experience since 1965 indicates.

5. All this clearly has monetary implications. The faster the rate of price increase, the faster the rise of GNP measured in current dollars. Since demand for money depends heavily on money GNP, the demand for money will be rising. So, an inflationary movement implies willingness of the monetary authorities to satisfy this demand by raising the money supply.

A rising price level, then, can always be ascribed to monetary causes in the sense that the monetary authorities *could,* by curbing the rate of increase in money supply and raising interest rates, bring on a recession that would decelerate the wage–price increase, but at the cost of unemployment and below-capacity output. This would be politically unpopular, and it is not surprising that the Federal Reserve System follows a complaisant or accommodating policy most of the time.

WAGES AND UNEMPLOYMENT: THE PHILLIPS CURVE

We want now to probe further into the behavior of the money wage level, and more specifically into the relation between labor market tightness and the rate of wage increase. This problem was first clearly posed by Professor A. W. Phillips of the London School of Economics. On the basis of British data from 1861 to 1957, Phillips concluded that there is a strong inverse relation between the rate of money wage increase and the unemployment rate.[1] This relation has since been tested and confirmed many times over for the United States and other countries. A curve exhibiting this relation, such as Figure 10–3, is commonly called a *Phillips curve.*

Figure 10–3 shows the curve as usually drawn, with the rate of full-time unemployment on the horizontal axis and the average rate of increase in the wage rates on the vertical axis. It would be more accurate to show, on the horizontal axis, a more sophisticated measure of labor market tightness; and on the vertical axis the rate of increase in *total* employee compensation per man-hour. But the shape of the curve would be little changed.

Behind the Phillips Curve: How Money Wages Rise

As the labor market tightens, the rate of increase in money wages rises. Can we explain this? And can we explain it as part of the normal operation of labor markets without resorting to union wage pressure? The answer is "Yes" to both questions.

---

[1] A. W. Phillips, "The Relation Between Unemployment and the Rate of Change of Money Wage Rates in the United Kingdom, 1861–1957," *Economica* (November 1958), pp. 283–99.

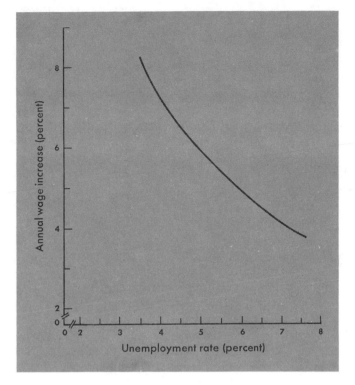

Figure 10–3

The Trade-off Between Unemployment and Inflation

Let us first explain why the money wage level normally rises even with substantial unemployment, why the wage system has a built-in upward bias. One reason is the strong tradition against money wage cuts, which were rare even in pre-1940 days and since then have fallen into almost complete disuse. Now combine this with the fact that "the labor market" comprises thousands of submarkets. Some of these will at any time have an excess of unemployed over vacancies, while others will have an excess of vacancies over unemployed. Suppose that, when one totals up, total vacancies and total unemployed are exactly equal. One might then think that the money wage level would remain unchanged. But it will not. In the markets with excess demand for labor, wages will certainly rise. But in the markets with excess supply, wages will not fall, or will not fall very much. Because of this asymmetric behavior, we come out overall with an increase in the average wage level.

A second consideration is that productivity is rising year by year, which by itself would mean falling unit labor costs. There are different possible adjustments to this situation. Money wages could be left unchanged, and the decline in unit labor costs could be passed on to consumers in lower prices. Alternatively, product prices could be left unchanged, and the productivity increase could be passed on to employees in higher money wages. On paper, these alternatives are equally possible. But there is a strong tendency to follow the second course, and it is easy to see why. The increase in money wages will please employees. Prices remain stable, so consumers have no cause to complain. (Price cutting, like wage cutting, is unfashionable, and tends to be stigmatized by competitors as "chiseling," "cutthroat tactics," and so on.) The company's profit margin is a high as before. So all is well. If you visualize the probable consequences of trying *not* to give money wage increases while consistently cutting prices, it is easy to see why this option is unpalatable.

The outcome is that a substantial positive rate of increase in money wages has come to be regarded as "normal," even if prices are stable and there is a large surplus of labor. In very few years since 1945 has the rate of wage increase been less than 3 percent. To break this expectation of regular and sizable increases would take massive unemployment, on a scale that hopefully we shall never again experience.

We have next to explain why, as unemployment falls and the number of vacancies rises, the rate of money wage increase also rises. Let us draw on our analysis of labor markets in Chapters 6 and 9 to explore what is going on in a period of rising labor demand:

1. As labor demand rises, workers find it easier to locate better jobs. The quit rate rises. Research studies indicate that workers who go directly from one job to another typically better themselves. This drift of labor from lower-wage to higher-wage jobs raises the *average* wage level in the area.

2. Quits are expensive and so, as the quit rate rises, some employers will decide to raise their wage rates to check the outflow. Low-wage companies will also find their queue of applicants growing shorter as the market tightens and will raise wages for recruitment reasons.

3. Unemployed job seekers will set their minimum wage expectations higher in a brisk labor market than in a slack market. Also, since jobs are found faster when demand is high, their initial demands will not be seriously eroded by passage of time. Thus the rates at which new employment bargains are concluded will tend to rise. An employer cannot, of course, openly pay new employees more than present employees; but he can do such things as classifying a worker in a higher labor grade than that to which he would normally be entitled, thus granting him more money per hour. At peaks of labor demand, such expedients are widely used.

4. Pressure to raise wages will impinge initially on the lowest-wage companies, as described in Chapter 9; and for a while the higher-wage companies may be content to see their wage premium narrow. Eventually, however, they too will raise wages to restore something like their customary advantage; and this will restore the pressure on the low-wage employers.

Thus the area wage structure moves upward hand over hand, and this will continue as long as labor tightness continues.

Other Influences on Wages

There have by now been many statistical studies [2] attempting to identify the determinants of the rate of increase in money wages and to assess their relative importance. Measures of unemployment or labor availability are always included. A second factor that always appears is the rate of increase in the Consumer Price Index. There is a marked feedback from living cost increases to wage demands, as one would expect. Most studies estimate this feedback in the neighborhood of 0.35 to 0.50, that is, a 1 percent higher rate of increase in the CPI means that the money wage level will rise by one-third to one-half of a percent faster than it otherwise would have risen.

The strength of the feedback, however, is not independent of the rate of inflation. At low levels of inflation, it may be quite moderate; but at higher levels of inflation, it becomes stronger. Some studies have concluded that there is a *critical* or *threshold* rate of price increase above which the feedback coefficient is close to 1.0. Thus Eckstein and Brinner find:

> The rate of increase of consumer prices influences wages, but with a coefficient of about one-half in normal times . . . [but] . . . a severe and persistent inflation results in greater wage sensitivity to prices. . . . In the specification adopted in this paper, every percentage point increase in prices above 2.5 percent is approximately reflected in a full percentage point increase in wage inflation.[3]

This hypothesis remains controversial. If correct, it would mean that beyond a certain point the wage–price spiral tends to become explosive.

In addition to cost-of-living changes and the unemployment rate, researchers have experimented with other variables in an effort to get a more complete explanation of money wage changes; but little consensus has been reached as yet. Perry's early study found that the level of *business profits* had a significant relation to money wage increases, but this variable does not figure in recent studies. The probable reason is that high profits reflect

---

[2] An early effort in this field was George L. Perry, *Unemployment, Money Wage Rates and Inflation* (Cambridge, Mass.: The MIT Press, 1966). More recent studies include the Perry article cited earlier, Robert J. Gordon, "Wage–Price Controls and the Shifting Phillips Curve," and William D. Nordhaus, "The World-Wide Wage Explosion," both in *Brookings Papers on Economic Activity,* No. 2 (1972).

[3] Otto Eckstein and Roger Brinner, "The Inflation Process in the United States," study prepared for the Joint Economic Committee, U.S. Congress (Washington, D.C.: Government Printing Office, 1972).

increases in output and demand for labor. Since measures of labor market tightness provide a good *direct* explanation of wage changes, there is no need to bring in profit rates, which simply reflect the same set of circumstances from a different standpoint.

Long-Run and Short-Run Phillips Curves

The immediate impact of a given unemployment rate on the rate of wage increase will differ from its effect over a longer period. The reason lies in the price–wage feedback already described. At any moment, workers will be anticipating a certain rate of inflation, perhaps that which has occurred in the recent past. Suppose they are expecting 2 percent inflation next year. Then on this assumption we can draw the short-run Phillips curve P_2 in Figure 10–4. If they had expected a higher rate of inflation, however, they would also have expected larger wage increases (for the *same* state of the labor market, as indicated by the unemployment rate). Thus there is a whole *family* of short-run Phillips curves, illustrated by P_1–P_5, lying one above the other and corresponding to different *expected* inflation rates.

Suppose the economy is at point 1, with 6 percent unemployment and a 2 percent expected inflation rate. An upswing now sets in and the unemployment rate falls to 4 percent. We move along the short-run Phillips curve to point 2. But now the workers get a surprise. They expected a price increase of 2 percent; but prices actually rise by 4 percent. What will happen? Wage demands will be revised upward on the next round. We travel up the vertical arrow toward point 3. Note that at point 3 the *expected* rate of inflation equals the *actual* rate, both being 4 percent. Point 3 is thus a stable position. By joining up all such points, at which expected and actual inflation rates are equal, we derive the *long-run Phillips curve, PP.*

Note that the long-run curve is considerably *steeper* than the short-run curves. The rate of wage increase corresponding to a given unemployment rate is *higher* in the long run, that is, after there has been time for price expectations to be adjusted to reality.

We can trace out a downswing in similar fashion. Suppose unemployment rises from 4 to 5 percent. We move along the short-run curve from point 3 to point 4. Inflation is slowed, but not very much. But this time workers get a pleasant surprise. The rate of price increase turns out to be *less* than they were expecting, and we move downward toward a stable position such as point 5. Thus over a complete cycle the economy can be visualized as traveling in a clockwise fashion around the "true" or long-run Phillips relation.

This mechanism rests on the existence of "money illusion," a focusing of workers' attention on money wage rates, and a lag in adjusting to

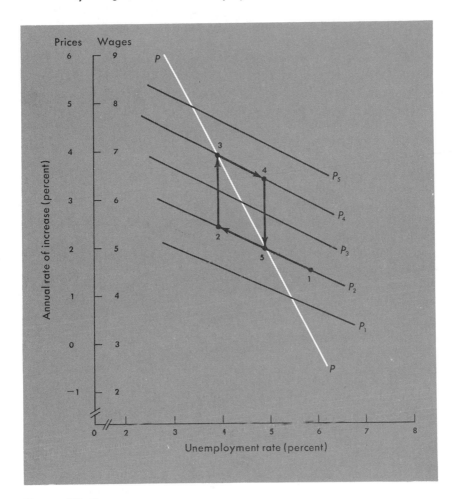

Figure 10–4

Long-Run and Short-Run Phillips Curves

price changes. People get fooled repeatedly—sometimes pleasantly, sometimes unpleasantly—but they never get smart. Some economists deny that money illusion exists, or that it can persist for any length of time. If there were no money illusion, if workers could foresee price movements exactly, and if they always demanded 100 percent compensation through higher wages, then the long-run Phillips curve would be simply a vertical line. The point at which this line cuts the horizontal axis has been termed the *natural rate of unemployment.*

This natural rate, its exponents contend, depends on frictional and structural features of the labor market and particularly on workers' search behavior. "Natural" unemployment is voluntary unemployment, arising from the fact that some workers prefer to continue searching the market for a better job. It can be reduced by improvements in labor market information. But it *cannot* be reduced simply by raising aggregate demand for labor and the rate of increase in money wages. In the short run, because of money illusion, this will cause more workers to accept jobs and reduce the unemployment rate. But as workers catch on, unemployment will return to its previous level.

On this view, the supposed trade-off between unemployment and inflation does not exist. Over any extended period, there is only one feasible unemployment rate, dictated by labor market characteristics. This unemployment rate is compatible with *any* sustained and fully anticipated inflation rate. This being so, why not choose zero inflation as a policy target?

The natural rate hypothesis, however, has been criticized by other economists on several grounds.[4] First, it is an argument about long-run equilibrium. But as Keynes remarked, "In the long run we are all dead." The economy is always passing through a series of disequilibrium positions, with no necessary tendency to approach a steady state. In this sort of world, expectations may well be disappointed year after year. Second, it is a highly aggregative argument, which runs in terms of total labor supply, total vacancies, a single wage level. But, as we argued earlier, there are a multitude of specific labor markets, some of which at any time will have excess demand for labor and others excess supply. The fact that excess demand raises wages while excess supply fails to reduce them helps to explain the inflational bias of the economy and also the characteristic tilt of the Phillips curve.

Third, the emphasis on voluntary job search blurs the existence of involuntary unemployment. Workers do get laid off as well as quitting voluntarily. They are unemployed, not because they are unwilling to take jobs at the prevailing real wage rate, but because of deficient demand.

The Worsening Trade-off

There is evidence that the U.S. Phillips curve today is in a less favorable position that it was in earlier times. A recent estimate [5] on this

---

[4] For the theoretical basis of the hypothesis, see Milton Friedman, "The Role of Monetary Policy," *American Economic Review* (March 1968), pp. 1–17; and several of the papers in Edmund S. Phelps (ed.), *Microeconomic Foundations of Employment and Inflation Theory* (New York: W. W. Norton & Company, Inc. 1970). For critiques, see James Tobin, "Inflation and Unemployment," *American Economic Review* (March 1972), pp. 1–18; and Albert Rees, "The Phillips Curve as a Menu for Policy Choice," *Economica* (August 1970), pp. 227–38.

[5] Michael L. Wachter, "The Changing Cyclical Responsiveness to Wage Inflation," *Brookings Papers in Economic Activity,* No. 1 (1976), pp. 115–59.

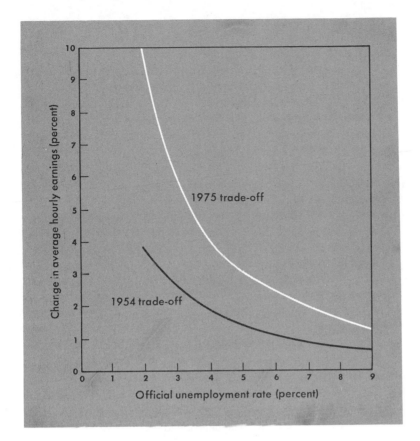

Figure 10–5

Shift in the Trade-off Between Unemployment and
Inflation

point by Michael Wachter is reproduced in Figure 10–5. The short-run
Phillips curve seems both to have shifted to the right and to have become
steeper. As unemployment declines into the inflationary range, the wage
response is sharper than it used to be.

The main reason for the rightward shift of the curve is the changed
composition of the labor force. Because of the "baby boom" of 1945–60,
plus the steady rise in women's labor force participation rates, the proportion of young people and women in the labor force is substantially higher
today that it was in the fifties. But women typically have higher unemployment rates, and teenagers have much higher unemployment rates, than
prime-age males. This by itself raises the average unemployment rate corresponding to any level of aggregate demand.

The noninflationary unemployment rate for prime-age males is usually estimated as in the neighborhood of 3 percent. In the early fifties this would have corresponded to an overall unemployment rate of 4.0–4.5 percent, and indeed 4 percent was widely accepted as the "full employment" target. Today, a 3 percent rate for prime-age males corresponds to an overall rate of about 5.5 percent. A decline of unemployment below that level will push up wages fast enough to generate a rise in the price level.

"Slumpflation": The Post–1973 Paradox

Some doubt has been cast on the Phillips curve concept by events since 1973. A recession began in late 1974. The unemployment rate shot up to almost 9 percent, and declined only slowly during the subsequent recovery, remaining near 7 percent at the end of 1977. Yet the Consumer Price Index also rose sharply—by 11 percent in 1974, 9 percent in 1975, and almost 6 percent in 1976. How can one have a simultaneous increase in both prices and unemployment? Does this not contradict the Phillips curve predictions?

A good part of the explanation lies in events outside the United States, operating independently of U.S. wage and employment levels. During the winter of 1973–74, the Organization of Petroleum Exporting Countries (OPEC) raised the price of crude oil from around $2.00 per barrel to $10.00 per barrel. Since oil goes into a wide variety of uses—power generating, auto use, truck and rail transport, plastics and petrochemicals—the shock effect was felt throughout the U.S. price structure. In addition, poor 1973 crops in the USSR and elsewhere led to a sharp increase in demand for American grain. Wheat went from $2.00 a bushel to $5.00 a bushel, corn from $4.00 to $7.50, and U.S. retail food prices jumped by about one-third.

Finally, the breakdown of the international monetary system in 1971 brought a shift from fixed exchange rates to flexible or floating exchange rates. Under this system the value of the dollar floated gradually downward, and by the end of 1974 was down about 20 percent relative to a "basket" of major foreign currencies. This meant that it took more dollars than before to pay for Volkswagens, French wine, and other foreign imports, and their U.S. price rose correspondingly.

The persistence of inflation through 1975 and 1976 must be attributed to the strong inertia of an inflationary movement. Once a strong uptrend in prices has been generated, this gets built into the next round of wage increases, which then become the basis for further price increases, and so on. But note that, while inflation did not go away, the *rate* of inflation declined during 1975 and 1976. This is what Phillips curve reasoning would predict.

Wachter and others have estimated that, if unemployment were to remain at 1976 levels for several years, the inflation rate would continue to decline toward zero. Squeezing out a strong inflationary movement, however, is a slow and painful process; and the price in terms of lost employment and output may well be judged too high.

ISSUES IN WAGE–PRICE POLICY

Choosing a Point on the Phillips Curve

Suppose we draw a Phillips curve for the American economy as of this year. Suppose also that the federal administration, by fiscal and monetary policy, can regulate aggregate demand and employment. How hard should it push toward fuller employment? Where should it try to land on the Phillips curve?

This is a typical economic problem in that it involves a choice among objectives: higher employment and output versus greater price stability. It involves weighing the damage done by unemployment against that done by inflation.

The people who suffer most directly from unemployment are the unemployed. Even in a mild recession, a couple of million people suddenly find themselves unemployed, and their income drops far below its normal level. Another million or two find themselves reduced to part-time work. Still others find themselves demoted, or blocked from promotion, because of insufficient demand for their services. These costs fall most heavily on black workers and on young people.

The output loss is considerably greater than the employment loss. As a rough rule, each 1 percent increase in the rate of full-time unemployment is accompanied by a 3 percent reduction in GNP. At present GNP levels, an output gap of 5 percent means a loss of about $100 billion a year. This is a lot of output, which might have been enjoyed by consumers or invested to raise productive capacity for the future. The consumers who do not get this lost GNP include not only the unemployed but business owners whose profits fall in recession and farmers whose prices are depressed by inadequate demand.

Unemployment also has undesirable side effects. It increases workers' feeling of insecurity and reduces the pleasantness of life on the job. It leads to dubious policy proposals, such as forced reduction of working hours, on the ground that they are necessary to eliminate unemployment. And it hampers desirable programs, such as retraining of the low-skilled to make them more fully employable. If jobs are not available for these people after they are trained, the programs will look foolish and the graduates will become frustrated.

Inflation involves no direct loss of output or income; but it may involve considerable redistribution of income among groups in the economy. Any group whose money income rises less rapidly than the price level suffers a loss of real income. Groups whose incomes rise faster than prices are the winners in the inflation lottery.

Who are the most likely losers? There are groups of salaried people, such as college teachers and civil servants, whose pay scales are adjusted rather infrequently and tend to lag behind increases in living costs. But the main losers are probably those unable to work—the aged, the disabled, the female heads of broken homes, the people of low mental or physical capacity. These people live on pensions, relief allowances, and other transfer payments that remain fixed for considerable periods. As the price level rises, their real income declines.

Inflation, like unemployment, has undesirable side effects. It undermines people's belief in the stability of money values. It thus undermines the basis of long-term lending, on which much of private investment and government financing depends. It may divert businessmen's energies from profit making through production efficiency to profit making through speculation on price changes.

Different individuals and interest groups will evaluate these disadvantages differently. The AFL–CIO Executive Council is unlikely to agree with the Board of Governors of the Federal Reserve System. Actual decisions depend on political pulling and hauling and will necessarily leave some groups in the economy unsatisfied.

Shifting the Phillips Curve

As one looks at the present-day curve in Figure 10–5, all feasible choices appear unsatisfactory. If we want to attain a 4 percent unemployment rate, which has often been taken as a "full employment" target, we would have to put up with substantial price inflation. If on the other hand we want price stability, this might involve unemployment of 6 percent or more.

Everyone would agree on the desirability of shifting the curve downward to the left, so that the feasible choice would be less unpalatable. But can anything actually be done about this?

1. *Making the economy more competitive.* It is usually thought that wage–price pressure at high employment would be less severe if there were less corporate power in product markets and less union power in labor markets. We have already raised a question as to how far such power actually intensifies inflationary movements. In addition, there are practical questions of how

much can be done to modify existing market structures. Few would disagree with the objective of increasing competitive pressures, but major advances on this front do not seem likely.

One important practical possibility is more frequent use of the pressure of international competition. Reduction or elimination of tariffs and import quotas on products where domestic prices seem to be getting out of hand could help to contain price pressure by letting in more imports and increasing total supply. In 1972–73, for example, the Nixon administration eliminated restrictions on meat imports to the United States and altered the oil import control system. It also released substantial amounts of metals and other raw materials from national defense stockpiles. The main reason was probably that these stockpiles had gotten above any reasonable estimate of needs, but an incidental effect was to moderate the rise of raw material prices.

2. *Manpower adjustment policies.* We have noted several times that unemployment arises partly from structural imbalance in submarkets for labor. If the labor force could be made more fungible, so that surpluses of labor in some markets could be fitted into excess demands in other markets, the overall unemployment rate might be reduced to 4 percent with no more wage-price pressure than we presently experience at 5 percent.

A good deal could doubtless be done along these lines, as was suggested in Chapter 7; but two warnings are in order. First, the job vacancies must actually be there. Total demand for labor must be held high enough so that people emerging from training and relocation programs can be fitted quickly into employment. Manpower programs, in other words, must be *validated* by macroeconomic policies designed to hold economic activity at a high level.

Second, the assumption that structural imbalance is mainly a matter of *job skills* is not entirely warranted. There is imbalance also in terms of *personal characteristics*—"too many" young workers, women, black workers, "too few" white men twenty-five to sixty-four. Blackness and femaleness cannot be changed, and age can be changed only with time. So correction of this kind of imbalance requires adjustment of employers' hiring preferences, to take in more of the (presently) less preferred groups.

3. *Special provision for unemployment-prone groups.* It has been argued recently that the overall unemployment rate is misleading as a policy guide. A better indicator of labor market tightness may be unemployment among white men twenty-five and over. An unemployment rate of 3.0 percent for this group indicates quite a tight market. Moreover, it is a level which can be regarded as largely frictional and as imposing no serious hardship on the workers involved.

In the 1950s, unemployment of 3.0 percent among prime-age white males would have corresponded to an overall unemployment rate of about 4 percent; and indeed 4 percent was widely accepted as a "full-employment" target. Today, however, the same level of white adult male unemployment corresponds to at least 5 percent overall. The reason is that the *relative* unemployment rates for young people, women, and black workers have risen, while at the same time these less preferred groups are a larger proportion of the labor force.

This presents several policy options: (1) Accept the 5 percent rate and redefine this as "full employment." This would involve considerable hardship and loss of output. (2) Reduce unemployment among the less preferred groups by monetary–fiscal measures to raise aggregate demand. This would make the market for white adult males *very tight*, (in the range of 1.5 to 2.0 percent unemployment), and would generate substantial inflationary pressure (3) Reduce unemployment among the less preferred groups by creating special public-service jobs. This would provide training and work experience, would produce useful public goods, and would not increase the tightness of the general labor market.

> Fellner, who favors the third approach, argues that

> unless we want to accept the high risk of generating . . . a level of activity from which the economy will have to be pulled back by a recession and a slow recovery, we should not be aiming at an unemployment rate of between 1.5 and 2 percent for white males aged 25 and over. Instead we should try to make a higher specific unemployment rate for this group compatible with a more moderate rate for workers outside the group. Reducing the discrepancy between specific unemployment rates calls for policies other than monetary–fiscal expansion.[6]

He estimates that, starting from 5 percent overall unemployment, provision of 400,000 to 500,000 jobs specifically for workers in the unemployment-prone categories would reduce *their* unemployment rate to where it normally is at a 4 percent overall rate.

DIRECT PRESSURE: INCOMES POLICY

Thus far we have not found any convincing formula for combining high employment with reasonable price stability. Some have concluded that the answer lies in bringing government pressure to bear directly on wages and prices. This approach is usually termed *incomes policy*. There has been considerable experimentation with it in Britain, the Netherlands, and the Scandinavian countries, and some experience in the United States. From 1962–66 the Kennedy and Johnson administrations tried to apply wage–price "guidelines," developed by the Council of Economic Advisers, through informal persuasion and "jawboning." In 1971–73 the Nixon administration applied a partial control system, in part to counter the inflationary impact of the devaluation of the dollar.

An examination of incomes policy raises several questions: can we define norms for desirable wage–price behavior? Are there effective administrative devices for ensuring closer conformity to such norms? Might not a control system have undesirable side effects which would make the remedy worse than the disease?

---

[6] William Fellner, *Employment Policy at the Crossroads* (Washington, D.C.: American Enterprise Institute, 1972), p. 11.

How Should Wages and Prices Behave?

A key question is what, ideally, one would like to accomplish. If one could wave a wand over wages and prices, how would one like them to behave? This question can usefully be explored in terms of the 1962–65 guidelines. These represent the most serious attempt to date to devise workable standards of behavior, and are thus of more than merely historical interest.

The guidelines concept was stated initially in the January, 1962, report of the Council of Economic Advisers, and was restated with modifications in subsequent CEA reports. The 1965 restatement read as follows:

> 1. *The general guide for wages is that the percentage increase in total employee compensation per man-hour be equal to the national trend rate of increase in output per man-hour.*
> If each industry follows this guidepost, unit labor costs in the overall economy will maintain a constant average.
> 2. *The general guide for price calls for stable prices in industries enjoying the same productivity growth as the average for the economy; rising prices in industries with smaller than average productivity gains; and declining prices in industries with greater than average productivity gains.*
> If each industry follows this guidepost, prices in the economy will maintain a constant average.[7]

The Council estimated that output per man-hour for the economy as a whole was rising at 3.2 percent a year. This would warrant an average annual increase of 3.2 percent in total employee compensation. It emphasized, however, that this is only an economy-wide average, and that individual industries may need to deviate from the average for good cause.

> Wage increases above the guidepost level may be necessary where an industry is unable to attract sufficient labor to meet the demand for its products, where wages are particularly low, and where changes in work rules create large gains in productivity and substantial human costs requiring special adjustment of compensation. . . . Wages should rise less than the guidepost rate where an industry suffers from above-average unemployment and where wages are exceptionally high for that type of work.[8]

These principles seem simple and plausible; but they are by no means as simple as they appear. It will be useful to review some of the difficulties in applying them to concrete situations.

---

[7] *Annual Report of the Council of Economic Advisers* (Washington, D.C.: Government Printing Office, 1965), p. 108.

[8] *Annual Report of the Council of Economic Advisers*, p. 108.

1. Suppose we can measure the rate of increase of man-hour output in the private economy. If hourly compensation, including fringe benefits, rises at this same rate, employers' labor cost per unit of output will remain unchanged. If prices also remain unchanged, then the *division of total output between labor and capital* will be constant. The statement that hourly compensation should advance at the same rate as man-hour output implies that constancy of the labor and capital shares is desirable.

In actuality, as we shall see in the next chapter, the labor and capital shares vary with fluctuations in business activity. Labor's share typically falls during an expansion and rises during recession. Over the longer run—say, from 1900 to date—there has been a moderate but unmistakable tendency for the labor share to rise and the capital share to fall. So, the "constant shares" formula cannot be taken as a rigid rule.

2. The trend of productivity differs widely from industry to industry. In industry *A*, man-hour output may be rising at 6 percent a year; in industry *B*, at only 1 percent. Suppose wage increases in each industry are guided, not by productivity changes *in that industry,* but rather by the average increase of productivity in the economy. If this is done, unit labor costs will be falling in industry *A* and rising in industry *B*. Industries of type *A* should presumably cut prices, while those of type *B* will be entitled to raise them, with these divergent movements averaging out to a stable price level.

One can doubtless count on rising prices in industries in which unit labor costs are increasing. But can one count on prices being reduced at an appropriate rate in the *A*-type industries? When there is monopoly or oligopoly in product markets, prices may be maintained even though costs are falling. The sight of large and growing profits in such industries may whet union appetites and lead to outsize wage demands. If union leaders are then accused of throwing the guidelines to the winds, they can retort that employers did it first.

3. The guidelines should probably be construed as applying to average behavior over the course of a business cycle. It is natural, and probably desirable, that wages should rise less rapidly in recession than in expansion.

4. What the guidelines really define is behavior that, starting from a position of price stability, will perpetuate that stability. But suppose the applecart has already been upset, as in 1976 when the Consumer Price Index rose 6.0 percent. What are workers entitled to expect in 1977? The usual 3.2 percent, which has already been canceled by rising prices? Or 9.2 percent (3.2 + 6.0), to enable them to catch up with last year's price increases? The latter figure will certainly help to perpetuate the upward movement of prices; but the former seems unfair, since it would mean a cut in real wages. The problem of getting back onto the rails once you have gotten off them is obviously difficult.

5. Part of the national increase in productivity comes about through the transfer of workers from low-productivity to high-productivity industries, notably from agriculture to manufacturing, in the course of economic development. This is presumably reflected in higher earnings of the transferred workers in their new occupations, and to use it also as a basis for a general increase in wage schedules would involve double counting. Increases in productivity from this source should be deducted, therefore, in calculating the tolerable rate of wage increase.

6. The guidelines apply to total *hourly compensation* rather than basic

wage schedules. Compensation, however, may rise considerably faster than base rates, especially during periods of sustained high employment. The reasons include rapid increase of fringe benefits, overrating of jobs to permit higher wage offers for recruiting purposes, loosening of time standards on piecework so that hourly earnings pull farther and farther above base rates, and straight overpayment of the official scale. This tendency for earnings to diverge above official wage schedules, often termed *wage drift,* has been noticeable in most industrial countries during the fifties and sixties. The moral is that the increase in basic wage schedules must be held below whatever target is accepted for employee compensation.

7. On the surface, a 3 percent (or any other) yardstick implies a uniform upward movement of employee compensation over time. But the pace of wage increases differs somewhat among occupations, industries, and regions. It is natural that wage increases should be above average in expanding companies, industries, and regions, and below average in stationary or declining areas and industries. Changes in relative wages help to speed reallocation of the labor force to the growth points of the economy. In addition, the wage structure always contains inequities and anomalies. A slice through the wage structure at a moment of time reveals groups that are underpaid and others that are overpaid, by standards of long-run equilibrium in a competitive labor market. The disadvantaged groups can catch up only if there is flexibility for specific wage rates to advance at different speeds.

The CEA recognized the need for flexibility and the desirability of above-average increases in certain cases. Once this is admitted, however, it is natural that everyone will try to squeeze through the loophole of "exceptional circumstances." What standards are available for determining which cases are really exceptional, and how large an exception is warranted? Administrative bodies with wage-fixing authority, such as the National War Labor Board in World War II, have found this question extremely difficult.

In sum, there are difficult conceptual problems of how wages should move, company by company, and industry by industry, to achieve the twin objectives of price stability and optimal resource allocation.

Can Controls Be Effective?

Even if one could get agreement on targets, there remains a question of how much can be accomplished in a far-flung, complex, and decentralized economy. One school of though contends that wage–price intervention, although it may have symbolic value, has little power to modify the course of events. If the system rests on volunary exhortation, it will simply be ignored, and employers and unions will continue to pursue their economic interests. If the controls have legal authority, loopholes will still be found; or, if controls last only for a short period of time, there will be "catching-up" increases in wages and prices as soon as controls expire.

It would be unwise, however, to be doctrinaire on this point. We have already had occasion to note the element of "play," of administrative discretion, in wage and price decisions, especially when there is substantial market power. Adding another voice to the dialogue, in the form of a public official, may conceivably lead to reconsideration and modification of private judgments. Several studies of the 1962–65 episode have concluded that wage and price changes were deflected downward, perhaps by as much as 1 percentage point, compared with what would have happened without government intervention.[9]

There are a variety of possible techniques for bringing direct pressure on wages and prices. These include:

1. *A wage–price freeze.* This can be used for a limited period to break the force of inflationary expectations. A complete freeze, however, cannot be maintained for more than six to twelve months. Groups that received wage or price increases just before the freeze may be content, but those who were not so foresighted or lucky feel that they have been dealt an injustice. Moreover, over any extended period, it is normal for wages to rise, and to rise at differing rates reflecting conditions in specific labor markets. Thus inequities and complaints accumulate as the freeze goes on, until eventually it has to be lifted. This does not mean that the technique is useless, but merely that it does not constitute a long-range program.

2. *Guidelines and "jawboning."* This was the main technique of the Kennedy and Johnson administrations. It involves presidential intervention in selected situations, usually involving large unions and large, concentrated industries, in which the decisions receive wide publicity and may be expected to have substantial economic influence. Although it relies mainly on persuasion, government does have a variety of economic instruments that can be used to support its "educational" efforts: release of raw materials from government stockpiles; use of government's position as a large purchaser to direct orders toward companies that hold that price line; reduction of tariff rates or import quota restrictions; and reduction of subsidies (such as those to the maritime industry) where cost increases are considered unwarranted.

3. *A wage–price review board: "jawbones with teeth."* Going further than the guidelines approach are proposals for a continuing federal board to review wage and price increases in industries with concentrated market power: steel, other basic metals, machinery and transportation equipment, other heavy manufacturing, perhaps building construction. Proponents of this procedure estimate that only about fifteen hundred corporations and a limited number of major unions would need to be brought under it. The Nixon control machinery in 1971–73 reflects elements of this approach.

The proposal comes in stronger and in weaker versions. The stronger version, favored by Kenneth Galbraith, Gardner Ackley, and others, would give the board power to scale down proposed increases that exceed what can

---

[9] George L. Perry, "Wages and the Guideposts," *American Economic Review* (September 1967), pp. 897–904. For a thorough review of other studies, see John Sheahan, *The Wage–Price Guideposts* (Washington, D.C.: The Brookings Institution, 1967). Robert M. Solow, "The Wage–Price Issue and the Guideposts," in F. H. Harbison and J. D. Mooney (eds.), *Critical Issues in Employment Policy* (Princeton: Industrial Relations Section, Princeton University, 1966).

be justified on economic grounds.[10] The weaker version would empower the board to delay proposed increases, require submission of supporting economic data, and hold public hearings, but would not confer a veto power. This would provide a breathing space, during which public attention could be focused on the issues and federal officials from the President downward could exercise their powers of persuasion.

4. *Tax or subsidy proposals.* One common objection to incomes policy is that it seems to imply a new federal bureaucracy overseeing private decisions. Partly on this account, some economists have proposed measures which would operate through the fiscal system and could be administered through a bureaucracy which already exists, the Internal Revenue Service.

Suppose the guideline for wage increases in a particular year is set at 5 percent. It could be provided that, if a company gave a larger increase, the excess could not be counted as a business cost in calculating the corporate income tax. The company would bear the full cost of the excess increase, which would be a powerful disincentive. There would be technical problems in applying such a rule: for example, should the 5 percent guideline apply to basic wage rates? to actual average hourly earnings? to total hourly compensation, including fringes? There would also need to be provision for exceptions in special circumstances.

Another interesting idea runs as follows: the real problem is to bring the wage level under control. If this can be done, prices will take care of themselves, either through the operation of competitive markets or through the conventional markups used in administered-price industries. (The notion that only wages and salaries need be controlled, of course, is a debatable idea, with which union leaders would disagree strongly.) Suppose, then, that the government made a grand deal with the labor movement to limit wage increases next year to 5 percent. Deducting the typical productivity increase of 3 percent, the expectation would be that prices would rise by no more than 2 percent, and government would in effect give a pledge to this effect. But surprise! The Consumer Price Index actually rises by 4 percent. Wage and salary earners have been robbed. As compensation, they could be allowed to count the 2 percent by which they have been robbed as a tax credit on their personal income tax, thus either paying less tax or receiving a refund of this amount.

A substantial body of opinion views direct wage–price intervention as either largely ineffective or, to the extent that it is effective, harmful to the economy. Opponents of wage–price controls argue that they interfere with the flexible movement of wages and prices that is central to a market economy. They stress the difficulty of developing criteria for wage and price behavior that will command general agreement and of applying these criteria to specific cases. The implication that wages and salaries should rise at a uniform rate ignores the variety of demand and supply movements in specific labor markets, and the need for differential wage

---

[10] For a statement of this view, see Gardner Ackley, "An Incomes Policy for the 1970's," *Review of Economics and Statistics* (August 1972), pp. 218–23. This symposium also contains papers critical of any form of wage–price control.

movements to reallocate labor to the growth points of the economy. There would be need for a sizable bureaucratic apparatus, which is costly in itself, in addition to the delay and distortion introduced into private decision making.

The force of these objections, of course, depends on the specific proposal under consideration. They apply most directly to a wartime type of control system, involving government review of every wage and price, which hardly anyone would propose seriously for peacetime use. A monitoring system, limited to areas of concentrated market power and depending heavily on publicity and persuasion, would be less open to objection. But one must concede a genuine dilemma: the more effective the system in altering private decisions, the greater the danger of rigidifying and distorting the wage–price mechanism.

Opponents of wage–price controls tend to favor monetary policy as the main antiinflation instrument. They believe that, if one is willing to apply the monetary brakes hard enough, inflation can *always* be controlled. But recent experience in this respect is not encouraging. The monetary authorities, to be sure, can always bring on a recession. But once a strong inflationary movement is underway, it apparently takes several years of high unemployment to reduce it to tolerable proportions. Advocates of incomes policy ask: Why punish ourselves in this way instead of facing the problem of wage–price pressure directly? No one denies that monetary–fiscal measures must form part of any antiinflation effort. But why reject what might turn out to be a useful auxiliary tool?

The one thing certain is that the problem will not go away. We do not yet have any proven technique for combining high employment with reasonable price stability. Considering that these are both valid policy objectives, inability to reconcile them is a serious defect in our economic institutions. Continued active discussion and experimentation are in prospect for the future.

DISCUSSION QUESTIONS

1. Does an increase in money wages necessarily mean an increase in real wages:
   (a) in a single industry?
   (b) in the economy as a whole?

2. In what sense can one speak of a "wage–price spiral?" Can the operation of such a spiral be explained independently of market power exercised by businesses and unions?

3. Why does the money wage level continue to rise even when there is a surplus of unemployed workers over vacancies?

4. Why does the rate of increase in money wages tend to rise as the unemployment rate falls?

5. Explain the distinction (and the relation) between "short-run" and "long-run" Phillips curves.

6. Why is the present location of the U.S. Phillips curve apparently less favorable today than it was in the 1950s? What morals, if any, can be drawn for public policy?

7. Explain and criticize the 1965 CEA guidelines for desirable wage and price behavior.

8. Would you favor a continuing wage–price review board? If so, would you favor veto power as well as review power? Explain.

9. "All the exictement over wage–price policy is much ado about nothing. Inflation is a problem which should be handled, indeed can only be handled, by monetary–fiscal policy." Discuss.

READING SUGGESTIONS

There is a voluminous literature on the causes and effects of money wage behavior. Most of this is reviewed and footnoted in GEORGE L. PERRY, *Unemployment, Money Wage Rates and Inflation,* Cambridge, Mass.: The MIT Press, 1966. The rationale and operation of the U.S. guidelines experiment were discussed in the annual reports of the Council of Economic Advisers from 1962 through 1966. The most thorough outside review of this experiment is JOHN SHEAHAN, *The Wage–Price Guideposts,* Washington, D.C.: The Brookings Institution, 1967. The best source for continuing evaluation of current money wage behavior and wage–price policies is the *Brookings Papers on Economic Activity,* published three times a year by the Brookings Institution.

11

Real Wages and
Labor's Income Share

The short-term fluctuations of money wages examined in the last chapter raise important issues of analysis and policy. Over a period of decades, however, greater importance attaches to the movement of *real wages,* that is, money wages corrected for changes in the price of consumer goods. Over the period 1947–75, average hourly earnings of employees in manufacturing rose from $1.21 to $4.81 per hour, a fourfold increase. Over the same period, however, the Consumer Price Index rose by about 140 percent. After adjusting for this price increase, real hourly wages—or wages in dollars of constant purchasing power—rose by about 70 percent.

This is a big increase. It means that employees were able to buy about 70 percent more goods and services in 1975 than they could buy a generation earlier. Nor is this anything new. The level of real wages in the United States has risen continuously for the past century or more. Real wages rise in good years and bad, whether money wages are rising rapidly or slowly.

What accounts for this strong and persistent uptrend? Real wages could rise because:

1. national output is increasing, or
2. labor's share of output is rising, or
3. for both reasons together.

In recent American experience, the first factor has been much the most important. National output per man-hour of labor employed has been rising at more than 3 percent a year. The reasons for this belong to the study of economic growth and cannot be detailed here. In addition, however, there has been a modest increase in labor's share of output in recent decades. So it is important to examine what determines labor's share of the output "pie."

THEORIES OF LABOR'S SHARE

Classical Distribution Theory

Speculation about what determines the share of income going to suppliers of labor, capital, and other factors goes back to the beginning of economics. British economists of the period from 1800 to 1830, especially David Ricardo and T. R. Malthus, regarded national income as divided among wage earners, capitalists, and landowners. Wages, they thought, must tend toward a minimum level of subsistence, that is, a level that would just enable the population to reproduce itself. If wages should rise temporarily above this level, workers would respond by having more children, and more of these children would be able to survive to maturity. The accelerated increase in labor supply would force wages down toward the subsistence level. This gloomy prognosis was termed *the iron law of wages,* and did much to earn economics its label of "the dismal science."

Agriculture was regarded as subject to *diminishing returns* or *increasing costs.* As the population grows, more and more food must be produced But this can be done only by bringing poorer land into cultivation or working the better land more intensively. In either case, if we assume no technical progress in agriculture, the amount of, say, wheat produced by a unit of labor and capital will fall. Or, putting this in reverse, the cost of producing a bushel of wheat will rise. But since the price of wheat depends on its cost of production, the price of wheat must also rise.

This has two consequences. First, rising food prices will bring an increase in landowners' incomes. Rent per acre, total rent, and rent as a percentage of national income will all rise over time. Economic growth, unaccompanied by technical progress in agriculture, means a continued enrichment of the land-owning class.

Second, *money* wages must rise in order to enable workers to buy as much food as before and thus keep *real* wages constant, and this will be harmful to employers of labor. The price of manufactured products has not risen, because there has been no change in the amount of labor required per unit of product. The manufacturers, then, are squeezed between a constant price level and a rising wage level, and the rate of profit must fall. It could conceivably fall to zero. But somewhere before this, the classics argued, the incentive to saving would have vanished and capital accumulation would cease. The capital stock would then remain constant, and the interest rate would remain constant at a low but positive level. Thus, with capital and labor both constant, we arrive at the famous *classical stationary state.*

Looking backward, it is easy to see why these predictions were not realized in Britain. Increased imports of grain from the New World after 1840 reduced the demands on Britain's farm land. Gradual spread of birth control methods in the late nineteenth and early twentieth centuries removed the specter of population pressure. Accelerated technical progress in all branches of the economy raised output fast enough so that workers, capitalists, and landowners could simultaneously enjoy higher returns.

Classical reasoning remains applicable, however, in many of the less developed countries. Some of these countries combined severe population pressure, inadequate food production, low rates of saving, and slow technical progress. It is not difficult to imagine them evolving toward a stationary state, with the great majority of the population living at subsistence levels.

The Neoclassical or Market Theory

By the late nineteenth century the British economy had changed substantially, and so had the complexion of economics. Land no longer appeared so important or so different from capital goods. The Malthusian theory of population had been generally abandoned. Economists no longer tried to determine the growth of factor supplies within their theoretical system, but concentrated simply on factor prices. Because of these and other differences, economists writing from about 1870 on are usually termed *neoclassical*.

The income distribution problem was reformulated as follows: Given fixed supplies of labor and capital, what determines the market price of each and hence the division of national output between them? The answer, worked out more or less simultaneously by John Bates Clark at Columbia, Alfred Marshall at Cambridge, and several European economists, is often called *the marginal productivity theory of distribution*.

Clark, for example,[1] constructed a hypothetical economic system with the following characteristics: (1) Free competition prevails throughout the economy, in both product markets and factor markets. Prices and wages are not manipulated by collusive agreements or government regulation. (2) The quantity of each productive resource is assumed to be given. Moreover, no changes occur in the tastes of consumers or the state of the industrial arts. The same goods therefore continue to be produced year after year in the same quantities and by the same methods. (3) The *quantity* of capital equipment is regarded as fixed, but it is assumed that the *form* of this equipment can be altered to cooperate most effectively with whatever quantity of labor is available. Although this seems at first glance a queer and unreal assumption, it makes a good deal of sense for long-

---

[1] John Bates Clark, *The Distribution of Wealth* (New York: The Macmillan Company, 1899).

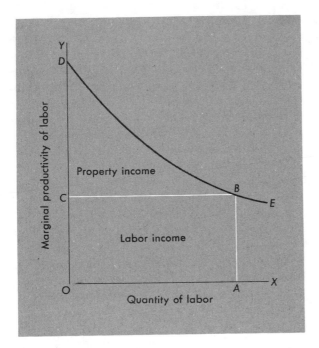

Figure 11–1

Determination of the General Level of Real Wages

SOURCE: John Bates Clark, *The Distribution of Wealth* (New York: The Macmillan Company, 1899), p. 201.

period problems. Over a period of decades plants *can* be adapted as they wear out and have to be replaced. If labor becomes more plentiful relative to capital, plants and machines can be redesigned to use greater quantities of labor. If labor becomes scarcer, equipment can be redesigned to use less labor. (4) Workers are assumed to be interchangeable and of equal efficiency. This assumption means complete absence of occupational specialization. The result is a single wage rate rather than a variety of rates for different occupations.

Clark summarized the operation of such an economy in a diagram, reproduced here as Figure 11–1. The line *DE* represents the marginal physical productivity of labor, that is, the amount added to the national product by the employment of additional workers. Clark showed this curve as falling steadily from the beginning. Actually, it might rise for some time, but this point is not important.

A represents the number of workers available for employment, which we assume to be given and constant. If all these men are employed, the last man added will have a marginal productivity of *AB*. His wage rate cannot be more than *AB*, for then it would not pay to employ him. The wage rate cannot be less than *AB*, for in this event some employer, seeing a chance to make a profit by hiring the worker for less than his marginal productivity, would try to lure him away from his present employer. Competition among employers for labor will ensure that the worker receives the full marginal product *AB*, but no more than this.

It follows next that no other worker in the system can receive a wage higher than *AB*. It may seem that the men above the margin—that is, the men to the left of *A* on the diagram—are being cheated by this arrangement. They seem to be producing more than they are getting. Actually, however, under the assumption of perfect interchangeability of workers, no man is more valuable than any other. If a man doing a particular important job were to drop out, a man could be taken from the margin to replace him. Hence one cannot earn more than another. If this were not so, and if each man were paid his specific productivity, nothing would be left over for the other factors of production. As it is, however, the workers as a group receive as wages the area *OABC*, that is, the number of workers multiplied by the wage rate. The triangular area *BCD* goes to the owners of land and capital.

The fact that there are thousands or millions of employers in the economy makes no difference to the argument. In a purely competitive labor market, each employer will be obliged to pay the market wage, *OC*. He will then adjust his hiring of labor so that the marginal productivity of the last man hired is also *OC*. Thus both the wage of labor and the marginal productivity of labor will be equal in all employing units; and it will not be possible to raise national output by transferring workers from one unit to another. Labor is ideally allocated.

Nor does it make any basic difference that there are in fact many skill levels in the economy. The assumption of a single skill level and a single wage rate is merely a convenient simplification. We could assume instead that there are several occupational levels, in which wages at any time bear a fixed relation to each other, and move up and down together. We could then regard *OC* as an average of these occupational rates. The conclusion would remain the same: the level of this average wage depends on the height of the productivity schedule and on the supply of labor.

Figure 11–1 was drawn for labor because labor is the subject of this book. But an exactly similar diagram could be drawn for capital. Units of capital supply would appear on the horizontal axis, and the rate of return to capital on the vertical axis. The rectangle at the bottom of the diagram would then represent property income, and the upper triangle would be labor income.

This suggests an interesting puzzle: Will the two diagrams be consistent? If labor is paid its marginal product, and capital is paid its marginal product, how do we know there will be just enough output to go around? To make sure that this will be so, we must make the further assumption that a small increase in input always produces a proportionate increase in output. A 1 percent increase in employment of labor and capital will add exactly 1 percent to output. The economy as a whole shows *constant returns to scale*. If this is true, it can be shown that paying each factor its marginal productivity will exactly use up the output of the economy.[2]

Monopoly and Monopsony Power

The competitive market explanation of factor shares has impressed many economists as too good to be true, or at least too simple to be true, and particularly since 1930 two lines of attack have been launched upon it. First, monopoly power is obviously present in many product markets, and monopsony power is thought to be quite prevalent in labor markets. Second, it seems rather odd to use microeconomic price theory to explain the *aggregate* distribution of national income, which might well be considered a problem in macroeconomics.

The first line of criticism,[3] associated particularly with the names of Michael Kalecki and Joan Robinson, is examined in this section. The second line of attack, suggested by Nicholas Kaldor but since developed by numerous other economists, is considered in the next section.

Consider first the implications of monopoly power in product markets. In Figure 11–2 we show the usual monopoly pricing diagram. *ATC* and *MC* are the firm's average total cost and marginal cost curves, while *D* and *MR* are its demand and marginal revenue curves. To maximize profit, the firm will produce the output for which $MC = MR$, in this case Q; and it can sell this output for price P.

Instead of price being equal to marginal cost as in pure competition,

---

[2] The functional relation between input and output is termed a *production function*. The assumption described above amounts to assuming a *linear homogeneous production function of degree one*. An example is the *Cobb–Douglas function* (named after Professor Paul Douglas of Chicago and a mathematician who collaborated with him), which has the form $Y = VK^\alpha L^{1-\alpha}$, where V is a constant, α is a constant fraction, K is capital, and L is labor.

The fraction α shows the effect on output of a small increase in capital, everything else remaining unchanged. Similarly, $1 - \alpha$ shows the effect of a small increase in labor. It can be shown that if factor markets are purely competitive, so that each factor is paid its marginal product, α *is the capital share of national income and $1 - \alpha$ is the share of labor*. Since $\alpha + (1 - \alpha) = 1$, the available product is precisely exhausted.

[3] For a review of the relevant literature and some efforts at statistical testing, see John R. Maroney and Bruce T. Allen, "Monopoly Power and the Relative Share of Labor," *Industrial and Labor Relations Review* (January 1969), pp. 167–78.

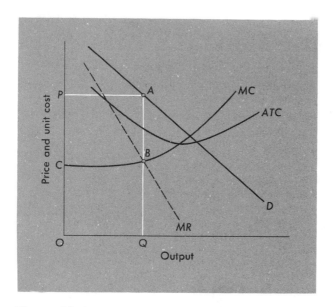

Figure 11–2

Monopoly Pricing and Factor Shares

there is a gap between them equal to AB. This gap as a proportion of the price itself—that is, the ratio AB/AQ—is termed the *degree of monopoly*. This measure is related to the elasticity of demand. The more inelastic the demand curve, the higher the degree of monopoly. It can be shown, in fact, that $AB/AQ = 1/e$, where e is the price elasticity of demand.

For present purposes, the important thing is that $OCBQ$, the area under the marginal cost curve, shows how much of the product price is paid for labor and other variable factors. $ABCP$ is the amount left for the fixed factors. While $ABCP$ is not precisely the capital share of output, it is very close to it. On this ground Kalecki and others have argued that anything increasing the degree of monopoly in the economy will raise the capital share, and conversely. If the degree of monopoly remains unchanged, and if business pricing practices remain stable, then the labor and capital shares will also remain unchanged.

Competition may also be restricted in the labor market. The exercise of *monopsony power* by a firm was analyzed in Chapter 5. The firm will restrict employment and output in order to profit from a lower wage level. This power to reduce the wage level is also a power to reduce labor's income share. Conversely, if the wage is raised to the competitive level by collective bargaining or legal regulation, labor's income share will rise.

There is considerable difference of opinion among economists as to how widespread monopsony power is in labor markets. But to the extent that it exists, it must operate to reduce labor's share below what it would be under fully competitive conditions.

Aggregative Distribution Theories

Finally, we must note a type of theory that does not start from the economics of the firm but from aggregative models of the economy. These models suggest that labor and capital shares are closely linked to the rate of economic growth. Nicholas Kaldor and other economists at Cambridge University have taken a prominent part in developing this line of reasoning. These theories return, in a sense, to the classical tradition of being interested in factor supplies as well as factor prices, and of trying to trace the course of events over time.

Kaldor's analysis [4] starts from the Keynesian proposition that, for any past period, saving must equal investment. He next distinguishes between saving from wage income and saving from property income. It is plausible to assume that recipients of property income have a higher propensity to save [5]—indeed, in some models of this type it is assumed that all saving comes from property income, while wage earners save nothing.

Call national income Y, investment I, the wage and property shares W and P, total saving from each of these shares S_w and S_p, and the proportion of each share that is saved s_w and s_p. Thus $S_p = s_p \cdot P$ and $S_w = s_w \cdot W$. The savings ratios, s_w and s_p, are assumed to remain constant for all levels of income.

The basic relations in the system are

$$Y = P + W$$
$$S = I$$
$$S = S_p + S_w$$

From this we can deduce that the investment level

$$
\begin{aligned}
I &= S_p + S_w \\
&= s_p \cdot P + s_w \cdot W \\
&= s_p \cdot P + s_w \ (Y - P) \\
&= (s_p - s_w) \ P + s_w \cdot Y
\end{aligned}
$$

---

[4] The original statement is in Nicholas Kaldor, "Alternative Theories of Distribution," *Review of Economic Studies,* 23 (1955–56), pp. 83–100.

[5] Evidence is scanty, but one study for France shows the following ratios of saving to income for different economic groups: employers in industry and commerce, 36.5 percent; senior management and professions, 24.3 percent; farmers, 16.8 percent; salaried workers, 1.2 percent; industrial workers, 2.4 percent. Jacques Lecaillon, "Changes in the Distribution of Income in the French Economy," in Jean Marchal and Bernard Duclos (eds.), *The Distribution of National Income* (New York: St. Martin's Press, Inc., 1968).

Dividing through by Y,

$$\frac{I}{Y} = (s_p - s_w) \frac{P}{Y} + s_w$$

and

$$\frac{P}{Y} = \frac{1}{s_p - s_w} \cdot \frac{I}{Y} - \frac{s_w}{s_p - s_w}$$

This means that, if the saving propensities are given and constant, *the profit share of income depends solely on the ratio of investment to output.* A high investment rate goes along with a high property share, and conversely. If we assume that wage earners do not save at all, so that $s_w = 0$, the above expression reduces to

$$P = \frac{1}{s_p} \cdot I$$

The level of property income depends on the level of investment and on the capitalists' own saving propensity In Kaldor's phrase, "capitalists earn what they spend, and workers spend what they earn."

Moreover, so long as s_p is greater than s_w, the system will be stable. An increase in I raises aggregate demand. If prices are flexible, this will raise prices relative to wages and thus increase the profit share of income. But since a higher proportion of profit is saved, this will increase total saving. The process will continue until saving has risen sufficiently to offset the increase in investment. A drop in investment will set off an opposite sequence of events—lower prices, lower profits, and lower saving. Thus as long as s_p is greater than s_w, and assuming prices flexible in both directions, the system will be stable in the vicinity of full employment.

The property share of income, in short, is linked directly to the investment rate and thus to the growth rate of output. A high-level growth path, such as that of Japan since 1950, goes along with a high investment rate and a large property share of income. A low-level growth path, such as that of Britain since 1950, is accompanied by a much lower investment rate and a smaller property share. What may cause an economy to be on one or the other path is a complicated question—indeed, the central problem of modern growth theory. Kaldorians would claim only that a consistent view of the economy must link income distribution to the behavior of the grand aggregates of the economy.

The Kaldor view of aggregate income distribution is not inconsistent with the view that the wage rate in each firm and industry must equal the marginal productivity of labor; and some economists have effected a satisfactory reconciliation of macro and micro distribution theories.[6] But this involves difficult problems that fall properly in a more advanced course.

CHANGES IN RELATIVE SHARES: ANALYSIS

The division of income between capital and labor at a particular moment is perhaps less interesting than the behavior of income shares over time. In a growing capitalist economy, will labor's share tend to rise, fall, or remain constant over the decades? This is a basic issue, which has been debated since classical times. Before looking at the statistical evidence, let us analyze on what the answer will depend. Throughout this section we assume competitive factor pricing.

Total labor income is the amount of labor in use (L) multiplied by the market wage (W), which we assume is equal to labor's marginal productivity (MP_L). Capital income is the capital stock (K) multiplied by its market rate of return (P), also assumed equal to the marginal productivity of capital (MP_K). The ratio of property income to labor income, then, is

$$\frac{P \cdot K}{W \cdot L} = \frac{P}{W} \cdot \frac{K}{L}$$

The distributive shares will remain constant if this expression remains constant.

The right-hand and left-hand terms are obviously related. A change in relative factor supplies will necessarily change their relative prices. Let us chart this relation, as in Figure 11–3. On the horizontal axis we measure the capital–labor ratio, K/L. Moving to the right on the axis means that each worker has more and more capital to work with. (This happens to have been the actual direction of movement in the United States and other industrial countries in modern times.)

On the vertical axis, we lay out the rate of return to capital (crudely, the rate of interest) relative to the wage rate, both defined in real terms. Moving *down* this axis means that the interest rate is falling relative to the wage rate—or, what amounts to the same thing, the wage rate is rising faster than the interest rate.

The relation between the two ratios is shown by the curve TT. Suppose we pick a point A on this curve, and lay out the rectangle $OCAD$. Then

$$OC = \frac{P}{W} \quad \text{and} \quad OD = \frac{K}{L}$$

---

[6] See several papers in *The Distribution of National Income,* cited in fn. 5, particularly those by Martin Bronfenbrenner and Robert Solow.

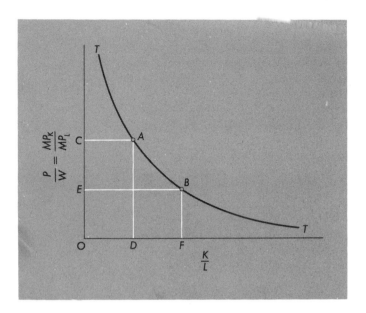

Figure 11–3

Capital–Labor Substitution: The Case of Unit
Elasticity

Multiplying,

$$OCAD = \frac{P}{W} \cdot \frac{K}{L} = \frac{W \cdot L}{P \cdot K} = \frac{\text{Property income}}{\text{Labor income}}$$

As we move down TT, we can see whether the relative share of property income is rising or falling by observing what is happening to the size of the rectangles under the curve.

Why is it plausible to draw this curve as sloping downward from left to right? Suppose the capital stock rises with labor supply constant—a rightward movement on the X axis. This will rise labor's marginal productivity schedule (Figure 11–1), and hence the market wage rate. As K/L increases, P/W will fall; so the curve relating them must slope downward.

The same result follows in the more realistic case when the supply of both factors is rising but at different rates. Suppose capital supply is rising faster than labor supply. Then the marginal productivity of both factors may be rising, but MP_L will still rise faster because capital is becoming relatively more abundant. If the factors are priced competitively, P/W will decline because MP_K/MP_L is declining.

This change in relative factor prices will react on methods of production. If capital is becoming steadily cheaper relative to labor, producers will be inclined to save labor by substituting capital. This will raise the demand for capital relative to labor, and will tend to check the fall of interest rates relative to wage rates.

The outcome, if we are comparing different periods of time, will depend on how easy it is to find ways of substituting capital for labor (or vice versa). This ease or difficulty is indicated by the *elasticity* of *TT*, which is termed the *elasticity of substitution*.[7] This elasticity might have various values, and its value might be different points on *TT*. One interesting case, however, and the case illustrated in Figure 11–3, is that in which the elasticity of substitution is one at any point on *TT*. (Geometrically, *TT* is a rectangular hyperbola, the area under which is constant for all points.)

This means that a small increase in K/L is always exactly offset by a decrease in P/W. Thus the expression $(P/W)(K/L)$ remains constant and hence the labor and property shares remain constant. The points *D* and *F*, for example, might represent dates thirty years apart, during which the capital–labor ratio has doubled. By our assumption, this causes the P/W ratio to fall to half its previous value. Thus *OACD*, which shows the property income–labor income ratio at the outset, has the same area as *OEBF*, which shows the ratio thirty years later. Relative income shares have remained unchanged.

The special feature of this case is that relative *rates of increase in factor supplies have no effect on income shares.* Capital supply can increase 50 percent faster than labor supply, or twice as fast, or three times as fast. Relative factor prices will always adjust, so that income shares remain unchanged. If, on the other hand, elasticity of substitution were *less than one,* the more rapidly growing factor would suffer a sharper fall in price and its share of national income would fall. Conversely, if elasticity of substitution were greater than one, the share of the more rapidly growing factor would rise.

There is of course no reason why *TT* in actuality should have the shape given it in Figure 11–3. The elasticity of substitution could readily be greater than unity or less than unity, and could differ at various points on the curve. Statistical investigation of actual elasticities presents complicated problems. Research results to date suggest that elasticity of capital–labor substitution differs substantially from one industry to another. Most of the estimates, however, fall within a range of 0.8 to 1.2. Thus an

---

[7] Algebraically, the elasticity of substitution is defined as

$$\frac{\Delta\,(K/L)}{K/L} \div \frac{\Delta\,(P/W)}{P/W}$$

assumption of unity for the economy as a whole seems a good working approximation for the time being.

So far we have concentrated on increase in factor supplies and have ignored the possibility of technical progress. Technical change, often referred to as innovation, shifts marginal productivity curves upward; but it is not necessarily neutral between the two factors. It may raise the marginal productivity of labor more than that of capital, or vice versa.

Here some definitions are in order. A *labor-saving innovation* is one that raises the marginal productivity of capital more that that of labor. *It acts like an increase in labor supply.* It provides opportunities to use additional capital without depressing its productivity. Mechanization and automation in manufacturing provide an abundance of illustrations.

A *capital-saving innovation* is one that raises the marginal productivity of labor more than that of capital. *It acts like an increase in capital supply.* Transmission of messages by radio instead of telegraph wires is an example of this sort. Another is the jet airplane, which can carry more transatlantic passengers per week than a large steamship, while costing considerably less to build.

A *neutral innovation* is the borderline case between these two.

Depending on which kind of innovation predominates at a particular time and place, one can say that technical change has a *labor-saving bias* or a *capital-saving bias.*

The character of technical progress in a particular economy has an obvious bearing on factor prices and factor shares. Neutral technical progress, by definition, raises MP_K and MP_L equally, and so would not change the P/W ratio. Progress with a labor-saving bias, however, would tend to raise P relative to W, while progress with a capital-saving bias would have the opposite effect.

There has been much discussion of the character of actual technical progress in the United States over the past century. It is usually argued that progress *should* have had a labor-saving bias, because there has been a strong incentive to labor-saving improvements. With labor supply increasing slowly relative to capital, and with labor becoming relatively more expensive, the problem of economizing labor has forced itself constantly on businessmen. It would be surprising if this were not reflected in the activities of inventors, engineers, and production managers. Some technical changes drop out of the blue as a by-product of basic scientific work; and there is no reason to expect that these *autonomous* inventions will be biased in one direction or the other. But to the extent that inventions are *induced* by an effort to lower production costs, one would expect them to have a labor-saving bias.

This surmise, however, has not yet been confirmed, or refuted, by research. It is very difficult to match the available statistics against theoretical concepts, and such evidence as we have is still indirect and fragmentary.

To sum up: The evolution of labor and capital shares over time is influenced by (1) relative rates of increase in labor and capital supplies, (2) elasticity of capital–labor substitution, and (3) the labor-saving or capital-saving bias of technical progress.

On general grounds, there is no reason why relative income shares should remain constant. But it is easy enough to find combinations of circumstances under which they would do so. This would happen, for example, if (1) L and K increase at the same rate, and technical progress is absent or neutral; (2) with technical progress still absent or neutral, factor supplies increase at different rates, but elasticity of capital–labor substitution is unity; (3) one factor, say K, increases more rapidly than the other, elasticity of substitution is too low to offset this entirely, but substitution is helped out by technical change with a labor-saving bias. Substitution and technical progress together operate to sustain returns to capital, so that P/W falls at about the same rate K/L rises. It is often asserted that something like this has happened in the United States over the last several generations.

CHANGES IN RELATIVE SHARES: EVIDENCE

Some Measurement Problems

When we turn to look at the evidence, we find a number of problems and difficulties. First, we must be clear about whether we are discussing income *earned* or income *received*. Recipients of profit income receive considerably less than they earn, because part is taken by the corporate income tax. The same is true on a smaller scale of wage and salary earners. Part of their compensation goes into private and public pension funds and other deferred benefits instead of being received currently.

When we come to consider household income distribution in Chapter 13, income received is the relevant concept. But here we are considering income *earned* or *produced*. We treat the total value product of each industry as divided between employee compensation and property income. Total profits before taxes, plus interest payments, are allocated to the property share. Labor income includes fringes and supplements as well as direct wage payments. The movement of the two shares, thus defined, tells us whether the price mechanism itself is redistributing income in one direction or the other.

A second problem arises from the shifting importance of different industries in the economy. In most countries, for example, government output has been rising relative to private output. The value of government output is conventionally defined as equal to the government payroll, so that the labor share of income produced is 100 percent. Thus if government output is increasing in relative importance, the national income statistics will show an increase in labor's share, even though factor shares in the private economy have not changed. Another illustration is agriculture, which has a relatively high property share because of the importance of land and mechanical equipment. Agricultural output as a percentage of national output has been declining for many decades, and this also tends to raise the labor share and reduce the property share for the economy as a whole. Because of these biases, most studies concentrate on the private nonfarm economy.

Third, certain groups in the economy—farmers, storekeepers, and other small business proprietors—have incomes that are a blend of labor and property income. They include payment for the proprietor's capital as well as his time. One can split these incomes apart statistically—for example, by assuming that an independent retailer's time is worth as much as that of an average chain-store employee, and treating the remainder of his income as attributable to capital. But such assumptions are always debatable, and so are the estimates based on them.

Short-Run Changes in Labor's Share

In the tangled literature of income distribution, it is encouraging to find something on which researchers agree. There is general agreement that labor's share of income produced in the private economy varies counter-cyclically. As output rises during an upswing, profits rise faster than output and labor's share declines. This is usually attributed to the *capacity effect,* that is, a decline in average fixed cost and average total cost as output rises.[8] Even if the product price does not rise, this permits a wider profit margin per unit. It is sometimes explained also by a presumed lag of wages behind prices during cycle upswings; but such a lag, if it exists at all, seems too small to make much contribution to profits.

During a decline in output, these tendencies are reversed. The profit share falls and the labor share of income rises. This is noticeable in Figure 11–4 for the recession years 1938, 1946, 1949, 1954, 1958, 1970, and 1974. One moral is that conclusions about long-run changes in labor's share should be based on averages for a period of years rather than one

---

[8] The underlying assumption is that, in recession years, many firms are operating to the left of the minimum point on their average total cost curves. For manufacturing, at least, there seems good warrant for this assumption. The minimum point on the *ATC* curve is usually estimated at about 90 percent of physical plant capacity. During recession years since 1945, output rates have typically been in the range of 80–85 percent of capacity.

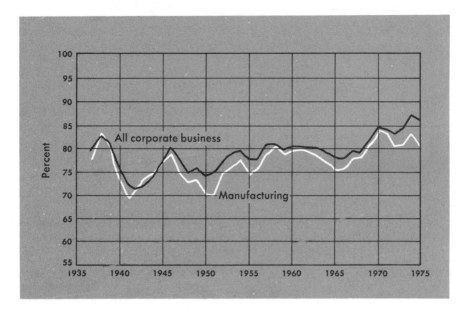

Figure 11–4

Employee Compensation as a Percentage of
Income Produced, 1937–75

SOURCE: U.S. Department of Commerce,
*National Income by Legal Form of
Organization, and National Income by
Industrial Origin: Manufacturing,* as reported
in the Survey of Current Business, July
1976. Employee compensation includes wages
and salary disbursements, other employee
income, and personal contributions for
social insurance.

single-year comparison. For example, a comparison of the boom year 1951
with the recession year 1958 would seem to show a marked rise in labor's
share. But this may be due entirely to differences in utilization of plant
capacity.

Long-Run Changes in Labor's Share

The evidence on long-run trends is less clear, partly because of the
statistical difficulties mentioned earlier. For a long time, it was customary
to say that the labor and capital shares are virtually constant, and theorists
worked at developing models that would explain this presumed constancy.

More recent studies suggest, however, that the share of labor has increased moderately since 1900 or so, while that of capital has fallen.

Three studies may be cited. A calculation by Irving Kravis, in which the incomes of independent proprietors are allocated in a constant proportion of 65 percent to labor and 35 percent to capital, shows the property share of national income falling from 30.6 percent in the years from 1900 to 1909 to 23.8 percent in 1949 to 1957.[9] Kendrick's calculations for the private domestic economy show the capital share of national income declining from 30.1 percent in 1899 to 18.6 percent in 1957, with the labor share rising from 69.9 percent to 81.4 percent.[10] Finally, Denison finds the labor share rising from 69.5 percent in 1909 to 1913 to 77.3 percent in 1954 to 1958, with property income declining accordingly.[11] Although these studies differ in detailed methodology, they all show property income shrinking from something like 30 percent at the beginning of the century to something like 20 percent today.[12]

A more recent study by William Nordhaus indicates that, using published accounting data, the profit share of income produced by U.S. nonfinancial corporations fell from around 20 percent in the late forties to about 12 percent in the early seventies. After adjusting for various biases in accounting practices, it appears that there was a genuine decline in the profit share, though less sharp than that shown by the crude data.[13]

There is similar evidence from other countries. Professor Simon Kuznets has made a wide-ranging inquiry covering several of the in-

---

[9] Irving B. Kravis, "Relative Income Shares in Fact and Theory," *American Economic Review* (December 1959), pp. 917–49. The tricky problem of splitting up proprietors' income (which is itself declining in relative importance over time) can of course be solved in several ways. Kravis applies three other methods in addition to the one described. All show the property share declining, but by somewhat different amounts.

[10] John W. Kendrick, *Productivity Trends in the United States* (Princeton: Princeton University Press, 1961), p. 121.

[11] Edward F. Denison, *The Sources of Economic Growth in the United States* (New York: Committee for Economic Development, 1962), p. 30.

[12] For other viewpoints on this problem, however, see Simon Kuznets, "Long-Term Changes in the National Income of the U.S.A. Since 1870," *Income and Wealth*, Series II (London: Bowes and Bowes, 1952); Edward C. Budd, "Labor's Share of National Income" (unpublished dissertation, University of California, Berkeley, 1954); Clark Kerr, "Labor's Income Share and the Labor Movement," in George W. Taylor and Frank C. Pierson (eds.), *New Concepts in Wage Determination* (New York: McGraw-Hill Book Company, 1957); Paul S. Sultan, "Unionism and Wage–Income Ratios, 1929–51," *Review of Economics and Statistics* (February 1954); and Norman J. Simler, *The Impact of Unionism on Wage–Income Ratios in the Manufacturing Sector of the Economy* (Minneapolis: University of Minnesota Press, 1961).

[13] William Nordhaus, "The Falling Share of Profits," *Brookings Papers on Economic Activity*, No. 1 (1974), pp. 169–208.

Table 1

Distribution of National Income Among Factor Shares, Selected Countries, Long Periods

	Compensation of Employees (Percent)	Income From Assets (Percent)
United Kingdom		
1860–69	54	46
1905–14	54	46
1920–29	66	34
1954–60	75	25
France		
1853	56	44
1911	66	34
1920–29	71	29
1954–60	81	19
Germany		
1895	53	47
1913	61	39
1925–29	79	21
1954–60	71	29
Switzerland		
1924	65	35
1954–60	74	26
Canada		
1926–29	81	19
1954–60	81	19
United States		
1899–1908	76	24
1919–28	73	27
1954–60	81	19

Source: Simon Kuznets, *Modern Economic Growth* (New Haven: Yale University Press, 1966), pp. 168–70.

dustrialized countries for periods of up to 100 years.[14] Some of his findings are reproduced in Table 1.

Two features of these estimates should be noted. First, they assume that the average labor income of independent proprietors was equal to the *average earnings of all employees in the economy*. This amount is then

[14] Simon Kuznets, *Modern Economic Growth* (New Haven: Yale University Press, 1966). See also several papers in Jean Marchal and Bernard Duclos (eds.), *The Distribution of National Income* (New York: St. Martin's Press, Inc., 1968).

deducted from total proprietors' income to obtain the capital share. Second, the estimates are not adjusted for interindustry shifts and so, for reasons noted earlier, they exaggerate the actual increase in the labor share. The trends are so marked, however, and so consistent from country to country, that it seems reasonable to conclude that labor's share has risen even on an adjusted basis.

There is considerable evidence, then, that the capital share of income produced has been falling gradually in the long run. If true, this could be explained along the lines of our earlier discussion. In the richer industrial countries, the K/L ratio has been rising quite rapidly. Capital supply has been rising at 3 to 4 percent a year, labor supply at about 1 percent (though there is a considerable range of variation in individual countries). This tends to depress the interest rate relative to the wage rate. This tendency has been offset by capital–labor substitution and (possibly) by a labor-saving bias in technical progress. But the offsets have apparently not been fully sufficient. Not merely has the return to a unit of capital fallen relative to the return to a man-hour of labor—given the above rates of increase in factor supplies, this would have been almost inevitable. The point is that relative returns to capital [15] have fallen so much that, even when multiplied by a rapidly growing capital stock, the total capital share has diminished.

Productivity and Wages: Some Qualifications

The modest increase in labor's share over the past half-century is much too small to explain the rapid rise in real wage rates. Suppose we had perfect measures showing that labor's income share rose from 65 percent in 1900 to 80 percent in 1970, a 23 percent increase in labor's slice of the income pie. If the pie itself had remained unchanged, this would have allowed wages to rise less than 0.25 percent per year, instead of the actual rate of about 3 percent.

The main reason for rising real wages, obviously, is that the pie itself has been growing. There has been a rapid rise in total output and in output per man-hour of labor employed. Labor earns more year by year mainly because, as a result of technical progress and additions to physical and human capital, labor is becoming steadily more productive.

---

[15] The word "relative" should be emphasized. The absolute return to capital, in physical units, has risen moderately since 1900; but it has risen much less than real wages per man-hour. For the United States, Kendrick reports that "between 1919 and 1957, average hourly labor compensation increased at an average annual rate of 4.0 percent—more than double the 1.5 percent average increase in the price of capital. . . . The total increase over the thirty-eight years was 346 percent in the case of labor rates compared with 77 percent in the case of unit capital compensation." *Productivity Trends in the United States,* p. 117.

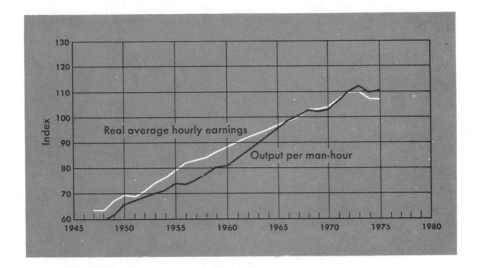

Figure 11–5

Indexes of Private Nonfarm Output per Man-Hour
and Nonfarm Real Average Hourly Earnings,
1947–75 (1967 = 100)

SOURCE: *Economic Report of the President* (Washington, D.C.: Government Printing Office, 1976), pp. 204, 206.

The notion that in the long run the rise of real wages is linked to the rise of productivity seems so obvious that it is in danger of being misunderstood. Wage changes show a good correspondence with the movement of the man-hour output, as is evident from Figure 11–5. This correspondence holds, however, only *over considerable periods of time and for the economy as a whole.* One cannot expect that wage movements and productivity movements will correspond within particular companies or industries.

The reason is that productivity trends vary widely from one branch of production to another. For the private economy as a whole, Kendrick's measure of total factor productivity rose at an average rate of 1.7 percent per year over the period 1899 to 1953. The rate of increase was 0.7 percent, however, in anthracite coal mining, 1.1 percent in farming, 2.0 percent in manufacturing, 3.2 percent in transportation, and 5.5 percent in electric utilities. Within manufacturing, the productivity increase averaged only 1.0 percent in lumber products but was 4.1 percent for rubber products.[16] When one considers that these rates of increase are compounded

---

[16] Kendrick, *Productivity Trends in the United States,* pp. 136–37.

annually, it is obvious that productivity levels had pulled very far apart by the end of the period. Taking 1899 as 100, the productivity index for anthracite coal had risen by 1953 to only 147, whereas for electric utilities it had risen to 1,764.

If, then, wage changes in each industry were geared to productivity changes *in that industry,* the wage structure would rapidly be pulled apart. Wages of workers in electric power companies would rise to fantastic heights, while miners' wages would stagnate. Because of the transferability of labor on the supply side of the market, such extreme divergence of wages is unnecessary and unfeasible. In fact, Kendrick's calculations for thirty-three industry groups over the period 1899 to 1953 show no significant relation between rate of increase in factor productivity and rate of wage increase in the same industry.

What happens is rather that the wage level rises more or less evenly in all companies and industries (though not *entirely* evenly, as will appear in Chapter 12). The rate at which the wage tide rises is geared to the *average* rate of productivity increase in the economy. The impact of this rising tide on a particular industry depends on how its own rate of productivity increase compares with the general average.

An industry in which productivity rises faster than the wage level will experience a fall in unit labor costs and, probably, in unit total production costs. Under competitive conditions, this would mean a drop in prices—not necessarily in absolute terms, but relative to prices of goods in general. Even for a monopolist, a decline in unit costs will lower the profit-maximizing price. Research studies show that industries with an above average productivity increase do in fact show a decline in relative prices. Recently, for example, this has been true of electric power and of such manufactured products as plastics, radio and television sets, household appliances, tires and tubes, and synthetic fibres. Partly because of these relatively low prices, output and employment in such industries rise faster than in other industries. There is a marked relation over long periods between an industry's rate of productivity increase and its rate of output increase.

Industries in which output per man-hour rises more slowly than the wage level are in a less happy position. Their unit labor costs and, probably, unit total costs will be rising. This will force a relative rise in their selling prices, which in turn will tend to reduce sales, output, and employment. This seems to be the situation in many of the service industries. Barbers' productivity has not increased very much over the years; and so, as the general wage level has risen, the price of a haircut has gone up within living memory from $0.50 to $3.50—much more than the general price level. Longer hair and less frequent haircuts is a rational consumer response. In the case of products to which consumers are not strongly attached, the steady rise of costs and prices may gradually extinguish the industry. The long decline of the "legitimate theater" is a case in point.

DISCUSSION QUESTIONS

1. How can the real wage per man-hour *rise* even in years when national output is *falling?*

2. What did the classical economists believe would happen in the long run to the *rates of return* to land, labor, and capital?

3. In neoclassical or market theory, what determines the level of real wages at a particular time? What assumptions underlie the reasoning?

4. Explain the meaning of elasticity of substitution. Can you think of industries in which one might expect elasticity of substitution to be:
   (a) unusually high?
   (b) unusually low?

5. What are the main factors determining whether labor's share of national income will rise or fall over time?

6. Do recent ideas about income distribution advanced by Kalecki, Kaldor, Robinson, and others, call for *substantial* modification of neoclassical reasoning?

7. What has happened in the United States since 1900 to:
   (a) the relative *prices* of labor and capital services?
   (b) the relative *shares* of labor and capital in national income?
What reasons can you suggest for the apparent increase in labor's share?

8. "Wages depend basically on productivity. So to determine how much wages should be raised this year in a particular company or industry, one need look only at the increase in man-hour output." Discuss.

9. How might one expect wages, prices, output, and employment to change over the course of time in an industry with zero productivity increase?

READING SUGGESTIONS

For original statements of neoclassical distribution theory, see JOHN BATES CLARK, *The Distribution of Wealth,* New York: The Macmillan Company, 1899; ALFRED MARSHALL, *Principles of Economics* (9th ed., Book VI), London: Macmillan & Co. Ltd., 1961. For more recent statements, see J. R. HICKS, *The Theory of Wages* (2d ed.), New York: St. Martin's Press, Inc., 1966; GEORGE J. STIGLER, *The Theory of Price,* New

York: Macmillan Publishing Co., Inc., 1966; and E. H. PHELPS BROWN, *The Economics of Labor,* New Haven: Yale University Press, 1962, Chap. 7.

For statistical analysis of real wages, productivity, and relative income shares, see the studies of Denison, Kendrick, Kravis, and Kuznets cited in this chapter. See also National Bureau of Economic Research, *The Behavior of Income Shares,* Princeton: Princeton University Press, 1964; U.S. Department of Commerce, Bureau of the Census, *Long-Term Economic Growth, 1860–1965,* Washington, D.C.: Government Printing Office, 1966; and JEAN MARCHAL and BERNARD DUCLOS, *The Distribution of National Income,* New York: St. Martin's Press, Inc., 1968.

Two important recent studies are MARTIN BRONFENBRENNER, *Income Distribution Theory,* Chicago and New York: Aldine-Atherton, Inc., 1971; and JAN PEN, *Income Distribution,* New York: Praeger Publishers, Inc., 1971.

12

Differences in Wages

The last two chapters examined the *average* level of wages; but this conceals wide differences in individual earnings. One can still find workers in the United States earning less than two dollars an hour, while some business and professional people earn a hundred dollars an hour.

There are two main reasons for being interested in these wage differences. First, their size provides clues to the operation of labor markets and the efficiency of labor allocation. For example, if, relative to other occupations, people in one occupation are earning more than can be explained on a competitive basis, one is led to suspect a supply blockage or some other market imperfection, which can be explored through further research. Second, the striking differences in income among families in the United States arise largely from differences in the earnings of family members. To the extent that one is interested either in understanding income distribution or in changing it, one is forced to explore the reasons for differences in earnings.

There are two apparently different and competing approaches to explanation of wage differences. The traditional approach, first developed by Adam Smith, focuses on wage differences among *occupations*. The economy is viewed as a network of labor markets for each of many occupations, differing in training requirements, regularity of employment, pleasantness of the work, and other respects. One can assume full information and freedom of choice among occupations; or one can admit the various impediments to free choice noted in earlier chapters. In either case, the key questions are of the type: How much more will an electrical engineer earn than a bricklayer? How much more will a bricklayer earn than a construction laborer?

More recently, this approach has been challenged by *human capital* theory, the general thrust of which was indicated in Chapter 3. The human capital approach emphasizes, not differences among *jobs,* but differences among *people.* It attempts to relate a worker's earnings directly to his personal characteristics, including age, sex, race, years of formal education, amount of on-the-job training, years of work experience, family background, and measures of inherent ability. The novelty of this view has stimulated a great deal of research. We shall examine the research results to date, and ask whether the new approach has displaced traditional labor market analysis, or whether instead it should be regarded as complementary to and compatible with earlier work.

OCCUPATIONAL WAGE DIFFERENCES

The theory of occupational differentials in a competitive labor market was developed in Chapter 5, and we need only remind the reader of what was said there. Occupations differ in numerous important dimensions—in the inherent pleasantness or unpleasantness of the work, in the social esteem it enjoys, in regularity of employment, in costs of learning the occupation, and in the chances of success or failure. Some of these characteristics are irremovable, while others change only gradually over long periods. The most flexible element in the system is rates of pay. Given free choice of occupations, then, the wage structure would adjust itself to equalize the *net advantage* of various occupations to people on the margin of decision, including young people entering the labor force. *Wage differences would be equalizing differences* and would serve to offset differences in job characteristics that cannot be readily changed.

When we ask how far the actual occupational wage structure corresponds to these competitive principles, however, there are awkward facts to be explained. At the level of manual labor, there is abundant evidence that workers with higher base rates of pay also receive larger fringe benefits. Supplementary benefit payments thus serve to accentuate wage differences rather than to offset them. It is notorious also that better-paid occupations are more desirable in terms of security, prestige, and working conditions. It is preferable in every way to be an accountant rather than a dishwasher in a restaurant; yet the accountant earns a good deal more. How does this square with the theory of competitive wage differentials?

At this point economists tend to fall back on a variety of *ad hoc* explanations: custom, limitations of natural ability in areas such as science and the performing arts, costs of education for professional and managerial occupations, inability of young people from poor families to finance the costs of higher education, union-induced distortions of relative wages, and other market imperfections. The magnitude of these effects is hard to estimate, and so we do not at this point have a good explanation of actual differences among occupations. Nor can we say with any precision what the wage structure would look like if universal pure competition could somehow be established.

Before pursuing these issues, it will be well to look at the evidence on occupational wage differences in the United States. A serious difficulty here is that our statistical measures do not correspond closely to theoretical concepts. What we should be comparing is *total employee compensation* per man-hour at different occupational levels, including the supplementary benefits which form a growing proportion of total compensation. The data most readily available, however, relate to current money earnings per hour, per week, or per month; and even this is less plentiful for white-collar than for blue-collar workers. The only information available for the whole range of occupations is on *annual earnings,* which is available every ten years from the decennial census. Between censuses, the Census Bureau conducts sample surveys that yield average annual earnings for broad occupational groups, but not for specific occupations within those groups. Annual earnings, which are influenced by time worked during the year, do not correspond closely to the price of labor; but we are nevertheless forced to rely heavily on them.

Table 1 shows the annual earnings from wages or salaries of male workers at various occupational levels who were employed from fifty to fifty-two weeks during the year. Using data for year-round workers rather than all workers should eliminate most of the variation arising fom irregularity of employment. Earnings are still not the same thing as rates of pay, because of the inclusion of overtime, bonuses, and other supplementary items. But they are the best indicator we have covering the whole range of occupations.

The year 1939 provides a pre–World War II base for comparison. The year 1955 is the first postwar year for which data are available on year-round workers. Data for 1975 are the most recent available at this writing. For each year, the earnings of higher occupational groups have been reduced to a percentage of laborers' earnings, to facilitate comparison of changes in occupational differentials.

The rank order of incomes in Table 1 is about what one would expect. Within the professional group, independent practitioners average much more than salaried workers. The main reason is that the salaried group is heavily weighted with schoolteachers, whose median earnings are still relatively low despite the rapid advance in recent years. Within the business group, on the other hand, the opposite relation holds: salaried executives earn substantially more than independent proprietors, most of whom operate stores, service establishments, and other small businesses. The reasons for this difference have not been thoroughly investigated. Is

Table 1

Median Annual Wage and Salary Income, Male Year-Round Workers, by Major Occupation Group, 1939, 1955, and 1975

Occupation Group	1939		1955		1975	
	Dollars	Index (Laborers = 100)	Dollars	Index (Laborers = 100)	Dollars	Index (Laborers = 100)
Professional and technical	2,100	212	5,382	174	16,133	178
Self-employed	n.a.	n.a.	n.a.	n.a.	24,763	273
Salaried	n.a.	n.a.	n.a.	n.a.	15,773	174
Managers, proprietors, and officials	2,254	227	5,584	180	16,093	178
Self-employed	n.a.	n.a.	n.a.	n.a.	11,283	125
Salaried	n.a.	n.a.	n.a.	n.a.	16,814	186
Clerical	1,564	157	4,162	134	12,152	134
Sales	1,451	146	4,937	160	14,025	155
Craftsmen	1,562	157	4,712	152	12,789	141
Operatives	1,268	128	4,046	131	11,142	125
Service, except private household	1,019	103	3,565	115	9,488	105
Farm laborers and foremen	365	37	n.a.	n.a.	5,935	66
Laborers (except farm)	991	100	3,105	100	9,057	100

SOURCE: Data for 1975 are from the Bureau of the Census, *Current Population Reports*, Series P-60, No. 103 (September 1976), p. 22. Data for 1939 and 1955 are from a 1960 census monograph by Herman P. Miller, *Income Distribution in the United States* (Washington, D.C.: Government Printing Office, 1966), p. 82.

Table 2

Indices of Annual Earnings of Male Wage and Salary Earners, Canada, 1931–61 (Laborers = 100)

Occupational Group	1931	1941	1951	1961
Managerial	514	368	232	277
Professional	412	268	189	245
Clerical	244	213	140	160
Carpenters	164	135	123	134
Laborers (nonprimary)	100	100	100	100
Laborers (agricultural)	68	64	52	62

SOURCE: Sylvia Ostry and Mahmood A. Zaidi, *Labour Economics in Canada*, 2nd ed. (Toronto: Macmillan of Canada, 1972), p. 266.
EDITOR'S NOTE: Nonprimary laborers excludes forestry and mine workers, as well as farmers.

the self-employed proprietor less capable, on the average? Does he value independence so highly that he deliberately sacrifices income to achieve it? Or is he a perennial optimist, always expecting to make more than he actually does make, and never learning from experience?

Looking at trends over time one notes that, during the period of very high employment and substantial inflation from 1939 to 1955, the two top occupational groups lost considerable ground relative to manual labor. Since 1955, on the other hand, the earnings of professional men have risen faster than those of any other group, and the relative position of the professional and managerial groups has improved. Clerical workers have also lost ground. Within the manual group, the earnings of skilled and semiskilled workers have fallen moderately relative to those laborers. Farm workers continue to be by far the lowest-paid group in the economy, though their relative position is better today than in the thirties.

Table 2 shows the relative weekly earnings of selected occupational groups in Canada at various dates. Note first that the earnings hierarchy is broadly similar to that in the United States. Note also that the income advantage of the higher occupational groups diminished considerably between 1931 and 1951. After 1951, on the other hand, the wage structure widened moderately, the higher groups improving their position somewhat but still falling well short of their prewar position. These trends are quite similar to those observed in the United States.

The decennial census makes possible a more detailed analysis of annual earnings. The tables, too voluminous to be reproduced here, rank more than 400 occupations in order, with separate rankings for men and women workers. They reveal that, within each broad occupational category, there is a wide range of earnings for specific occupations. In the professional group, for example, doctors are number 1 on the list, but high school teachers are 150 and clergymen are 316, at about the level of semiskilled factory workers. The highest-paid skilled craft, airline pilots, is number 8; but painters, because of irregular employment as well as lower skill, are number 321. In the sales category, advertising agents and salesmen are number 84, but retail salesmen are 214.

This means that the broad groupings, instead of being layered neatly above each other as Table 1 suggests, show a great deal of overlap. Airplane pilots earn more than most professional and managerial people. Tool- and diemakers earn more than most clerical workers. Many factory operatives earn more than retail salesmen.[1]

Returning to the problem of explanation, competitive theory does not do too badly in the lower occupational levels which comprise the bulk of the labor force. It makes sense that a routine clerical worker should earn less than a skilled craftsman, and that the craftsman should earn more than the unskilled laborer. The major trends over time, too, can be explained reasonably well on a supply–demand basis. As examples, let us consider the long-term decline of white-collar relative to blue-collar earnings, the shrinkage of the differential between craftsmen and laborers, and the failure of farm laborers to achieve anything like equality with city laborers.

On the first point, a key factor is that high school graduation has been a traditional requirement for white-collar employment; and conversely, graduates have tended to feel themselves entitled to white-collar work. There has been a sustained rise in the proportion of young people who complete high school, from about one fifth in 1910 to almost three-quarters today. This has swollen the supply of would-be white-collar workers. Demand for such workers has also been rising steadily, but apparently not fast enough to prevent a deterioration in their relative earnings.

Consider next the long-run decline of the differential between skilled and unskilled manual workers. In the early 1900s the craftsman received roughly twice as much as the laborer. Today this premium has fallen to only about 40 percent.[2] There may have been some effect of minimum wage legislation and of wage policies of industrial unions in manufacturing,

---

[1] For a summary of the 1960 census tables, see Max A. Ratzich, "A Ranking of U.S. Occupations by Earnings," *Monthly Labor Review* (March 1965). For similar tables from the 1970 census, see Dixie Sommers, "Occupational Rankings for Men and Women by Earnings," *Monthly Labor Review* (August 1974).

[2] Harry Ober, "Occupational Wage Differentials, 1907–1947," *Monthly Labor Review* (August 1948), pp. 127–34. See the review of this and other evidence in Lloyd G. Reynolds and Cynthia H. Taft, *The Evolution of Wage Structure* (New Haven: Yale University Press, 1956), Chap. 12; and also Melvin W. Reder, "Wage Differentials: Theory and Measurement," in *Aspects of Labor Economics* (Princeton: Princeton University Press for the National Bureau of Economic Research, 1962), pp. 257–311.

both of which have tended to raise the relative wages of the unskilled. In large measure, however, the shrinkage of differentials can be ascribed to supply–demand trends, and more specifically to the sharp decline in supply of unskilled labor.

In the past, high rural birthrates, plus a steady decline of labor requirements in agriculture, produced a large surplus of farm population, which moved into the lower levels of the urban labor force. The rate of migration from farms has not fallen (it has been consistently about 5 percent per year since 1940), but the absolute numbers have fallen because the farm population has been shrinking. Again, in the first quarter of this century European immigrants numbered more than a million a year. Most of these came from a rural background and entered American industry at the unskilled level. Because of changes in our immigration laws, the number of legal immigrants is now much smaller, and preference is given to occupational skills that are scarce in the United States.

Perhaps most important of all has been the broadening of educational opportunities already mentioned. The three-quarters of each age group who now finish high school certainly do not look to unskilled labor as a career. So recruitment is restricted to dropouts who can find no better alternative. Thus a shrinkage in supply of farm boys, immigrants, and poorly educated Americans has combined to shift the supply curve of unskilled labor to the left. The demand for unskilled labor has also been falling, for reasons noted in Chapter 4. Recall that, as recently as 1930, urban laborers formed 11 percent of the U.S. labor force, compared with about 4 percent today. The wage data suggest, however, that the supply curve has shifted leftward faster than the demand curve, leading to a relative rise in laborers' earnings.

Farm laborers, year in and year out, average only about half as much in earnings as do urban laborers. Why is this apparent disequilibrium not corrected by a flow of labor from country to city? Such a movement has been occurring on a large scale. Over the past several decades many millions of American farmers and their sons have given up farming for other activities. The supply of farm laborers, however, is continually renewed by immigrants, some legal but many illegal, for whom even a low wage in the United States is superior to even lower wages or unemployment at home. The farm lobby has managed thus far to exclude these workers from the minimum wage system; and only recently, mainly in California, has unionism made any appreciable headway. Farm workers' wages are largely market wages, set in markets where supply is abundant and the employer often has substantial monopsony power.

The main puzzles arise when we look at the upper occupational levels. Independent professional practitioners earn about three times as much as laborers, and salaried administrators about twice as much. These averages, moreover, fail to reveal the extremely high salaries of some individuals in these groups—the $200,000 a year surgeon, or the $500,000 a year president of a large corporation.

Educational costs can explain some of the wage premium of the higher occupations; but research studies have concluded that only part of the premium can be explained in this way. An early study by Milton Friedman and Simon Kuznets found that there was a difference varying from 85 to 180 percent between the average incomes of professional and nonprofessional workers in the same community who had been in the labor force for the same number of years. Educational costs, they estimated, could account for a differential of 55 to 70 percent, considerably less than that actually observed. They concluded that "there is nothing surprising about this finding. It is clear that young men are, in fact, not equally free to choose a professional or non-professional career. ... First, the professions require a different level of ability than other pursuits; second, the economic and social stratification of the population leaves only limited segments really free to enter the professions." [3]

We noted in Chapter 3 that limitations of knowledge, family background, and finance still prevent about half the ablest students from low-income families from going to college; and many of those who do go cannot finance the additional costs of an M.B.A., LL.B., or M.D. Moreover, in some professions, including medicine, there are not enough university places even for those able and willing to bear the cost.[4]

The very high salaries of top business executives may arise partly from special features of the market for such executives. This is in large measure an internal labor market, on which competitive forces impinge only indirectly. Intercompany movement at senior executive levels is relatively rare. More commonly, a young executive who has proven his worth to a company settles down to a lifetime career in that company, moving up gradually to successively higher levels in the hierarchy. Top executives, in effect, determine their own salaries, within limits of accepted business practice and stockholders' tolerance.

There is quite a close relation between top executives' salaries and *size* of company, as measured by assets, sales, or profits.[5] This can be

[3] Milton Friedman and Simon Kuznets, *Income from Independent Professional Practice* (New York: National Bureau of Economic Research, 1945), p. 88.

[4] Professor Tibor Scitovsky has hypothesized that there is a relation between the size of the professional differential, country by country and over time, and the proportion of young people admitted to higher education. This seems to be well supported by the evidence. See his "The Trend of Professional Earnings," *American Economic Review* (March 1966), pp. 25–42.

[5] See, for example, the analysis in Wilbur G. Lewellen, *Executive Compensation in Large Industrial Corporations* (New York: National Bureau of Economic Research, 1968). Lewellen found that correlations of salary level with company size over the years 1940 to 1963 were almost invariably significant at the 1 percent level.

rationalized on the ground that large companies require greater effort and ability. It may result also from the rules of thumb used in salary setting. A common principle is that those at one level in the hierarchy should receive a standard premium—say 50 percent—above those at the next lower level. The larger the company, the more levels in the hierarchy, and the higher a figure one comes out with at the top.

Wage Differences Within an Occupation

While part of the inequality of earnings is due to differences in *average* earnings of different occupations, an even larger part is due to differences in earnings *within* the same occupation. A study by Lydall [6] estimated that only one-quarter of the total variation in earnings in the United States could be attributed to the former source, leaving three-quarters attributable to intraoccupation differences.

There are many possible reasons for this rather surprising result. Differences in *annual earnings* arise partly from differences in amount of time worked. Some doctors, lawyers, and architects get a good deal more work during a year than others; and this is true also of carpenters, factory operatives, and farm laborers. This reflects mainly differences in work opportunities, but also to some extent personal preferences, as between income and leisure. To the extent that earnings differences reflect preference, they cannot be regarded as either abnormal or undesirable.

In addition, however, there are substantial differences in *hourly rates of pay*. We noted in Chapter 9 that some companies pay considerably more than others, in the same labor market and for apparently comparable labor. In Chapter 8 we saw that women often receive less than men, and black workers less than white workers, for similar kinds of work. Other differences arise from personal characteristics such as age, where pay rates move upward for a considerable time with increasing age and experience; and ability, where even at the level of routine factory or office work there is usually some variation in wages on a merit basis. These ability differentials are obviously even wider in professional practice and in business management.

One dimension of wage structure not previously examined is *geographic differences* among regions of the country and among different sizes of community in the same region. These differences are substantial. A careful analysis by Victor Fuchs reveals, first, that there are sizable wage differences by size of community, after adjusting for age, sex, color,

---

[6] H. F. Lydall, *The Structure of Earnings* (Oxford: Oxford University Press, 1968).

and education of the labor force.[7] Average hourly earnings rise steadily as one moves from rural areas through communities of increasing size up to the largest metropolitan areas. In the southern region, cities of more than a million population pay 40 percent more than towns of less than 10,000. In regions outside the South, the largest cities pay about 30 percent more than small towns. These differences are much larger than the differences in living costs revealed by Bureau of Labor Statistics surveys, so that there is a sizable difference in *real* wages.

How are these size-of-city differences to be explained? One possibility is that cost-of-living comparisons fail to capture all the costs and disadvantages of big-city life, such as the greater expenditure of time in getting from home to work and the reduced availability of costless outdoor recreation. Another possibility is that there may be differences in labor force quality that are not captured by such objective measures as age and education. It may be true, as tradition has it, that those who migrate to the big city to seek their fortunes are more capable and energetic than those who remain at home.

Still another possibility, as Fuchs points out, is "the existence of a disequilibrium in the supply of labor and capital. Surplus labor from agriculture may tend to move first to the small towns, and then later to the larger cities. Capital may be more readily available in the larger cities. If there is disequilibrium, we should observe a tendency for labor to migrate from small to large cities, and for industry to move in the reverse direction" (p. 34). Such labor and capital flows are actually occurring, but they are apparently too slow to eliminate intercommunity differences in wages.

For regional comparisons, the country may be divided into the northeast and north central states, the mountain and Pacific Coast states, and the southern states. The highest wages in the country are found in the western states, which average about 5 percent above the northeast and north central regions. The largest contrast, however, is between the South and all other regions combined. On a gross basis, the non-South averages about 25 percent above the South. But after adjusting for differences in labor force characteristics—age, education, sex, color—and for differences in city size (the South has a lower percentage of big-city population) Fuchs estimates that the true regional differential is only 9 percent.

A striking feature of the North–South differential is its variability among different kinds of industry and different categories of labor. For

---

[7] Victor R. Fuchs, *Differentials in Hourly Earnings by Region and City Size, 1959* (New York: National Bureau of Economic Research, Occasional Paper 101, 1967). See also Victor R. Fuchs and Richard Perlman, "Recent Trends in Southern Wage Differentials," *Review of Economics and Statistics* (August 1960), pp. 292–300; and James N. Houff, "Area Wages and Living Costs," *Monthly Labor Review* (March 1969), pp. 43–46.

example, in some manufacturing industries (furniture, food products, hosiery) the South has hourly wage rates 20 to 30 percent below the northern level. But in other industries (glass, rayon, bituminous coal, basic steel, pulp and paper) there is virtually no regional difference. The influence of unionism is clearly observable in some of these industries.

The North–South differential is *inversely* related to levels of skill and education; that is, it declines as one moves up the occupational ladder. Fuchs finds that white workers with zero to four years of schooling receive only 70 percent as much in the South as in the North. But white workers with high school education and above received 90 percent as much. This is compatible with a hypothesis that the geographic scope of the labor market broadens as one moves up the occupational ladder. Mobility and potential mobility serve to iron out geographic wage differences more effectively at higher occupational levels than at lower ones.

The regional differential is much wider for nonwhites than for whites. Even after standardizing for age, education, and city size, black male workers earn only 74 percent as much in the South as in the North, while white male workers earn 93 percent as much. The explanation may be partly that there are differences in skill level that are not captured by the years-of-education measure. Southern nonwhites may receive a lower quality of formal education, and also less on-the-job training. Further, market discrimination against nonwhite workers, while present in all regions, may be more severe in the South than elsewhere. This may force nonwhite workers down to occupational levels lower than would be predicted from their educational attainment, while at the same time lowering the market wage for these occupations because of supply pressure.

A NEW APPROACH: PERSONAL VARIABLES
AND THE EARNINGS FUNCTION

A different approach to explaining differences in earnings has recently come into fashion at both theoretical and research levels. This takes off from the "human capital" concept discussed in Chapter 3. It involves an attempt to explain individual earnings directly in terms of personal characteristics. Some of the characteristics which have shown up as significant in research studies are: age, years of schooling, quality of schooling, years of work experience, measures of native ability, father's occupation or other indicators of home background, geographic location, marital status, and union membership.

Note that neither the worker's occupation or industry appears in this list of explanatory variables. This approach appears to bypass the traditional reasoning about labor markets and occupational wage determination. The process by which various personal characteristics exert their influence remains hidden in the "black box" of the regression equation. The labor market and the occupational wage structure must still be lurking somewhere in the background. For example, the strong relation between earnings and years of education must be related to the fact that larger amounts of education prepare for, or at least serve as a screening device for, entrance into higher-paid occupations. But if measures of training, ability, and so on turn out to be good predictors of earnings, one could argue that this bypassing of the labor market is legitimate.

Decisions About Education and Training

Since the amount of education and on-the-job training which a worker acquires early in life has a major influence on subsequent earnings, one must first inquire what determines this amount. Why do some people end up with much larger amounts of human capital than others? In human capital theory, this is a matter of deliberate choice by young people (and their parents), based on a lifetime calculation of prospective benefits and costs. The choice is constrained, however, in two ways. One consideration is differences in individual ability, which can be interpreted as differences in *trainability*. The same investment in education and training will yield higher returns to more able people. The other consideration is access to capital in order to finance educational costs. Children from poor families have less access to finance or, what amounts to the same thing, will have to pay more for each dollar of borrowings.[8]

The returns to additional training can be analyzed in the fashion explained in Chapter 3. The gain to a person with x years of training is the amount the person will earn over and above what could be earned by a completely uneducated and untrained individual. Let us call the latter amount the *earnings base*. The problem, then, is to determine the *surplus* over the earnings base that can be attributed to formal and informal training.

The horizontal axis in Figure 12–1 shows differing amounts that might be invested in training, increasing from left to right in the usual way. The vertical axis shows how much an additional dollar invested in training will yield in future earnings, over and above the earnings base. Look, for example, at curve D_3, which relates to a particular individual. The first bit of investment in training yields a large return, indicated by G. As more and more money is devoted to education and training, however, the returns gradually decline. D_3 slopes downward to the right. Hu-

---

[8] For detailed development of this line of analysis, see Jacob Mincer, "The Distribution of Labor Incomes: A Survey with Special Reference to the Human Capital Approach," *Journal of Economic Literature* (March 1970), pp. 1–26.

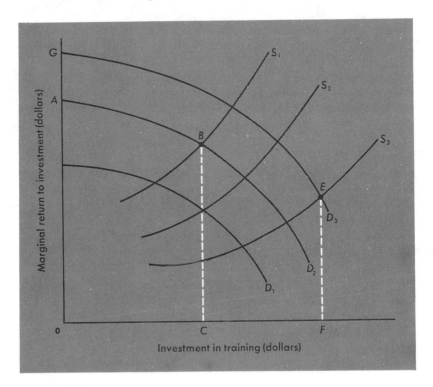

Figure 12–1

Effect of Training and Ability on Earnings

man capacities are limited, and hence successive units of investment yield diminishing returns.

The fact that some people's D curves are higher than others—as illustrated by D_1, D_2, and D_3—means that the same amount of investment in training yields larger returns to some individuals than to others. This reflects *differences in ability,* in the sense of trainability and potential productivity.

The D curves are *demand curves for training,* reflecting the additional income that it yields. The S curves, on the other hand, are *supply curves,* indicating how much the individual in question would be willing to invest in order to achieve a certain expected return. Look, for example, at S_3. Its upward slope indicates that, as the prospective return to training rises, the amount that will be invested in training also rises.

Why do the S curves differ? Why will some people invest more than others for the same prospective return? The most plausible explanation is differences in access to financing. Some people (or their parents) find it easier than others to finance additional investments in training. The *S* curves, then, can be interpreted as *opportunity curves,* while the *D* curves are *ability curves.*

An individual's investment in training, and the earnings level that flows from this, is determined by the intersection of his specific *D* and *S* curves. Thus, an individual whose situation is indicated by D_2 and S_1 would settle at point *B*. One with the curves D_3 and S_3 would settle at point *E*.

We can also determine from Figure 12–1 how much each individual will earn over the earnings base. Consider the man whose equilibrium is at *B*. The first little bit of investment in his training yields a return of *A*. Each additional unit of investment yields less than the previous one, as we travel down D_2. At the investment level *C,* the total addition to his earnings is the area *OABC,* that is, the *area under the returns curve.*[9] By the same reasoning, the man whose equilibrium is at *E* will earn an amount *OGEF* over the earnings base.

There are millions of intersection points such as *B* and *E,* one for each labor force member. The degree of inequality in labor incomes depends on how these intersection points are distributed over the diagram in a particular economy at a particular time.

To illustrate, consider three hypothetical cases:

1. Suppose one could establish *equality of opportunity*—equal access to finance for training, and equal willingness to borrow in response to a given rate of return. In terms of Figure 12–1, all those in the market would then have the same *S* curve. (It will be useful to sketch a revised Figure 12–1 in order to visualize the consequences.) It is clear that this would not bring about equality of incomes. A more able individual, one with a higher *D* curve, would still invest more and achieve larger lifetime earnings than a less able individual. But the degree of inequality would be less than if differences of opportunity were also present.

2. Suppose, on the other hand, that all people are of equal *ability*—they have the same *D* curve (and again, a sketch will be useful). Here inequality of earnings depends solely on differences in opportunity. The people with greater opportunity will invest more; but the marginal return to their investment will be lower, and their earnings may or may not be higher, depending on the slope of the *D* curve.

3. Suppose, finally, that the *D* and *S* curves are not independent of each other but are positively correlated—individuals with greater ability also have lower financing costs. It is not hard to find reasons why this might be so. Part of what appears as greater ability is doubtlessly not genetically determined but reflects greater motivation arising from a superior home environment. Here one has opportunity masquerading as ability. Parents with more education and

---

[9] Writing the earnings function as $E = f(I)$, the marginal return to investment is dE/dI. The total return to investment up to any level, *C,* is the integral of this function over the range in question. The reasoning is identical with that for the relation between marginal utility and total utility, or marginal cost and total cost.

larger incomes are likely *both* to encourage their children to persevere with education *and* also to be better able to finance the necessary costs.

A diagram illustrating this possibility would show the people having the most favorable (highest) *D* curves as also having the most favorable (farthest to the right) *S* curves. The outcome would be a strong positive relation between ability, amount invested in training, and level of earnings, which would produce marked inequality in the distribution of labor income.

The Earnings Function

Early work on personal determinants of earnings, inspired by the human capital approach, focused on the effect of years of schooling. As research has continued, however, it has become clear that other important influences are at work. These include quality of schooling, amount of on-the-job training after leaving school, personal ability, and family background. The statistical problem is to estimate the relative importance of these and other factors. One would also like to know just how they produce their effect. What do additional years of schooling do for the individual? How does superior home background raise a person's earning power? And so on. Let us look briefly at the state of knowledge on these points.

1. *Quantity of schooling.* The relation between years of formal education and subsequent earning power is by now firmly established. Schooling matters, even after taking due account of ability and other factors. But there is still uncertainty about just how education raises individual earning power.

The most obvious surmise is that education inculcates skills which raise potential productivity. This is clearest for high school vocational programs, for college training in engineering and other technical fields, for postgraduate training in law, medicine, or business administration. But what about academic curriculum in high school, or liberal arts majors at the college level? Supporters of liberal education maintain that it provides training in logical reasoning, in oral and written communication, in understanding and coping with one's physical and social environment. It may also be true that, apart from the specific subjects studied, completing an educational program develops qualities of persistence, initiative, responsibility, good work habits, skill in human relations, and ability to continue learning in later life, all of which are valuable for subsequent employment. The evidence on these points, however, is largely indirect, consisting in the fact that employers are willing to pay more for more highly educated people.

There are other ways in which education might contribute to higher earnings. There is evidence that more educated people, and particularly more educated women, have higher labor force participation rates; and also that the number of hours worked per year varies positively with education. This raises *annual* earnings, in addition to any premium in *hourly* rates. Education may also increase the worker's ability to find his way through the labor market maze. One study of a national sample of young men found that their scores on an occupational information test were positively related to years of education, as well as to measured intelligence and socioeconomic status of parents. A follow-up study two years later found that those with better information had also succeeded in getting higher-paid jobs.[10]

Another interesting hypothesis is that education serves as a convenient screening device for employers. An employer is interested in qualities of intelligence, teachability, good work habits, and so on. It is difficult, however, to test for these qualities directly. So employers use information about education, which is readily available and costless, as a proxy for desirable characteristics that are harder to determine, and specify some educational level as a prerequisite for employment. The result is that many of the less educated, who could perform satisfactorily in high-paying occupations, are screened out of those occupations and crowded into jobs lower down the wage ladder. The result is to increase the earnings gap. Taubman and Wales estimate that as much as half of the higher earnings associated with additional earnings may arise from the screening effect rather than from productivity differences.[11]

2. *Quality of schooling.* In a country as large and diverse as the United States, there are marked differences in school quality at every level from first grade through postgraduate education. Whatever it is that education does, some schools do it better than others. Thus years of education alone are not a satisfactory measure of educational input.

How can one measure school quality? The commonest procedure is to use school expenditures per pupil, which implies that more dollars must be buying more quality (though this supposition is disputed by some educators). Some studies have also used physical input indicators, such as class size and average educational level of teachers. At the college and postgraduate level, there has been some use of rankings of colleges and universities compiled by national associations. Most studies find that, for persons with the same number of years of education, there is a significant relation between earnings and indicators of school quality.[12]

This influence of quality shows up also in indirect ways. We noted in Chapter 8 that, for people aged thirty and upward, the rate of return to education is considerably lower for black workers than for white workers. But for those who have entered the labor force during the past ten years or so, this no longer seems to be true. Education now pays off as well for blacks as for whites. Reduction in labor market discrimination may be partly responsible. But another possible explanation is that the quality of education received by blacks has in recent years been rising more rapidly than that of whites, and

---

[10] Herbert S. Parnes and Andrew J. Kohen, "Occupational Information and Labor Market Status: The Case of Young Men," *Journal of Human Resources* (Winter 1975), pp. 44–55.

[11] The screening hypothesis is developed in Paul Taubman and Terence Wales, *Higher Education and Earnings* (New York: McGraw-Hill Book Company, 1974); and Paul Taubman and Terence J. Wales, "Higher Education, Mental Ability, and Screening," *Journal of Political Economy* (January/February 1973), pp. 28–55. For a critical view, see Richard Layard and George Psacharopoulos, "The Screening Hypothesis and the Returns to Education," *Journal of Political Economy* (September/October 1974), pp. 985–98.

[12] Studies emphasizing school quality include George E. Johnson and Frank P. Stafford, "Social Returns to Quantity and Quality of Schooling," *Journal of Human Resources* (Spring 1973), pp. 139–55; and Lewis J. Perl, "Family Background, Secondary School Expenditure, and Student Ability," *Journal of Human Resources* (Spring 1973), pp. 156–80.

that this reduction of the quality gap is partly responsible for reduction of the earnings gap.[13]

3. *On-the-job training.* Work-related training does not end when one leaves school. Many occupations are entered through apprenticeship programs, internship programs, or in-plant training programs, plus supplementary training and upgrading of skills as the person moves up a promotion ladder. Apart from formal programs, there is much learning by doing and learning under supervision, which accrues with additional years of experience on a job.

Entrance jobs differ widely in the opportunities for continued learning and advancement which they provide. This has always been taken into account in theorizing about occupational wage differences. Recently, however, Mincer and others have constructed more elaborate models of worker choice on this point.[14] A worker is regarded as being simultaneously in two markets: a market for current wages and a market for training opportunities. Alternative jobs offer different mixes of these two things. Some offer large (and valuable) training benefits, offset by a relatively low current wage, while other jobs offer a higher immediate wage but less training.

A young worker who takes a lifetime view of prospective income, and who is adequately informed, will choose among these opportunities according to his preference for present versus future income. Some may "take the cash and let the credit go." Others may accept a lower current income on a job whose large training component is expected to raise earnings in later life. Different preferences on this point will produce substantial dispersion of earnings both among young workers, some of whom are investing more heavily in training than others, and also among mature workers, who are now profiting in varying degree from their earlier investment.

One difficulty with testing these ideas statistically is that on-the-job training takes a variety of forms, and that direct measures of it are usually not available. This is commonly met by taking years of work experience as a convenient proxy. To the extent that training consists of learning by doing and learning under supervision, so that years of training and years of experience come to the same thing, this may be an appropriate procedure. But then there is a question whether this semiautomatic training is something which the worker chooses, or rather something which the employer chooses and indeed may insist on.

Length of work experience usually is positively related to earnings, after taking account of other variables; but the interpretation of this result is not entirely clear. We noted earlier that most jobs carry a range of wage rates or salary levels, within which workers tend to move up on a seniority basis. Promotion to higher-rated jobs is also strongly influenced by length of service, particularly in unionized establishments. The long-service worker has probably also learned more over the years, but even apart from this he will tend to earn more because of the hierarchical structure of jobs and salaries.

4. *Ability.* This is one of the more mysterious variables in the earnings function. One should probably speak of *abilities,* to take account of the many dimensions of personal capacity: mathematical ability, verbal capacity, health and physical vigor, nervous energy, personality characteristics which are help-

---

[13] See Finis Welch, "Black–White Differences in Returns to Schooling," *American Economic Review* (December 1973), pp. 893-907.

[14] See, in particular, Jacob Mincer, *Schooling, Experience, and Earnings* (New York: National Bureau of Economic Research, 1974).

ful or harmful in personal relations. It is not clear which of these (or others) are most directly related to productivity. Some studies have found that tests of mathematical aptitude were significantly related to earnings while other test scores were not; but there is little firm knowledge in this area.

Along with this variety of aptitudes, there is a wide variety of statistical indicators, and researchers have tended to lay hands on whatever was most readily available. IQ scores, class rank in high school or college, mathematical and verbal aptitude scores on college and graduate school entrance examinations, armed forces test scores, and other indicators have been used. It is not clear which of these is the best predicter of earnings. It is also unclear how far IQ and similar scores reflect "inherent ability" in the sense of genetic endowment, and how far they reflect early parental training and encouragement, school quality, and other environmental factors.

Even with the crude instruments available, however, one can conclude that ability is significantly related to earnings. Some studies have concluded that it is as important as education—that is, that the earnings variance among people of differing ability with the same years of education is as wide as that among people with the same measured ability but different amounts of education.

Ability and schooling, of course, are interrelated in a complex fashion. More able people tend to receive more years of schooling. Moreover, there is considerable evidence that differences in ability create greater differences in earnings at higher schooling levels, which could be explained on the ground that the more educated are employed in occupations where ability has a greater chance to show itself. There are indications also that differences in schooling create greater differences in earnings at higher levels of ability, which could be interpreted as meaning that the capacity-enhancing effects of education are greatest for the ablest people. We are still at an early stage in trying to sort out these interactions.[15]

5. *Socioeconomic status of parents.* Different studies have used such indicators as family income level, father's occupational level, father's years of education, and mother's years of education. However measured, the family's socioeconomic status shows up as having a significant influence on the subsequent earnings of children. There are several possible channels of family influence. More educated and affluent families are likely to push their children toward more years of education—it takes some time for young people's preferences to supersede those of their parents! Higher-income families can afford to buy more years of college and graduate education. Early training and encouragement in the home may raise children's IQ scores, motivation for learning, and school performance, enabling them to move more smoothly up the educational escalator. Finally, parental advice and influence may help young people to land better jobs after graduation. While we suspect that all these mechanisms are operative, their relative importance is unclear.[16]

---

[15] In addition to the studies cited earlier, see John C. Hause, "Ability and Schooling as Determinents of Lifetime Earnings, or If You're So Smart, Why Aren't You Rich?" in F. Thomas Juster (ed.), *Education, Income and Human Behavior* (New York: McGraw-Hill Book Company, 1975); and Paul Taubman, "Earnings, Education, Genetics, and Environment," *Journal of Human Resources* (Fall 1976), pp. 447–61.

[16] In addition to studies cited earlier, see Jere Behrman and Paul Taubman, "Intergenerational Transmission of Income and Wealth," *American Economic Review* (May 1976), pp. 436–40.

It cannot be overemphasized that the "earnings function" approach to an explanation of earnings differences is still at an early stage of development, and that it is beset by numerous problems and difficulties. It emphasizes the *supply* of personal characteristics to the labor market, leaving demand influences in the background. For most of the important variables, only proxy indicators are available, and it is not clear which proxies are most reliable. The theoretical predictions usually relate to comparison of *lifetime earnings streams,* involving a trade-off of lower income during the years of schooling and on-the-job training against higher income later on. Since we have little data on lifetime earnings, we fall back on comparisons of earnings in a *single year* by people with differing characteristics; but this is not really a satisfactory substitute.

The most basic difficulty, however, is that the ultimate determinants of earnings are interrelated in a complicated way, which so far has been rather resistant to statistical analysis. Some of the complications are suggested by Figure 12-2.[17] The influence of home background ramifies in several directions. Heredity has an effect on mental ability, physical stamina, and other personal characteristics. Further, what *appears* as intelligence in childhood IQ tests is partly cultural, and is influenced by parental encouragement to learning in the home. Parental education and income influences the child's years of schooling; and family influence may also help him acquire a job with superior earnings.

The child's ability, in turn, affects both his chances of getting admitted to higher educational institutions and his performance in those institutions.

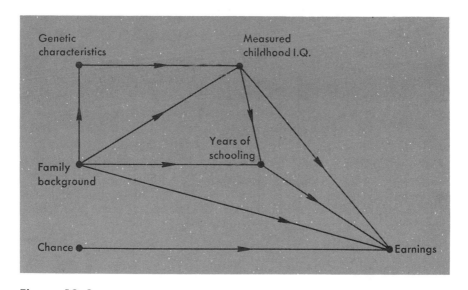

Figure 12–2

Influences on Individual Earnings

---

[17] Figure 12–2 is adapted from a similar figure in A. B. Atkinson, *The Economics of Inequality* (Oxford: Oxford University Press, 1975), p. 92.

Ability also affects earnings directly, independently of years of education. Nor should the arrow reflecting "chance" be neglected.

The statistical association between years of schooling and subsequent earnings is undoubtedly genuine, and has been confirmed by dozens of statistical studies. But it is not yet clear what this means in terms either of ultimate explanation or of how far inequality might be reduced by policy measures. Estimates of the separate effect—whatever that may mean—of education, ability, home background, and other factors show considerable variation in results. One can say only that here is a major research frontier, which should in time contribute importantly to our understanding of earnings inequality.

Substitute or Supplement to Market Reasoning?

What is the significance of the earnings function "revolution"? Is it a substitute for the traditional theory of occupational wage differences, rendering the latter unnecessary? Or it is a complementary approach, which can be fitted into the framework of market economics?

While it will take time for this issue to be resolved, the latter outcome seems more likely. No one doubts that workers and employers are participants in a labor market. No one doubts that demand and supply forces influence relative occupational wage rates at any point in time, and changes in these relationships over time.

What the earnings function approach mainly does is to provide a more penetrating analysis of supply decisions. In earlier writings, the worker was regarded as choosing among a spectrum of jobs on the basis of their characteristics and his own preference system. But this was viewed (unrealistically) as a one-time decision which could be reopened at any subsequent time, the basis of choice was not fully explored, and the constraints on choice were not clearly stated. The earnings function approach, with its strong emphasis on human capital, makes it clear that the most significant decisions are made early in life, that the key choice is how much education and training to acquire, that this choice is constrained by ability and access to capital, that the rational and informed individual will calculate in terms of lifetime rather than immediate earnings, and that differing time preferences are important in this realm just as they are in consumption and saving decisions. All this has enriched our understanding of educational and occupational choices.

It is equally clear, however, that earnings function analysis cannot explain everything. Regressions using education, ability, and other personal variables usually explain (in a statistical sense) only half to two-thirds of the observed variance of earnings. The remaining variance could be attributed simply to random forces. But it is more plausible to attribute it to factors which have always been considered important in labor market analysis.

To illustrate: a recent study [18] of a large sample of mature male workers started out by using the usual education and experience variables. Education, experience, and other personal characteristics (not, however, including measures of ability) explained about 40 percent of the observed variation in hourly earnings. There remained, however, wide variation in earnings even among men with the same amount of human capital.

To explain this residual variation, the authors ran a further analysis using traditional labor market variables. This revealed that, among men with the same amount of human capital, earnings were influenced significantly by (1) city size—residence in a standard metropolitan area is associated with a premium of about 15 percent in average hourly earnings; (2) region of the country, with western states relatively high and southern states relatively low; (3) occupation, with professional, technical, and managerial workers earning more, and farm laborers earning less, than their stock of human capital alone would warrant; (4) industry, where workers in government and in industries relatively sheltered from competition fare better than workers in trade, services, and other competitive sectors; and (5) union membership, where membership in an industrial union brought a wage premium of about 12 percent, and membership in a craft union about 24 percent.

Such results suggest that, while the earnings function approach has brought greater depth of analysis on the supply side, this does not deny the influence of labor market variables which have long been regarded as important.

DISCUSSION QUESTIONS

1. Explain the main reasons why occupational wage differences would exist in a purely competitive labor market.

2. To what extent are occupational differences in the United States today explainable in terms of competitive forces?

3. Suppose you were asked to organize a research project to determine whether there is a shortage of medical practitioners in the United States. How would you define "shortage," and what kinds of data would you analyze?

---

[18] Edward Kalacheck and Fredric Raines, "The Structure of Wage Differences Among Mature Male Workers," *Journal of Human Resources* (Fall 1976), pp. 484–506.

These plausible results suggest that, while earnings function analysis has brought a fresh perspective on earnings differences and greater depth of analysis on the supply side, it has not displaced the labor market variables which have long been regarded as important.

4. Do you expect that earnings of sales and clerical workers will continue to decline relative to those of manual workers? Why, or why not?

5. How can one explain the large difference in earnings between farm and factory workers?

6. Discuss the statistical problems involved in measuring the true wage differential between the southern and northern states.

7. Explain the determinants of individual earnings according to the "earnings function" approach.

8. Does the earnings function approach supersede the traditional theory of occupational wage differentials? Can the two be reconciled?

9. Considering the numerous factors influencing individual earnings, what realistic meaning can one give to the concept of "equal opportunity"?

10. Suppose that equal opportunity, in whatever sense you give to that term, were actually established. Why would there still be differences in individual earnings? Explain.

READING SUGGESTIONS

In addition to the Fuchs, Lydall, Meij, Reder, and Reynolds–Taft studies cited in the chapter, there are several recent books which use the earnings function approach: JACOB MINCER, *Schooling, Experience, and Earnings,* New York: National Bureau of Economic Research, 1974; BARRY R. CHISWICK, *Income Inequality,* New York: National Bureau of Economic Research, 1974; PAUL TAUBMAN and TERENCE WALES, *Higher Education and Earnings,* New York: McGraw-Hill Book Company, 1974; THOMAS F. JUSTER (ed.), *Education, Income, and Human Behavior,* New York: McGraw-Hill Book Company, 1975; GILBERT R. GHEZ and GARY S. BECKER, *The Allocation of Time and Goods over the Life Cycle,* New York: National Bureau of Economic Research, 1975.

13

Inequality, Poverty, and Public Policy

Inequality of income is a familiar fact of life. Some people in the United States have incomes of more than a million dollars a year. Many others have incomes of only a few thousand. But when we set out to measure the *degree* of inequality, and changes in this measure over the course of time, we run immediately into several difficulties.

1. *What is income?* The most obvious meaning is cash plus cash equivalents (such as farm produce consumed on the farm) actually received during a year or other time period. But what about increases in the value of homes, stocks and bonds, and other assets? Suppose that at the beginning of the year I have securities with a market value of $100,000. At the end of the year, because of a rise in the market, these securities are worth $110,000. The extra $10,000 constitutes *potential* income, which could be realized and (after paying taxes on the capital gain) could be spent without reducing my wealth. Most economists agree that such items should be counted as part of income; but statistical measurements usually count only income actually received.

2. *What time period?* The usual measures relate to income in a calendar year. But part of the inequality which appears in such tables arises from the fact that people are at different stages in the life cycle. Some are young people just entering the labor market, with relatively low earnings. Some are mature workers at the peak of their earning power. Some are older people living on a reduced retirement income. Thus even if *lifetime earnings* were completely equal, there would be considerable variation in annual earnings. Measures of inequality probably should relate to lifetime earnings; but in fact, we use annual earnings because this is all we have.

3. *Families or individuals?* Most people live as family members. While there may be two or more income earners in the family, their income is pooled and the family is a single unit for consumption purposes. It makes sense, therefore, to tabulate the amount of income received by each family unit rather than by each individual. This still omits one bit of information which is important for welfare judgments, namely, differences in family size. An income

which would yield a comfortable standard of living for two people may be quite inadequate when spread over a family of eight. Information on income by family size can be obtained from Census sources, but we shall not go into that degree of detail here.

In addition to members of family units, there were in 1975 some 20 million people living by themselves. The average income of these people was much below the average of family incomes because, first, there is by definition only one income earner and, second, they tend to be younger or older people whose incomes are relatively low for the reasons already mentioned. It is important, therefore, always to tabulate the incomes of unrelated individuals separately from those of families.

MEASURES OF INCOME DISTRIBUTION

The Census Bureau makes frequent sample surveys of household incomes from which estimates can be made for the population as a whole. The distribution of income for families and unrelated individuals in 1975 is shown in Table 1. The majority of families fall within an income range of $10,000 to $30,000 a year. They are "middle-income families" in the literal sense. But there is a long tail to the income distribution at either end. At the bottom are several million families and several million more unrelated individuals with the incredibly low income of $3,000 a year or

Table 1

Distribution of Families and Unrelated Individuals by Income Level, 1975

	Families		Unrelated Individuals	
Total Income	Thousands	Percent	Thousands	Percent
Under $2,000	1,209	2.1	2,863	14.1
2,000– 2,999	1,356	2.4	3,152	15.6
3,000– 3,999	1,908	3.4	2,518	12.4
4,000– 4,999	2,293	4.1	1,796	8.9
5,000– 5,999	2,310	4.1	1,468	7.2
6,000– 6,999	2,351	4.2	1,173	5.8
7,000– 7,999	2,444	4.3	1,159	5.7
8,000– 9,999	4,815	8.6	1,838	9.1
10,000–11,999	5,012	8.9	1,296	6.4
12,000–14,999	7,549	13.4	1,355	6.7
15,000–24,999	17,066	30.3	1,318	6.5
25,000 and over	7,931	14.1	298	1.5
Total	56,245	100.0	20,234	100.0
Median income	$13,719		$4,882	

SOURCE: Bureau of the Census, *Current Population Reports,* Series P-60, No. 103 (September 1976), p. 18.

less. At the top—not revealed by the rough classification in Table 1—are a substantial number of people with incomes of $100,000 or more, and a small number in the million-a-year range.

Suppose that, instead of Table 1, we want a single number summarizing the degree of inequality in the United States. Such a number is almost a necessity if we want to compare inequality among countries, or changes in the same country over the course of time. The measure most commonly used is illustrated in Figure 13–1. On the horizontal axis we measure percentages of household units, while the vertical axis shows percentages of total personal income. If income distribution were perfectly equal, then the first 20 percent of households would receive 20 percent of total income, the first 40 percent of households would receive 40 percent of income, and so on. Income distribution would be represented by points along the straight line *OY*.

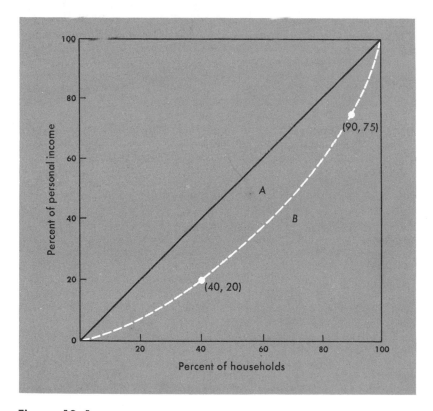

Figure 13–1

The Lorenz Measure of Income Distribution

We may imagine also the opposite extreme of complete inequality. Suppose that one household received all income in the economy, while the other 99.999 percent received nothing at all. Income distribution would then follow the path *OXY*.

Any actual income distribution will fall between these extremes. Suppose that a particular country in a particular year has the distribution shown by the broken line in Figure 13–1. This is called a *Lorenz curve,* after its originator. The curve shown represents a moderately unequal distribution of income. The lowest 40 percent of families receive only 20 percent of total income, while the top 10 percent receive 25 percent of income. If we call the area above the dotted line *A,* and the area below the line *B,* we can get a numerical measure of inequality by dividing *A* by *A + B*. This is termed the *Gini coefficient.* It can have any value between 0 (complete equality) and 1 (complete inequality).

A movement toward greater income equality is shown by a shallower Lorenz curve and a drop in the Gini coefficient. A move toward inequality means a bending outward of the Lorenz curve and a rise in the Gini coefficient.

While the Gini coefficient is the measure most frequently used, it is not the only number which might be considered significant. Use of the Gini coefficient implies that we attach equal importance to every level of the income distribution—we don't care whether a change in the coefficient arises from a change in the top 5 percent or in the bottom 5 percent of the distribution. But suppose instead that we are interested in the poorest groups in the population. A recent international comparison of income distribution, for example, focused on the percentage of personal income received by the poorest 40 percent of income recipients.[1] This gives us another set of numbers which is significant in terms of concern with poverty.

This yardstick shows that socialist countries have the highest degree of income equality. The proportion of income received by the poorest 40 percent of population is typically in the neighborhood of 25 percent—as, for example, Bulgaria (26.8), Poland (23.4), Hungary (24.0), and Czechoslovakia (27.6). The richer capitalist nations show somewhat less equality, the bottom 40 percent of the population typically receiving 15 to 20 percent of personal income—as, for example, Canada and Australia (both 20.0), United States (19.7) United Kingdom (18.8), and Japan (20.7). But some are lower, including France (9.5), Netherlands (13.6), Denmark (13.6), and West Germany (15.4). Most unequal of all is the distribution of income in the less developed countries. In these

---

[1] Hollis Chenery and others, *Redistribution with Growth* (Oxford: Oxford University Press, for the World Bank and the Institute of Development Studies, University of Sussex, 1974).

countries the income share of the poorest 40 percent is frequently below 10 percent and rarely rises about 15 percent. Again, there are exceptions: Pakistan, Thailand, Taiwan, and South Korea have an income distribution about as equal as that of the developed capitalist countries.

THE DETERMINANTS OF HOUSEHOLD DISTRIBUTION

We want first to examine what determines the amount of income received by each household. Next, we must consider that part of this income goes in tax payments to government. It is usually assumed that taxes bear more heavily on the rich than the poor, so that the posttax distribution is more equal than the pretax distribution. What is the evidence on this point? Finally, we must look at changes in inequality over the course of time. Is inequality increasing or decreasing? And can past trends safely be projected into the future?

The Pretax Distribution

It should be reemphasized that part of the inequality which appears in distributions of annual earnings is due to differences in age and consequent stage of the lifetime earnings cycle. Blinder estimates that about 30 percent of inequality comes from this source, and that when it is eliminated the U.S. Gini coefficient falls from about 0.43 to 0.30. The distribution of lifetime earnings, in other words, is considerably more equal than the distribution of annual earnings.[2]

The inequality which remains after this adjustment arises from several factors:

1. *Distribution of labor income.* This is much the largest source of overall income inequality. This has to be true, since wages and salaries constitute about four-fiths of all market-determined income. It follows that movement toward greater equality depends heavily on a reduction in wage differences between higher and lower occupations.

The sources of differences in wage rates were explored in Chapter 12. They include ability differences, unequal educational attainment, restrictions on entrance to occupations, race and sex discrimination, union pressure, and other influences. Differences in *annual* earnings, as distinct from wage rates, are influenced also by the incidence of unemployment. During recession years, many people get less work than they would like and drop into lower income brackets. Income inequality thus tends to increase during a recession and to decrease during an economic upswing.

2. *Distribution of property income.* Most income-yielding property is

---

[2] Alan S. Blinder, *Toward an Economic Theory of Income Distribution* (Cambridge, Mass.: The MIT Press, 1974), p. 139.

held by a small minority of the population. The top 5 percent of income recipients in the United States receive more than two-thirds of all dividend payments and about half of all property income. The concentration of property income is much greater than that of labor income. The top 5 percent of income recipients get only about 10 percent of total wage and salary payments.

Property income is unequally distributed because property itself is unequally distributed. But what determines the distribution of property? Here we have no real theory, perhaps because the answer depends on institutional factors that economists find hard to quantify and manipulate. Relevant factors in a particular society include whether rich families have more or fewer children than poor families; the extent to which rich boys tend to marry rich girls; whether property is equally distributed among children on death or whether the eldest takes all (primogeniture); how heavily government taxes gifts and inheritances; and the ease of accumulating property during one's lifetime, which depends partly on the tax structure.[3]

3. *The labor and property shares.* Here we are back on familiar ground and can rely on the analysis of Chapter 11. Since labor income is more equally distributed than property income, an increase in labor's share will make for a more equal overall distribution, and conversely. Since such shifts are gradual and moderate, however, they cannot explain a major part of changes in inequality.

4. *Demographic and related factors.* Reaching deeper into our bag of *ad hoc* considerations, we come up with several, related to labor force behavior. First, the distribution of labor income among female workers and among young workers is considerably more unequal than that among adult males, partly because these groups have higher unemployment rates and are in and out of the labor force more frequently. Thus the proportion that these groups form of the national labor force will affect the overall distribution of labor incomes.

The agricultural population also shows greater income inequality than the urban population, because farmers are entrepreneurs and capitalists as well as laborers, and American farms differ greatly in size, fertility, capital stock, and productivity. The average level of farm incomes is also relatively low. The ratio of farm families to urban families will thus affect the overall income distribution.

Further, when we move from analysis of *individual* earning power to analysis of *household* incomes, the number of wage earners per family becomes relevant. Particularly important is the growing tendency for married women to remain in the labor market or to reenter it after they are past the peak of child rearing. If married women's propensity to work were randomly distributed over all income brackets, it would not alter the national income distribution. But this is not the case. We saw in Chapter 2 that there is an inverse relation with the husband's income level, that is, the lower the husband's income, the greater the likelihood of the wife working. The fact that double incomes are more common at the lower occupational levels tends to pull up the bottom of the income distribution and to reduce inequality.

5. *Size of transfer payments.* Up to this point we have been examining reasons for differences in market-determined incomes, that is, incomes received

---

[3] See on this point Frederic L. Pryor, "Simulation of the Impact of Social and Economic Institutions on the Size Distribution of Income and Wealth," *American Economic Review* (March 1973), pp. 50–72.

in return for work or for ownership of capital. In addition, however, households receive large amounts outside the market system from government transfer payments. Such payments have been growing quite rapidly, both in absolute terms and as a percentage of personal income. The total in 1975 was $175 billion, or about 14 percent of all personal income in that year. More than half of this was retirement benefits to older people under the Social Security system. The remainder included veterans' benefits, other government retirement programs, unemployment compensation, aid to families with dependent children ("welfare"), and subsidies to low-income groups for consumption of food, medical care, and housing.

These transfers go heavily to the lower income brackets. For households with incomes below $3,000, income from government transfers is larger than income from all other sources. More than half of all transfer payments go to families that, without such transfers, would have been below the poverty line.[4] The result is to lift several million households and individuals (largely older people) out of the poverty group. Even so, other millions of families continue to be poor, for reasons to be examined later in this chapter.

Does the Tax Structure
Reduce Inequality?

Thus far we have been talking about the distribution of money received by households, from market transactions or from transfer payments. But over one-quarter of this income goes in tax payments to federal, state, and local governments. What matters to a household is how much it has left for personal use *after* tax payments. So we must ask how the tax burden is distributed among income brackets, and whether the tax system has an equalizing effect on posttax incomes.

This problem is complicated by considerable uncertainty over who actually pays a particular kind of tax. Some cases are clear. The personal income tax is paid by me, and I also pay the state sales tax when I go shopping. But what about the corporate income tax? Does this fall on stockholders through a reduction of corporate profits? Or is some of it passed on to consumers in higher prices, or perhaps passed back to employees in lower wages? What about payroll taxes on employers for Social Security and unemployment compensation? Are these passed on to consumers like other business costs, or passed back to employees via a reduction in the wage which the employer is willing to pay?

Because of these uncertainties, one cannot make any flat statement about how much of the tax burden falls on each income bracket. First, one must specify one's assumptions about who actually pays each tax in the system. A major study by Pechman and Okner [5] considers eight cases, each

---

[4] See studies cited in Robert J. Lampman, *Ends and Means of Reducing Income Poverty* (Chicago: Markham Publishing Company, 1971), Chap. 6.

[5] Joseph A. Pechman and Benjamin A. Okner, *Who Bears the Tax Burden?* (Washington, D.C.: The Brookings Institution, 1974).

Table 2

Effective Rates of Federal, State, and Local Taxes Under Various Incidence
Assumptions, by Adjusted Family Income Class, 1966

Adjusted Family Income (Thousands of Dollars)	Effective Total Tax Rate (Percent of Income)	
	Case 1a	Case 3a
0–3	19.5	23.6
3–5	21.7	22.9
5–10	23.5	25.1
10–15	23.6	25.3
15–20	24.0	25.0
20–25	24.7	24.9
25–30	25.4	24.4
30–50	26.8	23.9
50–100	31.2	26.8
100–500	38.5	34.0
500–1,000	41.5	38.2
1,000 and over	41.2	38.5
All classes	25.5	25.7

representing a different set of assumptions about tax incidence. The results
of two of their cases are shown in Table 2.

The assumptions of case 1a are as follows: the individual income tax
falls on taxpayers; the corporate income tax falls on property income in
general; sales and excise taxes are paid by consumers of the taxed commodities; a tax on land is paid by landowners; a property tax on buildings
falls on property income; employees pay their share of a payroll tax; the
employer's share of the payroll tax is shifted backward to employees in
lower wages.

In case 3a, five of these assumptions are the same, but two important
ones are modified as follows: only half the corporate income tax comes
out of dividends, while one-quarter is shifted forward in higher prices and
one-quarter is shifted backward in lower wages; and the property tax on
buildings is shifted forward entirely to consumers. These changes in
assumptions raise the tax burden on lower income brackets and reduce the
burden on higher brackets.

While the results of these cases differ in detail, the broad picture is
the same. The tax impact is nearly proportional over the income range from
zero to $50,000 a year, which includes the great majority of the population.
People with incomes of $5,000 a year pay about as large a percentage of
their income in taxes as do people with incomes ten times as high. The
progressive effect of the personal and corporate income taxes is about off-

set by the regressive effect of other taxes in the system. Only above $50,000 a year does the percentage taken in taxes rise appreciably, because of the heavier bite of the personal and corporate income tax.

It follows that the tax structure has only a slight equalizing effect on the distribution of household incomes. The Lorenz curve for the posttax distribution lies very close to that for the pretax distribution. In all of the Pechman–Okner cases, the reduction in the area of inequality is less than 5 percent.

This does *not* mean that the *fiscal system as a whole* has little effect on income distribution. It means merely that the equalizing effect comes mainly from transfer payments rather than tax collections. The fact that transfer payments go mainly to the lowest income brackets does shift the Lorenz curve and the Gini coefficient considerably. As Okner concludes in another study,[6] "transfer payments have a much greater effect on the after-tax and transfer distribution of income than do tax payments. For all families, transfer payments account for about three quarters of the reduction in the area of inequality, whereas taxes account for one fourth of the total change."

TRENDS IN INCOME INEQUALITY

What has happened to household distribution in the United States and elsewhere over the long run. Has inequality been increasing or decreasing, and why?

We have already noted that it makes a difference whether one looks at income before or after taxes. The tax structure has some equalizing effect, and this effect is stronger today that it was fifty years ago. More interesting, however, is the fact that the *pretax* distribution has also become somewhat more equal. Evidence of this for the United States and a number of other countries has been assembled by Professor Simon Kuznets.[7] As an indication of inequality he takes the percentage of national income received by the top 5 percent of households or tax units. Some of his results are summarized in Table 3. Note that for every country the share of the top income group is lower in the post–World War II period than in earlier periods. For some countries the decline of inequality can be traced back to before 1900. In other countries it seems to have begun with World War I, and in the United States the decline began still later, during the 1930s. The general direction of movement, however, is consistent for

---

[6] Benjamin A. Okner, "Individual Taxes and the Distribution of Income," in James D. Smith (ed.), *The Personal Distribution of Income and Wealth* (New York: National Bureau of Economic Research, 1975), p. 65.

[7] Simon Kuznets, *Modern Economic Growth* (New Haven: Yale University Press, 1966), pp. 208–11.

Table 3

Percent of Pretax Income Received by Top 5 Percent of Consuming Units, Selected Countries, Long Periods

United States		Netherlands	
1929	30	1938	19
1935–36	26.5	1949	17
1944–47	21	1954	13
1955–59	20	*Denmark*	
United Kingdom		1870	36.5
		1903	28
1880	48	1925	26
1913	43	1939	24.5
1929	33	1955	17.5
1938	31	*Norway*	
1947	24		
1957	18	1907	27
		1938	20
Germany—West Germany		1948	14
1913	31	*Sweden*	
1928	21	1930	30
1936	23	1935	28
1950	24	1948	20
1959	18	1954	17

all countries. It is interesting also that the share of pretax income received by the top 5 percent is now so nearly similar in the Western industrial nations.

Additional detail for the United States is provided by Table 4. This shows, for selected years over a forty-year period, the share of personal income received by the lowest 20 percent of income recipients, the next 20 percent, and so on up to the top 20 percent and top 5 percent of families. It is clear that there was a shift toward greater equality over this period. The proportion of personal income received by the top 5 percent of families fell from 30 to 15 percent, that of the top 20 percent from 54 to 41 percent.

At the bottom of the scale, the percentage of real income going to the poorest groups in the population has risen somewhat more than Table 4 suggests. The reason is that the Census Bureau surveys on which the table is based count *money income only*. In addition to cash, however, the poorest groups receive substantial transfers in kind through the food stamp program, the Medicaid program of free medical care, and subsidized hous-

Table 4

Distribution of Family Personal Income Among Consumer Units in Various Years

	Percent Distribution				
Quintiles	*1929*	*1935–36*	*1947*	*1962*	*1974*
Lowest	} 13	4	5	5	5
Second		9	11	11	12
Third	14	14	16	16	18
Fourth	19	21	22	23	24
Highest	54	52	46	45	41
Top 5 percent	30	27	21	20 .	15

SOURCE: Data for 1929–62 are from Bernard F. Haley, "Income Distribution in the Unted States," in the I.E.A. symposium volume, *The Distribution of National Income* (New York: St. Martin's Press, Inc., 1968). Data for 1974 are from Bureau of the Census, *Current Population Reports,* Series P-60, No. 103 (September 1976), p. 18.

ing rentals. Such transfers have risen especially rapidly since about 1960, and including them would show a larger increase in the low-income share.

The shift toward equality was particularly strong between 1935 and 1947. The Great Depression brought a reduction of property incomes and an increase in transfer payments to those at the bottom of the income structure. The forties brought a marked reduction in wage differences among occupations. Since the late forties the trend toward equalization has slowed down, and some statistical measures fail to reveal any significant change in income distribution. When we look below the aggregates to specific age and sex groups, we find that income inequality among adult males continued to decline quite rapidly during the fifties and sixties. But this has been partly offset by the fact that women and young people, whose income distribution is less equal than for adult men, have formed a growing proportion of the labor force.[8]

The reasons for the long-run trend toward greater equality are to be found in the determinants listed above, most of which have been operating in an equalizing direction. Occupational wage differences have been shrinking. Inequality in property ownership, while still high, is not as high as it was fifty years ago.[9] The property share of income has been falling and

---

[8] See T. Paul Schultz, "Secular Trends and Cyclical Behavior of Income Distribution in the United States, 1944–1965," in Lee Soltow (ed.), *Six Papers on the Size Distribution of Wealth and Income* (New York: Columbia University Press for the National Bureau of Economic Research, 1969).

[9] Simon Kuznets, *Shares of Upper-Income Groups in Income and Savings* (New York: National Bureau of Economic Research, 1953).

the labor share rising. The low-income agricultural sector is an ever smaller part of the total economy. Government transfer payments, which were very small in 1930, have risen rapidly since that time.

It is dangerous to project past trends into the future, but it does seem that future changes are more likely to be toward equality than away from it. This is not intended as an argument for complacency. The question whether movement toward equality can and should be accelerated by public policy will be examined at the end of the chapter.

POVERTY: MEANING, EXTENT, SOURCES

Turning to policy issues, it seems well to distinguish the poverty problem from the income distribution problem in general. Poverty will always be with us in the sense that those at the bottom of the income distribution will feel badly off. It would be possible, however, to establish a minimum income level below which no one in the United States would be allowed to fall. There is considerable consensus that this is a reasonable policy objective; and there has been much discussion of possible techniques.

A second issue is how hard we should work to reduce inequality above the poverty line. Here there is less agreement on objectives and techniques. We leave this issue for discussion at the end of the chapter.

What is poverty? How do we define and measure it? How many people in the United States are poor, and who are they?

The definition of poverty is necessarily conventional. When one gets above the minimum of food, clothing, and shelter necessary for physical survival, the adequacy of consumption levels becomes a matter of judgment. Where one sets the poverty line depends on one's beliefs about how people should be entitled to live. Moreover, conceptions of an adequate living standard change over the course of time. Conditions that were widely prevalent and accepted at one time may be regarded as unacceptable a generation later.

For this reason, Victor Fuchs has suggested that poverty be defined on a relative rather than an absolute basis. Any family whose income is less than, say, half of the median family income in the country might be regarded as poor. In support of this approach, Fuchs argues:

> Firstly, it explicitly recognizes that all so-called "minimum" or "subsistence" budgets are based on contemporary standards . . . and have no intrinsic or scientific basis. Secondly, it focuses attention on what seems to underlie the present concern with poverty, namely, the first tentative gropings toward a national policy with respect to the distribution of income at the lower end of the scale. Finally, it provides a more realistic basis for appraising the success or failure of antipoverty programs.

Fuchs points out that, if poverty is defined as an income of less than $3,000 a year (in constant 1965 dollars), the proportion of families who are poor fell from 30.0 percent in 1947 to 16.5 percent in 1965. The proportion of families with incomes less than one-half the median, however, remained virtually constant at about 20 percent.[10]

Most scholars and policy makers, however, continue to use an absolute standard of poverty. In the early sixties, this was commonly set at $3,000 for a family of four. Any such standards must ke kept up-to-date, however, as living costs change. The standard must be adjusted also for differences in family size. In the case of farm families, the fact that the family usually owns its home and grows part of its food should be considered. In 1975, the "poverty line" for a nonfarm family of four was estimated at $5,500.

After making these adjustments, the Census Bureau estimated that 12.0 percent of Americans were living in poverty in 1975.[11] This is an encouraging decline from earlier estimates of 31.7 percent in 1947 and 21.4 percent in 1959. But it is still about 25 million people.

Who are today's poor, and why are they poor? [12] The outlines of the picture are shown in Table 5. The first column shows the *number* of poor households with various characteristics. The second column shows the *percentage* of all households with a certain characteristic who were living in poverty in 1975.

Note that, of some 10 million poor nonfarm households, 3.3 million were headed by people aged 65 or over. These are older people who either failed to qualify for Social Security or whose Social Security payments arc too small to lift them above the poverty line.

Another 3 million poor households are headed by women under 65. These are women who have been widowed, divorced, or abandoned by their husbands. Many of them are unable to work because of the need to care for small children.

This leaves about 3.5 million households headed by men under 65. The sources of their poverty are not so clear. Many of these men, probably close to a million, are disabled and unable to work. The remainder are presumably men at the bottom of the labor force in terms of education and skill. Some are able to get little or no work and constitute the hard-core

---

[10] Victor Fuchs, "Comment," in Soltow, *Six Papers on the Size Distribution of Wealth and Income,* pp. 198–202.

[11] Bureau of the Census, *Current Population Reports,* Series P-60, No. 103 (September 1976).

[12] For other analyses of the poverty population, see Lester C. Thurow, "The Causes of Poverty," *Quarterly Journal of Economics* (February 1967), pp. 39–57; and James N. Morgan, Martin H. David, Wilbur J. Cohen, and Harvey E. Brazer, *Income and Welfare in the United States* (New York: McGraw-Hill Book Company, 1962).

Table 5

Characteristics of Poor Households, 1975

Characteristics of Head of Household	Number of Poor Households (Millions)	Incidence of Poverty (Percent)
Head 65 years and over	3.3	15.3
Unrelated individuals	−2.1	31.0
Families	−1.2	8.0
Heads under 65 years	7.2	13.2
Unrelated individuals	−3.0	22.1
White	2.2	19.8
Male	0.9	16.0
Female	1.3	23.8
Nonwhite	0.7	35.0
Male	0.3	29.7
Female	0.4	41.4
Families	−4.2	10.3
White	2.9	8.1
Male	1.6	5.0
Female	1.3	33.6
Nonwhite	1.3	26.2
Male	0.4	11.7
Female	0.9	53.2

SOURCE: Data for this table are from Bureau of the Census, *Current Population Reports: Consumer Income,* Series P-60, No. 103 (September 1976), pp. 34–35.

unemployed. Others are employed in the lowest-paid jobs in the economy, where even full-time work fails to yield an adequate income.

In every category the poverty percentage is much higher for nonwhite than for white households. Thus, for families with male heads under sixty-five, the proportion of poor is 5.0 percent for white families, 11.7 percent for nonwhite families. For families with female heads under sixty-five, the poverty percentage is 33.6 for whites, 53.2 percent for nonwhites. This is partly a reflection of low employability. Black workers, especially those reared in rural areas of the southern states, have been particularly disadvantaged as regards education and the kinds of work skill needed for urban occupations.[13] But it is also partly a reflection of continued hiring discrimination by employers. Black workers tend to get the least attractive and

[13] Thurow, "The Causes of Poverty," notes that in 1960 some 48.5 percent of nonwhite family heads had less than eight years of education, compared with only 19.2 percent of white family heads. He estimates that educational differences alone account for nearly half of the difference in incidence of poverty between white and nonwhite families.

lowest-paid jobs, even when their qualifications would entitle them to something better.

Old age, broken families, low employability, and color are the ingredients of the poverty problem. These characteristics are not mutually exclusive, but overlap in a complicated pattern. At a rough estimate, 30 to 40 percent of presently impoverished families contain employable members, and might be lifted out of poverty by better job opportunities. For the majority, however, transfer payments provide the only feasible source of income.

Poverty is clearly a complex problem, calling for action on many fronts. Many programs that are not aimed primarily at poverty nevertheless have an important impact upon it. Let us first look briefly at existing income maintenance programs, and then consider alternative proposals for the future.

REDUCING POVERTY: EXISTING PROGRAMS

Income maintenance programs should be distinguished from *social insurance programs,* of which the most important are the federal Old-Age, Survivors, Disability, and Health Insurance system (usually called OASDHI, or simply *Social Security* after the Social Security Act of 1935, which established it); and the federal–state unemployment compensation systems, initiated by the same act. Social insurance payments are a right earned in the course of employment rather than a charitable donation; and their size depends mainly on the worker's previous employment and earnings rather than on family need. For workers with a regular employment history, social insurance serves the important function of redistributing income *over time,* as between periods of earning and not earning. Many families are thereby held above the poverty level, particularly in old age. On the other hand, social insurance by its nature cannot help those who cannot or do not work regularly.[14]

Income maintenance programs, on the other hand, are unrelated to prior work experience and are based primarily on need. Some of these involve cash transfers, others free or subsidized provision of food, housing,

---

[14] At one time social insurance was included in courses on labor economics. But the subject is now sufficiently large and complicated that it is usually treated in separate courses and textbooks. See, for example, Eveline Burns, *Social Security and Public Policy* (New York: McGraw-Hill Book Company, 1956); William Haber and Merrill I. Murray, *Unemployment Insurance in the American Economy* (Homewood, Ill.: Richard D. Irwin, Inc., 1966); Valdemar Carlson, *Economic Security in the United States* (New York: McGraw-Hill Book Company, 1962); Margaret S. Gordon, *The Economics of Welfare Policies* (New York: Columbia University Press, 1963); Robert J. Meyer, *Social Insurance and Allied Government Programs* (Homewood, Ill.: Richard D. Irwin, Inc., 1965).

and medical care. Much the largest of the cash transfer programs is the program of aid to families with dependent children—AFDC, or *welfare*. Designed originally for widows, it now serves mainly women and children in broken homes. About three-quarters of welfare families are headed by women who are divorced, deserted, separated, never married, or otherwise living apart from their children's fathers.

The AFDC program is supported by matching federal grants to the states, but the states set benefit levels and administer the programs. The size of welfare payments varies widely from state to state, being about three times as high in Massachusetts, New York, and New Jersey as in some of the southern states. While able-bodied mothers whose youngest child is over five are required to register for training or employment, the system discourages work through what amounts to a high tax rate on earnings. In most states welfare payments are reduced by two-thirds of earnings over $360 per year, after deducting "work-related" expenses. The items covered vary from state to state, but may include payroll deductions, transportation, child care, union dues, food away from home, tools, and uniforms. Average allowances per family under this heading range as high as $1,000 per year in New York, California, and other high-income states.

The relative size of the main cash transfer programs is indicated by Table 6. Note that the Social Security program dwarfs all others in size. All programs have grown rapidly since 1950, and especially since 1965.

How much do these programs do to alleviate the poverty problem? Here we must introduce the concept of the "pretransfer poor," or those families and individuals who, in the absence of transfer payments, would have been below the poverty line. The existence of transfer payments raises many of these people above the poverty line, so that the number of

Table 6

Major Cash Transfer Programs, 1974

	Cash Benefits (Billions of Dollars)	Recipients (Millions of Persons)
Social Insurance		
Social Security pension payments	64.8	28.5
Social Security survivors' benefits	21.0	10.2
Unemployment insurance	6.7	2.7
Workmen's compensation	4.0	n.a.
Income Maintenance		
AFDC	7.9	11.0
Assistance for aged, blind, and disabled	5.3	3.7

posttransfer poor shown in Table 5 is substantially below that of pretransfer poor.

By no means all of these cash payments—indeed, only about half—go to the pretransfer poor; and this varies widely from program to program. In a recent year, only 21 percent of unemployment compensation payments and 33 percent of workmen's compensation payments went to the pretransfer poor; but the percentage was 58 for old age pensions and 87 for welfare payments. As a consequence, the posttransfer poor numbered only 12 percent of the population, in contrast to 19 percent who would have been counted as poor on a pretransfer basis.[15] The existence of transfer programs, in other words, lifted about 44 percent of the pretransfer poor above the poverty line; and about 78 percent of the pretransfer poor received one or another type of transfer payment.

It is striking that almost all the reduction in posttransfer poverty since 1965 has been accomplished through government transfer programs. The number of pretransfer poor has declined very little, by only about a million persons, while the dollar cost of bringing a family up to the poverty line has risen rapidly because of rising consumer prices. Thus despite a very rapid rise in transfer payments, the amount of posttransfer poverty has fallen by only a few percentage points.

This analysis, to be sure, somewhat overstates the size of the poverty population and understates its rate of decline. The reason, already noted, is that the Census Bureau's income surveys count cash income only. They do not count the value of free medical care for the indigent, subsidized food stamps, and subsidized rentals. These had a value in 1975 of about $12 billion, almost as large as cash relief payments. If these items were counted as part of income, many families which now appear to be below the poverty line would be raised above it.[16]

The food stamp program, unlike most others, has universal coverage of the population. It does not distinguish between families with or without children, with male or female heads, or between the employed and the unemployed. Eligibility depends solely on family income and family size. It amounts, in effect, to a universal negative income tax plan, but one whose benefits are confined to expenditure on a single item—food. For low-income families or very large families, the benefits are substantial. Thus a four-person family with an adjusted annual income of $3,000 can buy

---

[15] Robert J. Lampman, "Employment Versus Income Maintenance," in Eli Ginzberg (ed.), *Jobs for Americans* (New York: Prentice-Hall, Inc., for the American Assembly, 1976).

[16] A recent study by the Congressional Budget Office found that, when Medicaid, food stamp, and other in-kind payments are included in income, the number of families below the poverty line drops by about 40 percent, from 9.1 to 5.4 million families, or about 7 percent of all American families. [Reported in *The New York Times* (January 18, 1977, p. 10).]

$1,800 worth of food stamps for $852, an increase of almost $1,000 in its effective income. In recent years about 20 million people have been benefitting from this program, at an annual cost of some $5 billion.

There are two major medical programs, with similar names but differing in scope and purpose. Under *Medicare,* a federal program which covers old age pensioners under the Social Security system, medical and hospital care is heavily subsidized though not entirely free. The cost, like that of old age pensions, is borne by payroll taxes on employers and employees. Under *Medicaid,* the federal government pays at least half, and states the rest of the full cost of medical and hospital services for eligible low-income families. This money comes from general tax revenues. Virtually all AFDC recipients are covered by the program, as well as other families below a specified income level, who are classified as *medically indigent.* About 20 million people receive benefits under this program. The average cash value of benefits varies from state to state, but in the richer states is estimated at more than $1,000 a year. Unlike the food stamp and housing programs, Medicaid does not impose higher charges as income rises. Rather, when income rises above the eligibility threshold, benefits cease completely. This "notch" provision can turn a small increase in a family's cash income into a financial disaster.

Housing is a smaller program, costing currently about $3 billion a year. About 2.5 million people receive housing subsidies, either through living in low-rent public housing projects or through a more recent program of rent supplements which, for poor families, pays the difference between the market rental and 25 percent of family income. Eligibility for housing assistance depends on income, so some of the working poor are included. About half of those in public housing projects, however, are also receiving cash assistance. The amount charged the tenant rises as family income rises—again, a substantial tax on earned income. If income rises above a certain level, rent subsidies cease (under the rent supplement program) or the family must move out (in the case of public housing projects). The benefit to families covered by the subsidized housing programs is substantial, averaging more than $1,000 a year.

Some Criticisms of Present Programs

The present welfare system is a complex hodgepodge of uncoordinated programs, created at different times for different purposes, difficult to administer and even to understand, and subject to a variety of legitimate complaints. These include:

1. *Unevenness of coverage.* Families in the same circumstances receive very different amounts of support. The main reason is variation in eligibility levels and assistance standards from state to state. A second reason is multiple coverage—some families receive three or four kinds of assistance, others only

one. A recent survey of households in six low-income areas found that 40 percent were receiving no benefits at all. But of those receiving benefits, 66 percent received benefits from two or more programs, 43 percent were drawing on three or more, 29 percent benefitted from four or more, and 19 percent benefitted from five or more.[17] A family that is lucky or clever enough to gain coverage under several programs can live better than many of the working population; but an identical family that lives in the wrong place or hasn't filled out the right forms can find itself in desperate straits.

2. *Promotion of family instability.* The AFDC program has been much criticized for the provision that families with a husband present are normally not eligible for assistance. This contributes, it is claimed, not merely to genuine separations but to "fictitious desertions," in which the man simply lives elsewhere, or at any rate vanishes when the caseworker comes around. In this way he can earn an income, the family can receive welfare, and total income is higher than if he lived at home. But an absentee father system clearly has disadvantages in terms of child rearing and normal family life.

3. *Strong disincentives to work.* This arises in two ways:

a. A high implicit tax rate on earned income. As earned income increases, welfare payments diminish—normally by $2 for every $3 earned. But *in addition,* if the family receives food stamps, it must pay more for them; and if it is receiving housing subsidies, it must pay more rent. Aaron estimates that, for a family receiving all these types of assistance, the total tax on earned income is about 80 percent. One has to be quite devoted to the work ethic to earn $100 a week in order to keep $20.

b. The "notch effect," arising from complete cessation of benefits above a certain income level. When a family's income rises above the ceiling set by state standards, it becomes ineligible for welfare. Ineligibility for welfare normally means that the family also becomes ineligible for food stamps. Medicaid also suddenly vanishes when a certain income is reached. Thus a family with an income of $4,001 per year may be *much* worse off than if its income were $3,999 per year.

4. *Serious administrative problems.* Administrative costs of some programs are high, and overlapping of programs further increases these costs. The AFDC program involves large staffs of welfare administrators in the major cities. Despite these large staffs, investigations have turned up a substantial amount of fraud in AFDC and other programs—that is, receipt of benefits by people not entitled to them. Cost escalation has been a continuing problem under Medicaid. Government has raised the effective demand for medical and hospital care by guaranteeing payment of bills. The effect has been to encourage inflation of hospital costs and medical fees, with little control over quantity or quality of service.

REDUCING POVERTY: NEW PROPOSALS

No one likes the present welfare system. The term "welfare mess" has become conventional. Proposals for reform abound; and there is some possibility of major changes in the foreseeable future. It will be useful, therefore, to sort out the issues currently under debate.

---

[17] Irene Lurie (ed.), *Integrating Income Maintenance Programs* (New York: Academic Press, Inc., 1975), p. 11.

Cash Versus Goods

The present welfare system is a mixture of cash grants and subsidized provision of food, medical care, and housing. If one were starting from scratch to develop a new transfer system, what should it look like? If government wants to raise the living standards of the poor, why not simply give them cash that they can spend in accordance with their own preferences? The argument for this is the general argument for consumer preference as a guide to production. Those who take this view would prefer a "cashing out" of specific subsidy programs, replacing them with increased cash allowances.

Tobin has argued,[18] however, that transfers in kind should not be rejected out of hand. Specific programs should be examined on their merits. Transfers in kind make the most sense where there is fixity of supply, so that to give a minimum amount of the good to everyone may require limiting its use by some, as in the case of wartime rationing. On this ground, one might favor subsidized medical care, where supply limits are severe and where a voucher system would tend to equalize levels of service among income groups. At the same time one might be skeptical of housing vouchers or food stamps, where supplies are readily expansible.

There is also the consideration that Congress may be willing to approve a large total income transfer if at least part of this is transfer in kind. Congressmen are more impressed by the argument that people are hungry, or badly housed, or lack medical care than by arguments based on income alone. In addition, transfers of goods benefit powerful private interests— the farmers, the construction industry, and the health professions. Thus we cannot be *certain* that the poor would be better off if transfers in kind were abandoned, because cash transfers might not be increased correspondingly.

There is even a certain element of value judgment. Suppose the upper 80 percent of the income distribution take this position: "We want to make the poor better off by *our standards,* not necessarily by *their standards;* and after all, we are footing the bill." To what extent is this a valid preference, entitled to respect in the formulation of public policy?

The Negative Income Tax

Many of those who favor cash payments and deplore the complexity of the present system have proposed to replace it by a single system providing a minimum guaranteed income to all poor people, regardless of personal characteristics. This is often termed a *negative income tax.* At present, families above a certain income level make a tax payment to gov-

---

[18] James Tobin, "On Limiting the Domain of Inequality," *Journal of Law and Economics* (October 1970), pp. 263–77.

ernment. Under the proposed system, families below a certain level would receive a cash payment from government.

While a variety of plans have been proposed,[19] they have several common features:

1. A *basic allowance* or income guarantee, which is the amount paid to a family whose other income for the year is zero. It is the family's minimum disposable income. It could be adjusted to family size according to a prescribed scale.

2. An *offsetting tax*, which the family would pay on its income from work or other sources. The main issue here is the rate at which other income should be taxed—one-third, one-half, two-thirds, or whatever. The higher the tax rate, the less the scheme would cost the federal government, but the smaller also would be the incentive to work and earn income.

3. A *net benefit* to the recipient of the basic allowance less the offsetting tax. At low income levels, the government would be making net payments to the family—hence the term *negative income tax*. As the family's other income rises, the net benefit would decline. Eventually one reaches a *break-even* point, at which the offsetting tax just equals the basic allowance, and the family neither pays nor receives anything.

By combining various basic allowances with various tax rates one can derive numerous concrete programs. Suppose, for example, that one set a basic allowance of $2,500 for a family of four and a tax of 50 percent on other income. Then family income would behave as shown in Table 7. The

Table 7

Operation of a Negative Income Tax System

Basic Allowance (1)	Other Income (2)	Tax Payment (3)	Net Benefit (1) − (3) (4)	Disposable Income (2) + (4) (5)
2,500	0	0	2,500	2,500
2,500	1,000	500	2,000	3,000
2,500	2,000	1,000	1,500	3,500
2,500	3,000	1,500	1,000	4,000
2,500	4,000	2,000	500	4,500
2,500	5,000	2,500	0	5,000

[19] See, for example, Milton Friedman, *Capitalism and Freedom* (Chicago: The University of Chicago Press, 1963); James A. Tobin, Joseph A. Pechman, and Peter M. Mieszkowski, "Is a Negative Income Tax Practical?" *Yale Law Journal* (December 1967), pp. 1–27 (reprinted copies available also from The Brookings Institution); Christopher Green, *Negative Taxes and the Poverty Problem* (Washington, D.C.: The Brookings Institution, 1967); and George H. Hildebrand, *Poverty, Income Maintenance, and the Negative Income Tax* (Ithaca: New York State School of Industrial and Labor Relations, 1967).

break-even point under this program would occur at an income level of
$5,000. Income above that level would be subject to normal rates of per-
sonal income taxation.

How much would a negative income tax plan cost the government?
This depends heavily on the basic allowance schedule and on the rate of
offsetting tax. It depends on the size of the negative effect on labor supply.
It depends also on how "other income" is defined. For example, should
social security and public assistance payments be counted as other income
subject to tax? What about the rental value of an owner-occupied house,
or the value of food grown and consumed on farms? Finally, adoption of
a negative income tax plan would reduce the need for existing programs
of categorical assistance and general relief. Scaling down of these programs
would yield a substantial tax saving. Thus the net cost of the negative
income tax would be considerably less than its gross cost. After making
assumptions on these points, which can be checked in the original source,
the Tobin–Pechman–Mieszkowski paper estimates that the net cost of the
most plausible programs would have been in the range of $10 billion to
$20 billion as of 1967.

A welfare reform proposal incorporating some features of the guaranteed income idea was submitted to Congress by President Nixon in 1970.
It was caught in a cross fire, however, between liberals who considered the
income guarantee too low and conservatives who disliked the whole idea,
and after long debate was finally abandoned in 1972. The idea is very
much alive, however, and a new reform proposal was introduced by President Carter in 1977.

A major criticism of negative income tax proposals has been the possible adverse effect on labor supply. This arises in two ways. First, a
family can receive a basic allowance by doing nothing at all and, as we saw
in Chapter 2, this availability of "other income" reduces labor supply.
Second, if a family member does choose to work, he is penalized by a high
tax rate on earned income. There can be no doubt that tax rates in the
range of 50 to 75 percent, the range usually regarded as "practical," would
have an effect on the amount of work done.

The labor supply response of husband-and-wife families has been
tested by controlled experiments with samples of families in several states.
These families were given income guarantees at several levels, and were
subject to differing rates of tax on earned income. Their behavior over
several years was compared with that of "control families," similar in other
respects but without an income guarantee. It turned out that the income
guarantee had little effect on labor force participation or hours worked
by husbands. Wives in white families reduced their labor force participation appreciably, but wives in black families continued to work as much as
before. Rees concludes that

the added cost (of an income guarantee program) produced by the supply response is a rather small portion of the total cost—not over 10 percent and probably closer to 5 percent. The estimates suggest that a substantial part of this will, in effect, represent added benefits for mothers whose withdrawal from paid employment is likely to be offset by increased "employment" at home. There is a further suggestion that tax rates higher than 50 percent may lead to a more pronounced supply response and, consequently, a larger increment to total cost.[20]

The fact remains that there would be *some* reduction in labor supply and consequently in national output.

Separating Employable and Nonemployable

There is a natural concern about this potential reduction in employment and output. There is also a deep-rooted conviction, in Congress and among the general public, that those able to work *should* be drawing income from work rather than from relief payments. Indeed, many of the low-income population do work, though usually intermittently and at low-wage jobs. A Census survey for 1973 reports that, of the female heads of poor families with children under 18, 43 percent did some work during the year, though only 8 percent worked full-time. Further, among wives living with husbands in poor families with children under 18, 34 percent did some work but only 5 percent worked full-time.

It seems possible that, through a revision of present programs, employment of low-income women as well as men could be increased substantially. This has led to suggestions for a *binary* rather than a *unitary* program. This would involve separating potentially employable people from the nonemployable. The guaranteed income program would be limited to the latter group. The employable group would be handled by some combination of the following measures:

1. *A work requirement.* A family with one or more employable members would be declared ineligible for AFDC and other transfer programs. This is not a new idea. In 1972 Congress wrote into the welfare appropriation bill a provision that all welfare recipients, except the disabled and mothers with children under six, must register for job training or employment. Those who refused to register or to accept work would become ineligible for benefits. As we noted in Chapter 7, almost a million welfare recipients were registered under this "workfare" provision during its first year of operation; but only 256,678 were certified as able to work and, of the latter, only 82,075 were actually placed in jobs. The central problem is that employers will not hire people from this group except under conditions of severe labor shortage; and so most of them, after going through the formalities, remain on the welfare rolls. Lack of low-cost child care facilities is also a major problem.

---

[20] Albert Rees, "An Overview of the Labor-Supply Results," *Journal of Human Resources* (Spring 1974), pp. 158–80.

2. *A wage rate or earnings subsidy.* Most of the welfare population have limited work skills, and can find jobs only at the bottom of the wage structure. For these people, even full-time, year-round employment might still leave the family below the poverty line. To meet this by raising the minimum wage is counterproductive, since private employers will simply decline to hire people at a wage above their estimated productivity. As an alternative, government might undertake to subsidize low wage rates or earnings in the private sector.

One possibility is a *negative wage tax.* This would set a break-even wage, and would provide a negative tax on the gap between the actual and break-even wage. For example, suppose the break-even wage is $4.00 an hour, the tax rate is 50 percent, and a worker's actual wage is $2.50 an hour. Then he would receive from the government a payment of $(4.00 - 2.50) \times \frac{1}{2}$, or $0.75 per hour. His effective wage would rise from $2.50 to $3.25.

In calculating the cost of such a program, one cannot assume that the market wage rate would remain unchanged. If the labor supply curve is upward-sloping, the increase in the effective wage would call forth a larger supply of labor. This would tend to lower the market wage and, since the employer pays only the market wage, the amount of labor demanded would increase. The result, in short, would be a reduction in the market wage; an increase in labor supply, employment, and national output; and an increase in the hourly earnings of low-paid workers. An incidental benefit is that the minimum wage system would no longer be needed, since its protective function would be taken over by the wage subsidy.

An alternative proposal, which might be simpler to administer, would provide a subsidy to family *earnings.* One possible formula would be as follows: the earnings subsidy would be equal to 50 percent of regular family (sum of husband's and wife's) earnings from employment up to $3,000 a year. A family with earnings of $3,000 would receive a subsidy of $1,500, or a total income of $4,500. For earnings above $3,000, the subsidy would be reduced at a rate implying a marginal tax rate of 33 percent. Under this schedule, the break-even point would be $7,500 a year, and above that level the subsidy would cease.[21]

3. *A public service employment program.* There are many people of relatively low skill and education who, though they might be judged employable by the welfare authorities, have serious difficulty in finding steady employment in the private sector. Nor is this problem confined to the welfare population. It exists among the cyclically and structurally unemployed. It exists among young school dropouts, who need reorientation to the world of employment as well as job skills.

This is the rationale for proposals that government should become the employer of last resort. We saw in Chapter 7 that public service employment programs have existed on a limited scale since 1971. The question is whether they should be enlarged substantially and made a routine part of the employment structure. As Lampman points out, such a program would raise difficult problems:

Who should be eligible for—or required to take—PSE jobs? Should the emphasis be upon those who have the greatest need or those who can

---

[21] For an analysis of how such a program would operate, see Robert H. Haveman, "Earnings Supplementation as an Income Maintenance Strategy," in Lurie, *Integrating Income Maintenance Programs.*

make the greatest contribution to output? Should priorities be set to assume that some of the jobs go to long-term unemployed, heads of families, veterans, minority group members, youthful workers, and those in still other categories? Then there is the issue of wages. Should they be higher than welfare benefits to attract people off the welfare rolls, or lower than the minimum wage to avoid diverting workers out of the private sector? What about the work to be done? If it is socially valuable, can it be turned off when the recession abates? If it is not socially valuable, will the morale of the workers suffer? [22]

Administrative and political problems certainly would exist. But with some ingenuity it should be possible to remedy the anomaly of able-bodied people living in idleness while many public services are underdeveloped and understaffed because of financial constraints on state and local governments.

It should be reemphasized in conclusion that the success of any antipoverty program depends heavily on effective macroeconomic policies. Maintenance of high labor demand in the private sector is the single most effective antipoverty measure. It is needed to pull people at the tail end of the employment queue into regular employment. It is needed to validate training programs, whose gradates may otherwise find themselves as badly off as before. It is needed to break down employer resistance to employment of young people, women, and black workers, whose fuller employment would do much to alleviate poverty. It is needed to prevent the numbers falling back on public service employment from becoming unbearably large.

INEQUALITY AND INCOME REDISTRIBUTION

Suppose now that the poverty problem has been taken care of in one way or another. All families below the poverty line have been brought up to that level. Is there any reason to worry about the distribution of incomes above the minimum? If the poorest families can live decently, does it matter whether some television stars, surgeons, and business executives have very large incomes? This is the problem of inequality *per se*.

Equalizing Opportunities
To Earn Income

Let us distinguish at the outset between two ways of altering the distribution of income: by improving the operation of markets, and by revising the tax structure. The first would be generally regarded as desirable, while the second remains controversial.

---

[22] Lampman, "Employment Versus Income Maintenance," in Ginzberg, *Jobs For Americans*, p. 182.

The reluctance of many economists to tamper with income distribution arises from a belief that the pretax distribution mainly reflects the pricing of factors of production in competitive markets. An individual or family gets the market price for its labor and capital. Factor prices, like other prices, serve the *incentive* function of inducing work and saving, the *rationing* function of balancing total demand for a factor with available supplies, and the *allocating* function of distributing supplies among alternative uses. In a decentralized economy, which depends on prices as a signaling mechanism, efforts to redistribute income by manipulating prices, wages, interest rates, and so on should be viewed with suspicion.

This line of reasoning assumes, however, that markets are competitive and that the distribution of capital assets can be regarded as just; and both assumptions are open to question. One can scarcely argue that the earnings of low-skilled black workers and California lettuce pickers, or the earnings of surgeons, top corporation executives, and airline pilots are determined in perfectly competitive markets. Nor can one argue that all young people have effective freedom of occupational choice, which implies equal opportunity to acquire education and job skills.

There would be widespread agreement on the desirability of *equal opportunity to earn income from labor,* within the limits of individual ability and effort. Concretely, this means equal access to education by young people, without regard to parental background or income; equal access to employment opportunities on the basis of personal qualifications, without discrimination based on race, sex, or other grounds; and improvement of the operation of labor markets through vocational counseling, provision of job information, adult retraining programs, and other measures discussed in earlier chapters. All this would have an equalizing effect on labor incomes, which as we saw earlier are the largest single source of income inequality.

What about property incomes, which are presently very unequally distributed? This stems partly from differences in lifetime savings, but mainly from inheritance of wealth. It is no doubt impracticable to ensure that young people in each generation should start absolutely equal in the economic race. Young people from high-income families are bound to have advantages of home environment, greater opportunity for college and professional training, and placement in superior jobs through family connections. But should they in addition be allowed to inherit large amounts of wealth which they have done nothing to earn? There would seem to be a good case for heavier taxes on transmission of property to children and grandchildren through gifts and bequests. A common proposal is that the tax be levied on the recipient rather than (as at present) on the donor. Each individual would have a lifetime exemption entitling him or her to receive gifts and bequests of, say, $100,000 free of tax; but above that level the tax rate would rise fast enough to preclude transmission of substantial fortunes.

Any such program would no doubt have economic side effects. To the extent that high-income families now save to transmit an estate to their children, the national savings rate might be reduced, with effects on the rate of real capital formation. But this effect might not be very large; and in any event, one might judge it to be outweighed by a gain in equity.

Equalization via Income Taxation

Suppose now that these things have been done. There would still be substantial income inequality, mainly because of wage–salary differences. Is there a case for further efforts to reduce inequality?

There is no mystery about how this could be done. It would imply a steeper increase of the marginal tax rate on higher income brackets under the personal income tax, combined with a closing of the loopholes which now permit many people to pay much less than the nominal tax rates. This would not bring in a large amount of additional public revenue— the upper income brackets are not all that thickly populated. The gain, if it is judged to be a gain, would consist in a more equitable and defensible distribution of posttax income.

What does economics have to say about such a program? Can we say anything about the desirability of income equalization by *force majeure,* as distinct from equalization of opportunity? Can we say anything about the economic side effects of such equalization?

The first question has been debated for generations. The English classical economists thought they could prove that transferring income from richer to poorer people would increase total satisfaction. Consider a simple community consisting of two men, Mr. *A* and Mr. *B.* Suppose that their capacity to derive satisfaction from income is identical; that is, they have identical marginal utility schedules. Mr. *B,* however, has an income ten times as large as Mr. *A,* so that he is operating at a much lower point on his utility schedule. The satisfaction yielded by Mr. *B*'s last dollar is much less than that yielded by Mr. *A*'s last dollar. So, if we transfer a dollar from rich Mr. *B* to poor Mr. *A, A*'s satisfaction will be increased by more than *B*'s satisfaction is reduced. Total community satisfaction will rise.

People who advocate greater income equalization through government transfer have this argument in the back of their minds. They feel that an extra dollar means a lot to the poor, while to the rich man it means very little. But the argument has been undetermined by economic theorists, who point out that its assumptions are dubious and cannot be verified by observation. How do we know that marginal utility curves slope steadily downward? Perhaps appetite grows with eating, and utility curves may slope upward for a while. And how do we know that different people have the same capacity to derive satisfaction from income? Perhaps the well-to-do man, whose income has allowed him to cultivate expensive tastes, has a much higher utility curve than the poor man. Perhaps he derives just as much satisfaction from his last dollar as the poor man does from his. This aristocratic line of argument may seem unconvincing, but can one prove that it is wrong? There is no way to get inside the skins of Mr. *A* and Mr. *B*, or to compare their subjective satisfactions. This weakens the classical argument for income equality.

But in economics a major issue is rarely settled forever. Most recently, there has been a counterrevolution against the view that economics has nothing to say about distributive justice, and a variety of counterarguments have been advanced. First, individual utilities are interdependent in the sense that the satisfaction I get from my income depends, not just on the *absolute* size of my income, but on my position relative to others. This was pointed out many years ago by Thorstein Veblen, and appears more recently as a feature of James Duesenberry's theory of consumption. If I have $10,000 a year and everyone around me also has $10,000 a year, I will feel better off than if others have $100,000 or $500,000. Very high incomes arouse envy among those lower in the income scale. Some leveling of incomes might reduce envy and increase total satisfaction in the community.[23]

Second, in addition to preferences about work and consumption, individuals may have preferences about the social "rules of the game," and specifically about the desirable distribution of income. Even many of those in the higher income brackets might prefer greater equality than exists at present. As Thurow has noted,[24] this is not incompatible with normal selfishness in private economic behavior; that is, there is nothing inconsistent in trying to accumulate wealth within the existing rules of the game and at the same time believing that the rules of the game should be changed! Suppose a widespread preference for greater income equality does exist (though there is little evidence on this point at present). People with such a preference can do little about it *as individuals*. Just as in the case of public goods production, individual preferences can be made effective only through government action—in this case, revision of effective tax rates.

Third, marked inequality of incomes may pose dangers to life and property which could make it worthwhile for the well-to-do to consent

[23] For an analysis of this possibility, see Allan Feldman and Alan Kirman, "Fairness and Envy," *American Economic Review* (December 1974), pp. 995–1005.

[24] Lester C. Thurow, "Cash Versus In-Kind Transfers," *American Economic Review* (May 1974), pp. 190–95.

to some equalization of incomes *in their own interest*. A recent study of criminal activity concluded that "the rates of all felonies, particularly crimes against property, are positively related to the degree of a community's income inequality, and this suggests a social incentive for equalizing training and earnings opportunities across persons, which is independent of ethical considerations or any social welfare function." [25]

There is also the practical consideration that decisions about income distribution are going to be made anyway—by somebody. Virtually any government program alters the distribution of income to some extent. To say that, because of this, economists should not express any preference among alternative policies, comes close to ruling economics out of the realm of action. This point has been made by the noted Dutch economist, Jan Tinbergen:

> The contribution made to our problem by most of present-day economists has been to declare the comparison of different individuals' satisfactions an impossibility. This contribution is not very constructive, since it implies (i) that all feelings about social justice are meaningless, (ii) that the scientist cannot make any contribution, and (iii) that it is left to others, who often lack scientific education, to make such contributions. The first implication is especially important since it implies that the numerous decisions actually made about questions of distribution could just as well have been made differently. [26]

The "old-fashioned" view that economics can say something about income distribution has thus experienced a certain revival, and debate on the issue is not closed.

Whatever view one takes on this issue, it is clear that economics can say something about the side effects of a more progressive tax structure. The effect most commonly discussed is that on work effort. A higher effective tax on business executives, professional practitioners, and so on amounts to a wage cut. Now a wage cut has two opposite effects. On one hand the price of an hour of leisure, which is the wage which could have been earned by working that hour, is lower than before. So there is an incentive to "buy" more leisure by working less. This is the *substituton effect*. On the other hand, since the person is now poorer than before, he may try to work more in order to maintain his accustomed standard of living. This is the *income effect*. The two effects work in opposite directions, and there is no way to determine *a priori* which will predominate.

---

[25] Isaac Ehrlich, "Participation in Illegitimate Activities: A Theoretical and Empirical Investigation," *Journal of Political Economy* (May/June 1973), pp. 521–65. See also Llad Phillips, Harold L. Votey, Jr., and Darold Maxwell, "Crime, Youth, and the Labor Market," *Journal of Political Economy* (May/June 1972), pp. 491–504.

[26] Jan Tinbergen, *Economic Policy: Principles and Design* (Amsterdam: North-Holland Publishing Company, 1964), pp. 22–23.

There have been a few research studies of the subject. One study of independent professional practitioners in England found that some did work less in response to a tax increase; but others worked more, and the overall effect on work effort was small. These results accord with common sense. Successful business and professional men seem to be compulsive workers; and while they would certainly maintain that higher taxes were reducing their incentive, it is doubtful that they would change their activities materially.

A scaling-down of high incomes would probably reduce the amount of personal saving, which comes disproportionately from the higher-income brackets. The *incentives* for saving would not be altered, but the *ability* to save would be reduced. The size of this effect is hard to estimate, but it would probably be moderate. Much of our national saving comes from corporations and other institutional sources rather than from households. Still, some reduction in the national savings rate seems likely; and this would mean a reduction in the rate of capital formation and the growth rate of national output.

DISCUSSION QUESTIONS

1. "Inequality of family incomes is a persistent fact of our economy." Explain the main reasons for the present inequality of family incomes in the United States.

2. Would you expect family income distribution to be more equal, or less equal, in 2000 than in 1970? Explain.

3. "As wage and income levels continue to rise in the American economy, the poverty problem will largely take care of itself." Discuss.

4. "It is not a good idea for government to provide poor families with food, housing, medical care, or what not at cut-rate prices. Where subsidies are desirable, it is better to give a cash subsidy and let people spend it as they prefer." Discuss.

5. Would you favor a program of restricting welfare payments to the nonemployable and imposing a work requirement on the employable? How would you define "employability"? What would such a program imply in terms of provision of work opportunities?

6. Compare the operation of a negative income tax, a negative wage tax, and an earnings subsidy as ways of raising the incomes of the working poor.

7. What measures would help to equalize opportunities to earn income from work? Would you extend the idea of equal opportunity to property income as well, through heavier taxation of gifts and inheritance?

8. Assume that poverty has been eliminated and that equal opportunity to earn income has been established. Would you favor further equalization of incomes *via* the personal income tax? Explain your reasoning.

READING SUGGESTIONS

In addition to the extensive journal literature, good books on income distribution and the poverty problem include A. B. ATKINSON, *The Economics of Inequality*, Oxford: Clarendon Press, 1975; ALAN S. BLINDER, *Toward an Economic Theory of Income Distribution*, Cambridge, Mass.: The MIT Press, 1974; JOSEPH A. PECHMAN and BENJAMIN A. OKNER, *Who Bears the Tax Burden?* Washington: The Brookings Institution, 1974; LEE SOLTOW, (ed.), *Six Papers on the Size Distribution of Wealth and Income*, New York: National Bureau of Economic Research, 1969; James D. SMITH, (ed.), *The Personal Distribution of Income and Wealth*, New York: National Bureau of Economic Research, 1975; IRENE LURIE, (ed.), *Integrating Income Maintenance Programs*, New York: Academic Press, Inc., 1975.

Current data on household income distribution, and on the size and characteristics of the poverty population, are published frequently by the Bureau of the Census in its *Current Population Reports* series. Relevant discussion appears also in the annual *Economic Report of the President* and the annual *Employment and Training Report of the President*, both available from the Superintendent of Documents, Washington, D.C.

IV

TRADE UNION
INSTITUTIONS

This part marks a sharp turning point in our subject matter. Although we have made occasional reference to trade unions in earlier chapters, for the most part they have remained in the background. We now bring them on stage and ask how they operate, what terms they try to negotiate with employers, and how the outcome affects the operation of the economy. These questions are central to the study of industrial *relations*.

A country's industrial relations system is a complex and interrelated whole. It comprises the structure of worker and employer organizations; the coverage and content of collective agreements *(union contracts)*; and the framework of public control, which limits what the parties may bargain about and the tactics they may use. In Chapter 14 we discuss these features on an international comparative basis, pointing out the differences among countries and some of the reasons for them. This is instructive in itself; and it is also helpful in identifying special features of the American industrial relations system that are not found, or not found to the same degree, in other countries.

American trade unions have a long tradition, dating from the 1790s. In Chapter 15 we hit the highlights of this long development, emphasizing the rise of the national union of a particular trade or industry as the dominant organization in the trade world. We then describe the present coverage of union organization, the reasons for the recent slowdown in membership growth, and the prospects for future growth, with particular attention to white-collar employment and government service.

Chapter 16 analyzes the union as a political organization, with particular attention to relations between union members and union officials—*union democ-*

racy. This is a complex issue, often misunderstood and misinterpreted by outside observers. It affects the members' civil rights in the union and the work shop; it has a major effect on the behavior of union officials in collective bargaining; and it bears on the question of how far union demands can be regarded as reflecting the preferences and interests of the membership. Any model of the union as an economic institution must make assumptions on these points; and so it is important to examine the factual basis for these assumptions.

14

Industrial Relations Systems: A Comparative View

Trade unions exist in all parts of the world. There are unions in Senegal, in Pakistan, in Chile, in Rumania. But what a union is and what is does varies greatly from country to country. Collective bargaining in the American sense is limited largely to northern and Western Europe, the United States, Canada, Australasia, and Japan. Even within this range of countries, there are marked differences in union strength and bargaining procedures. In the USSR and the East European countries, trade union functions reflect basic differences in political structure. In most countries of the "third world," unions are weakly organized and highly political.

It will be instructive to look briefly at these intercountry differences. Without this we are apt to conclude erroneously that American practices are natural and inevitable. The American industrial relations system, like any other national system, has been shaped by a specific politicoeconomic matrix. Some features it has in common with other countries, but some are peculiar to the United States. Our practices are no more "natural" than those of Sweden, Italy, Australia, or Japan; and we shall understand them better by looking at them in world perspective.

What do we mean by an *industrial relations system?* [1] We mean such things as:

1. The politicoeconomic matrix that surrounds employer–employee relations: the industrial structure of the country, the characteristics of the labor force, the looseness or tightness of the labor market, management's personnel policies, and the balance of power in the political system.
2. The characteristics of trade unions: whether workers are organized by

---

[1] For an effort to answer this difficult question, see John T. Dunlop, *Industrial Relations* (New York: Holt, Rinehart and Winston, Inc., 1958).

plant, by craft, or by industry, whether power resides mainly in local or national unions, the degree of membership attachment, the strength of union finances and leadership.

3. Trade union tactics: whether they concentrate mainly on controlling the employer through collective bargaining or on influencing government through political action.

4. The structure of collective bargaining: the size of bargaining units, the subjects regulated by agreement, the duration of agreements, the method of resolving disputes over the application of the agreement, the use of strikes and other forms of economic pressure.

5. The framework of public control, which determines what the parties may bargain about and what tactics they may use.

THE POLITICOECONOMIC MATRIX

When we say that an industrial relations system reflects the setting in which it has developed, what do we mean? What aspects of the setting are important, and why are they important?

The Size of Employing Units

Where people work for themselves as farmers, storekeepers, or artisans, the problem of employment relations does not arise. Beyond this, unionism is associated with establishments of *substantial size*. Small workshops employing only a handful of workers are not very susceptible to union organization. Railroads, steel mills, government departments, and other large employing units are much more susceptible. This seems to be as true in India, Japan, or Uganda as it is in the United States or France.

In small shops the employer has somewhat the role of a family head. He is apt to know his workers rather intimately, and to take some part in their family festivities and social life. The simplicity of production organization does not require elaborate rules of procedure. Instead of formalized personnel policies, one has day-to-day decisions by the employer to meet situations as they arise.

The situation is different in an enterprise with hundreds or thousands of employees. The top manager, whose orders may be filtered through several layers of subordinates, is less of a person and more of an abstraction. It seems natural that his impersonal power should be countered by forming a separate workers' organization. The fact that there are many employees enhances their combined power—for example, by making them harder to replace in the event of a strike.

A large organization must either (1) have definite rules for production and personnel management, in which case workers can reasonably argue that they should have a voice in setting the rules; or (2) in the absence of definite rules, the differing decisions of individual foremen are likely to create injustices, or at least to provoke charges of injustice from the workers under them. This creates an atmosphere in which the argument for a union capable of protecting workers against arbitrary action becomes quite persuasive.

The size of the potential union *base* in a particular country is readily determined. First, subtract from the national labor force all farmers and other self-employed persons. (In the less developed countries of Asia, Africa, and Latin America, the great bulk of the gainfully employed are self-employed.) Then subtract those working for employers with fewer than, say, twenty employees. This leaves as (potentially) organizable the government employees; workers in transportation, power, and other public-utility-type enterprises; workers in sizable manufacturing and mining establishments; construction workers on large projects; possibly some agricultural workers on large farms or plantations.

Even in India, with its relatively large industrial base, this organizable area includes only about 5 percent of the labor force. In some countries of tropical Africa, the proportion would be only 1 or 2 percent. In the more developed Latin American countries, it might approach 10 percent. So even if *all* potential union members were actually enrolled, total membership would be relatively small.

At the opposite pole, the country with the highest percentage of its workers in large establishments is probably the United States. Three-quarters of our manufacturing workers are in establishments with upward of one hundred employees. If one adds to this miners, public utility workers, government employees, and half of those in construction, trade, and services, it appears that two-thirds of the American labor force is in what might be considered the normal area of union operation. The proportion is high also in Canada, Britain, several of the Western European countries, and Japan.

Characteristics of the Labor Force

A key characteristic of the industrial labor force in many countries is its newness. People very recently out of the bush or the rice paddy are being trained for employment in the "modern" sector of the economy. There is much evidence that, given proper training, supervision, and incentives, these new recruits can become efficient industrial workers within a few years. It seems to take longer, however, for them to develop attitudes and traditions that are compatible with strong union organization.

In the older industrial countries, the lag between the appearance of industry and the appearance of widespread unionism was long indeed. Britain's Industrial Revolution began before 1800, and there was limited unionism among skilled workers throughout the nineteenth century; but not until the 1890s was there mass unionization among the less skilled. The United States was building textile mills in the 1810s, and had a large industrial base by 1870; but again, large-scale organization of semiskilled and unskilled workers dates only from the 1930s. Japan was already industrializing in the 1880s and 1890s; but widespread unionism developed only after 1945, and then partly under the impetus of U.S. occupation policies.

One should not turn these examples into a historical law. The lag between industrial development and widespread unionization may well be shorter in today's industrializing countries. But one should not be surprised that few of these countries yet have sizable union movements.

Many employees in newly industrializing countries do not yet have a permanent commitment to industrial employment. In sub-Sahara Africa, the tradition of migratory labor is still strong. A young man may travel hundreds of miles to find employment in a Johannesburg mine or a Nairobi factory. He works there for two or three years, after which he returns home with his bicycle, transistor radio, and other modern necessities, and perhaps with enough money to pay a bride-price to his prospective father-in-law. Even in India, with its longer industrial tradition, it is reported that Bombay textile-mill workers return frequently to their native villages for family ceremonials and religious festivities. While they have one foot in the industrial economy, their social security still lies largely in their family and village connections.

The educational level of factory workers in the less developed countries is low and many are illiterate. Even if the impetus to unionism is present, it is hard to find people capable of running a meeting, keeping the union's books, or drafting written agreements with the employer. Partly for this reason, most union officials in India are "outsiders," often lawyers who have no direct connection with the industry. One of these men may serve a dozen or more local unions, giving each a minimal share of his time. This is a general problem throughout Africa, Asia, and many parts of Latin America.

Another important factor is the social status of the worker and his attitude toward the employer. In some countries the class structure is rigid and traditions of class hostility are strong. This is true, for example, in France, Italy, and most parts of Latin America. Union and political leaders preach constantly to the worker that the employer is his enemy. He is not to be reasoned with; he is to be overthrown. Most employers look down on their workers with equal distaste. This makes for guerrilla warfare in industrial relations rather than for peaceful bargaining.

In some countries, the gap is widened by caste and racial cleavages. How can a high-caste Hindu negotiate on equal terms with workers from the lowest strata of Indian society? How can a South African mine owner negotiate with African workers who by definition are second-class citizens?

(In the independent African state of Zambia, on the other hand, unions of African copper miners negotiate quite effectively with the major copper companies.)

Japan has an unusual and strong tradition of worker attachment to the company. Young people normally enter an enterprise on leaving school and expect to remain with it for the rest of their working lives, moving up the wage ladder primarily on the basis of age. Under these conditions, as Professor Alice Cook points out

> workers generally are reluctant to undertake actions which may endanger their job security or, equally important, their relationships with the firm. Strikes . . . tend, as one union leader put it . . . to differ from their counterparts in the West since "it is not our intention to hurt the enterprise, but rather to call the attention of the public to our grievances." The delicate arrangement of feelings, sentiments, and obligations which constitute the Japanese concept of loyalty are not to be seriously or lengthily disturbed by any anti-enterprise action.[2]

Tightness of the Labor Market

The labor market is often biased in favor of the employer, in the sense that there is a surplus of available workers over available jobs. Where this surplus is large, the conditions for unionism are unfavorable. In many of the less developed countries, there is substantial underemployment in the cities and an almost bottomless reservoir of underemployed farmers in the countryside. Those who have jobs in the modern sector, usually at wage rates well above what can be earned in agriculture, are a privileged class. They are not eager to jeopardize their jobs, and they are in a poor position to bargain, since they could be replaced instantly from the unemployed. This is undoubtedly one reason for the relative weakness of unionism in the less developed countries.

The same phenomenon was evident in earlier times in the presently "developed" countries. Japan, from the 1870s onward, had a large flow of labor from country to city and a consistent labor surplus in industry. Only in the 1950s did the reservoir finally run dry, and then only because of a sharp drop in the birthrate. This must be partly responsible for the fact that unionism was not a prominent feature of Japanese industry until after 1945. The United States had from the 1840s to the 1920s, in addition to a high rate of natural increase, a large influx of European immigrants, which created an ample supply of low-skilled labor. This seriously hampered union organization outside the skilled crafts.

---

[2] Alice H. Cook, *Japanese Trade Unionism* (Ithaca: Cornell University Press, 1966), p. 8.

But while unemployment is harmful to unionism in one way, it is helpful in another. It reduces the bargaining power of the individual worker, which consists essentially in his ability to change jobs. If there is either temporary unemployment or a continuing labor surplus, most workers will have difficulty in finding other jobs. How, then, can the worker protect himself against the employer *without quitting?* How can he ward off wage cuts and other adverse acts by the employer in bad years? One obvious way is to join his fellow workers in a mutual assistance pact, a trade union.

From this point of view, permanent prosperity might undermine union strength by reducing the worker's need for protection. Thanks partly to improvements in economic knowledge and national economic management, unemployment has been very low in the Western European countries since 1945. Except for the periods 1958–64 and 1975–77, it has been unusually low in the United States. In many countries labor has been so scarce that employers have bid up wages above the official union scale. The threat of wage cuts, layoffs, and so on has receded. It is thus natural for many workers to conclude that the union is not adding much to what they could win on their own. This may partly account for the fact that, both in the United States and Western Europe, the unionized percentage of the labor force has tended to decline.

The Political Structure

Finally, we must note the important influence of power relations among economic interests. The American–Western European systems of industrial relations have developed in a specific and rather unusual political context: a plural society with multiparty government, administrations changeable at the will of a broadly based electorate, economic groups that have independent bases of power and interact with the political regime in a complicated pattern.

Most countries do not have this kind of structure. About half of the less developed countries have military governments in which, while one general may replace another, the military remains in control. Most of the remaining less developed countries have one-party governments, with other parties either prohibited or in a permanent minority position. Only in a few countries does one find a functioning multiparty system. In a one-party state one can scarcely expect unions to enjoy much independence. They may be forbidden, they may be ignored and overridden, they may be (as in Argentina under Perón, Brazil under Vargas, or Italy under Mussolini) absorbed into the authoritarian structure of government and thus enabled to survive in emasculated form.

The situation is different again in the USSR and the Eastern European countries. There are trade union organizations which perform important functions. But their method of operation is conditioned by their being embedded in a one-party political system, with all producing enterprises owned by the state and subject to a central economic plan.

UNION ORGANIZATION

We now bring the unions onto the scene and raise such questions as: What is the meaning of union membership, at various times and places? Is there a tendency for some kinds of workers to become unionized earlier than others? Do workers most commonly organize by *occupation*, by *company*, or by *industry?* What are the main levels (local, regional, national) of organization, and what determines the balance of power among these levels?

The Meaning of Union Membership

Union membership is normally *permissible*, and it is normally *voluntary*; but neither statement is invariably true. In nineteenth-century Britain and the United States, judges imbued with laissez-faire economics often ruled that a union was an illegal combination in restraint of trade. Only after decades of legal and political struggle was the right of unions to exist clearly established. Even today there are countries in which to join a union is to commit a crime.

It is usually left to the union organizer to persuade workers to join; but this may be accompanied by various types of external pressure. American unions have devised the *union shop* clause, under which new workers hired by the company must join the union within a specified period. The union shop is common also in Japan, perhaps because of American influence during the occupation period, or perhaps because of the strong enterprise attachment already noted. The worker's lifetime commitment to the enterprise includes a similar commitment to the union organization within the enterprise. The union shop is not found, however, in some other strongly unionized countries, where worker solidarity is strong enough to make social pressure an effective weapon. In Britain, a nonunion man in a unionized shop is "sent to Coventry"; no one will speak to him, no one will eat or drink with him, no one will work alongside him.

Another specifically American concept is that of *exclusive jurisdiction* by a single union over a certain category of workers. AFL leaders of the eighties and nineties felt that the trade union movement was too fragile to weaken itself further by interunion competition. The principle of exclusive jurisdiction was accordingly written into the constitution of the Federation, and remains a cardinal principle of the AFL–CIO today. Each national union has a certain job territory within which it alone is permitted to enroll members. Disputed areas, which two or more unions claim are within their territory, are usually adjusted by negotiations under Federation auspices.

In most other countries, each union organizes wherever it is able. In Britain, union "territories" have grown up every which way over a century and a half of history. It is common to find half a dozen unions with members in the same plant. This happens also in countries where the union movement is split along political or religious lines. Thus in a French factory one may find members of a communist union, a socialist union, a Catholic union, even an independent union. This obviously creates complications in dealing with the employer. In Britain, unions with overlapping territories in the same industry have usually solved the problem by forming confederations for collective bargaining. In France and Italy, too, unions with differing political outlooks often collaborate in bargaining negotiations.

American unions require their members to pay regular monthly dues, and members may be dropped for nonpayment. A common union contract provision is the *checkoff,* under which the employer deducts union dues and transmits them directly to the union. Dues paying is also a regular practice in Canada, Australia, Britain, Germany, Scandinavia, and Japan. But that is about it. In Italy and France, even those who consider themselves members pay dues only sporadically and intermittently. The percentage of dues-paying workers is still lower in most of the less developed countries.

In such countries, *union membership* becomes hard to define. Does it mean the number of people who have a nominal affiliation with the union, who will attend a mass meeting or participate in a "quickie" strike? In this case the total numbers may be impressive. Or does it mean the number who contribute regular financial support? This may be a small fraction of the first total. In countries other than the few cited above, the number of members claimed by union leaders gives an exaggerated impression of union strength.

A union whose dues are low or nonexistent is seriously handicapped. It cannot accumulate enough funds to support its members during a strike. Nor can it afford to pay for full-time, salaried leadership. A practical reason for strong communist influence in the trade unions of many countries is that the party usually has money, while the unions do not. The party functionary, with a secure payroll behind him, can offer his time free of charge for union affairs; and a union with no other source of professional leadership may accept the offer.

The Propensity To Organize

The propensity to become unionized has not been thoroughly studied, but the evidence would probably support two hypotheses: first, unionism typically originates with the best-off workers rather than the worst-off. The skilled craftsmen organize earlier and more strongly than the less skilled. In the United States, the earliest unions were among printers, carpenters, and journeymen cordwainers (shoemakers). The first unions in Great Britain consisted of building and printing trades' workers, who were followed shortly afterward by unions of tailors and wool combers. The prosperous condition of the wool combers is indicated by the fact that they normally came to work in top hats and long coats. In Sweden, the first unions were formed by the printers, the next by the carpenters, and the next by the skilled metal trades' workers. These crafts have a tradition extending almost unbroken from the medieval guilds. Proud of their skill, financially able to pay dues, with a fraternal feeling based on common training and experience, these men are quick to resent and resist any worsening of their conditions of employment.

Second, there are indications that some *industries* are more union-prone than others. This seems to be true of coal and metal mining, where workers often live together in remote areas and work under unusually difficult conditions. It is true also of the transport industries. Even in countries where unionism is not generally strong, the railroad workers, dock workers, and merchant seamen are usually organized. This may be due partly to conditions of life and work in these industries, partly to the economic power of those who can bring transportation to a standstill.

Bases of Organization

In some industries most of the work force falls in a single occupational group. Most coal mine employees are miners, and their basis of organization is clear. But in many industries this is not true. An automotive assembly plant employs laborers, assembly line workers, machinists, tool- and diemakers, patternmakers, electricians, carpenters, and a variety of other skills. This raises a question whether the dominant principle of organization shall be by occupation or by industry. Should all workers in the plant belong to a single union, or should there be multiple unions representing the various skill groups?

This has been a continuing issue in the American labor movement, particularly during the 1930s, when the new CIO industrial unions were challenging the older craft-based AFL. Arguments were advanced purporting to show that one basis or the other was logically correct. Actual union structure from country to country, however, has been shaped more by history and practical expediency than by logical principles.

Very broadly, one can say that the industry principle predominates, and has tended to predominate increasingly with the passage of time. In the United States, Britain, and a few other countries one finds separate unions for each craft in industries where skills are clearly identifiable, such as printing, building construction, and railroad operation. Most countries, however, have single unions of railroad workers, construction workers and so on (though sometimes with subunits for the various crafts). In Sweden, Germany, France, and other European countries with a long union tradition, where a variety of union forms had grown up over the years, there has been a deliberate effort to merge these into a smaller number of units along industrial lines.

In some countries one finds multi-industry unions covering a complex of related activities. In Italy, for example, both employers and workers are organized by *categories* of employment. The "metal–mechanical category" covers steel, automobiles, shipbuilding, electrical apparatus, and a variety of other metal-fabricating industries. In West Germany the Metal Workers' Union, which has almost a quarter of total union membership in the country, includes workers in iron and steel plants, automobile factories, foundries, machine shops, electrical equipment factories, and many others. In Britain, the giant Transport and General Workers' Union takes in members from a wide range of industries.

Multi-industry unionism is not common in the United States, where the AFL–CIO has usually defined jurisdiction along industry lines or along narrower craft lines within an industry. The United Steelworkers, however, embraces a wide range of steel-fabricating industries. The United Automobile Workers extends beyond automobiles into aircraft and other industries, where it often encounters the even more wide-ranging Machinists' union. The Teamsters, while it has a solid core of truck drivers, has ranged far afield to take in members only distantly related—or not related at all—to transportation.

Levels of Organization

The basic units of the trade union world are local units, but these can be set up in two different ways. First, a local may include only employees of a single company. This is the main basis of organization in the United States. (Where employers are numerous and small, however, the same local may include employees of different companies, as is usually true of the building trades' union, the retail clerks, and so on.) In Japan, too, where worker attachment to the enterprise is very important, the enterprise union is typically the basic unit. Its company-oriented character is indicated by the fact that it usually includes white-collar workers up to the lower levels of management, and that many union officers are from the white-collar group.

In most countries, however, union organization is basically territorial. The local branch includes all members of a particular union, regardless of employer, in a particular city or district. There may be sublocals for members in a particular plant, but these groups do not have the independence and vitality of the U.S. plant local. This weakness, in most countries, of *union organization within the plant* is a serious handicap in handling issues arising at the plant level.

In France, Italy, Latin America, and some other countries the situation is complicated by political and religious cleavages. Thus instead of a single construction workers' local in a French city, one may have a communist-oriented local, a socialist-oriented local, and a Catholic-oriented local. Each of these will have members who work side by side for all construction employers in the area.

The superstructure of the union world is constructed along both industrial and geographic lines. The local union of construction workers belongs to a national union of construction workers, representing workers in this industry throughout the country. At the same time the construction workers' local will usually belong to a federation of all local unions in its city; and above this may be broader federations on a state or regional basis. At the top of the structure is an overarching federation, uniting both the industrial unions and the geographic federations in a single body. Thus in the United States most unions are affiliated with the AFL–CIO, in Britain with the Trade Union Congress (TUC), in Sweden with the Landsorganisationen (LO), in Germany with the Deutsche Gewerkschaftsbund (DGB). In France and Italy, because of the political cleavages noted above, there are three top federations, each with a full panoply of national industrial unions and territorial federations.

Where does power reside in this complex structure? The answers differ from country to country. Broadly, the relative importance of industrial as against territorial units is linked to the relative emphasis on collective bargaining as against political action in a particular country. If one wants to bring pressure on the city council, the local federation of all unions in the city is the strongest instrument. At the national level, top federations such as the AFL–CIO are useful for lobbying and other political activities. For negotiating a contract with all steel producers, on the other hand, it is the United Steelworkers which matters; and here the national industrial union comes to the center of the stage. Thus in countries where collective bargaining is well established, the national industrial unions are the core of the trade union world. In countries where labor activities are more politically oriented, the geographic federations are relatively more important.

UNION STRATEGIES: POLITICAL ACTION

Unions pursue their objectives in two main ways: by bargaining with employers and by political action. On a world scale, the latter technique is more widely used. In almost every country the trade unions are associated with one or more political parties; and they function as a pressure group to secure minimum wage laws, social security laws, and other things of benefit to their members. Direct bargaining with employers is the predominant activity in only a handful of countries: Britain, Germany, the Scandinavian countries, Canada, the United States, Mexico, Australia, New Zealand, possibly Japan. Even in these countries, political action is of substantial importance.

This bifurcation of union strategy raises fascinating questions, about which little is known: What determines the distribution of union effort between politics and collective bargaining in a particular country? How is this related to the importance of government in the country's economy? To what extent do unions turn to politics because they are too weak to deal directly with employers? Does growing union strength in a country produce a shift of emphasis toward collective bargaining?

In terms of union–party relations, countries can be divided into four groups: (1) one-party countries, in which the party is dominant and unions play a subsidiary role; (2) labor party countries, in which most unions are affiliated with a moderate socialist party on the British pattern; (3) fractionalized countries, in which there are several left-wing parties, with union support divided among them; (4) neutral countries, in which the unions have no official party affiliation.

One-Party Systems

The leading example of the one-party system is the Soviet-type economy, in which the Communist Party is the only recognized political organization. This is a relatively small, carefully selected, elite group, to which top figures in all branches of national life normally belong.

There are trade unions in these countries, with a typical structure of plant locals, industry-wide organizations, and national federations. The question whether these are "genuine" unions is perhaps a semantic one. They are certainly different from our unions, reflecting the institutional differences in the society. Most people are public employees, and a strike against the government is viewed with even more disfavor in the USSR than in the United States. Wage schedules for the entire economy are centrally determined. Individual plant managers operate within financial and other limits laid down by higher authorities, so that bargaining with them cannot have the same meaning as bargaining with the Ford Motor Company.

The top union federation, however, is involved in framing wage schedules and national regulations on hours, health, and safety standards, vacations, bonuses, and so on. The local union, as will be explained in a later section, plays an important role in handling worker grievances. Its leverage comes from the fact that the elected union officials are natural leaders in the plant and often members of the Communist Party. A plant manager who is unreasonable and uncooperative in labor matters will find his shortcomings discussed in the local party meeting, and reports may go back to Moscow, through both party and union channels, that will do him no good.[3]

Labor Party Countries

In labor party countries a moderate socialist party operates with trade union support. This group includes Britain, Australia, New Zealand, and the three Scandinavian countries.

The nature and closeness of affiliation varies from country to country. In Denmark, individuals can join the party only by enrolling in the party club of their district. In Norway and Sweden, it is common for local unions to affiliate as a group. About half the membership of the Norwegian Labor Party, and about two-thirds that of the Swedish Social Democratic Party, comes from unionists who have affiliated in this way. In some countries national unions may affiliate for their entire membership. In Britain, for example, some eighty national unions are affiliated with the Labour Party, and these unions provide more than four-fifths of the party's members. Where block affiliation is practiced, there is normally a legal provision that individual union members who favor another party may claim exemption from contributing money to support of the affiliated party.

Unlike the one-party countries, where the party is dominant and the unions subordinate, the union–labor party relation is conceived as an association of equal partners, with each organization performing its own functions under its own leadership. This does not mean that the relation is an easy one. The party, to win a national election, must present a program that will attract middle-class and white-collar voters as well as manual workers. Once in office, it is responsible for governing in the national interest. This may lead it to take positions that its union supporters regard as against their own interest. But if it goes too far in this direction, it will weaken its union base and will no longer be able to govern.

This dilemma is well illustrated by the problem of wage policy. In the era of high employment and continuing inflation since World War II, even labor governments have sought means of restraining the onrush of money wages. But it is hard to explain to union members why "their" government should be trying to hold down their wage increases. The result has been considerable union–party tension and considerable vacillation in policy. Another example is the 1969 effort of Labour Prime Minister Harold Wil-

---

[3] The best available description of labor relations in the USSR is Emily C. Brown, *Soviet Trade Unions and Labor Relations* (Cambridge, Mass.: Harvard University Press, 1966).

son to impose restraints on unauthorized (wildcat) strikes, which in long-shoring and elsewhere have done considerable harm to Britain's export trade. Union officials, of whom more than a hundred sit as Labour members of Parliament, took strong exception to this proposal, and the government withdrew it rather than face serious intraparty strife.

Fractionalized Countries

In many countries several left-wing parties compete for union support. There are often "right-wing" and "left-wing" socialist parties. Even the more disciplined communist group may be divided into pro-Moscow, pro-Peking, and (in Latin America) pro-Havana factions. Each group has its supporters in the union world.

The union–party relation is usually not a formal affiliation, but a looser and more personal relationship. Some union leaders move over to become party leaders, and conversely. A union collaborates with its chosen party in organizing demonstrations, providing election workers and election finance, and selecting candidates for office. The party provides trained leadership and other free services to the union. Strikes and demonstrations are called over political as well as economic issues.

In France and Italy, the largest union federations have close links with the communist parties of those countries. Several factors help to account for this. In both countries class lines are firmly drawn and class feeling is bitter. Employers typically look down on their workers to an extent that is difficult to imagine in the United States. They are bitterly opposed to dealing with trade unions, and collective bargaining is poorly developed. The unions are weakly organized, poorly financed, and the attachment of workers to them is so loose that one can scarcely speak of "union membership" in the American sense. A union may be able to call out a large number of workers for a short strike, but it cannot get these same workers to pay dues or participate in ordinary union activities. Seeing no way of rising through their own efforts and apparently blocked from advance through collective bargaining, not surprisingly, the workers turn to political activity. Economic and social reforms in these countries have been achieved almost entirely through legislation rather than through private collective bargaining. It is not surprising, then, that the political parties dominate the trade unions, and that the party with greatest popular appeal is the one that denounces employers in the strongest terms.

The situation is similar in many of the Latin American countries. The social gulf between employer and employee is wide, unions are rather weak and often led by men with primarily political interests, collective bargaining is poorly developed, and improvements in wages and other terms of employment are sought mainly through government. These conditions tend to produce a strong political orientation of the labor movement. Periodically, trade unions are suppressed by military or other dictatorships. In between, union strength is fragmented by rivalry among numerous left-wing groups.

An interesting exception is Mexico, where the unions are "in" rather than "out." Unions participated actively in the Mexican Revolution a half century ago, and are now a pillar of the dominant political party, which has governed continuously since the revolution. The leading union federation (the CTM) and most of its affiliates are solidly proadministration, though there is a communist-led minority. CTM leaders help to choose presidential candidates, are consulted on all relevant legislation, and appear frequently as legislators and administrators.[4]

In Japan there are right-wing socialist, left-wing socialist, and communist parties, each with its union supporters. In spite of the fact—or perhaps because of the fact—that workers have a rather paternalistic relation with the companies employing them, there is a strong "class struggle" atmosphere in Japanese politics. Antagonisms and frustrations that are muted within the enterprise break out in the political arena.

Union Neutrality in Politics

The leading example here is the United States. In modern times, left-wing political groups have not attained significant strength. Union groups with an ideological outlook, such as the Knights of Labor and the Industrial Workers of the World, have had little influence since World War I. The Socialist Party polled its largest presidential vote in 1912, but its strength has declined since then and is negligible at present. The Communist Party achieved some influence in the depressed conditions of the 1930s. A number of communists volunteered as organizers in the early CIO campaigns, and later served as officers of the new unions. After 1945, however, the foreign-policy split between the United States and the USSR produced a similar split between American communists (who continued to support the Soviet position) and noncommunist labor leaders. During 1949 and 1950, eleven national unions with some 900,000 members were expelled from the CIO on grounds of communist control. The present AFL–CIO constitution contains strong provisions against domination of unions by communists or members of other totalitarian groups, and communist influence has fallen to a very low level.

The earlier AFL and the present AFL–CIO have also refused to ally themselves permanently with either of the major political parties. They

---

[4] See two books by Robert J. Alexander: *The Labor Movement in Brazil, Argentina, and Chile* (New York: McGraw-Hill Book Company, 1962); and *Organized Labor in Latin America* (New York: The Free Press, 1965).

pick and choose among candidates from one election to the next, depending mainly on the individual's voting record on labor issues. Since the New Deal era, however, there has been a strong tendency to support the Democratic candidate in presidential elections.

In West Germany also there is a single major union federation, which is officially neutral among parties. This was not always so. Before World War II the German labor movement was divided among communist, socialist, and religious groupings. This fragmentation of the labor movement is believed to have weakened the basis of democratic government, contributing to Hitler's rise to power in 1933. Burned by this experience, postwar union leaders have resolved to avoid ideological cleavages in the interest of a united labor movement. In day-to-day politics, German unions lean toward the Social Democrats; but there is no direct party affiliation.

UNION STRATEGIES: COLLECTIVE BARGAINING

An important union activity in most countries, and the major activity in some, is negotiating with employers over wages and other terms of employment. This procedure is called *collective bargaining,* and its outcome is a *collective agreement* or *union contract.*

The arrangements for collective bargaining, like the structure of trade unions themselves, vary widely from country to country. We may note differences in the coverage of collective agreements, the content of these agreements, arrangements for handling grievances at the plant level, and use of the strike weapon.

The Area of the Collective Agreement

The collective agreement may cover a small number of workers or a very large number. It may be limited to employers of a single company or even a single plant. Alternatively, it may cover all workers of a certain type in a particular district, or all workers in an industry throughout the country. In a few countries, top union and management federations negotiate on broad issues for the whole union membership.

Single-company agreements are important in a few countries—the United States, Canada, Japan, Chile. On a world scale, however, the dominant form is the multiemployer agreement, negotiated with an employers' association. For local trade and service industries, building construction, and manufacturing industries catering to a local market, this may be a city-wide agreement. For national industries—mining, transportation, public utilities, most manufacturing—it will usually embrace workers and employers throughout the country. This is almost the exclusive form of bargaining in Germany, Holland, Italy, and the Scandinavian countries. It is the dominant form in Britain and France. It is prevalent practice also in Australia, in Mexico, and in the French-speaking areas of Africa. Even in the United States, the great majority of union members in building construction, garment manufacture, coal mining, transportation, retailing, and service industries (altogether, upward of 6 million workers) are covered by local or national multiemployer agreements.

There are several pressures making for multiemployer agreements. Where employers are numerous and small, as in retailing, hotel and restaurant employment, local trucking, or building construction, the individual employer is in a weak position to resist union demands. It seems clear that employers can increase their bargaining power by forming a common front. Even where employers are larger, they are in competition with each other; and labor costs are usually an important factor in this competition. Each employer has an interest in seeing that rival employers have to pay as much for labor as he does. Again, the logic points toward joint negotiation and a uniform wage scale.

Government intervention in the bargaining process also makes for larger bargaining units. These are more convenient from an administrative standpoint, and so government agencies usually prefer them. In Australia, for example, industrial disputes tend to end up before a government arbitration board, with power to make a binding decision. The procedure is rather time-consuming and expensive. So employers and unions, instead of processing dozens of small cases, usually band together to seek decisions with broad coverage.

In a number of countries, including Italy, France, Holland, Germany, and the French-speaking African countries, there is provision for legal "extension" of the terms of a collective agreement. An agreement that covers more than 50 percent of workers in an industry, or that has been negotiated by "representative" associations of employers and workers, is given the force of law throughout the industry. This places a premium on industry-wide negotiations covering enough workers to claim representative status.

The most highly centralized negotiations occur in the Scandinavian countries. These economies are small and compact, everyone who is anyone lives in the capital city, and leaders of all economic and political groups are well acquainted with each other. The top union and employer federations have strong disciplinary powers, and a union or employer group that engages in a work stoppage without federation approval receives no financial support. The bargaining season opens each year with consultation among top officials of the union federation, their opposite numbers in the employers' federation, and government economic officials who can judge the impact of prospective wage increases on the national economy. The object is to hammer out broad guidelines for the subsequent negotiations in each industry.

The individual industries are not strictly bound by the guidelines, and the ultimate wage increases tend to average out higher than the top leaders originally intend. But the procedure probably does moderate the pace of wage movements, and may also facilitate agreed readjustments of *relative* wages in the economy—for example, by restraining some of the highest-paid groups while the lower-paid are brought nearer to their level.

The Content of the Agreement

The content of the agreement varies greatly from country to country. Broadly, the larger the coverage of the agreement, the simpler its terms are likely to be. The European and British agreements, which cover an entire industry or even several industries, usually set only a minimum wage level. Individual employers may pay more than the minimum and, in the tight labor markets that have prevailed since World War II, they have usually done so. Rates for particular jobs, and other details of the wage structure, are not covered by the national agreement.

Such broad national agreements should logically be supplemented by more detailed agreements at lower levels; but the extent to which this is done varies from country to country. In Britain, there has been a considerable movement toward local agreements to set standards above the minimum. In most countries, however, local agreements are fragmentary. This is due basically to union weakness at the plant level, which leaves the employer in a dominant position. He conforms to the minimum standards laid down in the national agreement; but he declines to be bound beyond this.

Collective agreements in the United States are probably the most detailed and complex in the world. In addition to covering wages and hours, they usually include provisions for the union shop or some other form of union security; provisions governing layoffs, promotion, and discharge of employees; clauses requiring compensation for workers displaced by technical change; provision for health care, pensions, and other "fringe benefits"; and provision for handling employee grievances arising during the life of the contract. Canadian agreements, many of which are negotiated by U.S.-based unions, tend to resemble U.S. agreements. Mexico also has rather complex and complete union contracts. In other countries, however, most of the items included in U.S. agreements do not appear.

The reasons for this include: (1) Some of the matters covered in U.S.

contracts are covered in other countries by legislation. Examples are pensions, medical care, unemployment compensation, and other social insurance benefits. (2) Some items may not be of interest to unions in a particular country for special reasons. British unions, for example, are not interested in the union shop because they are able to isolate nonunion workers by social pressure. (3) Union weakness is a major contributing factor. Employers throughout the world are strongly opposed to being restricted on matters of employee selection, promotion, and discipline, and on questions of production methods and technical change. It takes a strong and aggressive union to impose such restrictions. In most countries the trade unions are not strong enough at the plant level to win concessions on these points.

Grievance Procedure

Once a collective agreement has been signed, the employer is bound by its rules. But suppose that the employer breaks the rules the following week? Or suppose that a question arises as to what a particular rule really means? How are such day-to-day problems to be settled?

American collective agreements normally provide that any worker who thinks he has been treated improperly under the contract may take the matter to his union representative. The representative discusses it with the man's supervisor, and the case is appealed if necessary through higher union and management levels. If there is still no agreement, the case is usually referred to an outside arbitrator whose decision is final. This is termed the *grievance procedure.* Its object is to provide for orderly day-to-day administration of the contract, and to avoid the possibility of strikes over individual grievances.

To anyone familiar with the American system, it is startling to find that few other countries have this kind of grievance procedure. (Canada and Mexico are exceptions, their agreements resembling U.S. agreements on this point as on others.) One reason is that few union movements have enough money to afford paid local officials. In Britain, for example, the grass-roots union representative is usually a "shop steward," who tends to become the *de facto* negotiator, grievance settler, and strike caller in the plant. But the stewards, who are locally elected and unpaid, are not really under the control of the national union. This fact, plus the absence of local contracts with a clear grievance procedure, helps to account for the large number of "quickie" strikes in Britain. This is a common situation in other countries. Local grievances fester and accumulate until they spill over into strike action.

A complicating factor in several European countries (and in some of the ex-British and ex-French areas of Africa and Asia) is legal provision for *plant committees* or *works councils*. These are elected by all workers in the plant and have legally defined functions. Although unions often sponsor candidates in these elections and thus try to infiltrate the plant committees, the committees themselves are not part of the union machinery. Yet they have grievance-handling and negotiating functions that in the United States would clearly be union responsibilities. For example, the German plant committees have: (1) a right of *co-decision* on "social matters," which include working conditions, methods of remuneration, establishment of piece rates, work schedules, vacation schedules, welfare services, and industrial discipline; (2) a right to be *consulted* on "personnel matters," such as recruitment, promotion and layoff.

From one standpoint, the existence of these committees reduces the need for union–management negotiation at the plant level. From another standpoint, they provide employers who wish to ignore the union with an effective means of bypassing it by carrying all issues to the plant committee.

We may add a word on the grievance-handling functions of local unions in the USSR. All workers in a Soviet plant are *de facto* union members and participate in electing a factory committee, which has the following functions: (1) the committee has a right to be *consulted* on production plans, plant expansion, and mechanization that might lead to displacement of labor; also, it must be consulted on appointments of managerial personnel; (2) the committee must *agree* on matters of overtime work, discharge of employees, penalties on any member of the factory committee, vacation schedules, distribution of housing, allocation of profits retained by the enterprise, and all details of the wage system and production standards.

Grievances of individual workers are processed through the following stages: (1) an effort is made to work out the problem directly with management; (2) unsettled cases go next to a commission on labor disputes, which has an equal number of members from the factory committee and from management; (3) a worker can appeal from this body to the full factory committee, but management has no appeal right; (4) the final appeal is to a district court. The emphasis of the system is on quick settlement, with deadlines of ten days or less for each stage of the procedure. Workers who are found to have been discharged illegally are ordered reinstated with back pay.

This machinery could be merely window dressing for one-man rule by the factory manager; but it does not seem to be so in practice. Managers often complain that they are hampered by pressure from the factory committee, and some express antiunion sentiments not unlike those heard in the United States. Removal of managers with a poor record in labor matters is not uncommon.

The Strike Weapon

The main weapon used to enforce union demands is the strike. There are several kinds of strike. First, there are strikes of indefinite duration over the terms of a new agreement. If negotiations do not produce a meeting of minds, the men walk out and stay out until, after further negotiations, a settlement is finally reached. This kind of strike seems to be declining gradually in the older unionized countries. In part, this may reflect the strength of union and employer organization. In Sweden, for example, a union whose strike is approved by the central labor federation can draw on the full resources of the federation. Similarly, employers are reimbursed by the employers' federation for profits lost during the shutdown. Neither side can starve out the other and a strike, once called, could continue forever. But just for this reason large strikes involving a whole industry are very rare.

Unions in most countries have low dues, small financial reserves, and cannot afford a long strike. A common device in such countries is the *scheduled strike,* called for a definite and short period, after which the union automatically returns to work. This is a standard technique in Japan. In France, Italy, and Latin America, there are frequent one- or two-day stoppages, sometimes involving a large segment of organized labor. This kind of strike seems to accompany union weakness in collective bargaining and heavy involvement in political party activity.

A third type is the *quickie* or *wildcat* strike, an impromptu stoppage over a localized issue. In the United States, union contracts normally prohibit this kind of strike and provide that detailed grievances shall be settled peaceably through the grievance procedure. But many such strikes do occur each year. Local union leaders and members who feel that the machinery is moving too slowly often take matters into their own hands. Quickie strikes are even commoner in countries where collective agreements do not include a grievance procedure. Such strikes are usually short; but if they occur again and again in the same plant, they can seriously disrupt production.

A special problem is strikes of public employees. In most of the "mixed economies," government now employs a substantial percentage of the labor force. Government employees are often strongly unionized; but a strike by public employees is usually considered illegal, as constituting an attack on the sovereignty of the state. Strikes nevertheless occur—either openly or in the disguised form of "calling in sick," observing every rule in the book, or otherwise slowing down production. How to resolve disputes when the rules of private bargaining do not apply is a growing issue in the United States.

THE FRAMEWORK OF PUBLIC CONTROL

We have noted a variety of ways in which government enters the industrial relations scene. Government regulates the general level of employment, with important effects on employers' and employees' bargaining power. Government often regulates wage rates and other terms of employment in greater or less detail. Government determines the legal status and powers of trade unions. It may regulate the procedures for union–management negotiation and the permissible content of collective agreements. It always limits use of the strike and other economic weapons and often prescribes procedures for resolving unsettled disputes. What government does, or fails to do, in each of these respects, affects the climate of industrial relations.

Government and the Wage Structure

In many countries government engages in extensive wage regulation. But wages are also the most important single issue in collective bargaining. To the extent that government takes over responsibility for wage decisions, the importance of collective bargaining is diminished, and union activities are directed toward influencing the wage-setting agencies.

France, for example, has an elaborate structure of legal minimum wages, providing graduated minima for higher occupational classifications, and geographic adjustments for different regions and sizes of city. These legal scales are the bony framework inside the actual wage structure. The French system has been imitated in most of the French-speaking countries of West and Central Africa. In India and some other ex-British colonial areas, government also has a decisive influence on the level and structure of wages.

Australia has a complex system, including two kinds of agency—the wage board and the arbitration tribunal—and including agencies of the various state governments as well as the Commonwealth government.[5] Wage boards have been set up to establish minimum wages in sectors where unionism is weak or absent. In strongly unionized industries, wage disputes usually end up before one of the arbitration tribunals, whose awards are binding. Purely private wage agreements are less numerous and important than in the United States, and union officials spend much of their time preparing and presenting cases before official bodies.

Most countries also have an elaborate body of social legislation cover-

---

[5] On the Australian system, see Kenneth F. Walker, *Industrial Relations in Australia* (Cambridge, Mass.: Harvard University Press, 1956); and J. E. Isaac and G. W. Ford (eds.), *Australian Labour Relations Readings* (Melbourne: Sun Books, 1966).

ing such things as hours of work, health and safety standards, retirement pensions, unemployment compensation, and medical and hospital care. To the extent that these matters are arranged by government, they do not have to be bargained about with employers. Government decrees are in this sense competitive with union contracts; and the greater their importance the more will union activity be directed into political channels.

The Status of Unions and Collective Agreements

In various countries unions are treated as: (1) prohibited organizations; (2) purely private associations; (3) organizations recognized, and in some measure controlled, by government; (4) official organs of the state.

At one extreme, British unions have traditionally been regarded as purely private bodies. They have the right to exist and to win concessions from employers through their economic power. But government does not intervene to protect, certify, or control them.[6]

More commonly, unions win the right to represent a certain body of employees through certification by a government agency. In the United States, the National Labor Relations Board certifies bargaining representatives through procedures described in a later chapter. Similar procedures operate in Canada. In most of the Western European countries, a government agency determines which is the "dominant" union in a particular industry, and this becomes the group authorized to negotiate with employers. In most of the less developed countries a union must be registered— "acquire a legal personality," as is said in Latin America—before its activities can have legal status.

Government recognition tend to bring varying degrees of public control. In some countries, including the United States, there is an elaborate body of law concerning internal union government, collective bargaining procedures, and legally permissible tactics of unions and employers.

There is a similar variation in the legal status of collective agreements. In Britain, these are purely private agreements between the parties. In the United States and some other countries, they have more nearly the status of a commercial contract, and one party can sue the other for damages resulting from violation of contract. Such suits are not common, but the courts will recognize them. In still other cases, the agreement has virtually the effect of a government decree. In Germany, Italy, France, and the French-speaking countries of Africa, an industry agreement negotiated by a "representative" union may be extended by decree to all employers and workers in the industry. In such countries figures on the coverage of col-

---

[6] This situation has been somewhat altered, however, by the Industrial Relations Act of 1971, which attempts to impose—with what success remains to be seen —a variety of statutory controls on union organizaion and collective bargaining.

lective agreements can be quite misleading. Wide coverage may result mainly from government procedures rather than from large union membership.

Adjustment of Industrial Disputes

There is a distinction here between disputes over the terms of a new contract and those over grievances arising under an existing contract. The former are disputes over *interests,* the latter disputes over *rights;* and the two are often treated differently in public policy. A common provision is that disputes over interests may be carried to the length of a strike after other possibilities have been exhausted, while disputes over rights must be settled by private arbitration or referred to a government tribunal. The reason is that, in disputes over what a certain contract clause means, or over whether a worker actually did the things for which he was discharged under the contract, judges and arbitrators can make findings of fact and rely on established precedents in similar cases. In a contract dispute over whether the wage increase should be twenty cents or twenty-five cents an hour, it is harder to find principles that an outside arbitrator can apply and that the parties are willing to accept.

The largest and longest strikes typically occur over new contract terms. In this area, there are several degrees of government intervention:

1. *Voluntary conciliation.* Most governments maintain experienced staffs who stand ready, with the consent of the parties, to step into a dispute and try to work out settlement. In the United States this kind of help is available from the U.S. Mediation and Conciliation Service in the Department of Labor, and from similar services in most of the larger states.

2. *Compulsory conciliation.* Under this, the parties *must* permit a government mediator to try and settle the dispute before taking strike action. This is a common procedure in Canada; but the situation varies from province to province, because main authority over industrial relations is vested in the provincial governments. In the United States, compulsory conciliation applies by statute to the railroad and airline industries, and can be applied to major disputes in other industries by presidential decision.

There is a wide variety of possible procedures. Conciliation may be undertaken by a single mediator, by a permanent conciliation board, or by a board appointed specially for each case. The board may or may not have a duty to file a report on the issues in the case, and this report may or may not be made public. The parties are sometimes required to wait for a certain length of time after a report has been filed (a *cooling-off* period) before taking strike action.

3. *Compulsory arbitration.* This is a procedure under which, after negotiation and conciliation have been exhausted, an unsettled dispute must be referred to a government arbitration board. The board's award is binding, and a strike against it is illegal. The countries with longest experience of compulsory arbitration are New Zealand and Australia, which have systems dating from the 1890s. Some of the Canadian provinces have compulsory arbitration procedures. There is no regular provision for compulsory arbitration in the United

States, though in a recent railroad strike Congress passed a special law sending the dispute to arbitration.

Experts have been arguing the merits of compulsory arbitration for decades. Broadly, the argument for it is that it provides a civilized way of settling disputes through a judicial process, without the loss of production and income associated with a strike. As a practical matter, the party that is weaker in a particular situation may be able to get more through a government board than through direct bargaining; and unions or managements have sometimes supported the procedure for this reason. Against compulsory arbitration it is argued that the parties know their own interests better, and are better able to write a workable agreement, than any outside body; and that if an outside board is available, the parties will cease to bargain seriously with each other and will refer all issues to the board. Even in Australia, after seventy years of experience, there is substantial difference of expert opinion on the merits of the arbitration system.

DISTINCTIVE FEATURES OF AMERICAN INDUSTRIAL RELATIONS

The theme of this chapter has been variety in institutions and procedures. Viewed in world perspective, many features of the American system appear unusual rather than typical. These features include:

1. The concept of exclusive jurisdiction
2. Substantial importance of craft organization
3. Substantial importance of single-company agreements
4. Complex agreements specifying employment conditions in considerable detail and restricting employers' managerial authority at many points
5. Strong grass-roots organization, with plant-based locals the predominant form
6. Well-developed grievance procedures culminating in arbitration
7. Predominance of collective bargaining over political activity
8. Absence of political party affiliation
9. Limited government influence on wage rates, fringe benefits, and other terms of employment
10. Extensive legal regulation of collective bargaining procedures and tactics
11. Absence of provisions for compulsory settlement of contract disputes

Why have these characteristics developed in the United States to a greater degree than elsewhere? This qquestion should be kept in mind as we examine the American system in more detail in the following chapters.

American unionism is often termed *business unionism,* because of the concentration on driving bargains with employers, the relative neglect of political action, and the disinterest in—or even scorn for—abstract ideologies. The conventional wisdom has it that this represents a "mature" stage of union development. Unions that are deeply involved in party politics, as in France, Italy and many of the less developed countries, are simply immature unions which, as they develop further, will shed their ideological trappings and concentrate increasingly on collective bargaining. Is this a valid theory of union evolution? Or does it simply reflect a cultural bias, a natural feeling that others should behave as we do? On these questions, too, we might well for the time being keep an open mind.

DISCUSSION QUESTIONS

1. "Unionism is a carryover from the period before full employment. Under conditions of substantially full employment, it no longer serves any major function and may be expected to decline in future importance." Discuss.

2. "Russian unions, which lack the ability to strike, have no real leverage over management. They are most nearly comparable to the 'company unions' that flourished in the United States before 1930." Do you agree? Why or why not?

3. In most countries, unions including all workers in an industry and collective agreements covering all firms in the industry are the general rule. What are the main reasons for this pattern of organization?

4. Does major involvement in political party activity represent an "immature" stage of union development? Explain.

5. Unions in the less developed countries are generally regarded as weaker than those in the advanced industrial countries. What are the main reasons for, and the main indications of, this weakness?

6. American collective agreements cover many more subjects, and have a more detailed grievance procedure, than agreements in most other countries. What would you surmise to be the main reason for this difference?

7. What limitations, if any, do you think government should place on the right to strike?

READING SUGGESTIONS

For a general survey of the issues raised in this chapter, see JOHN T. DUNLOP, *Industrial Relations Systems,* New York: Holt, Rinehart and Winston, Inc., 1958; JOHN T. DUNLOP, FREDERICK HARBISON, CLARK KERR, and CHARLES MYERS, *Industrialism and Industrial Man,* Cambridge, Mass.: Harvard University Press, 1960.

There are a large number of monographs on particular countries or groups of countries. Especially worth reading are ROBERT J. ALEXANDER, *The Labor Movement in Brazil, Argentina, and Chile,* New York: Mc-Graw-Hill Book Company, 1962; EMILY C. BROWN, *Soviet Trade Unions and Labor Relations,* Cambridge, Mass.: Harvard University Press, 1966; ALICE H. COOK, *Japanese Trade Unionism,* Ithaca: Cornell University Press, 1966; WALTER GALENSON (ed.), *Labor and Economic Development,* New York: John Wiley & Sons, Inc., 1959; WALTER GALENSON (ed.), *Labor in Developing Countries,* Berkeley and Los Angeles: University of California Press, 1962; J. S. ISAAC and G. W. FORD (eds.), *Australian Labour Relations Readings,* Melbourne: Sun Books, 1966; VAL R. LORWIN, *The French Labor Movement,* Cambridge, Mass.: Harvard University Press, 1955; CHARLES A. MYERS, *Labor Problems in the Industrialization of India,* Cambridge, Mass.: Harvard University Press, 1958; B. C. ROBERTS and L. G. DE BELLECOMBE, *Collective Bargaining in African Countries,* New York: St. Martin's Press, Inc., 1967; A. F. STURMTHAL (ed.), *Contemporary Collective Bargaining in Seven Countries,* Ithaca: Cornell University Press, 1957; and KENNETH WALKER, *Industrial Relations in Australia,* Cambridge, Mass.: Harvard University Press, 1956.

15

The Evolution of
American Unionism

More than fifty years ago Sidney and Beatrice Webb defined a trade union as "a continuous association of wage earners for the purpose of maintaining or improving the conditions of their working lives." This chapter is concerned with the development of such associations in the United States since their origin around the year 1790.

REASONS FOR THE DEVELOPMENT OF UNIONS

This history of American unionism is frequently dated from 1792, when a local union was formed by the journeymen cordwainers (shoemakers) of Philadelphia. Within the next ten years unions of shoemakers, carpenters, and printers were founded in Baltimore, Philadelphia, Boston, New York, and several other cities.

What accounts for the appearance of these associations? They cannot be traced to particular oppression of workers at that time. On the contrary most workers were better off in 1800 than they had been in 1780. It is significant also that unions did not appear at first among the most exploited groups—the cotton-mill workers, and home workers on piece rates —but among skilled tradesmen such as the printers, carpenters, and shoemakers. In the United States, as in most other industrial countries, the relatively skilled and prosperous workers organized first. The first unions in Great Britain, for example, consisted of building- and printing-trades workers, who were followed shortly afterward by unions of tailors and wool combers. In Sweden, the first unions were formed by the printers, the next by the carpenters, and the next by the skilled metal-trades workers.

Neither can the rise of unionism be traced to the introduction of machine production. None of the industries organized during the period

1790 to 1830 had been significantly affected by machine methods. An important stimulus to union organization in some industries, however, was the broadening of the domestic market for manufactures, which resulted from the improvement of transportation facilities. This expansion meant intensified competition in the sale of goods—shoes made in Philadelphia competed increasingly with shoes made in New York, Baltimore, and other cities. The merchant capitalist appeared, playing off small masters against each other and forcing them to cut wages in order to survive. This activity threatened the journeymen's customary standard of life and forced them into defensive organizations.

The growth of the market also fostered division of labor and development of larger production units. Even without mechanization of production, this meant that it took more capital to set oneself up in business and that it was increasingly difficult for journeymen to rise to the master class. The gulf between worker and employer widened. For the first time there appeared a group of permanent wage earners, who had little expectation of becoming masters in the future. Moreover, greater specialization of tasks reduced the element of skill in the production process. The semiskilled operative made his appearance and the need for fully skilled craftsmen diminished. This threat to the craftsmen's skill was unpleasant in itself and also threatened his earning power.

The extension of the market for manufactures can scarcely explain the rise of unionism in industries such as printing and building construction, which continued to cater to purely local markets. While product markets in these industries remained local, however, the labor market broadened steadily as improved transportation increased the mobility of labor. Printers, carpenters, and bricklayers began to move about the country in considerable numbers and were sometimes used by employers to undercut local wage scales. Some means had to be found for controlling this competition. Moreover, in local-market as well as national-market industries, employers were sometimes led by business depression or price competition to make a direct onslaught on established wage scales and working conditions. The development of local unions was a natural protective response to this pressure.

Until after the Civil War, almost all unions were local unions of workers in a particular trade or industry, and they were confined largely to a few cities along the Atlantic seaboard. These early unions were strikingly modern in objectives and methods. From the beginning, regulation of wages was the main issue and the strike was the main weapon. There was little, it is true, which could be termed "collective bargaining" during this period. In the beginning, the union simply decided on its "price" (that is wage rate), and the members pledged themselves not to work below this price. A little later, it became customary for a union committee to visit each employer and request his adherence to the union rate. Those who refused to agree were struck. There was still no written agreement with employers, and the procedure could scarcely be called bargaining. The wage scale was determined unilaterally by the union, and employers were given the choice of conforming or not conforming. When nonconforming employers were struck, the *walking delegate,* who at first was an unpaid worker but later became a paid official, went from shop to shop to make sure that all union members were out. Strikebreakers were termed *rats,* and later *scabs.* The locals of the same trade in different cities exchanged lists of scabs and agreed not to admit them to membership. This activity was almost the only contact between local unions in the early days. Strikes were financed by levies on the membership. They were relatively peaceful, and, except in depression periods, most of them were successful.

Another policy of the earliest trade unions was not to work with non-union men. The union shop, like the union wage scale, was enforced directly through a pledge by unionists "not to work for anybody who does not pay the rate nor beside anyone who does not get the rate." Nonunionists were also boycotted socially; union men would not live in the same boarding houses or eat at the same places as nonunion men. Thus the union shop, which is sometimes pictured as a new invention, actually dates from the earliest days of unionism in this country.

Apprenticeship regulations were another major concern of the early unions. Their main purpose was to prevent employers from replacing journeymen with learners, runaway apprentices, and women at wage rates below the union scale. The number of apprentices which an employer might train was usually limited to a certain proportion of the number of journeymen employed. They were required to serve a specified period of apprenticeship, and only journeymen who had completed this apprenticeship were admitted to the union and allowed to work in union shops.

These unions, though few in number, were sufficiently strong and aggressive to arouse consternation among employers. Editorial writers denounced unionism, employers' associations were formed to combat it, and conspiracy cases were launched against the unions in the courts. The antiunion arguments, like the union tactics of the day, have a surprisingly modern ring.[1] One hundred and fifty years have brought little change in

---

[1] The master carpenters of Boston, for example, when confronted in 1825 with a demand for a ten-hour day, replied that they could not believe "this project to have originated with any of the faithful and industrious sons of New England, but are compelled to consider it an evil of foreign growth, and one which we hope and trust will not take root in the favored soil of Massachusetts. . . . And especially that our city, the early rising and industry of whose inhabitants are universally proverbial, may not be infected with the unnatural production." John R. Commons and associates, *History of Labor in the United States,* Vol. 1 (New York: The Macmillan Company, 1918), p. 160. See also the antiunion statements on p. 271 of this same volume and those contained in E. W. Bakke and Clark Kerr (eds.), *Unions,*

the issues at stake and the arguments advanced on either side. Many of the arguments put forward today might easily have been copied from newspapers and speeches of a hundred years ago.

An important characteristic of these early unions was their inability to withstand business depression. They sprang up and flourished in good years but were nearly all wiped out during depression periods. After the Civil War, however, the situation began to change. The depression of the years 1873 to 1878 reduced union membership from about 300,000 to 50,000; but it did not wipe out unionism completely, as earlier depressions had done. With this development, and with the foundation of the American Federation of Labor (AFL) in 1886, we enter a new period of trade union history.

UNION GROWTH IN MODERN TIMES

The growth of unionism in the twentieth century is shown in Figure 15–1 and Table 1. Figure 15–1 shows the estimated number of union members year by year since 1897. The black line includes Canadian members of American unions, who have numbered about 1 million in recent years. The white line for recent years includes only members within the United States.

Table 1 shows union membership as a percentage of nonagricultural employment for selected years since 1880. Again, the years up to 1945 include Canadian members, while the figures from 1956 onward exclude them. Note that while the number of union members has increased moderately since 1956, the organized percentage of the labor force has fallen.

From 1880 until the early 1930s union membership rose gradually and intermittently, going up in prosperity periods and falling back in depression. Unionism was confined largely to the skilled crafts and did not succeed in penetrating the basic manufacturing industries. Except for a brief spurt during and after World War I, union membership never rose above 10 percent of nonagricultural employment. Membership declined gradually during the complacent twenties, and more sharply during the severe depression of 1929 to 1933.

The New Deal era brought a great upsurge of union strength. Between 1933 and 1939 union membership tripled, and unions for the first time became firmly established in steel, automobiles, and most other branches of manufacturing. Organization spread from the skilled crafts to the semiskilled and unskilled. The reasons included a federal administration favorable to unionism, new legislation guaranteeing the right to organize and improving the legal status of trade unions, a substantial re-

Management, and the Public (New York: Harcourt, Brace & World, Inc., 1948), pp. 272–80.

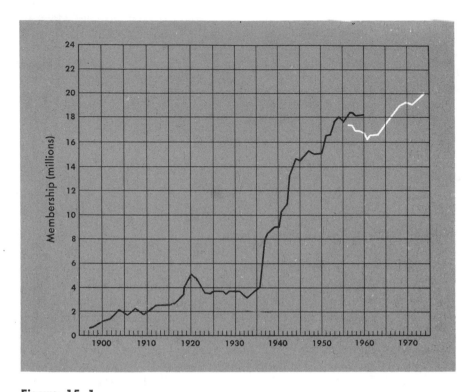

Figure 15–1

Trade Union Membership in the United States,
1897–1970

SOURCE: Data for the old series, 1897–1960, are from the Bureau of Labor Statistics, *Handbook of Labor Statistics,* 1950, p. 139, and Bureau of the Census, *Statistical Abstract of the United States,* 1962. Data for the new series are from the Bureau of Labor Statistics, *Directory of National and International Labor Unions in the United States* (Bulletin 1750, 1971). All are published by the Government Printing Office in Washington, D.C.

covery of employment from 1933 to 1937, and the vigorous organizing efforts of the Congress of Industrial Organizations (CIO).

By 1939 the organizing drive was losing momentum, and union membership might once more have stagnated or declined had it not been for World War II. During the war years administration policy remain favorable to unionism, and union leaders were enlisted both in the production drive and in the effort to stabilize wages and prices. The sharp increase of employment in war industries was favorable to enrolling more union members. Employers were more concerned with recruiting labor and getting out

Table 1

Union Membership as a Percentage of Nonagricultural Employment, Selected Years, 1880–1974

Year	*Average Annual Union Membership*		Year	*Average Annual Union Membership*	
	Thousands	*Percent of Nonagricultural Employment*		*Thousands*	*Percent of Nonagricultural Employment*
1880	200.0	2.3	1933	2,857	11.5
1890	372.0	2.7	1939	8,980	28.9
1900	865.5	4.8	1945	14,796	35.8
1910	2,140.5	8.4	1956	17,490	30.4
1920	5,047.8	16.3	1966	17,940	26.0
1930	3,392.8	8.8	1974	20.096	24.0

SOURCE: Data through 1945 are from Lloyd Ulman, "American Trade Unionism—Past and Present," in Seymour E. Harris (ed.), *American Economic History* (New York: McGraw-Hill Book Company, 1961), pp. 393 and 421. Data from 1956 on are from Bureau of Labor Statistics, *Directory of National and International Labor Unions in the United States, Bulletin* 1750 (Washington, D.C.: Government Printing Office, 1971).

production than with fighting the union, and employer resistance to organization subsided for the time being. So another 5 million union members were added. Unions came to include more than a third of the nonagricultural labor force and about 60 percent of all manual workers in the economy.

In retrospect, 1945 appears as a high watermark in union penetration of the economy. Membership has risen only slowly since that time, and the percentage of nonagricultural workers who are union members has been falling. What accounts for this decline in the unionized proportion of the labor force? What does it portend for the future? Is unionism over the hill, or will there be a fresh upsurge at some time in the future? We shall comment on these questions at the end of the chapter. But first we must examine the structure of union organization and how this has changed over the course of time.

THE EVOLUTION OF UNION STRUCTURE

There are four main types of organization units in the trade union world: local unions of workers in a particular trade or industry; city-wide and statewide federations of local unions, regardless of industry; national unions of workers in the same trade or industry; and peak federations of these national unions, such as the AFL–CIO.

The organizational structure may be visualized more readily by looking at a particular union. The printers' Local Number 6 in New York City is a branch of the International Typographical Union, and holds its charter and authority only from the international union. At the same time, Local Number 6 is a member of the New York City Federation of Labor and the New York State Federation of Labor. At the national level, the Typographical Union is affiliated with the AFL–CIO.

These organizational units did not develop overnight, nor did they develop simultaneously. They represent successive stages of development, comparable to strata in a geological formation. The first local union was the Philadelphia shoemakers' union, founded in 1792. Next in order of development came the city federations of local unions, the first of which were founded in New York, Philadelphia, and Baltimore in 1833. The first national union that has had a continuous existence up to the present day was the International Typographical Union, founded in 1850. The first federation of national unions that has had a continuous history to date was the American Federation of Labor, founded in 1886.

Numerous other forms of organization have also been tried during the past 150 years. There have been attempts to combine people from different trades and industries into a single local union, and to combine these "mixed locals" into an all-inclusive national organization. The outstanding example of this type of organization was the Knights of Labor, which flourished briefly during the 1880s. There have also been attempts to merge federations of local trade unions, local labor political clubs, and miscellaneous labor groups into a federation such as the National Labor Union, which flourished during the late 1860s. The reasons for the failure of these movements will be discussed below. Briefly, they suffered from a lack of homogeneity of interest among the underlying membership. Because of diversity of the membership, a chronic shortage of funds, an absence of systematic organizing tactics, and a lack of interest in continuous bargaining with employers, they made only slight headway on the economic front. Their activities were oriented mainly toward politics, and here they tended to dissipate their energies in broad middle-class reform movements of little immediate interest to wage earners. The organizational forms that we find in existence today are the survivors, which have proved their ability to survive by the concrete functions they perform.

These different organizational units are not of equal importance in the labor world. The key unit around which all else revolves is the national union of workers in a particular trade or industry. The national union is more important that the locals of which it is composed, and it is also more important than the federation with which it is affiliated. This has not always been the case, and we need to ask how the national union has come to occupy its present key position.

THE DOMINANCE OF THE NATIONAL UNION

The beginnings of local unionism around the year 1800 have already been described. These isolated locals soon found that they were in a relatively weak position compared with that of a strong employer. Consisting of workers in only one trade, with limited funds and no outside support, they often crumbled when forced to strike against a large employer or employers' association. The need for some kind of defensive alliance with other unions was felt almost from the beginning.

Such an alliance can be formed on either of two bases. The local may join with local unions of other trades in the same *area* to form a city-wide or statewide organization; or it may join with other local unions in the same *trade or industry* to form a national trade union. The first efforts were in the former direction. City-wide federations, called at the time *trade assemblies,* sprang up in Philadelphia, New York, and Baltimore in 1833, as we have noted, and in ten other cities during the next two years. The main function of these groups was mutual aid in strikes. Funds were obtained by taxing each local so many cents per member per month, and the tax was sometimes raised to meet emergency situations. A local that wished to go on strike usually had to secure approval either by a majority or by two-thirds of the member locals in order to draw strike benefits from the common fund. The trade assemblies also functioned as boycott organizations, lobbyists, propaganda bureaus, publishers of labor newspapers, and in some cities sponsored an independent labor party. The usefulness of the city federation is proved by the fact that it has persisted, with some change of functions, to the present day.

Why did the local unions find it necessary to go beyond this and to establish national unions of their respective trades and industries? One important reason was the nationalization of the market for many goods. Hoxie has laid down the principle that union organization tends to parallel the organization of the industry. In an industry in which employers compete on a national basis, the isolated local soon finds itself competing with local unions in other plants of the industry. In this sort of competition, wages tend to be leveled down to the lowest rates prevailing anywhere in the country. In some trades, too, migration of journeymen from one city to another early became a problem. The local unions of printers, for example, began to exchange lists of scabs, to regulate the conditions under which printers from one area might secure work in another area, and to provide "tramping benefits" to support the brother in the trade during his journeys in search of employment. A permanent national organization facilitated these exchanges and made it possible to enforce uniform apprenticeship and membership rules. With the passage of time, improved transportation facilities made it easier for delegates to assemble at national conventions and for organizers from the national office to travel throughout the country.

National unions date for all practical purposes from the Civil War. Two so-called national unions of shoemakers and printers were formed in 1835 and 1836, but they were confined to the Atlantic Coast and were wiped out almost immediately by depression. Three permanent organizations appeared during the 1850s: the printers (1850), molders (1859), and machinists and blacksmiths (1859). The first period of intensive national organization, however, was from 1863 to 1873. During these years some twenty-six new national unions were formed, many of which have survived to the present day. The present unions of locomotive engineers, locomotive firemen, carpenters, cigar makers, bricklayers, and painters date from this period.

The national unions showed much greater resistance to depression than the earlier local unions. The depression of 1873 to 1878 caused a great decline in union membership, but at least eleven nationals are known to have survived these years and eight new nationals were founded during the depression. The reasons for the greater permanence of a national union are not difficult to see. Even though many of its local unions are wiped out during a depression, the national headquarters can continue on a reduced scale and serve as a center for reviving the lost locals when prosperity returns. Moreover, a national union tends constantly to expand to the limits of its trade or industry. Its officers have the duty of organizing the unorganized; their prestige, and even their continuance in office, depend on successful performance of their function.

The national unions not merely survived, but gradually took over more and more functions from the local unions and city federations. They early began to build up war chests to aid in financing strikes. To prevent dissipation of these funds, it was necessary to forbid local unions to call strikes without the sanction of the national union. The national officers thus became involved in disputes between local unions and employers, with a view to preventing strikes except when absolutely necessary. From this it was a natural step for national officers to begin participating in the negotiation of new contracts with employers. This action was desirable also in order to keep some reasonable relation among the wage schedules and other contract terms secured by the various locals. These tendencies, to be sure, have been strongest in industries with a national product market. In industries where competition in confined to a locality, such as building construction, the local unions have retained a large measure of autonomy.

It was natural also that national officers with an intimate knowledge of the trade or industry should take over the work of organizing new locals. The great majority of full-time union organizers now draw their pay from the treasuries of the national unions. The benefit functions of the unions also become centralized increasingly in the national office. Uniform rules for sickness benefits, death benefits, strike benefits, and other types of payment were established throughout the union, and funds were paid to the national treasurer and were disbursed by him.

The expanding functions of the national unions tended to transfer the loyalty of local unions from the city federations to the national union of the trade. Most workers naturally have a sense of closer kinship with others in their own trade or industry. This feeling was now reinforced by the material benefits received from the national organizations. Dues payments to the national organization and cash benefits received from it soon amounted to many times the amounts paid to the city federations. The national unions benefited by the truth expressed in the maxim, "Where your treasure is, there will your heart be also."

The predominance of the national union was strengthened also by the turn that the labor movement took in the 1880s away from political action and toward direct bargaining with employers on the economic front. Had the labor movement taken a strong political turn, the outcome might well have been different. The city, state, and national federations are the natural units for political action. For reasons to be discussed below, however, political action has played a minor role in the labor movement over the past century. The state and city federations have accordingly fallen to a subordinate position. They continue to meet regularly, give a certain amount of support to member locals in strikes and organizing campaigns, approve legislative demands of member locals and lobby for them in city councils and state legislatures, conduct educational and propaganda activities, and in some cases support candidates for public office. The local union's real loyalty, however, is to the national union of its trade or industry. It is to the national union that it looks for support, and in any conflict of principles or policies it is the policies of the national union that will prevail.

The cornerstones of the trade union world today are the great national unions, which have a more lasting significance than any federation based on them. It was a question of less importance than one might think whether the old AFL and CIO survived as separate organizations, or whether they agreed to merge into a new federation, as actually happened.

The important thing is the growth and development of the national unions of steelworkers, automobile workers, textile workers, machinists, teamsters, carpenters, painters, mine workers, and other key groups.

PEAK FEDERATIONS:
THE AMERICAN FEDERATION OF LABOR

Federation of these national unions into an overarching labor organization dates from the 1880s. Several attempts at national federation were made in earlier years, notably by the ill-fated Knights of Labor established in 1869. This heterogeneous organization cut across industry lines and included large numbers of low-skilled workers, who joined enthusiastically but were easily discouraged and quick to drop out. The national unions of skilled craftsmen eventually concluded that they would do better to form their own federation. The American Federation of Labor, founded in 1886, quickly assumed a leading role in the trade union movement. It was a hard-hitting organization, led by Samuel Gompers and other energetic men in their thirties, who almost immediately launched the first successful strikes for the eight-hour day. The AFL also had a distinctive philosophy of unionism that appealed strongly to most organized workers.

What were the cardinal points of this trade-union philosophy? The first element that may be noted is group consciousness. Before this time workers had not distinguished their interests from those of farmers and middle-class people. They had joined in political reform movements that also drew support from these other groups. All this was changed by Gompers and his followers, most of whom had been reared as Marxian socialists. Although they later abandoned most of the tenets of Marxism, they retained a conviction that the interests of workers are distinct from those of other groups. Gompers argued that the workers must defend their own interests and must refuse to be drawn into middle-class reform movements. He asserted also that there is little hope of the workers' climbing out of their class through producers' cooperatives, antimonopoly campaigns, or other methods.

A second principle was that of organization by trades. Gompers believed that to lump together different trades, as the Knights of Labor had done, reduced the cohesiveness of the union. Greatest solidarity was obtained when each craft had its own union. The desirability of strong national unions, buttressed by large treasuries and extensive benefit systems, was stressed from the beginning. The Cigar Makers' Union, under Gompers' leadership, showed the way in this direction in 1879 by adopting a high scale of dues and benefits, and by giving the national officers complete control over the local unions. The Cigar Makers' organization was used as a model by most other national unions during the next ten years, and its prestige contributed to the election of Gompers to the AFL presidency. The marked success of British craft unions cut on this same pattern, and the influence of British immigrants in American unions, also helped to shape AFL thinking in these formative years.

Early AFL leaders insisted also that each national union must be autonomous within its own field of operation. The federation entered the scene only to define and enforce the jurisdictions of the member unions, and to perform certain political and educational functions. The federation, in short, was a confederation of sovereign bodies. Its chief power was that of granting jurisdiction over particular trades or industries: jurisdiction granted to one union must be observed by others, and dual unionism must be suppressed at all costs. This attitude toward dualism sprang partly from the unfortunate experience of the national unions in competition with the Knights of Labor during the 1880s. It sprang also from the fact that the AFL had to contend with strong and determined employer opposition. The existence of two unions in an industry gave the employer a chance to play each against the other, and the labor movement therefore has a strong practical interest in preventing dual organization. The bitterness of the rivalry between AFL and CIO from 1935 to 1955 can be understood only in terms of this long-standing taboo on dual unionism.

The third cardinal principle was that labor's objectives should be pursued mainly on the economic front through collective bargaining with employers. In spite of the socialist training of its founders, the AFL soon came to accept the main outlines of the capitalist order. Gompers believed that unions should not try to overthrow capitalism, but to get as much as possible for the workers by collective bargaining within the confines of the existing system. When someone asked Gompers what the aims of the federation were, he is reported to have answered, "More, more, more—now!" When another AFL leader was called before a Congressional committee in 1883 and asked about the ultimate objectives of trade unionism, he replied as follows: "We have no ultimate ends. We are going on from day to day. We are fighting only for immediate objects . . . we are opposed to theorists . . . we are all practical men." [2] There has never been a better summary of the traditional AFL position.

The device of the union contract or collective agreement, which had been used by a few unions in the 1880s, became during the 1890s the accepted method of dealing with employers. The AFL hammered out and wrote into union contracts a new conception of the union as a continuously operating organization, rather than a sporadic protest and strike movement.

---

[2] J. B. S. Hardman, *American Labor Dynamics* (New York: Harcourt, Brace & World, Inc., 1928), p. 99.

The union was to be a partner, though perhaps only a junior partner, in the conduct of industry. It was to be active every day in the year, representing the interests of its members on all fronts, winning small gains that would eventually mount up to an impressive total.

A corollary of the AFL's emphasis on collective bargaining was the avoidance of political organization, or at least of anything approaching an independent labor party. The labor movement had experimented with labor parties and political action since at least 1830. Gompers and his group felt that these activities had not gotten anywhere in the past and had served mainly to split the unions and divert them from their real business. They believed that the unions could get what they wanted through pressure on the established political parties—voting for candidates who had shown themselves to be "friends of labor," getting union demands written into party platforms, lobbying in Congress and the state legislatures, and so on.

Along with this avoidance of labor politics went a suspicion of intellectuals and of their tendency to foist abstract programs on the workers. There has been in the United States nothing of that close connection between intellectuals and the labor movement which exists in most European countries. Union leaders have had a similar distrust of socialists and other radical groups that attempt to divert trade union energy to revolutionary ends. This point of view is well expressed in Gompers' statement to an AFL convention:

> I want to tell you Socialists, that I have studied your philosophy, read your works upon economics. . . . I have heard your orators and watched the work of your movement the world over. I have kept close watch upon your doctrines for thirty years; have been closely associated with many of you, and know what you think and what you propose. I know, too, what you have up your sleeve. And I want to say that I am entirely at variance with your philosophy. . . . Economically, you are unsound; socially, you are wrong; and industrially you are an impossibility.[3]

All in all, then, the AFL provided a model of organization well suited to the requirements of the skilled trades. It stimulated the formation of new national unions. It acted as a stabilizer of union membership during depression periods. It shook the labor movement free of an incubus of unfruitful ideas and presented a practical operating program that proved very successful in winning gains on the economic front. Except for the short-lived Industrial Workers of the World, which flourished just before World War I, the story of American unionism for almost fifty years was the story of the AFL.

---

[3] *AFL Convention Proceedings, 1903*, pp. 188–98.

THE CIO: RIVALRY AND REUNION

While the AFL was quite successful in organizing skilled craftsmen, it made little progress in the mass-production manufacturing industries. These industries employ some skilled tradesmen, but the bulk of the plant labor force is semiskilled or unskilled. This poses a strategic choice between organization by occupation or *crafts,* under which carpenters employed by U.S. Steel would join the Carpenters' Union, toolmakers would join the Machinists' Union, and so on; and *industrial* unionism, under which everyone in a steel mill would belong to a single Steelworkers' Union.

The AFL leadership, dominated by craft unions which wished to preserve their right to enroll members of their craft who worked in manufacturing plants, favored the craft basis of organization while failing to implement it effectively. But this view was challenged in the early thirties by a group led by John L. Lewis of the Mine Workers, Sidney Hillman of the Clothing Workers, and David Dubinsky of the Ladies' Garment Workers, unions which themselves were industrial in form. After being outvoted at the 1935 AFL convention, six of these unions nevertheless set up a Committee for Industrial Organization (CIO) devoted to organizing industrial unions in the basic manufacturing industries and then bringing these new unions into the AFL. The AFL Executive Council, however, scenting a threat of dual unionism, first suspended and then expelled the unions that had formed the CIO. These unions then banded together in 1938, along with the new unions that they had fathered in the meantime, to form a rival federation—the Congress of Industrial Organizations.

The success of the CIO organizing drives is now a matter of history. During the late thirties one antiunion citadel after another capitulated. The list of employers organized by the CIO between 1936 and 1941 reads like a roster of Who's Who in American industry: Ford, General Motors, Chrysler, General Electric, Westinghouse, United States Steel, Bethlehem Steel, Republic Steel, Youngstown Sheet and Tub, Goodyear, Firestone, Goodrich, the major oil companies, the larger radio and electrical equipment manufacturers, the "big four" meat-packing companies, and so on down the list.

An important factor in this success was a favorable government attitude toward unionism throughout the Roosevelt era. Unions that formerly had to strike to win union recognition could now use the election procedures of the National Labor Relations Board, and the board also protected them against harassing tactics by the employer, which were now forbidden as "unfair labor practice." An additional factor was the prolonged rise in business activity after 1933. Except for the relapse of 1937 and 1938, employment and production rose steadily from 1933 to 1945. This provided a favorable setting for union organization.

But as CIO membership expanded, the AFL also continued to grow. By 1940 it was once more larger than its rival, and widened its lead in subsequent years. There were several reasons for this. First, the craft unions continued to enlarge their membership, taking good advantage of rising employment and the favorable attitude of government. Second, AFL leaders bent to the prevailing wind and themselves sponsored several new industrial unions in competition with the CIO. Third, several of the unions instrumental in forming the CIO, including the Mine Workers and the Ladies' Garment Workers, later withdrew from the CIO and rejoined the AFL. Finally, the CIO was weakened in 1949–50 when it expelled eleven left-wing unions containing almost a million members, following refusal of their officers to sign the non-Communist affidavits required by the newly enacted Taft–Hartley Act.

The cleavage in the labor movement after 1935 had disadvantages on both the political and collective bargaining fronts, and leaders on the two sides worked sporadically to close the breach. Negotiations looking toward unity were conducted by joint committees in 1937, 1939, 1942, 1943, 1947, and 1950. These negotiations broke down partly on substantive issues, particularly the insistence of CIO leaders that the new industrial unions be admitted to any merged federation "as is," with no concession to craft union jurisdictional rights. In addition, personal bitterness among John L. Lewis, William Green, Philip Murray, and other leaders who had been involved in the original split was an obstacle to unity.

In late 1952 Presidents William Green of the AFL and Philip Murray of the CIO died within a month of each other. The new presidents, George Meany and Walter Reuther, quickly reactivated the twenty-four-man Joint AFL–CIO Unity Committee. Over the next two years this body succeeded in hammering out first a "no-raiding agreement" between most of the national unions on both sides, and later the terms of a full merger. The key to the final agreement was a decision that all national unions in both groups would be taken into the new federation "as is." Mergers and other methods of eliminating overlapping jurisdiction would be encouraged but were not made compulsory. In December 1955, the AFL and CIO held their last separate conventions and then met jointly for the first convention of the new American Federation of Labor and Congress of Industrial Organizations (AFL–CIO).

The superstructure of the AFL–CIO is complicated, since it adds together the top management structure of the two predecessor bodies. In addition to a president and secretary–treasurer there are twenty-seven vice-presidents, distributed on an agreed basis between former AFL and former CIO affiliates. In addition to the trade departments of the old AFL (Building and Construction Trades, Metal Trades, Union Label Trades, Maritime Employees, and Railway Employees) there is now an Industrial Union Department, open to all unions organized wholly or partly on an industrial basis. This serves to maintain something of the identity and spirit of the old CIO.

The old AFL had quite limited powers over the affiliated national unions, and this remains basically true of the AFL–CIO. Two significant differences, however, should be noted:

1. The old AFL attached great importance to avoiding overlapping jurisdiction among the national unions, and asserted the right to draw clear jurisdictional boundary lines. This principle of exclusive jurisdiction was abandoned in 1955 for the sake of labor unity, and all national unions were taken into the new federation with the territory that they had managed to occupy at that time. Another new feature in the situation is the election procedures of the National Labor Relations Board, which give workers the ultimate right to decide whether they shall be represented by one union or another. The AFL–CIO retains the right to define the jurisdiction of new affiliates, to mediate jurisdictional disputes among its constituent unions, and if necessary to make decisions in such disputes. It has no enforcement powers, however, short of the drastic step of expelling an offending union. As a practical matter, jurisdictional controversies are now resolved mainly through National Labor Relations Board elections and through a large network of bilateral agreements between unions in neighboring fields.

2. The AFL–CIO constitution goes farther than its predecessors in prescribing standards of conduct for the national unions. No union that is controlled or dominated by communists, members of other totalitarian movements, or racketeers ("corrupt influences") may remain affiliated with the federation. The executive council has power to investigate situations where such control or domination is alleged, to make recommendations or give directions to the union in question, and to suspend the union from membership by a two-thirds vote. Council actions may be appealed to the biennial convention, which has final authority to reinstate or expel the accused union. But the threat of expulsion, while it may have some effect on small unions, is ineffective against the more powerful organizations. The outstanding example is the Teamsters' Union, which simply ignored federation orders to eliminate corruption, and accepted expulsion in 1957 with equanimity. Since then the union has continued to flourish on its own, while the federation had been deprived of valuable revenues and support.

The national unions, then, remain largely autonomous in managing their internal affairs and continue to be the real power centers of the labor movement. The national unions are not members of the AFL–CIO in the sense that Minnesota is part of the United States. Their position is more like that of countries within the United Nations, which by threatening to withdraw can veto actions contrary to their interests. They confer power on the federation much more than they draw power from it.

The United Automobile Workers, indeed, withdrew from the federation in 1968 because of policy differences, while, as previously mentioned, the Teamsters Union was expelled in 1957 on grounds of internal corruption. Neither union has suffered noticeably from its nonmembership; and there are several other large, independent groups, including the United Mine Workers. Thus the membership of AFL–CIO affiliates is considerably smaller than total union membership.

THE TRADE UNION WORLD TODAY

It is appropriate to close this survey of union development by indicating the centers of union strength at the present time. It is apparent from Table 2 that membership is highly concentrated in a few large organizations.

Table 2

Unions Reporting 100,000 or More Members, 1973

Union	Membership (Thousands)
Teamsters, Chauffeurs, Warehousemen, and Helpers (Independent)	1,854
Automobile, Aerospace, and Agricultural Implement Workers (Independent)	1,394
Steelworkers	1,400
International Brotherhood of Electrical Workers	957
Machinists and Aerospace Workers	758
Carpenters and Joiners	820
Retail Clerks	633
Laborers International Union	600
Meat Cutters and Butcher Workmen	529
Hotel and Restaurant Employees and Bartenders	458
State, County and Municipal Employees	529
International Ladies' Garment Workers Union	428
Service Employees International Union	484
Communications Workers	443
Operating Engineers	402
Amalgamated Clothing Workers	365
American Federation of Government Employees	293
International Union of Electrical, Radio, and Machine Workers	290
American Federation of Musicians	315
Railway, Airline, and Steamship Clerks	238
United Transportation Workers	248
Rubber, Cork, Linoleum, and Plastic Workers	183
Letter Carriers	220
Painters and Allied Trades	208
American Federation of Teachers	249

Union	Membership (Thousands)
Textile Workers Union of America	174
Oil, Chemical, and Atomic Workers	172
Retail, Wholesale, and Department Store Union	198
United Electrical, Radio, and Machine Workers of America (Independent)	165
American Postal Workers	239
Bakery and Confectionery Workers	146
Transport Workers	150
United Mine Workers of America (Independent)	213
Fire Fighters	160
Paperworkers	389
Bricklayers and Allied Craftsmen	149
Boilermakers, Blacksmiths, Forgers, and Helpers	132
Fraternal Order of Police	125
Railway Carmen	110
Graphic Arts International Union	106
Transit Union	130
Printing and Graphic Communications	123
Maintenance of Way Employees	142
Sheet Metal Workers	153
Typographical Union	115
Plate Printers, Die Stampers, and Engravers Union	228

SOURCE: Bureau of Labor Statistics, *Directory of National Unions and Employee Associations,* Suppl. 3 (January, 1976).

Three unions—the Teamsters, Automobile Workers, and Steelworkers—have more than a million members each. The ten largest unions have about 9 million members, or almost half of all union members in the country. At the bottom of the scale are about one hundred national unions with less than 25,000 members each. Although this group includes half the unions in the country, it includes only about 5 percent of all union members.

The degree of union penetration varies widely among sectors of the economy. In mining, construction, and transportation the great majority of wage earners are union members. In manufacturing, a substantial majority are members although the ratio varies in different branches of manufacturing—high in steel and automobiles, low in textiles. These four sectors —manufacturing, mining, construction, and transportation—account for more than 80 percent of total union membership. In the trade and service sectors, on the other hand, unionism has made much less progress.

The geographical distribution of union membership reflects in part the distribution of employment. States that have many workers in manufacturing, construction, and transportation also have many union members.

Five states (New York, California, Pennsylvania, Illinois, and Ohio) each with more than a million union members, account for about half of total membership.

In addition to the distribution of employment, however, regions differ in their susceptibility to union organization. The most recent survey shows the highest ratio of union members to nonagricultural employment in the state of West Virginia (44 percent), followed by Michigan and Washington (40 percent), Pennsylvania, New York, Indiana, Illinois, Ohio, Missouri, and Montana (34–37 percent). Union organization is strongest in the Middle Atlantic, East North Central, and Pacific Coast states. The Mountain and West North Central states, the South, and the Southwest are weakly unionized. The ratio of union members to nonagricultural employment is lowest in North and South Carolina (7 percent), South Dakota (10 percent), Mississippi (12 percent), Florida, Georgia, North Dakota, and Texas (14 percent), Virginia and Oklahoma (15 percent).

The weakness of unionism in the South is not just a matter of the industry mix. The same industries are less unionized there than in other parts of the country. An interesting calculation, made in 1953 near the peak of union strength, showed that union membership in the southern states was only 57 percent of what it would be *if each industry were as strongly unionized in the South as in the nation as a whole*.[4] The reasons for this weak showing include unusually active employer resistance to unionism, a generally unfavorable attitude in state legislatures and the courts, a new industrial labor force recruited largely from agriculture, and the complicating factor of racial divisions in the work force.

THE OUTLOOK FOR UNION GROWTH

The most striking feature of the past thirty years is the slow growth of union membership. After a period of rapid expansion, membership has leveled off and the percentage of the labor force in unions has dropped. In the traditional strongholds of manufacturing, mining, and transportation, most unions have lost members since the midfifties. The unions that have managed to swim against the tide and increase their membership are largely outside these areas. They include the Teamsters; Retail Clerks; Retail, Wholesale, and Department Store Employees; Letter Carriers; State, County, and Municipal Employees; Meat Cutters; Teachers; Government Employees; Musicians; and Building Service Employees.

There are several reasons for the leveling off of union membership. By the midfifties the most easily unionized people—manual workers in

---

[4]Leo Troy, "The Growth of Union Membership in the South, 1939–1953," *Southern Economic Journal* (April 1958), pp. 407–20.

large establishments in cities of the Northeast and Pacific Coast—had already been substantially organized. As unionism presses out into white-collar employment, smaller establishments, smaller cities and towns, and more heavily agricultural regions, it encounters increasing resistance.

The composition of employment has been changing in ways unfavorable to unionism. The number of production workers in manufacturing has been cut by technological improvements, and employment in mining and transportation has also fallen. The sectors with a strong uptrend of employment are trade, government, finance, and services; but, with the possible exception of government, these sectors are largely nonunion. Geographically, industry has tended to move from the Northeast to the South and Southwest, and from metropolitan areas to smaller communities, that is, to areas in which union organization seems inherently more difficult. For the time being, unionism seems to be confined within a shrinking area of the economy.

There has been a marked change in public attitudes and in the political climate over the past generation. The low wages, heavy unemployment, and other hardships of the 1930s have receded into the past. No longer can unions count on public sympathy for the underdog. On the contrary, they now attract part of the criticism and distrust of concentrated economic power formerly reserved for big business. The Taft–Hartley Act of 1947 and the Landrum–Griffin Act of 1959, apart from their direct effect on union operations, are symbolic of a changed climate of opinion that makes organization more difficult.

In addition to these external influences, some observers assert that the labor movement itself has become bureaucratic and complacent, and that the internal pressure for expansion has slackened. Although lip service is still given to the principle of organizing the unorganized, most union officers are in fact content to settle down within the area won in the past.

Further expansion of union membership, however, will have to come from moving outside existing frontiers. Geographically, the main frontier now lies in the South. Occupationally, the frontier lies mainly in white-collar employment. The prospect for further union growth, therefore, depends on the answer to two questions: Will unions be able to increase their coverage of employment in the southern states? Will the percentage of white-collar workers in unions rise substantially?

Prospects in the South

The organized percentage in the South has remained consistently at about half of the level in other regions, (Table 3). When one looks beneath such averages, however, the situation is very uneven. In Kentucky, where

Table 3

Percent of Nonagricultural Employment Organized

	1939	1953	1964
South	10.7	17.2	14.4
Nonsouth	21.5	34.1	29.5

SOURCE: Ray Marshall, *Labor in the South* (Cambridge, Mass.: Harvard University Press, 1967).

coal mining is important, the organized percentage is above 25. But in North and South Carolina, where the weakly unionized textile industry is important, only about 7 percent of nonagricultural employees are union members.

There is a similar unevenness among industries. Communications workers, longshoremen, mine workers, and the skilled crafts in printing, building construction, and railroad operation are about as well organized in the South as in other regions. Within manufacturing, the southern unionized percentage is high (that is, in the range of 75–95 percent) in basic steel, automobiles, aircraft, electrical equipment, rubber products, pulp and paper, and oil refining. These are oligopolistic industries in which most of the national output is produced by a few companies. Plants are large and mechanized; employee relations are impersonal. Southern plants are often owned by companies that operate throughout the country. Once a union has established collective bargaining relations in a company's northern plants, it is relatively easy to extend this relation to its southern plants.

In light manufacturing—food, beverages, textiles, clothing, boots and shoes, wood and furniture products—the situation is quite different. Here the unionized proportion is typically below 30 percent, and in the important textile industry it is only 14 percent. These industries are relatively small-scale and are often located in small towns or rural areas. Competition in the product market is severe, and labor costs are a large part of total costs. Thus employers have a strong economic incentive to resist the increase in labor costs which might result from unionization. In some cases, notably textiles, southern producers dominate the industry, depriving the union of a northern beachhead from which to expand.

Looking toward the future, several tendencies should be favorable to union organization:

1. The structure of manufacturing in the South is becoming more diversified. In 1939, the hard-to-organize light manufacturing industries provided three-quarters of southern manufacturing employment. Today the proportion is only one-half and is still falling. There has been a rapid increase of southern

branch plants of companies in heavy manufacturing, many of which are unionized from the outset. The strongly unionized building trades are also growing as a proportion of total employment.

2. In the South as in other regions, the percentage of the labor force employed in agriculture has dropped sharply since 1940. This drying up of the labor reservoir in agriculture removes a major source of "cheap labor" and a ready supply of strikebreakers to combat union organizing drives.

3. As the South becomes increasingly urban and industrial, with rural attitudes declining in importance the ideological and political climate should become less hostile to unionism than it has been in the past. This is one aspect of the vast "homogenization" of American society, the gradual erosion of regional differences.

There are other tendencies that may make union organization more difficult. Ray Marshall notes among other things,

> the tendency for plants to locate in smaller communities; the scattering of workers from the plant gates, making it more difficult to contact them; rising living standards and changed patterns of living . . . the workers' rising educational levels which make them more questioning of both management and unions . . . technological changes which increase employment in non-union areas and increase management's ability to operate during strikes; management's growing sophistication in fighting unions where it wishes to avoid them; the growing disenchantment with unions by intellectuals and union staff people.[5]

It is hazardous to predict how these conflicting tendencies will balance out in the future. There may possibly, over the next generation, be some reduction in the gap between the percentage organized in the South and in other parts of the country; but there seems little reason to expect a large reduction.

Prospects in White-Collar Employment

We noted in Chapter 4 the rapid rise of white-collar employment in all the industrial countries. These white-collar workers are by no means immune to union organization.[6] The percentage in unions, however, varies widely among countries, from a high of about 60 percent in Sweden to only about 11 percent in the United States. Comparative analysis of the industrial countries suggests several conclusions.

First, it appears that white-collar workers are best organized where unionism in general is strong. In Sweden and Austria, both strongly unionized, the percentage of white-collar workers in unions is unusually high.

---

[5] Ray Marshall, *Labor in the South* (Cambridge, Mass.: Harvard University Press, 1967), p. 351.

[6] For a good survey of evidence from a number of countries, see Adolf Sturmthal (ed), *White-Collar Unions* (Urbana: The University of Illinois Press, 1966).

In West Germany and the United Kingdom, where the degree of unionization is somewhat lower, white-collar unionism is also weaker. The United
States stands at the bottom of the range in both respects.

Second, the percentage of white-collar workers organized is always
(with the possible exception of Japan) below that for the blue-collar workers. In Sweden, for example, about 80 percent of blue-collar workers are
union members, compared with 60 percent of white-collar workers. In
West Germany the respective percentages are 42 and 23. In the United
States they would be about 40 and 11.

The reasons for this differential, which is especially large in the
United States, are not entirely clear. There seems no inherent reason why
unionism should not be as advantageous to white-collar employees as to
anyone else. Sales and clerical jobs now pay little more, on the average,
than manual labor. In government agencies, banks, insurance offices, and
elsewhere, large numbers of white-collar people work together under something like factory conditions. Problems of salary levels, fringe benefits, fair
treatment by supervisors, job tenure and promotion, threatened displacement by automation and technical change are presumably no less compelling for them than for manual workers.

On the other side stands the traditional feeling of white-collar workers that they are different from, and in some sense superior to, the manual
worker; and that trade unionism is *his* institution rather than theirs. White-
collar people normally have a superior educational background. At the
supervisory, technical, and professional levels, which set the tone of the
white-collar world, the orientation toward management is typically strong.
These people do enjoy an income advantage, and they also have chances
of promotion and professional advancement, based primarily on individual
performance rather than seniority. So they tend to think in terms of individual progress rather than group action.

The lower ranges of white-collar employment, the routine sales and
clerical workers, do not share these advantages. But most white-collar
workers at these levels are women, many of whom are supplementary earners rather than family heads. So while issues of employment are important
for them, they are not fighting issues as they may be for men. The lower
propensity of women to join unions shows up clearly in the statistics. In
Britain, for example, 36 percent of male white-collar workers are union
members, but only 25 percent of female white-collar workers are in unions.
In West Germany the percentage of white-collar workers in unions is 31
for men, but only 15 for women. While data have not been assembled for
the United States, they would undoubtedly show a similar discrepancy.

A third conclusion is that white-collar employees show a greater propensity to organize in public employment than in private employment. In
many countries the largest and strongest white-collar unions are those

of teachers and civil servants. In Sweden, the United Kingdom, and Japan, about three-quarters of government white-collar employees are unionized. In West Germany, which has a special civil servants association limited to white-collar workers, the percentage organized is very high. Even in the United States, six of the eleven white-collar unions with membership above 100,000 are unions of government workers.[7]

This greater propensity to organize among government employees has not been fully explored. It may be due partly to the large size of the employing unit and the impersonal, bureaucratic character of the employment relation. Research studies indicate that large plants and companies are more union-prone than small ones, and this tendency may operate in public as well as private employment. The fact that government, by definition, is a monopoly and not subject to product-market competition may be important. Next, there is the well-known sluggishness of civil service pay scales, which often remain unchanged for years at a time, while private wages and consumer prices are moving upward. In an economy that seems to have a persistent inflationary bias, civil servants may well find it advantageous to substitute collective bargaining for unilateral salary determination. Finally, unions of public employees are in an unusually strategic position to bring pressure on government. They can work through political channels as well as through bargaining. Strikes of public employees are unlawful, but by no means unknown; and even without striking, there are ways of reducing the normal level of service, attracting publicity, and bringing pressure on public officials.

What does all this signify for the United States? Is the proportion of white-collar workers in unions likely to rise substantially over the years ahead? The strongest prospects seem to be in public employment. At the federal level, union prospects were strengthened by an executive order of 1962, affirming the right of employees to join unions and providing for varying degrees of recognition corresponding to differing degrees of union strength. Where a union has been chosen by a majority of employees in an appropriate administrative unit, it may be granted exclusive recognition and then has the right to negotiate a written agreement. The status of unionism in state and local employment varies from state to state; but here, too, there has been a movement toward acceptance of union organization and collective agreements as a normal feature of employee relations. Seventeen states now have comprehensive labor relations laws for public employees.

Over the past twenty years or so, unions of government employees have shown a much higher rate of membership increase than unions in

---

[7] Sturmthal, *White-Collar Unions,* p. 340. These unions are the Postal Clerks, Letter Carriers, Teachers, Government Employees, Federal Employees, and State, County, and Municipal Employees.

general. Most of the leading unions have more than doubled their membership. The number of union members in government employment is now about 2.5 million, or one-eighth of total union membership. If present trends continue, the percentage of public employees in unions will soon exceed the percentage of private employees who are organized.

Another area in which union expansion may be expected is wholesale and retail trade. Gradual replacement of the small retailer by large supermarkets, chain stores, department stores, and discount houses has created favorable conditions for union organization. The largest union in the field, the Retail Clerks' International Association, has a membership of about half a million, with particular strength on the Pacific Coast and in the large food chains nationally. Total union membership in wholesale and retail trade is estimated at more than a million. But this is still small relative to the 10 million nonsupervisory employees in this sector.

Overall, it seems likely that the percentage of white-collar workers in unions will rise gradually over the years ahead. The expansion of white-collar membership may be about sufficient to offset the decline of employment and union membership in some branches of manufacturing, mining, and transportation. In this event, the unionized proportion of the labor force may level off at around 25 percent for the foreseeable future.

DISCUSSION QUESTIONS

1. To what factors can one attribute the beginnings of modern trade unionism around 1800?

2. In a depression, workers would seem to need special protection against wage cuts and loss of jobs. Why, in spite of this, has union membership usually declined in depression periods?

3. Explain why skilled workers have usually been the first to form stable trade unions.

4. What explains the dominance of the national union over the other forms of trade union organization in the United States?

5. The rise of the CIO was pictured at the time as a victory of *industrial unionism* over *craft unionism*. What do these terms mean? Is this a correct interpretation of CIO development?

6. Should union strength be defined in terms of the number of union members, or the percentage of the labor force in trade unions? Using the definition you prefer, would you expect union strength in 1990 to be greater or less than today? Explain.

7. "Union organization in a newly industrialized area is always slow

and difficult. This is the basic reason for the limited progress of unionism in the South." Discuss.

8. How would you appraise union prospects in the area of white-collar unemployment?

READING SUGGESTIONS

Classic studies in the history of American unionism include JOHN R. COMMONS and others, *History of the Labor Movement in the United States* (4 vols.), New York: The Macmillan Company, 1918; SELIG PERLMAN, *A History of Trade Unionism in the United States,* New York: The Macmillan Company, 1937; PHILIP TAFT, *The A.F. of L. in the Time of Gompers,* New York: Harper & Row, Publishers, 1957. The standard source for British unionism is SIDNEY WEBB and BEATRICE WEBB, *The History of Trade Unionism,* London: Workers Educational Association, 1919.

More recent studies relevant to this chapter include E. WIGHT BAKKE and CLARK KERR (eds.), *Unions, Management and the Public* (rev. ed.), New York: Harcourt, Brace & World, Inc., 1960; Section 1, "Sources of the Union Movement"; Section 2, "History of Unionism in the United States." See also IRVING BERNSTEIN, "The Growth of American Unions," *American Economic Review,* 44 (June 1954), pp. 301–18; RAY MARSHALL, *Labor in the South,* Cambridge, Mass.: Harvard University Press, 1967; ADOLF STURMTHAL (ed.), *White-Collar Unions,* Urbana: The University of Illinois Press, 1966; LLOYD ULMAN, *The Rise of the National Trade Union,* Cambridge, Mass.: Harvard University Press, 1955.

16

The Government of
Trade Unions

Collective bargaining is a relationship between organizations—the business firm and the trade union. The internal structure of these organizations affects the relations between them and helps mold the daily life of the worker. In this chapter we examine first the broad outlines of union government at the national and local levels. Next we shall consider some common criticisms of internal union management, and then review the efforts that have been made to correct these deficiencies through legislation.

MANAGING A NATIONAL UNION

A national trade union operates under a written constitution, which may run to forty or fifty closely printed pages. These constitutions are much more detailed than the charters of business corporations or of most other organizations. The duties and powers of union officers, the rights and duties of members, and all procedures for the conduct of union business are usually set forth at length.

The supreme governing body is usually the national convention. Most unions hold their conventions every year or every two years, though sometimes conventions are four or five years apart. The convention consists of delegates from the affiliated local unions. Each local is usually represented in proportion to its dues-paying membership, which means that the larger locals have a dominant voice. The convention has a number of functions and powers. It listens to reports by the national officers on their activities since the last convention, discusses these reports, and approves or disapproves them. It elects officers to serve until the next convention. It is free to debate any question of union policy or organization, and has power also to amend the basic constitution of the union.

The national convention provides a forum in which the views of local unions throughout the country can be expressed. Most of the delegates are local union officials. Many locals pass resolutions at their local meetings for submission to the national convention and frequently instruct their delegates on the stand they should take. The convention provides an opportunity for leaders of a particular local to learn about the problems facing other locals and the national organization as a whole. It thus widens the viewpoint of local leaders and makes them more cognizant of the part they play in a national institution. The convention debates also allow able local officials to display their leadership ability, thus giving them a channel into national office. Almost all national union leaders rise from lower ranks in the union, and must demonstrate their ability repeatedly before they attain high office.

The initiative in bringing business before the convention does not rest entirely, or even mainly, with the delegates. The national officials work out in advance their own policy proposals and seek support for them from the convention. The officers are also usually seeking reelection for another term. The union convention is therefore "stage-managed" in much the same way as the national convention of a political party. The top union officials appoint the key convention committees—the credentials committee, the resolutions committee, the committee on officers' reports, and so on. They determine the order of business and the time allowed for discussion of various subjects, and the union president from his position in the chair can do a good deal to influence the course of discussion. Much of the important business of the convention is done in private through individual discussions and committee meetings, and many key decisions are made in advance of any discussion on the convention floor. The delegates occasionally revolt and take decisions out of the hands of the union leaders. The leaders are usually astute enough, however, to appraise correctly the feeling of the delegates on each issue, and to shape their proposals to be sure in advance of a favorable vote. Their control is not arbitrary, but is based on a well-developed talent for keeping an ear to the ground.

A number of unions, primarily craft unions, that have been in existence for many years, use the referendum procedure, either alone or in conjunction with conventions. In some unions all national officers are elected by referendum vote of the membership, and all constitutional amendments must be ratified in the same way. In some cases, even though there is a national convention, all policy decisions of the convention must be submitted to a referendum vote. A few unions provide for initiation of new legislation directly by the membership. A petition signed by a certain number of union members or endorsed by a certain number of locals compels the national officers to submit the proposition in question either to the convention or to a referendum vote.

Administration of Unions

Administration of the national union's affairs is entrusted to an executive board, consisting usually of a president, secretary, treasurer, and numerous vice-presidents who are responsible for particular geographical areas or segments of the industry. Subject to any constitutional limitations, the executive board has full power to act for the union during the period between conventions.

The executive board, or in some cases the president acting for the executive board, appoints the salaried staff of the union and directs its day-to-day work. In the larger unions, the salaried staff includes several hundred people. At national headquarters there are usually departments for research, legal problems, education, the union magazine, organization, and other functions, plus a clerical staff to handle bookkeeping and correspondence. If legislation is important to the union, and if national headquarters are not located in Washington, there will be a branch office in Washington staffed by a legislative representative and frequently several assistants.

The field organization of the union usually consists of several regional or district offices, each headed by a regional director. If the union has jurisdiction over several industries, as in the case of the Textile Workers' Union, there may be a regional director for each industry. Under the regional directors are the field representatives or "organizers," who organize new local unions and assist existing locals in their dealings with employers. The field representatives are the cement that binds the locals to the national union. They move around their regions constantly, keep in close touch with grass-roots sentiment, report back to national headquarters, and at the same time interpret national union policies to local officials and the rank and file.

The salaries of most union officials are modest by business standards. A few of the larger unions pay their presidents $50,000 or more per year, but this is unusual. Most union presidents would be in the range of $25,000 to $50,000. Most second-echelon union officials would fall in the range of $15,000 to $25,000 per year. Local officers frequently serve without pay. Salaried local officers and field representatives usually do not receive much more than they could make by working in the plant. The practical reason for this is that union members are envious of anyone appointed to a job paying more than they earn themselves, and it is therefore poor politics to let the salaries of lower-level officials get much out of line with the members' earnings. In addition to salary, union officials usually receive allowances for travel and other necessary expenses.

Almost all of the top officials of American unions began as workers in the industry and rose to their present positions through the union's ranks. A man begins as a worker in the plant, is elected shop steward or shop committeeman, goes on to become an official of the local union, rises to international representative or district director, and finally becomes an officer of the international union.[1] A man rarely leaps from nowhere to high office in the union, just as he does not often become a candidate for President of the United States without having served his time in lesser political positions. Disappointing as it may be to college graduates who wish to contribute their talents to the labor movement, there is virtually no way of winning elective office in a trade union except by starting in the plant and coming up through the ranks.

In addition to its administrative functions, the executive board exercises supreme judicial authority during the period between conventions. It hears appeals of union members from actions of local officials, mediates disputes between local unions or factions within a local, and has broad authority to discipline local officials for maladministration or violation of the union constitution. Decisions of the executive board can usually be appealed to the next national convention, but there are a few cases in which this is not true. The president of the American Federation of Musicians, for example, has the right to perform any act on behalf of the union, including making amendments to the union constitution, with no appeal by the membership. There are historical reasons for this provision, connected with the unstable and migratory character of musicians' work, which created a special need for strong central authority. Instances of this sort, however, are very rare in the union world.

Union Finances

Dues paid by the members are the main source of union income. Although dues have tended to rise with wage levels, it remains true that "in most unions the monthly dues can be earned in less than two hours of work."[2] The highest dues are usually charged by unions of skilled workers whose earning level is higher. In the craft unions, too, dues fre-

---

[1] See Eli Ginzberg, *The Labor Leader* (New York: Macmillan Publishing Co., Inc., 1948), particularly Chaps. 5 and 6. See also Jack Barbash, *Labor Unions in Action* (New York: Harper & Row, Publishers, 1948); C. A. Madison, *American Labor Leaders* (New York: Harper & Row, Publishers, (1950); and Florence Peterson, *American Labor Unions—What They Are and How They Work,* rev. ed. (New York: Harper & Row, Publishers, 1952).

[2] Philip Taft, *The Structure and Government of Trade Unions* (Cambridge, Mass.: Harvard University Press, 1954), p. 81.

quently include an insurance premium to cover sickness, retirement, death, and other benefits provided by the unions. Dues are collected by the local union and divided between it and the national union in some specified proportion. The commonest basis is a 50–50 division, but in some cases the national office takes as little as 25 percent, and in a few cases it takes more than 50 percent.

As the functions of the national union have grown, there has been a tendency for its share of dues payments to increase. The level of dues has also risen in the course of time. Wage levels have also risen greatly, however, and it is doubtful whether dues are now as large relative to earnings as they were ten or twenty years ago. It is hard for national union officials to get dues raised fast enough to keep up with rising wage levels and the growing needs of the union. Convention delegates, who are tractable enough on other issues, frequently kick over the traces when it comes to approving a dues increase that they know will be unpopular with the members.

A secondary source of revenue is initiation fees for new members. These fees are generally less than $25 and in many cases around $5. Only seven of the eighty national unions Taft studied, all seven in the building trades, had initiation fees averaging as much as $75. There is considerable variation among local unions, which are usually allowed to set their own initiation fees within outside limits specified by the national. Reports by about 39,000 local unions under the Landrum–Griffin Act showed 325 locals with fees of $250 to $500, and 17 with fees ranging from $500 to a peak of $1,400.[3]

Where does the money go? A union economist has estimated that about one-third of national expenditures goes for organizing purposes, with benefits to members accounting for 22 percent, administrative expenses 15 percent, and strike benefits 13 percent.[4] Publications, research and legal expenses, and other minor items account for the balance. The major expense item for a local union is salaries of local officers, business agents, and clerical help.

The finances of the national union are carefully safeguarded. Officers who handle funds must be bonded, and there is usually a requirement that checks be signed by at least two officials. The union's books are normally audited at least once a year, and a statement of receipts and expenditures is usually printed either in the union magazine or in the proceedings of the national convention. Most national unions also require that the books of local unions shall be inspected periodically by a traveling auditor from

---

[3] Albert Rees, *The Economics of Trade Unions* (Chicago: The University of Chicago Press, 1962), p. 127.

[4] Cited in Jack Barbash, *The Practice of Unionism* (New York: Harper & Row, Publishers, 1956), p. 79.

the national office. Despite these precautions, embezzlement of local union funds still occurs occasionally, although it is very rare at the national level. Taft found that in any given year a certain proportion of local unions, ranging between 1 and 3 percent, will report shortages in their accounts. Some of this is of course due to inexperience and poor bookkeeping rather than deliberate misappropriation. After considering amounts recovered from surety companies and other bonding agencies, net losses are a very small percentage of total dues collections.[5]

Government of Local Unions

The government of local unions may be described more briefly. The local union is usually a branch of a national organization, though there are a few unaffiliated locals that have chosen to go their own way. An affiliated local operates within the constitution of its parent organization, which defines what it can and cannot do. In many unions, for example, a local cannot sign a contract with an employer until the contract has been approved by the national executive board. A local is usually forbidden to call a strike without national approval. If it does anyway, it is not entitled to funds or other support from the national organization and may be subject to disciplinary action.

The business of a local union is carried on in weekly or monthly meetings of the membership. When plants are very large, as in the automobile industry, some locals are so large that it is physically impossible to have a single meeting, and a delegate system has to be used. The typical local union, however, has at most a few hundred members, who can be brought together in a single meeting and can take a direct hand in union affairs if they wish to do so.

Only a small proportion of union members actually take an active and continuous interest in union affairs. On important occasions—the election of officers for the coming year, the formulation of demands to be presented to the employer, the ratification of a new contract, or the taking of a strike vote—a large percentage of the membership will appear at the meeting. Between crises, however, attendance shrinks to perhaps 5 to 10 percent of the membership.[6] The day-to-day work of the union is carried on by a few "wheelhorses" who are willing to put in the necessary time. These are the professional politicians of the labor movement, corresponding to the ward and precinct leaders in a political machine. This

---

[5] Taft, *The Structure and Government of Trade Unions,* Chap. 3.

[6] According to one survey the "normal" attendance in medium-sized established locals, i.e., of 200 to 4,000 members, is 2 to 8 percent. See George Strauss and Leonard Sayles, "The Local Union Meeting," *Industrial and Labor Relations Review* (January 1953), pp. 206–9.

active minority, however, is in close touch with the remainder of the membership. Even though only two men from a certain department of the plant show up at the meeting, they probably have a good idea of what the other men in the department are thinking. They also carry back and explain to their fellow workers the decisions that were taken at the meeting. There is thus a great deal of informal representation of the inert majority, and the government of the union is more democratic than might appear at first glance.[7]

The officers of the local union usually work in the plant along with the rest and receive no pay for their union activities. Exceptions are sometimes found in large locals, where union office may become a full-time job. The local officers carry on the day-to-day work of keeping the union running, persuading new workers to join, collecting dues, handling grievances arising in the plant, and so on. On major problems, such as the negotiation of a new contract, the handling of a strike, an important grievance, or an arbitration case, they are usually advised and assisted by a national field representative.[8]

The Local and the National

Over the past fifty years there has been a general tendency toward greater centralization of authority and responsibility in the national union. The main reason is increased centralization of bargaining negotiations with employers, which stems in turn from the broadening of competition in product markets and the increasing scope of employer organization. It is significant that local union autonomy is greatest in industries where the product market remains local, as in building construction, newspaper printing, local trucking, and the like. In such industries as steel, automobiles, clothing, and coal mining, on the other hand, competition is national, bargaining is in effect national, and union organization is correspondingly centralized. Key negotiations with major companies are conducted by the national officers, national field representatives typically sit in on local negotiations, all agreements are required to conform to national standards, and local policy decisions are closely monitored. A large national staff— a union "bureaucracy"—has been developed to service the local unions.

---

[7] See George Strauss and Leonard Sayles, "What the Worker Really Thinks of His Union," *Harvard Business Review* (May–June 1953), pp. 94–102, and "Patterns of Participation in Local Unions," *Industrial and Labor Relations Review* (October 1952), pp. 31–42.

[8] See George Strauss and Leonard Sayles, "The Unpaid Local Leader," *Harvard Business Review* (May–June 1952), pp. 91–104; Joel Seidman, Jack London, and Bernard Karsch, "Leadership in a Local Union," *American Journal of Sociology* (November 1950), pp. 229–37; and Eli Chinoy, "Local Union Leadership," in A. W. Gouldner (ed.), *Studies in Leadership* (New York: Harper & Row, Publishers, 1950), pp. 157–73.

Another significant tendency is the growth of intermediary bodies between the local union and the national office—regional or district councils on a geographic basis, conferences to deal with a major industry subdivision or a single major employer, and the like. For a million-member union operating in a variety of industries and in all parts of the country, some intermediate organization of this sort is essential.

Two aspects of local–national relations should be noted particularly, since they have given rise to considerable controversy and occasional charges of abuse. First, local union officers are subject to disciplinary action by the national officers. If the officers of a local union are accused by members of violating the national constitution, mishandling union funds, or other misdeeds, they may be brought to trial before the national executive board. If the verdict is against them, they may be removed from office and the national union may appoint a trustee or receiver to manage the affairs of the local until the situation can be rectified and new officers installed.

National officers are reluctant to take such drastic action because of the possibility of local opposition and schism, and in most unions the receivership device is used very sparingly. The commonest reasons for national intervention are financial irregularity, intense factionalism in the local, failure to organize the trade or locality, failure to reopen agreements on time, strikes in violation of contract commitments, communist domination and use of the local for political purposes, and toleration of racketeering in the local.[9] National intervention, in short, is typically a method of protecting the membership against incompetence, venality, or oppression by local leaders. The receivership device can also be used, however, to suppress local union democracy, to get rid of critics of the national machine, and to loot the local treasury. This has led to government regulation of trusteeships and receiverships, which will be considered in the next section.

A second issue concerns the adequacy of present procedures for protecting the "civil rights" of the individual union member. A member may be accused of having violated some working rule of the union, such as accepting pay below the union scale, doing piece work contrary to union policy, or working overtime without permission; or of misbehavior on the job—fighting, drinking, failure to perform job duties, or refusing to follow reasonable instructions of the shop steward. Less frequently, but more dangerously, he may be accused of antiunion activity, defaming a union officer, and so on. There certainly is such a thing as antiunion activity and the union constitution must provide against it, but such charges can also be a way of getting at men whose only real offense is criticism of the officers in power.

---

[9] For detailed evidence, see Taft, *The Structure and Government of Trade Unions,* Chap. 4.

Any charge against a member is heard and decided initially at the local level, either by a trial committee or by vote of the entire membership. The penalty, if guilt is established, is typically a fine appropriate to the offense. Expulsion from membership is regarded as a drastic measure and is rarely used. Either the member or his accusers may appeal the decision to the national president or the executive board, and there is usually a final right of appeal to the next national convention. Taft's study of the records of eight national unions indicates that the right of appeal is used quite frequently. The president and executive board typically review anywhere from twenty-five to one hundred appeals per year. The handling of appeals by national officers appears to be careful and conscientious. The ratio of reversals or modifications of local decisions is quite high—often between 30 and 50 percent of all cases considered. Even when a member's guilt is reaffirmed on appeal, the size of the penalty is frequently reduced. Emotion and personal vindictiveness run higher at the local level than in the national office. Taft concludes:

> The cases that arise out of what might be termed civil rights are relatively few . . . disciplinary penalties are usually imposed for the violation of trade rules and rather infrequently over issues such as free speech or publication of unauthorized materials. It is difficult for outsiders to evaluate the reasonableness of penalties, but the information does indicate that they are seldom severe or unwarranted. . . . On the whole, there is no evidence that the appellate machinery does not function effectively, that it is vain or useless, or that it would be improved by government supervision.[10]

PROBLEMS OF UNION STRUCTURE AND ADMINISTRATION

The internal procedures of trade unions have produced a variety of criticisms and complaints. In a minority of unions, officers have used their positions for self-enrichment and have been guilty of gross breaches of trust. More generally, it is charged that the officers typically dominate union affairs, and that members who oppose the leadership have inadequate protection against retaliation and arbitrary penalties. The proven instances of corruption, and the more general accusation of autocratic government, have led to increasing public control over union affairs. Let us first consider the criticisms before proceeding to the remedies.

Financial Malfeasance

Direct embezzlement of union funds mainly occurs at the local rather than at the national level and is relatively rare. The most important meth-

---

[10] Taft, *The Structure and Government of Trade Unions*, p. 180.

ods of self-enrichment are more subtle. They involve use of the union officer's position of power to secure special perquisites, while at the same time damaging—or at any rate failing to advance—the interests of the membership.

The union leader may negotiate a *sweetheart contract,* in which he settles for less than the union's strength would have allowed, receiving a kickback from the employer in return. Or he may own a share in the business with which he is negotiating on behalf of the union. Or he may set up a business of his own to sell supplies or services to the union at inflated prices. Or he may arrange for the union health and welfare fund to place its insurance with a company in which he has a financial interest.

Congressional investigations have turned up a wide variety of such practices. Here are a few examples:

1. Loans may be secured from the union to finance the officers' personal investments. Dave Beck, former president of the Teamsters Union, was found to have borrowed $270,110 from union sources. Vice-president Frank Brewster, operating at a lower level, confined his borrowing from the Western Conference of Teamsters to $77,660.[11]

2. Ownership of securities or other interests in a business with which the union deals in collective bargaining. In 1950 Peter Weber, business manager of Local 825 of the Operating Engineers, secured a one-eighth interest in Public Constructors Inc., a company under contract with the union, in exchange for a loan of $2,500. By September, 1957, the book value of these shares had risen to $108,677.[12] This is one way in which a company could bribe a union official to go easy on the company in bargaining or to avoid pulling strikes on company projects.

3. A less direct form of the same thing is interest in a business selling services or supplies to, or otherwise dealing with, a company involved in bargaining with the union. Mrs. Dave Beck purchased 40 percent of the stock of K and L Distributing Co., which distributed beer for Anheuser-Busch, Inc., a majority of whose employees are members of the Teamsters' Union. The territory of K and L was enlarged and it received preferential shipments of beer as a result of Beck's influence. Later the investment was sold at a 60 percent profit. A later Teamster president, James Hoffa (or his wife), held a substantial interest in companies that rented equipment to trucking concerns under contract with the Teamsters.[13]

4. Ownership of an interest in a business that buys from, sells to, or otherwise deals with the union itself. Dave Beck bought two lots that adjoined the Teamsters' Joint Council in Seattle for $39,000 and then sold them to the union for $139,000. He also, through a front man, had a hand in the National Mortgage Company, which handled $9 million of Teamsters funds.[14]

---

[11] Hearings before the Select Committee on Improper Activities in the Labor and Management Field (cited hereafter as "McClellan Committee Hearings"), 85th Cong., 1st sess., 1959, pursuant to Senate Resolution 74, part 4, pp. 1357, 1370.

[12] McClellan Committee Hearings, part 2, pp. 8134–40.

[13] McClellan Committee Hearings, part 7, pp. 2058–68, and 2099–2102; part 13, pp. 4933–50, and 4966–71; part 13, pp. 5543–57.

[14] McClellan Committee Hearings, part 5, p. 1671; part 7, pp. 2106–12.

5. Other business transactions with employers. The McClellan Committee hearings revealed that a number of union officials had sold equipment to, received loans from, or received other special payments from employers with whom they negotiated. These payments were presumably intended to influence the officers' conduct in organizing and collective bargaining.

These practices are concentrated in certain of the conservative craft unions. Unions with a strong welfare tradition, such as the Clothing Workers, Ladies' Garment Workers, and the newer industrial unions organized by the CIO, have been almost completely free of corrupt practices.

Racketeering

Racketeering is not a very precise term, but may be taken to include extortion from workers or employers under threat of physical violence, typically involving alliance with gunmen and local criminal syndicates. It has flourished principally in New York, Chicago, and a few other large cities, and in highly competitive industries catering to a local market, such as restaurants and other service establishments, local trucking, and building construction.[15]

The position of the union business agent in the construction industry is rather unusual. The business agent acts as an employment agency, and his control of jobs gives him power over the union membership. He also negotiates with employers, polices the terms of union contracts, and usually has the right to call an immediate strike when he believes the contract is being violated. This power enables him to make things easier or harder for the employer. An inopportune strike may prevent a contractor from finishing a building on time and subject him to a large penalty. The selling of "strike insurance" to employers has sometimes yielded incomes for union officials. The practice is by no means general in the building trades, but it has happened.

Racketeering sometimes results from the invasion of a union by gangsters who turn the union to predatory purposes. Instances of this sort were especially numerous after the repeal of Prohibition in 1933. Many gangsters had been employed in the bootlegging industry. When liquor became lawful, these men were left unemployed and had to find some other use for their talents. In Chicago and New York, in particular, they turned to control of local unions as a source of revenue. The main attempt was to control transport unions—drivers of milk wagons, coal trucks, oil trucks, laundry trucks, and so on. Control of transportation enables the gang to

---

[15] See on this point the interesting analysis in Philip Taft, *Corruption and Racketeering in the Labor Movement,* Bulletin 38 (Ithaca: New York State School of Industrial and Labor Relations, Cornell University, 1958).

"shake down" the businesses that depend on transportation for their existence. In some cases rival gangs tried to win control of the same union, and pitched battles were fought in Chicago for control of the milk-wagon drivers' and certain other locals. It was estimated that in the mid-thirties about two-thirds of the union members in Chicago were paying tribute in one way or another to the Capone organization. It must not be forgotten, of course, that a large proportion of the businessmen of the city were also paying tribute to the same organization.

An aggravated and long-standing example of racketeering involves the longshore industry in the Port of New York. Hearings before a special Crime Commission of New York State in 1952 revealed that numerous locals of the International Longshoremen's Association had been taken over forcibly by men with criminal records; that both rival gangsters and rebels within the union had been silenced by violence and even murder; that union funds had been spent and union business conducted with no effective control by the membership; that large amounts of money had been extorted from shipowners and other businessmen in the port by threats of strike action, damage to merchandise, and other forms of violence; that longshore workers had been forced to pay for their jobs through "kickbacks," "presents," and other payments to those in control; and that the gangsters involved had good political contacts in the cities surrounding the port.

As a consequence of the inability or unwillingness of top International Longshoremen's Association officials to correct these conditions, the AFL expelled the union from federation membership in 1953, and chartered a new longshoremen's union in the hope of winning away members from the expelled organization. The International Longshoremen's Association won a subsequent National Labor Relations Board election by a narrow margin, however, and has continued to maintain control of the port. Perhaps a more significant development was the establishment of a joint Waterfront Commission by the states of New York and New Jersey as a result of the 1952 hearings. The commission has endeavored to abolish the notorious "shape-up system" and to substitute hiring through commission employment offices, to reduce the amount of surplus labor on the docks by issuing longshore licenses only to reasonably regular workers, and to weed out racketeers by refusing licenses to men with criminal records. These measures may gradually weaken the economic basis for racketeering and provide a climate in which honest unionism can develop and survive.

Racketeering is a law enforcement problem rather than a problem of trade union government. The practices just described are already unlawful and can continue to exist only where the law is not enforced. Racketeering in unions is usually carried on in collusion with local political organizations and often with local business interests as well. It is not specifically a union sin, but stems from a generally low level of political and business morality.

Mills concludes that racketeering has been most prevalent in small-scale industries where intense competition has prevailed and where business has not yet grown large enough to maintain its own cartel arrangements. "In the main, these have been the building trades, cleaning and dyeing, restaurants, the garment trades, furriers, trucking, theaters, produce and live poultry markets." [16]

It should be reemphasized that racketeering is not of great quantitative importance in the labor movement. In most cases, union leaders maintain control of the organization by peaceable and lawful methods, by skillful use of the normal tactics of machine politics. This leads us to another line of complaint against trade unions—a complaint, not of wrongdoing, but of serious defects in internal structure.

Leadership Domination

Union government is democratic in the sense that officers at all levels are elected from below and are formally responsible to the membership. But in union elections, unlike elections for public office, there is usually only one recognized party. The Typographical Union, which has an old and successful two-party system, is a rarity in the trade union world. Normally all the political machinery of the union is controlled by the people in office, who naturally use it to remain in office. People who oppose them are "factionalists," "dual unionists," "union busters." The concept of a loyal opposition is not recognized.[17]

Strong leadership in a union seems unavoidable and even desirable for at least two reasons. The union is in part a fighting organization. It reaches crises in negotiating with employers that can be met only by a strike. It may have to fend off attacks by employers, government agencies, or others that threaten the very existence of the organization. Hardman has aptly said that a union is part army and part debating society,[18] but

---

[16] C. W. Mills, *The New Men of Power* (New York: Harcourt, Brace & World, Inc., 1948), p. 129.

[17] For discussions of this problem see Will Herberg, "Bureaucracy and Democracy in Labor Unions," *Antioch Review* (Fall 1943), pp. 405–17; Joel Seidman, "Democracy in Labor Unions," *Journal of Political Economy* (June 1953), pp. 221–31; Joel Seidman, *Union Rights and Union Duties* (New York: Harcourt, Brace & World, Inc., 1943); Philip Taft, "The Constitutional Power of the Chief Officer in American Labor Unions," *Quarterly Journal of Economics* (May 1948), pp. 459–71; and Philip Taft, "Democracy in Trade Unions," *American Economic Review Supplement* (May 1946), pp. 359–69.

[18] See J. B. S. Hardman, *American Labor Dynamics* (New York: Harcourt, Brace & World, Inc., 1928), particularly the articles by Hardman and Muste. See also Sylvia

it cannot be both things at once. Debate is all right before the battle is joined; but while the battle is on, someone must have authority to issue commands. A strike may be won or lost by a single decision, which has to be made so quickly that the members cannot be consulted, and on which the members might not be able to give an informed judgment in any case.

In addition to threats from without, unions are often threatened by factional strife within their own ranks. Unions are especially susceptible to penetration by doctrinaire political groups who are more interested in the establishment of their ideology than in the strength of the union. When a politically minded minority captures control of a union, the result is frequently the atrophy and eventual disappearance of the organization. Union officials must have sufficient authority to prevent schism and to defend the union against internal as well as external enemies. This is admittedly a delicate matter. It is hard to distinguish between a legitimate criticism of union officers and a movement to subvert the union's purposes. The charge of *union wrecking* has been used to crush a minority whose only real offense was differing with the leadership. One must recognize, however, that there is such a thing as antiunion activity by those professing allegiance to the union, and that a means of defense is necessary.

A striking feature of trade union government is the long tenure of office by national union officials, particularly national presidents.[19] John L. Lewis of the Mine Workers, David B. Robertson of the Locomotive Firemen, and William Hutcheson of the Carpenters were union presidents for more than thirty years. Daniel Tobin of the Teamsters, William Mahon of the Street Railway Employees, and George Berry of the Pressmen held office for more than forty years.

Long terms of office have advantages for the union as well as disadvantages. A union needs skilled and experienced leadership. Running a large union requires a detailed knowledge of the economics of the industry, wide acquaintance with management people and political officials, skill in speaking and writing, administrative ability, and experience in negotiation and in the management of men. A leader who is competent and experienced in these respects is a valuable asset to the union. This is a major reason for the long tenure of office by national union leaders. It is true, of course, that many union officials are continued in office beyond the point at which their usefulness has begun to diminish. After a man has been a union official for many years, there is scarcely anything else to which he can turn for a living. The union members, recognizing this

Kopald, "Democracy and Leadership," in E. W. Bakke and Clark Kerr (eds.), *Unions, Management and the Public* (New York: Harcourt, Brace & World, Inc., 1948), pp. 180–84.

[19] Mills, *The New Men of Power*, p. 46.

fact and appreciating the leader's past services, are usually reluctant to "turn the old horse out to grass."

On the other hand, long tenure of office presents certain problems. The viewpoint and objectives of the union leaders tend to diverge more and more from those of the rank and file. The leaders become increasingly interested in sheer perpetuation of the organization, in union-oriented demands rather than membership-oriented demands. Union-shop and checkoff clauses are a case in point. The members would frequently trade such objectives for immediate benefits. The leaders also become more skeptical about the possibility of rapid progress. The union members exaggerate business profits and believe that more money can always be had for the asking. The leaders know that this is not so. They tend to become conservative in their demands, to moderate the zeal of the membership, to settle for less than the members think possible. To the rank and file, this attitude often appears as a sellout to the employers; to the leaders, it means being realistic and practical.

The dilemma is this: in order to protect the long-run interests of the union, the leaders must have enough power to pursue union-oriented objectives, to make compromises with employers, and to override excessive and ill-advised demands by the membership. Given this power, however, it is difficult to prevent them from slighting the interests of the membership if they choose to do so.

Another problem is that union officers—like officeholders in industry, government, and elsewhere—become attached to their jobs and bend a good part of their energies to staying in office. The methods used are those of machine politics anywhere. The union leader makes friends with as many members of the organization as he can, performs various services for them, distributes salaried positions in the right quarters, stage-manages the union conventions, and makes full use of oratory and the other political arts. All this he does in perfectly good faith. He becomes convinced after a few years that he can run the union better than anyone else, and in many cases he is right. Indeed, unless he is able to "deliver the goods" year in and year out, no amount of political machination will suffice to keep him in office.

Where a strong leader has remained in office for twenty or thirty years, it will usually be found that he is an exceptionally able person with a profound grasp of the union's problems, and also that he has kept in close touch with membership opinion. The main function of the leader's political machine is not to suppress opposition, but rather to give an accurate report of rank-and-file sentiment that will enable the leader to develop a program commanding general approval. It will be found also that the successful and long-lived leader has achieved substantial gains for his membership in terms of wages and conditions.

The position of national union leaders, however, appears less secure today than it used to be. Several factors may have contributed to this: more frequent federal investigation of internal union affairs under the Landrum–Griffin Act and other regulatory statutes; the large influx into the labor force of younger workers, more aggressive in their demands on employers and union leaders; an increase of militancy and antiestablishment views dating from the civil liberties and antiwar movements of the sixties; and the increased rates of unemployment and inflation during the seventies, arousing concern over possible erosion of living standards. Hoffa of the Teamsters and Boyle of the Mine Workers ended up in prison. In 1977 there were bitterly contested elections for the presidency of the Mine Workers and Steelworkers. There have been threatened revolts in the Auto Workers and the Teamsters. Thus a union president can no longer count on remaining in office as long as he wishes and then passing on the mantle to his chosen successor.

The Meaning of Trade Union Democracy

In what significant sense may this structure of control be regarded as "democratic" or "undemocratic"? If one asks, "Are the forms of democracy observed?" the answer must be "Yes." Union constitutions are thoroughly democratic. The system of government is normally a one-party rather than a multiple-party system, but this is characteristic of virtually all private associations.[20]

If one asks, "Do the members determine union policy?" the answer is usually "No." Policy is determined by the national leaders and to a lesser extent by local leaders, within rather wide limits set by the members' interests and attitudes.

If one asks, "Are unions by and large operated in the interest of the members?" the answer is predominantly "Yes." Most union officers are honest and men of goodwill. They would rather do a good job for their members than not, and this is sensible also from a political point of view. It helps to keep the machine popular and reelection easy.

If one asks, "Can the members get rid of their leaders and install new ones whenever they wish?"—perhaps the most searching test of democratic control—the answer is "Yes and no." Contests over local office are frequent and the turnover of local officers is high. At the national level, it is possible to revolt against and overthrow an entrenched machine, but it is

---

[20] The only two-party system that has operated over a long period of time is found in the International Typographical Union. This is an unusual situation that is scarcely likely to develop in other unions. For a good analysis of the International Typographical Union case, see Seymour M. Lipset, J. S. Coleman, and M. Trow, *Union Democracy in the International Typographical Union* (New York: The Free Press, 1956).

certainly not easy. It requires organization and hard work, and involves a good deal of personal risk for leaders of the insurgent faction.

The most damaging criticism of union government in the United States is that it fails to recognize the right of legitimate opposition and to provide adequate protection for the dissenting member. A salaried union official who finds himself on the losing side of an internal power struggle is almost certain to be out of a job. A member who opposes the leadership will in some unions find himself exposed to physical violence. In others he will be expelled, with possible loss of employment; and if he appeals his case through union channels, he may find the very people he has opposed sitting in judgment upon him.

REGULATION OF INTERNAL UNION AFFAIRS

Self-Regulation

The labor movement itself has taken some steps toward meeting these criticisms. The United Automobile Workers in 1957 established a Public Review Board, composed of leading lawyers, professors, and clergymen. Members can appeal decisions of the union's international executive board to this outside body, and the review board can take up cases on its own motion. If the board finds that a worker's membership rights have been violated, it can revoke the penalties imposed on him, and the union is pledged to abide by the decision. The board has heard many cases, upholding the union's executive board in about three-quarters of these and reversing it in the remainder. It is regrettable that only two other unions, the Upholsterers and the Packinghouse Workers, have thus far adopted this promising technique.

The AFL–CIO constitution of 1955 pledged the organization "to protect the labor movement from any and all corrupt influences." An Ethical Practices Committee was appointed, which drew up six codes of ethical practice covering (1) issuance of local union charters; (2) operation of health and welfare funds; (3) the barring of racketeers, criminals, communists, and fascists from union office; (4) prevention of conflicts of interest between union officers and their organizations; (5) the setting up of adequate accounting and financial controls; and (6) establishment of minimum standards for union elections and disciplinary procedures. Any national union that, after hearings, is found guilty of violating these codes may be directed to mend its ways. If it declines to do so, the AFL–CIO Executive Council may suspend it from membership by a two-thirds vote. Suspension can be appealed to the next AFL–CIO convention, which has the ultimate right of expulsion. The executive council may also charter a new union to compete with the expelled organization and try to take over its membership.

This procedure has a good chance of success where there is a "clean" faction in the union that is willing to mobilize against a corrupt leadership. The Bakery Workers, whose president had been guilty of malpractice but where corruption was not deeply entrenched, was expelled at the 1957 convention and a rival union was chartered. The new union quickly took over the bulk of the membership in the industry. But where corruption is of long standing and is tolerated by the membership, as in the Teamster and Longshoremen cases, federation action can accomplish little. The Longshoremen were expelled by the AFL in 1953 and a rival union was chartered, but the new union did not succeed in winning mass support. The old union was eventually cleaned up somewhat and was readmitted to the federation in 1961; but this was due mainly to reforms instituted by the New York–New Jersey Waterfront Commission. When the powerful Teamsters Union was expelled in 1957, the federation did not even venture to charter a rival union, and the Teamsters continued to flourish as before. This case has done much to discourage AFL–CIO efforts against corruption.

Court Regulation

A member who has suffered damage from some union action can always go to court and seek redress under the common law. The legal status of unionism and collective bargaining is the subject of a later chapter; but we may comment here on court attitudes toward internal union affairs.

The courts have traditionally regarded a trade union as a private association, comparable to a lodge or social club. Like any club, the union could admit people or bar people as it saw fit, and could set up any rules it liked for internal government. So long as the union observed its own constitution, the courts would not intervene; and they were disinclined to intervene in any event. Only when it came to handling of union funds did the courts become interested, for here property was involved and analogies were available from trust and corporation law.

With the growing economic power of unions, however, this view has become less and less appropriate. Most collective bargaining agreements now provide for a union shop or its equivalent, under which a worker is expected to be a union member as a condition of continued employment. All workers are bound in any event by the conditions of employment which the union negotiates. A worker excluded from the union is thus bound by the actions of an organization in which he has no voice. Rules concerning admission, discipline, and expulsion can threaten a man's livelihood. So the courts have moved toward the view that a union resembles a public utility or government agency, and that its internal procedures are a matter of public concern. The new view is well stated in a California court decision:

> Where a union has, as in this case, attained a monopoly of the supply of labor by means of closed shop agreements and other forms of collective labor action, such a union occupies a quasi-public position similar to that of a public service business and it has certain corresponding obligations. It may no longer claim the same freedom from legal restraint enjoyed by golf clubs or fraternal associations. Its asserted right to choose its own members does not merely relate to social relations; it affects the fundamental right to work for a living.[21]

Following this doctrine, the courts have become more willing to probe into union affairs and to require not merely that the union abide by its own rules, but that the rules themselves should be reasonable. Courts have held, for example, that a closed-shop union must admit black workers to membership or else give up the closed shop; that union disciplinary procedures must meet the test of due process of law; that a union member may not be tried by people having a direct interest in the controversy; and that the union cannot prescribe support of a particular political candidate or otherwise regulate the member's private life.

An aggrieved member, then, may be able to bring a successful suit against the union under common law; but as a practical matter few people are willing to do this. Courts make most people nervous, lawyers are expensive, lawsuits are slow, and long before the worker can get redress he may be out of a job and even out of town. There has consequently been a demand for legislation to spell out standards of good union conduct, to ward off injury to members before it occurs, and to place enforcement responsibility on public officials. After exposure of serious malfeasance in the Teamsters and a number of other unions in the McClellan Committee hearings, Congress passed the Labor–Management Reporting and Disclosure Act of 1959, usually referred to as the Landrum–Griffin Act.

Statutory Regulation: The Landrum–Griffin Act

This Act contains five major sections. Title I, the "bill of rights" section, guarantees the right to vote in union elections and to oppose the incumbent leadership both in union meetings and by nominating opposition candidates. Disciplinary action cannot be taken against union members without proper notice of the charges and a full and fair hearing. Dues

---

[21] Cited by Joseph R. Grodin, "Legal Regulation of Internal Union Affairs," in J. Shister, B. Aaron, and C. W. Summers (eds.), *Public Policy and Collective Bargaining* (New York: Harper & Row, Publishers, 1962), p. 192.

cannot be raised or special assessments levied without a membership vote (at the local level) or a majority vote of duly accredited delegates (at the national level).

The free speech provisions of the Act have been liberally interpreted by the courts.[22] Members are free to voice strong, even untruthful, criticism of union leaders in speech and in writing. They can picket the leaders and make their displeasure known in other ways. They cannot, however, go to the length of creating a dual union or disrupting the union's contractual relations with employers. Thus a member who had incited fellow-workers to go on strike against an employer with whom the union had negotiated an agreement was held to have been properly disciplined by the union.

Title II requires that every labor organization adopt a constitution and bylaws, and file a copy with the Secretary of Labor. In addition, every labor organization must file an annual financial report, listing its assets, receipts and expenditures, salary payments to officers, and related data. It must also report direct and indirect loans to businesses, and any other loan in excess of $250. Union officers must report any holdings of securities and any financial transactions with the union or with companies with whom the union has bargaining relations. These provisions, designed to prevent embezzlement of funds and other financial malfeasance, are administered by an Office of Labor–Management and Welfare–Pension Reports (OLMWR) in the Department of Labor.

The OLMWR receives about 60,000 financial reports per year under this section. All international union reports are audited, and a sample of local union reports is also audited. The possibility that a return may be audited serves as a check on careless or false reporting. Misappropriation of funds is a federal offense, punishable by a fine up to $10,000 or imprisonment up to five years. Between 1959 and 1972, 888 persons were indicted under this provision, of whom 669 were convicted. The offenders came from seventy-nine different international unions, the Teamsters' Union leading the list with eighty-eight cases.

Third, Landrum–Griffin regulates the use of the trusteeship device. This is normally used for legitimate purposes, such as phasing out a declining local or correcting local mismanagement; but it has also been used on occasion to perpetuate a national union machine, or to milk funds from local treasuries. Landrum–Griffin prohibits transfer of funds, requires that any trusteeship be authorized by a proper tribunal after fair hearing, and provides that it automatically becomes invalid after eighteen months unless the union can make a convincing case for its continuation. The Secretary

---

[22] For discussion of the practical application of this and other sections of the Act, see Philip Taft, *Rights of Union Members and the Government* (Westport, Conn.: Greenwood Press, 1975).

of Labor has investigated hundreds of complaints from union members under this section, obtaining voluntary compliance in most cases of justified complaint, so that only a handful of court cases have been filed.

Title IV prescribes standards for local and national union elections. A member who wants to complain of election irregularities must first exhaust his remedies within the union. If still unsatisfied, he may complain to the Secretary of Labor. If investigation shows the complaint to be justified, the Secretary may ask the courts to set aside the disputed results and order a new election under the supervision of the Labor Department. Between 1969 and 1972, 1,289 union elections were investigated under this provision. In more than half of these, no violation was found or there was insufficient evidence that the actions complained of had influenced the outcome of the election. In about 20 percent of the cases, the union agreed voluntarily to hold a new election, usually under Department auspices. In another 20 percent (269 cases) the Department filed legal action, and the courts ordered new elections in 135 cases.

Most of these were local elections; but there have also been a few national cases, of which the most publicized involved the United Mine Workers. This union has traditionally been machine controlled, and there had in fact been no challenge to the national leadership since 1926. In 1969, however, an insurgent faction led by Joseph Yablonski challenged incumbent President Tony Boyle. After a bitter campaign, involving what the insurgents claimed to be illegal tactics, Boyle won the election by a vote of about two to one. Yablonski appealed to the Department of Labor, which at first declined to intervene. Matters changed, however, when Yablonski, his wife, and his daughter were murdered in their home early in 1970. The Department then intervened, conducted an intensive investigation, and sued successfully to have the 1969 election set aside. In the new election, held finally in 1973, the insurgents led by A. R. Miller defeated Boyle for the union presidency.

Finally, Title V establishes a fiduciary relationship of the union official to his union, enabling members to bring suit for improper monetary management, for conflict-of-interest situations, and possibly even for nonfinancial aspects of the leader's work. A union office cannot acquire personal interests that conflict with those of the union and, if conflicts develop, he must act in the union's interest rather than in his own. The Act puts the union official in the legal position of a bank trust officer managing the estate of a client. A substantial body of litigation and court decisions has developed under this section.

The results of Landrum–Griffin to date are scarcely as spectacular as the predictions made at the time of its enactment. On one hand, unionism has not been crippled. On the other hand, not all unions have been turned into the model organizations which the law might seem to require.

There have, however, been improvements in the competence and honesty of financial management, in the protection of dissident union members against arbitrary discipline and, in the regularity of election procedures. The growing tendency to challenge national as well as local union machines has been encouraged by the fact that union elections are now a matter of public record and public concern.

DISCUSSION QUESTIONS

1. What are the dangers and advantages of strong control over local unions by national unions?

2. What advantage does a national union derive from affiliation with the AFL–CIO? Is expulsion of a national union from the federation an effective disciplinary measure?

3. In what ways have some union officers used their positions for personal advantage? What remedies for this situation have been attempted, and what others might be tried?

4. "Unions are democratic in form, undemocratic in substance. Policy is determined by the leaders, and membership participation is at a minimum. There is urgent need of reforms to return the unions to membership control." Discuss.

5. Draw up specifications for a perfectly democratic national union.

6. "There is an inherent conflict between maximum democracy in a union and maximum effectiveness of the union in serving membership interests." Discuss.

7. Why do national union officers usually remain in office for long periods? Is this an undesirable tendency?

8. Why has racketeering occasionally developed in trade unions, and what remedial measures can be taken?

READING SUGGESTIONS

An authority on the subject of union government is Professor Philip Taft. See in particular his studies: *Corruption and Racketeering in the Labor Movement,* Bulletin 38, Ithaca: New York State School of Industrial and Labor Relations, Cornell University, 1958; *The Structure and Government of Labor Unions,* Cambridge, Mass.: Harvard University Press, 1954; and *Rights of Union Members and the Government,* Westport, Conn.: Greenwood Press, 1975.

Other general studies include JACK BARBASH, *Labor's Grass Roots,* New York: Harper & Row, Publishers, 1961; WALTER GALENSON, *Trade Union Democracy in Western Europe,* Berkeley: University of California Press, 1962; CLARK KERR, *Unions and Union Leaders of Their Own Choosing,* New York: The Fund for the Republic, 1958; WILLIAM LEISERSON, *American Trade Union Democracy,* New York: Columbia University Press, 1959; LEONARD R. SAYLES, and GEORGE STRAUSS, *The Local Union: Its Place in the Industrial Plant,* New York: Harper & Row, Publishers, 1953; MARTIN S. ESTEY, PHILIP TAFT, and MARTIN WAGNER (eds.), *Regulating Union Government,* New York: Harper & Row, Publishers, 1964.

A series of case studies of individual unions, sponsored by the Center for Study of Democratic Institutions, has been published by John Wiley & Sons, Inc. New York. Volumes in this series include MORRIS A. HOROWITZ, *The Structure and Government of the Carpenters' Union;* LEO KRAMER, *Labor's Paradox—The American Federation of State, County, and Municipal Employees;* MARK PERLMAN, *Democracy in the International Association of Machinists;* SAM ROMER, *The International Brotherhood of Teamsters;* MELVIN ROTHBAUM, *The Government of the Oil, Chemical, and Atomic Workers' Union;* JOEL SEIDMAN, *The Brotherhood of Railroad Trainmen;* JACK STIEBER, *Governing the UAW;* and LLOYD ULMAN, *The Government of the Steel Workers' Union.*

V

COLLECTIVE BARGAINING

The parties to collective bargaining—the business firm and the trade union—operate on different principles. As a first approximation, a business can be regarded as a cost-minimizing, profit-maximizing organization. Continued growth of assets, sales, and profits is also an important business objective. Business executives are convinced that efficient pursuit of these objectives requires a large degree of management autonomy in production and personnel decisions.

The trade union, on the other hand, is intrinsically a management-restricting organization. Responding in political fashion to membership pressures, it tries to check unilateral action by management on any matter importantly affecting the members' welfare, substituting a set of negotiated rules that has been termed "a system of industrial jurisprudence." Management dislikes and resists these restrictions on its authority. In Chapter 17 we explore these differing approaches of the two organizations, which are a source of continuing tension in industrial relations.

Chapter 18 deals with the standardized *procedures* used in collective bargaining. These include *contract negotiations,* in which negotiators selected by the parties hammer out changes in wages, fringe benefits, and other contract terms for one to three years ahead. Contract negotiation is a highly stylized game, proceeding through well-defined stages, and terminating normally in agreement but occasionally in deadlock and strike. Also important, though less dramatic, is the *grievance procedure* for handling day-to-day disputes over interpretation and application of the contract rules. This procedure, now almost universal in American industry, normally culminates in neutral arbitration of unsettled disputes.

Chapter 19 explores the elusive concept of *bargaining* power, seeking first an operational definition of this concept, and then an explanation of what determines the relative power of the parties in a particular case. We then look at the *negotiating tactics* of the parties—the effort to discover the other's true position, to conceal one's own position, to change the other's position by persuasion or coercion, to deploy bluff and threat to best advantage. The normal result of these tactics is to move the positions of the parties closer together, until eventually they overlap and agreement becomes possible. But this does not always happen, and we analyze the main situations in which negotiations may become deadlocked, leading to a strike.

17

Collective Bargaining: Union and Management Approaches

It is often said that collective bargaining is a relationship between a political organization, the trade union, and a business organization. Before plunging into the details of bargaining procedures, it is desirable to take a broad look at the objectives of the organizations involved. What is the general outlook and thrust of the trade union movement? On the other side of the table, what is the management group trying to accomplish? How does the appearance of a union on the scene alter management organization and policies?

ECONOMIC MODELS OF THE UNION

Economists, puzzling over how to get a handle on union behavior through familiar economic concepts, have tended to fall back on the concepts of *monopoly* and of *maximization*. Instead of the employer choosing his own wage rate, the union insists on a wage that has been bargained out with the union. Assuming that the union can prevent the employer from getting labor except at this wage, it would seem to be in the situation of a monopolistic seller of a commodity: "Pay my price, or else."

On closer examination, however, the monopoly analogy appears defective. If by saying that a union is a monopoly we mean simply that it has *market power,* that it can influence the level of wages, the statement is surely correct. But it is misleading if it connotes that union decision making closely resembles that of monopolistic sellers in product markets. The union does not itself sell labor; nor does it receive the proceeds. Rather, union–management negotiations establish a framework of rules within which the employer may buy labor from individual workers.

The maximization concept is also central to economics. The business concern maximizes profit; workers and consumers maximize utility. So, to the extent that the union is a purposive economic unit, must it not also be trying to maximize something? Let us look briefly at the possibilities of this approach.

Consider a union bargaining over wages in a locality (for local-market industries) or on a national scale (for national-market industries). There will be a demand curve for union labor, its elasticity depending partly on the degree of union organization in the industry. In cotton textiles, for example, only about 20 percent of total employment is under union contract. There are many producers selling their products under conditions approaching those of pure competition. In this situation, it is not feasible to push the wage level of union mills much above that of nonunion mills. At anything above the nonunion wage, the demand for union labor will be highly elastic. This is the prevalent situation in textiles, garment manufacture, and numerous other light manufacturing industries.

Let D and S in Figure 17–1 be the general supply and demand curves for labor in a particular industry; and suppose that employers at the outset are paying the competitive wage OW. A union coming into this industry may be able to raise wages of union plants moderately above OW. The

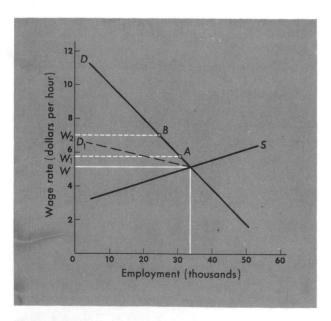

Figure 17–1

The Demand for Union Labor in an Industry

unionized mills may be able to increase efficiency somewhat to offset the wage pressure, or they may be willing in the short run to accept lower profit margins. But as the gap between the union and nonunion wage widens, more and more of the unionized companies will have to suspend operations. The demand for *union labor,* then, is shown by the dashed line D_1. The scope for union wage policy is limited.

Suppose on the other hand that the industry is fully unionized. The demand curve for union labor is then identical with the demand curve for all labor, that is, it is simply D. Suppose further that union officials know the location of this demand schedule. What will they do? The quantities that they might conceivably try to maximize include *the wage rate, the wage bill,* and *the level of employment.* Let us consider the plausibility of these various targets.

The Wage Rate

In the situation shown in Figure 17–1, wages could be raised to $10 an hour or even higher, while still retaining *some* employment for union members. Rational pursuit of this target might consist in pushing up the wage rate, and reducing the level of employment, at precisely the rate at which people retire from the industry. Eventually there would be a single employee left, working at an astronomically high wage! It is sometimes said that the policy of the United Mine Workers has tended in this direction. Especially after 1945, the union raised wages rapidly and tolerated a rapid decline in employment.

The difficulties of a rate-maximizing policy are clear. If pushed too aggressively, it could displace prime-age workers as well as those ready to retire. Since union members are interested in having a job as well as in how much they earn on the job, displacement would produce grass-roots dissatisfaction and bring pressure on union leaders to modify their policies. Moreover, the success of a rate-maximizing policy depends on an assumption that the industry can be kept organized. But as the union rate is pushed higher and higher, there is increased incentive for employers to break away from the union and for new firms to set up on a nonunion basis. A case in point is the construction industry, where escalation of union wage scales has contributed to a relative expansion of nonunion employment.

The Wage Bill

The union might conceivably try to maximize the total payroll of the industry, that is, the wage rate multiplied by the number employed. But there is no particular reason why it should do this, since the wage bill goes to the workers rather than the union. Moreover, this principle could lead to odd results. Over any section of the labor demand curve in which demand is elastic, the wage bill can be increased by *cutting* the wage rate. Union members would probably consider this rather odd and would not be consoled by a lecture on elasticity of demand.

The demand schedule in Figure 17–1 was drawn deliberately so that the upper portion (to the left of point *A*), is elastic, while the portion to the right of *A* is inelastic.[1] A wage of OW_1, corresponding to the point of unit elasticity *A*, would maximize the wage bill. If the union had somehow established or inherited a higher wage, say OW_2, it would have to cut wages in order to follow this maximizing principle.

Employment

Pursuit of this goal would require a wage of *OW*, the same wage that would exist under competitive conditions. At any wage below *OW*, the number of workers willing to enter the industry would fall short of the number that employers wish to hire. The wage *OW* thus yields maximum employment and (again assuming that the industry can be kept fully organized), maximum union membership of *OE*. But while union officials have some interest in the size of their membership, there seems no reason why they should take this as their *sole* objective.

The maximizing approach thus turns out not to be very helpful. So most writers, in the end, fall back on rather vague formulations: a union will try to set wages above the competitive level (how much above?), but at the same time it will take some interest in employment (how much interest?). There is no mechanical rule comparable to the profit-maximizing formula for a business concern.

Union policy is formulated by the leadership, subject to varying degrees of consultation and potential veto by the membership. We may gain additional insight by considering the main pressures impinging on the leaders as they go about their task. The most important of these are rank-and-file sentiment, the wage increases currently being won in "neighboring" occupations and industries, and the constraints imposed by the economic environment.

Union members at any time have some notion of whether they should

---

[1] As one moves down a linear demand curve from the *X*-axis, the curve will at first be elastic, will pass through a point of unit elasticity, and will be inelastic thereafter. The reason is explained in most elementary economics texts, or can be reasoned out from the formula for demand elasticity, which here is

$$e = - \frac{\% \text{ change in } E}{\% \text{ change in } W}$$

where *W* represents the wage rate and *E* is employment. As one moves down *D*, the numerator of this expression decreases steadily while the denominator increases, so that *e* falls continuously.

be getting more, and how much more. If the cost of living is rising, their wives will remind them of the inadequacy of the paycheck. If other workers in their area are getting increases, they will feel that their own wages should keep pace. Thus during a general economic expansion, there will be persistent membership pressure, which may be alleviated for a time after each wage settlement, but will then recur. On the downswing, however, few workers will concede that wages should be reduced. They are not impressed by the argument that, if the cost of living is falling, they can take a money wage cut and still have the same real wage. The principle of "no backward step" is firmly grounded in membership sentiment.

Members' opinions are brought home to the leadership through the normal processes of union government. Wage demands are discussed in local union meetings before negotiations begin. Rank-and-file members or lower-level officials in close touch with the membership usually sit on the negotiating committee. The terms tentatively agreed on with management must usually be submitted to a membership vote before the final ratification. This used to be regarded as a formality, since the members almost invariably voted to accept the settlement. But in recent years, this view has been less valid. During the sharp inflation of the years since 1965, union members have frequently rejected the terms recommended by their officers, forcing continued negotiations and often a continuation of strike action.

A second important consideration is interunion rivalry for members and prestige. Such rivalry is clearest where unions are competing for membership in the same industry. Thus some West Coast airframe plants are organized by the United Automobile Workers, others by the International Association of Machinists. Sailors on the East Coast belong to the National Maritime Union, those on the West Coast to the Sailors Union of the Pacific. East Coast and West Coast longshoremen also belong to separate organizations, which keep a close watch on each other. In the basic aluminum industry, some plants are organized by the United Steelworkers, others by the United Aluminum Workers. In such situations neither union can afford to settle for less than the other.

Political pressures may be important even within a single union. In the Teamsters' Union, for example, James Hoffa succeeded between 1940 and 1955 in building a firm power base in the Midwest, culminating in the negotiation of a uniform wage agreement with over-the-road truckers throughout the central states and most of the South. He then moved on to the East Coast and eventually to the Pacific Coast where, sometimes over the opposition of local officials, he attracted membership support by promising and delivering terms equivalent to those in the Central States' Agreement. This brought him the Teamsters' presidency in 1958, and unchallenged domination of the union thereafter.

In some cases two unions have an unusually close relation because of the physical proximity of their members. Longshoremen and sailors mingle on the docks. Truck drivers and warehousemen meet at freight terminals. Lumbermen and sawmill employees work close to paper-mill workers in the forested regions of the country. In centers of heavy manufacturing, the Automobile Workers, Steelworkers, Electrical Workers, and Machinists usually have sizable memberships in close proximity. The importance of interunion rivalry and imitation was first pointed out by Professor Arthur Ross, who coined the term "orbits of coercive comparison." More recently several cases of this sort have been documented by Professor Harold Levinson.[2]

A third factor that the union leader must consider is the economic situation of the industry at the time. If profits are high and the business outlook is good, he can afford to make large demands. If business is declining and profits are falling, he may have to be content with holding the present wage level. Most union presidents have a shrewd knowledge of the structure and financial prospects of their industry. This knowledge is derived from frequent discussions with employers throughout the country and long experience in negotiating with them, supplemented by the work of the union's research department and by governmental and trade reports. In many cases the union president knows more about the industry and has a broader view of its problems than does any single employer.

Although union leaders realize that there is an upper limit to what a company or industry can pay at a particular time, they do not necessarily take employers' statements about ability to pay at their face value. They believe that ability to pay is somewhat flexible; within limits, a company can pay more if it has to pay more. Any experienced union leader has had numerous experiences of wage increases that, according to the company's claim during negotiations, would cause bankruptcy but that the company later managed to bear. Employers have cried wolf so often that the union hesitates to believe them even when their plight is serious.

In the light of these various pressures, the union negotiators must decide on their (genuine) demands. The decision involves intuition and judgment, rather than application of a simple formula to clearly perceived economic data.

UNION OBJECTIVES IN COLLECTIVE BARGAINING

Wage demands get the headlines, partly because they can be expressed and dramatized in numbers. But this is by no means all that a union tries to

---

[2] Arthur M. Ross, *Trade Union Wage Policy* (Berkeley and Los Angeles: University of California Press, 1948); Harold M. Levinson, *Determining Forces in Collective Wage Bargaining* (New York: John Wiley & Sons, Inc., 1966).

accomplish. This can be shown by a brief review of the content of a typical collective bargaining agreement.

Union demands can be classified under the following headings: maintenance of the organization; rationing of scarce job opportunities; improvement of wages, hours, and other terms of employment; and development of a judicial system of deciding disputes over rights of individual workers.

The right to maintain a union organization is basic, since without this nothing else can be accomplished. The union's right to exist is usually challenged by employers at the outset, and conflict over this issue may continue for decades before the union is finally accepted as a permanent feature of the industry. During this time the union spends much energy in fending off employer attacks, developing experienced leadership and stable organizational forms, and persuading workers of the need to join the union, pay dues, and support union objectives. The right to organize is one of the few tenets that is accepted implicitly by all unionists everywhere and that will never be compromised. Even after the union's survival is no longer in doubt, much attention is still given to keeping the organization intact and strong.

A second facet of union activities, so important that Perlman has found in it the key to union policy, involves the control of job opportunities. Workers old enough to have lived through a depression are deeply convinced that there is never enough work to go around. Beyond this, there is clearly a shortage of "good" jobs, and the number of people trying to get into these jobs far exceeds the number of vacancies available. This poses the problem of who is to get the good jobs and who is to be left on the street or pushed into undesirable kinds of work.

In economic theory, this problem would be solved through employers' appraisal of workers' efficiency. The employer would select "the best man for a job" at a given time. In principle, he would be free to change his opinion from month to month—to promote or demote, to hire or discharge, on the basis of his most recent evidence concerning relative worker efficiency. It is not surprising that this solution does not commend itself to most manual workers. It implies great insecurity of job tenure, a constant threat of displacement if the employer can find someone else to do the job better. It also implies that nothing but efficiency should be taken into account in hiring and firing. Most workers would not agree. What about length of service, age, family responsibilities, membership or nonmembership in the union, and other considerations?

Faced with an assumed scarcity of jobs, and faced with the insistent demand of workers for security of job tenure, the union develops policies designed to maintain or increase the total number of jobs in its industry, to ensure that union members get first chance at these jobs, and to see that the different kinds of jobs are distributed among workers in a fair and reasonable way. The distribution of the available work is too vital to be left to the sole discretion of the employer, and steps are taken to control it by rules which the union has helped to formulate. In Perlman's words:

> *The group then asserts its collective ownership over the whole amount of opporunity,* and, having determined who are entitled to claim a share in that opportunity, undertakes to parcel it out fairly, directly, or indirectly, among its recognized members. . . . Free competition becomes a sin against one's fellows, anti-social, like a self-indulgent consumption of the stores of a beleaguered city, and obviously detrimental to the individual as well. A collective disposal of opportunity, including the power to keep out undesirables, and a "common rule" in making bargains are as natural to the manual group as "laissez-faire" is to the business man.[3]

The feeling that people already engaged in an occupation have a right to protection against outside competition, that experience on a job constitutes a kind of property that deserves equal protection with other forms of property, is strongest among the skilled crafts. Almost a century ago the leaders of a British craft union put the point as follows:

> Considering that the trade by which we live is our property, bought by certain years of servitude, which gives us a vested right, and that we have a sole and exclusive claim on it, as all will have hereafter who purchase it by the same means. Such being the case, it is evident it is our duty to protect, by all fair and legal means, the property by which we live, being always equally careful not to trespass on the rights of others.[4]

A third set of union objectives has to do with improvement of wages, hours, and other terms of employment. On this front, the unions are riding a flood tide. National output per capita has been rising for many decades in most countries of the Western world, and continuing improvement in wages and working conditions has come to be taken for granted. The unions may speed up this process in some respects. At any event, they usually take credit for the improvements that occur in the course of time, even though most of these may already have been in the cards; and they strengthen the workers' conviction that progress is normal and right. When an economist tells him that things are bound to get better for him because of the mysterious working of economic forces, he may have doubts; but

---

[3] Selig Perlman, *A Theory of the Labor Movement* (New York: The Macmillan Company, 1928), p. 242.

[4] Sidney Webb and Beatrice Webb, *The History of Trade Unionism* (London: Workers Educational Association, 1919), p. 564.

where the union tells him that things will be better next year because this is his right and the union will demand it, he is likely to believe. Thus normal economic progress takes on the aspect of a social movement, of something which is organized, planned, and inevitable.

It is above all in bargaining over terms of employment that unionism reveals its flexible and pragmatic character. There are no general principles determining how large the demands should be at a particular time, or what should be their specific character. At one time the unions will push for reductions in hours, at another time for pension plans or medical care funds, at other times for straight wage increases. In one year the wage demand may be ten cents an hour, in another twenty-five cents, as circumstances seem to warrant. The only firm principle is that the movement must always be in the same direction—forward.

A fourth sphere of union activity involves the process by which the general rules stated in the union contract are interpreted and applied to individual workers. The union is concerned, not only with a voice in making the rules, but also with seeing that they are equitably applied and that the rights of individual workers are fully protected. The grievance procedure through which this is typically done in the United States is described in Chapter 18.

A Concluding Comment

Outside observers often ask: "What are the unions really after?" Management people, in particular, often suspect some hidden objective of deep-rooted economic change. The truth seems rather to be that, at least in the United States, unions have no long-term strategy. In Strasser's words, they are simply "going on from day to day."

To a singular degree the American trade union movement is a movement without ideology. Its objectives are not deduced from broad principles of politics or economics. Union leaders have no picture in mind of an ideal future society.

It is clear that unionism brings important social changes. The trade union becomes a leading community institution, more central in the lives of many workers than the lodge, the company, the political party, or anything else. Other basic institutions must, so to speak, move over to make room for it. The union comes to play an important role in industrial management, particularly as regards wages and hours, working conditions, job tenure, and other personnel matters. Perhaps most important, unionism brings a considerable shift in the balance of political power in the community. It exerts effective pressure in the direction of what has come to be termed "the welfare state" and bars any return to

the governmental policies of the nineteenth century. In a strongly unionized democracy, every political party must take account of labor's interests
in order to survive.

One of the most important ways in which unionism tends to con-
serve and strengthen the social structure is by strengthening the worker's
attachment to his job, his work group, and his employer. It provides him
with a club, a fraternity, which helps to gratify the natural desire for
social bonds with one's fellows. It provides a channel through which he
can seek redress of grievances against supervisors or others, so that he
has the feeling of living in a self-governing society rather than in an autoc-
racy. It dramatizes the gradual improvement of wages and other conditions
from year to year. It strengthens his security in his job and, through the
influence of seniority rules, makes it more likely that he will stay with the
same employer in the long run. In all these ways unionism gives workers
a "stake in the system," a sense of belonging and participation, a feeling
that the existing setup of industry is reasonably satisfactory, and an an-
tipathy to proposals for radical change.

Some observers would disagree with this characterization of unionism as a conservative movement. In the light of the drastic changes in
Western capitalism over the past 200 years, however, and in the light of
the revolutionary political movements now sweeping the world, the demands and achievements of the trade unions seem modest. Certainly they
appear to be well within the range of tolerance both for private capitalism
and democratic government.

THE FUNCTION AND OUTLOOK OF
MANAGEMENT

Turning to management, we may begin by examining the economic function of the business firm. The picture of the business concern in economic
textbooks is considerably simplified, partly because of the emphasis that
economists have placed on the theory of pure competition. Under purely
competitive conditions, the prices which must be paid for all factors of
production are strictly determined by the market, and the prices of the
company's products are similarly determined. The only decision left to
management concerns the method of production to be used. On closer
investigation, however, it turns out that management has no real choice
even in this respect. By the definition of pure competition, new producers
are free to enter the industry at will. Unless a particular company uses
the most efficient possible methods, therefore, it will not be able to keep
pace with rival producers. It will find itself losing money and will eventually have to go out of business. Under purely competitive conditions, in
short, the business concern is a puppet maneuvered by the general forces

of supply and demand. Management discretion and judgment do not exist.

In practice, however, we know that management does do some managing. There is scope for initiative and judgment. The main reason is that actual business concerns operate under conditions of imperfect competition. They are sheltered in greater or lesser degree from the full sweep of market forces.

The price of labor, for example, is not completely determined by market forces; it can be altered within limits by management decision or union–management negotiations. Prices of purchased materials and equipment are frequently open to bargaining. The types, specifications, and prices of the products that the company sells can usually be adjusted within limits. Production methods can be altered somewhat. The upshot is that competing companies in the same industry may show quite different levels of cost and profit. Every industry has its high-cost and low-cost producers. This is due partly to factors other than management; but managerial skill and ingenuity do make a difference.

The extent of management's freedom, however, should not be exaggerated. First, management is bound by the simple accounting principle that you cannot make something out of nothing. A wage increase, to take the most relevant example, has to come from somewhere. Either product prices must be raised, or the volume of sales must be expanded, or money must be saved on material costs, selling expenses, or some other nonlabor item. If none of these things is done, profits will be reduced by the amount of the wage increase. Accounting logic allows no other possibilities.

Second, management is put under pressure by certain long-run tendencies that characterize our type of economy. The long-run tendency of wages is upward, for reasons that were discussed in Part Two. Any company must count, year after year, on finding more money to pay for the labor it uses. At the same time, however, the company is subject to downward pressure on the prices it can charge, because of the existence of rival producers and products, and because of continuing technical progress that makes better products possible at lower costs. Management is caught in a scissors between a steady expansion of its costs and at least a potential shrinkage of its revenues.

The only escape from this dilemma lies in managerial efficiency and inventiveness. In order to survive in a competitive world, management must continually search for new or improved products, better methods of merchandising, improved machinery and production techniques, and more efficient administrative organization within the company. These things can be neglected for a year or two, but any company that neglects them for ten or twenty years is headed for economic extinction.

These basic characteristics of business management help to account for certain attitudes that influence the process of collective bargaining.

Top management officials feel that the essence of their job lies in adjusting the conflicting pressures impinging on the company from competitors, customers, stockholders, wage earners, and others. The conflicting character of these pressures means that management cannot afford to respond fully to any one of them. It may, for example, have to resist certain union demands in order to ensure reasonable prices to consumers or reasonable returns to stockholders. Further, management people are inclined to feel that they, along with the scientists and engineers, are responsible for most of the improvement in products and production methods that constitutes economic progress and has made possible present living standards. Union demands are sometimes resented as an effort by a group that has contributed little to higher productivity to "cash in" on the fruit of management's labors.

The Significance of Profit

Our economy is sometimes described as a *profit system,* or as being guided by the *profit motive.* Economists often assume that each business concern tries to make as large a profit as possible. How much is there to this, and what is its significance for collective bargaining?

There is a large literature on the motivation of corporate executives and the objectives of the business firm. There is widespread agreement that to maximize profit at each moment of time is an impossible task, mainly because of continual changes in product and factor markets. Executives aim rather to achieve a "reasonable," or "normal," or "safe" level of profit.

Why is this considered necessary? First, profit provides a margin of security for the company. The higher the company's profit margin, the farther it can fall if business turns bad before encountering actual losses. Second, profit is important as a return to present and prospective investors in the company. Stockholders who find their dividends falling off seriously are likely to become discontented with the management and may try to do something about it. More important, a low rate of profit may make it difficult or impossible for the company to raise funds for expansion by floating new securities. Third, profits are themselves a source of funds for expansion of plant. Reinvested earnings are now the main source of capital for expansion. A low rate of profit may mean that the company will have insufficient funds to finance projects that would help to increase profit. Fourth, profits are an index of management success. A management that is not able to turn in as good a profit rate as other companies in its industry, or that finds its profit rate declining from year to year, is apt to feel this as a criticism of its own performance. Even though the profit rate may have no direct bearing on executive salaries, any manager likes to feel that he is "up to par" with others in his profession.

Some of the difficulties of collective bargaining arise from the difference in the way profits are regarded by management and by union officials. In the eyes of management, profit is not merely a legitimate form of income but an essential element in the operation of a private enterprise system. The expectation or hope of profit is a major incentive to managerial efficiency and serves to call forth capital investment in new enterprises. Realized profits are a major source of funds for expansion of existing businesses. A positive rate of profit is thus an essential condition for economic growth and development.

Most union leaders would not quarrel with this in principle. Their enthusiasm over profits is more restrained than that of management people, however, and their idea of a "reasonable" rate of profit is apt to be more modest. They sometimes talk as though the net income of a company were a simple surplus performing no function in the economy, a pool into which the union can dip at will without any economic consequence. Management people object strongly to this as a simplified and incorrect view of the situation.

There is also a general feeling among management people that profits are none of the union's business anyway. Management believes that the company should pay "fair wages," which usually means fair in comparison with what other employers are paying for similar work. If management can pay fair wages and still make large profits, this is purely management's business. Union officers and members, on the other hand, feel that high profits should be shared with workers in the enterprise through better wages. The workers have helped to produce these profits, it is argued, and hence should be entitled to a share in them. When a company is taking losses, however, the two parties usually switch sides in the argument. The union is apt to argue that the company should still pay fair wages and that its losses are of no concern to the union, while the company may now argue that losses should be taken into account.

A further source of difficulty is that the relevant profit figure in collective bargaining is the estimated profit for the year ahead. Past profits are bygones. The union and management are bargaining over how much the company can afford to pay *next year,* not *last year.* This involves forecasts of future sales volume, product prices, material costs, and numerous other things. Sales volume, which depends so largely on general business conditions, is especially hard to forecast in many industries, and a small change in volume may make a large difference in the firm's profit position. Faced with these uncertainties, management typically tries to play it safe, to leave some margin for a possible downturn in business, to make a conservative estimate of probable profits. Union leaders, on the other hand, have a strong interest in taking a rosy view of the future, estimating profits at a high level, and trying to get wages set accordingly. The union, in short, is constantly trying to get management to stick its neck out farther than management likes to do.

This is a serious complication in the path of collective bargaining. If sales and profits for the next year could be known with certainty, if management could be sure just how much it was giving away and how much it would have left after paying a specified rate of wages, negotiations would be simpler than they actually are.

MANAGEMENT AND THE UNIONS: SOME SOURCES OF TENSION

In the modern corporation, pursuit of efficiency requires coordination of the efforts of hundreds or thousands of individuals. The business manager is not just an expert in production techniques. He is the leader of an organization, the captain of a team. Successful performance of his functions requires that he have wide latitude in making decisions, and that he have "cooperation" or "teamwork" from those under him.[5] To most management people, teamwork seems to mean mainly fealty—a willing acceptance of managerial decisions and an earnest effort to execute them. It leaves room for tactful and "constructive" criticism of particular decisions, but no room for any challenge to management's right to make these decisions. The ideal situation is one in which the manager functions as a benevolent monarch. No one questions his authority, but his exercise of authority is so just and reasonable that his subordinates esteem rather than fear him. The feeling that one has been fair even when one did not have to be is probably one of the greatest satisfactions obtainable from a management position.

All this leads to a characteristic management view of satisfactory industrial relations, which has been summarized by Bakke in four major principles:

> Industrial relations are primarily and basically a matter of relations between management and employees, its own employees.
> The first objective of industrial relations, like that of every function of management, is the economic welfare of the particular company.
> Industrial relations arrangements must leave unimpaired management's prerogatives and freedom essential to the meeting of management's responsibilities.

---

[5] E. Wight Bakke and Clark Kerr (eds.), *Unions, Management and the Public* (New York: Harcourt, Brace & World, Inc., 1948), pp. 242–43.

All parties to industrial relations should be businesslike and re-sponsible.[6]

Trade unionism challenges these cardinal points in management's philosophy. It interposes between employer and employee the trade union, which many managers believe is more interested in its own growth and power than in the economic welfare of either workers or the company. It refuses to accept survival and profitability of the company as the sole aim of business management. It interferes with management's effort to achieve lowest money cost of production, and with the freedom of maneuver that most managers consider essential to successful performance of their functions. At point after point the union says, "You cannot do that," or, "You must consult us before doing anything." Many management people see in this a deliberate policy of union encroachment on management functions. They ask themselves where the process will end, and whether they may not be forced eventually to abdicate control of the plant to the union.

Management opposition to unionism is based partly on self-interest. Being human, managers dislike a reduction in their authority just because it is a reduction. Unionism also makes the manager's job harder by increasing the number of people whose agreement must be secured for a given decision, and by presenting the risk that agreement may not always be secured. If a lower executive of the company refuses to comply with a decision of top management, he can be removed from office; but management cannot fire the union or its officials. Unionism increases the number of conflicting pressures that converge on management. Between the insistent demands of organized workers for more money, customers for lower prices, and the board of directors for larger profits, the manager may be ground to pieces. In all these ways, unionism increases the amount of frustration, personal insecurity, and nervous wear and tear to which management is subjected.

It is too narrow a view, however, to regard management opposition to unionism as entirely self-interested. Most managers believe that unionism, by limiting managerial initiative and discretion, strikes directly at the roots of economic progress and rising national income. Unionism thus tends in the long run to reduce rather than raise the real income of the working class. This conviction is held just as firmly and sincerely as the conviction of union leaders that they are leading a drive for social progress.

Another element in the differing outlook of managers and unionists is the difference in their personal background and experience. Two-thirds of the top management officials in American corporations come from business and professional families. Three-quarters of them have been to

---

[6] E. Wight Bakke, *Mutual Survival,* (New York: Harper and Row, Publishers, 1946), pp. 2–3.

college. Only a small percentage have engaged in manual labor at any stage of their careers.[7] The day-to-day problems of the plant worker are something they have read about in business-school casebooks, but have not experienced directly. Contrast this with the background of the union official, almost invariably a former worker, short on formal training but long on plant experience. It is not surprising that the two groups view the world of industry differently and have different conceptions of "proper" personnel management.

The general outlook of management toward unionism, then, is critical and sometimes hostile. Concrete strategies, however, differ greatly from one situation to the next. They range all the way from forcible opposition and a determination to get rid of the union at one extreme, through various shades of reluctant acceptance, to positive cooperation with the union at the other pole. The commonest situation is one that might be termed "defensive endurance," a feeling that "if this is what our workers want, I guess we'll have to go along with it. But we don't understand why they want unionism. There's nothing in it for them. Perhaps they'll eventually see the light and the whole thing will go away."

Underlying this outlook are two assumptions that may be termed the "harmony of interests" assumption and the "management can do it better" assumption. The first asserts that there is no real divergence of interest between employer and employees. Prosperity for the worker depends on prosperity for the company. Management and workers have an equal interest in harmonious coordination of the enterprise and maximum productive efficiency. We shall have occasion in later chapters to examine both the element of truth in such statements and the qualifications that must be attached to them. Regardless of the truth of the matter, however, this attitude is sincerely held by large numbers of management people. It leads them to a conclusion that unions are stirring up conflict where no real conflict exists, and that they are useless or even harmful.

The second assumption flows logically from the first. It asserts that all legitimate interests of the employee can be protected adequately by management itself. The union can do nothing that management, with its greater technical skills and more reliable information, could not do even better. If the workers accept unionism, then, this must be due to some failure of management to organize itself effectively and to "put across" its story to employees. Unionism, in short, results from managerial failure and nothing else.

---

[7] Based on a sample survey of 8,300 top management people in 1952. See W. Lloyd Warner and James C. Abbeglen, *Occupational Mobility in American Business and Industry* (Minneapolis: University of Minnesota Press, 1955); and Mabel Newcomer, *The Big Business Executive* (New York: Columbia University Press, 1955).

Managements in this frame of mind accept unionism as a punishment for their sins and because it is legally obligatory. They continue, however, to regard it as an alien growth against which management must protect itself at every turn. They try to build dikes against the advance of union influence, to restrict the area of collective bargaining, to resist union intrusion on "managerial prerogatives."

These attitudes, however, are not immutable. After twenty or thirty years of collective bargaining (in some cases, only after the rise of a new generation of top executives!), a company may come round to a different view of unionism. It finds that the union, although it limits management at many points, can also be used to further the broad objective of profitable operation of the enterprise. Information about the economic situation and problems of the company, for example, may be accepted more readily by workers if funneled through the union organization than if disseminated directly by management. Union leaders who know the company's problems and have confidence in management may be able to "sell" the membership on new company policies and to elicit worker cooperation in production which could not be obtained in any other way. The grievance procedure to be described in the next chapter provides a sensitive instrument which top management can use to detect disturbances in lower levels of the organization. There are numerous ways in which a positive acceptance of the union, an effort to integrate it into the administrative structure of the enterprise instead of treating it as a thing apart, can contribute to efficient management.

Companies that take this point of view are probably still a minority. There are more of them today than there were a generation ago, however, and the number will probably continue to increase gradually in the future.

ORGANIZATION FOR INDUSTRIAL RELATIONS

Two kinds of management officials are involved in handling industrial relations: *line* officials who are directly responsible for production, and *staff* officials who function mainly in an advisory capacity.

In a manufacturing company, for example, line authority runs from the company president through a vice-president in charge of production to the superintendent of a particular plant. Under the superintendent are division heads, department heads, and so on down to the foreman. If the foreman has many workers to supervise, he may be aided by one or more assistant foremen or group leaders. The number of layers of supervision in the plant depends mainly on its size. The management of forty or fifty thousand people in a single plant, as in some of the giant automobile factories, requires a complicated hierarchy of production officials. This makes it difficult to get effective upward and downward communication, and to ensure uniformity of policy throughout the organization; and this gives rise to complicated problems in union–management relations.

The most important staff group involved is the industrial relations department. This group is charged with developing and recommending policies on such matters as employee recruitment and selection; training; employee rating and promotion; transfer, downgrading, and layoff; discipline and discharge; wage policies and wage administration; hours of work and shifts; services for employees; employee health and safety; and employee participation in production problems. There may also be a separate industrial engineering department responsible for analysis of job methods, time study, determination of output standards, and application of wage incentive systems.

People in the production line of command are responsible for issuing orders about what is to be done, how it is to be done, and who is to do it. They authorize changes in production schedules, methods, and personnel. They initiate layoffs, new hiring, discharges, promotions, and transfers of workers. Members of the industrial relations staff recommend overall company policies on these matters, check on how they are working in practice, and suggest changes as needed. But no orders can be issued until the production manager or some other line official has been sold on the policy in question. Indeed, people all the way down the chain of command must be sold on a policy to make it fully effective. Not least important is the foreman, who gives direct orders to the work force. The modern foreman has been shorn of much of the authority he once possessed, but he still has considerable power to sabotage policies that he does not understand and accept.

In theory, then, line officials are the doers, while staff officials look over their shoulders as advisers. The actual relation, however, is more complex and variable; and it is defined through day-to-day decisions in the plant rather than by the lines that appear on the organization chart. Suppose a foreman discharges a worker. The labor relations officer assigned to the department considers the discharge unwise and so reports to his superiors. There follow further discussions, perhaps between the industrial relations director and the plant superintendent. Eventually the decision is confirmed or reversed. If line officials find that too many of their decisions are reversed at higher levels under pressure from the industrial relations staff, they will become more hesitant about making decisions; and the *de facto* authority of the industrial relations department will have increased. Personalities are also important. If the industrial relations director is capable, assertive, and able to win the support of top management on disputed issues, the authority of those working under him is increased.

Union Impact on Management Organization

In preunion days, most managements did not attach major importance to the industrial relations function. The director of industrial relations, in those days commonly called the personnel director, was usually not an outstanding man and did not rank high in the management hierarchy. In large measure the line officials made personnel policy through their day-to-day decisions, which the personnel department had little power to influence. Many managements, either deliberately or through inadvertence, left wide latitude in decision making to lower levels of supervision. Thus actions on a particular subject might vary widely from one department to another; and top management might know little about what was actually happening at the grass roots.

The coming of a union changes the situation drastically. Personnel actions are no longer solely a matter of management discretion. They are governed by provisions of the union contract, and the union is there to police observance of the contract. It has its own information network throughout the plant, can detect discrepancies in management's actions, and is then likely to demand that the most favorable practice in any department be extended to all other departments—a tactic commonly known as *whipsawing*. Moreover, unsettled grievances between the union and management are normally referred to an outside arbitrator, under procedures to be described in the next chapter. So management must try to ensure that its decisions are consistent and will stand up under outside review.

Unionism, in short, compels *management by policy* rather than by off-the-cuff decisions. A newly unionized company usually reacts in three ways. First, it has to strengthen its industrial relations department, both because there is more work to be done and because top-flight people are needed to deal with the professional union leaders. Second, it may decide that personnel decisions should be made at higher levels of management, in order to ensure uniform interpretation of company policies and union contract provisions. Third, this normally means that industrial relations officials will have greater voice in decisions and line officials will have less. Some managements, indeed, have panicked to the point of virtually abolishing line authority over personnel actions and work standards and turning these matters over to the industrial relations department for handling.

Although greater centralization of decision making and greater staff authority are natural first reactions, they have their own disadvantages. Foremen know what is happening on the plant floor and are in closest touch with the facts on which correct personnel decisions should be based. They are also the people in charge of production. To hold them responsible for production results while depriving them of disciplinary authority over the work force is scarcely feasible in the long run. So in recent years many companies have been moving back toward decentralization, toward pushing decisions down to the plant floor, and toward reconstituting the authority of line supervisors.[8]

Both line supervisors and industrial relations people are involved in applying personnel policies to concrete situations and in handling grievances brought by the union. The problem is to work out the most effective cooperation between them. This must take account of characteristic differences of outlook arising from their differing functions in the organization. Line officials are naturally more production-oriented, while industrial relations people are more labor-relations-oriented. This does not necessarily mean that the former are "tougher" in holding the line on plant discipline and work standards. Foremen will often make special deals with a worker to secure his cooperation in getting out a rush production job, and it may be the staff people who have to insist on strict adherence to company policy. It is probably fair to say that the industrial relations people typically take a longer-range view and are more concerned with how decisions made today will affect company relations with workers and the union next month or next year.

But foremen and supervisors can also be trained to take a long-range view and to be concerned with the policy implications of specific decisions. This is essentially an educational task, a task of inculcating understanding and acceptance of the company's overall personnel policies. A foreman who has been trained in this way can and should be given the right to make initial decisions on all personnel matters arising in his department, which includes the right to make mistakes. It is important also that correct decisions based on established policy should be ratified and defended at higher levels of management. A foreman who finds his decisions constantly overturned because of union pressure or second-guessing by staff officials will soon cease to make any decisions and will pass all problems up the line. This is a common reason for "clogging up" of the grievance procedure and accumulation of problems in the front office.

DISCUSSION QUESTIONS

1. How does a union's wage-setting problem differ from the price-setting problem of a business monopolist?

---

[8] See on this point Sumner H. Slichter, James J. Healy, and E. Robert Livernash, *The Impact of Collective Bargaining on Management* (Washington, D.C.: The Brookings Institution, 1960), Chap. 29.

2. Describe the process by which union leaders typically formulate their wage demands. What are the main considerations that they must take into account?

3. "Trade unionism is basically a conservative institution, and does more to perpetuate private enterprise than to destroy it." Discuss.

4. "The profit motive no longer operates in the simple manner assumed by economic theory. The managers of a large corporation are interested in profit, to be sure, but their interest is quite different from that of the small owner–operator." Discuss.

5. What features of management's job produce a natural opposition to trade unionism?

6. "Whether the plant is already unionized, or whether it is merely liable to unionization in the future, management is forced to engage in a long, drawn-out competition with unionism for the attention and loyalty of its employees. In such a competition, the union has certain natural advantages that usually bring it out ahead in the long run." Discuss.

7. What does a management stand to gain, and to lose, by accepting the union as a permanent feature of its operations and trying to establish a cooperative relationship with it?

8. "A wise industrial relations director does not try to exercise authority—only influence." Discuss.

9. How is a company's problem of managing its industrial relations altered by the appearance of a trade union?

10. A foreman considers a worker in his department guilty of behavior warranting discharge. The union asserts that the discharge is unjustified. Analyze the proper functions of the foreman, an industrial relations officer attached to the department, the plant superintendent, and the plant director of industrial relations in handling this case.

READING SUGGESTIONS

A classic study of union objectives is SELIG PERLMAN, *A Theory of the Labor Movement*, New York: The Macmillan Company, 1928. A more recent study is RICHARD A. LESTER, *As Unions Mature*, Princeton: Princeton University Press, 1958. For analysis of management organization and objectives, see SUMNER H. SLICHTER, JAMES J. HEALY, and E. ROBERT LIVERNASH, *The Impact of Collective Bargaining on Management*, Washington, D.C.: The Brookings Institution, 1960; and two volumes by PAUL PIGORS, and CHARLES A. MYERS, *Personnel Administra-*

tion (rev. ed.), New York. McGraw Hill Book Company, 1960; and *Readings in Personnel Administration,* New York: McGraw-Hill Book Company, 1956.

For analysis of union wage policies, see JOHN T. DUNLOP, *Wage Determination Under Trade Unions,* New York: The Macmillan Company, 1944; H. GREGG LEWIS (ed.), *Aspects of Labor Economics,* Princeton: Princeton University Press, 1962; E. H. PHELPS BROWN, *The Economics of Labor,* New Haven: Yale University Press, 1962; ALBERT REES, *The Economics of Trade Unions,* Chicago: The University of Chicago Press, 1962; ARTHUR M. ROSS, *Trade Union Wage Policies,* Berkeley and Los Angeles: University of California Press, 1948; GEORGE P. SHULTZ, *Pressures on Wage Decisions,* New York: John Wiley & Sons, Inc., 1951. Company wage policies are discussed in RICHARD A. LESTER, *Company Wage Policies,* Princeton: Princeton University Industrial Relations Section, 1948; SUMNER H. SLICHTER, *Basic Criteria Used in Wage Negotiations,* Chicago: Association of Commerce and Industry, 1947; SUMNER H. SLICHTER, JAMES J. HEALY, and E. ROBERT LIVERNASH, *The Impact of Collective Bargaining on Management,* Washington, D.C.: The Brookings Institution, 1960. Other useful sources on wage determination at the company level include JOSEPH W. GARBARINO, *Wage Policy and Long-Term Contracts,* Washington, D.C. The Brookings Institution, 1962; JACK STIEBER, *The Steel Industry Wage Structure,* Cambridge, Mass.: Harvard University Press, 1959; GEORGE W. TAYLOR, and FRANK C. PIERSON (eds.), *New Concepts in Wage Determination,* New York: McGraw-Hill Book Company, 1957.

18

Collective Bargaining Procedures

Trade unions try to advance the interests of their members mainly by negotiating agreements, usually termed *union contracts* or *collective agreements,* with employers. The processes by which these agreements are negotiated, administered, and enforced are included in the term *collective bargaining.* The word *collective* indicates that the agreement is negotiated on behalf of a *group* of workers. The workers present a united front to their employer, and the terms of the bargain apply uniformly to all members of the group. Different employers may also band themselves together for the purpose of negotiating an agreement with a union. Such an agreement is frequently said to be *collective on both sides.*

From the union's standpoint, the object of collective bargaining is to prevent unilateral action by the employer. This is accomplished by requiring him to sign a contract fixing conditions of employment for a specified period and establishing a procedure for handling disputed issues arising during the period. Collective bargaining is thus an employer-regulating device, a method of guaranteeing certain rights and immunities to the workers by limiting the employer's freedom of action. The employer must now apply uniform procedures to all workers in the group; these procedures can be changed only at fixed intervals after negotiation with union officials; and any charge that the agreed procedures have been violated can be taken up through a series of appeal courts (the grievance procedure). There is thus created what has been termed a "system of industrial jurisprudence," a body of rights and obligations binding on workers, union officials, and management officials alike.

Collective bargaining includes two different kinds of union–management negotiation. General negotiations are entered into at regular intervals, usually every two or three years, to revise the basic agreement between the parties and extend it for a further period. At this time any term of the contract—wage schedules, work assignments, rules concerning layoff and promotion, union security provisions, and all the rest—may be reopened for discussion. These negotiations are usually carried on by top union and management officials. After the agreement has been signed, there are frequent discussions between lower union and management officials throughout the plant for the purpose of clarifying particular provisions and applying them to concrete situations. The method of resolving these day-to-day disputes, usually termed the *grievance procedure,* is specified in the contract itself. Although the negotiations for a new contract are more dramatic, the day-to-day negotiations may be equally important. Through them the contract is enforced, or, in the case of a new or weak union, not enforced. Through them the general provisions of the contract are given specific meaning and application.

These two aspects of collective bargaining—contract negotiations and the grievance procedure—will be discussed in turn. The present discussion is concerned with bargaining *procedures* rather than the substantive issues over which bargaining occurs. The main issues in bargaining will be discussed in Part Six.

BARGAINING STRUCTURE

The Labor–Management Relations Act requires an employer to bargain with representatives of a majority of his employees "in an appropriate bargaining unit." But what unit is appropriate? At one extreme, a single employer may bargain with representatives of a single skilled craft. At the opposite extreme, an employer's association may bargain with an industrial union over terms for all employees in the industry throughout the country.

We should distinguish first between the *election unit,* the *negotiating unit,* and the *impact unit.* The election unit is laid down by decisions of the National Labor Relations Board. The normal method of securing union recognition is to file a request with the National Labor Relations Board for certification as bargaining representative. If the union's claim to represent a majority of the workers is challenged by the employer, or if more than one union is seeking to represent the same workers, the board will conduct an election to determine the employees' wishes. In order to do this, it must decide on the appropriate bargaining unit. Depending on the wishes of the parties and on general board principles to be discussed in Chapter 25, it may select a single craft, or all employees in a plant, or several plants of the same company, or employees in a group of companies.

The *negotiating* unit will normally not be smaller than the election unit, and may be considerably larger. Even if elections have been held plant by plant, the union may prefer company-wide negotiations or may prefer to negotiate jointly with a group of employers. When an agreement is reached, it is applicable to all workers in the bargaining unit. The size of negotiating units thus determines the coverage of union contracts.

The *impact unit* may be still larger. A common union technique is to single out one leading employer—say, Ford or General Motors in the case of the United Automobile Workers—as the initial target in a particular year. After negotiations have been completed, the union insists that other employers in the industry sign up on the same terms under penalty of a strike. Under this technique, usually termed *pattern bargaining,* the impact unit is the industry even though the bargaining unit is a single company.

Our main interest here is the size of negotiating units. The most recent Bureau of Labor Statistics survey indicates that there are about 150,000 union contracts in the United States. The great majority of these units are small, covering only one company and a small number of workers. At the other pole, however, are 1,733 contracts covering one thousand or more workers each; and these contracts cover more than 8 million workers, or about half of all workers under contract. These large units are usually termed *major agreements.* The nine largest, each with more than 100,000 workers, cover almost 2 million workers in all.

The commonest type of agreement outside of manufacturing is the multiemployer agreement, including either all employers in a certain locality (building construction, printing, retailing, hotel and restaurant work, and other service industries), or all employers in a major region or in the entire country (coal mining, railroads, over-the-road trucking, merchant shipping).

In manufacturing, the single-company agreement is the dominant form. Multiemployer agreements are found in a number of manufacturing industries, however, including men's and women's clothing, baking, canning and preserving, brewing, glassware, pottery, lumber, furniture, and leather goods. And even where the union negotiates separately with each company, it can achieve some of the results of a multiemployer unit through the pattern-bargaining technique.

The main pressure for multiemployer agreements stems from competition among employers in product markets. If different companies organized by the same union are in competition with one another, the bargains between the union and various companies cannot be kept separate. The union cannot raise the labor costs of some plants so much above the general level that these plants are forced out of competition. Employers paying the highest wage rates in the industry are likely to demand that the union bring low-wage plants up to their level. Union members also compare wage rates in different plants. Members of one local who find their rates below those of certain other locals will be quick to protest and to demand that they be brought up to levels prevailing elsewhere. Apart from this political pressure, it seems natural to union officials that wages and conditions should be standardized for competing plants. The concept of the *standard rate, of equal pay for equal work,* is deeply engrained in union thinking. For all these reasons, unions seek some measure of uniformity among employers in the same competitive area.

Although the area of product market competition has great influence on the size of bargaining units, it is not the only determinant.[1] Other important influences include:

1. *The nature of bargaining issues.* Some issues, notably wages, have market-wide implications and tend to be resolved through large negotiating units. Other issues such as safety rules, plant working conditions, details of pension and insurance plans, application of seniority provisions, and time standards on piece-rate jobs are best handled at the company or even the plant level. When market-wide issues are predominant, there will be a tendency toward larger bargaining units and more centralized decision-making power within the union and management groups. But when local issues assume major importance, there will be pressure for local bargaining and decentralized decision making.

2. *Representational considerations.* The union is comprised of work groups, defined on a plant, department, occupation, age, or ethnic basis. These groups have common but also divergent interests. Up to a point, they can gain by pooling their strength in larger and larger bargaining units. But this involves losses in autonomy and attention to specific interests of the group. Thus in Weber's words:

> Each group will press for, or acquiesce in, the expansion of the worker alliance as long as the rate of substitution between the gains derived from the increment to bargaining power are greater than the perceived losses associated with the denial of autonomy in decision making. At some point, this rate of substitution will become negative, and tensions will develop within the union and the associated bargaining structures for the accommodation of special group interests or the fragmentation of the alliance.

Although representational considerations are especially important on the union side they arise on the management side as well. The interests of different companies in a bargaining unit are not identical, and there are numerous examples of companies that have withdrawn from an employers' association or have defected from the association's position in a particular negotiation when they found this to their advantage.

3. *Tactical and power considerations.* Bargaining power is hard to define but easy to recognize. Each side seeks a bargaining structure that will enhance its bargaining power. A common power enhancing tactic is *whipsawing.* When

---

[1] See on this point Arnold R. Weber, "Stability and Change in the Structure of Collective Bargaining," in Lloyd Ulman (ed.), *Challenge to Collective Bargaining* (Englewood Cliffs, N.J.: Prentice-Hall, Inc., 1967), pp. 13–36.

a company deals with several unions it may try to settle first with the union judged to be in the weakest bargaining position and then to extend these terms to the other unions. A union may tackle a company from which it believes it can secure the best terms and then try to extend this "pattern" to other companies. The obvious reply to whipsawing is counterorganization. This maneuvering and countermaneuvering tends to enlarge the size of bargaining units.

4. *Public policy.* This is a final influence expressed particularly through election district decisions of the National Labor Relations Board. Depending on his estimate of where the union has penetrated most effectively the employer may wish to include certain departments or plants and exclude others. The union's preference may be different. If two or more unions are involved, they may differ on the proper scope of the unit. The National Labor Relations Board officials, after hearing the parties and considering the pattern of bargaining elsewhere in the industry, must decide what is appropriate.

A particularly controversial issue has been that of craft versus industrial units. After 1935 the National Labor Relations Board often encountered situations in which a CIO industrial union urged a single unit covering all employees, while one or more AFL craft unions urged that groups of skilled workers be carved out as separate units. For some years the board showed a marked preference for industrial units—sufficiently so to permit the major companies in steel, automobile, electrical manufacturing, and other mass production industries to be organized on this basis. Yielding to AFL criticism and pressure, however, the board by the early forties was permitting craft groups to vote separately whenever they showed any marked inclination to do so. The Taft–Hartley Act increased the possibility of *craft severance* by providing that the National Labor Relations Board may not refuse a craft group's claim to separate representation simply because of some previous board decision conerning the bargaining unit. The general policy at present is that where there are indications that a skilled group may prefer separate representation, the board will allow them to vote separately from the rest. If a craft union wins out, it will be certified as bargaining representative. This policy has not been applied, however, to steel, aluminum, and a few other mass-production industries where the board has held that production processes are so highly integrated as to make craft severance impracticable.

During the critical period from 1935 to 1950, the board's preference for company-wide bargaining units contributed to the development of the many large units we observe today.

Product-Market Competition and Negotiating Units

Since the area of the collective agreement is strongly influenced by the area over which employers compete in the sale of their products, it will be well to explore this relation in greater detail. The basic distinction here is between local-market industries and industries in which competition is regional or national.

Where competition is limited to the immediate locality, city-wide agreements are likely to develop. This is the typical situation in building construction, hotel and restaurant work, newspaper and job printing, milk and bread delivery, local trucking and warehousing, retail trade, laundry and dry cleaning, and other local industries.

The individual employer in these industries is typically small and is in a weak position to negotiate separately with the union. So after a little experience, employers often decide to pool their strength in a bargaining association. The result is a single agreement reached by bargaining between representatives of the employer association and representatives of the union.

After the master agreement has been concluded, its administration and enforcement are usually left to the union and individual employers. In areas that have gone farthest in the direction of master agreements, however, such as San Francisco, the employers' association sometimes takes a continuing interest in the administration of the agreement. Several of the San Francisco associations maintain expert staffs to assist their members in processing grievances and handling other problems that arise, during the life of the contract. A few have even gone so far as to forbid members to settle grievances without association approval. The purpose of this policy is to prevent the union from *whipsawing* the employers—that is, as mentioned previously, securing more favorable treatment on a certain point in some plants than in others, and then using this as an argument to bring all plants up to the most favorable settlement achieved anywhere.[2]

A master agreement with the union has several advantages from the employers' standpoint. It enables employers to meet the union on more equal terms. It also places employers on an equal competitive footing as regards wage rates and other items in labor cost; the "chiseler" can no longer undercut the employer who pays a "decent" wage. Moreover, the agreement with the union can often be used to police price fixing and other monopolistic practices within the industry. Union and employers, instead of fighting each other, can unite with mutual benefit to levy tribute from consumers.

This situation has occurred from time to time in building construction. The building contractors' association generally agrees to employ only union men, thereby strengthening the building trades unions. The unions on their side agree to work only for members of the association. In some cases there has also been a tacit agreement that the unions will not supply labor to a contractor found guilty of departing from the established methods of figuring bids in the industry, that is, of cutting prices. The two main channels of competition—free price setting and free entrance of new firms to the industry—are thus effectively blocked.

Industries such as laundering and dry cleaning have frequently achieved the same results by allying themselves with the deliverymen, who usually belong to a local of the Teamsters' Union. Firms that cut prices or

---

[2] Clark Kerr and L. H. Fisher, "Multiple-Employer Bargaining: The San Francisco Experience," in R. A. Lester and Joseph Shister (eds.), *Insights into Labor Issues* (New York: The Macmillan Company, 1948).

engage in other "unethical" practices forbidden by the association are brought into line by strikes or threatened strikes. It has not been unknown for "accidents" to happen to the property of uncooperative employers; clothes get lost or misdelivered, acid gets spilled in the wrong places, or delivery trucks break down mysteriously.[3] In agreements between the Barbers' Union and the master barbers' association of a city, the price which must be charged for haircuts, shaves, and other services is frequently included in the agreement, so that any price cutter is guilty of a violation of contract and is struck automatically.

It should not be inferred that unions are mainly responsible for local price-fixing arrangements. In many cases, price agreements existed long before the union made its appearance. The union does, however, strengthen such agreements by providing an additional method of disciplining price-cutters.

While there is strong pressure in local-market industries to standardize terms of employment *within* each locality, there is no similar pressure for equalization *among* localities. Bricklaying in Pittsburg does not compete with bricklaying in Minneapolis, and there is no reason why the union scale should be the same. Union scales in building, printing, and similar industries vary a good deal throughout the country, and national union control over local settlements is loose.

Turning to companies that operate on a regional or national basis, one finds a variety of situations. First, there are the "natural monopolies" in transportation, power, communications, and so on. Here the bargaining unit is typically coextensive with the company. Each of the unionized electric power companies negotiates separately. So does each regional affiliate of the Bell Telephone system, although the union has pressed unsuccessfully for national negotiations. The main counterexample is railroading, where national negotiations have been customary for decades.

Second, there are some important nonmanufacturing industries where competition is regional or national. This is true, for example, of bituminous coal mining. It is increasingly true of major commercial construction, and of road and highway construction. Over-the-road trucking is another example. Longshoring is localized in each port, but there are coast-wide linkages arising from the movement of ships from port to port and the possibility of varying transportation routes to achieve a cost advantage. In such cases the union normally bargains with an employers' association covering a state, region, or occasionally the entire country. The basic pressure is the usual one of product-market rivalry. In some cases, however, the

---

[3] See in particular: C. L. Christenson, "Chicago Service Trades," in *How Collective Bargaining Works* (New York: Twentieth Century Fund, 1948), Chap. 15; and C. L. Christenson, *Collective Bargaining in Chicago* (Chicago: The University of Chicago Press, 1933).

bargaining unit has been influenced by other factors. The national contract for over-the-road truckers, for example, resulted partly from the effort of Teamster President Hoffa to obtain firm national control over the union.

In manufacturing, competition is usually regional or national, and the union must take an interest in securing similar contract terms from competing employers. But this effort takes different forms in different industries. In small-scale, highly competitive industries such as men's and women's clothing, hosiery, pottery, or canning, multiemployer bargaining is the general rule. Where there are many small employers, the union cannot find any firm prominent enough to establish an industry "pattern." On the other side, small employers cannot feel much confidence in their own strength and tend to band together for mutual protection. Both employers and the union find a master agreement convenient in enforcing minimum labor standards and "putting a floor under competition."

Quite different is the situation in heavy manufacturing, where companies are large and oligopoly the prevalent market form. Here employers usually feel powerful enough to go it alone, and also have a traditional resistance to industry-wide bargaining. While the unions often argue that industry-wide bargaining is desirable in principle, they have not pressed the point because pattern bargaining serves their purposes reasonably well.

The Electrical, Radio, and Machine Workers' Union for example, attempts to establish an industry pattern by dealing first with Westinghouse or General Electric. The United Automobile Workers directs its initial pressure at one or another of the "Big Three" companies. The Pulp, Sulphate and Paper Mill Workers traditionally open negotiations with the Great Northern Paper Company. The United Steelworkers negotiates first with the largest basic steel producers before proceeding to the hundreds of smaller companies.

The steel case may serve to illustrate both the procedures and problems of pattern bargaining. The contract terms to be presented to employers in a particular year are worked out initially by the Executive Board of the United Steelworkers. They are then presented for discussion to a Policy Committee, consisting of some 250 delegates from all parts of the country. After the program has been ratified by the Policy Committee, negotiations for a new contract are begun simultaneously with representatives of the major basic steel producers. After a settlement is reached with the major producers, the union proceeds to sign similar contracts with the other basic steel companies.

Negotiations with the hundreds of smaller companies engaged in steel fabricating are left mainly to district and local officials of the union. International headquarters, however, distributes to local officials a mimeographed list of the demands that are to be made on all employers. With respect to many contract terms, these instructions specify minimum as well as maximum terms of settlement. They tell local officials not only what they should demand to begin with, but also the minimum which they must get in order to have the agreement approved by the international office. The union's objective here is to prevent whipsawing by employers. If the union accepts a poor settlement in one plant, word will spread rapidly throughout the industry, and the case will rise to plague the union in another plant a thousand miles away.

In spite of this effort toward uniformity, the contracts signed with the fabricators show considerably more variation than the contracts with the basic steel companies. Wage levels in the smaller companies are both lower than those in basic steel and more variable from company to company.[4] The underlying reason is that the fabricators are operating in hundreds of specialized and distinct product markets—for wire, for pipe, for structural steel shapes, and so on—which may differ widely in demand trends, profit margins, and severity of competition. The union has to tailor its demands to these different situations. Thus the pattern tends to fray at the edges when transferred to product markets other than that for which it was designed.

This tendency is observable also in other industries. The United Automobile Workers develops its wage pattern for a particular year in negotiations with the major auto manufacturers. When it tries to transfer this pattern to the hundreds of automobile parts manufacturers, however, it runs into resistance. The parts manufacturers, who must bid for orders from the Big Three against strong competition from rival producers, have lower and more variable profit margins than the auto manufacturers themselves. The union adjusts to this by allowing greater intercompany variation of wages. The United Automobile Workers also has members in a variety of other industries, notably the West Coast airframe plants. At one stage the union attempted to apply the pattern of automobile wage changes to the aircraft plants as well, thus going beyond an *industry-wide* pattern to a *union-wide* pattern. This effort failed, however, because of the different market situation of the aircraft producers and also because of a different organizational situation in which some aircraft plants have been organized by the Machinists' Union.

An interesting question about oligopoly manufacturing is why employers are willing to accept single-company bargaining. Why do they not band together to resist the union's demands? Why will the other automobile companies, for example, allow the unions to single out one company to enforce concessions that will then be demanded of everyone? No outsider

---

[4] On this point, see George Seltzer, "Pattern Bargaining and the United Steelworkers," *Journal of Political Economy* (August 1951), pp. 319–31; and David H. Greenberg, "Deviations From Wage–Fringe Standards," *Industrial and Labor Relations Review* (January 1968), pp. 197–209.

can say. Traditional intercompany rivalry in product markets, fear that any concerted action may fall foul of the antitrust laws, and emotional resistance to industry-wide bargaining may all play some part. These attitudes may change in the course of time. Already there are limited arrangements in some industries for *strike insurance,* that is, payments to a struck company by other companies in the industry that continue to operate, to compensate the target company for its loss of sales and profits.

Centralization and Decentralization in Bargaining

From the thirties until the midfifties, the trend was strongly in the direction of larger bargaining units and greater centralization of negotiating power in the hands of top union and management officials. More recently, however, a reaction has set in. There has been pressure for greater attention to the interests of workers in particular plants or occupational groups, and a greater voice for the union membership in decision making. We may note particularly the increased influence of skilled craft groups in negotiations, and the relegation of numerous issues to settlement at a local level.

1. *Skilled craft representation.* During the rush to unionize mass-production manufacturing in the thirties and forties, skilled craftsmen were usually blanketed into plant-wide or company-wide units, where they formed a minority of the membership. Moreover, the new industrial unions during this period concentrated on bringing up the bottom rather than the top of the wage structure. It was common practice to negotiate a uniform cents-per-hour increase for everyone in the plant. Percentagewise, this meant larger increases for laborers than for craftsmen, and a reduction of the percentage differential between the two groups. This was an important source of craft discontent and of pressure for greater autonomy.

The effectiveness of this pressure varies from industry to industry, depending partly on the ratio of skilled workers to total employment. Where the percentage is high, as in electric utilities (48.5 percent skilled), the skilled men tend to dominate the union without ceremony. At the opposite pole, as in meat packing (10 percent skilled), they are too weak to make their voice heard. The interesting cases are those in which skilled workers form a substantial minority, not sufficient to dominate, but large enough to be influential. This group includes rubber products (18 percent), beverages (20 percent), electrical machinery (26 percent), motor vehicles (28 percent), and primary metals (35 percent).

Adjustment of the union machinery to accommodate craft interests takes a variety of forms.[5] Proceeding from weaker to stronger forms, we may note:
  a. Formation of a skilled trades department (or council), which conducts its own conventions and manages apprenticeship programs of special in-

[5] For a detailed discussion, see Arnold R. Weber, "The Craft Industrial Issue Revisited: A Study of Union Government," *Industrial and Labor Relations Review* (April 1963), pp. 381–404.

terest to craftsmen. Existence of such a department does not per se confer any special voice in wage negotiations.

b. Formal participation in decision making—for example, through a specified number of skilled representatives on the union's wage policy committee or negotiating committee. The United Automobile Workers, for example, deals with General Motors through a General Motors Council (there are corresponding councils for Ford and Chrysler). Under this are eleven subcouncils, two of which represent craft groups. Each subcouncil elects one representative to the National Committee of the General Motors Council, which represents the union in company-wide negotiations. In some unions, including the Brewery Workers and the Paper Workers, separate craft locals assure the skilled groups of representation on the joint committees created to negotiate with employers.

c. Most drastically, skilled groups may be given the right to approve or disapprove contract terms applying to them, and may autonomously exercise their right to strike. Since a strike of the skilled men would shut down the plant, this gives them an effective veto power. Only the Brewery Workers and the United Automobile Workers have gone this far, and there are still some controls and reservations. In the United Automobile Workers, craftsmen can vote separately only on issues that affect them alone (which would *not* include wage differentials vis-à-vis other occupational groups), and even this requires approval by the International Executive Board.

2. *Local negotiations.* A large manufacturing corporation may include dozens of plants, with quite different production operations and problems. Each plant has local problems of working conditions, work speeds and time standards, adjustment to technical change, application of seniority rules, scheduling of overtime work and vacation periods, calculation of fringe benefits, and so on. In the 1958 United Automobile Workers–General Motors negotiations, some 11,600 "local demands" were presented by the union. In the 1961 negotiations this had grown to 19,000 local demands, and in 1964 to 24,000. It is impossible to resolve these issues in a single national negotiation focused on general wage and benefit adjustments. Yet unless they are resolved there will be growing membership discontent, with a probability of wildcat strikes and slowdowns.

It is common practice, therefore, to provide for several levels of negotiation. In basic steel, there are industry–union, company–union, and plant–union committees at work simultaneously, and issues are sorted out for assignment to one or another of these levels. In the rubber industry, there is a company-wide master agreement plus local supplements negotiated at the plant level. The master agreement must be ratified by a majority of plants, each of which has a voice in proportion to its employment. Even if the master agreement is ratified, a local union can still strike over its local supplement. In the automobile industry, too, local unions have a qualified right to strike over local issues; and in some years there have been many such strikes even after national issues had been settled. The companies charge that this is a deliberate union tactic, designed to win maximum concessions at all levels. The union replies that it is a necessary adjustment to pressure from members and local union leaders.

The feasibility of permitting local issues to be resolved through strike action depends partly on characteristics of the industry. If a company's plants are carrying out parallel and independent operations, some can carry on while others are shut down. In the automobile industry, however, there is interdependence between parts suppliers and assembly operations. Strikes in a few plants can cripple the flow of materials and compel a company wide shutdown. The auto companies will probably insist more and more that local issues be resolved *before* the master agreement is concluded.[6]

CONTRACT NEGOTIATIONS

Collective bargaining is a highly stylized game, with ground rules that are understood and observed by both parties. These include rules about the timing of negotiations, the selection of the negotiators, the agenda for discussion, the main stages of negotiation, and the ratification of a new contract. We are concerned here solely with procedures, not with results. In the next chapter we shall examine why the outcome may be more favorable to the union or to management, the meaning and determinants of *bargaining power,* possible reasons for a deadlock in negotiations, and the cost of the strikes that result from such deadlocks.

Timing of Negotiations

Union contracts in the United States run for a specified period, usually either two or three years; and the approach of the contract expiration date triggers the beginning of new negotiations. There is nothing inevitable about this procedure. In Britain, for example, agreements have no expiration date, and negotiations may be requested by either party at any time. The U.S. procedure is simply a convention, which concentrates bargaining activity into periodic intervals, with periods of relative quiet in between.

The contract usually provides that, if either party wishes a change in contract terms, it must give notice to this effect so many days before the expiration date. Such notice is almost invariably given, since it is rare for a contract to be renewed without change. There is also a legal provision that the federal mediation service must be notified sixty days before the contract expiration date so that it may have an opportunity to keep in touch with negotiations in important cases.

A further ground rule is that, if agreement on terms of a new contract is not reached before the old one expires, a strike results automatically— "no contract, no work." This sets a deadline for the discussions, and negotiations become more intensive and more serious as this deadline approaches. The union may decide, however, to ignore this rule and to keep its members at work while negotiations continue. This might happen, for example, if the expiration date comes at a time of low activity in the industry, when a strike would put little pressure on employers. Or, if the

---

[6] On this range of issues, see E. Robert Livernash, "Special and Local Negotiations," in John T. Dunlop and Neil W. Chamberlain (eds.), *Frontiers of Collective Bargaining* (New York: Harper & Row, Publishers, 1967).

parties feel that they are very close to agreement when the deadline arrives, the old contract may be extended for a short time by mutual agreement.

Selection and Authority of Negotiators

The next important point is that negotiations are conducted by *delegates* of the parties, who usually do not themselves have power to conclude an agreement. This obviously complicates the bargaining process. Terms that the negotiators themselves would consider acceptable may be vetoed by higher company officials or the union membership. It also enlarges the room for tactical maneuvering. A negotiator on either side may resist certain terms on the ground (genuine or alleged) that he would not be able to "sell" these terms to his superiors.

Who are the negotiators, and how are they selected? On the union side, it will be simplest to begin with a local union negotiating with one or more employers in its area. As the expiration date of the old contract approaches, the demands to be served on the employer will probably be discussed at a general membership meeting. A committee will then be appointed to put the demands into better shape and to draft proposed terms for a new contract.

After the drafting committee has done its best, the proposed contract terms are taken back to another membership meeting. There they are discussed at length, perhaps revised, and eventually approved. A negotiating committee is then selected to meet with management. This will normally include the chief officers of the local, but may include other members as well. The national union representative for the area normally sits in on the negotiations and frequently plays a leading role. At some point prior to or during negotiations a strike vote of the membership will usually be taken. This does not necessarily mean that a strike is going to occur. The purpose is to strengthen the union representatives' hand by advance authorization to call a strike if negotiations with the employer break down.

After the union negotiators feel they have won as much as they can from management, they must come back to the membership for approval of the new contract before it becomes valid. In many unions the contract must also be approved by the national office. Participation by a national union representative is designed partly to ensure that the terms will be in conformity with national policy.

Preparation for regional or national negotiations, or for bargaining with a major pattern-setting employer, is considerably more complicated. National union officers normally take a leading role in such negotiations. Proposed union demands are hammered out by the national executive board, and then submitted for discussion to a conference of delegates from the local unions and district organizations. Depending on bargaining practices, this conference may cover the entire industry throughout the country, or all local unions dealing with a particular employer, or some other grouping. After revision and ratification of demands by the conference, the union negotiators begin discussions with management representatives. At the end of the process, the proposed contract terms must usually be reported back to the conference for further discussion and approval.

On the management side, contract negotiations are usually conducted by a small group of top management officials. In a small or medium-sized company, the president may serve as chief management negotiator. In large organizations, this responsibility is more likely to fall on the executive vice-president or some other line official. The chief counsel and the treasurer frequently participate and several top production officials normally sit in on the negotiations. The industrial relations director and members of his staff take part as expert advisers. Where the industrial relations director is a forceful individual with high status in the company, he may even serve as chief company spokesman.

The management representatives, like the union negotiating committee, begin to formulate their position well in advance of the start of negotiations. An effort is made to anticipate the main union demands and to determine a position on them. Management may itself want to take the initiative on certain points. Management initiative in presenting demands, instead of simply responding to union demands, is commoner today than it was ten or twenty years ago. Anything that requires a major change in company policy, such as agreement to a union shop, must normally be ratified in advance by the board of directors or the executive committee. Proposals involving money also require advance ratification. The management representatives go into negotiations with instructions that they may not raise the company's labor costs by more than a certain figure. If they are unable to reach agreement with the union within the specified limits, they must go back to the board for further discussion.[7]

Where there is multiemployer bargaining, representatives of the various companies involved will be called together for a preliminary conference. If there is a formal association, members of the association staff may take a prominent part in working out proposals to the union. Important conflicts of interest may have to be faced and resolved. Some companies, for example, may be in a comfortable profit position and able to afford substantial wage increases. Other companies closer to the margin may feel obliged

---

[7] In one case that came to the author's attention, the management negotiators were instructed by the board of directors that they could not concede more than five cents an hour. Agreement on this basis appeared impossible, so the vice-president conducting the negotiations came back to the board with an earnest plea that he be allowed to go up to eight cents. After he had made an eloquent statement of his case, the president burst out laughing and said, "Why, that's fine! We were willing to go to ten cents all along!"

to fight any increase in costs. These and other differences must be compromised in order to present a united front to the union. After policy has been determined, the actual conduct of negotiations is usually delegated to a small committee of the most experienced and influential company representatives.

The Agenda for Discussion

Negotiations in the international field are often two-stage negotiations. The parties first must agree on what they are going to discuss. Each side tries to put on the agenda items on which it hopes to score gains and to keep off the agenda items that might be harmful to its interests or on which it is determined to make no concessions. Only after the agenda is settled do the parties proceed to substantive negotiations.

In collective bargaining, on the other hand, these two stages are merged. There is no advance agenda. At the first negotiating session, the union representatives present their full list of demands, and the management representatives list the changes they would like to see in the new contract. The agenda is obtained simply by combining the "shopping lists" of the parties, and substantive discussion of these items begins at once. Occasionally one side objects that a certain topic "is not a proper subject for collective bargaining"; but such objections have not been very successful. In general, either side may raise any issue it chooses, and all these issues become part of the bargaining agenda.

We should note one legal point, which will be discussed further in Chapter 25. The National Labor Relations Act requires that both parties should "bargain in good faith." Suppose the union makes a demand on a point that management believes is within its sole discretion. Management says, "We do not want to discuss that issue." The union files a charge with the National Labor Relations Board that the employer has refused to bargain in good faith. The National Labor Relations Board then decides whether it is an issue that the parties must discuss, with a view to possible compromise and settlement, or whether it is an issue on which one or the other party may stand pat. The former is termed a *mandatory* subject of negotiation, while the latter is *permissive* only; and it is important whether an item falls in one category or the other.

The agenda usually includes dozens or scores of items. This leaves room to trade concessions on some items against gains on others. The agenda can be divided broadly into:

1. *Cost items,* including basic wages, fringe benefits, and rules that directly affect labor costs, such as overtime. These items can be reduced to a cents-per-man-hour equivalent and totaled, so that one can speak of a "20-cent package," or a "30-cent package."

2. *Noncost items,* such as union security arrangements or the seniority system, where the cost effect is so indirect that no measurement of it is attempted. Cost items are readily tradable against each other, since each side can measure approximately what it is yielding or getting. Trading between cost and noncost items is also possible, as indicated by the union official who said, "Every year I sell the union shop for a nickel."

A complete draft settlement, including tentative provisions on all major items, is known as a *package;* and both sides usually adhere to what may be termed *the package convention.* The items on the agenda are discussed one at a time—many of them more than once—with each side indicating the concessions and trades it might be willing to make. It is understood, however, that agreement on each item is tentative until agreement has been reached on the total package. If this proves impossible and negotiations break down, each party is free to withdraw these tentative concessions and start bargaining all over again. Realistically, however, the statements that have been made in the course of negotiations cannot really be erased from people's minds.

Stages of Negotiation

Although the course of negotiations is never the same in any two situations, one can distinguish several standard phases. The first of these—presentation of initial demands—typically reveals a wide gap between the positions of the parties. The union wants the moon, while management does not want to concede anything.

Next comes a period of probing, which in a large negotiation may last for weeks, during which each side questions the other's demands at length. Clause-by-clause questioning of the other party produces various kinds of information: the detailed contents of a particular proposal, the reasons it is considered necessary, the kinds of factual data that have been assembled to support it, sometimes a preliminary indication of the firmness with which the demand is held.

At this stage the negotiating group is usually scaled down to more manageable size—a few key people on each side who have authority to make concessions and decisions. Discussion can move more rapidly in such a group, and can also be more frank and informal. Each side continues to probe the other's position while trying to protect its own freedom of maneuver. There may be indications of willingness to make concessions on certain items. Some of the less controversial issues may be resolved and set aside, subject to the general rule that no one subject is regarded as settled until all items in dispute have been settled. For the key issues in dispute, each side may eventually indicate one or more *packages*—combinations of terms—that it would consider acceptable. The contents of these package proposals are significant in indicating which demands the parties are really serious about.

The packages put forward by the two sides, however, are likely still to be some distance apart. What forces further concessions and final compromise is the approach of the deadline date, after which a strike will occur. It is no accident that many contract settlements are reached after all-night conferences on the eve of a strike. The imminence of a strike, with the attendant costs and uncertainties for both sides, forces each party to re-examine its position realistically and to ask, "Is it really worth it?" This usually leads to a lowering of union demands and a raising of management offers to the point where they overlap and settlement becomes possible. Between 98 and 99 percent of the contract negotiations carried out in the United States each year result in agreement without a strike. The possibility of a strike, however, is a central feature of the bargaining process and the main force making for ultimate agreement.

A work stoppage, while marking a crisis, does not bring an end to negotiations. The issues in dispute must still be resolved. The only difference is that the costs of a stoppage, which previously were potential, have now become actual. As the strike lengthens and costs mount on both sides, there is growing pressure on the parties to make further concessions to bring the strike to an end. Occasionally a strike ends in closing down of the enterprise; and occasionally it just dies quietly, with the strikers trickling back to work or being replaced by strikebreakers. But the normal outcome is an agreement on new contract terms. A strike is one route to agreement.

Ratification of Agreements

At the end of the road comes ratification of the agreement by company and union. A few unions empower their negotiators to reach a binding agreement. In others, including the United Steelworkers, the agreement is ratified by a policy committee operating at one remove from the membership. By far the commonest procedure, however, is ratification by membership vote. A recent study found that more than 90 percent of union officers and members consider this to be the correct procedure.

Ratification by referendum vote involves the possibility of rejection. Although there are no statistics on the frequency with which members reject the terms recommended by their leaders, experienced observers place it at 5 to 10 percent of the cases.

Rejection does not always mean what it appears to mean. The union negotiators may pretend to agree to certain terms, submit them to the membership, but openly or secretly urge the members to reject them. The membership vote is a bargaining gambit, used to justify additional demands. In other cases the negotiators may submit a tentative agreement to the

members without any recommendation, simply to test membership sentiment. A negative vote in this case is an instruction to the negotiators to try
for more.

But there are also genuine rejections. The union leaders believe that
the terms they have secured are reasonable and acceptable, they recommend them to the members, and the members proceed to vote them down.
When this happens, it is usually because the package lacks certain components highly valued by the membership. Contracts have been voted down
because of provisions relating to work assignments, seniority rights, shift
preferences, rotation of job assignments, work scheduling, and specific
working conditions. The commonest reason for rejection appears to be a
failure of communications within the union, so that the leaders' conception of what is acceptable fails to accord with reality. In some cases factional strife within the union is a contributing factor. Leaders aspiring to
union office urge members to reject terms recommended by those in office,
as a step toward displacing the existing leaders.

A study of the problem by Professor Clyde Summers concludes that
membership ratification serves a constructive purpose in explaining and
legitimizing a proposed agreement. Even those who vote against it will
usually accept the principle of majority rule. Conversely, if an agreement
is imposed by the negotiators and turns out to have unpopular provisions,
it is likely to generate quickie strikes and other forms of protest. But proper
use of ratification votes requires procedural safeguards. Misuse of the procedure, as a bargaining ploy or as an abdication of leadership, should be
avoided. The vote on ratification should be tied to a vote to strike (which
is often not true at present), so that the price of rejection is clearly evident;
and those who vote on the issue should be the ones who will actually have
to strike, which again is not always the case.[8]

The Technique of Continuous Negotiation

A prominent feature of contract negotiations in the United States is
their crisis atmosphere. Discussion usually begins only a few weeks before
the contract expiration date, and not until a few days before the deadline
do the negotiators begin to reveal their basic positions. Hence the familiar
sight of weary negotiators working right down to the deadline in day-and-

---

[8] Membership of a local, for example, may include workers in several plants,
while the negotiation in question involves one plant only. If the proposed agreement
is submitted to a vote of the entire local, employees in other plants are free to vote
it down without having to strike in consequence. For a review of this and other
problems, see Clyde Summers, "Ratification of Agreements," in Dunlop and Chamberlain, *Frontiers of Collective Bargaining*.

night sessions, and finally signing an agreement at the last possible moment. This may not work too badly for wage issues, where the positions of the parties can be stated and compromised in quantitative terms. But it is not a good way of resolving more intricate problems, such as rewriting the company's seniority rules, or compromising management's desire for flexibility in production methods with the union's desire to protect the job security of its members.

There has been a growing tendency, therefore, to refer such problems to special committees, whose mission is to work on them continuously between contract negotiations, and to have agreed proposals ready in advance of the next contract deadline. These are sometimes tripartite bodies, including neutrals as well as union and management representatives. In other cases they include labor and management representatives only. In either event they have leisure to undertake thorough exploration of the issues, to commission special studies and expert reports, to test the acceptability of various possible solutions, and to draft clauses for inclusion in the next contract.

After the long and bitter steel strike of 1959, the parties agreed to set up two special committees. The controversy over management's right to change established working methods was referred to a tripartite study group, the labor and management members of which were to agree on a single neutral member to serve as chairman. It proved impossible to agree on a chairman, and this venture came to nothing. More successful was a "Human Relations Research Committee," which included union and management representatives only and which was assigned to look into matters touching on job security, particularly "seniority, including maximum practicable protection for long-service employees against layoffs and for recalls after layoffs." This committee worked continuously from 1960 to 1962, and both parties give it much of the credit for the fact that the 1962 negotiations were concluded three months before the old contracts expired.

It is not surprising that the technique of continuous negotiation should have been used most frequently to deal with problems arising from technical change. Here basic interests of both parties are deeply involved. Management feels that without freedom to close and open plants, to introduce new machinery, and to make other changes in production methods it cannot control costs and maintain the company's competitive position. The union wants to protect workers' rights in their jobs, which it considers akin to property rights, and to hold displacement or downgrading of workers to a minimum. Compromise of these interests is possible, but workable compromises require inventiveness and the drafting of intricate contract provisions. There is an advantage in handling such complicated problems through leisurely and thorough analysis rather than hurried improvisation.

ADJUSTMENT OF GRIEVANCES

Collective bargaining does not end with the signing of an agreement. Union and management officials must live under the agreement during the ensuing year, and the agreement must be applied to concrete situations arising in the plant. Contract provisions must at best be rather general. They are often unduly vague, even self-contradictory, because of unwillingness of the parties to face and resolve an underlying difference of opinion. It is easier to compromise on a vaguely worded clause that each party may interpret differently. The necessities of plant administration, however, compel specific decisions in particular cases. For this reason virtually all collective agreements contain a grievance procedure providing for adjustment of disputes arising during the life of the contract.

The grievance procedure serves a variety of functions in a collective bargaining relationship.[9]

1. The most obvious function is that of interpreting the terms of the agreement and applying them to particular cases. Two or more sections of the agreement may be in conflict. Which is to govern? The contract may be silent on a particular problem, so that grievance adjustment involves closing a gap in the agreement. The language of a particular section may be unclear. What does the section actually mean? Even where the wording is clear, its application to a particular case frequently involves a finding of fact. The agreement may say that smoking on duty is a valid reason for discharge. A foreman discharges a man on this ground. The man says that the foreman's charge is incorrect. Was the man smoking, or was he not? Shall he be discharged, or not?

2. The grievance procedure is also a means of *agreement making* in two senses. To the extent that it reveals problems that are not covered clearly enough or not covered at all in the existing agreement, it helps to build up an agenda of issues for the next contract negotiation. Further, the body of decisions on past grievances itself forms part of the agreement in the broadest sense. There gradually develops, case by case and precedent by precedent, an impressive body of shop law. In long-unionized industries such as railroading and coal mining, this body of precedents is much larger than the formal union agreement and is understood by both sides to be in effect incorporated in the agreement.

3. The grievance procedure can be a sensitive device for locating sore spots in the plant organization and for pointing up inadequacies of particular foremen or union committeemen. The fact that an unusual number of grievances ic filed in a particular department or on a particular issue may be more significant than the intrinsic merit of the grievances. Several leading students of industrial relations have urged the wisdom of taking a clinical rather than a legalistic

---

[9] For a good discussion of this matter, see Van Dusen Kennedy, "Grievance Procedure," in Arthur Kornhauser, Robert Dubin, and Arthur M. Ross (eds.), *Industrial Conflict* (New York: McGraw-Hill Book Company, 1954), Chap. 21. See also Slichter, Healy, and Livernash, *Impact of Collective Bargaining,* Chaps. 22–26.

view of the grievance procedure, of seeking to remove sources of conflict rather than to score points or win cases.

4. Where relations between the parties are good, the grievance procedure may be used to adjust virtually all day-to-day difficulties between workers and supervisors, whether covered explicitly by the agreement or not. It can become an orderly and systematic way of examining any disputed personnel action.

5. Conversely, where relations are poor, the procedure may become an instrument of conflict. It may be used

> not to settle problems between workers and supervisor or union and management but to promote the interests of either or both parties in connection with a future test of strength. . . . In unusually incompatible relationships the grievance process may operate as a sort of guerilla warfare during which the parties keep sniping at each other and endeavor to keep their forces at a martial pitch in preparation for the open conflict which will follow expiration of the contract.[10]

Most grievances relate to rights and duties of individual employees. Discharges, or even less severe disciplinary penalties, are frequently appealed. The application of complicated seniority rules to a particular worker may be questioned. Any choice by a supervisor that involves giving preference to one worker over another—distribution of overtime work, assignment to day work rather than night work, assignment to a preferred type of work and work location—may become a subject of grievance. Classification of a worker or his job for wage purposes—whether a job should be rated as Machinist A rather than Machinist B—may be disputed. On occasion, considerable number of workers may become involved in a grievance case: it is alleged that the assembly line is being run too fast, or that a foreman is speeding up those under him or that work loads throughout a department are too heavy, or that piece rates on a certain operation have been set too low. A multitude of such issues, each of them minor from a top management standpoint but important and emotionally explosive to the workers concerned, get worked out peaceably through the grievance process.

The procedure for handling grievances varies with the nature of the industry. In building construction, for example, the work sites are scattered, jobs are often of short duration, and disputes have to be adjusted quickly or not at all. Each union normally has a *business agent* who makes frequent visits to building sites in his area to check that only union men are employed, to ensure that other contract terms are being complied with, and to hear any complaints by the members. The business agent goes over any grievances with the employer then and there. If no agreement is reached, the men simply leave the job. This is quite different from the lengthy grievance procedures in manufacturing or railroading.

---

[10] Kennedy, "Grievance Procedure," p. 282.

In most manufacturing industries, the basic union official concerned with grievances is the *shop steward* or *grievance committeeman.* He is usually elected by the union members in his department, and is normally a plant employee; but he is allowed time off from his job to handle grievances, which in a large department can become almost a full-time job. The time spent in handling grievances is often paid for by the company, but in some cases the union bears the cost.

The normal first step in a manufacturing plant is for the worker who is "grieving" to consult his shop steward, who discusses the matter informally with the foreman. Most grievances are and must be disposed of at this level. If this is not done, higher union and management officials face a hopeless burden of cases, settlements are long delayed, and the procedure becomes a source of annoyance rather than relief. An experienced foreman eventually learns the wisdom of bargaining things out informally with the union, trading concessions that he can afford for offsetting concessions from the union when he really needs them.

A grievance that is not adjusted between the steward and the foreman is generally reduced to writing and then goes to the shop committee on one side and the plant superintendent on the other. The next appeal stage may be discussion between a national field representative and the labor relations director of the company. The final step before arbitration may be discussion between a vice-president of the company and a national union representative. The number of stages in the grievance procedure varies somewhat with the size of the company, and the complexity of its organization. When the procedure is working properly, the case load is gradually whittled down at successive levels, leaving only a small percentage of "hard core" cases for the final arbitration stage.

The Arbitration of Grievances

Unions generally favor arbitration as the final step in disposing of unsettled grievances. Many newly unionized companies in the thirties and forties opposed it because it allowed outsiders to intervene in personnel decisions. Experience has gradually convinced most managements of the value of the procedure and its use has increased steadily. Today between 90 and 95 percent of union contracts provide for arbitration as the final step in the grievance procedure.

Both management and the union take a risk under arbitration that they may lose decisions on matters that they consider important. Arbitration has the decisive advantage, however, of making possible a final settlement of grievances without a stoppage of work. Arbitration is also in some cases a convenient face-saving device, particularly for the union. Union officials sometimes have to push a case up through the grievance procedure to satisfy a group in their membership, even though they know that the members' demands are unreasonable. If such a case goes to arbitration and is decided against the union, the blame can be put on the arbitrator. Part of the arbitrator's function is to serve as a shock absorber for decisions that are unavoidable, but for which one side or the other is reluctant to take responsibility.

It should be noted that we are talking here about voluntary arbitration, agreed to in advance by the parties and limited to interpreting an existing agreement. The arbitrator under a grievance procedure is there solely to say what the existing agreement means. He has no authority to change the terms of the agreement or to rule on issues not covered by the agreement.

There are several types of voluntary arbitration clauses. The most common practice is for the parties to appoint an arbitrator each time the occasion arises. It is frequently provided that, where the parties cannot agree, the arbitrator shall be designated by the American Arbitration Association, the head of the Federal Mediation and Conciliation Service, the head of the state department of labor, or some other public official. In some industries it is customary to use three-man or five-man arbitration boards; each party appoints one or two members to the board, and these members select a neutral chairman. In large companies, or in agreements between a union and employers' association, there may be enough arbitration work to justify a permanent arbitrator on a full-time or part-time basis. Such an official is frequently termed an *umpire* or *impartial chairman*.

A properly constructed grievance procedure capped by arbitration should in principle render work stoppages unnecessary during the life of the agreement. In recognition of this fact, most contracts contain clauses denying or limiting the right to strike during the contract year. For example, "Under no circumstances shall there be any strike, sympathy strike, walkout, cessation of work, sit down, slow down, picketing, boycott, refusal to perform any part of duty, or other interference with or interruption of the normal conduct of the company's business during the term of this agreement." [11] What happens if a worker engages in a wildcat or "outlaw" strike during the term of the agreement? Some contracts do not contain any penalty provisions. Many contracts, however, provide that instigators of an outlaw strike may be subject to discharge, and that participants may be fined or suspended from work for a time. If there is disagreement over whether a man did instigate a work stoppage, this is taken up through the grievance procedure in the usual way.

In the thirties and forties wildcat strikes were a serious problem in

---

[11] Agreement between the Turbo Engineering Corporation, Trenton, New Jersey, and Local No. 731, United Automobile Workers.

many manufacturing companies. Newly organized workers were still enjoying the excitement of being able to talk back to the boss. Finding that the grievance procedure operated slowly, they often tried to get quick settlement of a disputed issue by direct action. In some plants the slowdown and the quickie strike virtually replaced the official grievance procedure. Managements inexperienced in labor relations got into the habit of yielding on disputed issues to avoid interruptions of production; and this success of wildcat tactics encouraged their continued use.

By the late fifties, however, increased experience and a different economic climate had brought a change in management attitudes. Companies found that constant yielding on work speeds, output standards, and shop discipline had raised production costs to a dangerous extent. With the ending of the postwar boom in the midfifties, costs once more became a matter of concern. Many employers, therefore, decided to stand up to the situation. They began to penalize participants in outlaw strikes; and they refused to settle disputed issues while such a strike was in progress, insisting that work be resumed first and the normal grievance procedure followed thereafter. Once management resistance was apparent, most of the unions accepted it in good spirit. The national unions had never sanctioned the unofficial tactics of their more exuberant local members, and now took steps to tighten internal union discipline. The problem of outlaw strikes receded to minor proportions.

DISCUSSION QUESTIONS

1. What procedures and activities are covered by the term *collective bargaining?*

2. Why may there be differences in the size of the election unit, the negotiating unit, and the impact unit? Can you think of cases in which the three are identical?

3. Explain clearly, giving examples, why the scope of product markets has an important influence on the size of negotiating units.

4. Why are multiemployer bargaining units less common in manufacturing than in nonmanufacturing industries?

5. "The divergent interests of local and occupational groups pose a serious problem for a union engaged in nationwide bargaining."
    (a) Why is this a problem?
    (b) What are some steps that have been taken to deal with it?

6. What are the main functions of the grievance procedure in collec-

tive bargaining? What are the characteristics of a satisfactory grievance procedure?

7. "Without the strike threat in the background, real collective bargaining cannot exist." Discuss.

READING SUGGESTIONS

Comprehensive discussions of collective bargaining include NEIL W. CHAMBERLAIN, *Collective Bargaining,* New York: McGraw-Hill Book Company, 1951; JOHN T. DUNLOP, *Collective Bargaining: Principles and Cases,* Homewood, Ill.: Richard D. Irwin, Inc., 1955; JOHN T. DUNLOP, and NEIL W. CHAMBERLAIN (eds.), *Frontiers of Collective Bargaining,* New York: Harper & Row, Publishers, 1967; JAMES W. KUHN, *Bargaining in Grievance Settlement,* New York: Columbia University Press, 1961; ROBERT M. MACDONALD, "Collective Bargaining in the Postwar Period," *Industrial and Labor Relations Review,* July 1966, pp. 533–57; and SUMNER H. SLICHTER, JAMES J. HEALY, and E. ROBERT LIVERNASH, *The Impact of Collective Bargaining on Management,* Washington, D.C.: The Brookings Institution, 1960.

19

Bargaining Power, Deadlocks, and Strikes

Why do the terms of settlement come out as they do? Why are they sometimes more favorable to management's position and in other cases more favorable to the union? Can one develop any theory of bargained wage rate comparable to the theory of market-determined wages?

APPROACHES TO BARGAINING THEORY

We assume at the outset that the bargain can be expressed in quantitative terms. Without this we cannot graph the positions of the parties or frame hypotheses capable of statistical tests. This is, of course, a considerable simplification of reality. Conversion of demands to a common denominator is easiest for wages and other monetary benefits, such as pensions, paid vacations, or health care. But what about a demand for a union shop? Or a demand for a change in the bargaining structure, which one side or the other believes will work to its advantage in future negotiations? Such demands are often considered matters of principle, which are not capable of compromise. We assume nevertheless that any principle has its price, and that all the items in the settlement package can be reduced to dollar equivalents.

The Contract Zone

Consider a single buyer of a certain kind of labor confronting a single union, a situation known as *bilateral monopoly*. In Figure 19–1, D is the employer's labor demand curve, while S and MC are his labor supply and

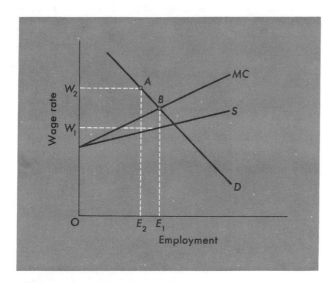

Figure 19–1

The Contract Zone under Bilateral Monopsony

marginal cost curves. The diagram is identical with that for the monopsonistic buyer of labor in Chapter 5. We now face two problems: (1) What are the outside limits within which the bargained wage must fall? (2) What determines where it will fall within these limits?

The limits within which the bargain must fall is usually termed the *settlement range* or the *contract zone*. Its location depends on the policies of the parties. As regards the employer, we usually assume that he will try to maximize profit. In the present case, by the reasoning used in Chapter 5, this will mean operating at point B. The most profitable employment is E_1, where the marginal cost of additional labor (shown by MC) just equals the marginal revenue product of additional labor (shown by D). We see from the supply curve that E_1 workers can be recruited at a wage W_1.

Concerning the union we cannot be so definite. Union negotiators will certainly give some weight to employment as well as wages. They may be influenced also by political and "pattern-following" considerations. Such determinants of union wage policy were examined in Chapter 17. Here we need assume only that the union negotiators do have a policy; that is, that they can select a wage that is preferred to any other wage. Suppose that this preferred wage is W_2 in Figure 19–1.

Have we now defined the limits of the contract zone? Not necessarily. The contract zone cannot be *wider* than W_1W_2 because neither party would want to go outside these limits; but it may be narrower. Suppose the union considers a wage of W_1 so unattractive that it would sulke indefinitely rather than accept it. Then the bottom of the contract zone, the lowest wage that the union could be forced to accept, will be above W_1. Similarly the wage W_2 may be so high that the employer would close down permanently rather than pay it, so that the top of the zone is below W_2. But there will normally be a contract zone, and it will often be wide enough to leave substantial scope for bargaining.

At this point earlier economists, such as Edgeworth, were inclined to leave the matter. They said, in effect, "We cannot answer the second question raised above. Within the limits of the contract zone, the actual wage rate is indeterminate." But this means only that *the market variables usually included in economic theory* are insufficient to determine the outcome. A wage rate does get decided, after all, through the negotiating process. In this sense the outcome *is* determinate.

The Hicks Approach

Not all economists were happy with the Edgeworth pronouncement; and intermittently they have tried to find paths to a determinate solution. One such attempt, by Professor Sir John Hicks of Oxford, is sketched in Figure 19–2. The central idea is that there is a functional relation between

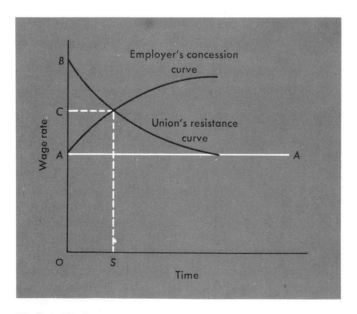

Figure 19–2

Hicks' Solution of the Bargaining Problem

the wage that one or the other party will accept and the length of strike that would be necessary to establish that wage. The horizontal axis in Figure 19–2 is a time axis, along which various possible lengths of strike can be measured. *A* is the wage that the employer would prefer if the union were not in the picture. He will concede more, however, in order to avoid a strike; and up to a point, his concessions will rise with the length of strike he anticipates. Thus we derive the *employer's concession curve,* each point on which shows the maximum amount the employer would pay rather than face a strike of specified length. This curve eventually levels off; that is, there is an upper limit beyond which the employer will not go under any circumstances.

The union's preferred wage would be *B,* provided this could be obtained without a strike; but the prospective costs of a strike may lead it to accept less. The *union's resistance curve* shows the minimum that the union would accept rather than face a strike of the length indicated, and this minimum declines as the prospective strike becomes longer. The resistance curve eventually intersects *AA;* that is, there is some maximum length of strike beyond which the union would prefer simply to accept the employer's terms.

It seems natural to think that the intersection of the two curves yields a determinate solution to the bargaining problem. *Both* parties would agree to the wage *C* rather than face a strike *S* weeks in length. But what does Figure 19–2 really tell us? If it applies to the negotiation period *before* a strike has been called, then the determinate solution rests on assumptions about knowledge and foresight. *If* each party knows the other's curve, and *if* each expects that a strike when called would last at least *S* weeks, the path to settlement is clear. But these assumptions are not very plausible. The essence of collective bargaining is uncertainty about the other party's intentions and about the course of events if negotiations break down.[1]

Alternatively, the Hicks diagram might be interpreted as charting the course of events over time *after* negotiations have broken down and a strike has begun. With each succeeding week of strike, the union's minimum demand falls and the employer's maximum offer rises, until after *S* weeks agreement is reached at *C.* This may be a useful way of looking at the history of

---

[1] Hicks recognized this difficulty: "If there is a considerable divergence of opinion between the employer and the Union representatives about the length of time the men will hold out rather than accept a given set of terms, then the Union may refuse to go below a certain level, because its leaders believe that they can induce the employer to consent to it by refusing to take anything less; while the employer may refuse to concede it, because he does not believe the Union can hold out long enough for concession to be worth his while. Under such circumstances, a deadlock is inevitable, and a strike will ensue; but it arises from the divergence of estimates, and from no other cause." *The Theory of Wages,* 2nd ed. (New York: St. Martin's Press, Inc., 1966), pp. 146–47.

a strike; but it does not provide a theory of negotiation in advance of strike action.

The Concept of Bargaining Power

Bargaining power is a slippery concept, which can be defined in different ways. One interesting definition, developed by Professor Neil Chamberlain, starts from the concept of the *inducement to agree.*[2] Two parties, *A* and *B,* are in a bargaining situation. *A* makes an offer to settle on certain terms. *B*'s inducement to agree is defined as the cost of disagreeing on *A*'s terms/the cost of agreeing on *A*'s terms. This will usually be a positive fraction, greater than zero, but not necessarily greater than one. Only if and when it becomes greater than one—that is, when the cost of continued disagreement exceeds the cost of agreement—will *B* be willing to accept *A*'s offer.

The size of the ratio depends partly on the terms. By making his terms more and more attractive, *A* can raise *B*'s inducement to agree and eventually bring about a settlement. Concession is one route to agreement. But there are other things that *A* can do without altering his offer. *A* may try to persuade *B* that the cost of accepting *A*'s terms is less than it seems, thus reducing the denominator of the ratio. Or he may, by bluff or threat, cause *B* to raise his estimate of the cost of disagreement, and thus raise the numerator.

This leads to a definition: "Bargaining power can be defined as the capacity to effect an agreement on one's own terms; operationally, one's bargaining power *is* another's inducement to agree. If *X* and *Y* are in a contest over the terms of their cooperation, *X*'s bargaining power is represented by *Y*'s inducement to agree . . . while *Y*'s bargaining power is *X*'s inducement to agree . . ."[3] While the two are inversely related, *Y*'s bargaining power tending to be less as *X*'s is greater, the relation is not a simple reciprocal. It is possible, for example, that at some point in a union–management negotiation *both* parties may find themselves with an inducement to agree greater than one. All that is necessary for a settlement, however, is that *one* party find itself in this position.

While Chamberlain's concept is useful, and has been adopted in one form or another by most later writers, it carries us only part of the way. We need to examine the costs of agreement and disagreement in more detail and to look at the tactics that the parties may use to manipulate these magnitudes.

---

[2] Neil W. Chamberlain, *A General Theory of Economic Process* (New York: Harper & Row, Publishers, 1955), pp. 80–82.

[3] Chamberlain, *A General Theory of Economic Process,* p. 81.

The Bargainer's Utility Functions

It is useful to think of each bargainer as having in mind not a single wage target, but a variety of possible settlements yielding varying degrees of satisfaction. Let us call this the *utility* of the settlement to the negotiator in question. In Figure 19–3, let the vertical axis measure utility and the horizontal axis various sizes of wage increase. O indicates the existing wage level. Then the utility function of, say, the union negotiators will have a shape such as U_L. Any increase of less than B would yield negative satisfaction. Increases above B yield increasing satisfaction up to L, at which U_L reaches a maximum. Still larger increases, in the range LC, would be acceptable but would yield decreasing satisfaction for reasons to be noted in a moment.

The union negotiator must consider not only the potential benefits of various wage settlements but also the potential costs of attaining them. The costs are mainly strike costs, and are positively related to the size of the wage demand. The larger the increase on which the union insists, the more likely is it that a strike will occur and the longer its probable duration. The cost function, then, will be upward sloping to the right, as indicated by AS. By deducting this potential cost from the potential benefit of each wage increase we derive the *net* utility function U'_L.

Note that U'_L reaches a maximum at an earlier point, L' instead of L. It also becomes negative at an earlier point, C' instead of C. We conclude

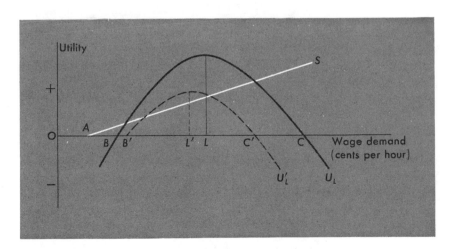

Figure 19–3

The Union Negotiator's Utility Function

that, when costs are brought into the picture, the range of outcomes that could benefit the union becomes narrower, and the union's *preferred* increase (*L'*) is lower. Moreover, an increase in the probability of a strike or in its estimated cost will increase the slope of *AS*—the steepness of the *strike gradient*, if you will. Any such shift will move *L'* to the left.[4] Thus if management can convince the union that probable strike costs are greater than it originally thought, this will reduce the union's (preferred) wage demand.

In Figure 19–4 we construct a similar picture of the management negotiator's gross and net utility functions. Since the logic is identical with the foregoing, we can abbreviate the discussion. Note that management's cost function slopes upward to the *left*—the *smaller* the increase management is willing to concede, the greater the probability of a strike and the greater its estimated cost. Introduction of costs, then, raises management's preferred settlement from *M* to *M'*. Moreover, any increase in the strike gradient *FS* will move *M'* to the right.

It is the net utility functions, U'_L and U'_M, that are significant for bargaining. Several features of these functions should be noted. First, they are utility functions for the *negotiators* rather than for the organizations they represent. One can scarcely think of a corporation feeling varying degrees of satisfaction from a wage bargain; but one can do this for the executives in charge of negotiations. Second, each negotiator's utility function is *un*-

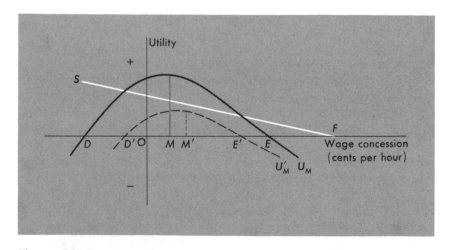

Figure 19–4

The Management Negotiator's Utility Function

---

[4] *L'* is the point at which the rates of increase in benefits and costs are equal; i.e., the slopes of *AS* and U_L are equal. An increase in the slope *AS* will shift *L'* leftward to a point where the slope of U_L is greater by a corresponding amount.

known to his opponent. If each party knew at the outset where the other stood, most of the phenomena observed in collective bargaining would never arise. Third, the utility functions *shift* in the course of negotiations. A major tactical objective in bargaining is to shift the opponent's utility function in a way favorable to oneself.

The points corresponding to the maxima of the net utility functions can be interpreted as *strike points*. The union will call a strike rather than accept an increase of less than L'. Management will take a strike rather than concede more than M'.

The Contract Zone Once More

We concentrate now on these strike points rather than on the net utility functions as a whole. Remember that neither party knows the true position of the other. Indeed, to discover this is a major objective in bargaining. So with a slight change in lettering, let us call the union's real strike point or minimum wage demand L_R, and management's real maximum offer M_R. And let us use L_N and M_N for the nominal or "shadow" positions put forward by the parties.

Several possible relations among these quantities are shown in Figure 19–5. The union's real demand might be below the employer's real offer, as in Figure 19–5 (a). The range $L_R M_R$ is a *positive contract zone,* any point within which will be acceptable to both parties. This does not mean, however, that a bargain can be struck immediately. The nominal positions of the parties are far apart. It may take much hard bargaining before the true positions are disclosed; and it is even possible to have a deadlock and a strike because of the difficulty of "backing down" from the nominal positions. If and when the true positions are revealed, there is still a problem of just where the bargain will be struck within the range $L_R M_R$. We return to this in discussing negotiating tactics.

Second, the true positions of the parties might coincide, as in Figure 19–5(b). This is what Boulding terms the "bare bargain" case, since agreement is possible at one point only. Again, the existence of a point of (potential) agreement does not ensure that this point will be reached quickly or at all.

Finally, in Figure 19–5(c), the union's demand is above management's offer. The range $M_R L_R$ is a *negative contract* zone in the sense of a gap between the true positions of the parties. But this does not mean that a breakdown of negotiations is inevitable. Indeed, we know that the great majority of contract negotiations are concluded without a shutdown. One reason is that, in the course of negotiations, the positions M_R and L_R are shifted toward each other by tactical maneuvers of the parties.

With this framework in hand, we can give more operational content to the concept of bargaining power. The union's ability to win increases is

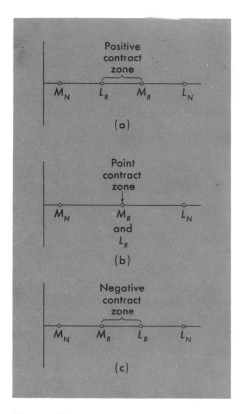

Figure 19–5

Possible Positions at the Outset of Bargaining

higher (1) the higher the value of M_R at the outset of negotiations, and (2) the greater the union's ability to shift M_R upward over the course of negotiations.[5]

BARGAINING POWER AND NEGOTIATING TACTICS

Determinants of Bargaining Power

Bargaining power may seem to imply personal forcefulness, shrewdness, or tactical skill. So we should emphasize that bargaining power depends mainly on objective circumstances, economic and organizational. Such famous negotiators as John L. Lewis of the Mine Workers and James

---

[5] For an approach quite similar to that adopted here, see Bevars D. Mabry, "The Pure Theory of Bargaining," *Industrial and Labor Relations Review* (July 1965), pp. 479–502.

Hoffa of the Teamsters achieved their results, not mainly by superior poker-playing ability, but because they actually held good cards.

The costs of a shutdown are a key factor in the power relation between the parties. In part, these costs depend on the nature of the product and the industry. If the company is producing a service or a perishable commodity, sales lost during a strike can never be regained. In an industry that produces a durable good and that normally operates below capacity, such as coal mining, what is not produced during the strike will be produced later on. But if potential imports are important, as in steel or automobiles, a shutdown may mean a loss of sales to foreign producers; and if U.S. customers find the foreign goods acceptable, this loss can become permanent. In the construction industry, builders normally contract to complete a building by a certain date, with a substantial penalty charge for each day beyond this. A strike called close to the completion date thus becomes very expensive.

Apart from these intrinsic industry characteristics, each party may maneuver to reduce strike costs to itself and raise costs to its opponent. The United Automobile Workers prefers that a strike, where one eventuates, be confined to one of the auto companies. This reduces the cost to the union, since most of its members continue to work and pay dues while only a minority are drawing strike benefits. And it increases the cost to the company, since if Ford alone is shut down many customers will switch to Chrysler or General Motors.

In some cases this tactic has led employers to band together and insist on industry-wide bargaining. In other cases companies have established a system of *strike insurance*. The airline companies, whose strike hazards are increased by the multiplicity of unions with which they bargain, have a mutual assistance pact dating from 1958. A company that is shut down by strike is entitled to receive payments from other airlines which continue to operate. The method of calculating benefits, and of assessing the cost against other airlines, is specified in great detail.[6] Transfers under the program have been substantial, totaling about $183 million in the years 1971 to 1974. In 1967 the five major tire producers formed a similar agreement, details of which have not been made public, and used it to sustain a two-month strike against three of the companies. The American Newspaper Publishers' Association provides strike insurance for a specified premium. An annual premium of $50,000, for example, buys strike benefits of $20,000 per day per strike. The association of American railroads has a similar scheme operated through Lloyd's of London.[7]

---

[6] For the detailed provisions, see S. Herbert Unterberger and Edward C. Koziara, "Airline Strike Insurance: A Study in Escalation," *Industrial and Labor Relations Review* (October 1975), pp. 26–45.

[7] John S. Hirsch, Jr., "Strike Insurance and Collective Bargaining," *Industrial and Labor Relations Review* (April 1969), pp. 399–415.

An interesting power tactic developed by the Teamsters' Union is the *open-ended grievance procedure.* Unlike the usual grievance procedure terminating in arbitration. Teamsters' contracts provide that any grievance that cannot be adjusted by discussion between the parties may become a subject of strike action. This increases the union's leverage in contract negotiations. An employer who does not accede readily to union demands may be informed none too gently that he is likely to have an unusual number of grievances in the year ahead. The union's ability to cut off the flow of freight from other unionized companies is also a powerful bargaining weapon.

A shutdown brings losses to workers and the union as well as to the employer. Striking members are usually excused from dues payments and entitled to draw strike benefits, so that a long strike drains the union treasury. On this score, union bargaining power fluctuates over time. A union that has just been through an expensive strike has reduced bargaining power because the treasury is low and the memory of lost paychecks is fresh in the members' minds. As time passes, the union's ability to strike recovers and its bargaining power rises.

The prospective losses are usually serious enough to serve as a substantial deterrent to both sides. But how can one estimate the probability that insisting on a certain position will actually lead to a strike? It is here that uncertainty becomes critical. If the union negotiator knew the management negotiator's utility function, he would know that up to some point the probability of a strike is zero, and that above some point a strike is a certainty. But the union negotiator does not know where these points are. So he will estimate the probability of a strike at something between zero and one, rising toward the upper limit as the wage demand becomes larger.

In an uncertain situation, attitudes toward risk influence the outcome. A cautious bargainer may settle for less than he could have gotten. A negotiator who enjoys taking chances may try to see just how far he can go, sometimes overstepping the mark. Instances of both sorts can be found in the history of collective bargaining. This determinant, unlike those discussed previously, depends partly on the personalities of the negotiators. Increasing experience, however, is likely to moderate extremes of behavior. Negotiators who persist in being too cautious or too reckless will find themselves eliminated from the game.

The Tactics of Negotiation

How does the union (or management) negotiator endeavor to improve the opponent's offer? We noted earlier that the first step in negotiations is usually "the big demand"—deliberate overstatement by the union of how much it wants, deliberate understatement by management of how much it will concede.

A long and ambitious list of demands has advantages. It conceals one's true demands and "keeps the other fellow guessing," which is an important element in bargaining strategy. It provides ample room for negotiation and maneuver, for trading elimination of some items against concessions on others. It serves as protection against a marked change in economic conditions during the course of negotiations. Some negotiations go on for months, during which prosperity may change to recession or vice versa. If one's initial demand turns out to be less than would be feasible several months later, one is bound to be criticized for ineptitude or worse.

Although initial demands are expected to be large, they must not be so large as to lose credibility. If the union's minimum demand is twenty cents an hour, it may be good strategy to ask for forty cents. But to ask for a dollar an hour would not be taken seriously and would be equivalent to saying nothing. Similarly, in a period of rising prices and profits, a company's insistence on no wage increase would not be credible and could arouse anger rather than amusement.

Although the big demand is usual, it is not invariable. In rare cases management states its maximum offer at the outset and adheres to it firmly thereafter. This technique is often termed "boulwarism," after a former vice-president of the General Electric Company, who was one of its early exponents. In this case, M_R and M_N are identical. If the union's (true) demand is above M_R, it must do all the adjusting required for a settlement. If the union is unable or unwilling to adjust, management will take a strike rather than yield.

This tactic is resented by union leaders, not because it necessarily leads to smaller wage increases, but because it is a refusal to play the bargaining game and to allow the union to take any credit for the settlement. Management is saying to its employees, "We are prepared to make a fair adjustment in wages for the year ahead. We will not give a penny more because of the presence of a union. So what is the union really doing for you?" The probable result is increased antagonism between union and management officials, and more frequent breakdown of negotiations. Union resistance to this tactic has contributed to several work stoppages at General Electric.

Starting from the initial positions, each negotiator is trying to accomplish certain things. The union negotiator is interested in: (1) representing (or in some measure misrepresenting) his own preferences; (2) trying to discover management's preferences; (3) trying to shift management's preferences; and in some cases (4) attempting to alter the preferences of third parties such as the general public, or executive and legislative officials. The management negotiator is trying to accomplish the same things vis-à-vis the union.

The available tactics are persuasion and coercion. The union may try to persuade management that a certain wage increase will be more beneficial than management thinks—because labor productivity will rise along with wages, because the economic outlook is brighter than management expects, and so on. Management may argue that the benefit of a large increase is *less* than the union thinks, because it would reduce employment or even force the company out of business.

Such arguments amount to saying to the other party, "You don't really know your own interests." This is not likely to be very palatable. But persuasion should not be dismissed as entirely ineffective. It may convey factual information that the other party did not have at the outset, possibly leading to a shift of preferences. The rationalizations set forth by one side may also provide the other with a ladder by which to climb down gracefully from a position that no longer seems defensible.

The object of coercive tactics is to change the other party's estimate of the costs of disagreement. The union negotiator implies that a strike will result unless certain minimum terms are met. The management negotiator may state that the company will have to shut down or move to another location if the increase exceeds some maximum.

Following Carl Stevens, we may distinguish between bluff and "not-bluff." [8] Not-bluff consists in announcing what you intend to do ("we will strike at anything less than ten cents an hour"), with the intention of actually doing it if the contingency develops. The difficulty is that even though your intention is firm, the other party may not believe it. So one can have the following sequence of events: the union announces a certain demand. The employer, if he believed the strike threat, would be willing to concede rather than take a strike. But he does not believe it, and refuses to concede. The result is a strike that nobody wants.

Bluff consists in announcing a certain course of action even though you do *not* intend to follow it if the contingency arises. Again, there is a problem of credibility. To be effective, the bluff must be believed. If the bluff is called and the bluffer backs down, this will reduce his credibility in future negotiations.

One possible method of increasing credibility is *commitment*. Thomas Schelling has argued that a negotiator can strengthen his bargaining position by committing himself in such a way that he cannot later retreat without disastrous consequences.[9] The union negotiator can whip up membership sentiment behind certain minimum demands, take a strike vote, mobilize a strike fund, and make other visible and dramatic strike preparations.

---

[8] See his *Strategy and Collective Bargaining Negotiations* (New York: McGraw-Hill Book Company, 1963).

[9] Thomas C. Schelling, "An Essay on Bargaining," *American Economic Review* (June 1956), pp. 281–306.

The management negotiator may state that the board of directors will not go beyond a certain limit, thus laying their credibility on the line along with his own.

This is a dangerous tactic, because events can get out of hand. What started out as a tentative commitment on one or both sides may harden into a firm commitment, leading to a strike that was not necessarily in the cards at the outset. It is a little like playing a game of "chicken" with the steering wheel locked in position.

Tactical maneuvering on both sides over a period of weeks usually leads to concessions that bring the stated positions of the parties closer to their true positions and also brings the true positions closer together. Making concessions is delicate, since it may be interpreted as weakness, and so concessions are usually signaled indirectly. One side may simply remain silent about a point on which it has been insisting; or it may suggest that the point be set aside for the time being, implying that eventual agreement will not be too difficult. One party, having made such an implicit concession, may then wait for the other to take reciprocal action, so that negotiations proceed through a series of moves and countermoves.

Eventually the approach of the contract expiration deadline forces a final reexamination of positions. As the probability of a shutdown rises, the costs of shutdown are estimated more carefully and taken more seriously. It is no accident that many contracts are renewed at the eleventh hour after hectic all-night bargaining sessions. The fact that it *is* the eleventh hour moves the parties toward a possible agreement.

There are several possible cases:

1. The final positions of the parties may still fail to overlap, even after shutdown costs have been fully weighed. In this case the parties will continue to go through the motions until the deadline, but a strike is inevitable.

2. The final positions may have shifted sufficiently so that they coincide. Here agreement appears easy. Remember, however, that neither party knows the true position of the other. The stated positions are probably still some distance apart. Someone must take the first step toward a solution; and this step, like any concession, is subject to misinterpretation.

Consider the following sequence: The company states it will give no more than ten cents but is actually willing to give fifteen rather than face a shutdown. The union is still asking twenty cents but is willing to take fifteen. As the deadline nears, the union reduces its nominal demand to the true figure of fifteen cents. The management negotiator takes this as indicating that "the union is caving in," and reduces his maximum offer to twelve cents. The union does not cave in, and a strike follows.

This problem, which Stevens terms "coming clean without prejudice," is quite difficult. A strike remains a possibility until settlement has been reached; and if there is a strike, bargaining will continue from the final announced postions of the parties. This may lead one or both parties, even at the eleventh hour, to announce positions somewhat more favorable to themselves than the true positions. Thus overt agreement may not be reached despite the existence of covert agreement.

3. The final positions of the parties may overlap, yielding what we termed earlier a positive contract zone. The union would take ten cents, but the employer would concede fifteen; so any settlement between these figures is feasible. What will determine the actual figure? There are various possibilities. One party, under the pressure of the strike deadline, may reveal its true position, in which case the bargain will be struck at that level. Here the party that moves first loses. Perhaps more commonly, the parties will cast around for precedents that might justify a settlement at some intermediate level. Under *pattern bargaining,* the level already accepted by comparable companies may point the way toward compromise. The standard *wage criteria* employed in collective bargaining may also suggest a certain figure as plausible.

These wage criteria deserve brief comment. The criteria most commonly urged in negotiations are: (1) the wage currently paid by other employers for the same type of labor; (2) wage increases in the recent past by other employers of the same type of labor; (3) cost-of-living increases since the date of the last wage increase; (4) the average rate of increase in labor productivity and real wages in the economy; and (5) the recent and prospective movement of labor productivity, unit labor cost, prices, and profits in the company for which the bargain is being made—*ability to pay.*

These criteria are often derided on several grounds: that each yields a different figure, so that they do not point to a unique solution; that some of them are not proper criteria; that the union and management positions are in fact shaped by other considerations; and that the supposed criteria are used merely to "dress up" or rationalize these positions.

This view, however, is too extreme. The wage criteria do serve several useful functions: (1) Some of them—current wage levels of other employers competing for the same grade of labor, cost-of-living changes, the average movement of wages in the economy—are valid criteria, both in the sense that they would be operative in a nonunion economy and in the sense of having significant influence on union and management positions. (2) In a bargaining setting, the criteria chosen and the strength with which they are asserted provide useful clues to the true positions of the parties. (3) The arguments developed in support of one or another criterion may provide a line of retreat for a party that wishes to make concessions. Here the fact that different criteria point in different directions and can be used to justify a range of possible settlements is a positive benefit. (4) Finally, they can rationalize an eventual compromise figure within a positive contract zone. If different criteria yield increases varying from zero to twenty-five cents an hour, a negotiator who agrees to twelve cents can claim some objective justification.

STRIKES, STRIKE COSTS, AND STRIKE PREVENTION

It has been said that war is a continuation of diplomacy by other methods. Similarly, the strike is a continuation of bargaining by other methods. Why do strikes happen? How much harm do they do? Under what circumstances, if any, should unions and managements be prohibited from "slugging it out"? What methods might be developed for settling disputes without a stoppage of production?

Why Strikes Occur

In an average year during the period 1970–75, about 2.5 million workers were involved in strikes. This was about 13 percent of union members, and 3 percent of all employed workers. The average length of strikes was about three weeks. The amount of time lost through strikes, as a proportion of total working time in the economy, varied from about 0.37 percent in 1970 to 0.14 percent in 1973.[10] How far this represents an actual loss in output will be considered in a later section.

Why did these strikes occur? It is customary to classify strikes according to the leading issue in a particular dispute—so many strikes over wages, so many over working conditions, and so on. This is not a meaningful classification. The issues involved in a dispute are always interrelated, and to single out one as the primary issue is an arbitrary procedure. Moreover, the important thing is not what the issue was, but why the parties were unable to reach agreement on it. In order to discover the "causes" of strikes, one must discover the kinds of circumstances in which agreement between the parties becomes impossible.

Drawing on our previous analysis, we can distinguish between *avoidable* and *unavoidable* strikes. An avoidable strike is one in which the true positions of the parties overlap, so that an omniscient observer could prescribe a solution acceptable to both. An unavoidable strike is one in which the final positions of the parties fail to overlap, so that each prefers a shutdown to further concessions.

In the last section we noted several reasons why a potentially avoidable strike may nevertheless not be avoided. First, inexperienced or clumsy negotiators may stake out firm positions from which it is later difficult to retreat, may misread the signals from the other side, may be unable to surmount the tactical difficulties of graceful concession, and so on. Second,

---

[10] *Monthly Labor Review* (December, 1976).

even the tactics of experienced negotiators may misfire on occasion. The not-bluff that is not believed can lead to a strike that no one wants. So can excessive commitment to a threatened course of action, which may build up an equally firm commitment on the other side. Third, there is the tactical difficulty of "coming clean" about one's true position in the crucial final stages of negotiations. This can lead to an impasse even when there is a positive contract zone.

Unavoidable strikes, where the contract zone is still negative when the deadline arrives, may also occur for several reasons. First, the basic issue may be not the terms of the new contract, but the framework of bargaining itself. We noted earlier that the size of the bargaining unit, the degree of cooperation among employers and unions, and the timing of contract expiration dates can influence the balance of power between the parties. One party may decide that the time has come to force a change in the bargaining framework that will improve its bargaining position in future years. Such a power struggle is less easily compromised than a dispute over terms of employment.

An example is the 114-day strike of the Printers' Union against the New York newspapers in 1962 and 1963. Prior to this time the employers' contract with the Newspaper Guild had expired five weeks before that with the printers and other pressroom crafts. The newspapers first negotiated new wage terms with the guild, which then became the pattern for other employee groups. The printers felt that this deprived them of any independent negotiating power. They demanded, and eventually won, a common contract expiration date that enabled them to enter negotiations on an even footing.

Second, one party may attach positive value to a strike. An employer may think that a prolonged strike will break the union and free him from the necessity of collective bargaining. A union leader may consider an occasional strike desirable to maintain the members' morale and to impress the employer with the union's willingness to fight. Unused weapons become rusty. A union that never strikes may lose its ability to make the strike threat credible and may have to accept unfavorable settlements in consequence.

Third, we have assumed that all terms of the contract can be reduced to a dollar equivalent, which can be compromised by small stages. But this is not always true. It is hard for the employer to concede "half a union shop." A demand that does not have a clear dollar dimension, that must be granted in full or denied in full, and that is considered a matter of principle by one or both sides, can readily lead to an impasse.

Fourth, the negotiators are delegates of their respective organizations. Even when their own judgment would lead them to compromise, they may be prevented from doing so by institutional constraints. An absentee corporation president or board of directors may order a plant manager to take a position that the latter knows will lead to a strike. A union leader may privately consider the union's demands untenable; but to retreat might jeopardize his own position and split the union. A rival leader, for example, may have convinced the bulk of the membership that the demands are attainable. If the negotiator settles for less, he will be accused of a "sellout," the settlement will be voted down by the membership, and a strike will result in any event.

Finally, a strike may result from misjudgment of the cost of disagreement. Even where compromise is possible, one side may be unwilling to compromise because it has a low opinion of the other's strength and thinks it can win its point easily and quickly. The employer may underestimate the membership, solidarity, and financial strength of the union; the union may underestimate the determination of the employer to resist further concessions. One frequently finds an employer who, by conceding wage increases and restrictive working rules year after year, has got his production costs seriously out of line with those of competing companies. He may finally decide to hold the line and prevent further cost increases. Union leaders, however, have got in the habit of securing easy concessions from him and will not take him seriously. When they find out too late that he is serious, they are confronted with a strike.

To discover which of these situations was responsible for a particular strike requires careful analysis of the circumstances. The union normally makes the first overt move, and the public therefore tends to regard it as the aggressor. The employer can cause a strike by doing nothing; the union has to take the positive step of calling out the workers. But all one can conclude from the fact of a strike is that there was a failure to reach agreement. The reasons for the failure can be learned from an inside knowledge of the people and issues involved.

The Role of Mediation

Most of the strongly unionized countries, including the United States, maintain staffs of experienced, full-time neutrals, usually called *mediators* or *conciliators,* to assist in resolving industrial disputes. Some countries require that mediators be given a chance to settle a dispute before strike action is lawful. In the United States, except for the railroad and airline industries and for the "emergency dispute" provisions of the Taft-Hartley Act and some state acts, use of mediators is entirely voluntary. But when the Federal Mediation and Conciliation Service or a state mediation body proffers its services, the offer is rarely refused.

The mediator may come in at an early stage of negotiations, at the critical eleventh-hour stage, or after a strike has begun. Whenever he enters, he tends to become the main communication channel between the parties. A common technique is to separate the parties physically, while the medi- ator carries information and proposals back and forth between them.

The possible functions of the mediator can be analyzed in terms of our earlier discussion of negotiating tactics. A common function is to save face for one or both parties when they have gotten locked into a position from which there seems no graceful retreat. As Stevens points out

> the mediator may supply a party with arguments which the party may in turn use to rationalize a position (or retreat from a position) vis-à-vis his own constituents . . . the mere fact of a mediator's entrance into a dis- pute provides the parties with a means of rationalizing retreats from previously held positions, particularly if the mediator can be made to appear to take a part of the "responsibility" for any settlement.[11]

The mediator may help in a situation where a not-bluff by *A,* which is not believed by *B,* creates the possibility of an unwanted strike. Each party is more likely to believe the mediator than to believe the opposing party. The mediator may be able to convince *B* that the not-bluff is genuine, thus averting the strike danger.

The mediator's function in the event of a bluff is less clear. Consider this situation: *A* is bluffing. *B,* if he believed the bluff, would make con- cessions sufficient to settle the dispute. If the mediator can convince *B* that *A* is *not* bluffing, this will contribute to a settlement. What is more impor- tant for the mediator: to be truthful or effective? Another possibility, of course, would be for the mediator to convince *A* that his bluff is not be- lieved and that he should abandon it.

As the strike deadline approaches, it becomes increasingly important that each side reveal its true position; but this raises the tactical difficulty of "coming clean without prejudice." Each side fears that, if it reveals that it is willing to compromise, this will be interpreted as weakness and will cause the other side to stiffen its position. They may be willing, however, to reveal their true positions to the mediator. When the mediator discovers that the potential compromises coincide or overlap, he may call the parties to a joint session and propose a settlement that each has privately indicated it will accept.

Where positions overlap and there is a positive contract zone, the question arises of where the bargain should be struck within this zone. In this situation the mediator can help to focus the attention of the parties on one solution as most plausible, incidentally providing a rationalization for it and taking a measure of responsibility. The union negotiator can now go back to his members and say, "We were holding out fine, but that un- mentionable mediator made us give in."

---

[11] Stevens, *Strategy and Collective Bargaining Negotiations,* p. 130.

Finally, an ingenious mediator can sometimes think of compromise proposals that have not occurred to either of the parties. This is particularly useful in demands that have become matters of principle.

Frequency of Strikes

The number of strikes fluctuates with the movements of the business cycle. Strikes fall off during depression and the percentage of strikes won by the union also declines. Rees concludes from this that union strategy rather than company strategy dominates the scene and that strikes behave as one might expect on economic grounds—they are more frequent when the chances of success are high, and vice versa.[12] If employers could choose when to have strikes, the number would presumably rise during depression when employers are relatively strong.

There are also marked differences in the strike proneness of individual industries. Kerr and Siegel, on the basis of strike statistics from eleven countries for varying periods of time between 1919 and 1950, found a consistently high propensity to strike in mining, shipping, longshoring, lumber, and textiles. The lowest strike propensities were found in clothing, public utilities, hotel and restaurant service, trade, railroad transportation, and agriculture. They attribute the high incidence of strikes in the first group of industries to: [13]

1. An isolated position of the worker in society. Workers in these industries typically form an "isolated mass," living apart from other people in company towns, at sea, in the woods, and so on. All do the same work, have the same grievances, and mingle with each other. There is little or no opportunity to rise to higher occupational levels. The employer is often landlord and governor as well. Under these circumstances, all grievances focus on the (usually absentee) employer. The union becomes a kind of working-class party or even a subgovernment. "The strike for this isolated mass is a kind of colonial revolt against far-removed authority, an outlet for accumulated tensions, and a substitute for occupational and social mobility."

Workers in the low-strike industries are in an opposite situation in these respects and are integrated successfully into the larger community.

2. A subsidiary but important factor is the nature of the work and the workers. "If the job is physically difficult and unpleasant, unskilled or semiskilled, and casual or seasonal, and fosters an independent spirit (as in the logger in the woods), it will draw tough, inconstant, combative, and virile workers, and they will be inclined to strike."

---

[12] Albert Rees, "Industrial Conflict and Business Fluctuations," in A. Kornhauser, P. Dubin, and A. M. Ross (eds.), *Industrial Conflict* (New York: McGraw-Hill Book Company, 1954), Chap. 15.

[13] Clark Kerr and Abraham Siegel, "The Interindustry Propensity To Strike—An International Comparison," in Kornhauser, Dubin, and Ross, *Industrial Conflict,* Chap. 14.

There are also wide differences among countries in the extent of strike activity.[14] Interestingly enough, some of the countries in which unionism is very strong—the Scandinavian countries, Holland, West Germany—have few strikes. Threats are sufficiently effective that resort to strikes is not necessary. On the other hand, France, Italy, and India, where unions are relatively weak, have had high proportions of union members involved in strikes. But in some countries that have many strikes (France, Italy, Australia), the average strike lasts only two or three days, so that time lost is not great. Canada and the United States have had moderately high rates of strike activity in the postwar period, the American rate being typically about double the Canadian one.

In most countries the level of strike activity today is well below the level in earlier decades; and in some of the most strongly unionized countries resort to strikes is approaching the vanishing point. Ross and Hartman suggest three main reasons for this "withering away of the strike":

> First, employers have developed more sophisticated policies and more effective organizations. Second, the state has become more prominent as an employer of labor, economic planner, provider of benefits, and supervisor of industrial relations. Third, in many countries (although not in the United States), the labor movement has been forsaking the use of the strike in favor of broad political endeavors.[15]

Dunlop has suggested several additional factors. In some industries— oil refining, chemical plants, telephone communication, electric utilities— technical progress has made it increasingly possible for supervisors and technicians to keep the plant in operation during a strike. This obviously reduces the usefulness of the strike weapon. In other industries—rail and bus transportation, maritime transport, steel, automobiles—strikes have led customers to shift to other sources of supply, including imports. This increases the cost of a stoppage to both parties, which discourages its use. In other newly unionized areas, such as atomic energy, military procurement and construction, public-school teaching, and public employment generally, strikes are either illegal or severely frowned on by public opinion.[16]

The Cost of Strikes

Here one must distinguish between *private* and *social* cost, between cost to the parties and cost to the national economy. The striking workers lose some wages and the company loses some profit. These are losses that

---

[14] For a statistical comparison, see Arthur M. Ross and Paul J. Hartman, *Changing Patterns of Industrial Conflict* (New York: John Wiley & Sons, Inc., 1960).

[15] Ross and Hartman, *Changing Patterns of Industrial Conflict*, p. 42.

[16] John T. Dunlop, "The Function of the Strike," in John T. Dunlop and Neil W. Chamberlain (eds.), *Frontiers of Collective Bargaining* (New York: Harper & Row, Publishers, 1967).

the parties consider it worthwhile to bear rather than settle on adverse terms. The loss to the economy consists in a reduced output of goods and services available for consumption or investment.

A strike may not involve any loss in national output. In a seasonal industry, a strike may simply change the location of the slack season. A strike in men's clothing factories early in the spring season means only that the factories will have to work longer at the end of the season to make up for lost time. In this case there is not even a loss of income to the parties, merely a postponement of income to a later date.

The impact of strikes is mitigated also by the fact that most industries in most years operate below full capacity. This is true, for example, of the basic steel industry. Every three years when the steel contract expires, raising the possibility of a strike, users of steel stock up heavily in advance and the industry works full blast for a while to meet these orders. If a strike actually develops, steel buyers can sit it out for two or three months by drawing on inventories. After the end of the strike, the mills may again work full blast for a time to restore inventories throughout the industry. But the main effect is a shift in the *timing* of production rather than the *amount* of production.

A similar shift occurs when a union strikes selectively against part of an industry. If Ford is shut down, Chrysler and General Motors will sell more cars. Ford and its workers have less income, but other companies and their workers have more income. This assumes, of course, that the other companies have unused capacity and can absorb the additional business. If all plants are operating at full capacity throughout the year, a strike anywhere in the industry will reduce national output.

The main output losses occur in two situations. First, in industries producing services for immediate consumption, production lost today is lost forever. If I do not buy a newspaper or a subway ride today, I am not going to buy two tomorrow to catch up. The seriousness of such losses depends on the kind of service in question. A strike of radio announcers would not affect most people's lives materially. A strike of hospital attendants, public-school teachers, garbage collectors, or truckers delivering perishable food to market is a more serious matter. In some cases, availability of close substitutes may mitigate the impact on consumption.

Second, there are industries, such as electric power production and rail transportation, whose continuous operation is essential to steady production in other industries. A strike in such an industry may, by crippling production in many other industries, cause a disproportionate drop in national output. Strikes in merchant shipping and longshoring can have a serious effect on countries that depend heavily on foreign trade.[17]

---

[17] Donald E. Cullen, *National Emergency Strikes* (Ithaca: New York State School of Industrial and Labor Relations, 1968). Chapter 2 surveys research studies that have tried to measure the losses caused by specific strikes.

A third possibility, which has become increasingly important with reduction of tariff rates and growth of world trade, is that foreign output may be substituted for domestic output. If American automobile production were shut down for any length of time, sales of foreign cars would rise substantially. Moreover, the trade relations established during the strike do not necessarily cease when it ends. The level of imports may remain permanently higher than before. In national terms, this means a worsening of the U.S. balance of payments. In private terms, it means a loss of markets to the companies and an employment loss to union members.

This factor, plus the undesirability of frantic production in advance of a steel strike followed by months of slack production and employment after the end of the strike, led to an unusual 1973 agreement between the United Steelworkers of America and the basic steel producers designed to prevent a steel strike in 1974. The three-year contract in effect at the time was not due to expire until August 1, 1974. The parties nevertheless negotiated a basic agreement in March 1973, with the following main provisions:

1. The cost-of-living escalator clause, under which wage rates are adjusted upward automatically for increases in living costs, will remain in effect.
2. In addition, steelworkers will receive general wage increases of *at least* 3 percent on August 1, 1974, August 1, 1975, and August 1, 1976. (Larger increases remain permissible by joint agreement.)
3. In addition, each worker will receive a one-time bonus of $150 on August 1, 1974.
4. Within this framework, contract negotiations will proceed in 1974 according to the usual procedures and timetable; *but,* in the event of failure to reach agreement on one or more issues, these issues will be submitted to binding outside arbitration. The possibility of a strike is thus precluded.

This procedure worked well, a strike was avoided, and it was agreed that a similar procedure would be used in preparation for the 1977 steel negotiations.

DISCUSSION QUESTIONS

1. What is meant by the statement that, under collective bargaining, a company's wage level becomes indeterminate?

2. Explain the merits and limitations of J. R. Hicks' approach to wage bargaining.

3. Explain the meaning, and outline the main determinants of bargaining power.

4. Construct a bargaining situation in which all elements would contribute to maximum bargaining power for the union negotiator.

5. Can the tactical skill of a negotiator appreciably influence the outcome of bargaining? Explain.

6. Why may it be impossible to reach a settlement even when the eleventh-hour positions of the parties coincide or overlap?

7. What is an "unavoidable" strike? What are the main reasons for such a situation?

8. Why does the United States have a higher level of strike activity than Britain, Germany, or the Scandinavian countries?

9. Under what circumstances will a strike reduce national output?

READING SUGGESTIONS

The best modern statements of bargaining theory as applied to union–management negotiations are probably J. PEN, *The Wage Rate Under Collective Bargaining,* Cambridge, Mass.: Harvard University Press, 1959; and CARL M. STEVENS, *Strategy and Collective Bargaining Negotiation,* New York: McGraw-Hill Book Company, 1963. See also ALAN CODDINGTON, *Theories of the Bargaining Process,* Chicago: Aldine Publishing Company, 1968; GEORGE DE MENIL, *Bargaining Monopoly Power Versus Union Power,* Cambridge: The MIT Press, 1971; and ORLEY ASHENFELTER and GEORGE E. JOHNSON, "Bargaining Theory, Trade Unions, and Industrial Strike Activity," *American Economic Review,* March 1969, pp. 35–49.

For statistical studies of strike activity, see K. G. J. C. KNOWLES, *Strikes—A Study in Industrial Conflict,* Oxford: Blackwell, 1952; ARTHUR M. ROSS, and PAUL T. HARTMAN, *Changing Patterns of Industrial Conflict,* New York: John Wiley & Sons, Inc., 1960; and D. W. OXFORD, "The Incidence of Strikes in Australia," in J. E. ISAAC, and G. W. FORD (eds.), *Australian Labor Relations Readings,* Melbourne Sun Books, 1966, which contains international comparisons as well as Australian data.

VI

THE IMPACT OF THE UNION

In Parts I to III we examined how labor markets allocate the labor force among thousands of specialized occupations and determine wage rates for these occupations. But in the unionized sector of the economy terms of employment are set by the union–management negotiation described in Parts IV and V. The results may differ from those that would be reached in a nonunion market. The purpose of Part VI is to explore how far collective bargaining actually does alter market results. It thus serves as a capstone to the preceding parts.

Who is first in line for a vacant job? What are the tenure rights of an employee in his job? Under what conditions may he be transferred, demoted, laid off, or discharged? Chapter 20 examines union contract rules on these points and their possible effects on worker satisfaction and production efficiency. We consider also the union shop and other devices for union security, a subject that falls more logically here than at any other point.

Working conditions and work methods are regulated partly through contract rules, partly through the grievance procedure. Physical conditions of work often become a matter of dispute. Work speeds are usually regulated by formal or tacit agreement. This issue takes different forms, depending on whether workers are paid on an hourly basis, an output basis, or some combination of the two; and so we review union policies toward piece-rate or "incentive" payment. Unions in such industries as building construction, printing, and railroading have often required hiring of unnecessary labor (feather-bedding) or insisted on time-consuming methods (make-work rules). Unions in manufacturing have usually not opposed mechanization, but have tried in various ways to cushion its labor-displacing effects. Issues in these areas, which typically involve both production efficiency and worker welfare, are discussed in Chapter 21.

457

The wage effects of collective bargaining can be analyzed at both macro-economic and microeconomic levels. Macroeconomic studies usually conclude that the effect of unionism on the general level of either real or money wages is conjectural in direction and probably minor in size. With rather more confidence we can assert that unionism does have a significant impact on relative wage rates, on the *national wage structure*. The dimensions of wage structure that may be affected include relative wage levels of companies in the same industry, of different industries, of different occupational groups, and of different geographic regions. Chapter 22 reviews the evidence on actual union impact in each respect.

The concluding Chapter 23 attempts an overview of the effects of unionism and collective bargaining on our political economy. These effects are numerous, complex, and often uncertain. Even when an effect is clear, its desirability often remains a matter of judgment. Thus when one seeks an overall judgment of the social utility of unionism, reasonable men may reach different conclusions. The writer has tried not to impose his own scale of preferences on the reader, but to provide the raw materials from which the student can fashion his own conclusions.

20

Job Tenure and Job Security

The matters regulated by the collective agreement, or *union contract,* vary
greatly from one situation to the next, depending on the age of the agreement, the nature of the industry, the structure and policies of the union,
and the attitudes and objectives of management. Speaking generally, unions
attempt to regulate every kind of managerial action that directly affects the
welfare of the membership or the strength and security of the union itself.
Almost every aspect of personnel administration, and many aspects of
production management, eventually become matters of collective bargaining. A list of the subjects covered in the more than 100,000 union contracts
in the United States would include hundreds of items; and with respect to
each of these, many different contract provisions have been worked out to
meet differing circumstances.

To do justice to this wealth of issues and variety of solutions would
require a separate book.[1] In the limited space available here it is necessary
to concentrate on a few key issues and, with respect to each issue, to discuss
the general objectives and attitudes of the parties rather than detailed differences in contract arrangements The student who wishes to examine the
variety of contract provisions currently existing on any subject can find this
information in a number of convenient sources.[2]

---

[1] For a survey of the detailed issues that arise in collective bargaining and the
alternative methods of handling them, see Neil W. Chamberlain, *Collective Bargaining* (New York: McGraw-Hill Book Company, 1955); and John T. Dunlop and
James J. Healey, *Collective Bargaining: Principles and Cases,* rev. ed. (Homewood,
Ill. Richard D. Irwin, Inc., 1953).

[2] Notably the file of current union contracts maintained by the Bureau of Labor
Statistics of the Department of Labor, and the current labor services issued by
Prentice-Hall, Inc., and others.

Union contracts normally contain a number of procedural provisions, designed to set the general framework of relations between the parties. These include provisions concerning recognition and status of the union, rights and prerogatives of management, duration of the agreement and the method of extending or renewing it, prevention of strikes and lockouts during the life of the agreement, and handling of grievances arising under the contract.

The substantive provisions of the contract may be organized into three broad groups:

1. *Job tenure and job security.* This includes all provisions concerning hiring, training, assignment to work, promotion and transfer, layoff and recall, and discharge. Since length of service (seniority) is an important criterion in some of these decisions, the contract must specify how seniority is to be calculated and applied.

2. *Work schedules, work speeds, and production methods.* This includes determination of the standard workday and workweek, and payment for work in excess of the standard schedule. It covers also the determination of proper work speeds—size of machine assignments, proper speed of assembly lines, time standards and work quotas under incentive systems, and similar matters. Working conditions of every sort—including health, safety, sanitation, heating and lighting, and ventilation—are included. Finally, the agreement may touch on certain aspects of production methods—methods of work that may be used, the number of workers to be used on a particular job, and introduction of new machinery and production processes.

3. *Amount and method of compensation.* This includes provisions concerning the basic wage schedule and general changes in this schedule; the method of wage payment, and, if a piece-rate or incentive system is used, the extent of union participation in the administration of the system; setting of wage rates on new or changed jobs; wage increases for individual workers on a seniority or merit basis; and a wide variety of indirect or supplementary wage payments to workers, including pension funds, health and welfare funds, and supplementary unemployment benefit plans.

In this and the next two chapters, we shall examine these three groups in turn. Note that they are increasingly economic, in the sense of affecting labor costs per unit of output. Methods of hiring, promotion, and layoff doubtless affect costs, but the effect is indirect and hard to estimate. Work speeds and production methods have a clearer effect, since they determine how much output the worker delivers in exchange for his wage. The wage itself, including supplementary, or *fringe,* benefits, bears directly on costs. So all three groups are of concern to the employer; and for different reasons, each is important to the worker as well. The first affects his employment opportunities and job security; the second affects the pleasantness of his daily life on the job; and the third sets limits to his standard of living.

CONTROL OF HIRING:
APPRENTICESHIP; THE CLOSED SHOP

Economic reasoning suggests that it is natural for unions to take an interest in the supply of labor. Reducing the supply of a particular kind of labor is one way of raising its price.

One way of reducing supply might be through control of training opportunites. Training is important mainly for a limited number of skilled trades. Semiskilled jobs can be learned quickly and are normally learned on the job. The skilled crafts require longer training and experience, and are often learned in advance of employment either through vocational school courses or apprentice training programs. Control of the number admitted to such programs could conceivably be used to restrict the supply of labor.

This has not happened in practice, partly because there are so many other ways in which one can learn a skilled trade. Many men learn trades during service in the armed forces. Semiskilled workers are often trained and upgraded to skilled jobs within the plant. Many people simply pick up a trade by getting a smattering of it, finding someone willing to hire them, and improving their competence as they go along. Every farmboy naturally becomes something of a carpenter, painter, and auto mechanic. Only a minor part of the supply of skilled craftsmen comes from formal apprenticeship programs. The number completing such programs has varied recently between 25,000 and 30,000 per year.[3] Thus apprenticeship can scarcely form an effective method of restricting labor supply.

Unions have nevertheless taken an active interest in apprenticeship programs for several reasons. Skilled workers have pride in their craft and would like to see the next generation get a thorough training. They want to make employers pay high enough wages to apprentices so that they do not become a source of cheap labor that could undercut the union scale. There is usually a contract provision that the apprentice shall start out at, say, 40 percent of the journeyman's rate, and work up to this rate by steps over his period of training. Craftsmen also want adequate opportunity for their sons to gain admission as apprentices. It is as customary for a plumber's son to become a plumber as for a doctor's son to become a doctor.

The Machinists, Electrical Workers, Typographers, Plumbers, and Boilermakers have been particularly active in developing apprenticeship programs in cooperation with employers in their respective industries. The

---

[3] *Manpower Report of the President* (Washington, D.C.: Government Printing Office, 1969), pp. 235, 251.

Bureau of Apprenticeship and Training in the U.S. Department of Labor has national responsibility for fostering such programs and setting minimum standards for their operation. The main problem is not union reluctance to permit more apprentices to be trained, but rather employer reluctance to take on as many apprentices as union regulations allow. The employer puts considerable investment into each apprentice, but has no assurance that the worker will stay with him beyond the apprenticeship period. So it is to each employer's interest to persuade *other* employers in his industry to train apprentices whom he will later be able to hire away from them. Heavier investment in training, with each employer bearing his proper share of the cost, might well benefit employers as a group; but to sell this idea and work out an acceptable program is often difficult.

Granted that a union can rarely control the number of persons who learn a particular trade, it might still control the number admitted to the union. Then if it could get employers to hire only people who are already union members (a *closed shop* arrangement), it would have effective control of the labor supply. Admission to the union could be regulated either by closing the books when the number of union members equals the number demanded by employers at the union wage rate, or by charging an initiation fee high enough to reduce applications to the desired level.

Suppose that the demand and supply curves for a particular craft are shown by the solid lines in Figure 20–1. The wage rate in a competitive

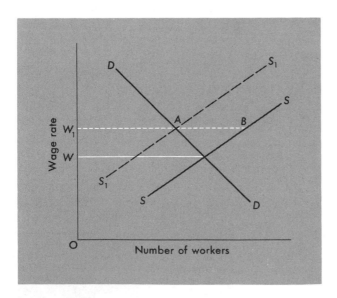

Figure 20–1

Methods of Controlling Labor Supply

labor market would be W. The number seeking employment just equals the number desired by employers, and the market is cleared. The union is strong enough, however, to secure a wage of W_1 and to insist on a closed shop rule. At this wage, the number seeking work in the trade exceeds the number employers will hire by the distance AB. The union might do one of two things. It might say: "We will admit only W_1A people to the union, and the rest must remain outside." This requires some way of selecting the lucky people to be admitted. Alternatively, it might charge a stiff initiation fee for admission to the union. A charge for admission, by reducing the net returns from the occupation, will reduce the number seeking employment at a given wage; that is, it will shift the labor supply curve to the left. The union could discover by experiment an initiaition fee just high enough to shift labor supply from SS to S_1S_1. Then the number spontaneously seeking employment would once more equal the number desired by employers.

Unions actually do not make much use of either method. That they do not use the second method is shown by the moderate level of union initiation fees. Out of 39,000 local unions filing reports under the Landrum–Griffin Act, only 342 reported initiation fees of more than $250, and the highest fee reported by any local was $1,400. This must be well below the value of union membership in many cases. Becker reports that "New York City taxicab medallions have sold for about $17,000 in recent years, and San Francisco papers in 1959 reported a figure of $16,000 for the transfer of licenses to operate a taxicab in that city. The value of entry to a union with a 20 percent effect on relative earnings would be of this order of magnitude even at fairly high interest rates." [4] One reason for not using high fees as a job rationing device is doubtless that it would outrage public opinion and publicize the monopolistic level of the union wage.

One finds occasional cases of arbitrary closing of the union books to exclude labor and buttress a high wage scale.[5] But these cases are exceptional. To leave a surplus of eager applicants (shown by AB in Figure 20–1) outside the union is a standing invitation for employers to hire these people at less than union wage rates. It is safer to take into the union every-

---

[4] Albert Rees, *The Economics of Trade Unions* (Chicago: The University of Chicago Press, 1962), p. 128; as taken from Gary S. Becker, "Union Restrictions on Entry," in Philip D. Bradley (ed.), *The Public Stake in Union Power* (Charlottesville: University of Virginia Press, 1959). Professor Rees adds in a footnote: "Membership in a union with an effect of 20 percent on annual earnings would increase earnings $1,000 a year for a man whose alternative earnings were $5,000. The present value of an annuity of $1,000 a year for 40 years is over $15,000 at an interest rate of 6 percent."

[5] An example of a closed union is the Newspaper and Mail Deliverers' Union of New York, which for years has maintained an illegal closed shop in violation of the Taft–Hartley Act. Memberships in it are reported to have sold for as much as $5,000, although about $500 is said to be the usual price. Sumner H. Slichter, James J. Healy, and E. Robert Livernash, *The Impact of Collective Bargaining on Management* (Washington, D.C.: The Brookings Institution, 1960), p. 41.

one who applies, and this also brings in more dues revenue. Then, if there is less than enough work to go around, the union can devise rules for allocating this work among the membership.

When an exceptional rise in labor demand is expected to subside in the near future, a local union sometimes decides to meet this rise, not by enlarging its regular membership, but by allowing outsiders to work temporarily under a *permit card* system. This is a legitimate way of covering seasonal peaks of employment in irregular industries such as food processing or construction, or of meeting labor needs on a large construction project in a remote locality where the regular labor force is small. Some locals, however, have abused the permit system by refusing admission even to regularly employed workers, and then charging them high fees for the right to work. National unions almost invariably discourage such practices, and they are also regulated by legislation. The Landrum–Griffin Act requires local unions to report on their permit fees, and the Taft–Hartley Act prohibits the charging of fees higher than the union's normal dues.

The main examples of labor supply restriction occur in certain occupations covered by state licensing regulations. A law is passed providing that barbers, say, can be admitted to the trade only after passing an examination set by a state licensing board. (For "barbers" read also "plumbers" or "elecricians," or, for that matter, "accountants," "lawyers," or "doctors.") To no one's surprise, the licensing board turns out to consist of representatives of the barbers' union and the master barbers' (employers) association. The number of candidates who "pass" is held down to a level that does not endanger the jobs or wage scale of those already employed in the industry. This is typically part of a broader pattern of monopolistic control over prices, wages, and admission of new employers as well as new workers.

If the closed shop is ordinarily not used to control the number admitted to an occupation, what is the point of the closed shop? First, it is traditional in many of the skilled trades. In Britain, the principle that a union craftsman will not work alongside a nonunion man is so well established that no formal closed-shop rules are necessary. Second, it strengthens the union organization. If nonunion men cannot even get hired, the employer has no opportunity to undermine and weaken the union. In addition to this defensive function, the closed shop enables the union to ration job opportunities among members of the craft on some equitable basis; and it often furnishes employers with a central employment agency.

The closed shop is typically accompanied by an arrangement under which the union acts as an employment agency for the industry and provides workers to individual employers on request. This is convenient where employers are small, as in clothing manufacture or job printing, or where jobs are of short duration and each employer's needs fluctuate widely, as in building construction. Central hiring is useful also in industries where there is a good deal of seasonal or casual unemployment, such as longshoring and merchant shipping. Where there is regular year-round employment, as in most manufacturing industries, the unions have taken little interest in closed-shop clauses or central hiring facilities.

In 1946, just before passage of the Taft–Hartley Act, the closed shop appeared in about one-third of all union contracts. The Taft–Hartley Act forbade the closed shop, and it has almost vanished from union contracts; but this is not to say that the practice has disappeared. In building construction, the closed shop continued in open defiance of the Taft–Hartley Act and was eventually (in effect) relegalized by the Landrum–Griffin Act. In other cases the former contract provisions have been replaced by new clauses intended to have the same effect. For example, the contract may provide that the union shall have first opportunity to fill job vacancies, and that only if the union cannot provide workers within a certain period will the employer look elsewhere; or that preference in employment will be given to workers employed in the industry before a certain date, that is, during the closed-shop period, hence necessarily union members; or that preference will be given to graduates of a training program operated by the union; or simply that preference will be given to "experienced" or "qualified" workers. There are additional cases in which a bootleg closed shop has continued by tacit agreement between the union and employer with no contract provision. Where there is a long tradition that union members will not work alongside nonunion men, it is simpler for the employer to accept this tradition than to assert his rights and lose his labor.

The main practical problem associated with a closed shop is that of union admission requirements. Where there is a tacit closed shop, and where the union declines to admit certain kinds of workers—women, non-whites, or whatever—these people are barred from employment in the industry. This has not been an important problem in industrial unions, since they rarely have the closed shop and rarely discriminate in membership. Some of the craft unions have followed discriminatory policies, however, and this has made it hard particularly for nonwhite workers to get into the building trades, railroad trades, and some other areas of employment. The situation is all the more difficult because employers and the union are usually in full agreement on this policy.

COMPULSORY MEMBERSHIP: THE UNION SHOP

More than four-fifths of all union contracts contain some provision for union security. Much the commonest provision is a straight *union shop*. This leaves the employer free to hire at will; but after the worker has served his probationary period and becomes a regular member of the plant

labor force, he is required to join the union. If he declines to do so, or if
he drops out of the union, the employer must discharge him. A variant of
the union shop is the *maintenance-of-membership* clause. This does not
compel any worker to join; but if he chooses to join, he must remain in for
the duration of the contract as a condition of employment. Another rather
rare variant is the *agency shop,* under which a worker who declines to join
is obliged to pay the union a fee—usually set at the level of the monthly
dues—in return for the collective bargaining service that it is rendering him.

In earlier times the union shop gave union leaders a powerful disciplinary weapon over recalcitrant members. Anyone who fell foul of the
existing leadership could be expelled from the union and would then be
out of a job. This doubtless contributed to the growth of oppressive or corrupt practices in some unions. To correct this, the Taft–Hartley Act provided that the employer is not obliged to discharge a worker who has been
expelled from, or denied admission to, the union on any ground other than
failure to tender the regular dues and initiation fees.

The union shop itself is legal under the Taft–Hartley Act. But the act
contains a curious provision that, where any state has passed a law forbidding the union shop, the state law shall take precedence. This reverses
the normal rule that federal law has precedence as regards workers in
interstate commerce. Twenty states have laws (usually labeled *right-to-
work laws*) that prohibit both the closed and union shop. These states are
almost all in the South and West (Indiana is the only major industrial state
with such a statute), and include only about 15 percent of industrial employment in the country. Unions have fought these laws vigorously on the
ground that they will destroy trade unionism, while employer and farm
groups have hailed them as the Magna Carta of the working man. It is
doubtful that either claim could be substantiated. Research studies suggest
that the practical effect of these laws has been small.[6] Employers who want
good relations with their unions have usually winked at the law, just as
employers in traditional closed-shop industries have winked at the Taft–
Hartley Act. Where relations are bad, however, and where the employer
wants to mount a drive against the union, an antiunion-shop law may give
him an additional weapon.

Some Pros and Cons of the Union Shop

The legitimacy of the union shop has been argued for generations,
and the issue arouses strong emotion on both sides. Unionists argue that,
since everyone in the bargaining unit benefits from the contract terms
established by the union, everyone should be required to contribute to the

---

[6] See, for example, Frederic Myers, *"Right to Work" in Practice* (New York:
Fund for the Republic, 1959).

union's support. If this is not the case, some workers will receive a "free ride" at the expense of their fellow workers. This situation is as unfair as one in which citizens of a community could decide whether or not they wish to pay taxes.

A more powerful argument for the union shop is that only if the union's existence is secure can it afford to cooperate with management and play a constructive role in the operation of the enterprise. The union interprets management's denial of the union shop as a lack of complete acceptance of collective bargaining, an indication that management does not consider the union a permanent part of the enterprise and hopes in time to be rid of it. The union must, therefore, devote much of its energy to keeping its fences mended against employer attack. It must try to hem in the employer by contract restrictions at any point where he might try to discriminate against union men; it must limit his power to select, promote, transfer, lay off, and discharge. It must manufacture enough grievances to keep the workers convinced that the employer is a tricky fellow and that the union is essential for their protection. It must give good service on grievances to its members, and poor service or no service to nonmembers, in order to emphasize the practical advantages of union membership; this discrimination makes for unequal treatment and ill-feeling within the labor force.

Employer acceptance of the union shop, it is argued, would make all this unnecessary. The time of union officials could be put to constructive use in ironing out personnel problems and production difficulties, giving prompt attention to genuine grievances, performing educational functions, and cooperating with management in other ways. Freed of any necessity to stir up antagonism to the employer in order to hold their members in line, union leaders could afford to take a reasonable position on disputed issues.

This general point of view is supported by a number of careful students of the subject. Slichter, for example, concludes that the union shop is desirable for the contribution it can make to stable industrial relations. He points out that a union whose security is beyond question can afford to be more reasonable on other matters—notably promotions, layoffs, and other points at which discrimination might be practiced against union members. A union that fears for its life must necessarily try to restrict the employer at all these points. Slichter concludes, therefore, that the employer can secure a generally more favorable contract by conceding the union-shop issue at the outset.[7]

On the other hand, many management officials argue that the union shop is coercive and involves an undue encroachment on the liberty of the individual worker. In a free society, a worker should be able to seek and

---

[7] See Sumner H. Slichter, *Union Policies and Industrial Management* (Washington, D.C.: The Brookings Institution, 1941), Chap. 3.

accept employment with any employer who is willing to hire him, without paying tribute to a third party. The union shop forces him to join an organization of which he may not approve, and forces him to pay for the right to work, a right which he should enjoy as a citizen.

This argument that the union shop coerces workers into unionism against their will appears to have been overdone. Few workers seem to have any conscientious objection to unionism. Most of those who stay out of the union do so simply out of inertia or to avoid dues payments. The coercion involved in requiring them to join the union is mainly financial, and is no greater than that involved in levying payroll taxes on them for social security or other purposes. There is abundant evidence that where the union shop has been in effect in the past, the great majority of workers favor its continuance. The Taft–Hartley Act originally provided that a union-shop clause could not be included in a union contract unless a majority of the employees in the bargaining unit voted in favor of it in a secret ballot conducted by the National Labor Relations Board. During the first year of the act's operation, some 22,000 elections were held under this section. The union shop was upheld in more than 98 percent of these cases and secured more than 95 percent of all ballots cast. It soon became clear, in fact, that these union-shop referenda were simply an unnecessary expense to the government, and the act was subsequently amended to eliminate the referendum requirement.

Beneath the arguments over the union-shop issue lies the hard fact of a power struggle. A union security clause strengthens the union's position in the shop, renders it less vulnerable to attack by the employer or rival unions, and helps to make it a permanent institution. It also makes the position of union officials more secure and less arduous. Management opposition to the union shop is based mainly on a recognition of these facts. Most managements see no reason to go out of their way in helping the union to become a permanent fixture. This does not necessarily mean that they have any hope of breaking the union. Their strategy may be merely to fight an effective delaying action. If the union can be kept busy holding its membership together, it will be in a weaker position to press fresh demands on the employer.

One's attitude toward the union shop is bound to depend on how one answers the following question: Is it desirable to maintain strong, stable, and permanent unions in American industry? If one answers "no" to this question, the open-shop position follows automatically. If one answers "yes," a strong case can be made for a union-shop clause. There seems little doubt that a union is better able to function in a peaceful and constructive way if it embraces most or all of the labor force. It is unreasonable to demand that unions be "responsible" while at the same time denying union officers the control over their membership that would make group responsibility effective.

An issue related to the union shop should be noted in conclusion. Union demands for a union- or closed-shop clause have usually been accompanied by a demand for the *checkoff*. This is an arrangement by which the regular weekly or monthly dues of union members are deducted from their paychecks by the employer and transmitted in a lump sum to the union. Most unions prefer the checkoff, partly because it saves them a good deal of effort and unpleasantness in collecting dues from delinquent members, and partly because it still further regularizes and entrenches the position of the union in the plant. Most managements oppose the checkoff because it involves the company in effort and expense for the primary benefit of the union.

In general, where one finds a closed-shop, union-shop, or maintenance-of-membership provision, one is likely to find the checkoff as well. About two-thirds of all union contracts contain this provision. There are many detailed variations in checkoff clauses. Under some contracts, dues are checked off automatically for all union members; under others, they are checked off unless the worker asks the company in writing not to deduct his dues; in still other cases, the dues are deducted only if the worker makes a positive request in writing that this be done. The Taft–Hartley Act provides that a dues checkoff requires the written consent of each employee; but this consent is rarely refused. The whole issue, while presenting many possibilities for technical arguments, is subsidiary to the broader argument over the union shop. The outcome of that argument usually determines the outcome of the checkoff argument as well.

JOB TENURE: SECURITY AND OPPORTUNITY

An important group of provisions in union contracts concerns the conditions under which individual workers shall have access to vacant jobs, the rules governing their tenure of the job, and the conditions under which they may be separated from employment. So important is this matter that Perlman and others have found in it the key to the growth and persistence of trade unionism. Workers are continually faced with a scarcity of available jobs, and consciousness of this scarcity molds union philosophy and tactics. The union is a method of controlling the job opportunities in a craft or industry and of distributing these opportunities among union members according to some equitable principle.

The union tries to introduce into industry a "civil service system" of job tenure. The worker ceases to be so many units of productive power, which can be shifted about in the plant or dispensed with altogether at the pleasure of the employer. He becomes an individual with a system of rights, which the employer is bound to observe and which can be defended through the grievance procedure. The different matters regulated by this system of rights will be examined briefly in this section.

The Seniority Principle

Over the past thirty years there has been increasing acceptance of the principle that a worker's job rights should be related to his length of service. Commonsense ideas of equity suggest that a man who has devoted more years to the company deserves more of the company in return. Seniority is objective, relatively easy to measure and apply, and easy to defend before workers and outside arbitrators.

Seniority appears in the union contract in two main ways. First, it usually governs eligibility for fringe benefits: vacations, paid holidays, pensions, severance pay, sick-leave provisions, insurance and health services, profit sharing, supplementary unemployment benefits, and the rest. In bargaining over these issues, employers have usually insisted, and unions have accepted, that a man's entitlement to benefits should vary with length of service. The twenty-year man gets longer paid vacations, larger pension rights, more sick leave, and so on, than the two-year man. Slichter, Healy, and Livernash call this *benefit seniority.*

The second area they term *competitive status seniority.* Here the problem is one of ranking workers relative to each other. Several workers are in competition to get a promotion or avoid a layoff, and the seniority principle is used to resolve the competition. The most obvious applications are to layoff, transfer, and promotion; but there are also many others. The senior worker may be given first choice in picking vacation periods. He may be given first chance to earn more money through overtime work. He may lay claim to the newest of a group of machines, or to the machine in the pleasantest location. Spaces in the company parking lot may be allocated on a seniority basis. In one company the senior men are allowed to punch out first on the time clock at the end of the day.

Benefit seniority is almost always calculated from the date of first employment wth the company; but competitive status seniority is harder to calculate and apply. Suppose Bill Jones has been with the company fifteen years, working five years in department *A,* five years in department *B,* and five years in his present job in department *C.* Layoffs now become necessary in department *C,* and it is agreed that they should be in order of seniority. What is Bill Jones' seniority in Department *C?* Is it fifteen years, or only five years? If he is laid off from department *C,* can he go back to his previous job in department *B* and displace ("bump") some less senior worker? And how much seniority does he have in department *B?* The rules have to be spelled out in the contract; and the rules may be different for different problems—one principle for promotion, another for layoff, and so on. These fine details have important effects on employee security and on management's freedom to deploy its work force to greatest effect.

Sharing of Work Opportunities; Irregular Industries

In some industries, continuous attachment to a single employer is impossible by the nature of the industry. Seamen are often paid off at the end of each voyage and, after a shorter or longer period "on the beach," sign on with another vessel for a new voyage. In longshoring, the amount of work coming into a particular pier is irregular, depending on what ships happen to arrive on a particular day. When a cargo comes in and has to be unloaded, it is necessary to hire a gang of longshoremen on the spot; when the vessel is unloaded, their job ends. In other industries, production is highly seasonal. Building construction tapers off in the late fall and revives in the early spring. Each worker naturally wants to be the last man laid off in the fall and the first man hired in the spring. The men's and women's clothing industries have two production seasons during the year, one for the spring trade, the other for the fall trade. During each of these seasons activity begins slowly, mounts to a peak of production and employment, and then declines. Again, each worker in the industry wants to be the first hired and the last laid off.

In the absence of contract rules concerning hiring, the bulk of the work in such industries would go to men who were of superior efficiency or who had special "pull" with foremen and hiring officials. Workers who got relatively little work would feel that the union was not serving them effectively and would be tempted to drop out. Partly to preserve the organization, partly out of consideration of equity, the union attempts to ensure that the available work is shared more or less equally among the membership.

Where employers are numerous and small, this attempt may require union control over the referral of workers to jobs. It is no accident that the union office has been used as an employment agency in the building, printing, and clothing industries, or that the union *hiring hall* has developed in longshoring and merchant shipping.

The devices used to ensure something like equal division of work vary from one industry to the next. In the shipping industry, the man who has been longest "on the beach" gets the first opportunity to sign up for a new voyage; all job vacancies and referrals to work are cleared through the union hiring hall. In longshoring work in Pacific Coast ports, a regular list of *gangs* (work teams) is maintained at union headquarters, and gangs are dispatched to work in the order in which they appear on this list. When a gang comes off the job it must go to the bottom of the list and wait until its number comes up again before being dispatched to a new job.

The hiring-hall arrangement has traditionally been a closed-shop arrangement as well, and was therefore rendered unlawful by the Taft–Hartley Act. The maritime unions, however, have succeeded in developing formulas that have maintained the hiring hall relatively unchanged. In merchant shipping, preference in hiring is no longer given to union members as such, but is given to men who have sailed previously on the ships of members of the employers' association. Since the great majority of seamen had been unionized in the past, this amounts to almost the same thing. The new arrangement appears to have had little effect on hiring-hall practices. The Taft–Hartley Act requires that, if nonunion workers do come to the hiring hall, they must be given the same service as union members and referred to work on a nondiscriminatory basis.

In the clothing industries, the unions have favored reduction in working hours rather than layoffs as work tapers off toward the end of a season. In this way all workers in a shop get an equal amount of work as long as work is available. In building construction, there has been some experimentation with "first off, first on" rules, under which the first man laid off in the fall would be dispatched to the first job opening in the spring. This sort of rule, however, presents certain difficulties. The first men laid off in the fall may be chronic drunkards or undesirable for other reasons. Experience has shown that, where the first employer who starts building work in the spring is forced to hire those undesirables, there is a good deal of jockeying among employers to avoid this unpleasant necessity. Whether for this or other reasons, the building trades have done less than most other unions to enforce formal work-sharing rules.

Sharing of Work Opportunities: Reductions in Production Schedules

Even in stable industries the labor requirements of a firm may vary somewhat from month to month. It may fail to secure a large order on which it has been counting, the sales of a new product line may be disappointing, or a general business recession may develop. This situation causes a reduction in production schedules and man-hours worked. Several questions then arise: Who is to bear the brunt of the reduction in employment? How shall the work that is left be distributed among those who want it?

A reduction in production schedules can be met either by laying off workers, by reducing the number of hours worked per week, or by a combination of these methods. One possibility is to keep everyone on the payroll but to work the plant fewer hours per week. This policy is beneficial to the short-service employees, since it gives them some work, whereas layoffs based on length of service would put them out of work completely. Even the long-service workers are likely to consider it equitable that work opportunities be shared among the entire labor force. A policy of work sharing also has certain advantages to management, since it enables the plant labor force to be held together and eases the problem of increasing production when demand revives.

It is necessary, however, to set some limit to a work-sharing policy. If hours fall below thirty per week, most workers will feel that they are sharing poverty rather than opportunity. They will in fact be earning little more than the unemployment compensation they would receive if totally unemployed. If the drop in demand is severe and prolonged, therefore, it will be necessary to go beyond hours reduction to layoff of workers. Many union contracts provide for something like the following combination of procedures to meet a decline in production: first, lay off all temporary and probationary employees; second, reduce hours of work as required down to some minimum—say thirty-two hours per week; third, if these measures are insufficient, begin to lay off members of the regular work force.

Where layoffs have to be made, unions typically and successfully insist that they should be made on a seniority basis. They argue that the workers with greater length of service will, in general, be more efficient at their jobs and more valuable to the company. In addition, the long-service workers will usually be men with family responsibilities, whose incomes should be protected on social grounds. Primarily, however, unions like the simplicity and definiteness of a seniority system, which makes it impossible for the employer or the foreman to use layoffs as an occasion for "taking it out" on certain workers. In some industries, such as the railroads, the older men are dominant in union affairs, and this may have something to do with union adherence to the seniority principle. By the same token, a straight seniority rule runs the risk of alienating the young men by forcing them to bear the brunt of cyclical unemployment. This situation may cause serious factional conflict between younger and older men in the union, as has happened more than once in the railroad trades.

It is easier to defend the seniority principle than it is to work out detailed regulations for applying it. A central issue here is the size of the *seniority district*. Should seniority be considered as the man's length of service in a particular occupation, or in a particular department of the plant, or in plants as a whole, or in all plants of a multiplant company? Under plant-wide seniority a man laid off in one department may be able to shift over and bump a worker in an entirely different department whose seniority is less than his own, who in turn may bump someone in a third department. A single layoff may thus set off a chain of displacements throughout the plant. The more narrowly the seniority unit is defined, the smaller is the possibility of bumping and consequently the smaller the protection afforded to long-service employees. The union will typically argue for broad seniority units in order to achieve maximum employee protection, while management will argue for narrower units in order to minimize the disruption of work teams and the added training time that may result from excessive bumping. Arguments over the drafting of seniority clauses and their application to individual workers consume a good proportion of union and management time in collective bargaining.

Whatever procedure is chosen for layoffs normally applies also to rehiring. Workers are recalled to work in reverse order from that in which they were laid off—"last off, first in." The brunt of unemployment is thus borne by those with the shortest period of service.

Some agreements provide that "key men" may be exempted from the operation of the seniority rule. These men are designated by management, and it is usually provided that they may not exceed a certain percentage of the total labor force. The argument of management for this provision is that it is desirable during depression to hold together a skeleton force of men trained for strategic positions in the plant. If this force is broken up through strict application of a seniority rule, it may be difficult and costly to rebuild it. The union sometimes makes a similar argument that, if key union officials are laid off during depression, smooth administration of the union contract will be seriously hampered. On this ground they urge *superseniority* for shop stewards and other union officials; that is, that these men be placed automatically at the top of the seniority lists in their respective departments. Management frequently objects to this provision on the ground that it creates a privileged class and places too high a premium on running for union office. Despite the objections, superseniority clauses appear in an increasing percentage of union agreements.

Promotion and Transfers

It is increasingly the practice in modern industry to fill "good" vacancies in the plant by promoting members of the present work force. New workers usually enter the plant in the least desirable jobs and work their way up as vacancies arise. The concept of "promotion" has more dimensions than might occur to an outside observer. Most obvious is movement to a job involving greater skill and a higher wage. But movement from the night shift to the day shift on the same job would also be considered a promotion by most workers, as would transfer to a lighter but equally well-paid job, or even movement to the newest machine or the pleasantest location in a particular work group.

The nonunion employer is free to decide whether to fill a vacancy from the outside or from within and, in the latter case, to decide who should be promoted. Decisions are made unilaterally and without advance notice. A union typically insists, as a minimum, that notice of vacancies shall be posted and that present employees shall have opportunity to apply. This enables each worker to know about vacancies as they arise, to decide whether a particular job would be a promotion *for him,* and to make his bid for it if he wants to.

Most unions try to make length of service the dominant consideration in promotion as well as in layoffs. Employers naturally resist this demand, which they feel would hamper them in rewarding merit and in selecting the most efficient man available for each job. Few contracts outside the railroad industry specify seniority as the *sole* criterion for promotion. The usual outcome is a compromise providing that where ability is relatively equal the senior man shall be promoted, or that the senior man shall be promoted if competent to do the job, or simply that both ability and length of service shall be considered in making promotion decisions. The meaning of these general statements is then worked out through the grievance procedure in individual cases. The practical outcome is usually that seniority governs in the absence of marked differences of ability among the candidates, and that where management believes there is a marked difference of ability, it must be prepared to prove its case. Emphasis on the seniority factor is increasing in the course of time.

The Economic Impact of Seniority

Increasing emphasis on seniority in both layoffs and promotions has caused some apprehension concerning the long-run economic consequences.

We rely heavily on free worker choice in the labor market both to get the right man to the right job and to correct serious discrepancies in the terms offered by different employers. Anything that reduces workers' ability to make a free choice among alternative employers hampers the market in performing these functions. Heavy emphasis on seniority, it is argued, ties the worker increasingly to his present employer, reduces actual and potential labor mobility, and thus interferes with the market mechanism. If new employees are hired only for the least attractive positions while "good" vacancies are filled from within, the worker who seeks to change employers runs a serious risk. He may have to step down to the bottom of the occupational ladder and work his way up again slowly and painfully, meanwhile being subject to the risk of layoff as a short-service employee. The obvious moral is to stay where you are and accumulate as much seniority as possible, thus insuring yourself against layoff and strengthening your chances of promotion.

Seniority, however, is only one of numerous factors making for strong attachment of workers to their present jobs. Most people prefer stability to change in any event. Accumulated pension rights and other company benefits make it increasingly worthwhile to stay on with the same employer. Long service typically confers certain privileges even where strict seniority does not govern. It is questionable whether seniority does much more to reduce labor mobility.

Moreover, labor mobility can be too high as well as too low. It is not desirable that everyone in the labor force shuttle about constantly from job to job. Efficient operation of the market requires only a mobile minority, which may be made up largely of new entrants to the labor force plus the unemployed. For the bulk of the labor force, stability has advantages in terms of productive efficiency as well as personal satisfaction. Thus even if it could be shown that seniority reduces labor mobility, one could not conclude that this result is necessarily harmful.

Seniority in promotions is often criticized on efficiency grounds. If capable young men find that promotion comes only through serving time and bears no relation to effort, they may decide to exert less effort and initiative. The efficiency of the economy will suffer also through failure to assign the most productive worker to each job.

There is a problem here, but it may not be as serious in practice as it may appear on paper. Many low-skilled, machine-paced jobs leave little scope for differences of ability or effort. There is likely also to be some positive correlation between length of service in a plant and ability to perform successively higher jobs. On many production operations one finds a natural promotion ladder within a work team, and it is reasonable for men to work up from one rung to the next as vacancies occur. The fifth hand on a large paper machine becomes a fourth hand, then a third hand, and finally a machine tender in charge of the crew. Promotions to foremanships and other supervisory jobs are almost always at the sole discretion of management and are made on a merit basis.

As regards seniority in layoffs, it is argued that to give a long-service employee complete job security may cause him to work less diligently than he would with the possibility of layoff hanging constantly over his head. This argument implies that fear, or at least uncertainty about the future, will stimulate maximum effort. On the other hand, it is argued that people work best when they feel secure about their future and that seniority protection will therefore increase efficiency instead of reducing it. This whole question reduces to a difference of opinion over why men work well, a matter on which there is little reliable evidence.

Seniority rules prevent employers from following the traditional practice of "weeding out" the labor force during depression periods. They may even compel an employer to keep relatively inefficient people on his payroll indefinitely. The union replies to this, however, that the employer had ample opportunity to weed out these people during their probationary period in the plant. If he chose to keep them on, he made a mistake and must abide by the consequences. Supporters of seniority argue further that the inability of the employer to correct his hiring mistakes in later years will in time lead him to be more careful and make fewer mistakes, with benefit to all concerned.

It should be noted also that the employer retains the right, even after the probationary period, to discharge an employee for gross inefficiency, insubordination, or violation of plant rules. This is normally sufficient to prevent workers from abusing their seniority protection.

Even if it were decided that seniority rules make it more difficult for the individual employer to run his plant at minimum cost, this would not settle the matter from a social standpoint. The workers whom one employer "weeds out" in his search for efficiency must be hired by someone else or must become public charges. Seniority systems may be regarded as a method of distributing the less efficient workers more or less equitably among employers. Slichter points out that if employers were allowed to make layoffs on a strict efficiency basis, men over forty-five or fifty would be laid off in large numbers and would have great difficulty in finding new jobs.[8] Seniority rules may prolong their working lives to the age of sixty or sixty-five, with benefit both to themselves and to the economy. Apart from this, the peace of mind engendered by seniority rules must be counted as a positive benefit, albeit one that cannot be measured in monetary terms. Even if seniority did lead to a reduction in total physical output, which is doubtful, this reduction might be more than offset by psychological gain to the workers.

With respect to seniority in layoff and rehiring, then, one may conclude that the positive advantages probably outweigh any adverse effects. One cannot speak so confidently about seniority in promotions, and employers are probably wise in resisting this principle for skilled jobs, where unusual ability can really show itself.

Discipline and Discharge

One of the most delicate areas of day-to-day administration is the application of discipline, including use of the ultimate weapon of discharge. Because seniority now carries so many accumulated rights, discharge is a drastic economic penalty that requires careful consideration. The union is forced to defend its members against discharge except in the most flagrant circumstances. Yet management must retain reasonable latitude to apply discipline and to enforce minimum standards of efficiency.

The union contract normally recognizes management's right to discipline the work force and to take the initiative in applying penalties "for

---

[8] Slichter, *Union Policies and Industrial Management,* pp. 160–61.

just cause." What constitutes "just cause" may be spelled out in the contract itself or in supplementary rules issued by the company. Standard grounds for discipline include continued failure to meet production standards, disobeying instructions of the foreman, persistent absence from work without excuse, participating in wildcat strikes or slowdowns, fighting, gambling, drinking, smoking in prohibited areas, and other personal misdemeanors. For each kind of offense there is usually a graduated series of penalties, which may begin with an oral reprimand by the foreman for the first offense, and then go on to written reprimand, a brief suspension from work without pay, a longer suspension from work, and finally discharge. The worker has thus usually had a number of warnings before incurring the ultimate penalty. Some offenses, however, may be considered so serious that suspension or discharge follows immediately.

If a worker contends that he is not guilty of the offense with which he is charged, or that the penalty imposed was too severe, the case is taken up through the grievance procedure. Discharges, because of their serious consequences for the worker, are invariably appealed and a large percentage of them are carried all the way to arbitration. Arbitrators have been reluctant to uphold discharges, especially for long-service workers, unless the offense is serious and the evidence clear. The box score of discharge arbitrations shows that in a substantial majority of cases the arbitrator has either reversed management's decision or scaled down the penalty to a temporary suspension from work.[9]

The union check on management's unfettered right of discipline has doubtless improved plant administration in addition to benefiting employees. In preunion days the right of discharge was often grossly abused. The foreman could take out his temper on those under him without recourse, and favoritism and bribery were common. This produced much injustice without necessarily promoting efficiency. Protection against arbitrary discipline and discharge is probably the most important single benefit that the worker derives from trade unionism. More than anything else, this serves to make him a free citizen in the plant.

DISCUSSION QUESTIONS

1. Explain the main ways in which a union might try to restrict the supply of labor. Why is there little use of these methods in practice?

2. What are the advantages of a closed shop to the worker, the employer, and the union?

---

[9] For a detailed analysis, see Orme W. Phelps, *Discipline and Discharge in the Unionized Firm* (Berkeley and Los Angeles: University of California Press, 1959).

3. "The Taft–Hartley prohibition of the closed shop has had little practical effect and has simply encouraged law violation. It would be better to repeal this section of the act." Discuss.

4. What are the main arguments for and against the union shop?

5. Is there a conflict between the goal of stable collective bargaining, which is furthered by union-shop agreements, and the goal of maximum freedom for the individual worker? If so, how do you think the conflict might best be resolved?

6. What is the difference between *benefit seniority* and *competitive status seniority?* What are some of the difficulties in measuring seniority for the latter purpose?

7. What are the advantages and limitations of the seniority principle in making:
      (a) temporary layoffs?
      (b) permanent layoffs?
      (c) promotions?

READING SUGGESTIONS

In addition to general works on collective bargaining, the issues discussed in this chapter are examined in ORME W. PHELPS, *Discipline and Discharge in the Unionized Firm,* Berkeley and Los Angeles: University of California Press, 1959; ALBERT REES, *The Economics of Trade Unions,* Chicago: The University of Chicago Press, 1962; SUMNER H. SLICHTER, *Union Policies and Industrial Management,* Washington, D.C.: The Brookings Institution, 1941: SUMNER H. SLICHTER, JAMES J. HEALY, and E. ROBERT LIVERNASH, *The Impact of Collective Bargaining on Management,* Washington, D.C.: The Brookings Institution, 1960; PAUL SULTAN, *Right-To-work Laws,* Los Angeles: Institute of Industrial Relations, U.C.L.A., 1958.

21

Work Schedules, Work Speeds, and Production Methods

Unions are less directly concerned with production management than with personnel management. Their concern is limited to points at which production decisions affect the security or satisfaction of workers on their jobs. Unions are concerned that hours of work should be reasonable, that work speeds and work loads should be moderate, and that physical working conditions should be safe and comfortable. They are interested in avoiding sudden and large-scale displacement of labor as a result of technological change. They have sometimes encouraged the use of relatively expensive production methods in order to create additional employment.

The points at which union objectives impinge on production management are the subject of this chapter. The issues discussed have only one thing in common: All involve some aspect of production management, and all have a direct effect on production costs.

WORK SCHEDULES

The Fair Labor Standards Act establishes a normal forty-hour week for most industries, and prescribes time-and-a-half payment for overtime work. Union contracts, however, often go beyond this legal requirement. First, the contract regulates daily as well as weekly hours: for example, it may specify an eight-hour day and a five-day week. Thus a worker who put in forty hours during a certain week, but who worked ten hours on one day of that week, would not be entitled to overtime under the Fair Labor Standards Act but is entitled to two hours overtime under the union contract. Second, the union contract may set a weekly limit of less than forty hours. A number of unions now have standard workweeks in the range of thirty-two to thirty-seven hours, and even fewer hours are encountered occasionally. Third, the contract may impose heavier overtime penalties. Double time is often required for work on weekends and on specified holidays, and even triple time is not unheard of.

The intent of these provisions is to prevent overtime work by making it unduly expensive. The statistics of actual working hours suggest that this intent is usually realized. Weekly hours worked in manufacturing and most other industries have hovered around the forty-hour level since World War II. In contract construction, however, the average week is about thirty-seven hours, while in retail trade it has fallen gradually to below thirty-five hours.

During periods of peak demand, many employers face the question of whether to lengthen working hours or hire additional workers. Lengthening the workweek beyond the limit prescribed by the Fair Labor Standards Act or by union contract requires overtime payment. But recruiting, screening, and training new workers also involves costs, usually estimated at several hundred dollars per man. So, if the abnormal demand is expected to continue for only a short time, some employers will find it less expensive to offer overtime to the existing work force.[1] In the years from 1965 to 1969, the average workweek for all plants in durable goods manufacturing was about forty-two hours. This means that some plants were working substantial amounts of overtime.

We noted in Chapter 2 that some workers prefer a longer workweek than others. Those with low hourly earnings or high consumption goals or large family responsibilities may be unable to meet their income requirements in forty hours. So, when overtime is available, they are eager to apply for it. Indeed, the demand for overtime typically exceeds the amount available, requiring some method of rationing. Union contracts usually specify seniority as the basis for rationing, although some attempt to ensure an equal division of overtime, and some give weight to family responsibilities.

There are situations, however, in which the amount of overtime that employers require exceeds the amount that workers are willing to supply. This happened in the automobile industry during the peak production years of 1972 and 1973. Management, exercising its right to require overtime whenever needed to meet production schedules, assigned many workers to six-day weeks and sometimes to double shifts. Some workers concluded that the extra income did not compensate for the extra fatigue and complained strongly through union channels. In the 1973 contract negotiations the United Automobile Workers urged that overtime work be made voluntary rather than compulsory, and won some concessions.

---

[1] For an analysis of this choice problem, see W. Oi, "Labor as a Quasi-fixed Factor," *Journal of Political Economy* (December 1962), pp. 538–55.

Strong unions have occasionally demanded a short workweek, not to reduce actual working hours, but to raise members' incomes. The New York local of the International Brotherhood of Electrical Workers, for example, has established a basic twenty-five hour week on construction jobs. This presumably does not mean that electricians will sit idle the rest of the week. Some of them will continue to work longer hours on their regular job, drawing time and a half for the hours beyond twenty-five. Others may devote time to private electrical repair work or other sideline activities. The twenty-five-hour week is mainly an income-raising rather than work-spreading device.

A special scheduling problem arises in continuous-process industries where plants must operate around the clock. Such a plant may work a day shift from 8 A.M. to 4 P.M., a second shift from 4 P.M. to midnight, and a third or "graveyard" shift from midnight to 8 A.M. Even where continuous operation is not essential, two- or three-shift operation produces more output from the same plant, thus lowering overhead costs per unit. Against this must be set the fact that labor cost per unit is likely to increase. Workers on second shifts typically produce somewhat less than on the day shift, while third-shift output is substantially lower.

When two or three shifts are operated, the question arises of who will man the later shifts, which most workers consider less attractive because they interfere with sleep, recreation, and family life. The contract usually provides a premium of so many cents per hour for second-shift workers, and a still higher premium for those on the third shift. The contract also typically provides that, as vacancies occur on the more desirable shifts, workers may apply for transfer to them on a seniority basis.

Shift differentials under collective bargaining are probably not much larger than the employer would have to pay anyway to induce workers to accept the less desirable shifts. If they were, one would find a surplus of workers applying for second- and third-shift jobs, and this one usually does not find.

Another group of contract provisions relates to payment for time not worked. In coal mining, for example, it may take considerable time to travel from the pithead to the coal face. Miners used to be paid only for time spent actually working at the face. In the 1940s, however, the United Mine Workers negotiated a "portal-to-portal" clause, under which men are paid from the time they enter the mine until they leave it. There is often provision for paid lunch periods, and for "wash-up time" at the end of the day's work. Another common provision is for "call-in time" under which, if a man reports for work and is not needed on that day, he must be paid for a minimum number of hours.

In some industries, such as trucking, the worker may lose working time for reasons beyond his control. Over-the-road drivers are usually paid on a mileage basis; but to protect men assigned to short runs, they are normally guaranteed payment for a minimum number of hours per day, regardless of distance driven. Drivers paid on a trip basis are sometimes guaranteed a certain number of runs per week. The Teamsters' contracts also protect against numerous contingencies inherent in trucking, such as payment for layover time and lodging while waiting for a truck in which to return home; "deadheading," when a man returns as a passenger; equipment breakdown; and impassable highways.

Union influence on work schedules raises two main questions. First, are working hours today shorter than they would be in the absence of trade unionism? The answer is not self-evident. With the sustained rise of real wages over the past century, workers would have preferred to "buy" more leisure as well as more goods and services. Evidence on this point was presented in Chapter 2. Even without unions, there would have been pressure for reduction of hours. It is probable, however, that unions helped to crystallize this sentiment and to speed up the reductions, which employers usually opposed. Unions of skilled craftsmen were in the forefront of the ten-hour movement of the 1860s and the eight-hour movement of the 1880s and 1890s. Labor provided the main political support for the Fair Labor Standards Act of 1938, which generalized the forty-hour week. Extension of paid vacations and holidays, which has brought a continued reduction of annual hours, has also been speeded by union pressure. It seems likely, then, that unionism has reduced total labor supply, that is, the number of man-hours of labor available to the American economy.

A second question is whether unions tend to press for shorter hours than their members would prefer. Are leaders' preferences biased toward leisure as against income, compared with the average preference of the membership? There is little evidence on this point at present, but such a bias may well exist. The belief that hours reduction is a remedy for general unemployment, and that hours reduction can be costless if accompanied by offsetting wage increases, is deep-rooted in union ideology. The history of union agitation for shorter hours produces strong institutional momentum in this direction; and so does the desire of union officers to take care of unemployed members in industries where labor demand is declining. The employed members, who may stand to lose by hours reduction, are apt not to see the issue clearly or to put up effective opposition.

WORK SPEEDS AND WORK ASSIGNMENTS

Workers have an interest in how much they must produce in return for their wage. In addition to the desire to avoid "working themselves out of a job," workers enjoy a moderate work speed for its own sake. Too rapid a pace not only robs the worker of any pleasure during the day but leaves him drained of energy and incapable of enjoyment after working hours. But what is a "moderate" pace of work in a particular situation? The workers may have one conception, while supervisors and top management may have quite another. When there is disagreement over proper work speeds, the union is bound to get involved in bargaining over the issue.

Speed Under Piecework

The problem of work speeds takes a somewhat different form depending on whether the worker is paid solely on a time basis or whether his earnings are related to the amount produced. Suppose that a plant is operating under the simplest type of piecework system, in which a worker's earnings vary directly and proportionately with his output. Suppose also that it has been decided that a worker of average proficiency on a certain job should earn $4 per hour. This is a wage decision, the basis for which will be examined in the next chapter. It is necessary next to make a work-speed decision. How many units of output should the worker be required to produce per hour in order to receive $4? If it is reasonable to require twenty pieces in an hour, the piece rate will be 20 cents; if the worker should turn out twenty-five, the piece rate will be 16 cents. Thus the question amounts to asking how many seconds or minutes should reasonably be allowed for the worker to produce a unit of output. At this point the time-study man and the stopwatch enter the picture.

Ideal time-study procedure, not always adhered to in practice, is about as follows. The first step is to standardize conditions on the job and to determine the best way of doing it through a methods' analysis, including a study of workers' motions on the job. Operators on the job are then trained to use the proper methods until they do so naturally and automatically. This first step is essential to accurate time study, and can often by itself yield large increases in productivity. The next step is to select an operator who appears to be of average speed and ability, and to time his production over a long enough period so that variations in his speed of work can be averaged out. The worker will hardly ever take exactly the same time for two successive units of output. The only way to eliminate these irregular fluctuations in work speed is to time a considerable number of units and take an average.

The actual work of timing jobs is a good deal more complex than this brief statement suggests. The timer does not simply measure the time required for the whole process of turning out a unit of output. He breaks the production process down into each separate movement of the worker's hands and body. The time required for each of these movements is recorded separately. This enables the observer to determine whether the worker is using the proper methods, whether he is using them consistently, whether certain motions are taking more time than they should normally take, and even whether the worker is deliberately holding back during the time study.

After the time-study man has determined the average time required to turn out a unit of product, certain adjusments must be made in this result. If it seems that the operator was above or below "normal" ability, or that he was working above or below "normal" speed during the study, an adjustment must be made on this acount. In addition, allowances are usually added for fatigue, unavoidable delays, necessary personal time, and other possible interruptions to production. At the end of the process one obtains a total of, say, three minutes per unit. This indicates a normal hourly output or "task" of twenty units. If expected earnings on the job are $4, the piece rate must be 20 cents.

It is clear that this process is not mathematically precise and that it involves numerous judgments by the time-study observer. Was the man timed actually of average ability? Was he using the best methods available? Was he working at the right rate of speed? There is an almost unavoidable tendency for workers to slow down while being timed, even when they do not mean to do so, and the time-study man must correct for this as best he can. Again, what allowance should reasonably be made in the circumstances for fatigue, personal time, unavoidable stoppages of production, and other factors?

Unions naturally insist that work speeds cannot be left to the sole judgment of management, and that the union must have a voice in the setting of time standards and piece rates on individual jobs. The procedure under most union contracts is that management has the right to make the initial time study of a job and to set a temporary piece rate on it. The temporary rate automatically becomes permanent unless protested by the union within a certain length of time. If the rate is protested by the union, the job is usually retimed, and the dispute can be carried up through the regular grievance procedure. Some union contracts provide that a piece rate cannot be put into effect at all until it has been approved by the union, but such provisions are rather rare.

In a few industries, the union sets the piece rate and management has the right to protest rates that it believes are unfair. This is the usual procedure in the men's and women's clothing industries, and is due to the special characteristics of those industries. Employers in the clothing industries are usually small, and many of them are transient. They could scarcely afford the engineering staff necessary to determine new piece rates on a great variety of styles and types of clothing. The union, being much the largest organization in the industry, can afford to maintain a staff of rate-setting experts. Piece-rate determinations are made in the first instance by the union rate setters, with the employer having the right to appeal any decision within a certain period of time.

Piece-Rate Changes

The other main problem in the administration of an incentive system is to determine the conditions under which management shall be entitled to retime a job and alter the piece rate. The generally accepted principle, written into most union contracts, is "no change in the rate without a change in the job." It is not easy, however, to get agreement on the application of this principle to specific cases. Where management has the upper hand, it will frequently try to take away from the workers the benefit even of their own greater effort or increased skill. A strong union, on the other hand, will often take the untenable position that piece rates cannot be changed unless there is a complete reengineering of the job. This stand produces inequities in the wage structure because of differing rates of technical progress on different jobs. A job on which management has made many minor improvements or the workers have discovered numerous short-cuts may gradually come to yield earnings twice as high as those on another job that requires the same skill and effort but which has undergone no changes in method. When these discrepancies have become sufficiently glaring even the union will frequently agree to a general overhaul of piece rates. It is politically difficult, however, for a union to subscribe to a step that reduces the earnings of any of its members. The rank-and-file worker regards anything that reduces his earnings as a rate cut, and he holds the union leaders responsible.

The difficulty of getting agreement on piece-rate changes leads to a good deal of tactical maneuvering by workers and management. Management tries to "sneak up" on jobs where it believes earnings have become too high, and to make just enough changes in the job to justify a new time study. Workers try to hold down their rate of production while a time study is in progress. The time-study man tries to guess how much they are holding back and to correct this in his results. Determination of time standards thus becomes to some extent a battle of wits between the worker and the engineer, in which the latter does not always come out victorious.

There is also a strong tendency for incentive workers to hold down their production at all times, and for different workers on a job to maintain about the same rate of output. Workers who rise much above the accepted rate are called "speed artists," "rate busters," and other uncomplimentary names. Unless they desist from their high rate of production, they are likely to find that things happen to their machines, that wrenches fall accidentally on their heads, and that they are ostracized by their fellows. The result is that incentive systems usually fail to obtain maximum effort from the faster workers. Their rate of production is limited by social pressures exerted by their fellow workers, while an incentive system requires completely individualistic behavior to produce its full effects.

The agreed rate of output on a job is usually set slightly below the level that the workers think would cause management to retime the job and cut the piece rate. Workers with long experience under incentive systems develop a keen sense of what is a "safe" amount to earn on a particular job, and are careful not to exceed this amount. If too much work is done one day, part of it is hidden overnight and turned in the next day, during which the worker takes it easy. Some workers prefer to work rapidly for several hours, produce their "quota," and then take it easy for the rest of the day. The most serious aspect of these output standards is that they become fixed by custom and persist even after improved methods have made a higher level of output appropriate. When this happens, the main effect of improvements in methods is to increase the amount of leisure that workers have on the job rather than to increase their output.

Restriction of output by incentive workers is not due specifically to union organization and seems to be as prevalent in nonunion as in union plants. It is not at all certain, therefore, that unionism results in slower work speeds than would prevail without it.

Speed Under Timework

The oldest form of wage payment, and still a very common one, is at a flat rate of so much per hour. It has often been pointed out that under timework the employment contract is incomplete. There is an understanding as to how much the worker shall be paid, but no understanding as to how much he must produce. It is left to the foreman to get as much work out of him as he can after the wage agreement has been made. When the job is essentially a hand operation, the foreman has to rely on instruction, admonition, example, cajolery, sarcasm, and the ultimate threat of discharge. In a unionized shop, however, the foreman must stay within limits generally acceptable to the workers under him. Anything that the workers regard as undue driving or pushing by the foreman is likely to be raised as a grievance by the union.

When the work is machine-paced, and the worker is mainly a machine tender, the problem becomes how fast the machinery should run, or how many machines one worker should be expected to tend. Two examples may be cited. In preunion days, automobile assembly lines were run at a speed that was determined solely by management and that many workers regarded as too fast. When the United Automobile Workers was organized, one of its first actions was to seek determination of assembly-line speeds by the company and the union together. The companies first contended that determination of these speeds was a "management prerogative" that should not be made subject to collective bargaining. The matter was of such great importance to the workers, however, that the union kept pressing the issue and gradually succeeded in bringing assembly-line speeds under joint control in most plants.

Another illustration is the size of machine assignments in the cotton textile industry. A weaver, for example, usually tends a considerable number of looms. As looms have become more nearly automatic, and as improved production methods have been developed, textile companies have tended to increase the number of looms assigned to each worker—sometimes on the basis of systematic engineering studies, sometimes without such studies. The workers usually object on principle to any "stretch-out" of their work assignment, and many spontaneous strikes have occurred over the issue even in nonunion plants. Management usually contends that machine assignments should be made and altered at the sole discretion of management. The unions in the textile industry have never conceded this right, and the size of work assignments has become a major issue in collective bargaining.

The problem of work speeds is intrinsically difficult, because there is no way of determining the proper pace of work with anything like mathematical precision. A faster pace of work means more discomfort to the worker, but lower unit production costs and lower prices to consumers. At some point there must be a proper balance between the interest of workers in a pleasant job and the interest of consumers in high production at low prices. Determination of this optimum, however, seems inevitably to be a matter of judgment. It is neither fully determined by market forces nor is it capable of scientific measurement. Unions may press for a pace of work below the socially desirable optimum, just as management is likely to set a work pace above the optimum point. The outcome in a particular case depends on the relative strength and bargaining skill of the parties, and actual achievement of the optimum work speed would appear to be only a lucky accident.

Incentive Work Versus Timework

Because of these difficulties, the basic question of whether workers are to be paid on an hourly or an incentive basis is an important feature of the union contract. Union policy on this point is variable. A few unions, which have experienced employer abuse of incentive systems or have found them unsuited to the conditions of their industries, have refused to work under any sort of incentive plan. The outstanding example among the older unions is the International Association of Machinists, which has long had a constitutional provision against introduction of an incentive system in any shop where it has not previously been used. The building trades unions have also refused flatly to work under piece rates. Among the newer industrial unions, opposition to incentive payment has probably been strongest in the United Automobile Workers, which has succeeded in abolishing this type of payment throughout most of the automobile industry. Some unions that at one time opposed piece-rate payment, such as the International Ladies' Garment Workers' Union, later reversed themselves and now favor this type of payment. The reversal occurred when the union became strong enough to control the employers' administration of wage incentives, so that its members could enjoy the benefit of higher incentive earnings without risking a speed-up of their work.

Unions have frequently opposed the use of particular incentive formulas, such as the original Bedaux system and other plans under which the amount paid for extra units of output decreases as the worker's output rises. In addition to being inequitable from the worker's point of view, these plans have often been remarkably complicated. It is hard to see how a worker can be motivated to greater output by a system that makes it impossible for him to understand the basis of his paycheck.

The use of incentive payment varies widely from industry to industry. A Labor Department study found that in some manufacturing industries (basic steel, men's suits and coats, women's outerwear, boots and shoes) more than 60 percent of production workers are paid on an incentive basis.[2] There is moderate use of incentive payment—30 to 40 percent of production workers—in textiles, carpet manufacture, pottery workers, steel foundries, electrical apparatus, and industrial machinery. Industries in which less than 10 percent of production workers are on an incentive basis include chemicals, scientific instruments, aircraft and parts, cigarettes, cement, and commercial printing.

In some cases, such as motor vehicles and equipment (13 percent on incentives), one can see a clear effect of union policy. In general, however, there is no statistical relation between the percentage of workers in an industry covered by collective bargaining and its use of incentive payment. The significant determinants appear to be:

1. The nature of the work. Where quality rather than quantity is important, as in diamond cutting or instrument manufacture, piecework is not appropriate.

2. The ratio of labor cost to total cost. Where the labor-to-total cost ratio is high, as in clothing and footwear, incentive payment may be preferred as a way of standardizing unit labor cost throughout the industry. Where labor cost is a minor factor—as in cigarettes, chemicals, cement, oil refining—there is little interest in incentives.

---

[2] Robert B. McKersie, Carroll F. Miller, Jr., and William E. Quartermain, "Some Indicators of Incentive Plan Prevalence," *Monthly Labor Review* (March 1964), pp. 271–76.

3. Age of the industry. Incentive payment is "old-fashioned" in the sense that it was developed in an era of primitive management and little knowledge of worker motivation. Many of the newer industries, such as aircraft manufacture, have never resorted to it because of the availability of other motivational techniques.

PRODUCTION METHODS AND EMPLOYMENT OPPORTUNITIES

An important reason for union interest in production methods is their effect on employment opportunities. Most workers are convinced that jobs are always scarce; it is important, therefore to protect existing jobs and to create new ones if possible. This belief leads unions to combat technical changes that threaten to displace labor and to seek opportunities for the employment of additional workers.

These practices are particularly likely to develop in industries in which the total number of jobs is declining, such as railroading and live musical performances. In such industries, rising unemployment leads the union to seek desperate means of providing a livelihood for its members. Industries with rapidly increasing employment opportunities are less likely to suffer from restrictive practices. Craft unions are also more likely than industrial unions to resist technical change and to adopt make-work rules and policies. Skilled workers stand in particular danger of having their skill undermined, their job opportunities reduced, and the very basis of their craft whittled away by new production methods. An industrial union is less likely to be concerned over whether a particular operation is done by skilled men in one way or semiskilled men in a different way, since in any event the work will be done by members of the same union.

Make-work Rules and Policies

The effort to create employment, or to prevent a shrinkage of employment, takes many forms. The practices described in this section, however, all have the intent of increasing the number of man-hours of labor that employers must hire. For this reason they are often termed *make-work policies.*

1. *Limiting daily or weekly output per worker.* This is a widespread practice in both nonunion and union shops, particularly where the workers are paid on a piecework or incentive basis. The motive for limitation of output is partly to make work, partly to avoid rate cutting and speeding up by the employer.

The output limitations are frequently reasonable at the time they are set but tend rapidly to become obsolete. It is natural for the output of a work group to rise gradually in the course of time, as a result of improvements in machinery, materials, and methods. If workers continue to produce at a rate determined years in the past, the gap between actual and potential output becomes larger and larger with the passage of time. The consequence is an ever greater volume of unnecessary labor and a progressive inflating of production costs.

2. *Limiting output indirectly by controlling the quality of work or requiring time-consuming methods.* These techniques are best illustrated in the building trades. Although the unions have done a useful service in combating shoddy construction by the less reputable contractors, they have frequently insisted on needlessly high quality in order to justify spending more time on the job. The gradual decline in the number of bricks laid per hour by bricklayers, for example, is usually justified by the union in terms of the care that must be taken to ensure perfect accuracy and soundness in the product. It would seem, however, that this argument has been overworked. Plastering, lathing, and other processes are often done more thoroughly than necessary in order to create additional work.

Another frequent device of the building trades is to require that work be done on the construction site rather than in the factory. Painters often require that all window frames and screens be primed, painted, and glazed on the job. Plumbers in many cities prohibit the cutting and threading of pipe in the factory, and refuse to install toilets and other fixtures that have been assembled at the factory. There has recently been a growing movement toward prefabrication of plumbing fixtures, kitchen cabinets, and even whole kitchen units as a means of reducing production costs. This movement has been resisted by the organized construction workers. The prefabrication of the whole house structure has been resisted even more vigorously.

The restrictiveness of union policies in the building trades, however, should not be exaggerated. Haber and Levinson point out that many new techniques and materials have been introduced into the industry over the past generation. Union opposition to new methods was not nearly so strong during the high-employment fifties as it was during the depressed thirties. The trades in which restrictive practices are mainly concentrated—painting, plumbing, electrical work, and sheet metal work—represent only about 20 percent of on-site labor costs on a typical house. Haber and Levinson estimate that the total effect of opposition to new techniques, make-work rules, and other restrictive practices is to raise on-site labor costs by from 8 percent at a minimum to as much as 24 percent in areas where all union regulations are severely applied. Since labor costs form approximately 30 percent of the selling price of a house, this means that house prices are raised by from 2 to 7 percent.[3]

The difficulty of drawing general conclusions, however, is illustrated by another study of two Michigan cities.[4] The author found that the number of man-hours required to build a standard house was considerably *lower* for union than for nonunion contractors. True, the wage bill for the union-built house was higher; but this was due entirely to the higher union wage scale, which more than offset the saving in man-hours. The author surmises that the

---

[3] William Haber and Harold M. Levinson, *Labor Relations and Productivity in the Building Trades* (Ann Arbor: University of Michigan Bureau of Industrial Relations, 1956), particularly Chaps. 7–9.

[4] Allen B. Mandelbaum, "The Effects of Unions on Efficiency in the Residential Construction Industry: A Case Study," *Industrial and Labor Relations Review* (July 1965), pp. 503–21.

higher man-hour output of the union contractors may have been due to some combination of higher labor force quality, use of more or better equipment, greater cost consciousness of employers in an effort to offset the high wage scale, and (in the case of the strongly unionized Ann Arbor area) potential competition from nearby contractors in Detroit.

3. *Requiring that unnecessary work be done, or that work be done more than once.* Switchboards and other types of electrical apparatus, for example, were in the earlier days always wired on the job. The recent tendency has been to have this equipment wired in the factory, where the work can be done at considerably lower cost. The New York City local and certain other locals of the International Brotherhood of Electrical Workers have refused to install switchboards and other apparatus unless the wiring done in the factory was torn out and the apparatus rewired by union members.

Another example is the "bogus" rule of the International Typographical Union. This provides that when a newspaper uses ready-made plates or matrices, as is often done when the same advertisement is run in several papers, the copy must nevertheless be reset, read, and corrected in each paper's composing room. The reset copy is known as *bogus*. Although this is mainly a makework rule, it is sometimes used for bargaining purposes. A publisher may be exempted from the bogus rule in exchange for an outsize wage increase or a guarantee of a certain number of jobs.

4. *Requiring stand-by crews or other unnecessary men.* This practice is often termed *featherbedding*. The Musicians' Union, for example, attempted to enforce a rule that radio stations that broadcast recorded music or that rebroadcast programs originating elsewhere must employ a standby orchestra to be paid for doing nothing. This led eventually to passage of the Lea Act of 1946, which made it unlawful to compel a licensee under the Federal Communications Act to employ unnecessary people, or to refrain from using unpaid performers for noncommercial programs, or to limit production or use of records.

The theater is especially vulnerable to featherbedding because picketing can so easily interfere with attendance. The Stagehands' Union requires a minimum crew to be hired for any theatrical performance, regardless of whether their services are actually needed, and so does the Musicians' Union, the Electricians', and other groups. The resulting inflation of production costs and ticket prices has contributed to the disappearance of commercial theaters in many cities.

The Motion Picture Projectors' Union has tried for years to require two operators for each projection machine, and has succeeded in some cities. The Operating Engineers asserts jurisdiction over all machines and engines used in building construction, regardless of their source of power. Even if the power is purchased from an electric company, a union member must be there to push the button or turn the switch, which may constitute his whole day's work.

5. *Requiring crews of excessive size.* This is a common practice among the printing pressmen, longshoremen, musicians, and a number of other unions. By far the most ambitious and successful efforts, however, have been made by the railroad-running trades. They have worked through the state legislatures to get full-crew laws and train-limit laws. The full-crew laws usually provide that the crew shall consist of an engineer, fireman, conductor, and a number of brakemen varying with the length of the train. Seventeen states had such laws in 1960. The train-limit laws limit the number of cars per train, and are

intended to make more jobs for engineers and firemen. The Arizona train-limit law, however, was invalidated by the U.S. Supreme Court as having no reasonable relation to safety; [5] and while several states have train-limit laws on the books, they are not enforced.

A major controversy in this area concerned the use of firemen on diesel locomotives. On high-speed passenger trains, safety considerations might dictate having a second man in the cab as a backstop for the engineer. But the union insisted also on use of firemen in freight trains and even in yard switching. This controversy continued for decades, causing several railroad strikes, and was not finally settled until 1972. The union agreed to eventual elimination of fireman positions on diesel freight locomotives through attrition. The existing force of about 18,000 firemen on freight trains were guaranteed jobs until they were promoted to engineer, retired, resigned, or died.

6. *Requiring that work be done by members of a particular occupational group.* The object is to enlarge the job territory of the group so that there will be the maximum amount of work available to be divided among its members. Pursuit of this objective takes various forms. A common rule prohibits employers or foremen from working at the trade. This prevents supervisors from reducing the amount of work available to employees by doing it themselves, and from acting as pacesetters by working alongside the men. Another common rule requires that skilled men be used for semiskilled or unskilled work. The Typographical Union frequently requires that proof be read and revised by union members before going to anyone outside the composing room. The building trades often require that material handling be done by craftsmen rather than laborers.

Some Teamsters' locals, on the other hand, prohibit drivers from assisting helpers in unloading their trucks. This does not make more work for drivers, but creates more jobs for helpers, so that total employment is increased. Longshoremen in some ports refuse to shift from ship to dock work, or even from one ship to another of the same company, thus compelling use of multiple crews. In this, as in other aspects, the railroad unions

> have gone to unbelievable extremes in restricting duties, taking the position that every item of work *belongs* to some employee. If that employee is deprived of the opportunity to do the work, he is entitled to compensation first. In addition, the one who does the work is entitled to compensation. In many instances the amount of compensation given to both is a day's pay. The result is that two days' pay may be given as compensation for a trivial amount of work.[6]

What can one say about the economic effects of make-work rules and policies? Pressure for them arises mainly from the threat of unemployment, but they are clearly not a desirable method of coping with unemployment. Seasonal and intermittent unemployment can best be dealt with through efforts to regularize production, supported by adequate public

---

[5] *Southern Pacific Company* v. *Arizona*, 325 U.S. 761.

[6] Sumner H. Slichter, James J. Healy, and E. Robert Livernash, *The Impact of Collective Bargaining on Management* (Washington, D.C.: The Brookings Institution, 1960), p. 319.

employment services and unemployment compensation systems. Cyclical fluctuations must be countered by fiscal policy and other types of governmental action. A long-run decline in the demand for a product requires that workers be transferred out of the declining industry.

It may be said that this is a harsh view. Why not cushion a drop in the demand for labor by creating additional jobs? Why not have everyone in an industry somewhat underemployed, instead of some workers totally unemployed? If the expedients adopted were temporary, and were used only until more basic remedies could be devised, one might make out a case for their use. The difficulty is that restrictive work rules and practices are scarcely ever discarded. They persist even during periods of full employment, when they are clearly inappropriate. They tend to freeze in each industry the maximum number of people ever employed there in the past. In the long run, therefore, they create all sorts of anomalies in the structure of employment and production.

It is by no means clear that make-work policies are beneficial even to the group imposing them. There is a limit to the costs that a union can impose on an industry, set by the demand curve for the industry's products. If the union adds to the industry's costs through excessive employment, it must accept a lower level of wages. If restrictive practices were abandoned and excess employment eliminated, employers could be obliged to pay higher wages to the workers remaining in the industry.

The Industrial Unions and Technical Change

The quickened pace of mechanization and automation [7] since World War II has reduced employment opportunities in coal mining, basic steel, automobiles, and numerous other industries, and has caused unions in these industries to be concerned for the job security of their members. In general, their reaction has not taken the form of trying to block technical change, a policy that would have had little chance of success. The new equipment in these industries is so labor-saving and cost-reducing that employers have a powerful incentive to install it, and the unions could at most fight a delaying action for a limited period. So they have concentrated instead on ways of cushioning the impact on their members.

In bituminous coal mining, mechanization has proceeded very rapidly both through mechanization of underground mines and acceleration of strip mining. The amount of mechanical equipment per worker has more than doubled, and so has output per man-hour. Employment has dropped

---

[7] The meaning of *automation* is discussed is Chapter 4, in connection with trends in labor demand and employment. The writer is inclined to regard it as complex mechanization, differing in degree, but not in kind, from mechanization in earlier decades.

sharply. The United Mine Workers did not oppose the mechanization movement. Indeed, the union encouraged mechanization by raising wages rapidly even in the face of severe unemployment. It also secured substantial employer contributions for medical and hospital care, insurance, and pensions.[8]

In automobile production, the United Automobile Workers has not opposed technical change as such. The industry has a tradition of annual model changes, rapid technical innovation, and wide management flexibility in production methods (except for the joint control of assembly-line speeds already noted). The union has tried, however, to cushion the decline of auto employment by speeding the exit of older workers from the industry and by spreading the available work among those remaining.

Exit is speeded through liberalization of retirement benefits and a reduction of the retirement age. In the 1973 negotiations the parties agreed to a "30 years and out" principle for retirement, with "25 and out" for foundry and forge workers, regardless of the worker's age. A major objective in the 1976 negotiations was to spread employment by reducing the days worked per year by each employee. In the second year of the 1976–79 contract, each worker will be entitled to five days off, and in the third year seven days off, in addition to all preexisting vacations and paid holidays. This will require the hiring of more workers than otherwise to maintain production schedules.

In meat packing, the Armour Company maintains a joint program with the union, under a neutral chairman, who has usually been a labor economist. The program includes research on the company's future manpower requirements, advance notice of plant closings or cutbacks in employment, preferential hiring rights for displaced workers in other plants of the company, assistance with moving and relocation costs, and assistance in finding other work for those who prefer to remain in their home community.

In the mass-production industries, then, things have moved in the direction of a trade, in which management gets reasonable flexibility in changing production methods while the union gets provisions to cushion the impact on its members' jobs. The cushioning devices include liberalized pension provisions, a reduction of the retirement age, and other efforts to encourage early retirement; severance pay for workers released permanently; work sharing through reduction in the number of days and hours worked per year; outright guarantees of lifetime employment in some cases; and arrangements under which workers in a plant that is closed down permanently can "follow the work" to other plants of the same company, with

---

[8] For a thorough analysis of mechanization in this industry, see C. L. Christenson, *Economic Redevelopment and Bituminous Coal* (Cambridge, Mass.: Harvard University Press, 1962).

preferential hiring rights. The assumption is that the number of production jobs in these industries will continue to decline; and the object is to ensure that the shrinkage of employment will be orderly and will do minimum damage to the present labor force.

This trade-off of greater freedom for the employer against employment guarantees for the worker is not limited to manufacturing, but has occurred also in other industries.[9] The diesel fireman agreement has already been noted. In the printing industry, the New York newspaper publishers had long sought to introduce modern composing-room technology, which would reduce both the number of employees and the level of skill required. After many years of opposition, the International Typographical Union in 1974 agreed to a settlement. Management got a free hand with regard to automation, manning requirements, job assignments, and elimination of bogus type. In return, all regular and substitute employees received a guarantee of employment until retirement. Retirement provisions were liberalized, and a bonus of $2,500 was provided for anyone retiring within six months of the contract date.

From its unionization in 1934 until the late fifties, the West Coast longshore industry was marked by poor union–employer relations, chronic guerrilla warfare, and a host of inefficient work practices designed to use as much labor as possible. These included overmanning, dual handling of cargo, limitation of sling loads, and resistance to containerization and bulk-cargo handling methods. Eventually, however, union leaders became convinced that this delaying action could not succeed indefinitely, and that they would do better to make a trade. In 1960 they negotiated an agreement that gave employers virtually a free hand in overhauling work rules, installing labor-saving devices, and increasing efficiency generally. The *quid pro quo* for the union was a promise that no registered longshoreman would be laid off as a result of the changes, a guaranteed annual wage, and a pension fund permitting voluntary retirement at sixty-two. These guarantees are underwritten by a fund to which employers will contribute 4 to 5 percent of longshore payrolls. "But their savings are considerably greater. During negotiations, an estimate was presented showing that the elimination of *only* the multiple-handling rules, in Los Angeles *alone,* would save the employers more than their total fund contributions." [10]

This agreement proved so successful that it was renewed in 1966 and subsequent agreements. A similar agreement has since been negotiated for

---

[9] For a review of cases, see Joseph P. Goldberg, "Bargaining and Productivity in the Private Sector," in *Collective Bargaining and Productivity* (Madison, Wis.: Industrial Relations Research Association, 1975), pp. 15–44.

[10] Charles C. Killingsworth, "Cooperative Approaches to Problems of Technological Change," in G. G. Somers, E. I. Cushman, and N. Weinberg (eds.), *Adjusting to Technological Change* (New York: Harper & Row, Publishers, 1963), p. 83.

the East Coast ports. Employers received greater flexibility in manning and a reduction in the size of work gangs. The union received liberalized retirement benefits to encourage exit from the industry plus an income guarantee for those remaining. This was set initially at 1,600 hours of wages per year, but has since been raised to 2,080 hours or fifty-two 40-hour weeks.

PHYSICAL CONDITIONS OF WORK

Union officials spend much time negotiating with management over various aspects of physical working conditions—heating, lighting, ventilation, and cleanliness of the plant; safety arrangements; sanitary facilities; dangerous or objectionable features of particular jobs; provision of adequate cafeterias and rest rooms; and many other matters. Most of these matters are discussed informally in the plant from day to day, since they are usually too small to arise as issues in contract negotiations. Taken as a whole, these matters are very important to the workers; but they are so varied and heterogeneous that it is difficult to find any way of generalizing about them.

The nearest one can come to generalizing is to distinguish three kinds of improvement in working conditions. The first involves plant improvements that produce an increase in labor productivity more than sufficient to cover the cost of making the improvements. It is usually assumed that management will be alert to such opportunities and will seize them of its own accord, but this is not always the case. Unions can do valuable work by pointing out improvements that perhaps should have been obvious to management but were not, and that, once discovered, can be installed with a net gain to the company as well as the workers.

Second, one may distinguish improvements that are a matter of *degree,* and where beyond a certain point the additional cost outweighs the gain in labor productivity. Consider a plant using very hot processes, the natural temperature of which would be 130 degrees Fahrenheit. By installing an air-cooling system the plant can be cooled to any desired temperature. The lower the temperature, however, the greater the cost of the system. Suppose also that worker productivity increases steadily as the temperature falls. It will pay the employer to reduce the temperature of the plant down to the point at which the additional cost of cooling just equals the additional revenue obtained from increased output. If this point turns out to be 95 degrees, this is the optimum plant temperature from the employer's standpoint.

The workers, however, might feel happiest at a temperature of 70 degrees. There is a divergence here between the interest of workers and management. In a perfectly competitive labor market, management would presumably have to pay a higher wage rate to compensate for the unpleasant working conditions. In practice, however, competitive forces are not fully effective. One cannot be sure, therefore, that unpleasant conditions will actually be offset by a wage premium.

Suppose now that a union comes on the scene and compels the employer to reduce the temperature of the plant from 95 degrees to 80 degrees. Depending on the circumstances of the case, the added cost of doing this might or might not be absorbed out of existing profit margins. For the sake of argument, however, suppose that the cost is entirely transferred to buyers of the product through higher prices. The union, in effect, has taxed consumers a certain amount in order to improve the daily lives of its members in the plant. Is this action economically beneficial or harmful?

The problem appears even more clearly in a third type of case, where there is no effect on productivity, and the only consequence of the improvement is pleasanter "plant living-conditions" for the workers concerned. The money cost of the improvement is felt initially by the employer, later by buyers of the product. The social cost consists in the economic resources that were used in making the improvement. How can one say whether, in a particular case, the benefit to the workers was worth the expenditure of resources? How far should consumers be taxed in order to pay for improved working conditions? How far should the satisfaction of man as consumer be reduced in order to increase that of man as producer?

There seems no way of giving any general answer to these questions. One is certainly not entitled to assume that all plant improvements of this type are economically harmful, or that all are beneficial. A separate decision must be made in each case on the basis of informed judgment.

DISCUSSION QUESTIONS

1. What would be the main economic consequences of reducing the standard workweek in manufacturing from forty to thirty hours?

2. What would be the effect of amending the Fair Labor Standards Act to require double time rather than time-and-a-half for overtime work?

3. Suppose you were asked to design a research study to determine whether union leaders prefer a shorter workweek than their members, on the average, would prefer. How would you proceed?

4. How much would you estimate that make-work rules and policies reduce the potential output of the economy? Can anything be done to reduce the frequency and impact of such rules?

5. Why is it difficult for unions to resist technical changes in mass-production manufacturing? What provisions have unions negotiated with employers to cushion the labor-displacing impact of such changes?

6. "Work speeds and work assignments are a matter for management decision. Union interference in these matters is fatal to productive efficiency and harmful to the public interest." Discuss.

7. "Time study is a scientific procedure that leaves no possible room for argument or bargaining over work speeds." Discuss.

READING SUGGESTIONS

Classic early studies include GEORGE BARNETT, *Chapters on Machinery and Labor,* Cambridge, Mass.: Harvard University Press, 1926; STANLEY B. MATHEWSON, *Restriction of Output Among Unorganized Workers,* New York: The Viking Press, Inc., 1931; GLADYS L. PALMER, *Union Tactics and Economic Change,* Philadelphia: University of Pennsylvania Press, 1932. For more recent studies of union policy, see C. L. CHRISTENSON, *Economic Redevelopment in Bituminous Coal,* Cambridge, Mass.: Harvard University Press, 1962; G. G. SOMERS, E. L. CUSHMAN, and N. WEINBERG (eds), *Adjusting to Technological Change,* New York: Harper & Row, Publishers, 1963. There is a large literature on time study and incentive wage systems, references to which will be found in any standard text on personnel management. For specific discussion of union attitudes and policies, see WILLIAM A. GOMBERG, *A Trade Union Analysis of Time Study* (2d ed.), Englewood Cliffs, N.J.: Prentice-Hall, Inc., 1955; VAN DUSEN KENNEDY, *Union Policy and Incentive Wage Methods,* New York: Columbia University Press, 1945.

22

The Impact on Wage Structure

The wage effects of collective bargaining can be analyzed at either a macro-economic or a microeconomic level. At the macroeconomic level, unionism might alter the general level of real wages and the short-term behavior of money wages. This chapter, however, is concerned with the microeconomic effects of collective bargaining on *relative* wage rates for particular companies, industries, occupations, geographic areas.

INTERCOMPANY DIFFERENCES WITHIN
AN INDUSTRY

How does collective bargaining affect the relative wage levels of companies competing in the same product market? Where an industry is partially organized, are wages of unionized companies typically above those of nonunion companies? Within the unionized sector, does the union try to enforce the same wage level on all companies? Or does it tailor its demands to the individual company's ability to pay?

Statistical studies of partially unionized industries usually show a wage differential between union and nonunion establishments. Vernon Clover found that Bureau of Labor Statistics studies of thirty-one manufacturing industries during the years 1960 to 1965 showed an average earnings differential of 18 percent between union and nonunion plants. These differences were not fully explained by community size, region, or ratios of men and women employed. When the surveys were broken down by region, the average union–nonunion differential was still 12 percent, and appeared in seventy-one out of seventy-six cases.[1]

---

[1] Vernon T. Clover, "Compensation in Union and Nonunion Plants, 1960–65," *Industrial and Labor Relations Review* (January 1968), pp. 226–33.

Such results must be interpreted with caution, however, because of the difficulty of controlling for all the variables affecting a company's wage level. For example, wages are normally higher in large plants and companies than in smaller ones. But large establishments are also more susceptible of unionization. So a new union coming into an industry may first organize the large establishments, which already had higher wages in preunion days. The specific impact of unionism cannot be inferred without controlling for plant size, labor force quality, and other relevant variables.

Moreover, the bargained wage in union establishments will probably affect the wage policies of nonunion companies. They may set a higher wage than otherwise in the hope of avoiding unionization. This has been termed the *threat effect* of unionism. To the extent that this effect is important, the observed wage differential between union and nonunion plants will *understate* the true impact of the union.[2]

There is clear evidence that unions try to reduce wage differences *among unionized companies* in the same industry, and that they in good measure succeed. The principle of "the standard rate" for men doing comparable work is firmly grounded in trade union history. It stems partly from considerations of equity and from political pressures within the union, but economic considerations are also important. If some companies in an industry are allowed to pay less than others, there is a danger that the low-wage companies will underbid their competitors in the product market, forcing down prices and wages throughout the industry. A uniform wage level for firms selling in the same product market is regarded as a way of "putting a floor under competition" or "taking wages out of competition."

Application of this principle, as we noted in Chapter 18, varies with the geographic scope of the product market. In local-market industries there is a tendency toward wage equalization within the city, though there may be considerable variation in wage levels from one city to the next. In manufacturing industries where employers compete on a regional or national basis, there is a tendency toward leveling up of wages throughout the country. We shall be concerned in this section mainly with the economic effects of national wage equalization in manufacturing industries.[3]

---

[2] For an interesting analysis, see Sherwin Rosen, "Trade Union Power, Threat Effects and Extent of Organization," *The Review of Economic Studies* (April 1969), pp. 185–96. Rosen surmises that the threat effect is strongest in the early stages of unionization, and tapers off when the percentage of unionization passes a certain point. This might help to explain the fact that some unions seem to have raised the relative wage level of their industries most rapidly during the early stages of unionization.

[3] See the chapter entitled "The Standard Rate" in Sidney Webb and Beatrice Webb, *Industrial Democracy* (London: Longmans, Green & Co. Ltd., 1902); D. A. McCabe, *The Standard Rate in American Trade Unions* (Baltimore: The Johns

It should be noted at the outset that *wage equalization* has several possible meanings: equality of the *lowest wage rate* in each plant, often termed the *common labor rate;* equality of all job rates in each plant; equality of *piece rates* in each plant; and equality of *labor cost per unit of output.* Each of these objectives has been pursued by one or another union at various times. Equalizing wages in one of these senses, however, will not produce equality in the other senses; and pursuit of these differing objectives will clearly have different economic consequences. Imposition of uniform hourly rates, for example, may work serious hardship on a plant with relatively inefficient workers, equipment, or management; its lower output per man-hour means that its unit labor costs are above the remainder of the industry. Uniform piece rates work no such hardship; if the workers in a particular plant produce little, by the same token they are paid little. This does not mean that the latter arrangement is necessarily preferable, but it is certainly different.

Since it is not possible to discuss each type of wage equalization in the space available here, we limit ourselves to a few remarks on the effects of installing a uniform scale of hourly job rates throughout an industry. This is in some ways the clearest case, and it is probably the most important in practice.

Effects of Wage Leveling

The effects of wage leveling will depend on why wage rates formerly differed in different plants of the industry. The reasons are usually complex and vary from one industry to the next.[4] The wage-paying ability of plants may differ because of variations in technical efficiency. Some plants may be newer, closer to optimum size, better designed, better located relative to materials and markets, or have other advantages. Managerial capacity also varies, and two mangements may get different results from very similar plants. An additional reason—differences in geographic location—we leave for a later section.

The first effect of union pressure for wage equality is to test whether the low-wage firms are actually paying as much as they are able to pay. Allegations of inability to pay are not always well founded, and the union requires convincing evidence. Second, union pressure frequently forces

---

Hopkins Press, 1912); R. A. Lester and E. A. Robie, *Wages Under National and Regional Collective Bargaining* (Princeton: Princeton University Industrial Relations Section, 1946); and Thomas Kennedy, *Significance of Wage Uniformity,* Industry-wide Collective Bargaining Series (Philadelphia: University of Pennsylvania Press, 1948).

[4] For a more thorough analysis than can be given here, see Lloyd G. Reynolds and Cynthia H. Taft, *The Evolution of Wage Structure* (New Haven: Yale University Press, 1956), Chap. 7.

management to step up efficiency and increase the firm's ability to pay. It may be objected that this "shock effect" works only the first few times it is applied, but a few times may be sufficient to raise the firm's efficiency substantially.

But what happens when everything possible has been done in this direction and the union comes up against irremovable differences in plant efficiency? Continued pressure for wage equalization will then tend to eliminate some of the less efficient plants from the industry. Elimination of these plants will make more business available for the more efficient plants and encourage them to expand their operations. In the end, there may be little change in total output and employment in the industry, but there will be considerable redistribution of employment. Jobs will disappear at some places and new jobs will open up at other places, possibly far distant from the first. The long-run effects may be economically beneficial; the immediate effects will be disturbing to the employers who are shut down and to their workers. Indeed, if union members in a particular plant become convinced that to bring their wages up to the national level will cost them their jobs, they will usually vote to accept a lower wage and keep the plant in operation. This is particularly true when the plant is geographically isolated and the members would have to travel some distance to find new employment. In such cases even the national union officers may be willing to tolerate some departure from wage equality.

This is one reason why, even in a strongly organized industry, one rarely finds complete uniformity of wage scales. Most plants will cluster closely around a single wage level, but one will usually find that the union has left a few plants at lower levels because these plants are unable to pay the standard rate and yet it seems expedient to keep them in operation. One may also find that in some of the most efficient plants the union has yielded to the temptation to extract a little more than the prevailing scale. In general, however, unions hew closer to the principle of the standard rate than to the principle of ability to pay.[5]

INTERINDUSTRY DIFFERENCES

The commonest question raised by both scholars and laymen is this: Does unionization of an industry tend to raise the industry's wage level relative to nonunion industries? Many consider this *the* key question about the wage impact of collective bargaining.

The nature of this effect is illustrated in Figure 22–1. Consider an

---

[5] For a good analysis of the ways in which a union may make concessions to firms with low wage-paying ability, see David H. Greenberg, "Deviations from Wage–Fringe Standards," *Industrial and Labor Relations Review* (January 1968), pp. 197–209.

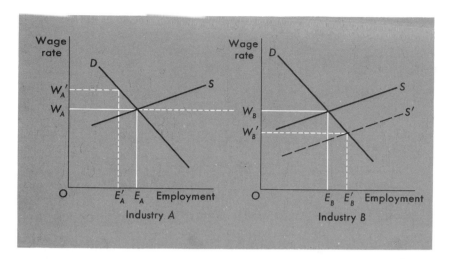

Figure 22-1

A Possible Wage–Employment Effect of
Collective Bargaining

economy consisting of two industries, A and B, with identiical labor supply and demand curves. (This assumption is not necessary, but simplifies
the exposition.) If we assume a competitive labor market, both industries
will pay the same wage, $W_A = W_B$.

Industry A now becomes unionized. The union compels employers
to pay a higher wage, W'_A. At this wage, employers find it profitable to
hire only E'_A workers. So some of these previously employed in the industry, shown by the distance $E'_A E_A$, are out of work.

These workers would presumably rather work in industry B than
remain unemployed. So labor supply to industry B increases from S to S'.
The wage level of industry B falls to W'_B, while employment rises to E'_B.
This increase just equals the decrease of employment in industry A, and
everyone is once more employed.

Note that the allocation of labor between the two industries is no
longer optimal. The marginal product of labor in industry $B (= W'_B)$ is
substantially below that in industry $A (= W'_A)$. So national output is
reduced. This effect is similar to that of monopoly power in product
markets.

How is the wage effect of unionism to be measured? At first glance,
the answer might seem to be $W'_A - W_A$. This is the wage increase in industry A relative to the wage rate in that industry before unionization.
But this overlooks the fact that wages in the nonunion sector have at the
same time been *reduced*. The significant measure, then, is $W'_A - W'_B$, the

size of the wage gap between the union and nonunion sectors. It is useful to reduce this to a *percentage* of the average wage level for the economy, that is, to calculate $W'_A - W'_B/[(W'_A + W'_B)/2]$. Alternatively, one could use the nonunion wage level, W'_B, as the base.

So far we have been discussing *possibilities*. But what about actualities? Is there evidence that unions in the United States have raised the relative wage level of their respective industries? There have by now been many research studies aimed primarily at this issue.[6] They are of two kinds:

1. *Cross-section studies at a point in time.* Take an industry such as hotels and restaurants, barber shops, or men's clothing manufacture, in which the degree of unionization in different areas ranges from zero to one hundred percent. Suppose one has data for 1970 on percentage of unionization and on average hourly earnings, area by area. One can then examine whether there is a systematic relation between unionization and earnings. It is of course necessary to control for other variables that have an influence on earnings, such as labor force characteristics (age, sex, color, education), region of the country, and size of community.

A variant of this method is to use some other group of workers as a reference group. In one study of construction wages, for example, the wage rate for carpenters in each area was divided by the average wage of common laborers in the area (excluding laborers employed in the construction industry). The problem then becomes: Is the carpenters' premium over the common laborer, area by area, related systematically to the degree of unionization among carpenters?

2. *Studies of change over time.* Suppose we have data on average hourly earnings and percentage of unionization in fifty industries, year by year over the period 1950 to 1970. We then examine whether industries with a higher degree of unionization have had a more rapid rate of wage increase. Again, it is necessary to control for changes in other variables that may have influenced an industry's wage level, notably labor force quality, geographic location, profit level, and rate of increase in employment.

Alternatively, one can examine a single industry, using one or more other industries as a reference point. A study of bituminous coal mining, for example, used the average wage level in all manufacturing industries as its base. The question then was whether the ratio of coal mining wages to manufacturing wages was related systematically to changes in coal mine unionization.

Both types of studies face serious difficulties. First, as we emphasized in Chapter 12, there are many economic reasons for wage differences, and for changes in wage relations over time. An industry's relative wage level may change because of changes in the skill mix of the labor force, shifts in geographic location, changes in the ratio of men and women workers or

---

[6] For a review of such studies, a reestimation of some of their findings, and an effort to draw general conclusions, see H. Gregg Lewis, *Unionism and Relative Wages in the United States* (Chicago: The University of Chicago Press, 1963).

of white and nonwhite workers, and a variety of other factors. Careful studies try to measure and adjust for all such influences, to isolate the independent effect of unionism. But this can never be done with perfect precision.

Further, it is usually assumed for statistical convenience that union power is a linear function of percentage of workers organized. A union with 100 percent coverage of its industry is assumed to have twice as much wage influence as one with 50 percent coverage, and four times as much as one with only 25 percent membership. But the actual relation is probably more complex. A union with 25 percent coverage may have zero influence on wages, because the nonunion firms have a dominant effect on price and wage levels in the industry. At some point in its expansion, however, the union "gets over the hump" and itself becomes the dominant force in the industry, with the remaining nonunion firms as the tail on the dog. Suppose this occurs at around 60 percent unionization. Then over the range of 0 to 50 percent the increase in wage influence will be less than proportionate to the increase in unionization; over the range of (say) 50 to 70 percent it will be much more than proportionate; and from 70 to 100 percent it may again be less than proportionate. Testing such a complex hypothesis is more difficult than testing a supposed linear relation and has rarely been attempted.

Recognizing these limitations, it is still interesting to look at the general drift of the statistical studies. As analyzed and summarized by Lewis, they suggest three conclusions:

1. Looking broadly at the economy, the wage gap created by union pressure seems normally to be of the order of 10 to 15 percent. Lewis's summary of past studies concludes:

> These figures imply that recently the average wage of union workers was about 7 to 11 percent higher relative to the average wage of all workers . . . than it would have been in the absence of unionism. Similarly, the average wage of all nonunion workers was about 3 to 4 percent lower relative to the average wage of all workers than in the absence of unionism.[7]

It should be noted, however, that other economists have arrived at different estimates. Weiss concludes that "unions that organize their entire jurisdictions seemed to raise earnings by 7 to 8 percent for craftsmen and 6 to 8 percent for operatives, compared with poorly organized industries."[8] Throop estimates that the average union–nonunion differential was 22.3 percent in 1950 and 26.0 percent in 1960, but concedes that there is probably an up-

---

[7] Lewis, *Unionism and Relative Wages in the United States,* p. 5.

[8] Leonard W. Weiss, "Concentration and Labor Earnings," *American Economic Review* (March 1966), pp. 96–117.

ward bias in his results.[9] Reder, in a careful review of the Lewis volume, finds the basic data so faulty that "one cannot reject the null hypothesis that the relative wage effect of unionism has been zero for most of the period since 1920." [10] Despite these differences of judgment, there is more consensus today than there would have been twenty years ago that unionism has a significant, though moderate, effect on interindustry differentials.

2. The average effect of unionism has varied considerably in the course of time, and particularly between periods of inflation and deflation. Union influence is felt most strongly in depressions, when unions maintain wages or even keep them moving upward, while nonunion wages stagnate or decline. Lewis estimates that at the bottom of the Great Depression in 1932 to 1933, the relative wage effect of unionism may have been above 25 percent. During an inflationary period, such as from 1940 to 1948 or from 1965 to 1969, on the other hand, nonunion wages are pulled up rapidly by rising labor demand, while the fact that union wages are set by contract for a fixed period may actually retard their advance. Lewis estimates that in the late forties the relative wage effect of unionism fell below 5 percent. In some unionized industries, including basic steel, there were sizable labor shortages at this time. This demand–supply gap suggests that the union contract rate was below the rate that would have prevailed in a competitive market.

3. Some unions have had more success in raising wages than others; and the same union has had differing degrees of success at different times.[11] Bituminous coal miners seem rather consistently to have earned 35 to 50 percent more than they would have in the absence of unionism. Commercial airline pilots and East Coast merchant seamen seem to have gained 35 percent or thereabouts. The relative gain of skilled construction workers has been estimated at around 25 percent. Although there have not been comparable studies of the teamsters or the railroad operating crafts, their relative wage gain has probably been substantial. On the other hand, groups for which unionism seems to have produced wage gains of less than 10 percent include building construction laborers, employees of year-round hotels, and production workers in a wide range of manufacturing industries including cotton textiles, footwear, furniture, hosiery, womens dresses, and (in recent years) men's clothing.

The same union has done better in some periods than in others. Thus in 1921 and 1922 bituminous coal miners are estimated to have earned more than twice what they would have earned without the union. Their wage advantage then declined as union strength declined, but recovered during the thirties; by the late fifties it was estimated at 48–58 percent. Less happy is the experience of the men's clothing industry, where the union is estimated to have secured a wage advantage of 20 to 30 percent for its members during the 1920s. This advantage has now almost completely disappeared, partly because of the difficulty of maintaining union organization throughout this small-scale and highly migratory industry.

---

[9] Adrian W. Throop, "The Union–Nonunion Wage Differential and Cost-push Inflation," *American Economic Review* (March 1968), pp. 79–99.

[10] Melvin W. Reder, "Unions and Wages: The Problem of Measurement," *Journal of Political Economy* (April 1965), pp. 188–96.

[11] See the summary table in Lewis, *Unionism and Relative Wages in the United States,* pp. 184–86.

These research findings suggest two questions. First, why has the overall impact of unionism apparently been rather moderate? Considering that elasticity of demand for labor varies widely among industries, and that some industries are much more expansive and profitable than others, one might have expected the most favorably situated unions to run away with their industry wage level, leaving the others far behind. Why has this apparently not happened?

The answer is not entirely clear, but several possible reasons may be suggested. One reason may be that many union officials function as "lazy monopolists" rather than aggressive monopolists. The politics of unionism compels them to keep up with the wage procession, but not necessarily to forge much ahead of it. They would prefer to keep out of trouble both with employers and with their members, and this dictates a certain conservatism in wage demands.

Further, even in an organized economy ideas of equity and reasonable wage relationships retain considerable force. If wages for a particular group, instead of being 20 percent above the competitive level, came to be 50 or 75 percent above it, other groups of workers might be resentful. Employers would feel on strong ground in resisting such demands and would have public support in doing so.

Finally, during periods of high employment the labor market limits the wage differences that can exist among industries for similar types of work. If certain industries fall too far below the level of the highest-wage industries, they will no longer be able to recruit and hold an adequate labor force. When this limit has been reached, the unions in the high-wage industries, while they may continue to push up their absolute wage rates, will no longer be able to improve their relative positions. Instead, they will simply pull up the wage levels of the low-wage industries at the same rate at which their own wages are rising. It is as though one had two men tied together by a rope in which there is at the moment a certain amount of slack. If one of the men decides that he wants to go in a certain direction, he can walk forward until the rope is pulled taut. After that he can go no farther unless the man on the other end of the rope moves in the same direction at the same rate.

Because of these various checks, the tendency toward wage distortion under collective bargaining may not be so serious as some have feared.

A second question arises from the observation that some unions have raised the relative wages of their members considerably more than others. What explains these differences in union success?

The economic environment is clearly important. An industry in which productivity is rising sharply, product demand curves are moving rapidly to the right, and profits are high and rising presents a favorable situation for outsize wage increases. Since profit margins are tending to widen, employers can concede large increases without cutting into profit, and this may weaken their resistance to union demands. Moreover, the tendency of wage increases to reduce employment, which might normally give the union pause, is cushioned by the rapid rightward shift of the labor demand curve.

One cannot say, however, that a favorable economic climate is *essential* to wage gains. Witness the large gains won since 1945 by the maritime unions and the bituminous coal miners, despite severe competitive pressure, low profits, and a rapid decline of employment in these industries.

A familiar hypothesis is that industrial concentration is favorable to a high wage level. A monopolistic or oligopolistic product market, a high degree of unionization, and a relatively high wage level tend to go together. But this does not reveal the chain of causation. Two separate issues are involved. First, is industrial concentration favorable to a high degree of unionization? Second, given the same degree of unionization, is a competitive or monopolistic market structure more conducive to union wage gains? [12]

The answer to the first question seems to be positive. Segal has argued that large-scale, highly concentrated industries (basic steel, automobiles, aluminum, heavy electrical equipment, aircraft manufacture, and so on) are especially susceptible to organization for several reasons. There are economies of scale in an organizing campaign. Where establishments are large, organizing cost *per capita* will be low. Workers in large establishments are likely also to be more alienated from management and hence more union-prone. These industries are much in the public eye, and thus vulnerable to criticism if they engage in overt antiunion activity. Having a heavy investment in fixed plant, they cannot run away to escape the union. Barriers to entrance are high, so that once the union is ensconced in the industry, it is relatively safe from new, nonunion competitors.

In relatively small-scale industries with numerous firms (textiles, clothing, leather goods, furniture, and so on), the opposite conditions prevail. The multiplicity of small producers presents organizing difficulties. There is greater turnover of firms and, since all new firms are nonunion at the outset, the task of organization is never finished. Firms with little fixed plant are freer to move about the country in search of low-wage, nonunion locations. Even if the nonunion sector constitutes only a minority of employees, it imposes a critical limit on wage and price levels.

---

[12] There is a large literature in this area. Recent contributions include Harold M. Levinson, "Unionism, Concentration, and Wage Changes: Toward a Unified Theory," *Industrial and Labor Relations Review* (January 1967), pp. 198–205; Martin Segal, "The Relation Between Union Wage Impact and Market Structure," *Quarterly Journal of Economics* (February 1964), pp. 96–114; and Leonard Weiss, "Concentration and Labor Earnings," *American Economic Review* (March 1966), pp. 96–117.

Why, then, does one sometimes find a high degree of unionization even in industries with a multiplicity of employers, such as longshoring, merchant shipping, and over-the-road trucking? Levinson has suggested that the basic factor is not industrial concentration per se, but rather "the ease of entry of new firms into production outside the jurisdictional control of the union." In oligopolistic manufacturing industries, the barriers to entrance take the form of large optimum scale of plant, heavy selling costs, patent protection of products or processes, and so on. But in other cases the barrier may lie in "the spatial limitations of the physical area within which new entrants could effectively compete." [13] Shipping and longshoring firms must have access to the docks. Long-distance trucking concerns must use certain terminals to make local deliveries and interchange freight with other lines. So once the union has effective control of these locations, the operation of nonunion firms can be prevented. By similar reasoning, Segal suggests that a union is in a stronger position in a competitive local-market industry than in a competitive national-market industry. Organizing is less costly when all potential recruits are in the same area, and geographic movement of firms to escape the union is no longer a possibility.

The second question remains: given the same degree of unionization in two industries, is there any independent relation between wage level and structure of the product market? *A priori*, one can argue this issue either way. In a concentrated industry, the fact that the price level is controlled by tacit agreement may reduce downward pressure on wages during recession and may enable wage increases to be translated more smoothly into price increases during expansion. This should be favorable to union wage gains. But on the other side one can argue that the managerial expertise and financial staying power of large oligopolistic concerns puts them in a better position to resist union demands. When the industry includes scores or hundreds of relatively small firms, no one company or group may be able to stand up effectively against the union.

There is difference of opinion also on the statistical evidence. Recent research findings suggest that when degree of unionization, labor force characteristics, and other relevant variables are held constant, the "pure" relation between concentration and wage level is either insignificant or slightly negative. The significant relation, in other words, is between concentration and ease of union penetration. But a 100-percent union is *not* likely to achieve greater wage gains under monopoly or oligopoly than under competition. A further complication is that increasing concentration is accompanied by increasing average size of plant, while large plants tend to pay higher wages than smaller ones. The wage effects sometimes attri-

---

[13] Harold M. Levinson, *Determining Forces in Collective Wage Bargaining* (New York: John Wiley & Sons, Inc., 1966), pp. 265–66.

buted to concentration, therefore, may in fact be due to the plant-size variable.[14]

OCCUPATIONAL DIFFERENCES

We concluded in the last section that unionism may have raised the average earnings of union members, relative to nonunion workers, by 10 to 15 percent. Union membership consists predominantly of blue-collar workers in manufacturing, mining, transportation and public utilities, and construction. It would seem to follow that unionism has raised earnings of unionized blue-collar workers relative to those of clerical, professional, and managerial workers. But since the rising level of education and other factors discussed in Chapter 12 has been working in the same direction, the *independent* influence of unionism is not easy to judge.

One must remember also that the bulk of the least skilled and lowest-paid workers are nonunion: most farm laborers, domestic servants, store clerks, hotel and restaurant employees, laundry workers, and other low-skilled workers throughout the service sector. The wages of these people are presumably *lower* relative to those of the unionized groups than they would be in the absence of unionism. Overall, then, it is not clear whether unionism has increased or decreased occupational differences in wages.

A more limited question concerns the effect of unionism or occupational differentials *within* the unionized sector. What might one expect to have happened? Is there satisfactory evidence as to what actually has happened?

Two preliminary comments are in order. First, how do we measure occupational differentials? Should the premium of one group over another be measured in *cents per hour,* or in terms of *percentage* relations? Suppose that in 1950 laborers in industry *A* earned $1.00 an hour and skilled men $1.50. In 1970 we observe that laborers in this same industry earn $2.00 an hour and skilled men $3.00. Do we say that the differential of the skilled men has *widened* from $0.50 an hour to $1.00 an hour? Or do we say that it has *remained unchanged* at 50 percent in both years? The second statement seems more nearly correct. The worker is concerned mainly with how well he can live on his earnings relative to other groups in the community. In this illustration the skilled man in 1970 can live 50 percent better than the laborer, just as he could in 1950.

The behavior of occupational differentials over time depends on how general wage increases are made in a company. If all workers receive a 5

---

[14] See in this connection Stanley H. Masters, "Wages and Plant Size: An Inter-industry Analysis," *Review of Economics and Statistics* (August 1969), pp. 341–45.

percent increase, then occupational differentials (measured, as they should be, in percentage terms) will remain unchanged. But if all workers receive an increase of ten cents per hour, this will be a larger *percentage* increase for the laborer than for the craftsman. Occupational differentials will narrow. Thus the issue of whether differentials should be narrowed or maintained often takes the form of an argument over how general wage increases should be applied.

Our second preliminary comment is that collective bargaining is not the only determinant of occupational differentials. We saw in Chapter 12 that market forces have been tending to reduce the percentage premium for high-skilled jobs over low-skilled ones. So if we find that differentials have narrowed in an industry where rates are set by collective bargaining, we cannot conclude that union pressure was responsible. It is difficult to distinguish the impact of unionism from that of other factors in the situation.

Where skilled, semiskilled. and unskilled workers are employed in the same enterprise, one can assume that demand for the skilled men will be more inelastic. Their wages form a small proportion of total cost; it is less easy to replace skilled men with semiskilled men than vice versa; and skilled men are also less easily replaced by machinery.

One might expect this economic fact to be reflected in bargained wage structures; but the outcome will depend also on the form of organization. For example:

1. If the skilled men organize in one or more craft unions, while the others are unorganized, one might expect the skilled men to exploit their demand curves and to widen their differential over the other groups. To test this hypothesis, however, one would have to go back to the period before 1930, when craft unionism was dominant and most low-skilled workers were unorganized.

2. A common situation is that in which the skilled men have one or more craft unions, which bargain separately from another union of the lower-skilled workers. Thus in building construction the carpenters, bricklayers, and so on, are organized separately from the laborers and hod carriers. In the railroad industry, the train-operating crafts are organized separately from the shop crafts and the maintenance-of-way workers. In paper manufacturing, the skilled machine tenders usually belong to the Papermaker's Union, the maintenance men to craft unions of their respective trades, and everyone else to an industrial union, the Pulp, Sulphite, and Paper Mill Workers.

In this case, too, one might reason that the skilled groups will exploit their demand curves and raise differentials to some equilibrium level beyond which, barring major changes in technology or labor supply, differentials would remain stable. But maximizing models may not yield correct predictions. One can find cases, such as the printing industry, where the premium of compositors over bindery workers and other low-skilled groups has been well maintained. But there seem to be more cases, including building construction, railroading, and paper, where differentials have fallen substantially over the past several decades despite the prevalence of craft organization.

One can argue, of course, that this reflects simply the *general* tendency toward narrowing of occupational differentials throughout the economy. But in some cases it has been furthered by union policy. The skilled Papermakers, who normally bargain jointly with the Pulp, Sulphite, and Paper Mill Workers, have collaborated with the latter group to raise the common labor rate rapidly, even though this meant a narrowing of occupational differentials. They seem to have reasoned that the labor rate is a protective floor underneath their higher rate structure, and that raising this floor improves their own long-run position.

3. Perhaps the most interesting case, and the one most frequently studied, is that of the industrial union including all levels of worker from laborer to craftsman. If the union behaved as a monopolist—trying, for example, to maximize the wage bill—it might still exploit the demand situation by establishing a relatively higher wage for the skilled men than would exist under nonunion conditions. It is a familiar principle that a monopolist selling in two or more distinct markets will maximize profit by charging the highest price in the market whose demand is least elastic.

On the other hand, the union is a political body, whose leaders must be responsive to membership sentiment. Since the bulk of the members are low-skilled, they might be expected to press for policies which would bring them closer (percentagewise) to the skilled wage level. On the basis of this "democratic" reasoning, it has often been assumed that industrial unionism makes inevitably for a narrowing of occupational differentials.

But this view is also rather simplistic. The skilled men will certainly feel that their "traditional" differential over the less skilled is right and proper, and should be perpetuated; and since custom has considerable weight in workers' thinking about wages, many of the less skilled will accept this reasoning. The skilled men also, because of their standing in the plant hierarchy and their personal qualities, will usually carry more than proportionate weight in union discussions and furnish more than their share of the union leadership. Finally, the skilled men can exert leverage by threatening to form their own union and bargain separately if their views are not given sufficient weight.

So while speculative reasoning might lead one to expect a narrowing of differentials under industrial unionism, in fact the pressure in this direction has not been strong. In the basic steel industry, for example, some narrowing did occur during the 1940s (as happened in virtually every industry during this period). During a period of rapid price inflation, which put particular pressure on the living standards of low-paid workers, equal cents-per-hour increases for all seemed equitable. This was also the formula favored by the National War Labor Board, whose rulings had extensive influence on the wage structure from 1941 to 1946. Since the late forties, however, percentage differentials in the industry have been fairly stable. General wage increases have taken the form of roughly equal *percentage* additions throughout the wage structure.

The United Automobile Workers also attached great importance in the early years to raising the bottom of the wage structure and insisted on equal cents-per-hour raises for all workers. The effect was to reduce the *percentage* differential between various grades of labor.

By the midfifties this trend had produced considerable restiveness among the skilled toolroom and maintenance workers, who constitute about one-quarter of automobile employment. Some craft groups threatened to withdraw from the UAW and bargain separately. The union responded to this pressure by negotiating larger cents-per-hour increases for the skilled men from 1955 onward, and by giving craft representatives a direct voice in wage negotiations and an opportunity to vote separately on issues involving the crafts only. Since that time the percentage differential between skilled and less skilled workers has not changed appreciably.

Sherwin Rosen has analyzed union–nonunion differentials for major occupational groups, using cross-section data for 1960.[15] He concluded that the relative wage effect of unionism was largest for laborers, probably somewhat less for craftsmen, and decidedly less for semiskilled operatives. Put differently, unionism may have narrowed the laborer–craftsman differential slightly. The really significant effect, however, was a reduction in the position of the semiskilled relative to both the other groups. This conclusion was tested for several industries by using the regression equations to predict earnings in the industry and then comparing with actual earnings. Good results were obtained for automobiles, steel, farm machinery, rubber, clothing, electrical equipment, and textiles, indicating that these industries conform well to the model described above.

To sum up: A decline in the earnings of skilled and semiskilled workers relative to laborers has been a general tendency in the United States and other industrial countries over the past half century. Unionism may have accentuated this tendency. But the impact of union policy is not very striking—certainly less than would be deduced from an economic model in which each skill-group maximizes its own wage bill. The impact has also varied considerably from industry to industry.

GEOGRAPHIC DIFFERENCES

We saw in Chapter 12 that wage levels in the South are considerably lower, and those on the Pacific Coast somewhat higher, than in the North–Central states. There are also considerable differences among communities of varying size within each region.

Union efforts to apply "the standard rate" should have tended to reduce geographic differentials; but this depends on the market structure

---

[15] Sherwin Rosen, "Unionism and the Occupational Wage Structure," *International Economic Review* (June, 1970), pp. 269–286.

of the industry and the scope of the collective agreement. Where competition is limited to a locality, as in house building and repair, retailing, and the service industries, and where bargaining is conducted locally with little supervision by the national union, there is no reason to expect wage equalization among localities. On the contrary, it may well be that unionism, by entrenching itself first in the high-wage regions and communities, has for the time being widened differentials in such industries. This may be one reason why building-construction wages in the South today are further below the northern level than they were forty years ago.

In manufacturing industries selling in a national market, on the other hand, geographic differentials have usually been reduced and in some cases virtually eliminated. In addition to the economic pressures for wage equalization, there is usually political pressure from union members. Bargaining is typically on a national basis, and delegates from all parts of the country serve on the wage-policy committee. Delegates from lower-wage areas are bound to feel that their members should receive as much as workers in the highest-wage plants of the industry; and national union leaders are under pressure to effect a gradual leveling-up of area differences.

Employers, on the other hand, tend to feel that wages in a particular plant should be in line with the *community* wage level. If a company has been lucky or astute enough to locate in a low-wage area, it should be entitled to reap the benefit.[16] So where geographic leveling has occurred under collective bargaining, it must be attributed to union pressure overriding employer resistance.

Where differentials have been eliminated, as in basic steel and flat glass, there has typically been a combination of favorable circumstances: a high degree of unionization, a high degree of industrial concentration, and a situation in which the southern plants were subsidiaries of northern companies. It is easier in such a situation for the union to force acceptance of wage equalization, and for the industry to adjust to it, than in an industry with many small, independent producers.

Elimination of geographic differentials in basic steel production was an early objective of the United Steelworkers. After twenty years of effort, this goal was substantially achieved in 1954 with the elimination of the "Birmingham" differential favoring the southern mills.[17] In automobile assembly, the union has succeeded in substantially eliminating geographic differentials among Ford and Chrysler plants, though some area differences

---

[16] This is true, at any rate, in heavily capitalized and hard-to-enter oligopolistic industries, where wage differences do not threaten the price level. It is not necessarily true of more footloose and competitive industries such as textiles and clothing. Northern employers in such industries often urge the union to make a maximum effort toward raising southern wage levels.

[17] For an examination of the union impact in steel, railroad transport, pulp and paper, and cotton textiles see Reynolds and Taft, *The Evolution of Wage Structure.*

remain in General Motors. In pulp and paper, unions have largely succeeded in equalizing company wage levels *within* each of the major producing regions (South, Pacific Coast, Northeast and Midwest); but because
wood costs and other production costs are higher in the older Northeast
and Midwest mills, their average wage level remains below that in the
South and the Pacific Coast.

In some industries the union has not been able to control geographic
differentials because of unevenness in its own strength from region to region.
This has been true of textiles, hosiery, clothing, furniture, leather goods—
indeed, most of light manufacturing industry. We saw in Chapter 15 that
unions have been relatively unsuccessful in organizing these industries in
the South. Their influence on geographic differentials is thus necessarily
small.

Finally, we may note the interesting case of the trucking industry.
This is not a "national" industry in the true sense. Some over-the-road
truckers, to be sure, operate routes across the country. But most confine
their operations to a particular state or region, while local truckers operate
within a single city. From the product-market side, then, there is no reason
for interregional wage equalization. The pressure came rather from within
the union, and was associated particularly with Hoffa's drive for national
leadership of the Teamsters and a single nationwide trucking contract.

By the end of Hoffa's regime a uniform *basis of payment*–mileage
rates plus a minimum hourly guarantee—had been established for over-
the-road truck drivers throughout the country; and the *level* of mileage
rates and hourly guarantees in different regions had been brought much
closer together. This was true also of local truck drivers. In 1949 rates in
some Southern cities were only 60 percent of those in New York. By 1964,
the lowest city rates were about 90 percent of the highest.

These differing experiences cannot be summarized in any simple
formula. Most unions in the majority of industries have probably had little
effect on geographical differentials, either because of the local-market
character of the industry, or because of union weakness in one or more
regions, or because the union (as in the paper case) has not found it expedient to aim at geographic equality. On the other hand, in truck driving,
coal mining, basic steel, automobiles, and some other branches of heavy
manufacturing, geographic differentials have been reduced and in some
cases eliminated.

Where differentials have been reduced, this might be expected to exert
some influence on the location of industry. The fact that some communities
have lower wage levels than others is an inducement for new plants to locate
in those communities. Specifically, there is an inducement for new plants
to spring up in small towns rather than in large cities, and in the southern
states rather than in the North. Wage leveling reduces this inducement. If

the union insists on the same wage level in all parts of the country, and if labor quality is substantially the same, there is no longer any reason for employers to prefer one locality on *grounds of labor cost,* though there may still be tax, marketing, or other advantages. The effect is to discourage movement of industry from North to South and from large cities to small towns. Or, to put the point in reverse, the effect is to increase congestion in established manufacturing centers.

This point may be less important in practice, however, than it appears in principle. It applies most strongly to small-scale, labor-intensive, foot-loose industries, in which labor costs are a large part of total costs. The "runaway garment shop" is the classic example. But these are precisely the industries in which unionism has had greatest difficulty in penetrating the low-wage areas. So where unionism might conceivably have had significant locational effects, it has in fact had relatively little influence. At the other pole, it seems unlikely that national wage uniformity will have much effect on the location of steel mills, oil refineries, auto assembly plants, and so on.

DISCUSSION QUESTIONS

1. You are asked to design a research study to determine whether wages in the automobile industry are higher than they would have been in the absence of unionism. Outline at least two ways in which you might approach this problem.

2. Some unions seem to have had a much larger effect than others on the relative wage level of their industries. What are the possible reasons for such differences?

3. You are national president of an industrial union, whose membership consists of 25 percent skilled workers, 60 percent semiskilled workers, and 15 percent unskilled workers. What policy would you pursue for occupational wage differentials?

4. You have data on average earnings in each occupation in an industry, year by year from 1940 to 1970. The industry has been unionized throughout this period, and you have full records of the union's internal discussions. How would you proceed to estimate the impact of union policy, relative to the effect of economic forces, on occupational differentials?

5. What conditions are most conductive to reduction of geographic wage differences through collective bargaining?

6. What are the probable effects of eliminating geographic wage differences in a national market industry where such differences were previously substantial?

7. The man in the street would probably say that unions have had a large effect on the average wage level in the economy. This chapter suggests that the effect has been quite moderate. Why this difference of opinion?

READING SUGGESTIONS

In addition to the references listed in Chapter 22, see H. GREGG LEWIS (ed.), *Unionism and Relative Wages in the United States,* Chicago: The University of Chicago Press, 1963; HAROLD M. LEVINSON, *Determining Forces in Collective Wage Bargaining,* New York: John Wiley & Sons, Inc., 1966; ROBERT M. MACDONALD, *Collective Bargaining in the Automobile Industry,* New Haven: Yale University Press, 1963; and LLOYD G. REYNOLDS and CYNTHIA H. TAFT, *The Evolution of Wage Structure,* New Haven: Yale University Press, 1956.

23

The Balance Sheet of
Trade Unionism

Earlier chapters have explored the effects of particular union policies. It is now time to put the pieces together. The economic effects of union activity can be classified under five headings: (1) the structure of labor and product markets; (2) the general level of real and money wages; (3) the relative wages of union and nonunion workers; (4) the nonmonetary terms of employment; (5) the social structure of the shop.

STRUCTURE OF LABOR
AND PRODUCT MARKETS

It is commonly said that unionism substitutes "monopoly" for "competition." The implication is that, in the absence of unionism, market competition for labor would force employers to offer equivalent wages and working conditions for a particular occupation; and that wage differentials among occupations would be no larger than necessary to equalize the net advantage of each occupation to workers on the margin of choice. Thus unionism could be regarded as at best a fifth wheel, and at worst a force distorting the wage structure and the allocation of labor away from competitive standards.

This view, however, does not take account of two well-known defects in nonunion labor markets. The first is the presence of monopsony power. Many employers are large relative to the local labor market in which they operate, and can alter wage rates rather than taking them as given. Tacit collusion among employers on wage levels and hiring practices is also common.

Second, our economy usually operates below full employment. There are fewer vacancies than there are workers seeking jobs. As Alfred Marshall and others have emphasized, this tilts the balance of bargaining power in favor of the employer. Because of the scarcity of jobs, and because of his limited resources, the worker is more anxious to get a job than the employer is to attract or retain any particular worker. A further consequence is that pressure on employers to bring wages and other terms of employment up to a common level varies with the level of aggregate demand for labor. It is strong at business cycle peaks, weak during recession periods.

Trade unions, in short, do not intrude into a situation in which terms of employment have already been perfectly aligned by competitive forces. They come into a situation in which relative wages may already have been distorted by monopsony and by weak labor demand. How far do unions correct previous distortions of the wage structure, and how far do they create new distortions? This is a factual question which requires examination of evidence rather than *a priori* judgment.

The economy might, in principle, be made to operate closer to full employment; and monopsony power might conceivably be reduced. But the difficulties with the competitive labor market model go deeper than this. Job characteristics are complex. They include hours and shift arrangements, a variety of employee benefits, physical conditions of work, work speeds, security of job tenure, and fairness of treatment by supervisors. Even if market competition worked reasonably well in determining wage rates, would it work equally well in regulating these other things?

A nonunion worker dissatisfied with some condition of employment has two alternatives. He can complain to the foreman or the personnel office; but this may endanger his job, and so direct complaint is discouraged. Alternatively, he can quit. So, why isn't this a satisfactory solution? If a company finds its quit rate rising, won't this bring adequate pressure to improve its conditions of employment?

From the worker's standpoint, quitting may or may not be a viable course of action. A job is an asset, whose value typically increases with length of service. Quitting imposes a heavy penalty on a long-service worker, who usually has fixed home costs and family responsibilities, and whose age may be a serious barrier to new employment. Quitting is also less viable when demand for labor is low than when it is high. In any event, quitting is usually not the preferred alternative. What the worker wants is some way of bringing pressure on management without quitting.

From the employer's standpoint, too, there are some disadvantages in relying on quits as a signaling device. When an experienced worker leaves, the company loses what it has invested in recruiting and training him. Turnover is costly, and is something to be discouraged rather than encouraged. Further, the information transmitted by quits is limited and ambiguous. An abnormal rise in the quit rate signals that something is wrong in the multidimensional employment relation; but it does not indicate just where the trouble is. Exit interviews, in which a departing worker is asked why he left, are notoriously unreliable, since there is no incentive for the worker to give a reasoned explanation.

Unionism provides the worker with a way of expressing dissatisfaction without quitting, and also provides a different—and possibly superior —information source for management. Union representatives can pinpoint sources of discontent, and can also suggest possible remedies, which may be applied unilaterally by management or may eventually be incorporated in new contract terms. To the extent that this alternative channel proves satisfactory, one would expect a negative association between unionization and quit rates. Further, if quit rates are reduced, the employer has a stronger incentive to invest in careful selection and job training, since he is less likely to lose this investment in the future.

There seems in fact to be a syndrome in which stronger unionization is associated with lower quit rates, heavier investment in training, and higher wage rates.[1] This association does not reveal the causal sequence involved. There is a distinct possibility, however, that unionism may in this way make a positive contribution to productivity, which can be set against the negative productivity effects noted in Chapter 21.

While the main impact of unionism is on labor markets, it probably tends also to strengthen monopoly power in product markets. Unions tend to favor "orderly" or quasi-collective determination of prices as well as wages. In industries with a few large companies which are able to control competition effectively, unions simply insist on a share of the proceeds. In industries with many producers, where control of competition is difficult, unions may take the lead in forming and policing restrictive argreements. The union will also typically line up with employers in support of legalized price fixing and restriction of new competitors, such as the controls exercised by the Interstate Commerce Commission and the Civil Aeronautics Board over the transportation industries.

As between its own industry and the remainder of the economy, in short, the union lines up with employers and strengthens their hand against outside competition and against the consuming public.

---

[1] On this range of issues, see the references cited in Richard B. Freeman, "Individual Mobility and Union Voice in the Labor Market," *American Economic Review* (May 1976), pp. 361–68. See also John F. Burton, Jr., and John E. Parker, "Interindustry Variations in Voluntary Labor Mobility," *Industrial and Labor Relations Review* (January 1969), pp. 199–216.

THE GENERAL LEVEL OF WAGES

Let us talk first about possible union influences on the real wage level, and then about effects on money wages and inflation.

If we grant the neoclassical model of Chapter 11 some degree of validity, the real wage level depends on the size of the labor force and on the height of labor's marginal productivity schedule, and unionism could influence real wages only *via* one or other of these routes.

The productivity effect is quite conjectural. Previous chapters have pointed out some ways in which unionism may raise labor productivity, and other ways in which it may lower it. Considering that the effects run in both directions, and considering also that only one-quarter of the American labor force is unionized, it seems unlikely that the net effect on the productivity schedule has been substantial.

It does seem likely, however, that unionism has produced a considerable reduction in labor supply. The labor movement was influential in the enactment of restrictive immigration laws in the 1920s, which reduced immigration from a flood to a trickle. Trade unions have also been in the forefront of movements to reduce weekly and annual hours of work, and to encourage retirement through private and public pension systems. A major device here is the provision of the Social Security Act which sets a ceiling on the amount that a retired worker may earn annually without reduction of Social Security benefits. More recently, unions in industries where emploment is declining have tried to speed the exit of older workers from the industry by lowering the retirement age.

It is impossible to measure the total effect of these policies, but it would not be surprising to find that labor supply in the United States is 10 percent lower than it would have been in the absence of union activity. The effect is to reduce national output because of the reduction in labor inputs, and to raise the real wage rate per man-hour of work. This may raise labor's share of the reduced output, but will not necessarily do so, the result depending on the elasticity of labor–capital substitution.

Suppose now that we depart from competitive assumptions and accept that employers sometimes have monopsony power in the labor market. In this situation the employer has an incentive to restrict employment in order to lower the wage rate. The effect (as compared with what would happen in a perfect labor market) is to reduce the wage rate, employment, and the wage bill; to increase the employer's profit margin per unit and his total profit; and to reduce labor's share of value added. A minimum wage enforced by law or collective bargaining restores the conditions of a perfect labor market in the sense that labor supply becomes perfectly elastic at the prescribed wage. Up to a point, wages can be raised with a simultaneous *increase* in employment, hence in the wage bill, and also in labor's share of value added. Here, then, is a case in which unionism clearly can alter the distribution of income in labor's favor.

What we do not know is the practical importance of this case. How extensive is monopsony in nonunion labor markets? How fully do employers recognize and exploit their monopsony power? Differences of opinion on these points can lead to widely differing estimates of the union impact. The writer's hypotheses would be that (1) monopsony is important for large firms in towns of, say, 10,000 or less located at some distance from a metropolitan center; (2) many employers do take advantage of their monopsony position; (3) a union entering such a situation for the first time can often secure a large initial wage increase, which wipes out part or all of the previous monopsony gain; (4) this is a once-for-all increase, wages thereafter moving in line with regional or industry trends; (5) for the economy as a whole, it seems unlikely that such transfers could total more than a small percentage of the wage bill. The *direction* of the impact, however, is toward an increase in labor's income share.

Finally, a union may go beyond simply offsetting employers' monopsony power and use its own market power to set a wage above the competitive level. The gains made in this way, however, are only to a limited extent at the expense of the employer. Most of the burden is borne by buyers of the product in higher prices, or by nonunion workers, whose wage level is depressed by the reduction of employment in the unionized sector and the consequent increase of labor supply to the nonunion sector. Thus there may be little or no increase in the average level of real wages for all workers in the economy.

Overall, then, we come out with an impression that unionism probably has increased the *real wage rate* per man-hour of labor, mainly through a reduction in labor supply; and that it may have increased labor's *share of national income,* partly through the once-for-all gain from organizing monopsonistic employers. These effects are small, however, amounting at most to a few percentage points; and they are almost insignificant relative to the long-run rise of real wages resulting from productivity growth.

It is startling that public opinion polls show a large majority of the American public believing that labor's long-run gains have been due *mainly* to union organization. There is no economic evidence for this belief. It is a natural optical illusion, however, since a union president always takes full credit for wage gains, just as a U.S. president takes credit for business cycle upswings (but not downswings!). The situation is similar to that of the rooster in the fable who, observing that his crowing always coincided with the rising of the sun, concluded that his efforts were causing the sunrise.

There is a similar optical illusion concerning union influence on the money wage level and the rate of inflation. Unions doubtless make some difference, but the difference is much less than popularly supposed.

The clearest impact of unionism is in recession periods, when unions not merely prevent wage cuts but keep wages moving upward despite growing unemployment. The main mechanism here is the multiyear contract, with built-in wage increases scheduled in advance. Three-year contracts negotiated in 1973, a year of high employment and substantial inflation, provided for large wage increases in the years 1974 to 1976. These increases automatically went into effect, even though business had turned downward in the fall of 1974, and 1975 and 1976 saw substantial unemployment. The momentum of a past inflationary period is thus carried forward into the future.

Nonunion wages do not fall either during a recession; but their rate of increase is slower, and the union–nonunion gap widens.

It is less clear what happens during business cycle upswings. Probably the commonest view, advanced originally by H. G. Lewis, is that unionism makes wage rates more sluggish on the upswing. This could result from the three-year contract cycle, where a low increase negotiated two years ago during a recession goes into effect automatically, even though today's boom conditions would make a higher increase appropriate. Nonunion rates, on the other hand, tend to rise more rapidly because of active employer competition for labor in a tightening labor market. The result, Lewis argued, is that the union–nonunion wage gap tends to narrow at business cycle peaks, just as it widens during recession.

This view, however, is by no means universally accepted. Studies by Perry, Pierson, and McCaffree have concluded that, at a given level of unemployment, there is some tendency for wage rates to rise faster in strongly unionized industries.[2] Pierson, for example, states: "To conclude . . . it appears that union strength significantly worsens the trade-off between unemployment and inflation. At 5 percent unemployment the wage rate advantage to strong unionism is in the range of 0.6 to 1.7 percentage points."

Whichever view turns out to be correct, the impact of unionism is clearly less than it appears in popular writings, where union leaders are often cast as villains in the inflationary drama. A quite believable explanation of wage–price behavior can be developed without bringing these actors onto the stage. The popular view may in part represent a confusion between *levels* and *rates of change*. It is one thing to argue that union wages tend to be *higher* than nonunion wages for the same kind of work. This apparently is true, as later evidence will suggest. But it is quite another thing to argue that union wages *rise faster* than nonunion wages. This would have

[2] See George L. Perry, "Changing Labor Markets and Inflation," *Brookings Papers on Economic Activity* (1970), pp. 411–41; Gail Pierson, "The Effect of Union Strength on the U.S. Phillips Curve," *American Economic Review* (June 1968), pp. 456–67; Kenneth M. McCaffree, "A Further Consideration of Wages, Unemployment, and Prices in the United States, 1948–58," *Industrial and Labor Relations Review* (October 1963), pp. 60–74.

to mean that the gap between the union and nonunion wages is increasing constantly over time, which is something we do not observe.

UNIONISM AND RELATIVE WAGE RATES

The clearest effect of unionism is to alter the relative wages of particular groups of workers. Since Chapter 22 was devoted to this subject, we need do little more than restate the conclusions reached there.

1. At the plant level, unionism tends to reduce differences among people doing the same kind of work by establishing standard job rates or rate ranges. The economic effect of this depends on how far the workers concerned differ in personal efficiency, and on just what is equalized—a simple hourly rate, a range of hourly rates, a schedule of piece rates, or whatever.

Members of a work group usually differ somewhat in productive capacity. In a perfectly competitive labor market, these capacity differences would be reflected in differing rates of pay. The market would tend to equalize, not earnings per worker, but wage rates *per efficiency unit of labor*. If a union required that every worker receive exactly the same amount, the wage per efficiency unit would be unequal, being highest for the least efficient workers. Such a result could be criticized as both inefficient and inequitable. In practice, however, this effect is usually attenuated either by a piece-rate system or by setting a rate range rather than a single rate for the job, so that superior workers can advance beyond their fellows.

A side effect of union pressure for wage uniformity is to make employers more conscious of, and more careful about, their hiring standards. An applicant will not be hired, or will not survive the probationary period, unless he can produce enough to justify the standard wage. Thus the "layering" of the wage structure, with some plants and industries paying more than others, leads to a corresponding "layering" of the labor force. High-productivity individuals tend to be allocated to high-wage industries. This makes the difference in wages-per-efficiency unit of labor somewhat less than the crude wage differences.

2. Unionism tends to equalize the wage levels of companies competing in the same product market. In the case of local-market industries, such as retailing, repair and service industries, job and newspaper printing, and most building construction, this usually means equalization within a city or metropolitan area. In the case of manufacturing and other industries that compete on a national basis, it usually produces efforts at national wage equalization. This is not always true, however, as witness the paper industry case. And even where the union tries, it cannot succeed unless it is able to maintain a high degree of organization in all parts of the country.

The effect of bringing competing employers to the same wage level depends partly on the reasons for the previous wage differences. To the extent that monopsony power was responsible, there is simply a transfer from profit to wages. (There is also an incidental benefit to the higher-wage employers, who are freed of the threat of low-wage competition.) To the extent that low wages reflected low productivity resulting from lack of managerial capacity or effort, there will probably be a "shock effect" leading to a rise in productivity and some reduction in employment. On the other hand, companies suffering from irremovable disadvantages of location or antiquated equipment, and that were previously able to offset this by a lower wage level, will find their profit margin permanently reduced. Returns to capital may fall to the point at which the company cannot survive. Unions are reluctant to put a company out of operation, however, particularly where reemployment possibilities for their members are poor; and they often make concessions to firms with low wage-paying ability.

3. To the extent that unions reduce intercompany differentials in regional- or national-market industries, this means a reduction in geographic wage differentials. This might be considered desirable as a long-run goal. Existing geographic differences in real wages, however, presumably reflect a disequilibrium situation, a more abundant labor supply (relative to demand) in some areas than in others. This situation requires labor migration out of the low-wage areas and capital migration into them, which will gradually reduce geographic wage differences. "Premature" wage equalization under collective bargaining, which reduces the incentives to both types of movement, may thus be considered undesirable.

4. There is considerable evidence that unionism has raised the wage level of unionized industries relative to earnings of nonunion labor. The effect varies, however, between inflationary and depression periods, among industries, and within the same industry at different periods of time. Estimates by Lewis and others suggest that the overall effect is of the order of 10 to 15 percent, though there are occasional instances in which the union has gained a wage advantage of 25 percent or more.

This "monopolistic distortion" of the wage structure is an undesirable effect of collective bargaining. The size of the effect, however, is smaller than has often been alleged. Why unions have not achieved larger distortions by exploiting differing elasticities of labor demand is one of the more intriguing questions in the economics of collective bargaining.

5. The fact that collective bargaining establishes standard rates for each job means that unions are necessarily concerned with occupational wage differences. It is difficult to frame general hypotheses about the outcome, because this depends partly on the form of union organization in each industry. There has also been less study of this problem than of inter-industry wage relations.

The most interesting hypothesis to emerge recently is that unionism may raise the relative wage level of *both* laborers and skilled craftsmen, with little effect on the percentage differential between them. In this view, the main effect would be a relative *decline* in the position of semiskilled workers. There is some statistical support for this hypothesis, but more investigation is needed to support any firm conclusions.

If one looks at the whole range of occupations in the economy, it appears that unions have raised the average earnings of organized manual workers relative to *both* the white-collar groups higher up in the wage structure *and* the lowest-paid, unorganized groups at the bottom. It is not clear whether this has increased or decreased the overall inequality of earnings from labor.

NONWAGE BENEFITS AND THEIR COST

Unions try to win for their members a wide array of benefits in addition to wages. Some of these involve little cost or may even reduce costs and add to productive efficiency. Others, however, do involve costs that must be weighed against the benefits provided.

In some cases the costs are borne mainly by the workers themselves. For example, a reduction of working hours means a reduction in potential national output and part of this will fall on workers in the form of lower real incomes and consumption levels. Here one encounters the problem of workers' valuation of income versus leisure. Up to the present there has probably been no serious discrepancy between union-established working hours and those which workers would have chosen voluntarily; but the problem of conflicting objectives may become more serious in the future.

The workweek and workyear will probably continue to decline gradually in unionized industries. Workers will go along with a policy of hours reduction, partly because they do not understand the income costs involved, partly because shorter hours are plausibly urged as an unemployment remedy. Actually, hours reduction is not a suitable remedy either for general unemployment or for overstaffing of a particular industry. There is also reason to doubt whether a further substantial shortening of hours would be in accord with workers' preferences. Several million people are now holding more than one job, indicating that for them the standard workweek is already too short. The eagerness of many workers to put in overtime whenever possible testifies in the same direction. It is quite possible, therefore, that unions may force down hours faster than most workers prefer, and that what used to be counted a major benefit of unionism may turn into a disadvantage.

The cost of some union benefits falls partly or mainly on consumers, among whom workers are of course included. Union efforts to control work speeds increase production costs by increasing the amount of labor time required per unit of product. Improvements in physical working conditions usually cost money. Resistance to technical improvements, insistence that promotions be made strictly on a seniority basis, and insistence that the union's consent must be given before certain management decisions can be carried out—these and other things tend to reduce production efficiency and raise costs.

Critics of unionism sometimes imply that any union policy that reduces man-hour output or increases unit production costs is economically harmful. This is not a tenable position. The question that must be asked in each case is this: Do the benefits that workers obtain from a particular union policy outweigh the additional costs imposed on consumers of the product? This question can be answered only with respect to a particular situation; and the answer will usually depend not on the kind of policy involved, but on the degree to which it has been carried. Down to a certain point, for example, a reduction in work speeds does more good than harm; beyond that point it becomes undesirable. The problem in each case is to strike a proper balance between the interests of a particular producer group and of society at large.

There is strong reason to think that, in the absence of trade union organization, the balance is tilted too far in the direction of minimizing money costs of production, that is, of sacrificing the interests of workers to those of employers and consumers. There is equally little doubt that unions, in attempting to redress the balance, sometimes overshoot the mark and saddle industry with unduly high costs. On the whole, however, it seems likely that one comes closer to a proper balancing of producer and consumer interests with collective bargaining than without it.

It should be recognized also that collective bargaining yields important benefits involving little or no addition to production costs. Many improvements in working conditions and personnel methods can be accomplished with little expense; yet unless workers point out the possibilities and are in a position to insist on them, the changes may not be made. The greatest single benefit that unionism brings the worker is protection against arbitrary discharge. The involves little direct cost and seems as likely to raise workers' efficiency as to lower it. Seniority rules concerning layoff and retiring are also much appreciated by workers and may well have a neutral or even favorable effect on efficiency. Where benefits accrue to the worker at little or no social cost, they would seem to be advantageous from every point of view.

SOCIAL STRUCTURE OF THE SHOP

A major consequence of collective bargaining is to change the foreman from an absolute to a constitutional monarch, who must operate within the framework of the union agreement and whose decisions can be appealed to higher authority. To the worker, this appears as an unmitigated gain. To the foreman, it appears as an increase in the difficulty and a reduction in the attractiveness of his job. It is one thing to maintain production standards when the men under you are fully subject to your authority. It is quite another when your every decision, large or small, may be taken up as a grievance by the union and you may be forced into ignominious retreat. The foreman is part of management; yet he must live with the workers and with the union. Nor can he be sure that higher management will back him up in a grievance proceeding. Management must save its powder for crucial issues and must view each case in the light of overall strategy vis-à-vis the union. The individual foreman is expendable. The trying nature of the foreman's job under union conditions has created a real problem of persuading qualified men to accept promotion to foremanships. Many workers understandably reason, "Why should I have everybody hating me for an extra ten cents an hour?"

The degree of personal harmony and productive efficiency in the shop depends a good deal on the relation that the foreman is able to work out with the union steward in his department. A skillful foreman can use the steward as an aid to management, an informal consultant and go-between in dealing with the workers. Foreman and steward may work out flexible interpretations of personnel rules and may trade enforcement on some points for concessions on others. Carried too far, of course, this may lead to erosion of the foreman's authority. One finds situations in which the union steward is the *de facto* head of the shop and the foreman's position is secondary. The foreman's central problem is to maintain effective control while winning consent and cooperation.

Whatever difficulties the grievance procedure may pose for the individual foreman, it has important advantages from an overall management standpoint. It provides a channel through which complaints and problems arising in the plant can be transmitted rapidly up the line to top management. In theory, the regular management chain of command already provides a means for upward communication of information and problems as well as downward communication of directives and instructions. It was pointed out in Chapter 17, however, that upward communication is apt to be heavily censored with a view to passing on only favorable news to one's superiors. Top management thus get the impression that everything is running smoothly in the plant, when in fact discontent may have risen almost to the point of explosion.

Under collective bargaining, pressures accumulating in the plant that do not find expression through regular management channels can travel up the line through the grievance procedure. This procedure provides a supplementary, and frequently more rapid, line of communication from the bottom to the top of the management structure. Selekman has advocated that management make full use of this method of keeping its finger on the pulse of the labor force.[3] Management, he contends, should adopt a clinical rather than a legalistic approach to the grievance procedure. The first question to be asked about a grievance should not be, "Is it a valid grievance under the contract and does the worker have a legal case for adjustment?" The question should be rather, "What does the filing of this grievance, whether valid or invalid, indicate about the state of human relations in the shop? What can be done to improve the situation?"

Finally, collective bargaining makes a fundamental difference in the determination and administration of personnel policies. Under nonunion conditions these can be regarded as analogous to any other group of management functions—marketing, finance, engineering, and so on. They are subject to unilateral management control, and the only question that

---

[3] Benjamin Selekman, *Labor Relations and Human Relations* (New York: McGraw-Hill Book Company, 1947).

arises is whether a particular procedure will contribute to greater efficiency of the business. Under collective bargaining, this is drastically changed. A few functions—notably the selection and training of new employees, and certain welfare activities—remain under primary control of management. With respect to the great majority of personnel functions, however, both the determination and execution of policy become a bipartisan matter. With respect to any policy, management must ask not only, "Does it contribute to efficiency?" but also, "Can it be sold to the union?" Skill in negotiation and personal contacts, rather than skill in engineering and other managerial techniques, becomes the primary requirement for an industrial relations officer. An incidental effect is usually to raise the status of the industrial relations group in the management hierarchy, and to bring about the hiring of better industrial relations personnel.

We have dwelt a good deal in earlier sections on wage rates and other economic consequences of collective bargaining. One should never lose sight, however, of the effects just described. It is these that most directly affect the daily lives of everyone in industry, from laborers to corporation presidents. These effects must consequently bulk large in an overall appraisal of trade unionism.

CONCLUDING COMMENT

Unionism and collective bargaining are doubtless here to stay. Judgments on the merit of trade unionism are thus in a sense academic, but are still of intellectual interest. The author has tried to provide the reader with facts, ideas, and arguments on which to base his own evaluation.

One's evaluation of unionism should not be too narrowly economic in character. It is a curious fact that both the critics and defenders of unionism have based their arguments mainly on the wage–employment effects outlined in the first few sections of this chapter. Actually, there is little evidence that unionism has any striking effects on productivity, money wage levels, real wage levels, or the distribution of industry's receipts between wages and profits. These subjects bulk large in textbook discussion mainly because we have theories about wages and employment, while we have no equally precise theoretical framework for analyzing working conditions and social relations in the plant. But the fact that we have conceptual difficulty in grappling with these problems does not mean that they are less important than wage issues.

A good case can be made that the wage effects of unionism are harmful on balance, and that the economy would function better without them. A positive case for unionism has to rest mainly on its (probably) favorable effect of nonwage conditions of employment, and on its protection of the worker's job tenure. These effects may well be judged to outweigh distortions in the structure of wages and employment. But this is necessarily a matter of judgment rather than scientific demonstration.

DISCUSSION QUESTIONS

1. "Unionism substitutes 'monopoly' for 'competition' in wage determination." Discuss.

2. What are the effects of unions on competition in product markets?

3. What are the determinants of productivity? Do labor unions, on balance, raise or lower labor productivity?

4. What are the main noneconomic consequences of collective bargaining in terms of the plant and the individual worker?

5. "When all is said and done, the chief sufferer from union economic activity is the consumer." Discuss.

6. Can one imagine a system in which unions would perform all their present functions *except* the setting of wage rates?

VII

THE FRAMEWORK
OF PUBLIC CONTROL

Collective bargaining operates within a framework of legal rules, imposed partly by state and federal statutes, partly by rulings of administrative bodies such as the National Labor Relations Board, and partly by court decisions. Chapter 24 describes the way in which public policy has evolved from strong hostility toward unions before 1930, through a brief prounion period from 1933 to 1947, toward greater neutrality combined with increasingly detailed regulation of industrial relations.

The next two chapters outline the main principles of contemporary labor law. The treatment is necessarily too brief to do justice to such a complex subject; but we have tried to convey the flavor of legal thinking and a sense of the dynamic, evolving character of legal rules. Chapter 25 deals with the rights and responsibilities of the parties to collective bargaining: the right to free and unrestrained organization; the determination of bargaining representatives; the duty to bargain in good faith; the legal status of collective agreements and arbitration awards; and issues of the union's relation to its members.

Chapter 26 deals with the use of economic weapons—strikes, picketing, boycotts. The line between lawful and unlawful tactics is thin and controversial, with many issues still in dispute. A particularly difficult problem is what can be done about "emergency strikes" that cut off an essential service such as railroad transport, electric power production, food deliveries, health and sanitation services. Such strikes cannot be allowed to continue for any length of time. Yet the disputes that give rise to them must somehow be resolved. We examine the main devices that have been used in this area, and also some new and experimental proposals.

The most rapid growth of unionism since 1960 has been in the public sector. Particularly at the state and local levels, collective bargaining is rapidly becoming the standard method for determining wage and other terms of employment. In Chapter 27 we examine the differences between private-sector and public-sector bargaining, the ground rules that have been laid down in federal and state statutes, the ways in which state and local government units are reorganizing themselves to bargain more effectively, and the problems of reconciling collective bargaining with preexisting organizations such as the Civil Service Commission. Here, too, we face the problem of the strike. If strikes by public employees are declared unlawful, as they usually are, what alternative procedures can be used to obtain final settlement of disputes? If strikes still occur, as they do, what effective penalties can be imposed?

24

Public Policy: Development and Administration

Unionism everywhere operates in an environment of legal and political controls. Through statute, through administrative regulation, and through judicial decision, the larger community enforces its will in *public policy*— a large and amorphous body of rules, yet a potent force.

Around the world there are quite different types of public policy toward unionism. At one end of the spectrum unions exist and operate free of government controls, as private bodies. At the other end unions are brought into a close relationship with government agencies, so that economic decisions on wages and related matters are carried out under direct government supervision. The United States is somewhere in the mid-range. Historically, American public policy has moved from a position of complete freedom of action and absence of direct government controls to one of increasingly detailed regulation of union activities.

As the American continent was settled and developed, legal institutions inherited from the English system altered as they adjusted to the problems of governing on a continental scale. Unions learned how to develop and exercise political power. They engaged in a continuing conflict with employers on the political level no less than in collective bargaining. Each side adopted in turn the weapons and tactics of the other. The prize was control over the rules of the game, for these rules affected the growth, power and operation of organized labor. The relative fortunes of each side fluctuated, and the balance of power tilted with changes in the external environment.

Elements of consistency can be identified amid the zigzags of policy. These include, first, a consistent assertion of the public interest; the two sides could not be left completely free to fight out their differences. Second, American policy has implied a basic approval of conflict, as a healthy and creative force, which should be curbed only as it becomes disruptive. Third, there appears a consistent narrowing of the area of conflict. Fourth, there is a consistent invocation of the principle of equality of treatment.

Major shifts in labor policy are marked by acts of Congress and the state legislatures. The legislature is the proper body for defining social policy; but under the American Constitution the judicial and executive branches of government have elements of independent authority. American courts, through judicial review, have a considerable power of veto. The courts say that they merely interpret the law and the Constitution; but as one student of labor law has said, this only means that they are reserving the freedom to change their minds. Landmarks of policy change thus appear in Supreme Court decisions. The tremendous power of the American President, and to a lesser extent of the state governors, means that the executive branch also has a powerful voice in labor policy. The National Labor Relations Board, the National Mediation Board, and other agencies charged with administering the statute law of industrial relations have elements of independent power, and some of their major decisions stand for a long time.

This fragmentation of power and rivalry between separate units of government, which could happen in few other countries, has made it possible for the contest between labor and management to be shifted from one arena to another, as one side saw some advantage to be gained. Loss of ground at the bargaining table may be regained by an appeal to the government. *Law* becomes a weapon in the struggle for power.[1] The intrusion of government ever deeper into industrial relations has created an increasingly large, complex, and often contradictory body of rules.

JUDICIAL CONTROL OF UNION ACTIVITIES

A review of the turning points in American labor policy begins with a long period of a century or more when the power of the judiciary was unchallenged. Trade unions have been subject to comprehensive government control through the courts from the very beginnings of union organization.

There are two main types of legal rule: statutory rules enacted by the legislature, and common law rules, which are unwritten and are based on consistent lines of previous court decisions. The courts have the final word in administering both types of rules. Statutory law is applied first by administrative agencies, such as the National Labor Relations Board, but decisions of the board can be appealed by the losing party to the lower courts and eventually to the Supreme Court. Thus the practical effect of a

---

[1] Archibald Cox, "The Role of Law in Labor Disputes," *Cornell Law Quarterly*, 39 (1954), p. 592.

law is tested in a series of hearings, first administrative and then judicial, and in the end the judges often decide what the statute means.

Common law rules, on the other hand, are rules that have developed solely or primarily through the accumulation of judicial decisions. Instead of interpreting the language of a statute, the court decides a dispute on the basis of a line of precedents, a logical sequence of decisions in previous cases where the court finds elements of similarity. In the absence of statutory law, judicial application of common law principles shaped the growth of unionism for almost a century.

To enforce their decisions, the courts have three types of legal remedies. The first of these is criminal prosecution. If it can be shown that union members have broken laws concerning theft, trespass, assault and battery, arson, and other crimes, or even that they have violated local ordinances prohibiting loitering, obstructing traffic, or disturbing the peace, they may be subject to fine and imprisonment. The number of workers who have been punished for real or alleged misdemeanors runs into the hundreds of thousands. The second type of remedy is civil suit for damages. If union members cause damage to an employer's property, suit can be brought against the workers and in some circumstances against the union. The third and perhaps most important type of remedy is the injunction. This is a court order restraining the party against whom it is issued from doing specified acts. If the person goes ahead and does these things anyway, he may be ruled in contempt of court and punished by fine or imprisonment. The speedy and powerful character of this procedure has caused it to be widely used in labor cases.

The long period of judicial control was repressive and negative in character. Judges for the most part concluded that unionism was an undesirable activity that, if it could not be prevented altogether, should be held within narrow limits. This view was due partly to the nature of law itself and partly to the personal predilections of the judges. Law is necessarily a conservative force. It exists to protect established rights. The common law of Great Britain, carried over in large part into American practice, gives special weight to rights connected with property ownership. Unionism, however, attacks the rights of the owners of industrial enterprises to manage them as they see fit. It seeks to curb property rights in order to establish new rights of workers in their jobs. The common law also regards freedom of contract and freedom of trade as desirable social objectives. The union, however, exists to restrict competition and establish a quasi-monopolistic position for its members. Unionism thus seemed contrary to the spirit of the common law, and it was easy for judges to find rules and precedents that would repress the activities of organized labor.

The judges' legal training in common law principles was buttressed by their political preferences. They came mainly from the propertied class, mingled more freely with employers than with workers, and tended naturally to sympathize with the interests of property owners. Their political thinking was influenced also by classical and neoclassical economics, which could find no useful place for joint action by wage earners.

The Doctrine of Criminal Conspiracy

In the early nineteenth century a number of court cases declared union activity of any sort illegal as a criminal conspiracy under the common law, punishable by fine or imprisonment. In other cases it was held that union actions designed to raise wages or reduce hours were lawful, but that other objectives such as the closed shop were unlawful. The basic legality of trade unionism was not settled until the case of *Commonwealth* v. *Hunt,* decided in 1842. In this case, Chief Justice Shaw of Massachusetts held that union activities were not *per se* unlawful, their legality depending rather on the objectives they sought to attain. Workers who were powerless as individuals could, he said, combine lawfully for mutual assistance. They might increase their control over their own livelihood by bargaining as a group with their employer. He held further that the closed shop was a legitimate union objective and that a strike to obtain it was not illegal. The case was not appealed to the Supreme Court of the United States, perhaps because it was recognized as a policy that would reduce labor violence and thereby benefit the expanding industries of Massachusetts. Labor peace required some show of equal treatment before the law. At any rate, the doctrine of criminal conspiracy disappeared from American labor policy after this decision.

Trade Unions "Lawful" for What?

Unions thus came to be regarded as lawful associations, but the question remained open as to what kinds of activity a labor union could legally pursue and what actions were forbidden to it. To this question the courts applied the common law rule that harm intentionally inflicted on another is actionable unless it can be shown that the harm was justifiable. This idea arose out of business disputes, where the courts developed a line of precedents ruling that pursuit of economic self-interest by normal business methods is sufficient justification for harm done incidentally and without malice to the interests of others.

A strike or boycott clearly harms the employer and frequently other groups and individuals as well. This provides a ground for finding such activity unlawful unless the union can justify it as necessary to promote the economic interests of the workers. A judgment of fact must be made as to what tactics really advance the economic interests of the workers and under what conditions their claims are strong enough to justify the damage inflicted on the employer and on third parties. In the absence of a legislative statement of policy, the courts decided these questions case by case.

During this period the common law of labor relations developed somewhat differently in the different states. The courts of New York, for example, allowed considerably more scope for union activities than did the courts of Massachusetts or Pennsylvania. But in most states legitimate union activity was narrowly confined to peaceable strikes for improved wages, hours, or working conditions. Strikes for the closed shop, sympathetic strikes in aid of workers in related industries or trades, strikes against one employer to compel him to bring pressure on another employer (secondary boycotts), and many other types of activity were held unlawful. Once the objective of a strike had been ruled illegal, even peaceable actions in support of the strike came under the ban. And when the object of the strike was lawful, a court might nevertheless find that the tactics used were unduly coercive or injurious.

In the efforts of employers to seek court protection against strikes and boycotts, the favored weapons were criminal prosecution of union leaders and suits for damages. But in the 1880s a speedier and more effective instrument was developed—the labor injunction, which spread rapidly and continued unchecked until the 1930s.

Government by Injunction

The injunction was originally a court order designed to prevent threatened physical damage to property, under circumstances in which later action through regular court processes would be too slow. This device also came from English law.[2] The injunction was presumed to be a temporary restraining action to prevent irreparable damage to tangible property interests. It "froze" the relative position of two antagonists until the dispute could be settled in court. But once applied to *economic* damage, and to *intangible* property, in practice the necessity of later legal action was forestalled. The injunction is one of the speediest of legal remedies. Requiring only the judge's signature and backed by the court's full authority of fine and imprisonment, it could close down a picket line and bring a strike to a halt within a matter of hours.

When American courts extended the idea of safeguarding property

---

[2] The injunction developed as one of the remedies in *courts of equity*, which in England are separate courts with separate judges and a body of precedents different from the *courts of law*, where disputes between two adversaries are tested in open trials with judge and jury. But American courts sit simultaneously as trial courts and equity courts, the judge applying the different bodies of precedent according to the type of action taken by the plaintiff.

interests to such intangibles as "justifiable expectation of profit" from the continuous operation of a business, the entire strategy of the union was undercut. Under such an interpretation it could be shown that any strike was *ipso facto* injurious to property. American courts also tended to accept unsubstantiated allegations that the strikers were threatening physical damage, and to take affidavits from only one side of the controversy. This was a clear abuse of the equity procedure, which should obviously be applied without favoring one antagonist over the other. Yet the existence of many such cases has been well documented.

The injunction procedure operated usually as follows.[3] The company would go to a judge, usually one already known to be antiunion, and present a written complaint, stating that the union was threatening imminent damage to the employer's property and that this damage could be prevented only by issuing an order restraining the union from certain specified actions. Many injunctions were actually drawn up by a company attorney and simply signed by the judge. Even if the judge decided to take evidence from the union, this would be limited to an affidavit replying to the employer's charges; the union could not call witnesses or present oral testimony. After considering the employer's and possibly the union's statements, the judge decided whether to issue the injunction.

The temporary injunction, or *restraining order,* was usually drawn in sweeping terms, restraining anyone from interfering with the employer's business in any way. Judges occasionally went into detail, specifying that there must be only one picket at each plant entrance, that he must be standing so many feet from the gate, and so on. But the general vice of injunctions was their vagueness. Drawn in broad terms, anyone who supported the strike in any way could be held guilty of a violation, tried without a jury for contempt of court, and severely punished.

In theory there was a later hearing by the court, at which witnesses were heard, after which the temporary injunction was either vacated or made permanent. But the strike was usually won or lost in the intervening months. Even when the injunction was not strictly enforced, its application to a labor dispute brought the weight of law down against the strikers. With the union stigmatized before the public, its members became demoralized and intimidated, its treasury melted away, and its drive was weakened. In the more usual case where the injunction was broadly drawn and vigorously enforced by the police, it was an almost unbeatable method of strikebreaking.

An indirect result of the injunction procedure was to stimulate union interest in political activity. Many state judges were elected, and the others were appointed by elected officials. Unions saw the point of taking an

---

[3] The classic study is Felix Frankfurter and Nathan Greene, *The Labor Injunction* (New York: The Macmillan Company, 1930).

active role in this process. They also appealed repeatedly to Congress and the state legislatures to pass statutes legalizing trade union activities and forbidding the courts to interfere with them. These efforts were largely unsuccessful. Few laws were passed, and even these were unfavorably interpreted in hostile court decisions.

LEGISLATIVE POLICY: FIRST PHASE

The Antitrust Acts of 1890 and 1914

Legislative action in labor relations is part of a general trend toward increased government regulation of industry. After a century of rapid industrial development, in which business competition was restrained only by the courts under the common law rules of contract and tort, the legislative branch of government began to assert the public interest in a series of antitrust laws, which attached criminal penalties to agreements that created monopolies and market controls.

The Sherman Antitrust Act of 1890 was the first major step toward a federal economic policy. The Sherman Act sought to prohibit monopolistic control over the production and marketing of commodities. It applied, under the federal Constitution, only to "interstate trade and commerce"— that is, to activities not wholly within a single state. It is not certain whether Congress ever meant the Sherman Act to apply against big unions as well as big corporate interests. At any rate, the Supreme Court in 1908 *did* apply the act to union activities in the *Danbury Hatters* case.[4] The United Hatters Union, in a drive to organize the manufacturers of felt hats, had called a strike against Loewe, a small hat producer in Danbury, Connecticut. It tried to force a settlement by cutting off the flow of orders for his hats from merchants in other states. Loewe successfully sued the union membership for triple damages, and the award of the court (which amounted to half a million dollars) sent a shock wave of fear through organized labor.

Within a few years the Sherman Act was amended by the Clayton Act of 1914. The unions believed that they had scored a great victory, for Congress wrote into this act a long list of normal strike activities, forbidding the federal courts to issue injunctions against such acts so long as they were "peacefully" and "lawfully" carried on. Samuel Gompers and other AFL leaders called the act a Magna Carta of American labor. But it soon appeared that the legislators had drafted the act in less than precise terms. The new labor law did not say plainly that the Sherman Act should not apply to labor unions. Instead, it referred to "labor, agricultural, or horticultural organizations, instituted for the purposes of mutual help, and not having

---

[4] *Loewe* v. *Lawler,* 208 U.S. 274 (1908).

capital stock or conducted for profit." Moreover, the ambiguous words "lawfully" and "peacefully" opened up a loophole wide enough to drive a truck through, which the Supreme Court soon did, in the 1921 case of *Duplex* v. *Deering*. The Court nullified the act for all practical purposes, by limiting its application to disputes where employer and workers were in the direct relationship of master and servant. Leaders and friends of organized labor might rage, but the decision stood as a precedent for all federal courts, which would be changed only by a later Supreme Court decision or by an act of Congress.[5]

Two subsequent decisions are important. The 1922 *Coronado Coal* case arose out of a highly destructive strike by the United Mine Workers against a mine owned by the Coronado Coal Company. The company, ignoring the clear grounds for a damage suit in the state courts, elected to sue the union in federal court for triple damages under the Sherman Act. The Supreme Court ruled against the company, distinguishing the case from the *Danbury Hatters* and *Duplex* cases by noting that the strike had shut down only the *mining* of coal and had not directly interfered with interstate marketing or distribution. The company then brought a new suit, at which a disgruntled union official testified that the union's *intention* had been to eliminate competition between union-mined and nonunion-mined coal in interstate markets. On this showing, the Court ruled against the Mine Workers.[6]

A few years later, in the *Bedford Cut Stone* case of 1927, the Court applied the Sherman Act to a secondary labor boycott by the national stonecutters' union, and struck down their attempt to organize the Indiana limestone quarries by refusing to handle nonunion Indiana limestone.[7] In these four cases the entire program of organized labor was threatened. If strikes and boycotts were to be interpreted as restraints on interstate commerce, the logical extension of this view would lead to workers being forced to work at whatever terms the employer set, since few industries by this time did not have some interstate aspect.

In this period another weapon was added to the antilabor injunction and the antilabor interpretation of the antitrust laws. This was the *yellow-dog contract,* a promise that the employee would not join a union, which many employers began to require as a precondition of employment. In the absence of statute law, employers were free to exact whatever terms of employment they could; workers were legally presumed free to accept or reject the job as offered. Such an antiunion pledge was usually informal

---

[5] *Duplex Printing Press Co.* v. *Deering,* 254 U.S. 443 (1921).

[6] *United Mine Workers* v. *Coronado Coal Co.,* 259 U.S. 344 (1922); and Coronado Coal Co. v. *United Mine Workers,* 268 U.S. 295 (1925).

[7] *Bedford Cut Stone Co.* v. *Journeymen Stone Cutters' Association,* 274 U.S. 37 (1927).

and, since the employer did not promise a fixed period of employment in return, it is doubtful whether it could properly be called a contract. In the *Hitchman* case in 1917, however, the Supreme Court granted an injunction against the United Mine Workers to forestall organization of a mine in West Virginia where miners had secretly signed up with the union after having given the employer an antiunion promise. The union was forbidden to induce workers to violate their legitimate contract with the employer. This was a landmark decision in the use of the injunction, and still more on the buildup of belief that Court control of industrial relations was weighted heavily against the workers.[8]

The Railway Labor Act of 1926

Meanwhile the railroad industry had taken the first step toward recognizing the value of collective bargaining and peaceful settlement of labor disputes. Arbitration boards, made up equally of labor and management representatives with a neutral referee, had come into use on a voluntary basis. When these were incorporated into the machinery of the Railway Labor Act of 1926, the country's first important piece of labor legislation was on the books.[9] The administrative machinery created by this act is described in a later section.

The Norris–LaGuardia Act of 1932

The last phase of the period in which labor leaders favored government neutrality closed with the passage of the Norris–LaGuardia Act of 1932. This legislation set up for the first time a national policy in labor relations. Carefully drafted, its provisions specifically removed the judicially built obstacles to union organization and peaceable union activities.

The act, which is still in effect, declares that as a matter of sound public policy the individual worker would "have full freedom of association, self-organization, and designation of representatives of his own choosing, to negotiate the terms and conditions of his employment, and that they shall be free from the interference, restraint, or coercion of employers of labor, or their agents, in the designation of such representatives or in self-organization or in other concerted activities for the purpose of collective bargaining or other mutual aid or protection." Activities that the courts are forbidden to enjoin are listed: (1) a concerted refusal to work; (2) membership in or support of a labor organization; (3) peaceable urging of

---

[8] *Hitchman Coal Co.* v. *Mitchell,* 245 U.S. 229 (1917). For a comprehensive review of these issues and cases see Charles O. Gregory, *Labor and Law,* 2d rev. ed. (New York: W. W. Norton & Company, Inc., 1958), Chaps. 7, 8, and 10.

[9] The amended Railway Labor Act can be found in U.S. Code, Title 45, Chap. 8.

others to leave work; (4) publicizing a trade dispute by any method not involving fraud or violence; (5) peaceable assembly; and (6) payment of strike benefits and aid to anyone interested in a labor dispute who is party to a lawsuit. Moreover, yellow-dog contracts were made unenforceable in the courts.

The issuance of labor injunctions by the federal courts was further controlled by procedural requirements. The employer was required to prove that the regular police force was either unwilling or unable to protect his property. He also had to be innocent of violating any labor law. The judge, in issuing a temporary injunction, had to hear witnesses from both sides and could not rely solely on affidavits. A jury trial was permitted if contempt-of-court proceedings followed issuance of an injunction.

The provisions were essentially negative and neutral. The intent and effect of the law was to remove certain legal restraints by which trade union action had been controlled, and to leave the unions free to exert their full economic power against the employer. The Norris–LaGuardia Act was followed by antiinjunction acts in most of the major industrial states (Wisconsin had passed a similar law in the preceding year). The state courts would thus tend to follow the policy and procedures laid down by Congress for the federal courts.

GOVERNMENT INTERVENTION: PROTECTIVE LEGISLATION

A major change in direction came only three years later, with the passage of the National Labor Relations Act of 1935, commonly known as the Wagner Act from its principal sponsor, Senator Wagner of New York. From this date onward, government was to take an active part in labor relations.[10]

What made the difference after 1935? Government had scarcely been absent from collective bargaining in the preceding century. The judicial branch had taken an active hand from the beginning; the legislative branch had laid down basic rules to govern the contest. But the Wagner Act took the additional step of creating an administrative agency to implement the legislative policy and to oversee the collective bargaining process.

This step was the result of experience. In other areas of federal economic policy it had been found that mere passage of a law, with enforcement left to the initiative of the attorney general and the decisions of the courts, was not enough. A useful instrument had been devised in

---

[10] The National Labor Relations Act of 1935 can be found in 49 Stat. 449; the Taft–Hartley amendments are in 61 Stat. 136 (1947), and the Landrum–Griffin Amendments in 73 Stat. 519 (1959). The full text of the act with amendments is found in 28 U.S.C. 151 *et seq.*

the quasi-administrative agency, which performs the administrative functions of fact finding, just as a division of the Justice Department would do, but which also makes a preliminary judgment between contesting parties in which it exercises judicial power, subject to review by the federal courts.

Passage of the Wagner Act, and its subsequent approval by the Supreme Court, marked a change in direction so revolutionary that it can only be understood by recalling the atmosphere of the early 1930s, when worldwide depression had brought stagnation to the American economy. Underlying the provisions of the act was a belief that unionization would bring higher wages and greater purchasing power, which would contribute to economic recovery.

The philosophy of the Wagner Act was essentially as follows: it is desirable that terms and conditions of employment be regulated by collective bargaining. It is also desirable, therefore, that workers should organize strong and stable unions as rapidly as possible, without the crippling effects of bitter organizational strikes. This objective will not be accomplished if government follows a hands-off policy, since employers have many effective methods of resisting union organization. It is necessary, therefore, that government should restrain the use of certain types of coercion by employers for a long enough period to allow unions to be formed throughout industry.

Workers were not required to join unions, but the union organizer was to be given full freedom in presenting his case to them, while the employer was required to remain silent and inactive. The act took the position that a worker's decision concerning union membership is none of the employer's business. The role of government, through the National Labor Relations Board, was to ensure that union organization was not hindered by employer action. It was assumed that, if employer pressure were removed, most workers would choose to join unions. The growth of union membership from about 4 million in 1933 to 15 million in 1948 seemed to confirm the accuracy of this forecast, although it must be remembered that high employment and excess demand for labor during and after World War II also did much to promote unionization.

The Wagner Act gave employees the right to organize unions, to bargain collectively through representatives of their own choosing, and to engage in other concerted activities for the purpose of mutual protection. Employers were prohibited from engaging in *unfair labor practices,* which included: (1) interference with, restraint of, or coercion of employees in the exercise of their rights under the act; (2) domination of, interference with, or financial support of a union organization; (3) discrimination to encourage or discourage union membership, except where a closed or union shop was established by agreement with a majority of the employees; (4) discrimination against an employee for filing charges or giving testimony under the act; and (5) refusal to bargain in good faith" with the legal representative of the employees.

The act provided that, where doubt existed as to the majority status of a union, the matter could be decided by a secret ballot of the workers involved, or by some other suitable method. Such elections and other fact-finding aspects of the act were to be administered by the National Labor Relations Board, which was also given responsibility for prosecuting unfair labor practices by employers.

The Supreme Court's long record of antilabor decisions created expectations that the Wagner Act would be declared unconstitutional. But the Court had finally decided to accept the authority of Congress and the President in determining national economic policy. The great popularity of President Roosevelt, and his unprecedented landslide victory in 1936, were doubtless a factor in the Court's change of attitude.

At any rate, the constitutionality of the Wagner Act was upheld by the Supreme Court in 1937, in the case of *National Labor Relations Board* v. *Jones and Laughlin Steel Corporation,* by a vote of five to four.[11] For a decade thereafter, it was the unchallenged law of the land. It was still not generally accepted by employers, however, and in the early years there were serious difficulties in administering the act. The staff was inadequate and inexperienced for handling the flood of unfair labor practice charges that came in 1937 and 1938. But the board developed informal and increasingly effective administrative procedures and, by concentrating its effort on key cases, was able to bring about widespread observance of the act. In the twelve years from 1935 to 1947 over 45,000 unfair labor practice cases and over 59,000 representation cases were handled either formally or informally. Colllective bargaining became the accepted method of conducting industrial relations.

Acceptance of the Wagner Act soon led to passage of "little Wagner Acts" in many of the industrial states. State labor relations acts were enacted by Utah, Wisconsin, New York, Pennsylvania, and Massachusetts in 1937, Rhode Island in 1941, and Connecticut in 1945. These state laws are important, because the Wagner Act (and its successors) cover only establishments engaged in interstate commerce. A third or so of the non-agricultural workers in the country are subject primarily to state regulation.

Government protection of union-organizing activities, combined with the rising level of employment after 1933, led to a rapid increase in union membership. The CIO, which was not in existence when the Wagner Act was passed, quickly unionized most workers in the mass-production industries. This was not accomplished, however, without a number of large

---

[11] *National Labor Relations Board* v. *Jones and Laughlin Steel Corp.,* 301 U.S. 1 (1937).

and bitter strikes, culminating in the wave of sit-down strikes during 1937. Regardless of the reason for these strikes, middle-class opinion tended to label the sit-down as a sign of "radicalism" in the new unions. Instances of violence or irresponsibility during strikes, and occasional malfeasance by union officials were publicized by newspaper editors, columnists and commentators. Public opinion, particularly in small towns and rural areas, became increasingly critical of union objectives and tactics.

The strongest criticism of the Wagner Act, if one ignores the attacks of those who rejected it altogether, was that its treatment of unions vis-à-vis management was inequitable. Employer tactics were severely restricted, but no comparable restrictions were imposed on the unions. There was also criticism that the rights of individual employees were not sufficiently protected under the act. This objection is not surprising, since the purpose of the act was to favor collective action in all cases in which a majority had voted for it.

GOVERNMENT INTERVENTION: RESTRICTIVE LEGISLATION

The unfavorable public reaction did not lead to repeal of the federal and state labor relations acts, though this was the hope of many employers. It resulted rather in the passage of additional laws intended to control certain types of union activity. In an effort to achieve a workable balance of power between unions and employers, government was projected ever farther into the labor relations scene

The first of the new acts, which Killingsworth has termed "restrictive laws" as contrasted with "protective laws" on the Wagner Act model, was passed as early as 1939, when Pennsylvania amended its state labor relations act. In the same year Wisconsin repealed its act, substituting a new measure with controls on union activities; and Minnesota and Michigan passed new labor relations acts of a restrictive type. Kansas and Colorado followed in 1943, and Utah in 1947. In addition to these comprehensive labor relations acts, the years 1937 to 1947 saw a multitude of state acts imposing specific restrictions on trade unions. These laws dealt with, among other things, sit-down strikes, use of force and violence in strikes, mass picketing, jurisdictional strikes, sympathy strikes, strikes in the absence of an agreement, strike votes, picketing in the absence of a labor dispute, picketing of agricultural premises, picketing by nonemployees, primary and secondary boycotts, refusal to handle nonunion materials (the secondary labor boycott), coercion or intimidation of workers by trade unions, prohibition of the closed or union shop and the dues checkoff, licensing of unions and their officers, registration and submission of information by unions to the state government, filing of financial reports, control of mem-

bership requirements, control over expulsion of workers from membership
regulation of strikes in public utilities, and regulation of strikes in public
employment. By the late 1940s, there was scarcely a state that did not have
one or more union control laws on its statute books.

The Taft–Hartley Act of 1947

The movement toward restrictive laws was less rapid on the federal
level. Numerous amendments to the Wagner Act were introduced in every
session of Congress; but the Democratic majority in Congress and the opposition of President Roosevelt prevented enactment. During the war years
amendments were pressed less vigorously, since labor disputes were handled under special emergency provisions by the national War Labor Board.

After the war the campaign to curb union power gained momentum.
When government control of wages ended with the war, there was no accepted plan for resolving the difficult issues of wages and hours in the
reconversion period. Unions demanded higher wage rates to compensate
for reduced earnings due to shorter workweeks and less overtime pay.
Serious strikes over this issue occurred in the steel, coal, and automobile
industries in 1946, and there was also a nationwide railroad strike. Public
alarm over these strikes was partly responsibile for election of a Republican
majority to Congress in 1946. In 1947 Congress passed the Labor–Management Relations Act of 1947, commonly known as the Taft–Hartley Act
after its two principal sponsors.

The new law was in form an amendment of the Wagner Act, most of
of the provisions of the earlier law being carried over intact. But there were
many new provisions, and the total effect was to establish a different philosophy of labor relations. The Wagner Act assumed that most workers
prefer to join unions; that the interests of unions and their members are
identical; that restricting certain employer tactics will ensure sufficient
equality of bargaining power between unions and management; and that,
once the parties have been brought to the bargaining table, they should be
left free to write whatever contract provisions they choose. Government
should not try to shape the content of collective agreements.

In contrast, the Taft–Hartley Act reflects a distrust of collective action,
regardless of majority sanction. Its outlook may be summarized as follows:
(1) Workers may or may not wish to join unions. Their right to stay out
should be protected against coercion from any quarter, including the unions;
and workers already in unions should be given reasonable opportunity to
get out if they so desire. (2) The interests of members and of the union
organization are not necessarily identical. Workers need protection against
the union as well as against the employer. Government may have to regulate
internal union affairs for this purpose. (3) Unions are not necessarily the

weaker party in collective bargaining. In some areas of the economy the employer may be the underdog. To ensure true equality of bargaining power, the law must restrain unfair tactics of unions as well as of employers. (4) There is a public interest in the terms of union contracts. It may be necessary to prohibit some contract provisions; government is entitled to scrutinize bargaining results as well as bargaining procedures. (5) The public also requires protection against crippling strikes in essential industries, and special procedures are needed to deal with such strikes. (6) Union political power should be specially controlled; it is necessary to prohibit unions from contributing to federal election campaigns.

The Taft–Hartley Act thus moved away from the policy of protecting unions toward a policy of protecting employers, individual workers, and the general public. A variety of restrictions were imposed on union operations. The unions strongly opposed the act and later worked energetically to secure its repeal. These efforts were unsuccessful, however, and the Taft–Hartley Act continues as the main federal legislation governing labor relations.

Most provisions of the act can be related to three professed objectives:

1. To equalize bargaining power by restraining certain tactics of both unions and employers. To this end the act lists certain unfair practices on the part of unions, paralleling the list of unfair employer practices that was carried over intact from the Wagner Act. Unions may not interfere with the individual employee's right not to participate in collective bargaining. They may not attempt to cause employers to discriminate against non-unionists, except as may be required by a valid union-shop agreement. They may not refuse to bargain collectively with an employer. They may not engage in secondary boycotts or jurisdictional strikes, nor in strikes to force recognition of one union when another has already been certified as bargaining representative. They may not extract money from an employer for work not needed or not actually performed.

2. Second, the act attempts to protect individual employees against the union in a variety of ways. Union contracts may no longer establish a closed shop or any other system of preferential hiring. A union may not charge excessive dues or initiation fees. Although it remains free to discipline and expel members, it cannot cause the employer to discharge a worker under a union shop contract if the worker was denied membership or dropped from membership for any reason other than nonpayment of dues and initiation fees. In addition, employees are given a way of getting rid of a union that they no longer wish to represent them. If 30 percent of the employees in a bargaining unit file a petition requesting decertification of the union representing them, the National Labor Relations Board must conduct a secret ballot to determine the wishes of the majority.

The checkoff system of collecting union dues is regulated by a proviso that dues can be deducted from the paycheck only with the written consent of the individual employee. Employer payments to union welfare funds are only permitted if certain conditions are observed, such as separation of the welfare funds from general union funds and joint union–management administration. The act provides further that union funds may not be used for political purposes.

3. A third professed objective is to protect innocent bystanders against the consequences of interunion or union–management strife. The innocent party may in some cases be the employer. Under the Wagner Act, an employer sometimes found himself caught in the cross fire of two rival unions, each seeking to organize his plant and each threatening to shut it down, unless granted recognition. Since the employer could not petition for a National Labor Relations Board election to settle the issue, his hands were tied. The Taft–Hartley Act accordingly provides that employers as well as unions may petition the National Labor Relations Board for a representation election. A similar situation often arises in jurisdictional disputes where two unions—say, the carpenters and machinists—each demand that the employer assign a certain type of work to its members under penalty of shutdown. The Taft–Hartley Act forbids strikes in such situations and provides that they be decided by the National Labor Relations Board unless the rival unions work out their own arrangements for settlement. This has stimulated the growth of private settlement machinery, notably as between the various building trades' unions.

We have already noted the act's restrictions on the secondary boycott, an old union device of putting pressure on one employer so that he will exert pressure on another employer whom the union is really after. The practical effect of this provision, as applied and interpreted by the courts, will be examined in the next chapter. While secondary boycotts have not been eliminated by the act, they have probably been considerably reduced.

Strikes often cause inconvenience to another neutral party, the consuming public. The Taft–Hartley Act contains no limitations on strikes in general, but it does provide a procedure for use in so-called "national emergency" disputes. Strikes that, in the opinion of the President, imperil the national health or safety are made subject to injunction for a maximum period of eighty days. The President is authorized to appoint a special board of inquiry, which makes a preliminary investigation prior to the time an injunction is sought, and must turn in a final report when the injunction has been in effect for sixty days. If the parties, with the aid of the Federal Mediation and Conciliation Service, have not been able to settle the dispute by this time, the National Labor Relations Board is required to poll the employees as to whether they are willing to accept the employer's last offer. After this step the injunction is dissolved and the President may, if he wishes, refer the dispute to Congress and recommend a course of action concerning it. The board of inquiry is specifically prohibited from recommending terms for settlement of the dispute. These provisions do not apply to government employees, who are prohibited by the act from striking; nor do they apply to railroad workers, for whom a special procedure is provided by the Railway Labor Act.

The Landrum–Griffin Act of 1959

In the decade from 1947 to 1957 there was continued complaint of corruption and high-handed procedures in trade union government. Such practices may not have been widespread in the sense of involving large numbers of union members; but the complaints were genuine, they had high publicity value, and were sometimes supported by sensational testimony.

In 1959 Congress passed the Labor–Management Reporting and Disclosure Act, usually referred to as LMRDA or the Landrum–Griffin Act. This legislation broadened the area of federal regulation to include most of the internal affairs of labor unions. This was not a totally new departure. The Taft–Hartley Act was in effect a declaration of principle that government might regulate internal union affairs. Under it, a union that wished to use the facilities of the National Labor Relations Act, including National Labor Relations Board election procedures, was required to file with the Secretary of Labor a copy of its constitutional bylaws, an annual financial report, a list of its officers (including their salaries and allowances), and an affidavit by each officer that he was not a member of the Communist party or any other subversive organization. This last provision was particularly offensive to the unions, and a number of unions, including the vigorously anti-Communist United Mine Workers, declined to comply. A union that had its industry substantially organized could readily operate outside the protection of the act.

Several amendments to the Taft–Hartley Act were written into the final version of the 1959 bill just before passage. One of these eliminated the non-Communist affidavit. Secondary boycotts were restricted, but the building trades unions and clothing workers unions were permitted to curb subcontracting in their respective industries by negotiating, if they could, *hot-cargo agreements,* which controlled their employers' dealings with non-union manufacturers, contractors, and jobbers. The union practice of advertising the names of secondary parties to a dispute, such as distributors selling goods produced by a manufacturer, in the hope of enlisting public support for boycott of such goods, continued to be legal. The closed shop, prohibited by the Taft–Hartley Act, was in effect relegalized in the building industry. These amendments softened the opposition of some politically powerful unions sufficiently so that the leaders of organized labor, already deeply divided, were unable either to mobilize effective opposition or to unite on proposals for substitute provisions.

The main thrust of the Landrum–Griffin Act, however, was an effort to increase the power of the individual union member vis-à-vis his officers. The relevant provisions were described and appraised in Chapter 16 on internal union government.

ADMINISTERING PUBLIC POLICY

The basic statute controlling the conduct of industrial relations today is the amended National Labor Relations Act (NLRA). The administrative structure created in 1935 has been continued by successive Congresses, with amendments added in 1947 by the Taft–Hartley Act and in 1959 by the Landrum–Griffin Act.

The National Labor Relations Board

The agency charged with administering the law is the National Labor Relations Board, usually abbreviated to NLRB, or "the board." The prime responsibility of the National Labor Relations Board is rule making, and its rulings have the force of law. Its functions are half administrative, through its authority to make investigations, and half judicial, through its power to adjudicate disputes. The board's rules and decisions taken together have established a line of precedents through which there has come into being a common law of industrial relations. Across the United States unions and employers conduct negotiations on a relatively uniform pattern. Orderly procedures and settled precedents make it possible for both sides to know what to expect in most situations.

The board consists of five members, appointed by the president but not removable by him, with a five-year term of office. This arrangement, which is typical of federal regulatory commissions, tries to combine elements of responsiveness to public opinion expressed through presidential elections with elements of stability and independence of political controls. The board will usually include individuals of different political views, and the expectation is that they will consult reasonably on cases coming before them. The president designates one member of the board as its chairman.

The board acts as a group in the hearing and disposition of cases. These are of two types: (1) those arising from disputes over unfair labor practices, as defined in the act, and (2) those arising from representation disputes under the act's election procedures. A case may be heard by all five board members, or by three members. Majority agreement is needed for decision.

The administrative powers of the board are concentrated in the office of the general counsel. He is appointed by the president, with senate consent, for a four-year term. He is also removable by the President, but only for malfeasance, and this provision has not been used to date. Day-to-day administration of the act is carried out by regional offices, established at key industrial centers throughout the country, under the direction of the general counsel.

The duties of the general counsel are impressive. He has final authority over investigations; complaints in unfair practice cases issue only over his signature; he is responsible for all litigation involving the board; and his office supervises the regional offices across the country, with their large staffs of attorneys and other employees.

In addition to these statutory responsibilities, the general counsel has certain duties assigned him by the board. These include the conduct of all elections and all matters of personnel administration. The general counsel has a large administrative staff. Trial examiners, who are appointed from the register of the Civil Service Commission, conduct hearings and issue decisions called "Intermediate Reports." Their decisions become the final order of the National Labor Relations Board unless one of the parties carries an appeal to the board within twenty days. They have broad powers in hearings, and can rule on all motions and questions raised by attorneys for the disputing parties. Heading up this structure is the chief trial examiner and two associate trial examiners.

The regional offices, each a replica of the national, are headed by a regional director who is assisted by a chief law officer and a staff of field attorneys. In the larger regional offices there are field examiners; and in some regions there are subregional offices headed by an officer-in-charge.

National Labor Relations Board procedure in unfair labor practice cases involves three stages: (1) complaint; (2) hearing; and (3) issuance of a board order. The board cannot initiate a complaint but must wait until a charge has been filed. The regional office will then schedule a hearing before one of the trial examiners. The rules of court procedure apply in general to these hearings, but the aim is to collect facts as expeditiously as possible, and any party can introduce evidence or request evidence to be produced under subpoena. The trial examiner files his report with recommendations, which the board can accept, reject, or modify. It can also require the case to be reopened for further evidence. But in most cases the trial examiner's report is approved and becomes the basis for an order issued in the name of the board. In form this will be a *cease-and-desist* order, including a requirement of affirmative action (legally, a *remedy*). If the order is issued against an employer, there will also be a requirement of posting in the plant so that employees can be informed of the board's action.

At this point the board's authority ceases. It has no enforcement powers of its own. If either party to the dispute ignores or refuses to comply with the order, an action must be brought in the U.S. Court of Appeals in whichever of the eleven federal judicial circuits the dispute originated. Legal action may be started by the board; or the respondent may ask the court to review the board's order. The court can enforce, modify, set aside, or order further evidence to be taken; but it cannot simply substitute its own judgment. The board's findings of fact "if supported by substantial evidence" are conclusive. Only questions of law are reviewable.

The weapon of enforcement is a contempt-of-court proceeding. The officers of a corporation can be held personally responsible for obedience to a National Labor Relations Board order upheld by court review. The board has another weapon, the temporary injunction, which can be sought in a federal district court as a means of freezing the dispute pending a decision. If this is used in a strike or boycott case where the dispute concerns assignment of work between two unions, the board need only show a *prima facie* case. If the strike or boycott has been called to force the employer to recognize an uncertified union, or in violation of the board's prior certification, the board is obliged under the law to ask the district court for an injunction.

When a dispute has been appealed to the courts, the issue can go eventually to the Supreme Court. Reviewability is limited; otherwise the volume of appeals could clog the Court calendar and frustrate enforcement of the act. For example, the board's certification of elections has been defined by the Supreme Court as not within the meaning of *final orders* under the act, and hence not reviewable.[12] Other rulings that fall short of being final orders include negative decisions by the general counsel in unfair labor practice complaints; that is, the general counsel cannot be compelled to issue a complaint. His discretion on this point is final.

Court review aims to ensure a balance between forceful support of National Labor Relations Board decisions on the one hand, and protection of constitutionally guaranteed individual rights on the other. Ruling by ruling, the board's decisions hammer out a pattern that holds industrial conflict within predictable lines of action. To the extent that the contestants feel they cannot expect a better deal by appealing to the board, or by appealing from the board to the courts, they are encouraged to reach agreement through private collective bargaining.

As a piece of social machinery, the National Labor Relations Board can be given a good rating on both purpose and structure. It is reasonable that the courts should have given the board wide latitude and support over the years. Recent cases suggest, however, an increasing judicial concern to protect private rights against arbitrary board action. Indeed, after more than thirty years of operation, there remain basic unsettled questions about the board's role in making national labor policy. The Supreme Court, confronted with the necessity of deciding substantive issues on which Congress has remained silent, does not always show a high degree of confidence in the National Labor Relations Board. Instead of accepting the board's expertise and authority, the Court sometimes appears to limit the board's role to fact finding. Final decisions on substantive policy come down to a battle of Court precedents versus board precedents. As one authority has said, "Who's in charge here?"[13]

Why should there be, after three decades, so much oscillation and apparent inconstancy of purpose? Partly because Congress defaults by its silence. But the trouble stems too from lack of data about the board's effectiveness; also, from its infrequent use of formal rule making for the

---

[12] *AFL* v. *National Labor Relations Board,* 308 U.S. 401 (1940).

[13] Clyde Summers, "Labor Law in the Supreme Court: 1964 Term," *Yale Law Journal,* 75 (1965), p. 59.

clear articulation of settled policies. There are statistics on the number of cases "settled" at various levels of the board. But there have been hardly any empirical studies of the *impact* of board policies.

One such study was an investigation of nine cases in the Chicago area. All were discrimination cases, on which the issue and the remedy were quite clear, but the investigators found it impossible to obtain data about what had happened after the board's decision. The employers were reluctant even to discuss the cases. The union officials, due partly to the high turnover of union personnel, could not or would not identify the official who had been directly involved in the cases. The employees themselves, who had been the subject of the controversy, simply could not be located. Thus the study could not answer such a simple query as how many individuals had returned to work as a result of the board's decision. The investigators concluded that in most substantive fields the difficulty would be still greater.[14] For example, the most flagrant cases of secondary boycotts may escape the board's procedures because of an imbalance of power between union and employer, which deters the employer from bringing a complaint.

The board, seeking flexibility in developing its policies, has made little use of its power to announce rules after formal notice and hearing; and in its adjudications, written opinions often do not accompany the decision. Thus uncertainty about the *grounds* for board decisions is common. Sometimes an issue is raised twice before two differently constituted boards and a complete reversal occurs. Such reversals occur also in the courts; but when they do, and especially in Supreme Court cases, the reasons are stated carefully in the Court's opinion. Development of a line of *reasoned* precedents, and more courageous rule making, might cause the Supreme Court to give greater weight to board decisions.

At any rate, despite the declared purpose of Congress that the expertise of the board should be considered, the courts continue to grant entirely new trials. The National Labor Relations Board has more "business" in the appeals courts than all other federal administrative agencies combined. So long as the board and the lower courts do not regard each other's decisions as in any way binding, there are many areas in which it is not possible to say exactly what can be done and what cannot be done.

The National Mediation Board and National Railroad and Airlines Adjustment Boards

The transportation industry operates under a regulatory system different from the rest of American industry. This is partly because the government regulates fares and other matters through the Interstate Commerce

---

[14] Douglas V. Brown, "The Impact of Some N.L.R.B. Decisions," Industrial Relations Research Association, *Proceedings* (1960), pp. 18–26.

Commission and the Federal Aviation Commission; but this last cannot
fully explain the separate treatment. The Railway Labor Act, with its
amendments, sets up machinery altogether different from that provided in
the National Labor Relations Act. The act classifies disputes as "major"
and "minor," and separate but related procedures are followed for each
type. Minor disputes are those arising under an existing contract or from
unforeseen circumstances—in effect, grievance cases. Major disputes are
those arising in contract negotiations. The statute requires in both cases
that the parties first negotiate with each other. If the parties cannot agree,
in disputes under existing contracts the dispute is submitted to the National
Railroad Adjustment Board, whose award is binding.

If the parties are unable to agree in a major dispute, the next stage
is mediation by the National Mediation Board. The National Mediation
Board may also move into the case without waiting for a request by the
contending parties. If the National Mediation Board cannot settle the dispute, it requests the parties to submit the case to arbitration. If the parties
reject arbitration (as they almost invariably do), and if the National Mediation Board certifies the dispute as threatening to deprive the country of
essential transportation, the President appoints an emergency fact-finding
board. Meanwhile, the dispute is frozen for thirty days from the date of
formation of the emergency board, which means that a strike during this
period can be enjoined by the courts.

The Railway Labor Act's provisions go no further. After the cooling-
off period, the parties are free to engage in a trial of strength. Experience
shows, however, that when the statutory procedures fail, there will be
rapid intervention, by the President and possibly also by Congress.

The National Railroad Adjustment Board is made up of thirty-six
members, eighteen selected by the carriers and eighteen by the unions.
They are paid by the parties they represent and are organized in four
divisions, each with jurisdiction over a stated group of transportation employees. When the act was extended to air transportation in 1936, Title 2
created a four-member National Air Transport Adjustment Board on the
same pattern as the Railroad Adjustment Board.

The National Mediation Board, at the apex of the structure, consists
of three members appointed by the President, with senate approval, and
removable only for cause. Not more than two may be of the same political
party. Their term of office is three years, with the terms overlapping so
that one new appointment is made annually. One member of the board is
chosen by the others to act as chairman.

The Railway Labor Act of 1926 was drafted after long consultation
with the railroad brotherhoods and representatives of the carriers. This
may help to explain the success of its grievance arbitration machinery.
Arbitration of major disputes, however, has been consistently resisted by

the unions; and the issues have often been passed on to Congress for settlement. Presidential requests for Congressional action were made by Wilson in 1916 and 1919, by Roosevelt in 1944, by Truman in 1946 and 1952, and by Kennedy in 1963. Three of these resulted in special legislation that sought to avert specific work stoppages, two of them nationwide. Most recently, in a dispute over use of firemen on diesel locomotives, Congress in the Railroad Arbitration Act of 1963 made arbitration of the dispute compulsory for a period of two years. In all three cases the threatened strike was postponed, but within a year there followed renewed Presidential intervention. In no case has Congressional action really resolved the dispute.

Awards in arbitration cases have frequently been set aside by federal district courts, new trials often being granted where money awards were claimed. In June 1966, amendments to the Railway Labor Act for the first time prescribed specific standards for judicial review. The district court may now set aside an arbitration award only for failure to comply with the requirements of the act, for exceeding the scope of the board's jurisdiction, or for fraud or corruption. These standards still leave considerable scope for judicial review. In particular, "failure to comply with the requirements of the act" opens the door to judicial intervention.

Collective Bargaining: A Multistage Process

State and federal statutes have established a pattern of self-organization and majority rule, closely resembling the political process, as the basis for economic relationships in American industrial life. For unionized workers, wages and working conditions are determined by group action rather than by individual negotiation. A whole class of contracts, those of employment, have been removed from the application of the traditional law of contracts. Negotiations remain private, however, and the signed agreement that determines the conditions of employment for a whole plant, industry, or other bargaining unit, is a contract enforceable in the courts. Although it is no longer an individual contract, it is a private contract, in contrast to countries where the terms of employment are determined by a government ruling.

The process goes through a predictable series of stages beginning with the confrontation of union officials and employer representatives in bargaining negotiations. In theory, the two sides are free to negotiate as they see fit, about any subject either side wishes to bring up. In practice, both sides know that previous rulings of the National Labor Relations Board and the courts have defined certain limits of action. They may abide peacefully within these limits or they may decide to test the limits by doing something different. Out of previous contests have come scores of rulings

which, taken together, make up a kind of common law of industrial relations. The vast majority of negotiating sessions operate within the framework of this new common law and proceed to the writing of a contract.

Beyond the private negotiations, however, is the possibility of appeal
by one side to the National Labor Relations Board, or to the equivalent
state tribunal, or to the Railroad Adjustment Board, for an interpretation
of the basic law as it applies to a particular set of facts. The final stage,
and one in which it is sometimes possible to bypass the National Labor
Relations Board, is appeal to the courts.

The multistage process has created a legal structure of great diversity.
Perhaps diversity is a source of strength in our circumstances, for the
structure of American industry scarcely permits of simple, uniform solutions to employment problems. What is appropriate for electronics manufacturing may be unsuitable for the trucking industry or for longshoring
or automobile manufacturing. Legally, of course, it is untidy. Indeed, the
most remarkable aspect of the system may be that there are so many areas
of what the experts call *settled law,* areas in which the parties are willing
to accept previous rulings and to do things as they have been done by an
earlier generation of negotiators. In the next two chapters we explore the
main issues and areas of action, both settled and unsettled, in contemporary
collective bargaining.

Discussion Questions

1. "Until recently there were practically no statutes affecting labor
relations; yet public control over labor relations is as old as trade unions
themselves." Explain, giving examples.

2. Why have unions taken strong exception to the injunction procedure? How did the Norris–LaGuardia Act alter the use of this device?

3. Explain why union organization was easier after passage of the
Wagner Act than before that time.

4. Compare the philosophy and objectives of the Taft–Hartley Act
and those of the Wagner Act.

5. Does it make sense to have a special set of rules for industrial relations in the railroad and airline industries? Explain.

6. "Experience since 1933 proves that it is impossible to legislate good
labor relations. The best thing that could be done would be to repeal all
federal and state statutes on the subject and turn the matter back to the
regular courts." Discuss.

7. Suppose the National Labor Relations Act had been passed *with-*

out creating a National Labor Relations Board. Would the act have been equally effective? Explain.

READING SUGGESTIONS

References on current labor law are given at the end of the next chapter. Studies with a historical orientation include IRVING BERNSTEIN, *The New Deal Collective Bargaining Policy,* Berkeley and Los Angeles: University of California Press, 1950; FELIX FRANKFURTER and NATHAN GREENE, *The Labor Injunction,* New York: The Macmillan Company, 1930; CHARLES C. KILLINGSWORTH, *State Labor Relations Acts,* Chicago: The University of Chicago Press, 1948; HARRY A. MILLIS, and EMILY C. BROWN, *From the Wagner Act to Taft–Hartley,* Chicago: The University of Chicago Press, 1950; MARJORIE S. TURNER, *The Early American Conspiracy Cases; Their Place in Labor Law,* San Diego: San Diego State College Press, 1967.

There are a number of useful general discussions dealing with the problems and institutions of American labor policy. Book-length studies include ROBERT EVANS, *Public Policy Toward Labor,* New York: Harper & Row, Publishers, 1965; ROBERT C. MCCLOSKEY, *The American Supreme Court,* Chicago The University of Chicago Press, 1960; LLOYD ULMAN (ed.), *Challenges to Collective Bargaining,* Englewood Cliffs, N.J.: Prentice-Hall, Inc., 1967; JOSEPH SHISTER, BENJAMIN AARON, and CLYDE W. SUMMERS (eds.), *Public Policy and Collective Bargaining,* Industrial Relations Research Association Publication 27, New York: Harper & Row, Publishers, 1962; and *The Public Interest in National Labor Policy,* New York: Committee for Economic Development, 1961. Shorter general discussions include BERNARD D. MELTZER, "The Supreme Court, Congress, and State Jurisdiction over Labor Relations," in *Columbia Law Review,* 59 (1959), p. 6; L. C. RUTLEDGE, "Justice Black and Labor Law," *U.C.L.A. Law Review,* 14 (1967), p. 501; HARRY WELLINGTON, "The Constitution, the Labor Union, and 'Government Action,'" *Yale Law Journal,* 70, (1961), p. 345; ARCHIBALD COX, "The Role of Law in Labor Disputes," *Cornell Law Quarterly,* 39 (1954), p. 592; DAVID ZISKIND, "Standards for Evaluating Labor Legislation," *Cornell Law Quarerly,* 51 (1966), p. 502: and BENJAMIN AARON, "The Labor Injunction Reappraised," *Labor Law Journal* (January 1963), pp. 41–81.

25

Rights and Responsibilities

What are the main outlines of American labor law? What are the parties to collective bargaining required to do, what are they free to do, what are they prohibited from doing? As in other areas of law, the answers are not entirely clear-cut. We shall try to distinguish between what appear to be settled principles and frontier issues on which legal opinon is evolving and inconclusive.

The issues examined in this chapter fall into five groups:

1. The right of free and unrestrained organization
2. The determination of bargaining representatives
3. The duty to bargain in good faith
4. The status of collective agreements and arbitration awards
5. The individual's relation to his union

Another range of issues, involving the use of economic weapons such as strikes, picketing, and boycotts, will be examined in Chapter 26.

THE RIGHT OF
FREE AND UNRESTRAINED ORGANIZATION

The law governing the establishment of a new collective bargaining relationship looks first to the adoption of standards for union organizing campaigns and elections. In principle, certain items are paramount: (1) The employees should have a free choice between competing unions, and the right of rejection of unionism. (2) The union campaign should be conducted with propriety, without undue attacks on the employer, or on rival union groups, or on those employees who wish to abstain altogether.

(3) The employer is similarly restricted in the tactics he may use to combat the union campaign. (4) The personal and property interests of employers and employees alike should be respected. (5) The election process as administered by the National Labor Relations Board should be above reproach.

Election standards are set forth in the National Labor Relations Act. The employee is protected from coercion and from various forms of interference with his free choice [Sec. 8(a)(1)]. He is protected from employer domination [Sec. 9(c)(2)], and employer assistance to a company-dominated union is forbidden [Sec. 10(c)]. The courts under these provisions have prohibited a wide variety of discriminatory actions. The act also defines certain unfair practices of unions in elections [Sec. 8(b)(1) and (4)]; and the union winning the election may be certified by the National Labor Relations Board as exclusive bargaining representative [Sec. 8(a)(5) and 9(a)].

The National Labor Relations Board procedure in representation cases may be formal or informal. When there is no doubt about the scope of the bargaining unit and no dispute with the employer, a *consent election agreement* is prepared by the company and the union, specifying the name of the bargaining unit, the eligibility of voters, and the date of the election. On the other hand, if there is doubt as to whether the union has an actual majority, or disagreement over the bargaining unit, the regional director (through his agents) conducts hearings on these issues. A formal order is then issued (*direction of election*), ordering an election to be held in a specified unit within a certain period, usually very brief. The procedure from this point resembles in all respects a local political election. If votes are challenged when the ballots are counted and the challenges cannot be settled at once, the ballots will be set aside. If there are enough challenged votes to affect the outcome, the regional director will hand down a ruling on the disputed ballots.

The volume of elections is great and has been growing steadily. Final authority and responsibility rests with the National Labor Relations Board in Washington, but has increasingly been delegated to the regional directors. Since 1961, appeal to the board occurs only when there are compelling reasons either for reconsidering a board policy or for believing that there has been a factual error.

The two principal issues in representation elections are (1) who is eligible to vote and (2) what constitutes majority choice. Eligibility of employees engaged in an economic strike has been a troublesome issue. The 1959 amendments to the National Labor Relations Act permit such employees to vote for a twelve-month period following the beginning of the strike, even if they have taken other jobs and are not entitled to reinstatement with the company.

What constitutes majority choice? As in other American elections, it is not necessary to have a majority of all employees but only a majority of the valid ballots cast. If more than one union is involved and no union wins a majority, a runoff election is conducted in which the employees choose between the two highest candidates, one of which may be the choice "no union."

The final count of ballots is not necessarily decisive. Elections may be set aside by the board, either on generalized grounds such as interference with employees' freedom of choice, or on allegations of specific union or employer unfair practices. There is also the possibility of judicial review of the board's certification, though this has been used rarely and on a limited basis. In a 1965 case the Supreme Court overruled the court of appeals and indicated that the courts must accept the board's discretion in appraising factual situations to determine the bargaining unit. The Supreme Court said, "For reviewing courts to substitute counsel's rationale or their discretion for that of the Board is incompatible with the orderly function of the process of review." [1]

The present law provides little control of tactics in union organizing campaigns, and it is not uncommon to see bitter no-holds-barred contests. Under the Wagner Act, employer free speech was strictly limited. No matter how innocent his remarks, under the board's definition of "strict neutrality" they would be ruled coercive. In the Taft–Hartley amendments of 1947, the employer was allowed to make statements seeking to influence the election, provided they contained no threat of reprisal or promise of benefits. Subsequently the board adopted the concept of a framework of coercive behavior based on the "totality of conduct" by the employer. The courts have never fully accepted the board's rationale of this policy, however, and judicial rulings have allowed greater latitude to the employer in elections.

After 1961, with a change in membership of the National Labor Relations Board, there appeared more detailed restrictions on the content of employer campaign statements. It became accepted practice that the employer might take various forms of action against the union, and might freely express his antiunion beliefs, provided he did not either threaten the employees or promise benefits as a condition of rejecting the union. In the *Dal–Tex Optical Company* case in 1962 the union lost by a vote of 101 to 96, and asked the board to set aside the election on the grounds that hostile speeches by the employer had been coercive.[2] The speech complained of had included a statement that the employees' interests were not necessarily the union's interests, the employer was not afraid of a strike, the

---

[1] *National Labor Relations Board* v. *Metropolitan Life Insurance Company,* 380 U.S. 438 (1965).

[2] *Dal–Tex Optical Company,* 137 NLRB 1782 (1962).

union had nothing to lose, and the ones actually hurt would be the employees. The board ruled this to be a misrepresentation of the consequences of unionism and thus that it went beyond the free speech privilege of the Taft–Hartley amendments.

In the same year, the board set aside a Mississippi election because the employer had circulated handbills containing appeals to racial prejudice. In the *Hollywood Ceramics* case, the board ruled that an election might be set aside because of statements that involved "a substantial departure from the truth" and that were circulated at a time when the other side could not reply effectively—that is, the action must have had a significant effect on the election. The Hollywood Ceramics election was invalidated because a leaflet distributed by the employer just before the balloting made a dramatic but erroneous comparison of the comparative wage situation between his plant and unidentified "other union plants." [3]

It is well settled that employees shall have access to relevant information and shall be free to act on it. The employer must furnish information about the company's operations when requested by the union; and the employer may not unreasonably limit either the employees or outside union organizers from meeting, even on company property, to discuss unionization. The employer cannot use plant rules against solicitation to bar union organizers from communicating with the employees. The principle was laid down in 1945 in the *Republic Aviation* case. It was reinforced in 1949, when the board ruled that a company cannot deny the union use of a meeting hall if this is the only public space available in a company town.[4]

The board, in short, has very considerable discretion. Unlike the situation in political campaigns, the burden of proof has been on the party making a speech to establish that it was truthful and relevant. There has also been a tendency toward inconsistency in applying the board's own precedents, particularly as turnover of membership has resulted from new political administrations in Washington. In 1953 the Eisenhower-appointed board had ruled that letters to employees could not be made the basis for setting aside an election; ;but in 1962 (the *Dal–Tex* decision) a Kennedy-appointed board ruled that hostile speeches by the employer, even though they contained explicit disclaimers of coercive intent, were not privileged as "employer free speech."

Three regulations of recent years have aimed at equal opportunity for the parties. First, the *equal opportunity rule* requires that the union must be given an opportunity to reply if the employer makes a speech on company time and property. In the *Elson Bottling Company* case in 1967, the employer was required to give the union space and time for a one-hour meet-

---

[3] *Hollywood Ceramics, Inc.,* 140 NLRB 221 (1962).

[4] *Republic Aviation Corp.* v. *National Labor Relations Board,* 324 U.S. 793 (1945); *National Labor Relations Board* v. *Stowe Spinning Co.,* 336 U.S. 226 (1949).

ing to "redress the imbalance" following a preelection speech by the employer. Second, the *captive audience rule* requires that the employer refrain altogether from addressing the employees on company time in the twenty-four hours immediately preceding the election. Third, neither side may engage in "material misrepresentation."

Both employer and union statements in organizing campaigns are subject to the protection of free speech guaranteed by the First Amendment, as well as the standards set by the National Labor Relations Board. In political campaigns, the right of free speech has been jealously protected by the courts. In the late 1960s some fairly extreme expressions of employer views have been held to be privileged free speech. In a 1966 case, descriptions of violence and reference to "union goons who trampled a nonstriker to death in a tavern" were ruled noncoercive. In the same year it was held that a statement that unions "blew up homes and kidnapped children" was a mere expression of opposition to unionism.

In recent years, the free speech issue has been raised chiefly in a context of racial prejudice in organizing campaigns in the South. In the *Sewall Manufacturing* case the board set aside an election, lost by the union, on the grounds that the employer's literature had "inflamed and tainted the atmosphere." In two 1965 cases, where the employer had asked that an election be set aside because of union statements asking the employees not to act like "Uncle Toms," the board ruled that such statements were not prejudicial but rather an appeal to "racial self-consciousness," which was germane to the issue. But in a 1966 case involving far less inflammatory union statements than the Uncle Tom references, a National Labor Relations Board ruling was overturned by the circuit court on the ground that the union could have no other purpose than the inflammation of racial feeling.[5]

Misrepresentation designed to influence the election was the basis for setting aside an election in a case in which the union had offered to waive initiation fees if the union won, at the same time stating that employees hired after the election would have to pay. There was an element of misrepresentation, the court ruled, in that the fee was rumored to be $300 without any union denial. But the crucial fact was the conditional nature of the offer, its dependence on union victory. A similar ruling against employer action came from the Supreme Court in 1964. Six days after the National Labor Relations Board had ordered an election, the employer offered a "floating holiday" and a "birthday holiday" for all employees, combined with a summary of past benefits and the suggestion that these might not be continued if the union won. The Court ruled that, to avoid the taint of mis-

---

[5] *Sewall Manufacturing Co.,* 138 NLRB (1962). For a review of these and other cases see Daniel H. Pollitt, "The NLRB and Race Hate Propaganda in Union Organization Drives," *Stanford Law Review,* 17 (1965), p. 373.

representation, economic benefits must be "conferred unconditionally and permanently." [6]

DETERMINATION OF BARGAINING REPRESENTATIVES

To win certification as bargaining representative, a union must demonstrate that it is the choice of a majority of employees "in an appropriate bargaining unit." But what is the appropriate unit? There is frequently disagreement on this point between the employer and the union, and there may also be disagreement within the labor force. Groups of skilled workers may prefer to be represented by separate unions of their own craft, while semiskilled production workers may prefer a single plant-wide unit. Resolving such disputes is one of the board's important functions, both in terms of volume of work and the influence of board decisions in shaping the collective bargaining structure.

In most cases the appropriate bargaining unit is determined informally by a stipulation between the regional director and the parties. When voluntary agreement cannot be reached, there is a formal hearing procedure. Since 1961, power to make unit determinations has been delegated to the regional director, subject only to limited review by the National Labor Relations Board.

The most controversial issue has been that of granting separate bargaining rights to particular groups of skilled workers. During the period of AFL–CIO rivalry in the thirties and forties, the board was under strong pressure from both sides, and there was considerable shifting of policy. In an early case (*Globe Machine Company*, 1937) the board ruled that the question of separate craft representation should be put to a vote of all employees in the plant.[7] With low-skilled workers in a decided majority, this policy tilted the scales against craft unionism.

A few years later, in the *American Can* case, the board ruled that a minority group could not have separate representation when a larger unit had already been established by board determination, and where bargaining had been carried on actively by the larger unit. But as pressures from powerful craft unions continued, exceptions to the *American Can* doctrine were made and *craft severance* was granted when certain conditions were met. These conditions were summed up in the board's opinion in the *General Electric* case of 1944. The essential elements were a demonstration that

---

[6] For a general discussion of the board's policies in regulating representation elections see Derek Bok, "The Regulations of Campaign Tactics in Representation Elections Under the National Labor Relations Act., *Harvard Law Review*, 78 (1964), p. 38.

[7] *Globe Machine and Stamping Co.*, 3 NLRB 294 (1937).

the group was truly a craft, not merely a dissident faction; that it had main
tained its identity throughout the period of bargaining on the comprehensive unit basis and had protested being included in the larger unit; or that
the comprehensive unit had been established without its knowledge and
without previous consideration of the merits of a separate unit. In the 1946
Allied Chemical case, craft severance was granted even though the craft
had not been in existence when the earlier determination was made and
subsequently had not protested against inclusion in the larger unit.

The craft unions seemed to have won a victory when the Taft–Hartley
Act in 1947 forbade the board to decide "that any craft unit is inappropriate . . . on the ground that a different unit has been established by a prior
board determination" [Sec. 9(b)(2)]. In the 1948 *National Tube* case,
however, the board interpreted Section 9(b)(2) as permitting prior history
to be considered as long as it was not the only ground for preventing creation of a craft unit. A group of bricklayers asked severance from a long-
established industrial unit in basic steel. The board examined the traditional
bargaining pattern in basic steel and concluded that, for this reason and
because of the highly integrated production process, a craft unit would be
inappropriate. This precedent was later used to deny craft severance in the
milling, lumber, and aluminum industries.

In summary, the board's rulings on separate craft representation take
into account the past history of bargaining in the plant and industry, the
degree of industrial integration and the company's organization for personnel management, the degree of skill involved in the work for which
separate representation is asked, and finally but not solely, the expressed
wishes of the employees. When the group in question has a well-established
craft skill, and when there is clear evidence of its desire for separate representation, this will usually be granted.[8]

The issue of single-employer versus multiemployer bargaining units
has proven less controversial. Where multiemployer units have been established, this is usually because both parties prefer them for the reasons
discussed in Chapter 18.

Once a bargaining unit has been defined and a bargaining representative certified, how long does the decision last? Can the employer or a rival
union come in next month and demand a new election? The board early
adopted a rule that certification of a representative bars any new election
for at least a year, and this policy was confirmed by the Taft–Hartley Act.
The board also requires an employer to continue bargaining with the certified union for a year even if employee sentiment has changed. In a 1954
case, an election had been won by the Machinists Union. A week after the

---

[8] Development of the board's policy in making unit determinations is summarized
in Archibald Cox and Derek Bok, *Cases and Materials on Labor Law*, 6th ed.
(Brooklyn: The Foundation Press, Inc., 1965), pp. 346–48.

election and before the union had formally been certified, the employer received a letter from nine of his thirteen employees stating that they did not wish to be represented by the union. The employer thereupon refused to bargain with the union, and the National Labor Relations Board declared the refusal an unfair labor practice. The Circuit Court of Appeals upheld the board's order, but in another district precisely the opposite ruling had been made. The Supreme Court thereupon made a comprehensive ruling that the employer may not refuse to bargain, though he may petition the board to revoke the certification, during a one-year period following the selection of the bargaining agent.[9]

The presence of an existing collective agreement will also bar a new election or certification until the old contract runs out. But in the course of time this rule has frequently been amended, and a substantial list of circumstances is now required to keep a contract in force against the apparent wishes of a majority of the employees. If it has no fixed duration, it will not be a bar for any period. If it has a fixed term of years, a petition may be filed by a rival union after only three years have passed. It may not contain provisions violating any section of the National Labor Relations Act; and in 1962 the board ruled that no contract could bar an election petition if it discriminated against employees on racial grounds. Procedural requirements also exist. The rival union must file its petition not more than ninety nor less than sixty days before termination of the existing contract. But if the bargaining representative has become "defunct" or if a "schism" is found to exist, or if changes in the employer's operations through merger or relocation have brought major changes in personnel, an existing contract will not bar a new election.

The Taft–Hartley Act, while it continued the Wagner Act certification procedures, established a new procedure for decertification, that is, a way by which employees can get rid of a union that they no longer wish to represent them. If a "substantial number" (interpreted as 30 percent) of the employees in a bargaining unit file a petition requesting decertification, the National Labor Relations Board must conduct a secret ballot to determine the wishes of the majority. More than a hundred such elections are held each year, most of which are lost by the union. This is not surprising, since the very filing of a decertification petition is an indication of serious dissatisfaction.

THE DUTY TO BARGAIN IN GOOD FAITH

Once a bargaining representative is certified, the National Labor Relations Act places on both parties a legally enforceable duty to bargain. The reason

---

[9] *Brooks* v *National Labor Relations Board*, 348 U.S. 96 (1964).

is partly that without this the other provisions of the act would be meaningless. Organization is of no avail unless it leads to joint determination of conditions of employment. Further, it is believed that serious exchange of proposals and the reasoning behind them has an educational effect. Each side comes to understand the other's position better, ways may be found of bridging initially irreconcilable positions, and the chances of peaceful agreement are increased.

Refusal to bargain may be remedied by an affirmative order of the National Labor Relations Board; and if the board's order to bargain has been properly issued, the United States Court of Appeals is required to compel enforcement under contempt-of-court penalties. Moreover, certain kinds of bargaining behavior may be held to constitute an unfair labor practice.

But what does this duty actually mean? Does it mean going through the motions, or does it mean serious bargaining? And what is "serious" bargaining? In Congressional debate on the Wagner Act it was stated that this provision "only leads the employees to the door of the employer . . . what happens behind those doors is not inquired into." But this view turned out to be untenable. As one party or the other did not like what was going on behind the doors and complained to the board, the duty to bargain began to be defined in depth by board and court decisions.

Some of these decisions were codified by the Taft–Hartley Act in 1947. The parties must meet at reasonable times. They must confer "in good faith" about terms of employment; and they must go beyond discussion to negotiation of an agreement. Points on which agreement has been reached must be put into a written contract. The obligation to bargain, however, does not compel either side to make concessions on specific points. Bargaining may be as hard as the economic power of the parties can make it.

The test of good faith is thus partly a procedural test. The board cannot look into the hearts of the parties and discern there a cooperative or antagonistic spirit. Nor can it require that the proposals put forward by one side or the other be "reasonable." This would go too far in the direction of government interference with the content of collective agreements. What it can do is to infer, from the behavior of the parties, whether they are trying to avoid agreement or whether their negotiating posture is sufficiently genuine to meet their legal obligation.

On mandatory bargaining subjects (to be defined in a moment) each party must listen to the other's proposals, make counterproposals, and advance facts and arguments in support of its position. The employer must furnish relevant data to the union on request. In the *Truitt* case the board held that: "It is settled law that when an employer seeks to justify the refusal of a wage increase upon an economic basis, . . . good-faith bargaining under the act requires that upon request the employer attempt to substantiate its economic position by reasonable proof." [10] The Supreme Court upheld this ruling.

The two sides do not have to agree, but they must "bargain to impasse." When both sides have exhausted their stock of proposals and arguments, and still no settlement has been reached, either party is free to break off negotiations and call a strike or declare a lockout.

A key case in this area involved the General Electric Company's use of the "boulwarism" techniques described in Chapter 18. In 1960 the company opened negotiations with the International Union of Electrical Workers by bringing in a comprehensive three-year contract, with the announcement that this was both its first and last offer. There followed a professional public relations campaign, in which management sent 246 separate bulletins to employees in its Schenectady plant and 277 communications to the Pittsfield plant employers. Meanwhile, the company was prepared to go on talking indefinitely. It claimed that the proposed contract had been carefully researched and represented the very best that could be done. In effect, it relied on the ability of managment to forsee all claims that the union could rationally make, and also on the workers being motivated more by a desire for uninterrupted work than by a desire to support their representatives in contract negotiations.

The National Labor Relations Board ruled against this take-it-or-leave-it technique. [11] Management, the board said, must fulfill the requirement of good-faith bargaining by affirmatively demonstrating its willingness to resolve differences and reach common ground. Four types of actions were cited as evidence of bad faith: (1) failure to furnish information requested by the union; (2) attempts to deal separately with local unions on matters that were properly within the scope of national negotiations, while at the same time the local unions were solicited to refrain from supporting the threatened strike; (3) the take-it-or-leave-it presentation of proposals, with specific mention of a clause involving personal accident insurance; and (4) the company's general approach to the conduct of bargaining, which relegated the union to a merely advisory position.

The National Labor Relations Board did not prohibit any specific action by General Electric. Its complaint was that the General Electric policy "devitalized negotiations" and sought to discredit the union. In March of 1970 the Supreme Court refused to review the board's ruling on boulwarism, a decision which had little practical effect since the company itself, following a fourteen-week strike in 1969, had backed away from the policy.

In the *Reed and Prince* case, negotiations were with the Steelworkers. The company, which is family-owned, submitted a signed contract as a

---

[10] *Truitt Mfg. Co.*, 110 NLRB 856 (1954); *National Labor Relations Board* v. *Truitt*, 351 U.S. 149 (1956).

[11] *General Electric Company,* 150 NLRB 192 (1964).

"final offer." Simultaneously, management sent all employees a letter calling the union's bargaining position "CIO sabotage of their wage-earning capacity." The National Labor Relations Board ruled this an unfair practice, interpreting the letter as evidence of a concealed determination to avoid agreement. Meanwhile, the union had called a strike. The company then hired a public relations consultant and carried through a publicity campaign aimed at discrediting the union. Subsequently, more than half the employees signed petitions authorizing acceptance of the company's contract offer, and the strike was broken. The National Labor Relations Board decided that in the "total context" the Reed and Prince communications to their employees were evidence of bad faith, and again ordered management to resume bargaining.[12]

The local union collapsed without a contract having been signed. Five years later, the Steelworkers won an election by a vote of 449 to 304. Negotiations following certification proved fruitless and the National Labor Relations Board, by a divided vote, found a breach of the duty to bargain. This time, five specific grounds were given: (1) delay in scheduling the first negotiating session and delay in furnishing the union with data on the company's wage structure; (2) insistence on a stenotypist recording the sessions; (3) withholding agreement on "trivial" matters, such as permission for the union to post its notices on company bulletin boards; (4) giving a wage increase after the negotiations had broken down; and (5) refusing a checkoff of dues. None of these actions individually was declared an unfair practice. Rather, they were cited as a test of motive on the part of management.

The company held off the union for thirty-nine months and finally signed an agreement that merely wrote into contract form the existing wage scales and company personnel policies. In fifteen years, this contract has never been renegotiated. The *Reed and Prince* case suggests that, if a weak union fails to secure its first contract, a stubborn management can avoid the burden of collective bargaining even though the National Labor Relations Board and the courts have ruled against the employer.[13]

The National Labor Relations Board and the courts would say that their function is not to strengthen one side or the other but only to assure fair play. Whether the unions can in fact compel good faith bargaining within this framework is still an unsettled question.

While the courts have emphasized, and would prefer to hold to, a

---

[12] *National Labor Relations Board* v. *Reed and Prince Mfg. Co.*, 205 F. 2d 131 (1st Circuit, 1953); certiorari denied, 346 U.S. 887 (1953).

[13] J. Cross, D. Cullen, and K. C. Hanslow, "Good Faith in Labor Negotiations: Tests and Remedies," *Cornell Law Quarterly*, 53 (1968), p. 1009. See also Herbert R. Northrup, "The Case for Boulwarism," *Harvard Business Review* (October 1963), pp. 86–97.

procedural test of good faith, the board has edged into applying also a *substantive test*. The central issue here is what *subjects* the parties are obliged to bargain about. The act refers to "wages, hours, and other terms and conditions of employment," which the courts have ruled to be mandatory subjects for bargaining. But these concepts have considerable elasticity. Unions steadily try to enlarge the mandatory area by giving a broad interpretation to "terms and conditions of employment." Employers naturally contest this at every stage, claiming an area of "management prerogative" in which efficient operation requires unilateral decision.

Occasionally the shoe is on the other foot. One employer proposed a contract clause under which, before the union could call a strike, it must take a secret ballot of all employees on the employer's last offer. In the event of employees rejecting the offer, the company was to have seventy-two hours to present a new proposal. The union refused to bargain on this issue, on the ground that it related to internal union affairs, and this position was upheld by the board.

An issue on which the parties are not required to bargain is termed a nonmandatory or *permissive* issue.[14] Either party is free to raise such a subject, but the other party is under no obligation to discuss it, and his refusal to do so is not an unfair labor practice. Nor may the party who raised the subject insist on it to the point of a strike or lockout. This is permissible only in the case of disagreement on mandatory subjects.

The board, and ultimately the courts, are responsible for drawing the line between permissive and mandatory subjects. The consequences are important. Matters that are ruled to be mandatory will be subjected to joint control through collective agreements, not only in the industry where the issue first arose, but in other industries that rely on the first as a precedent. A ruling that a subject is permissive only will tend to exclude it from collective agreements. The broad phrase, "other terms and conditions of employment," can be used either to restrict or to expand the scope of bargaining.

The most controversial area involves the employer's right to close down or relocate plants, to subcontract work previously done by company employees to an outside contractor, or to make other labor-displacing changes in production schedules and methods. Unions argue that such decisions directly affect the job security of their members, and should therefore be subject to joint control. Management replies that these matters have traditionally been reserved for management decision, and that without this orderly and efficient management becomes impossible.

---

[14] In addition to *mandatory* and *permissive* subjects, there is a small category of *prohibited* subjects that may not be included in a collective agreement. The leading examples are the *closed shop* and the *hot-cargo clause,* under which the union requires the employer to refrain from dealing with third parties.

A few cases may illustrate the variety of situations that arise. Can an employer cease operations and move without first consulting the union? The National Labor Relations Board in 1965 held that this constituted a denial of good faith bargaining when Garwin, a New York manufacturer of swimsuits, closed down and formed a new Florida corporation to produce the same items with funds and machinery from the defunct New York firm and under a management in which only the executive titles had been changed. The board's ruling required that the New York employees be offered jobs in Florida and be compensated for lost wages if they decided not to accept. Moreover, the employer must either return to New York or bargain with the old union at the new plant regardless of whether the union represents a majority of the Florida employees.

Can an employer threaten to close the plant and subsequently go out of business if the union wins an election? In the *Darlington Manufacturing* case, the National Labor Relations Board ruled that if the plant is one unit in a large business, and if closing results from antiunion animus, the employees must be compensated or put on preferential hiring lists. In a 1965 decision on this case the Supreme Court held that, if the employer terminated his entire business, this could not be considered an unfair labor practice. But a partial closing, which is what occurred here, was held to be an unfair labor practice if the motive was to deter unionism in any of the employer's remaining plants.[15]

These cases again suggest that determined refusal to bargain can sometimes be successful. In the *Garwin Swimsuit* case, even assuming full enforcement of the board's order, the company would be able to resist the union more easily in a largely nonunion state like Florida.

In the *Fibreboard* case, where the company had "contracted out" an operation without first consulting the union, the Supreme Court undertook to define those "terms and conditions of employment" that are as basic as wages and hours. In so doing, it had to balance management's function of adopting technical changes and increasing production efficiency against the rights of the workers to security and stability in their jobs. A narrow interpretation of the statutory phrase would give the company an unrestricted right to eliminate jobs through technological improvements. A broad or vague definition would give the union a veto on technical change. The ruling of the Supreme Court in effect included in the protected "terms and conditions of employment," the termination rights and posttermination pension rights of present employees. The Court requires that *all* management decisions representing a departure from prior practice that significantly impair (1) job tenure, (2) employment security, and (3) "reasonably anticipated

---

[15] *Textile Workers Union* v. *Darlington Mfg. Co.*, 380 U.S. 263 (1965). For a discussion of the Garwin case see the Comment in *Harvard Law Review*, 79 (1966), p. 855.

work opportunities," must be negotiated as mandatory subjects before the management decision becomes effective.[16]

The board is not supposed to prescribe the outcome of the bargain; at times, however, it has come close to doing so. In the *Porter* case, the board ruled in 1963 that the employer must concede a proposal for check-off of union dues, *in return for some reasonable but unspecified concession* by the union. The checkoff of dues was in this case a matter of life or death for the new union. The board's ruling, though upheld by the court of appeals in 1967, was struck down by the Supreme Court in March 1970 with a strong statement that any extension of the board's remedial powers to enforce mandatory bargaining must come from Congress. Meanwhile a similar ruling in the *Roanoke Iron and Bridge Works* case had also been upheld by the court of appeals.[17]

The legal and practical difficulties of establishing a group of subjects on which refusal to bargain would be *prima facie* evidence of bad faith are great, for it is hard to discern any inherent logic in the placement of specific contract provisions inside or outside the mandatory area. The principle of freedom of contract, which is the foundation of collective bargaining, requires the government to stay out of the terms of the contract; yet it has another mandate, sometimes conflicting, that requires the establishment of collective bargaining relationships to promote industrial stability. In applying this mandate the board has influenced both the scope of collective agreements and, by altering the relative strength of the parties, the outcome of the bargain. Some legal opinion holds that the board has intruded too far into the subject matter of bargaining, that the whole effort to distinguish mandatory from permissive subjects is misguided, and that the parties should be left to bargain about any issue which either side wishes to raise.[18]

---

[16] *Fibreboard Paper Products Corp.* v. *National Labor Relations Board,* 379 U.S. 203 (1964).

[17] *United Steelworkers* v. *National Labor Relations Board,* D.C. Circuit, December 27, 1967. The Steelworkers reached their first agreement with Roanoke in 1951, with the checkoff of dues not included. During the term of this first contract the union lost its majority, and in 1961 the company negotiated an agreement with a local union that did not include the checkoff. This second union also disappeared by the time its agreement expired. In 1964 the Steelworkers returned and gained National Labor Relations Board certification. After lengthy negotiations and a strike, agreement was reached but with no provision for dues checkoff. The Steelworkers appealed to the National Labor Relations Board charging refusal to bargain in good faith; the board ruled that the company"s purpose in denying the checkoff was the belief that this would break the union, and ordered bargaining resumed. This ruling was subsequently upheld by the court of appeals on the grounds that the checkoff is now the normal method of collection (83% of all contracts in 1967) and is not an arrangement affecting allocation of economic values between worker and employer.

[18] On this point, see the interesting discussion in Harry Wellington, *Labor and the Legal Process* (New Haven: Yale University Press, 1968), Chap. 2. Wellington

PRIVATE AGREEMENTS AND PUBLIC POLICY

The collective agreement, in addition to regulating wages and other terms of employment, usually contains two procedural provisions. First, grievances arising during the life of the contract that the parties are unable to resolve by negotiation are usually referred to a neutral arbitrator, whose decision is final. Second, the parties agree that there will be no strike or lockout during the contract period.

Is this just a gentleman's agreement between the parties, enforceable only by private methods? Or can one party or the other go to court to compel enforcement? In practice, lawsuits are not likely to promote good industrial relations, and the parties will normally prefer to avoid them. But can they go to law as a last resort?

It appears that they can. Before 1947 there was considerable doubt in most states whether the trade union, which is an unincorporated association, could be sued for breach of contract. But Taft–Hartley included a specific provision on this point: "Suits for violation of contracts between an employer and a labor organization . . . may be brought in any district court of the United States having jurisdiction of the parties. . . ." The courts have shown themselves willing to entertain such suits, and so by this route also government has been projected farther into the details of industrial relations.

Both the National Labor Relations Board and the courts have taken a favorable view of grievance arbitration. The board generally will not accept an unfair labor practice charge unless the contract procedures, including arbitration, have been exhausted. The Supreme Court has also held that, where there is an arbitration clause in the contract and the employer refuses to observe it, the union can bring suit to compel him to do so.

Suppose, however, the employer maintains that the issue in question does not fall within the scope of the arbitration clause. This question arose in a case in which the company had contracted out some of its maintenance and repair work, causing a layoff of several of its employees. The union challenged this action and, when the dispute was not resolved through discussion, filed suit to compel arbitration. The company replied that con-

---

concludes that ". . . the totality of effects which stems from the mandatory–nonmandatory distinction makes law much too important in terms of the statutory goal of freedom of contract . . . The Borg-Warner rule, that insistence on hard bargaining over a nonmandatory subject is itself an unfair labor practice, is indefensible and should be rejected. It, more than any other rule, makes sharp the distinction between mandatory and nonmandatory subjects: the Borg–Warner rule keeps such subjects from collective bargaining and out of the contract. To this extent the institution of collective bargaining develops by government fiat; the terms of collective contracts through government intervention" (pp. 76–77).

tracting out was strictly a function of management, and that the agreement provided that "matters which are strictly a function of management shall not be subject to arbitration." The Supreme Court ordered that the case go to arbitration, explaining: "An order to arbitrate the particular grievance should not be denied unless it may be said with positive assurance that the arbitration clause is not susceptible of an interpretation that covers the asserted dispute. Doubts should be resolved in favor of coverage . . ." [19]

The arbitrator himself might rule that the issue in question was not arbitrable. The Court was saying, in effect, that a qualified arbitrator is better able to make this kind of technical judgment than a group of judges who are amateurs in industrial relations.

A different situation arises after an arbitration award has been made. Can the losing party appeal to the National Labor Relations Board or the courts to upset the decision? Here again the tendency has been to rely on the arbitrator's judgment. In a 1955 case the National Labor Relations Board laid down a set of conditions under which it would accept an award as final: first, if the proceedings had been "fair and regular"; second, if the parties had made an advance agreement to accept the award as binding; and third, if the decision was not "clearly inconsistent" with the purposes of the National Labor Relations Act. The board in effect gave up its primary jurisdiction over arbitrable grievances involving breach of contract, and possibly to some extent over arbitrable grievances involving unfair labor practices.

The Supreme Court also has tended to hold that court review of arbitration awards is inappropriate. In one leading case it stated: "The refusal of courts to review the merits of an arbitration award is the proper approach to arbitration under collective bargaining agreements. The federal policy of settling labor disputes by arbitration would be undermined if courts had the final say on the merits of the awards." [20]

---

[19] *United Steelworkers* v. *Warrior and Gulf Navigation Co.*, 363 U.S. 574 (1960). For a critical review of the issues see Donald H. Wollett, "The Agreement and the National Labor Relations Act: Courts, Arbitrators and the NLRB—Who Decides What?" *Labor Law Journal*, 14 (1963), p. 1041; and Dallas L. Jones and Russell A. Smith, "Management and Labor Appraisals and Criticism of the Arbitration Process: A Report with Comments, *Michigan Law Review*, 62 (1964), p. 1115.

[20] *United Steelworkers* v. *Enterprise Wheel and Car Corporation*, 363 U.S. 593 (1960). See also *United Steelworkers* v. *Warrior and Gulf Navigation Co.*, 363 U.S. 574 (1960); and *United Steelworkers* v. *American Mfg. Co.*, 363 U.S. 564 (1960). These cases are commonly referred to as the "Steelworkers Trilogy," and are a landmark in the law of arbitration. The case of *Warrior and Gulf Navigation* contains the fullest expression of the Court's viewpoint.

There has been widespread comment by students of labor law on the implications of these cases. See A. Bickel and H. Wellington, "Legislative Purpose and the Judicial Process," in *Harvard Law Review*, 71 (1957), p. 1; B. Meltzer, "The Supreme Court, Arbitrability and Collective Bargaining," *University of Chicago Law Review*, 28 (1960), p. 464; H. Wellington, "Judicial Review of the Promise To Arbi-

This judicial modesty is no doubt commendable. The effect, however, is to compel the sending of disputes to arbitration and to compel acceptance of the award without serious court review of the circumstances. Wellington has argued that it would be better to withhold legal enforcement of arbitration clauses, leaving this to the economic strength of the parties

> under present law the major function of courts in the labor arbitration area . . . is blindly to approve and make official the actions of private decision-makers whose authority to decide is frequently itself the issue in dispute . . . It seems to me quite improper, where contempt of court and ultimate imprisonment may be at stake, for a court so to rubber-stamp the decision of a private arbitrator." [21]

Finally, it is now clear that the courts will order enforcement of a no-strike clause. Indeed, the Supreme Court did this in one case where the contract did not contain a no-strike clause but did provide for grievance arbitration. The reasoning was that a promise to settle all grievances through arbitration *implies* a promise to refrain from direct action.[22] A union that violates the no-strike clause, then, can be sued for damages, though practical considerations may deter the employer from bringing suit. In the rarer case of an employer lockout during the life of the contract, the union could presumably bring a similar suit.

INDIVIDUAL RIGHTS AND UNION POWER

The union has traditionally been regarded as a voluntary organization, and as such outside the scope of public regulation. Like religious organizations and private clubs, the operation of trade unions has been in theory and largely in practice the sole responsibility of the membership. But as unions increasingly took on powers conferred by state and federal laws, the ground work for public regulation was laid. The growing size and financial strength of unions also invited regulation, for union officers increasingly controlled the economic destinies of members while their dependence on the goodwill of the membership diminished. When such power was used in an arbitrary or discriminatory fashion, redress was sought first through the courts and finally through the legislature.

---

trate," *New York University Law Review,* 37 (1962), p. 471; and Benjamin Aaron, "Strikes in Breach of Collective Agreements: Some Unanswered Questions," *Columbia Law Review,* 63 (1963), p. 1027.

[21] Wellington, *Labor and the Legal Process,* pp. 122–23.

[22] *Local 174 Teamsters* v. *Lucas Flour,* 369 U.S. 95 (1962).

The Right to Fair Representation

The principle of majority rule in industrial relations, first stated in the Railway Labor Act of 1926, is now firmly established.[23] The terms established by the collective agreement cannot be modified unilaterally by the employer to grant or deny certain benefits to individual employees.

In 1944 the Supreme Court invoked this principle to bar the J. I. Case Company from undercutting a recently certified union. The company had obtained from about 75 percent of its employees signed one-year individual contracts of employment. It then notified the union that these contracts had legal effect and refused to bargain on any matters covered by the individual contracts. The Supreme Court refused to permit this. In its decision, the Court defined the collective agreement as different from a contract of employment. "The negotiations between union and management result in . . . a trade agreement rather than a contract of employment." Although there is still room for an individual contract, even in industries covered by the National Labor Relations Act, such contracts cannot be used to defeat or delay the law's procedures, or to exclude the contracting employee from a properly established bargaining unit, or to obtain individual advantages. "The practice and philosophy of collective bargaining looks with suspicion on . . . individual advantages. The workman is free, if he values his own bargaining position more than that of the group, to vote against representation, but the majority rules." [24]

If individuals can no longer bargain for themselves, it becomes important that the union bargain effectively and impartially on their behalf. The union in return for its position as sole bargaining representative, has a clear duty to represent fairly all workers within the bargaining unit. But this is not easy of accomplishment. Two issues of special importance are discrimination against nonmembers of the union and discrimination on racial grounds.

Nonmembers. It is well settled that the bargaining agent cannot legally cause any disadvantage to workers who are not members of the union. This is true both in negotiating the contract and in handling grievances under the contract. The union cannot secure special advantages for its members to the disadvantage of nonmembers.

Questions of discrimination arise chiefly in industries where employees do not work regularly for any one employer, and where the union acts as an employment agency. The main examples are building construction, ship-

---

[23] A leading case is *Order of Railroad Telegraphers* v. *Railway Express Agency,* 321 U.S. 342 (1944).

[24] *J. I. Case Company* v. *National Labor Relations Board,* 321 U.S. 322 (1944).

ping, and longshoring.[25] In 1957 the National Labor Relations Board declared that a contract of construction workers with the Mountain Pacific Chapter of the Associated General Contractors, Inc., was invalid unless the contract explicitly provided that selection of applicants for referral to jobs would "not be based on, or in any way affected by, union membership, bylaws, rules, regulations, constitutional provisions, or any other aspect or obligation of union membership, policies or requirements." [26]

In several more recent cases the board has intervened to require that hiring halls be operated in a nondiscriminatory manner.[27] But it is unclear whether these rulings have had much practical effect. It is obviously easier to detect the presence of discrimination than to prescribe a workable remedy short of public operation of the dispatching service.

Minority Groups. Union membership is not always open, even to qualified applicants. In spite of the good record of the labor movement as a whole, and despite the efforts of most national union leaders, there remain pockets of racial discrimination. Here, the conflicting economic interests of white and black workers have resulted either in Jim Crow locals with no black members, or in discriminatory systems that give priority treatment to white union members at the expense of black members. As early as 1944, in a case arising under the Railway Labor Act, the Supreme Court declared these practices illegal. The majority union may not sacrifice the rights of the minority of a craft who are outside the union. "The use of the word representative," the Court said, "in all contexts in which it is found plainly implies that the representative is to act on behalf of all the employees which, by virtue of the statute, it undertakes to represent."

The National Labor Relations Board did not move vigorously to apply this doctrine until 1964. In that year, in the *Hughes Tool Company* case, the board refused to certify a discriminatory union. The board's opinion said, "We hold that the board cannot validly render aid under Section 9 of the act to a labor organization which discriminates racially when acting as a statutory bargaining agent." [28] In the case of unions still struggling for recognition, the fact that the board will no longer certify a union guilty of racial discrimination is a rather strong weapon. But in areas where unions are already strongly entrenched, such as railroading and construction, this weapon loses most of its force.

A more direct approach was provided by the Civil Rights Act of 1964,

---

[25] See "Unilateral Union Control of Hiring Halls: the Wrong and the Remedy," Note, *Yale Law Journal*, 70 (1961), p. 661.

[26] *Mountain Pacific Chapter, Assoc. Gen. Contractors, Inc.*, 119 NLRB 883 (1957).

[27] Wellington, *Labor and the Legal Process*, pp. 141–44.

[28] *Independent Metal Workers Union, Local No. 1, Hughes Tool Co.*, 147 NLRB 1573 (1964).

when for the first time Congress declared racial discrimination to be contrary to national labor policy. Under this act, a court can now issue an order forcing a union to admit an employee to membership.

The root of the problem, however, is that few discriminatory systems are written into collective agreements. Most of them are informal "understandings," which are made effective by manipulating the job classification system or the seniority rosters. Although such policies are clearly discriminatory, they may be set up on paper so that bias is difficult to prove. The employer can accomplish a good deal also by defining "ability to do the job" as he sees fit, and the union has only to agree.[29]

Union Membership and Discipline

Since membership in a union can affect a worker's status in the plant or industry, the fact of membership itself takes on significance. Freedom to join, freedom not to join, and the status of workers dropped from union membership become important.

A standard objection to the union shop used to be that, where union membership is compulsory, a worker who is expelled from the union for any reason is thereby deprived of his job. The Taft–Hartley Act provided, however, that the employer shall not discriminate against a nonmember if (1) he was denied membership on the terms and conditions open to other employees, or (2) if his membership was terminated for reasons other than his failure to pay the standard dues and initiation fees. The latter provision as Wellington points out, "means that an employee can break every minor rule in the book . . . be expelled from the union, and under the statute retain his job if he tenders his dues to the union. Good union membership . . . and job rights are separated, or at least that is the statute's aim." [30] The union may still pressure the employer in one way or another to get rid of the offending worker; but if the employer yields, he is guilty of an unfair labor practice.

From rules concerning expulsion from union membership, it is a short step to regulating fines, suspensions, and other lesser penalties. In recent years there has been increasing concern for the individual member's ability to hold his own against a growing concentration of union power. Decision by decision, in cases arising under the Railway Labor Act and the National Labor Relations Act, lines have been drawn between permissible and nonpermissible forms of union discipline.

1. The union may not discipline employees who cross a picket line to work during a strike, if the disciplinary action affects their job rights. In the

---

[29] "Seniority Discrimination and the Incumbent Negro," *Harvard Law Review*, 80 (April 1967), p. 1260.

[30] Wellington, *Labor and the Legal Process*, pp. 132–33.

case of the *National Labor Relations Board v. Bell Aircraft Corporation*, three
hundred employees who crossed picket lines during a strike were charged by
the union with violating their union responsibilities. Under the contract, union
members against whom charges were pending were ineligible for promotion.
The union sent management a list of these employees and one of them, Finch,
was denied promotion to a foremanship solely on the basis of the union's action.
He appealed to the National Labor Relations Board, which upheld the union's
position. But Finch was not in arrears on his union dues. The circuit court of
appeals ruled that under the amended Section 7 of the National Labor Relations Act, protecting the employee's right to strike *or not to strike*, the job
rights of Finch and the others could not be made an instrument of union
discipline.[31]

2. But the union may use coercive discipline as long as it does not strike
at the individual's job or working conditions. Fines have been the preferred
method. In a Wisconsin case, the National Labor Relations Board upheld fines
on members who had exceeded production ceilings set by a union rule designed
to limit incentive earnings.[32] This form of discipline is permissible also in
strikes. The United Automobile Workers, in 1964, was upheld in imposing
fines on workers who had worked during an economic strike. The board's
majority opinion said, "Just as the First Amendment to the United States
Constitution protects the right to speak but does not insulate the speaker
against all consequences of having exercised the freedom of speech, in like
fashion the act . . . protects the right of an employee either to support a
lawful picket line or to refuse to do so, but does not insulate the employee
from all consequences flowing from his choice." [33] But the union may not exercise this power in "arbitrary" fashion. It must have procedures that do not
deprive the member of his basic rights under the law, and that also give the
individual a fair hearing and impartial treatment. For example, a union that
had imposed a fine for filing charges with the National Labor Relations Board
before the union's own remedies had been exhausted was ruled in violation of
the act.

3. Union discipline for intraunion political activities is restricted, although it is permissible under some circumstances. This was already true at
common law, but previous provisions were codified and strengthened by the
Landrum–Griffin Act.

The right to electioneer against the union officers, and to criticize their
actions even to the point of libel, is apparently beyond the reach of union
discipline. In the case of *Salzhandler* v. *Caputo*, the financial secretary of a
local union attacked the president, circulating election handbills accusing the
president of fiscal malfeasance and even of larceny. The union district council,
after a trial, found Salzhandler guilty of "acts inconsistent with the duties and
obligations of a member of the brotherhood," removed him from the post of
financial secretary, and suspended him for five years from all participation in
union affairs. The district court held that the circulated leaflet had been libel-

---

[31] 206 F. 2d 235 (1953). For a detailed review of the issues and cases, see two
articles by Clyde W. Summers: "Legal Limitations on Union Discipline," *Harvard
Law Review,* 63 (1951), p. 1049; and "The Law of Union Discipline: What the
Courts Do in Fact," *Yale Law Journal,* 70 (1960), p. 175.

[32] *Wisconsin Motor Corp.,* 145 NLRB 109 (1964).

[33] *Automobile Workers Union,* 149 NLRB 10 (1964).

ous and that the Landrum–Griffin Act was not designed to protect libel and slander. But the court of appeals rejected this view, and ruled that "although libelous statements may be made the basis of a civil suit between those concerned, the union may not subject a member to any disciplinary action on a finding . . . that such statements are libelous." [34]

4. The right of free speech, it appears, will be upheld by the courts against any provision of the union constitution. In a 1964 case involving removal of officers for electioneering against the incumbent union management, the court refused to allow their discharge although they had not been elected by the membership and had in fact been appointed by the union president whom they opposed.

In external political activity also, union discipline cannot infringe on the constitutional right of free speech. In 1964, however, a New York union with an anti-Communist provision in its constitution was upheld in a severe disciplinary action, a five-year suspension of a member who had arranged speeches and rallies for a well-known Communist party member. [35]

DISCUSSION QUESTIONS

1. What are the present ground rules for union and employer behavior in representation elections? Are these rules fair to both parties?

2. "The effort to distinguish between mandatory and permissive issues has produced undue government intervention in the substance of collective bargaining. This concept should be abandoned, and both parties left free to raise any issue they wish." Discuss.

3. What are a union's duties toward black workers employed in the bargaining unit that the union represents? What difficulties are involved in actual enforcement of these duties?

4. Does present law adequately protect the rights of workers who may dissent from and campaign against local or national union officials?

READING SUGGESTIONS

Case materials and general discussions of the substantive issues in labor policy can be found in CLYDE W. SUMMERS, *Cases on Labor Law,* Brooklyn: The Foundation Press, Inc., 1969; ARCHIBALD COX and DEREK C. BOK, *Cases and Materials on Labor Law,* Brooklyn: The Foundation Press, Inc., 1965; CHARLES O. GREGORY, *Labor and the Law* (2d rev. ed.),

---

[34] 316 F. 2d 445; certiorari denied 375 U.S. 946 (1963). See Benjamin Sigal, "Freedom of Speech and Union Discipline: The 'Right' of Defamation and Disloyalty," New York University Conference on Labor, 17 (1964), p. 367.

[35] *Rosen* v. *District Council No. 9, Brotherhood of Painters,* Southern District of New York (1964).

New York. W. W. Norton & Company, Inc., 1958; and HARRY H. WELLINGTON, *Labor and the Legal Process,* New Haven: Yale University Press, 1968. A useful comparative survey will be found in OTTO KAHN-FREUND (ed.), *Labour Relations and the Law,* Boston: Little, Brown and Company, 1965.

Among the many specialized studies, a few recent titles may be cited. Good-faith bargaining is discussed in PHILLIP ROSS, *The Government as a Source of Union Power,* Providence: Brown University Press, 1965. A detailed account of the problems of contracting out is MARGARET CHANDLER, *Management Rights and Union Interests,* New York: McGraw-Hill Book Company, 1964. A comprehensive study of the effect of industrialization on union organization and growth in the southern United States is F. RAY MARSHALL, *Labor in the South,* Cambridge, Mass.: Harvard University Press, 1967. A comprehensive survey of the Labor Management Reporting and Disclosure Act of 1959 is MARTIN S. ESTEY, PHILIP TAFT, and MARTIN WAGNER (eds.), *Regulating Union Government,* New York: Harper & Row, Publishers, 1964. See also the "Symposium on Labor Law," *Northwestern University Law Review,* 63 (1968), and the "Symposium on the LMRDA of 1959," *New York University Law Review,* 43 (1968).

26

The Use of Economic Weapons

The ultimate source of bargaining power is the ability to inflict economic damage on the opponent. Thus the ground rules regulating the use of economic pressure have always been a hotly disputed area of labor law. After summarizing the present state of the law, we turn to two special topics: (1) "emergency strikes," which threaten immediate damage to health and welfare and are usually thought to require special treatment; and (2) the status of union tactics under the antitrust laws.

ECONOMIC WEAPONS:
STRIKES, PICKETING, BOYCOTTS

Public control operates in this area as in others. Actions that are entirely legal as individual rights become a subject of state and federal regulation when they are part of a pattern of group action. The right to strike is based on the individual's freedom to leave his job. Underlying the boycott is the principle that anyone is free to withhold his labor or his purchasing power. Picketing, insofar as it involves the communication of information about a labor dispute to potential employees or potential customers, involves the right of free speech. But it would be overcredulous to assert that an individual could or would undertake these activities by himself, as an individual, without the intention of persuading others to join him in "concerted activity." Thus concerted action by employees or employers is never free from government control absolutely and as a matter of right.

The Right to Strike

Before 1935 public policy was largely negative. The force of law operating through the courts was weighted on the employer's side. There was a shift toward neutrality with the Norris–LaGuardia Act of 1932, which restricted employer use of the federal courts in breaking strikes. Positive recognition of the right to strike came in 1935, when Congress declared in the National Labor Relations Act that employees have the right to undertake a concerted work stoppage, and that strikers retain their employee status. Subsequently the Supreme Court carried this statement of policy to its logical conclusion, ruling in the *McKay Radio* case that, if the strike has been called because of an employer's unfair labor practices, the strikers must be reinstated even if replacements have been hired.[1]

The National Labor Relations Board distinguishes between "unfair-practice strikers" and "economic strikers," that is, workers involved in a normal contract dispute over wages and other terms of employment. Unfair-practice strikers have a right to reinstatement with back pay "so long as the labor dispute is current." Wtihout this protection an employer determined not to deal with a union could readily bring on a strike, declare that the strikers had left his employ, and hire permanent nonunion replacements. In some cases where the union has remained officially on strike for years, and where the employer has eventually been judged guilty of an unfair labor practice, he has been faced with a large bill for back pay to the striking workers.

Economic strikers receive less protection. The employer is entitled to hire temporary strikebreakers to keep production going, even though he intends to take back the strikers after the end of the dispute. Moreover, he may hire a permanent replacement for a striking worker. This ends the worker's employment connection, and he is no longer entitled to reinstatement.

Replacement hiring raises both legal and practical problems. If the strike has been long, many workers will have given up and taken permanent jobs elsewhere. Those who lasted the course and who reclaim their old jobs will have to work beside some individuals who crossed the picket line during the strike. It is in the nature of the conflict that the employer will press for favored treatment of the newly hired replacements, and that the union will resist such action. Some employers have tried to give the replacements an automatic "bonus" of so many years' seniority as a reward for their co-operation with him during the strike. In the 1963 *Erie Resistor Corporation* case, however, the Supreme Court ruled against granting such extra seniority rights.

Various qualifications have been added to the basic policy protecting the right to strike. Thus the Taft–Hartley Act amended Section 7 of the National Labor Relations Act to protect the right *not* to strike. Certain types of strike—notably strikes to short-circuit or upset the results of National Labor Relations Board elections—were declared unfair labor practices. The law also requires written notice by either party of intention to

---

[1] *National Labor Relations Board* v. *McKay Radio and Telegraph Company,* 304 U.S. 333 (1938).

modify or terminate an existing contract at least sixty days prior to the termination date. During this period the party serving notice must inform the appropriate federal and state mediation agencies and must observe all terms and conditions of the existing contract without resort to strike or lockout.

Federal law dominates this field of policy. For interstate industries there can be no state regulation of peaceful strikes over wages, hours, or conditions, whether by legislative or judicial action. The Supreme Court has ruled that even local utilities are subject to federal policy if interstate commerce is affected. Employment in intrastate industries is under state control, and in most states the right to strike is protected either by state statute or at common law.

Unlawful Strikes

There is no absolute right to strike. This principle was first laid down by the Supreme Court in a Kansas case in which the strike, though orderly and peaceful, was ruled "illegal because of its purpose." [2] The Mine Workers had called a strike, not over terms of employment, but to compel the company to pay a claim for $180 due to one of the local union's members, Brother Mishmash. The claim had been pending for two years, there was no provision for arbitration, and in fact Brother Mishmash had changed jobs and left the company. Union discipline was so tight, however, that the strike succeeded in forcing payment of the claim. Criminal proceedings were brought against the union vice-president, Dorchy, on the basis of a Kansas antistrike law; Dorchy claimed as a defense that the Kansas law was unconstitutional as a denial of the liberties protected under the Fourteenth Amendment. The Supreme Court, in an opinion by Justice Brandeis, ruled that "to collect a stale claim due to a fellow member of the union who was formerly employed . . . is not a permissible purpose."

A strike may be *tainted,* or ruled illegal, either because of its purpose or because of the way it is conducted. The "illegal purpose" doctrine most commonly means that the right to strike is in conflict with some other established policy, either state or federal. Thus a strike to obtain wage demands that would violate wartime wage-control legislation was held illegal. A strike creating a national emergency in coal mining was ruled illegal. [3] Strikes of public employees are normally held unlawful as conflicting with the sovereignty of the state. A strike in violation of a contract made under federal law was ruled illegal. [4] State law also can supersede the right of

---

[2] *Dorchy* v. *Kansas,* 272 U.S. 306 (1926).

[3] *United States* v. *United Mine Workers,* 330 U.S. 258 (1947). For an excellent discussion of this historic case, see John L. Blackmen, Jr., *Presidential Seizure in Labor Disputes* (Cambridge, Mass.: Harvard University Press, 1967), pp. 33–36.

[4] *National Labor Relations Board* v. *Sands Mfg. Co.,* 306 U.S. 332 (1939).

workers to strike, provided the state policy does not conflict with national labor policy. The leading example is a case in which a Missouri antimonopoly law was held to be a proper exercise of state authority. Union action that forced a company to violate the state law thereby became illegal. A union of ice peddlers picketed the Empire Storage and Ice Company to prevent the sale of ice to nonunion distributors. The company claimed that, under the state antimonopoly law, it was required to sell to all distributors alike. On this basis it obtained an injunction against the union's activities, in a decision later upheld unanimously by the Supreme Court.[5]

Most of the cases in which state law has been controlling have involved the *conduct* of a strike. Under the federal constitution, the states are responsible for the health and safety of their citizens. This is known as the states' *police power,* and under it either individual actions in a strike or the entire strike pattern may be called to account in the state courts. Moreover, state labor laws control employer–employee relations as long as they do not conflict with applicable federal law. They may, and in most cases do, control the conduct of strikes and other union activities. These controls will be illustrated as we consider the definition and limits of "peaceful picketing."

Picketing

For a brief period after 1937, the Supreme Court took the view that picketing was almost exempt from state control by the free speech guarantees of the Fourteenth Amendment. A Wisconsin law authorizing peaceful "stranger" picketing by a union attempting to organize a nonunion shop was challenged by an employer, but was ruled constitutional by the Supreme Court on the grounds that the Fourteenth Amendment gives union members a constitutional right to "make known the facts of a labor dispute." [6] Picketing, in this view, is "communication." A few years later an Alabama law that made every sort of picketing a misdemeanor was declared unconstitutional in a decision that broadly identified peaceful picketing with free speech. Subsequently the Court applied this principle to strike down a state court's injunction against peaceful picketing, where no state law but rather a state policy based on common law forbade picketing if there was no immediate dispute between employer and employee.[7]

---

[5] *Giboney* v. *Empire Storage and Ice Co.,* 336 U.S. 490 (1949).

[6] *Senn* v. *Tile Layers' Union,* 301 U.S. 468 (1937).

[7] *AFL* v. *Swing,* 312 U.S. 321 (1941). For a comprehensive discussion of the "free speech doctrine" see Charles O. Gregory, *Labor and the Law,* 2d rev. ed. (New York: W. W. Norton & Company, Inc., 1958), Chap. 11, "Rise and Decline of the Thornhill Doctrine."

But the tide receded from this high point of the "free speech doctrine." The Supreme Court later ruled that picketing, even though peaceful, involved more than just communication of ideas and could not be totally immune from state regulation. "Picketing . . . involves patrol of a particular locality and . . . the very presence of a picket line may induce action of one kind or another, quite irrespective of the nature of the ideas which are being disseminated." Since 1957, the Court has relied increasingly on the facts of each case, balancing the competing interests of unions, employers, their employees, and the public at large. There is no absolute right to strike. In a Texas case, an injunction had been granted under a state antitrust law against picketing of a restaurant by unions protesting the use of nonunion labor, not by the restaurant itself but by a contractor who had done some work for the restaurant. The contractor's dispute had nothing to do with the restaurant being picketed. The Supreme Court ruled that Texas was not violating the Fourteenth Amendment in "insulating" this neutral establishment from the dispute. In cases where picketing involved more than "publicity," or where the element of "communication" was less important than the element of pressure, the states might issue injunctions in support of valid state policy.[8]

State policies thus upheld by the Supreme Court have included a common law policy against the union shop; a California policy against employment on racial lines, upheld against union picketing of a place of business solely to demand that employees be hired in proportion to the racial origin of customers; a statutory policy against employer coercion of employees' choice of bargaining representative, in an injunction against picketing a hotel with signs declaring the owner unfair to organized labor after an unsuccessful attempt at unionization; a state right-to-work law, upheld as the basis for an injunction against picketing a general contractor to eliminate nonunion men from the job; and a Wisconsin statute prohibiting picketing "in the absence of a labor dispute," upheld against picketing a nonunion gravel pit in an effort by the Teamsters' Union to organize the company's drivers. The Wisconsin case, decided in 1957, has become the leading case because the Court specifically restated the principles governing interpretation of the Fourteenth Amendment as applied to state regulation of picketing.[9]

Control of strike violence is the commonest area of state regulation under the police power. A strike that occurs in a context of destruction of property and personal injury will be declared illegal, with consequent loss by the employees of their protection under the National Labor Relations Act. Individual strikers guilty of serious violence may be discharged and

---

[8] *Carpenters' and Joiners' Union* v. *Ritter's Café*, 315 U.S. 722 (1942).

[9] *International Brotherhood of Teamsters, Local 695, AFL* v. *Vogt, Inc.*, 354 U.S. 284 (1957).

local laws against destruction of property can be applied. The employer may also refuse reinstatement to workers against whom violence on the picket line can be specifically proved.[10]

The National Labor Relations Board is responsible for determining whether acts of violence are the responsibility of the union and thus an unfair labor practice. In a 1948 decision, the board made the union responsible for incidents of violence and misconduct even by unidentified pickets. When a strike against the Sunset Line and Twine Company followed the breakdown of contract negotiations, the company reopened the plant with nonstrikers, and called local law-enforcement officers to protect the cars transporting men across the picket line. In the presence of the first vice-president of the local union, the business agent of the local, and the regional director of the international, a crowd of two to three hundred men succeeded in blocking off some of the cars and closed the plant down for that day. There was considerable jostling, and pickets crowded against the cars. The sheriff made arrests and threatened to use tear gas. The vice-president actively urged on the pickets, while the other officers stood by and said nothing. Nonstrikers were followed home by a parade of pickets shouting abuse and threats. The National Labor Relations Board ruled these acts illegal and held the union officers responsible.[11]

Misconduct by strikers, even if nonviolent, may be ruled "coercive" by the board and therefore a ground for removing National Labor Relations Act protection from the strike and for refusing reinstatement to individual employees. In a Massachusetts case, the circuit court of appeals held that visits to the homes of nonstrikers by several carloads of strikers were coercive in nature because they were calculated to instill fear of physical harm.[12] But while the states may regulate the methods by which a strike is conducted, it is important to note that the National Labor Relations Act cannot be superseded by any form of state regulation. The state court's determination that a strike is an illegal breach of the peace will not necessarily deprive the strike of the protection of Section 7 of the National Labor Relations Act, or the employees of their rights to reinstatement.

Disputes Over Organization and Recognition

The recognition strike has presumably been made unnecessary by the certification procedures of the National Labor Relations Board. When the union claims to represent a majority of the employees, it can file a representation petition with the board. Informational picketing is then permitted. The union's claim can be tested either by an election or by other evidence,

---

[10] *Berkshire Knitting Mills* v. *National Labor Relations Board,* 139 F. 2d 134 (1943).

[11] *Sunset Line and Twine Company,* 79 NLRB 1487 (1948).

[12] *National Labor Relations Board* v. *Thayer Co.,* 213 F. 2d 748 (1954).

such as signed authorization cards demonstrating to the satisfaction of the board that it is the free choice of the majority of the employees. Once a decision has been reached, a union that has failed to win certification, or a union that has lost out to another in an election, is barred from further picketing of the employer's premises.

There is some uncertainty over whether a union can picket for recognition when no election has been held. This might happen because the union has been unable to obtain enough signed authorization cards, or because it has not tried to do so. Such a situation was not covered explicitly by the 1959 Landrum–Griffin Act amendments. It is also unclear whether the union defeated in an election can continue picketing if the wording on the picket signs is changed from a demand for recognition to some other "informational" wording.

As a result of this ambiguity, unions have developed a tactic of picketing for *area standards*. If the union's sole purpose is to advertise the fact that the company is paying wages below the standards prevailing in the area, or to publicize some other valid labor issue, it appears that picketing is permitted even though it may cause some employees to refuse to work. Picketing may also be aimed at the consumer public. In a 1961 case, the Hotel and Restaurant Employees' Union had been picketing a cafeteria with signs stating that the establishment was nonunion. No election petition had been filed. The board at first ruled that since the evidence indicated that the cafeteria employees did not want to join the picketing union, the picket line, regardless of the wording of the signs, was "concealed recognitional picketing." But subsequently the board reconsidered this decision and ruled that "purely informational picketing cannot be curtailed," even if it is done for the purpose of recognition or organization, provided that it does not cause a work stoppage.[13]

Secondary Pressures

An old and controversial union tactic is the *secondary boycott*. This involves putting pressure on one employer so that he will exert pressure on another employer whom the union is really after. The Carpenters' Union, for example, has jurisdiction over factories making millwork and other lumber products. These plants are numerous, small, and often difficult to organize. One way to organize them is for the union carpenters on construction jobs to refuse to install millwork from nonunion factories. This forces the building contractors to buy from union plants only. The nonunion plants find their market reduced or even destroyed, and are forced to recognize the union.

The legitimacy of such "billiard shot" tactics has been debated for decades. Boycott activities have usually been held illegal at common law.

---

[13] *Crown Cafeteria,* 130 NLRB 570 (1961).

The Taft–Hartley Act reinforced this view by making it an unfair labor
practice to encourage a strike or a concerted refusal to handle a company's
goods when the purpose is to force the company to stop doing business
with another company. This has led to complicated litigation over who is
the "primary" and who is the "secondary" employer in a particular case,
whether the secondary employer is actually neutral or whether he is in
effect an ally, and so on. For example, construction unions trying to organize a subcontractor have taken the position that they are in fact engaged
in a dispute with the general contractor. Is it possible to distinguish between
different kinds of secondary boycotts, some more undesirable than others?
Will collective bargaining be impaired by a restriction on the use of economic pressure to the detriment of third parties?

The traditional refusal of union workers to work on the same site with
nonunion men was a central issue in the *Denver Building and Construction
Trades' Council* case, which came to the Supreme Court soon after passage
of the Taft–Hartley Act. The Court held that a strike to force the general
contractor on a construction project to cancel its contract with a nonunion
subcontractor was an unfair labor practice. Doose and Lintner, the general
contractor, had given a subcontract for electrical work to a firm (Gould and
Preisner) that for twenty years had employed nonunion workmen. The
construction project was brought to a halt when the Denver Building
Trades' Council placed a single picket at the site. The union claimed that
its objective was to force Doose and Lintner to make the construction site
an all-union job; and indeed, if Doose and Lintner themselves had employed nonunion labor, the union's right to strike would have been clear.
But the Court ruled that the existence of a business relationship between
independent contractors restricted the union's use of economic pressure.[14]

Congress amended the basic act in 1959 to close loopholes that had
been exposed by actions brought before the National Labor Relations
Board and the courts. One change in the wording of the secondary boycott
provisions made the prohibition applicable to refusals to work by workers
who were not technically "employees." Another was intended to make
clear that inducement to even a single individual to refrain from work was
proscribed. General threats of "labor trouble" made to the secondary employer had previously been held to be outside the range of prohibited action.
Now Congress made such conduct unlawful, if it could be shown to
"threaten, coerce, or restrain" any person.

These provisions were interpreted by the Supreme Court in a 1964
case. A union of delivery drivers and salesmen was conducting a strike

[14] *National Labor Relations Board* v *Denver Building and Construction Trades'
Council,* 341 U.S. 675 (1951). For a general discussion of the effect of the Taft–
Hartley Act on secondary boycotts see Howard Lesnick, "The Gravamen of the
Secondary Boycott," *Columbia Law Review,* 62 (1962), p. 1363.

against Servette, Inc., a wholesale food distributor in California. The union sought to support the strike by picketing supermarkets that bought food from Servette. Handbills were passed out in front of the supermarkets asking customers not to purchase Servette's merchandise. The handbills were carefully limited to named products, and were not worded as an attack on the supermarkets themselves. When Servette complained to the National Labor Relations Board, the board dismissed the charges on the grounds that the managers were not being induced to refrain from performing their managerial duties. Rather, they were being asked to make a managerial decision to discontinue accepting merchandise from Servette, and they remained free to do so or to go on as before. The Supreme Court interpreted as informational and nonthreatening the union's warning to the supermarket managers that handbills would be distributed.[15]

The central issue in secondary boycotts, as in organizational disputes, has thus come to turn on the question of whether the union's pressure on third parties is limited to a peaceful publicity campaign. The 1959 amendments specifically legalized publicity, other than picketing, for the purpose of truthfully advising the public about a labor dispute, so long as such publicity did not have the effect of inducing any individual to stop transporting goods or performing services for a secondary employer. In a 1964 case, the Supreme Court ruled that this mention of publicity other than picketing had not been intended to outlaw picketing itself in all circumstances.

In this case, the Fruit and Vegetable Packers' Union sought to support a strike against fruit packers in Yakima, Washington, by instituting a consumer boycott against their apples in Seattle. The union picketed Safeway Stores and other supermarkets, with a carefully worded appeal to refrain from buying Washington State apples, which were only one of many food products sold in the stores. The limited nature of the boycott was explained in a letter to the store managers before the picket line was set up, and the pickets were expressly forbidden to request customers not to patronize the store, and also to avoid interfering with the Safeway employees or with deliveries or pickups. The National Labor Relations Board, ruling against the union, held that consumer picketing in front of a secondary establishment is prohibited by the 1959 amendments. But the Supreme Court, reviewing the legislative history of the act, rejected this view: "In the sensitive area of peaceful picketing Congress has dealt explicitly with isolated evils which experience has established flow from such picketing." Justice Black, in a concurring opinion, felt that if the statute had intended to prohibit such picketing it would be unconstitutional under the free speech protection of the First Amendment.[16]

---

[15] *National Labor Relations Board* v. *Servette, Inc.*, 377 U.S. 46 (1964).

[16] *National Labor Relations Board* v. *Fruit and Vegetable Packers Local 760*, 377 U.S. 58 (1964).

Hot-Cargo Clauses

Closely related to the secondary boycott is the *hot-cargo clause,* by which an employer agrees with a union not to handle or use the goods of another employer. For a long time it was argued that a *voluntary agreement* not to handle nonunion goods was a valid expression of support for proper union objectives. The Supreme Court had ruled that an employer might voluntarily support a boycott, and hence might legally agree to do so. "The board has no general commission to police collective bargaining agreements," said the Court, "and to strike down contractual provisions in which there is no element of an unfair labor practice." [17] In reaction to this Supreme Court decision, Congress in 1959 amended the National Labor Relations Act to outlaw agreements to support secondary boycotts. Such action by an employer is now an unfair labor practice.

Exceptions were permitted, however, for the construction and clothing industries, in which refusal to handle nonunion work was deeply embedded in past practice. The first exemption applied only to agreements between union and employer relating to the contracting or subcontracting of work to be done at the site of construction. The second exemption permitted enforcement of agreements relating to both the premises of the manufacturer and the stages of an integrated process of production in the clothing industry. These exemptiions were challenged as unconstitutional, but the circuit court of appeals accepted the argument that Congress was justified in not disturbing long-standing tradition in these industries. [18]

National policy is now clear. The National Labor Relations Act makes unenforceable and void any agreement, express or implied, by which one employer agrees to cease from handling, transporting, or dealing in the goods of another employer. It is an unfair labor practice for an employer to grant, or for a union to demand, such an agreement. Nevertheless, some powerful unions, such as the Teamsters, continue to have a working relationship with employers on this point. And in industries where hot-cargo clauses were a feature of collective bargaining in the years before they were outlawed by Congress, efforts have been made to write contracts that will give the union some measure of protection without coming under the Congressional ban.

The Amalgamated Lithographers union, for example, has negotiated agreements that contain a *struck work* clause, providing that the employer will not render assistance to any lithographic employer engaged in a strike

---

[17] *Local 1976, United Brotherhood of Carpenters and Joiners* v. *National Labor Relations Board,* 357 U.S. 93 (1958).

[18] *Employing Lithographers of Miami* v. *National Labor Relations Board,* 5th Circuit, 301 F2d, 20 (March 1962).

with the union, and that the employees shall not be requested to handle any work not already begun for an employer whose plant was struck by any Amalgamated local. The struck work clause in this form embodies the *ally doctrine*—that employees cannot be compelled to handle work farmed out by another employer who is engaged in a strike with their union. It would be unreasonable to force one local to help break a strike by another local. The Supreme Court has held that such an arrangement by itself is not prohibited by the 1959 amendments.

Work Assignment Disputes

A common situation is the jurisdictional dispute in which two unions —say, the Carpenters and the Machinists—each demand that the employer assign a certain type of work to their members under penalty of shutdown. The Taft–Hartley Act prohibited strikes in such situations and provided for decision by the National Labor Relations Board unless the parties could work out their own arrangements for a settlement. This has stimulated the growth of private settlement machinery, notably as between the various building trades' unions. It has also led to an increase in litigation before the National Labor Relations Board and the courts.

A key case arose out of a dispute in the Columbia Broadcasting System in 1961. CBS had assigned the lighting work for a major telecast in New York City to the Stage Employees rather than to the "technicians" who were members of the Electrical Workers (IBEW). Both unions were certified bargaining agents for their respective CBS employee members, but neither the National Labor Relations Board certification nor the contracts subsequently negotiated had apportioned clearly the areas of work for each group. Particularly acrimonious was the question of "remote lighting," when telecasts away from the home studio took place. When the rival locals could not agree, CBS claimed the right to divide the dispute work on improvised criteria, keeping the peace on a day-to-day basis. This broke down when the technicians refused to operate the cameras unless the entire lighting assignment was given to their members. A major program had to be canceled, and CBS filed unfair practice charges claiming a violation of the amended National Labor Relations Act.[19]

The National Labor Relations Board held the strike illegal, not on the factual basis of the dispute, but on the ground that a strike over work assignment is illegal unless the union is entitled to the work under a board order, a board certification, or a collective bargaining agreement.[20] The

---

[19] *National Labor Relations Board* v. *Radio & Television Engineers Union, International Brotherhood of Electrical Workers,* 364 U.S. 573 (1961).

[20] For a review of the issues, see James B. Atleson, "The National Labor Relations Board and Jurisdictional Disputes: The Aftermath of CBS," *Georgetown Law*

union refused compliance, contending that this ruling was too narrow an interpretation of the board's statutory duty "to determine the dispute." The union claimed that the board's ruling should have been a final determination of the work assignment issue and should have been based on broad criteria derived from the practices and custom of the industry. The question of what kind of decision is required of the National Labor Relations Board under the law had come up also in other circuit courts, some of which had taken one view and some another.

When the CBS case reached the Supreme Court, the Court ruled that the board cannot limit its determination to a legalistic finding concerning the "guilt" of the parties. Rather, the board has the responsibility of actually allocating the disputed work on the facts and merits of the case before it The board defended its narrow construction on a variety of grounds, which added up to a reluctance to assume loosely defined yet very broad powers, which had been given in the act without clear standards to govern their application. In such circumstances, the board felt, it would be exercising the functions of an arbitrator rather than its proper function of rule making. The board obviously believed that this area would best be left to private settlement. The Supreme Court, however, was unsympathetic to this view, saying that with the board's long experience "and a knowledge of the standards generally used by arbitrators, unions, employers, joint boards and others in wrestling with this problem," the board could do the job.

Following the CBS decision, the board adopted criteria to be considered in making affirmative awards in jurisdictional disputes.

> The board will consider all relevant factors in determining who is entitled to the work in dispute, e.g. the skills and work involved, certifications by the board, traditional practice in the company and the industry, agreements between unions and between employers and unions, awards of arbitrators, joint boards and the AFL–CIO in the same or related cases, the assignment made by the employer, and the efficient operation of the employer's business.[21]

Subsequent decisions have been aimed mainly at encouraging the disputing unions to settle jurisdictional disputes by private agreement. Existing agreements between unions, or between employers and unions, have generally been given greater weight than other criteria.

Journal, 53 (1964), p. 93; and Guy Farmer and N. Thompson Powers, "The Role of the National Labor Relations Board in Resolving Jurisdictional Disputes," *Virginia Law Review,* 46 (1960), p. 660.

[21] *International Association of Machinists* v. *J. A. Jones Construction Co.,* 135 NLRB 1402 (1962). For a general review of the problem see Bernard D. Meltzer, "Organizational Picketing and the N.L.R.B.: Five on a Seesaw," *University of Chicago Law Review,* 30 (1962), p. 78.

Employer Behavior in Strike Situations

Where should the line be drawn between the right of the employer to operate his business and the right of the employees to strike? Under the National Labor Relations Act, the employer is prohibited from interfering with the right to strike. This ended a long period in which the employer could exact reprisals for striking or for other union activities. But this apparently clear-cut provision, like other sections of the act, has raised many problems of interpretation.

The employer is entitled to hire strikebreakers to keep the plant in operation. Moreover, he is entitled to promise them permanent jobs, so that, if and when the strikers return to work, the new men must be fitted into the work force. If, however, it can be shown that his real purpose is to get rid of some of the strikers because of their union activities, he may be held guilty of an unfair labor practice.[22]

May an employer lock up his plant when the union calls a strike? There appears to be no simple answer. The legality of the lockout, like that of the strike, will be judged on the factual situation rather than on abstract principles. Generally, the Court has limited the right to lock out employees to situations in which, at the very least, the possibilities of settlement through collective bargaining have been exhausted.

The National Labor Relations Board rule, formulated in the *Quaker State* case, is that a lockout does not violate the act when it is used "to safeguard against unusual operational problems or hazards or economic loss where there is reasonable ground for believing that a strike is imminent." Lockouts have been approved to prevent seizure of a plant by a sitdown strike,[23] to forestall repetitive disruptions of an integrated operation by quickie strikes,[24] to avoid spoilage of materials in case of a sudden work stoppage,[25] and to prevent the immobilization of customers' automobiles brought in for repair.[26]

The board approved the use of the lockout by a multiemployer bargaining unit as a response to a whipsaw strike against one of its members, in a ruling later upheld by the Supreme Court. Subsequently the lockout was used as a defensive measure against the whipsaw strike by four operators of retail food stores who locked out their employees when the local union struck a fifth employer during contract negotiations.[27] All five em-

---

[22] *National Labor Relations Board* v. *Mackay Radio and Telegraph Company,* 304 U.S. 333 (1938).

[23] *Link Belt Co.,* 26 NLRB 227 (1940).

[24] *International Shoe Company,* 93 NLRB 907 (1951).

[25] *Duluth Bottling Association,* 48 NLRB 1335 (1944).

[26] *Betts* v. *Cadillac-Olds,* 96 NLRB 268 (1951).

[27] *National Labor Relations Board* v. *Brown,* 380 U.S. 278 (1965).

ployers were able to operate with the help of temporary replacements and management personnel. The dispute reached the Supreme Court in 1965, where the hiring of temporary replacements during the lockout was ruled to be not discriminatory. The Court argued that the union could have returned its members to work by ending the strike, and that the employer motivation, a union shop being in effect, was only the protection of legitimate business interests. The first nationwide lockout occurred in the trucking industry in March 1967.

The National Labor Relations Board has been reluctant to put the legality of the lockout on the same level as the legality of the strike, possibly feeling that this would tip the scales too far in the employers' favor and defeat the statutory purpose of ensuring equality at the bargaining table. In a 1965 case involving a Great Lakes shipbuilding company,[28] the board ruled a lockout illegal as an unfair practice. The Supreme Court, in a unanimous decision, overruled the National Labor Relations Board, saying that the right to strike does not carry with it the right exclusively to determine the timing and duration of all work stoppages. To find a violation, the Court said, the board must show that the employer has acted for a proscribed purpose—that is, to discourage union membership, or to discriminate against the union. The tools of economic self-help available to the employer—replacement of strikers, stockpiling, subcontracting, maintaining his operations while the strikers go without pay, and especially the right to institute his own conditions unilaterally when his contract with the union has expired—also include the lockout, provided it is used in nondiscriminatory fashion.

Discharge and disciplinary measures are protected against board orders for reinstatement under Section 10(c) of the National Labor Relations Act if the individuals have been suspended or discharged "for cause." The employer's right to manage his business in his own interest has been a common defense to union charges of bias and discrimination. There is an important exception. When a strike has been caused by the employer's unfair labor practices, National Labor Relations Board policy has usually prohibited discharge even to the point of requiring reinstatement at the expense of replacements hired during the strike.[29] Even unfair labor-practice strikers, however, lose their protected status if violence or other misconduct occurs during a strike. The sitdown strikes and plant seizures of the late 1930s came within this category. In a Massachusetts case in 1954, the appeals

---

[28] *American Shipbuilding Company* v. *National Labor Relations Board*, 380 U.S. 300 (1965). The leading authority on lockouts is Professor Bernard D. Meltzer; see his review of the problems and cases in "Single Employer and Multi-employer Lockouts under the Taft–Hartley Act," *University of Chicago Law Review*, 24 (1956), p. 70; and discussion of the 1965 cases in *Supreme Court Review, 1965* (Chicago): The University of Chicago Press, 1965), p. 87.

[29] *Brown Shoe Company*, 1 NLRB 803 (1936).

court required the National Labor Relations Board to distinguish between employees in an unfair labor-practice strike who had restrained and coerced other employees, ruling that those who were guilty of misconduct might legally by discharged by the company.[30] The employer is free to refuse reinstatement to striking workers against whom violence on the picket line can be specifically proved.

GOVERNMENT'S ROLE IN MAJOR STRIKES

Most strikes cause little permanent loss of output, for reasons examined in Chapter 19. But it is equally clear that some strikes do cause serious economic damage. These are often called *emergency strikes,* and there is a strong case for government intervention to avert or settle them.

What is an *emergency strike?* The common answer is: one that causes dangerous curtailment of a necessary service. But what services are *necessary?* At what point does curtailment of service become dangerous rather than merely inconvenient? At one pole, a strike in a toy manufacturing plant would be recognized as minor. At the other pole, a nationwide railroad strike is clearly dangerous. But in between there is a continuum of situations, and the point at which danger sets in is a matter of judgment. It is probably better to speak of *major strikes,* recognizing that there will be differences of judgment on the proper content of this category.

One approach to a definition is to observe the kinds of cases in which government has intervened in the past. Rail and air transport are considered essential, and there is special statutory provision for disputes in these industries. (There are no comparable provisions for road transport, although a trucking strike could interrupt the flow of foodstuffs and other essential supplies.) The emergency dispute provisions of the Taft–Hartley Act were invoked twenty-eight times between 1948 and 1967. Twelve of these cases involved direct defense industries: atomic energy, aerospace, aircraft and aircraft engines, shipbuilding. Another nine involved longshoring or merchant shipping, which affect the overseas flow of military supplies as well as commercial exports and imports. Other scattered cases involved bituminous coal (three cases), basic steel, telephone service, and meat packing. At the local level (excluding for the moment strikes of public employees), strikes in bus and subway service, electrical utilities, hospital services, and newspaper publishing have been held to require government intervention.

A common feature of all such disputes is that they generate political pressure. If the dispute has high visibility, either because it causes wide-

---

[30] *National Labor Relations Board* v. *Thayer Co.,* U.S. Court of Appeals, First Circuit, 213 F. 2d 748 (1954).

spread inconvenience or because there is a dramatic potential for claiming danger to public health or safety, pressure will inevitably build up for government intervention. The President, the governor, or the mayor will be expected to settle the dispute—whether or not he actually has power to do so. Either of the contending parties may try to use government intervention to win concessions they could not gain by collective bargaining. Meanwhile, the focus of public wrath may be shifted away from union or management representatives to a politically vulnerable elected official. The appeal for government intervention marks a shift of the dispute from the economic to the political arena, with the elected executive having willy-nilly a large personal stake in the outcome.

Existing Settlement Machinery

Techniques of government intervention may be divided into *ad hoc* procedures versus *continuing,* or *statutory,* procedures. At the federal level, the Railway Labor Act and the Taft–Hartley Act authorize presidential intervention in certain circumstances. Several states have laws specifying the procedures to be used in emergency situations. But Presidents, Congress, governors, and mayors have also improvised measures to deal with specific situations.

Under the Railway Labor Act, the National Mediation Board may intervene in *major* (new contract) disputes at the request of either party or on its own motion. If mediation is unsuccessful, the board must request the parties to submit the dispute to voluntary arbitration, which they almost always decline to do. The President may then appoint an emergency board to investigate the dispute and make recommendations concerning it. During the thirty days that the emergency board is allowed for its investigation, and for another thirty days after the board's report is filed, neither party may make any change in the conditions out of which the dispute arose. The parties are not obliged to accept the recommendations of the emergency board, however, and a strike at the end of the waiting period is entirely legal.

Before World War II labor disputes on the railroads seem to have been settled quite successfully within the framework of the act. Between 1926 and 1941 only sixteen emergency boards were appointed, most of these disputes were settled along the lines of board recommendations, and only two minor strikes occurred. Since 1941, however, few major disputes in the industry have been settled successfully through the procedures of the Railway Labor Act. In most cases the President has had to intervene to avoid a crisis. In 1941, for instance, the unions were dissatisfied with the recommendations of an emergency board and appealed to President Roosevelt, who negotiated a settlement that gave the unions more than the emergency board had proposed. In three cases, one from 1942 to 1943, one in 1947, and one in 1951, both the emergency board recommendations and the terms proposed by the President were repudiated by one of the parties, and service was maintained only by government seizure of the railroads under the President's emergency powers. In 1963 and again in 1967, special legislation by Congress was required to settle major railroad disputes.

The Taft–Hartley Act also provides a special procedure for cases in which "in the opinion of the President of the United States, a threatened or actual strike or lockout affecting an entire industry or a substantial portion thereof . . . will, if permitted to occur or to continue, imperil the national health or safety." In such cases the president, after preliminary investigation by the board of inquiry, may ask the Attorney General to seek an injunction against the strike. If the injunction is granted, strike action becomes unlawful for an eighty-day period, during which the parties may continue to negotiate. If no agreement is reached by the end of the period, the injunction is dissolved and the strike may proceed.

There is considerable difference of opinion about the usefulness of this procedure. Cullen has analyzed twenty-eight cases in which it was used between 1948 and 1967. In twenty of these cases a strike was already in progress when intervention occurred. Injunctions were issued in twenty-four cases. When a strike was already in progress, the injunction halted it in all except two cases, both involving the bituminous coal industry. Most significant is what happened during the compulsory waiting period. Here the record is mixed. When a strike was halted by injunction, settlements were achieved without renewal of the strike in about three out of four cases. The act did fail to ward off a strike, however, in eight cases—a 1949–1950 coal case in which a strike continued until President Truman threatened seizure, and seven disputes in longshoring and shipping, where union–management relations are unusually bitter and interunion rivalry is strong.[31]

Such statistics, of course, are not a conclusive test of the Taft–Hartley procedure. There is continuing controversy over such matters as whether existence of this procedure leads to its being used more often than necessary; whether the injunction is really a neutral device; whether likelihood that the procedure will be used in a particular case encourages union and management negotiators to stall in the earlier stages of bargaining; and whether the procedure could be improved by giving the boards of inquiry power to make recommendations for settling the dispute, which the act presently prohibits them from doing.

When it is not considered desirable to invoke the statutory procedures, or when a strike continues after these procedures have been exhausted, or

---

[31] For a more detailed review, see Donald E. Cullen, *National Emergency Strikes* (Ithaca: New York State School of Industrial and Labor Relations, 1968), Chap. 3.

when (as in many states and most cities) there is no specific legislation, the executive is forced to improvise. He seeks a good solution by any means available, or by a combination of several techniques in sequence. For example, *ad hoc* intervention may begin with an announcement that mediation services have been offered to the parties, followed by appointment of a fact-finding board and distribution of press releases describing the board's assessment of the issues. There may follow conferences with the Secretary of Labor, persuasion to accept arbitration, and even dramatic meetings of the leaders of both sides with the Chief Executive. The essence of the *ad hoc* approach is that it looks neither backward nor forward. It attends only to the specific dispute at hand.

Dissatisfaction with existing statutes and with hastily improvised procedures has led to a continuing search for improved methods of dispute settlement. The policy objective is not just to prevent stoppages of production, which can always be done by use of force. The objective is rather to prevent strikes by methods that are orderly and uniform in their application, that involve a minimum of direct compulsion, that do not impose greater pressure on one party than on the other, and that leave maximum scope for settlements to be reached through direct negotiation between the parties. These subsidiary requirements make the problem extraordinarily difficult.

Possibilities for the Future

It would be constructive, first, to improve collective bargaining machinery wherever possible. To the extent that this leaves fewer unsettled disputes, the need for emergency procedures is reduced.

Greater use might be made of the technique of *continuous bargaining,* described in Chapter 18. Calm discussion of technical issues over a period of months or years may lead to agreements which could not have been reached in the crisis atmosphere of a contract expiration deadline.

The parties might also be encouraged to submit unsettled disputes to neutral arbitration. Both unions and companies have been reluctant to accept arbitration of new contract terms. A good number of agreements in public employment, however, contain arbitration clauses. The 1973 steel agreement also provided for ultimate arbitration of any unsettled contract issues.

A perennial proposal is that, if the parties to a major dispute will not accept arbitration voluntarily, they should be compelled to do so. The main argument for compulsory arbitration is that, unlike the techniques described earlier, it *does* secure an adjudication of the disputed issues. It does prescribe terms of settlement. True, the terms may be rejected and a strike may still ensue, as has happened frequently in Australia despite its widespread arbitration system'. But in this event the executive has a clear mandate to enforce the award by legal procedures and can expect strong support from public opinion.

The main argument on the other side is that compulsory arbitration, rather than serving as a supplement to collective bargaining, tends to supplant and eliminate any genuine bargaining. As in the case of board-of-inquiry proceedings, but even more strongly, the parties will decline to reveal their true positions or to compromise their shadow positions. Rather than make concessions on a disputed issue, they will pass the buck to the board in the hope of a favorable decision.

Compulsory arbitration is a legal procedure, a special kind of court trial. The outcome of a trial is a victory. The outcome of bargaining is an agreement. There is strong reason to believe that terms that have been agreed to voluntarily, rather than imposed by government, will be accepted with better grace and complied with more completely. In addition, the process of mutual persuasion is educational to both parties.

Whatever the merits, union and employer opposition make it unlikely that compulsory arbitration will become a regular feature of emergency dispute procedures. This has led to a search for techniques which fall short of compulsion but still bring public pressure to bear effectively on the parties.

One interesting possibility, the *choice-of-procedures* approach, was devised originally by a tripartite committee headed by the late Professor Sumner Slichter, and subsequently enacted into law in Massachusetts. The Massachusetts law applies to production and distribution of food, fuel, water, electric light and power, gas, hospital care, and medical services. It does not cover local transportation or telephone service. When the governor finds that a dispute in these industries threatens public health and safety, he may take any or all of the following steps:

1. Require the parties to appear before a moderator to show cause why they should not submit the dispute to arbitration. The moderator may also perform mediation functions. If he fails to get a settlement or a submission to arbitration, he makes a public report on responsibility for the failure but may not comment on the merits of the case.

2. Request the parties voluntarily to submit the dispute to a tripartite emergency board empowered to recommend terms of settlement. If a submission is arranged, the board must submit its findings and recommendations to the governor within thirty days.

3. If the governor finds these procedures inappropriate or if the dispute remains unsettled after using them, he may declare an emergency and arrange with either or both parties for continuing production to the degree necessary for public health and safety.

4. He may also seize and operate the plant or facilities. During the seizure period he may at his discretion put into effect the recommendations of the emergency board if there has been one, or he may appoint a special commis-

sion to recommend terms of employment and may put these into effect at his discretion. Seizure ends when the parties notify the governor that the dispute has been settled, or he may terminate it when he considers it no longer necessary even though the dispute remains unsettled.

This law seems to have yielded broadly satisfactory results, partly because the governor has wisely refrained from intervening in every situation. When intervention has occurred, the eventual settlement has usually been reached either through continuation of collective bargaining or through a submission to voluntary arbitration. The settlements do not appear to have been biased consistently in favor of labor or of management.

Some experts have urged that the choce-of-procedures approach be adopted at the federal level. No one settlement technique, it is argued, can be equally effective in all situations. Moreover, the very specific procedure under the Railway Labor Act and the Taft–Hartley Act lets the parties know precisely what to expect, and enables them to outwit or outsit the government. Instead, policy should aim to keep the parties guessing as to what will happen next. Holding over their heads a variety of possibilities, most of them distasteful, will generate maximum pressure on them to settle their own disputes.

LABOR RELATIONS AND THE ANTITRUST LAWS

The possibility that unions might be penalized under the antitrust laws was a live issue from the enactment of the Sherman Act in 1890 until the 1930s. With the passage of the Wagner Act and the creation of the National Labor Relations Board, however, it appeared that the courts had effectively lost their power to apply the antitrust laws to union activities, since machinery now existed to handle possible abuse of union power.

This view was supported by Supreme Court decisions in two early cases—*Apex Hosiery* [32] (1940) and *Hutcheson* [33] (1941)—in which the Court held that a strike in support of normal union objectives could not be attacked under the antitrust laws, even though a side effect was interference with interstate commerce. The Court's opinion in the latter case, delivered by Mr. Justice Frankfurter, ruled that the only test of legality is whether the union was acting out of self-interest and without combining with nonlabor groups.

Five years later, however, a case reached the Supreme Court that for the first time raised the issue of unions controlling the product market in collusion with nonlabor groups. In New York City, Local 3 of the International Brotherhood of Electrical Workers had greatly enlarged the em-

---

[32] *Apex Hosiery* v. *Leader,* 310 U.S. 469 (1940).
[33] *United States* v. *Hutcheson,* 312 U.S. 219 (1941).

ployment opportunities of its members by first obtaining closed shop contracts (at this time not illegal) with local concerns manufacturing electrical equipment, and then using the pressures of strike and boycott to persuade contractors to purchase equipment only from these manufacturers. Subsequently these arguments were expanded from individual contracts into an industry-wide "understanding" covering New York City, in which a committee of union, manufacturers', and contractors' representatives acted to exclude from the metropolitan area all electrical equipment manufactured elsewhere—indeed, excluding even the output of factories with contracts with other International Brotherhood of Electrical Workers' locals. Allen–Bradley, Inc., a Milwaukee manufacturer of electrical equipment, brought suit in federal court against the New York union. The district court found Local 3 in violation of the Sherman Act and issued an injunction; but this was reversed by the court of appeals on the grounds of the *Hutcheson* case—that is, that activities not forbidden to Local 3 if it were acting alone could not be prohibited merely because other groups had joined with the union to accomplish the same purpose.

But the Supreme Court took a different view. It held that the Sherman Act had indeed been violated and that an injunction could be issued, provided it were limited to activities in which the union had combined with nonlabor groups to control the product market. The opinion, written by Mr. Justice Black, reasoned that the immunity claimed by Local 3 could not be found in any language of Congress, nor could it be inferred from the union's undoubted right to make bargaining agreements with employers. Standing alone, the contract of Local 3 was not a violation of the antitrust laws; but it did not stand alone. On the contrary, the facts of the case showed such collective agreements to be only one element in a larger program to monopolize all the business in New York City and to charge prices above a competitive level. "When the unions participated with a combination of businessmen who had complete power to eliminate all competition among themselves and to prevent all competition from others, a situation was created not included within the exemptions of the Clayton and Norris–LaGuardia Acts." [34]

The case involved open and flagrant restrictions on competition. But what if the effects on pricing and competition are less clear? There appears to be a gray area, in which the courts reserve the right to balance legitimate pursuit of union interests against damage to competitors and the public.

In *United Mine Workers* v. *Pennington,* the union and the major coal producers were alleged to have conspired to drive out of business the smaller and less efficient coal producers by establishing a uniform, industry-

---

[34] *Allen–Bradley* v. *Local 3, International Brotherhood of Electrical Workers,* 325 U.S. 797 (1945).

wide wage rate act deliberately at a level higher than the small companies could afford to pay. The union claimed that an antitrust action could not be brought against a wage agreement; as a mandatory bargaining subject, the companies' "duty to bargain" was paramount. But the Supreme Court declined to ignore the purpose of the wage pact. Legality under the antitrust laws becomes an issue, said the Court, when as a precondition of the wage bargain the union agrees to "secure the same wages, hours or other conditions of employment from the remaining employers in the industry." In making a multiemployer agreement, the union may indeed attempt on its own to get the same terms from employers outside the unit. But the duty to bargain exists only on a unit-by-unit basis; there can be no compulsion to negotiate about standards outside the unit. "We think a union forfeits its exemption from the antitrust laws when it is clearly shown that it has agreed wih one set of employers to impose a certain wage scale on other bargaining units." The Court ruled the Mine Workers guilty of conspiracy, but allowed reargument and in 1968 the union won its case; but meanwhile, in an identical case, a jury awarded triple damages of $1.5 million to the Tennessee Consolidated Coal Company. Using the *Pennington* rationale the Supreme Court upheld this award in March 1970, and the door was clearly opened to control of union activities under the antitrust laws.[35]

A companion case, *Amalgamated Meat Cutters* v. *Jewel Tea Company,* was decided on the same day. Jewel Tea, a retail chain, had sued the Meat Cutters' union under the Sherman Act, alleging a conspiracy between seven unions and nine thousand retailers to prevent the sale of meat in the Chicago area after 6 P.M. The union argued that the matter was entirely within the regulatory powers of the National Labor Relations Board and therefore outside the court's jurisdiction. But the court of appeals ruled that a conspiracy in restraint of trade had been shown, the marketing hours clause being classified as a product-pricing provision. The conspiracy ruling was rejected by the Supreme Court, but they also rejected the union argument that the case was exclusively a matter for the National Labor Relations Board. Exemption of the union's actions from the antitrust laws was held to depend not on the form of the agreement—the fact of bargaining on wages, hours, or working conditions—but on its relative impact on the product market balanced against the interests of union members in labor standards.[36]

[35] *United Mine Workers* v. *Pennington,* 281 U.S. 657 (1965). For a discussion of the issues, see Theodore St. Antoine, "Collective Bargaining and the Antitrust Laws," Industrial Relations Research Association, *Proceedings* (1966), p. 66, and Archibald Cox, "Labor and the Antitrust Laws: Pennington and Jewel Tea," *Boston University Law Review,* 46 (1966), p. 317. The 1970 decision was one of four damage suits that reached the Supreme Court; see *The New York Times* (March 3, 1970), p. 22.

[36] *Local 189, Amalgamated Meat Cutters* v. *Jewel Tea Company,* 381 U.S. 676 (1965). For a detailed empirical study of the problems underlying the case, see

So the application of antitrust to labor agreements, which on several occasions in the past has seemed to be settled, is once more in dispute. The courts seem to be saying that, whenever a collective agreement encroaches on product-market competition, it may be held unlawful unless the effect is outweighed by the union's legitimate interest in wages, hours, and conditions. And who is to say which effect outweighs the other? Naturally, the courts. The door thus seems open to extensive judicial intervention in the substance of collective bargaining.

DISCUSSION QUESTIONS

1. What are the main legal restrictions on the right to strike? What practical difference does it make whether a strike is ruled unlawful?

2. Under what conditions may picketing of an employer's premises be held unlawful? Are present rules governing picketing too lenient? Too severe? About right?

3. Which measures may an employer take, and which may he not take, against a striking employee? Are the rules reasonable?

4. What kinds of situation come under the heading of *secondary pressures?* Is the policy of treating such pressures as unlawful:
(a) reasonable?
(b) effective?

5. In what industries would you consider a stoppage of production serious enough to warrant special treatment by government? Give your reasons in each case.

6. Why is a national railroad strike a very uncommon event in the United States?

7. Review the main arguments for and against compulsory arbitration of major disputes.

8. Suppose you were asked to draft a new federal statute to replace the "emergency" provisions of the Taft–Hartley Act. What would you include in the statute?

9. In what ways might collective agreements serve, either deliberately or inadvertently, to restrict competition in product markets?

10. Draft an amendment to the antitrust laws specifying the kinds of bargained agreements that shall be considered unlawful because of their effect on product-market competition.

Herbert R. Northrup, *Restrictive Labor Practices in the Supermarket Industry* (Philadelphia: University of Pennsylvania Press, 1967), Chaps. 5 and 6.

READING SUGGESTIONS

On the subject of national policy toward major strikes, the student may consult the following titles: IRVING BERNSTEIN, HAROLD L. ENARSON, and R. W. FLEMING (eds.), *Emergency Disputes and National Policy,* New York: Harper & Row, Publishers, 1955; DONALD E. CULLEN, *National Emergency Strikes,* Ithaca: New York State School of Industrial and Labor Relations, Cornell, 1968; NEIL CHAMBERLAIN, "Strikes in Contemporary Context," *Industrial and Labor Relations Review* (July 1967), p. 602; C. V. SMYTHE, "Public Policy and Emergency Disputes," *Labor Law Journal* (October 1963), p. 827; and A. P. MARSHALL, "New Perspectives in National Emergency Disputes," *Labor Law Journal,* 18 (1967), p. 451. The definitive study of the use of presidential power in major disputes is JOHN L. BLACKMAN, JR., *Presidential Seizure in Labor Disputes,* Cambridge, Mass.: Harvard University Press, 1967. On compulsory arbitration and settlement machinery, see DAVID L. COLE, *The Quest for Industrial Peace,* New York: McGraw-Hill Book Company, 1963; also HERBERT R. NORTHRUP, *Compulsory Arbitration and Government Intervention in Labor Disputes,* Washington, D.C.: Labor Policy Association Inc., 1966.

On the application of antitrust laws to collective bargaining, see ARCHIBALD COX, "Labor and the Antitrust Laws; a Preliminary Analysis," *University of Pennsylvania Law Review,* 104 (1955), p. 252; BERNARD D. MELTZER, "Labor Unions, Collective Bargaining and the Antitrust Laws," *Journal of Law and Economics,* 6 (1963), p. 152; GEORGE HILDEBRAND, "Collective Bargaining and the Antitrust Laws," in JOSEPH SHISTER, BENJAMIN AARON, and CLYDE W. SUMMERS (eds.), *Public Policy and Collective Bargaining,* New York: Harper & Row, Publishers, 1962, pp. 152–82; THEODORE ST. ANTOINE, "Collective Bargaining and the Antitrust Laws," *IRRA Proceedings,* 1966, p. 66; and RALPH WINTER, "Collective Bargaining and Competition: The Application of Antitrust Standards to Union Activities," *Yale Law Journal,* 73 (1963), p. 14.

27

Bargaining in the Public Sector

The last three chapters have outlined the legal framework of collective bargaining in private employment. Here government is formally a neutral, laying down rules of conduct for unions and employers.

We turn now to the large and growing sector in which government itself is the employer. What accounts for the rapid rise of unionism among public employees? How does public-sector bargaining differ from bargaining in the private sector? What has been the impact of collective bargaining on government organization and on wages and conditions of public employees? Are strikes of public employees ever permissible? If not, how are unsettled disputes to be resolved?

PUBLIC EMPLOYEES AND THEIR UNIONS

In Chapter 4 we noted the rapid expansion of government employment, which, as a proportion of all employment in the economy, rose from 8.8 percent in 1929 to 17.1 percent in 1975. In absolute numbers government employees increased from 3.2 to 14.5 million. Four-fifths of these are employed by local and state governments.

How many of these workers are regarded as unionized depends on whether one includes associations, such as the National Education Association, which have been acting increasingly like unions in recent years. Including such groups, the number of organized government employees is now in the neighborhood of five million. The degree of organization is substantially higher than in the private sector. About one-quarter of private wage and salary earners are union members. But more than half of all federal employees are now in units for which a union has been recognized as exclusive bargaining agent. Virtually all of the nation's 2 million schoolteachers belong either to the National Education Association or the American Federation of Teachers. About 40 percent of state and local government employees, exclusive of teachers, are members of employee organizations.

The reasons for rapid growth of public employee unionism during the sixties and seventies are unclear. Contributing factors may have included the demonstration effect of the gains won by unions in private employment; the relative backwardness of personnel administration in the public service; the growing size, bureaucratization, and impersonality of government departments and agencies; the continuing pressure of inflation on living standards; and the tendency for salaries of many public employees to lag behind the general advance.

A more tolerant public attitude must also have made some contribution. Before 1940, unionization of teachers, policemen, firemen, and other public employees was regarded as highly irregular, even unlawful. Today numerous federal executive orders and state public employee relations acts, almost all enacted since 1960, have endorsed the legality of collective bargaining by public employees and provided orderly procedures for union recognition, bargaining relations, and resolution of bargaining deadlocks. The growing strength of public-employee unionism doubtlessly stimulated passage of these acts; but once on the books, they gave another booster shot to union growth.

Organization of public sector employees takes a variety of forms.[1] These include:

1. *All-public unions.* The largest of these is the American Federation of State, County, and Municipal Employees (AFSCME), which in 1972 had 550,000 members and must be considerably larger today. An industrial type of union affiliated with the AFL–CIO, it includes state and local government employees in all occupations, except for teachers, firefighters, and most police officers, who have chosen to organize separately.

The American Federation of Teachers, also an AFL–CIO affiliate, had a 1973 membership of 375,000. While it admits teachers in private as well as public institutions, including college and university teachers, it is dominated by teachers in public elementary and secondary schools. Firemen are organized in the International Association of Firefighters, with a membership of some 130,000. The nation's quarter million police officers are organized in a variety of ways, the largest bodies being the Fraternal Order of Police and the International Conference of Police Associations. The police and firefighters organizations typically bargain together at the local level, and parity of pay for the two uniformed services is an important bargaining issue.

At the federal level, unionization of postal workers is virtually complete. The United Federation of Postal Clerks and the National Association of

---

[1] For detailed discussion, see Jack Stieber, *Public Employee Unionism* (Washington, D.C.: The Brookings Institution, 1973), Chaps. 1–4.

Letter Carriers have a combined membership of about 375,000. The American Federation of Government Employees has more than 300,000 members in the classified federal service.

2. *Mixed Unions.* Many unions whose membership is predominantly in the private sector also admit public employees within their respective jurisdictions. Blue-collar workers in federal employment tend to join the unions of their trades. Craftsmen in arsenals and navy yards, for example, have long been organized in District 44 of the Machinists' Union.

At the state and local level, the most important bodies are the Service Employees International Union (SEIO), the Laborers' International Union, and the Teamsters' Union. The SEIO claims a very wide jurisdiction, and competes actively with the AFSCME and other unions. By 1971, government employees accounted for about one-third of the SEIO's 450,000 membership. The Laborers' Union, basically a union of semiskilled and unskilled construction workers, has expanded into numerous areas of public employment. Government workers now constitute about 10 percent of its 550,000 membership. The Teamsters' Union has been especially active in organizing city sanitation departments and county and state highway departments; but this wide-ranging organization stands ready to take in almost any occupations, including sheriffs, registered nurses, X-ray technicians, school principals, and parking-meter maids. In 1970 it already had over 57,000 public employee members.

3. *Associations.* Much the largest of these is the National Education Association, with a membership of about 1,500,000 school teachers. This was initially a professional organization, seeking to improve the status of education and the level of professional accomplishment, working mainly on and through state legislatures, and with a constitutional provision against strikes and other forms of economic pressure.

During the 1960s, however, in response to the militant advance of the American Federation of Teachers, the NEA began to act like a traditional union where local membership demanded it do so. The constitutional provision against strikes was dropped in 1965. The NEA began to compete with the AFT in representation elections, typically winning a good majority of these. As a result, the climate of opinion in the teaching profession has undergone a profound transformation, with widespread acceptance of the life-style of organized unionism, its "demands," bargaining, negotiation, and striking as the ultimate resort.

The American Nurses' Association has experienced a policy evolution much like that of the NEA and is increasingly taking on collective bargaining functions. While most of its 200,000 members are in nonprofit hospitals or in private practice, about 50,000 are public employees.

Most states and many localities have associations of government employees. These were founded mainly between 1920 and 1950, to provide retirement and other benefits, and to initiate or protect a civil service system. Most of them are affiliated with the Assembly of Government Employees (AGE), a loose confederation which in 1969 had 618,000 members. Some of these associations continue to perform mainly benefit and lobbying functions; but others have been converted into full-fledged bargaining organizations, espousing normal union objectives and tactics.

Because of this transformation of association functions, the number of public employees engaged in collective bargaining is substantially larger than the number of union members in the conventional sense.

SPECIAL FEATURES OF PUBLIC-SECTOR BARGAINING

How different is collective bargaining in the public sector from the private bargaining discussed in earlier chapters? The answer has important practical implications. For example, should unions of public employees be allowed to strike? Those who say "yes" usually argue that collective bargaining serves essentially the same functions in the private and public sectors, and that the strike weapon is essential to compel serious bargaining. Those who favor prohibition of strikes in public employment argue that the politicoeconomic context is decidedly different, and that an unlimited right to strike tilts the balance of bargaining power too far in the direction of the union.

Economic Differences

1. A major argument for private collective bargaining is that it serves as an offset to employers' monopsony power. Some students of public employment argue that monopsony power is less prevalent in the public sector, or at any rate less likely to be exercised. Many of the skills needed by government—typists, bookkeepers, truck drivers, skilled maintenance crafts, building laborers—are demanded also by private employers, and the bidding of these numerous competitors can be counted on to prevent government from paying less than the market rate. Even where government is the sole or major employer—as for teaching, firefighting, or police work—there are private occupations requiring the same general abilities and qualifications. No one has to become a policeman; and unless the employment package offered by government is competitive with that in alternative occupations, the supply of recruits will dry up. Further, even if government had substantial monopsony power, it might not take full advantage of this for political reasons. Government employees are also voters, and so are their relatives and friends. Marked unfairness in terms of employment would probably lead to retaliation at the polls.

To the extent that these arguments are valid, they suggest that the wage-protective functions of unionism may be less necessary in public than in private employment. It would follow that the union has less need of economic weapons.

2. Turning to the *product* market, the wage-raising power of a union in private industry is constrained by market forces. There are usually a number of employers competing in the same product market. Unless a union can organize them all, it cannot force wage rates in union plants much above the nonunion level. Further, wage increases in one industry relative to others tend to reduce employment in that industry, both by stimulating mechanization and by raising product prices. This wage–employment trade-off has some influence on union wage demands. The question is whether there are equally strong constraints on union behavior in the public sector.

Several points are relevant. First, government is normally a monopolistic seller of public services. A citizen who regards the price of these services—that is, the level of tax rates—as too high does not have the option of seceding and ceasing to pay taxes. In the long run, however, freedom of householders and businesses to move produces a limited competition among local government units. Second, demand for public services may be more inelastic than that for private goods and services. The amount of fire protection or elementary education demanded by the citizens may not be much affected by their cost. To the extent that this is true, demand for labor in public employment is also inelastic, and wages can be pushed up with little loss of jobs.

Third, it can be argued that public services are more essential than most private goods and services. Interruption of police and fire protection, of hospital service, and of sanitation service have an immediate effect on citizens' welfare. Even where continuous production is less essential, as in public education, park and recreation facilities, or transit systems, the citizens suffer definite inconvenience from a stoppage. They are likely to react by bringing pressure on government officials for a quick settlement, even at the cost of abnormal wage increases. Thus public employers, it is said, are unusually vulnerable to economic pressure, which tends to be translated into political pressure; and union use of the strike weapon is correspondingly dangerous. This essentiality argument is disputed by others, however, and we shall return to it later in discussing the strike issue.

3. The method of *financing* employee compensation is characteristically different in the public and private sectors. Some government agencies, to be sure, sell their services at a price and can respond to wage increases by price increases. Most government operations, however, are financed from tax revenues. There are, of course, a variety of constraints on tax increases: the natural resistance of the citizens, the consequent hesitancy of officials interested in reelection, fear of losing business and employment to other cities or states, occasional constitutional restrictions on states and cities, occasional requirements for a public referendum. But these constraints are different from, and may possibly be weaker than, those operating to restrain price increases by private employers.

The overall issue is whether a union of public employees armed with the full panoply of political and economic weapons, including the strike threat, is in a stronger position vis-à-vis the public employer than the typical union of private employees. If so, this might warrant different treatment in public policy.

Organizational Differences

Governmental units had systems for managing employee relations long before the appearance of unionism. These older managerial structures have posed serious problems for the development of collective bargaining. We shall comment particularly on practices in local government, where some of the most complex problems arise.

In a private corporation, lines of authority are usually clear. The union knows with whom it must bargain; and it knows also that the management bargainer can make good on any commitments he makes. Neither of these factors is necessarily clear in bargaining with local government units.

Cities differ, to begin with, in their basic organization. Some have strong-mayor systems, others weak-mayor systems, others a city-manager system. Under any of these systems, the all-important authority over budgets is usually divided between the executive and legislative branches. The mayor or city manager may recommend a budget, but the city council can usually modify or veto it. Which has the dominant influence varies from city to city. The fiscal authority of local officials may be restricted by legislation. Sometimes tax increases beyond a certain size must be approved by the state legislature or submitted to popular referendum. Frequently, important fringe benefits such as pensions, vacation, and sick-leave arrangements are regulated either by state law or by the city charter. Local ability to pay is influenced also by availability of state and federal grants.

This situation presents the union with both difficulties and tactical opportunities. It is often unclear whether the bargainer for the city can actually commit the city to a proposed increase, which implies a corresponding budget appropriation. The bargainer may try to hide behind his limited authority or to pass the buck to other levels of government. Thus one finds the mayor of New York saying to a union group, "I'd be glad to give you the money if the governor would first give it to me" (these two gentlemen often being political rivals). In other cases the bargainer is incapable of making a binding commitment because someone else will have to ratify the budget.

But the division of fiscal authority can also be turned to union advantage. If the city manager or his representative is proving a tough bargainer, the union can sometimes go around him to friends on the city council who will ratify a larger settlement. Collective bargaining is thus intertwined with personal and party rivalries in city politics.

A different kind of problem arises from the fragmentation of government units. One often finds semiautonomous agencies with independent authority over wages and benefits. These agencies may have their own taxing power, or may be supported by state and federal grants. They are often under no compulsion to coordinate their wage struggles with other city departments or to follow directives of the mayor and council. Los Angeles, for example, has six independent salary-setting authorities, and the mayor and council set salaries for less than 60 percent of city employees. An example from Michigan is the Wayne County Road Commission, which operates in virtual independence of the Wayne County Board of Supervisors. Of its $100 million budget, only $1.8 million comes from the county, the remainder from state grants and other outside sources.

It has complete authority over this budget, including authority to enter into contracts with employees.

Another important body is the civil service commission, well established at the state and federal levels and in many of the major cities. Created as a reaction against the earlier *spoils system,* it attempts to substitute merit for political patronage in public employment. It normally has authority to esablish basic job classifications and descriptions; to compile lists of applicants for entry jobs, and to select from these lists through competitive examination or some other objective basis; to lay down rules for training, retention, and promotion of employees in each classification, making further use of competitive examination as required; and to hear employee appeals from supervisors' decisions. Occasionally the commission's jurisdiction extends to salary administration and recommendation of salary increases; but more usually its authority is limited to nonsalary matters.

The existence and strength of civil service commissions creates additional confusion over who can bargain for the public, and on what issues. The Michigan legislature in 1965 passed a Public Employment Relations Act confirming the right of public employees to organize and the duty of public employers to bargain with union representatives. But who is "the employer"? In Wayne County, this status was claimed by (1) the County Board of Supervisors; (2) the three-man civil service commission appointed by the Board; and (3) the Road Commission (for its employees). This dispute has made collective bargaining difficult.

Unions also regard the civil service commission as an arm of the employer, rather than as a neutral agency. Commission administration of personnel matters in accordance with its own judgment of merit runs counter to two union principles outlined in earlier chapters: (1) the principle that procedures for recruitment, promotion, layoff or discharge of employees must be bargained out with the union and administered jointly through the grievance procedure, rather than determined and administered unilaterally by the employer; and (2) the principle that seniority should be given dominant weight in personnel decisions. Promotions and demotions based on merit only, with merit decided by the employer, are not acceptable.

BARGAINING ARRANGEMENTS: FEDERAL LEVEL

The growth of public-sector unionism has raised much the same issues as were faced earlier with respect to private employment. Should employees have the right to organize and designate their own representatives? Should public employers be required to negotiate with such representatives? Should negotiations cover the full range of "wages, hours, and other conditions of work" found in private-sector bargaining? If public employee strikes are prohibited by law, what alternatives can be provided for the resolution of a bargaining impasse? These questions have been faced, with varying success, at all levels of government in the United States over the past twenty years or so. Coming through the back door, collective bargaining has become a working reality in the public service in the United States, as it has been for many years in most European countries.

Federal authorities long took a negative if not hostile view of employee organization. Federal employees, along with state and local employees, were excluded from the coverage of the Wagner Act, while the Taft–Hartley amendments of 1947 specifically outlawed strikes by federal employees: ". . . Any individual employed by the United States or any such agency who strikes shall immediately be discharged from his employment, and shall forfeit his civil service status, if any, and shall not be eligible for reemployment for three years. . . ."

The first positive statement of policy came in two executive orders issued by President Kennedy in 1962, after investigation by a task force under the chairmanship of Arthur Goldberg. These laid down a "Code of Fair Labor Practices" in federal employment, and also "Standards of Conduct for Employee Organizations." Agencies excluded from these orders include those which had already set up their own labor relations programs, such as the Tennessee Valley Authority, and those involving national security, such as the Central Intelligence Agency, FBI, and Atomic Energy Commission. But the "old line agencies," the regulatory commissions, and the "independent" agencies are now covered.

The orders guarantee the right of federal employees to join unions, although this right is defined to exclude the right to strike. Unfair labor practices by unions or employing agencies are prohibited in much the same terms as the National Labor Relations Act. A union that receives a majority of votes in an election participated in by at least 60 percent of the employees eligible to vote is to be granted exclusive recognition. Disputes over the scope of the "appropriate unit" are to be resolved by the Secretary of Labor, who may resort to advisory arbitration for this purpose. There is provision also for two lower levels of recognition: formal recognition, when the union includes at least 10 percent of the employees in a unit where no other union has been granted exclusive recognition; and informal recognition, for organizations with less than 10 percent membership.

Unions with exclusive recognition have the right to negotiate agreements. (Formal recognition confers a right to be consulted on personnel matters, while informal recognition gives a union the right to be heard on matters affecting its members.) The subjects of bargaining, however, are severely restricted by a provision reserving certain matters for management decision. These include the right to hire, transfer, promote or demote, suspend, lay off, discipline, or discharge employees; and to determine the methods and personnel by which operations are to be conducted. The order also provides that the obligation to negotiate "shall not be construed to extend to such areas of discretion and policy as the mission of an agency, its budget, its organization and the assignment of its personnel, or the technology of performing its work." A grievance procedure is established, with provisions for appeal of administrative decisions adversely affecting employees.

The limited scope of collective bargaining reflects the contrasting philosophies of the two federal agencies most closely concerned with the subject. The Department of Labor believes in encouragement rather than mere toleration of collective bargaining, and supports extension of bargaining rights to the fullest extent compatible with law. In this view, people work better if they exercise genuine control over their conditions of work. The Civil Service Commission, on the other hand, supports the hierarchical view of the public service in which responsibility for efficient performance is fixed in the agency head, authority is delegated to subordinates, and daily tasks are set and performed under duly established rules. In this view the work relationship is to be judged primarily by criteria of efficiency in performance rather than job satisfaction, and the existence of a merit system for hiring and promotion is regarded as a fully satisfactory substitute for employee representation and collective bargaining. Thus, on the one hand, the Code of Fair Labor Practices invites federal employees to organize and try to bargain with their supervisors. But the broad definition of "management prerogatives," reflecting the traditional Civil Service Commission attitude, at the same time holds bargaining within a narrow range of subjects; and the absence of impasse-resolving machinery, along with the Congressional prohibition against striking, tends to keep the union representatives in the position of petitioners rather than allowing them to bargain on equal terms.

Since the 1962 executive orders there has been a marked increase in union activity in the federal service. Postal employees, who have the longest tradition of unionism within federal employment, have achieved "exclusive recognition units" covering 90 percent of postal workers. Elsewhere, exclusive representation rights have been achieved in some 800 units, covering some 835,000 employees, or about one-third of all federal employees. Some 430 agreements have been negotiated, about half of which are with the Department of Defense, covering 750,000 workers. The Department of Labor has processed over 150 requests for advisory arbitration to define bargaining units.

The unions of federal employees, however, are by no means satisfied with the operation of the system. The commonest grounds of complaint are that top personnel managers in each agency have been unwilling to delegate enough authority to local management to permit meaningful negotiation; that agencies restrict the scope of bargaining even more narrowly than the executive order requires; that too many matters are excluded from the grievance procedure, and that few agencies have been willing to submit unsettled issues to advisory arbitration; that only 10 percent of agreements provide for outside mediation, and only 25 per cent for fact finding and referral to higher authorities in the agency when an impasse occurs in bargaining—an important matter where the strike is forbidden; and that unfair practice charges are usually heard by hearing officers from within the agency itself, who tend to rubber-stamp management decisions.[2]

The lack of a central agency to administer the code means that each agency has developed its own rules and procedures. Legislation has been proposed to create a board comparable to the National Labor Relations Board, which would administer the code impartially and uniformly in all departments to which it applies. But Congress has shown little inclination to pass such legislation.

BARGAINING ARRANGEMENTS: STATE AND LOCAL LEVELS

Recognition, Bargaining Units, Union Security

Until recently there was little legislation concerning unionization of state and local employees. State legislatures, particularly in the more agricultural states, were usually critical or hostile to the idea; and some states prohibited unionization of policemen, firemen, or even public employees in general. But usually the decision of whether to bargain was left up to city, county, or state officials. Unions had to make their way by politics and persuasion. Just as in the private sector, this led to numerous strikes over the basic issue of union recognition.

This situation has now greatly changed. Several federal circuit court and Supreme Court decisions have held that states may not prohibit free association of state and local employees,[3] although they may regulate bargaining procedures and tactics. Most of the larger industrial states have now passed comprehensive labor relations statutes covering state and

---

[2] See Jack Stieber, "Collective Bargaining in the Public Sector," in Lloyd Ulman (ed.), *Challenges to Collective Bargaining* (Englewood Cliffs, N.J.: Prentice-Hall, Inc., 1967).

[3] Harry H. Wellington and Ralph K. Winter, Jr., *The Unions and the Cities* (Washington: the Brookings Institution, 1972), Chap. 5.

municipal employees. States with such statutes include Alaska, California, Connecticut, Delaware, Florida, Hawaii, Maine, Massachusetts, Michigan, Minnesota, Missouri, Nebraska, New Hampshire, New York, Oregon, Pennsylvania, Rhode Island, Vermont, Washington, and Wisconsin. Most other states have statutes restricted to particular employee groups, such as teachers, policemen, or firemen. Only half a dozen states still have no legislation of any sort.[4]

A comprehensive statute usually contains an explicit declaration of the right of public employees to organize, to be represented by associations of their own choice, and to negotiate with their employers. Administration is usually in the hands of a public employee relations board, or some equivalent title. This board has the general powers, and follows the general procedures, of the National Labor Relations Board in defining bargaining units, conducting elections, certifying bargaining representatives, and enforcing the right to bargain. In the larger states the volume of election activity is high; and as a result of the new procedures, recognition strikes have almost disappeared in these states.

There is often a question of specifying who is the employer in a particular instance. Board decisions on this point are not necessarily accepted by the other public agencies involved, and there is often considerable confusion, which will presumably be reduced gradually over the years. The fragmentation of local government decision making has also led to a corresponding fragmentation of bargaining units. Where there are half a dozen budgetary authorities with independent wage-setting powers, there will usually be at least that number of bargaining units. Police unions almost always negotiate independently of anyone else, and so do the firefighters and public school teachers. Bargaining units are influenced also by the accident of which union organized which groups at a particular time. The city of Milwaukee, for example, has fifteen separate units. In Philadelphia, on the other hand, all the nonuniformed city employees bargain as a group.

In most areas there are certainly too many units, and this creates several problems. It consumes the time of city officials in multiple negotiations. It tends to produce a crazy-quilt pattern of wages and benefits, differing among units, and subject to no central oversight or rationale. It can pose barriers to ready transfer of city employees among departments using the same kinds of skill. It leads to whipsawing in the bargaining process, as one union wins superior terms on a particular front, and other unions then press for similar treatment. The tradition that city employees should be treated equally in general wage increases, pension rights, holidays and vacations, and other benefits makes it difficult for city officials to resist this kind of

---

[4] For details and state legislation as of 1970, see Wellington and Winter, *The Unions and the Cities,* Appendix A.

pressure. These disadvantages are widely recognized, and public employee relations boards lean in the direction of wider rather than narrow units. But any consolidation and rationalization of bargaining units will probably be very gradual.

Public employee unions usually press for a union security provision, either in the form of a union shop or an agency shop, under which non-members must pay a specified fee for the union's bargaining services. Such clauses are appearing in a growing number of public-employee agreements. Some state courts have cast doubt on their legality, and, because of differences in state constitutions, this issue will have to be litigated on a state-by-state basis. In practical terms, however, the arguments for and against the union shop do not seem to differ materially from the corresponding arguments in the private sector, which we examined in Chapter 20. Those who favor union-shop provisions in private employment can reasonably argue for them in public employment as well, and vice versa.

Employer Organization for Bargaining

We have already noted the complex structure of authority in local government units. The first reaction of city governments to the appearance of unionism is usually to improvise, to add collective bargaining agreements on top of the existing structure without really modifying it. The result, however, is an unstable situation. Some union aims and some collective bargaining procedures run counter to the preunion pattern, and gradually compel modifications of it.

In cities where bargaining has been going on for some time, several trends are becoming apparent:

1. A shift of authority for labor relations toward the executive branch, as against the legislature and the civil service commission. This has clear practical advantages. The executive branch normally prepares and recommends the budget. When it also does the bargaining, any agreements involving money can be coordinated with the timing and content of the budget. Moreover, it is mainly the executive officials who will have to live with the agreement and participate in its administration. They are in the best position to anticipate administrative problems and inefficiencies that may be created by union requests on hours of work, shift arrangements, staffing requirements, transfers of personnel, and other restrictions on managerial authority. City councillors are often part-time, usually nonexpert in labor matters, and unavoidably political in outlook. This does not make them good bargaining representatives. So where the legislature has attempted to become the bargaining agency in the early stages, this approach has usually been abandoned after a short time.

2. Increased centralization of authority within the executive branch. This is needed to coordinate city policy across the board and reduce whipsawing. It also permits hiring of expert personnel to carry on the bargaining.

3. Transfer of bargaining authority from existing staff officers, such as

the budget director or personnel director, to full-time labor relations specialists. The first reaction has often been to assign bargaining responsibility to an existing staff member; but this creates difficulties. Apart from the fact that these officials usually lack expertise in labor relations, the bargaining function involves them in a conflict of roles. The budget director may want to reach agreement with the union; but his main function is to hold down costs to the city. A personnel director, on the other hand, may be willing to make outsize wage concessions if the union will go easy on interfering with personnel management. Increasingly, therefore, the bargaining function is located directly under the mayor or city manager. In smaller communities, the city manager himself may do the negotiating. In larger cities, there is usually a labor relations office with specialized, full-time personnel, such as the Detroit Labor Relations Office and the New York City Office of Labor Relations.

4. One of the more difficult issues has been what functions remain to the state and city civil service commissions. These bodies normally have statutory authority over job and salary classifications, recruitment, promotion, and other aspects of job tenure. The unions, however, insist that all important aspects of job tenure be regulated by the collective agreement. To the extent that this creates conflicting rules and overlap of authority, the unions contend that the agreement should prevail. Most states have not tried to resolve this conflict, leaving it to be fought out case by case. When there is a statute, it usually reaffirms the role of the civil service commission. The Wisconsin law, for example, provides that "nothing herein shall require the employer to bargain in relation to statutory and rule-provided prerogatives of promotion, layoff, position classification, compensation and fringe benefits, examination, discipline, merit salary determination policy and other actions provided for by law and rules governing civil service." Somewhat similar provisions appear in the Massachusetts, California, Oregon, and Washington laws. The Connecticut Municipal Employee Relations Act, on the other hand, severely limits the role of civil service and the range of issues that may not be bargained about: "The conduct and the grading of merit examinations, the rating of candidates and the establishment of lists from such examinations and the appointments from such lists and any provision of any municipal charter concerning political activity of municipal employees shall not be subject to collective bargaining." On all other issues, where there is a conflict between the terms of a collective agreement and the rules of the civil service commission, the terms of the agreement shall prevail. The strong prounion position, however, has not yet been followed by any other state. One can predict that this issue will continue to generate tension in state and municipal employee relations. A possible outcome is that civil service commissions will be restricted increasingly to initial recruitment and selection of employees, and that personnel procedures beyond that point will be dominated by the collective agreement.

The Content of Bargaining

Public employee agreements read very much like union contracts in private industry. They cover such standard subjects as wage rates and fringe benefits; hours and overtime; shift arrangements; transfer, promotion, discipline, and discharge; and procedure for processing grievances.

Two points, however, require special content: questions of the *scope of bargaining*, and occasional complications in the *grievance procedure*.

The question of the scope of bargaining arises most frequently with respect to quasi-professional groups such as teachers, policemen, nurses, social workers. How far should teachers' unions be entitled to bargain over issues of educational policy? Is class size a legitimate bargaining issue? What about arrangements for student discipline? What about curriculum content, including special programs for underprivileged children? How far should teachers' unions become involved, as the New York City union has done, in the issue of "home rule," or decentralization of school administration? These subjects affect teachers' "terms and conditions of employment." But they also affect educational standards, administrative efficiency, pupils' welfare, and parents' attitudes and interests. The issue is whether collective bargaining on such matters provides adequate protection for third parties who have a legitimate interest in the outcome.

Similar problems arise with respect to other professional groups. Can a union of social workers bargain over standards and procedures in a city's welfare system? Can a police union bargain for a clause prohibiting establishment of a civilian police review board? This is an issue with strong racial and class overtones, which has polarized public feeling in many communities.

In private industry, bargainability is determined through the procedures described in Chapter 25. A long series of NLRB and court decisions has drawn a line between *mandatory* subjects and *permissive* subjects of bargaining. But these precedents are not directly transferable to the novel issues that arise in the public sector; and state public employee relations acts are usually silent on the subject. The typical state act obligates the employer to bargain about "wages, hours, and other terms and conditions of employment"; but what is included in "terms and conditions" is left to be decided by the public employee relations board or by the courts. These may not be the best bodies for resolving such socially explosive issues. Further clarification by state and city legislatures would appear preferable.

The beginnings of such legislation are already found in some states. Thus the Maine statute requires local school boards "to confer and negotiate in good faith with respect to wages, hours, working conditions and contract grievance arbitration . . . (and to) meet and consult but not negotiate with respect to educational policies." Some state statutes, and many public employee agreements, contain a *management rights* clause, confirming the employer's authority to direct employees, to determine the methods and personnel by which operations shall be conducted, to maintain the efficiency of governmental operations, and to hire, promote, classify, transfer, suspend, demote, discharge, or otherwise discipline employees. The implication is that union demands which clearly reduce efficiency, restrict service to the public, or encroach on normal supervisory authority are suspect.

Grievance procedures are often complicated by the fact that state and local governments had already established procedures for employee appeals. The collective agreement sets up a new procedure without eliminating the old ones. Thus in some government units an aggrieved employee may have as many as four channels for processing his grievance. He can use the procedures specified in the collective agreement; or he can go up through administrative channels, possibly as far as the mayor's office (which may appeal to employees with political connections); or he can use procedures established by the civil service commission; or he can resort to the courts. Which channel should be regarded as "normal," and which takes precedence over others, is often unclear.

This is part of a larger problem already underlined at several points. Collective bargaining in the public sector is not moving into a vacuum, but into well-established systems of employee relations, often with statutory authority, covering the same subject matter. The process of choosing among, reconciling, and synthesizing the old and new procedures is still in its early stages.

DO PUBLIC EMPLOYEE UNIONS RAISE WAGES?

Before commenting on this question, let us raise a related question: Do public employees, whether unionized or not, tend to earn more than comparable private employees? The federal government and most lower governmental units have legislation requiring them to follow the *prevailing wage principle*—that is to adjust their rates of pay to those prevailing for comparable work in the private sector. Experienced observers have argued, however, that there are biases in government wage-setting procedures which tend to produce a higher wage level for public employees.[5]

First, there is usually a range of private wage rates for any occupation. The wage surveys used in ascertaining the "prevailing wage" tend to exclude the smaller, relatively low-wage employers, and thus contain an upward bias. Second, for occupations with active unions (such as the building trades), the prevailing wage is almost invariably interpreted as the union scale, regardless of the actual prevalence of that scale in the private sector. Third, focusing attention on equality of wage *rates* ignores other important characteristics of public employment, such as year-round work and greater security of job tenure, which might under competition lead to a

---

[5] See in particular Walter Fogel and David Lewin, "Wage Determination in the Public Sector," *Industrial and Labor Relations Review* (April 1974), pp. 410–31.

compensating wage differential in favor of the private sector. Finally, some argue that there is a political bias in wage-setting procedures. Public employees are also voters, who can penalize elected officials at the polls for adverse wage decisions. The general body of voters has an interest in holding down wage rates and tax rates, but this interest is more diffused. Candidates for office are thus likely to be more responsive to the views of the minority directly concerned, and to tilt decisions in their direction.

This hypothesis seems to be supported by a number of statistical studies, which have found an appreciable wage advantage for public employees both at the federal level and in most (though not all) localities.[6] This bias is especially marked at the lower occupational levels. In the top managerial and professional occupations, on the other hand, government tends to pay less than the private sector.

There remains the question whether unionization of public employees introduces a second bias so that, within the public sector, organized employees earn more than the unorganized. Evidence on this point is limited and inconclusive. A study by Ashenfelter of union and nonunion firefighters concluded that the union had achieved a considerable reduction in working hours plus an appreciable increase in annual earnings. The combined effect was to raise the average *hourly* wage of unionized firemen by somewhere between 6 and 16 percent above the hourly wage of nonunion firemen.[7] There have been numerous studies of schoolteachers, some of which find no significant effect of union organization.[8] Those which do find a union effect usually estimate it as small, of the order of 2 to 4 percent. More research is needed; and the results will doubtless differ from one occupational group to another, as is true in private industry.

THE STRIKE ISSUE

Should unions of public employees have the same right to strike as unions in private employment? There is a marked division on this point among both practitioners and students of labor relations.

---

[6] In addition to the data in Fogel and Lewin, see Sharon P. Smith, "Pay Differentials Between Federal Government and Private Sector Workers," *Industrial and Labor Relations Review* (January 1976), pp. 179–97; and *Unions and Government Employment* (New York: Tax Foundation, Inc., 1972).

[7] Orley Ashenfelter, "The Effect of Unionization on Wages in the Public Sector: The Case of Fire Fighters," *Industrial and Labor Relations Review* (January 1971), pp. 191–202. For somewhat different results, see Ronald G. Ehrenberg, "Municipal Government Structure, Unionization, and the Wages of Fire Fighters," *Industrial and Labor Relations Review* (October 1973), pp. 36–48.

[8] Several of these are summarized in David B. Lipsky and John E. Drotning, "The Influence of Collective Bargaining on Teachers' Salaries in New York State," *Industrial and Labor Relations Review* (October 1973), pp. 18–35.

Those who favor retaining the strike as the ultimate sanction in bargaining rely on the following arguments: (1) Collective bargaining serves the same protective functions in public as in private employment. (2) Without the potentiality of a strike, the employer is under little pressure to accede to union demands. Collective bargaining becomes "collective begging." The strike possibility is needed both to force serious bargaining and to ensure that disputes will eventually be settled. (3) Both in the private and public sectors, some services are essential, while others are not. Whether government intervenes forcibly to ensure continuous operation should depend on the essentiality of the service, not on whether the employer is a business or a government agency.

Burton and Krider suggest that public services can be divided into three categories: "(1) essential services—police and fire—where strikes immediately endanger public health and safety; (2) intermediate services—sanitation, hospitals, transit, water, and sewage—where strikes of a few days might be tolerated; (3) nonessential services—streets, parks, education, housing, welfare and general administration—where strikes of indefinite duration could be tolerated." [9] They doubt that legal prohibition of strikes should be extended beyond the first category. Other scholars, however, take the view that it is impossible to draw a clear line between strikes which create an "emergency" and those which do not, and point out that this has never been done sucessfully in the private sector.

Those who favor continued prohibition of strikes by public employees tend to argue: (1) Public sector bargaining is not closely analogous to private bargaining, for reasons suggested in an earlier section. Public employers are less likely to have monopsony power; and even when they do have it, there are political reasons why it may not be fully exercised. (2) Even without the strike weapon, public employee unions have substantial economic and political power to advance their demands. (3) To give them the strike power in addition makes them unduly powerful relative to other groups in the community and distorts the political process.

Representative of this view is the following statement by Wellington and Winter:

> Distortion of the political process is the major, long-run social cost of strikes in public employment. The distortion results from unions obtaining too much power, relative to other interest groups, in decisions affecting the level of taxes and the allocation of tax dollars. This distortion therefore may result in a redistribution of income by government, whereby union members are subsidized at the expense of other interest groups. And where nonmonetary issues, such as the decentralization of the gov-

---

[9] John F. Burton, Jr., and Charles Krider, "The Role and Consequences of Strikes by Public Employees," *Yale Law Journal,* 80 (1970), pp. 418–43 (reprinted as Brookings Institution Reprint 176).

ernance of schools or the creation of a civilian board to review police
conduct, are resolved through bargaining in which the strike or threat
thereof is used, the distortion of the political process is no less apparent.[10]

Whatever the merit of these two lines of argument, in practice strikes
of public employees are almost universally prohibited. Such legal prohibitions raise two questions: (1) If a bargaining impasse cannot be resolved
through a strike, how can a final solution be assured? (2) What sanctions
can be applied successfully against unions and union members who go on
strike in spite of the ban?

To the first question there are two broad answers. Issues that cannot
be resolved through bargaining could be submitted to final and binding
arbitration. The difficulty with this, already noted in Chapter 26, is that it
tends to undercut the bargaining process. With arbitration in the offing,
the parties may not reveal their true positions, since this might prejudice
them in later arbitration proceedings. Moreover, an award that the union
regards as substantially unfair may still not be accepted, and a strike may
result.

For these reasons compulsory arbitration is not very widely used.
Wyoming provides for binding arbitration of disputes involving firemen,
while Pennsylvania and Rhode Island provide for compulsory arbitration
of police and firemen's disputes. The final step in New York State under
the Taylor Act of 1967 amounts, in a sense, to compulsory arbitration by
the state legislature—an unusual and probably not very workable procedure. Some state laws also encourage the parties to submit unsettled disputes
to *voluntary* arbitration by a neutral of their own choice, which obviously
increases the chances of the award being accepted.

Much the commonest approach in practice is to process unsettled
disputes through a series of stages. Although no final settlement mechanism
is provided, most impasses are resolved at one stage or another, leaving only
a small residue of "hard core" cases. Mediation by professional staff members of a state mediation agency is usually the first step. Even when this
does not settle all issues in dispute, it normally reduces their number.

The commonest next step is *fact finding* by a publicly appointed individual or board. *Fact finding* in this connection does not mean academic
research, and what it actually means varies from case to case. The fact
finder usually has authority to mediate, and may be able to bring about a
settlement by informal negotiation. Alternatively, he may ask the parties
to present views and evidence in briefs and oral hearings, and then draft
a report with recommendations on each of the disputed issues. In so doing,
he is not functioning as a judge applying clear principles, which often do
not exist. Rather, he is trying to devise contract terms sufficiently palatable

---

[10] Wellington and Winter, *The Unions and the Cities*, p. 167.

to the parties that they will prefer to settle on these terms rather than have the dispute drag on. A high proportion of the disputes submitted to fact finding—in some states as high as 90 percent—are settled on the basis of the fact-finding report.[11]

Wellington and Winter comment:

> While any evaluation is difficult because one does not know what would have happened without the existence or employment of the post-impasse procedure, the evidence shows that many disputes are resolved without the issuance of formal recommendations; that recommendations usually are accepted; that while there are strikes after recommendations, they are few; that in most jurisdictions the parties do not resort to fact-finding too frequently; and that, by and large, the parties regard these impasse tribunals as helpful.[12]

Even after all available procedures have been exhausted, some disputes remain unsettled and some strikes do occur. The number of work stoppages by state and local government employees rose from 42 in 1965 to 409 in 1969, involving several hundred thousand employees. About half of these were strikes by schoolteachers; but there were also a substantial number of strikes in sanitation departments, hospitals, and administration and protective services. Strikes were relatively short, averaging only about ten days, and in police and fire departments less than five days. In about 80 percent of the cases, government was able to maintain partial operation during the strike by using supervisors and others.[13]

What penalties should be, or can be, applied in such cases? One difficulty is that there are devices that, although technically not strikes, can slow down production and bring pressure on the public employer. Teachers have sometimes resigned or threatened to resign en masse, knowing that the school board could not replace them all, and that in the end the resignations would not be accepted. In other disputes, teachers have appeared and performed their classroom duties, but have declined to perform such auxiliary but customary duties as supervising lunchrooms and playgrounds or attending PTA meetings. Air traffic controllers, transit employees, postal workers, and other groups have used the device of *working to rule,* following all standard operating procedures in minute detail, carefully, thoroughly —and slowly. This can effectively tie up operations without involving any illegal action.

A further difficulty is that penalties must be neither too light, in which

---

[11] See the analysis in Jean T. McKelvey, "Fact Finding in Public Employment Disputes: Promise or Illusion?" *Industrial and Labor Relations Review* (July 1969), pp. 528–43.

[12] Wellington and Winter, *The Unions and the Cities*, p. 177.

[13] Wellington and Winter, *The Unions and the Cities*, Appendix B.

case they will be ignored, nor so severe as to offend the public's sense of justice, in which case they will not be applied. New York State in 1947 passed the Condon–Wadlin Act, which provided that a striking public employee was to be discharged immediately. If reemployed, he was to be in probationary status for five years and to forgo any pay increase for three years. These penalties were too strong to work. In New York City the law was deliberately not invoked in thirteen cases, and the penalties were scaled down in two others.

Political difficulties apart, to discharge all employees in a particular category in the face of a tight labor market is not a very practical procedure. So the act was repealed and the Taylor Act of 1967 provided that sanctions be applied instead to the union organization. A union striking illegally could be fined up to $10,000 or one week's dues, whichever is less, for each day of the strike, with a minimum fine of $1,000 and loss of checkoff privileges for up to eighteen months. The New York Teachers' Union subsequently had its checkoff privileges revoked on two separate occasions.

It is possible also to move against unlawful strikes via the injunction procedure. Once a judge has enjoined a strike, all actions in support of the strike are punishable as contempt of court, and union officers may be subject to fine or imprisonment. But even if they then order the men back to work, this may not be effective if the strike has strong grass-roots support.

Although it may be easier to punish organizations than individuals, it is still difficult to act against a strong union in a strongly unionized city. In the end, main reliance must be placed on the impasse-resolving procedures discussed earlier.

DISCUSSION QUESTIONS

1. What are the main *economic* differences between collective bargaining in the public and private sectors?

2. If your college is in or near a city, what unions of public employees exist in this city? With whom in the city government does each union bargain? Appraise the effectiveness of present bargaining arrangements.

3. What changes in municipal *organization* for collective bargaining seem to be occurring in response to union growth?

4. Is it desirable, and feasible, to restrict the scope of collective bargaining between unions and public employers? If so, indicate the kinds of restriction you consider desirable.

5. Explain the main points of conflict between union policies and civil service commission procedures. How, in your judgment, could this conflict best be resolved?

6. "There is no reason for any legal distinction between union activities in the public sector and in the private sector. In both sectors, strike activity should be limited only where it interrupts production of an essential service." Discuss.

7. Should impasse procedures in state labor relations acts specify compulsory arbitration as a terminal stage?

8. What penalties should be imposed for unlawful strikes, and against whom should they be assessed?

READING SUGGESTIONS

A major program of studies in public employee unionism is presently under way at the Brookings Institution. The Burton and Wellington, and Stieber studies cited above are early results of this program. Additional studies in this series will be appearing in the near future.

See also the symposium "Collective Negotiations in the Public Service," in *Public Administration Review,* (March–April 1968); and the symposium "Labor Relations in the Public Sector," in *University of Michigan Law Review,* 67 (1969). Two recent studies of collective bargaining in education are ROBERT E. DOHERTY and WALTER E. OBERER, *Teachers, School Boards, and Collective Bargaining,* Ithaca: New York State School of Industrial and Labor Relations, 1968; and MICHAEL H. MOSKOW, *Teachers and Unions,* Philadelphia: University of Pennsylvania, Wharton School, 1966.

Index

629